Andreas Herzig · Andrei Popescu (Eds.)

Frontiers of Combining Systems

12th International Symposium, FroCoS 2019
London, UK, September 4–6, 2019
Proceedings

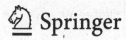

Editors
Andreas Herzig ⓘ
CNRS, University of Toulouse
Toulouse, France

Andrei Popescu ⓘ
Middlesex University London
London, UK

ISSN 0302-9743   ISSN 1611-3349 (electronic)
Lecture Notes in Artificial Intelligence
ISBN 978-3-030-29006-1   ISBN 978-3-030-29007-8 (eBook)
https://doi.org/10.1007/978-3-030-29007-8

LNCS Sublibrary: SL7 – Artificial Intelligence

This Springer imprint is published by the registered company Springer Nature Switzerland AG
The registered company address is: Gewerbestrasse 11, 6330 Cham, Switzerland

Lecture Notes in Artificial Intelligence 11715

Subseries of Lecture Notes in Computer Science

Preface

These proceedings contain the papers selected for presentation at the 12th International Symposium on Frontiers of Combining Systems (FroCoS 2019). The symposium was held during September 4–6, 2019 in London, UK, at Middlesex University. It was co-located with the 28th International Conference on Automated Reasoning with Analytic Tableaux and Related Methods (TABLEAUX 2019).

FroCoS is the main international event for research on the development of techniques and methods for the combination and integration of formal systems, their modularization and analysis. Previous FroCoS meetings were organized in Munich (Germany, 1996), Amsterdam (The Netherlands, 1998), Nancy (France, 2000), Santa Margherita Ligure (Italy, 2002), Cork (Ireland, 2004, as part of the International Joint Conference on Automated Reasoning, IJCAR), Vienna (Austria, 2005), Seattle (USA, 2006, as part of IJCAR), Liverpool (UK, 2007, co-located with the International Workshop on First-Order Theorem Proving, FTP), Sydney (Australia, 2008, as part of IJCAR), Trento (Italy, 2009), Edinburgh (UK, 2010, as part of IJCAR), Saarbrücken (Germany, 2011), Manchester (UK, 2012, as part of IJCAR), Nancy (France, 2013, co-located with TABLEAUX), Vienna (Austria, 2014, as part of IJCAR), Wrocław (Poland, 2015, co-located with TABLEAUX), Coimbra (Portugal, 2016, as part of IJCAR), Brasilia (Brazil, 2017, co-located with TABLEAUX), and Oxford (UK, 2018, as part of IJCAR). Thus, if we also count the IJCAR editions, in 2019 FroCoS celebrated its 20th edition.

FroCoS 2019 received 30 high-quality paper submissions, which were evaluated by the Program Committee on the basis of their significance, novelty, technical soundness, and appropriateness for the FroCoS audience. Reviewing was single-blind and each paper was subjected to at least three reviews, followed by a discussion within the Program Committee. In the end, 20 papers were selected for presentation at the symposium and publication. We have grouped them in this volume according to the following topic classification: (1) automated theorem proving and model building, (2) combinations of systems, (3) constraint solving, (4) description logics, (5) interactive theorem proving, (6) modal and epistemic logics, and (7) rewriting and unification.

We were delighted to have three outstanding invited speakers. The abstracts of their talks were included in this volume:

- Maria Paola Bonacina: "Conflict-Driven Reasoning in Unions of Theories"
- Stéphane Graham-Lengrand: "Recent and Ongoing Developments of Model-Constructing Satisfiability"
- Uli Sattler: "Modularity and Automated Reasoning in Description Logics"

Uli Sattler's invited talk was shared with TABLEAUX 2019. Conversely, one of the TABLEAUX invited talks, "Automated Reasoning for the Working Mathematician" by Jeremy Avigad, was shared with FroCoS.

The joint FroCoS/TABLEAUX event had two affiliated workshops:

- The 25th Workshop on Automated Reasoning (ARW 2019), organized by Alexander Bolotov and Florian Kammueller
- Journeys in Computational Logic: Tributes to Roy Dyckhoff, organized by Stéphane Graham-Lengrand, Ekaterina Komendantskaya, and Mehrnoosh Sadrzadeh

It also had two affiliated tutorials:

- Formalising Concurrent Computation: CLF, Celf, and Applications, by Sonia Marin
- How to Build an Automated Theorem Prover – An Introductory Tutorial (invited TABLEAUX tutorial), by Jens Otten

The program committee has offered two awards for outstanding submissions. The Best Paper Award went to "A CDCL-Style Calculus for Solving Non-linear Constraints" by Franz Brauße, Konstantin Korovin, Margarita Korovina and Norbert Müller. The Best Paper by a Junior Researcher Award was shared between "On the Expressive Power of Description Logics with Cardinality" by Filippo De Bortoli as junior co-author and "Verifying Randomised Social Choice" by Manuel Eberl. The awards have been financially supported by Springer.

We would like to thank all the people who contributed to making FroCoS 2019 a success. In particular, we thank the invited speakers for their inspiring talks, the authors for providing their high-quality submissions (all 30 submissions!), revising and presenting their work, the workshop and tutorial organizers for the interesting and engaging events, and all the attendees for contributing to the symposium discussion. We thank the Program Committee members and the external reviewers for their careful, competent reviewing and discussion of the submissions on quite a tight schedule.

We extend our thanks to the local Organizing Committee chaired by Franco Raimondi and to the Middlesex University staff, especially to Nicola Skinner, for offering their enthusiastic support to this event.

We gratefully acknowledge financial support from Amazon, Springer, and Middlesex University. The Association for Symbolic Logic (ASL) has kindly included FroCoS among the events for which students can apply to them for travel funding. Finally, we are grateful to EasyChair for allowing us to use their excellent conference management system.

September 2019   Andreas Herzig
                                                        Andrei Popescu

Organization

Program Chairs

Andreas Herzig   CNRS, University of Toulouse, France
Andrei Popescu   Middlesex University London, UK

Local Organizing Chair

Franco Raimondi   Middlesex University London, UK

FroCoS Steering Committee

Franz Baader (President)   TU Dresden, Germany
Clare Dixon   University of Liverpool, UK
Marcelo Finger   University of São Paulo, Brazil
Pascal Fontaine   LORIA, Inria, University of Lorraine, France
Carsten Lutz   University of Bremen, Germany
Silvio Ranise   Fondazione Bruno Kessler-Irst, Italy
Renate Schmidt   University of Manchester, UK

Program Committee

Carlos Areces   FaMAF - Universidad Nacional de Córdoba, Argentina
Alessandro Artale   Free University of Bolzano-Bozen, Italy
Franz Baader   TU Dresden, Germany
Christoph Benzmüller   Free University of Berlin, Germany
Jasmin Christian Blanchette   Vrije Universiteit Amsterdam, The Netherlands
Torben Braüner   Roskilde University, Denmark
Clare Dixon   University of Liverpool, UK
Marcelo Finger   University of São Paulo, Brazil
Pascal Fontaine   LORIA, Inria, University of Lorraine, France
Didier Galmiche   LORIA – Université de Lorraine, France
Silvio Ghilardi   Università degli Studi di Milano, Italy
Jürgen Giesl   RWTH Aachen University, Germany
Andreas Herzig   CNRS, University of Toulouse, France
Moa Johansson   Chalmers University of Technology, Sweden
Jean Christoph Jung   Universität Bremen, Germany
Cezary Kaliszyk   University of Innsbruck, Austria
Ekaterina Komendantskaya   Heriot-Watt University, UK
Roman Kontchakov   Birkbeck, University of London, UK
Alessio Lomuscio   Imperial College London, UK
Assia Mahboubi   Inria, France

Stefan Mitsch	Carnegie Mellon University, USA
Cláudia Nalon	University of Brasília, Brazil
Andrei Popescu	Middlesex University London, UK
Silvio Ranise	Fondazione Bruno Kessler-Irst, Italy
Christophe Ringeissen	LORIA-Inria, France
Philipp Rümmer	Uppsala University, Sweden
Renate Schmidt	University of Manchester, UK
Viorica Sofronie-Stokkermans	Universität Koblenz-Landau, Germany
Christian Sternagel	University of Innsbruck, Austria
Andrzej Szalas	Linköping University, Sweden
Cesare Tinelli	The University of Iowa, USA
Ashish Tiwari	SRI International, USA
Christoph Weidenbach	Max Planck Institute for Informatics, Germany

External Reviewers

Martin Avanzini
Haniel Barbosa
Alexander Bentkamp
Rasmus Blanck
Elena Botoeva
Martin Bromberger
Ugo Dal Lago
Warren Del-Pinto
Santiago Escobar
Mathias Fleury
Florian Frohn
David Fuenmayor
Carsten Fuhs
Lorenzo Gheri

Alessandro Gianola
Ping Hou
Boris Konev
Panagiotis Kouvaros
Chencheng Liang
Andrew M. Marshall
Johannes Marti
Aart Middeldorp
Julian Parsert
Andrew Reynolds
Anders Schlichtkrull
Sophie Tourret
Rakesh Verma
Sarah Winkler

Abstracts of Invited Talks

Conflict-Driven Reasoning in Unions of Theories

Maria Paola Bonacina

Dipartimento di Informatica, Università degli Studi di Verona
Strada Le Grazie 15, 37134, Verona, Italy
mariapaola.bonacina@univr.it

As the development of automated reasoning has brought to relative maturity multiple reasoning paradigms and tools, a general challenge is that of *interfacing*, *combining*, and *integrating* them, in *reasoning environments* that are more powerful and easier to use. Reasoning in a union T of theories $T_1, \ldots, T_n$ is a context where this challenge arises naturally, and many applications of automated reasoning require to handle a union of at least a few theories. This talk advertises a recent paradigm named CDSAT (*Conflict-Driven SATisfiability*) for *conflict-driven reasoning* in a union of theories [4].

Reasoning in a union of theories can be approached in more than one way. The *equality sharing scheme* by Nelson and Oppen, and its integration in the well-known DPLL(T) framework, combine decision procedures for T_i-satisfiability ($1 \le i \le n$) into a decision procedure for T-satisfiability. Decision procedures are combined as *black-boxes* that only exchange entailed (disjunctions of) equalities between shared variables. Superposition reasons in a union of theories by taking the union of their axiomatizations: under suitable conditions the termination of superposition is *modular*, so that termination on T_i-satisfiability problems ($1 \le i \le n$) implies termination on T-satisfiability problems [1]. *Model-based theory combination* by de Moura and Bjørner is a variant of equality sharing, where the T_i-satisfiability procedures build candidate T_i-models, and propagate equalities true in the current candidate T_i-model rather than entailed. DPLL($\Gamma + T$) integrates superposition and DPLL(T) with model-based theory combination to handle unions mixing axiomatized and built-in theories [5].

DPLL(T) and DPLL($\Gamma + T$) are built around the CDCL (*Conflict-Driven Clause Learning*) procedure for propositional satisfiability (SAT) pioneered by Marques Silva and Sakallah. CDCL builds a candidate partial model of a propositional abstraction of the formula, and applies propositional resolution only to *explain* conflicts between the model and the formula, so that the conflict explanation tells how to update the model and solve the conflict. CDCL inspired several T_i-satisfiability procedures for fragments of arithmetic (e.g, using Fourier-Motzkin resolution only to explain conflicts in linear real arithmetic), and was generalized to first-order logic (without equality) in a theorem-proving method named SGGS (*Semantically-Guided Goal-Sensitive* reasoning) [6]. Methods that perform nontrivial inferences only to explain conflicts are called *conflict-driven*.

In DPLL($\mathcal{T}$) and DPLL($\Gamma + \mathcal{T}$) the conflict-driven reasoning is only propositional as in CDCL: conflict-driven $\mathcal{T}_i$-satisfiability procedures could be integrated only as black-boxes, so that they could not participate in the model construction on a par with CDCL. The MCSAT (*Model-Constructing SATisfiability*) framework by de Moura and Jovanović shows how to integrate CDCL and a conflict-driven $\mathcal{T}_i$-satisfiability procedure, called *theory plugin*, so that *both* propositional and $\mathcal{T}_i$-reasoning are conflict-driven. A key idea is to abandon black-box combination: open the black-box, pull out from the $\mathcal{T}_i$-satisfiability procedure clausal inference rules that can *explain* $\mathcal{T}_i$-conflicts, and enable CDCL and the $\mathcal{T}_i$-plugin to cooperate in model construction.

CDSAT generalizes MCSAT to the multi-theory case, solving the problem of how to combine multiple $\mathcal{T}_i$-satisfiability procedures, some of which are conflict-driven and some of which are black-boxes. The theories are assumed to be equipped with theory inference systems called *theory modules*, with propositional logic viewed as one of the theories in the union. CDSAT provides a framework for the theory modules to cooperate as peers in building a candidate $\mathcal{T}$-model and explaining $\mathcal{T}$-conflicts. Thus, reasoning in a union of theories is achieved by putting together inference systems, rather than procedures or axiomatizations: of course, theory modules are abstractions of decision procedures, and inference rules may correspond to axioms. A black-box $\mathcal{T}_i$-satisfiability procedure is treated as a theory module with only one inference rule that invokes the procedure to check $\mathcal{T}_i$-satisfiability. CDSAT encompasses the previous approaches: it reduces to CDCL if propositional logic is the only theory, to equality sharing if propositional logic is absent and all $\mathcal{T}_i$-satisfiability procedures are black-boxes, to DPLL($\mathcal{T}$) if propositional logic is one of the theories and all other theories have black-box $\mathcal{T}_i$-satisfiability procedures, and to MCSAT if there are propositional logic and another theory with a conflict-driven $\mathcal{T}_i$-satisfiability procedure. Under suitable hypotheses, CDSAT is *sound, terminating,* and *complete.*

CDSAT opens several exciting directions for future work, including an integration, or at least an interface, between CDSAT and SGGS, or SGGS enriched with conflict-driven superposition to handle equality. Descriptions of all these approaches appear in recent surveys [2, 3] where the references can be found.

References

1. Armando, A., Bonacina, M.P., Ranise, S., Schulz, S.: New results on rewrite-based satisfiability procedures. ACM TOCL, **10**(1), 129–179 (2009)
2. Bonacina, M.P.: On conflict-driven reasoning. In: Shankar, N., Dutertre, B. (eds.) Proceedings of the 6th Workshop on Automated Formal Methods (AFM), Kalpa Publications, vol. 5, pp. 31–49. EasyChair (2018)
3. Bonacina, M.P., Fontaine, P., Ringeissen, C., Tinelli, C.: Theory combination: beyond equality sharing. In: Lutz, C., Sattler, U., Tinelli, C., Turhan, A,Y., Wolter, F. (eds.) Description Logic, Theory Combination, and All That. LNCS, vol. 11560, pp. 57–89. Springer, Cham (2019). https://doi.org/10.1007/978-3-030-22102-7_3

4. Bonacina, M.P., Graham-Lengrand, S., Shankar, N.: Conflict-driven satisfiability for theory combination: transition system and completeness. J. Automat. Reason. 1–31 (2019, in press). http://doi.org/10.1007/s10817-018-09510-y
5. Bonacina, M.P., Lynch, C.A., de Moura, L.: On deciding satisfiability by theorem proving with speculative inferences. J. Automat. Reason. **47**(2), 161–189 (2011)
6. Bonacina, M.P., Plaisted, D.A.: Semantically-guided goal-sensitive reasoning: inference system and completeness. J. Automat. Reason. **59**(2), 165–218 (2017)

Recent and Ongoing Developments of Model-Constructing Satisfiability

Stéphane Graham-Lengrand

SRI International

Model-constructing satisfiability is an approach to SMT-solving developed by Jovanović et al., generalising work on satisfiability in non-linear arithmetic [9]. The approach lifts the principles of *Conflict-Driven Clause Learning* (CDCL) from classical propositional reasoning to theory reasoning. It is incarnated by the MCSAT calculus [4, 8] and is implemented in the Yices SMT-solver [5].

Model-constructing satisfiability constitutes a reasoning scheme within the more abstract framework of *conflict-driven satisfiability* (CDSAT) for theory combination [2]. It is more specific than conflict-driven reasoning in that it is tailored to theories that have a standard model, such as arithmetic theories. Using that standard model to evaluate terms and formulae is a central part of model-constructing satisfiability, and allows the reduction of ground satisfiability problems to (series of) interpolation problems, as explained below.

Given some (quantifier-free) *constraints* to satisfy, MCSAT successively guesses assignments of first-order values to first-order variables, with the invariant that none of the constraints evaluates to false, given the assignments made so far. If the invariant can be maintained until all variables are assigned, then the constraints are satisfied by these assignments. But if at any point the invariant cannot be maintained, it means that, for some first-order variable y, every possible choice of value makes one of the constraints evaluate to false. This means that, for a subset $\{C_1, \ldots, C_m\}$ of the constraints with free variables among $x_1, \ldots, x_n, y$, the assignments $\Gamma = \{x_1 \mapsto v_1, \ldots, x_n \mapsto v_n\}$ made so far make the formula $\exists y(C_1 \wedge \cdots \wedge C_m)$ evaluate to false, i.e., $[\![\exists y(C_1 \wedge \cdots \wedge C_m)]\!]_\Gamma = \texttt{false}$. This situation is called a *conflict*, with *conflict constraints* $C_1, \ldots, C_m$.

After hitting a conflict, MCSAT backtracks over some of the guessed assignments and tries new ones. For this, MCSAT requires from the theory solver a symbolic explanation of the conflict, namely a quantifier-free formula I, such that (i) $(\exists y(C_1 \wedge \cdots \wedge C_m)) \Rightarrow I$ is valid in the theory and (ii) $[\![I]\!]_\Gamma = \texttt{false}$. Formula I is the *interpolant of* $(\exists y(C_1 \wedge \cdots \wedge C_m))$ *at* Γ. Any other pick Γ' of assignments such that $[\![I]\!]_{\Gamma'} = \texttt{false}$ will lead to a conflict for the same reason Γ did, so after the backtrack, MCSAT will seek to satisfy the interpolant.

This notion of interpolation relates to *quantifier elimination*, where any formula of the form $(\exists y(C_1 \wedge \cdots \wedge C_m))$ above can be transformed into a quantifier-free formula F such that $(\exists y(C_1 \wedge \cdots \wedge C_m)) \Leftrightarrow F$ is valid in the theory. Property (i) of interpolation is weaker than such an equivalence, and property (ii) makes the production of the interpolant "model-driven", i.e., driven by assignments Γ.

MCSAT applies for instance to linear and non-linear real arithmetic, where the interpolants are respectively produced using Fourier-Motzkin resolution and Cylindrical Algebraic Decomposition (CAD). These key mechanisms of quantifier elimination are used in MCSAT on demand, in response to a particular conflict.

MCSAT is also being applied to the theory of bit-vectors. The difficulty there is the diversity of bit-vectors operations that may occur in conflict constraints. While bit-blasting provides a default interpolation mechanism, the interpolants are not very good for the efficiency of MCSAT, being closer to the bit level than to the word level. Current research and implementation efforts in Yices aim at better interpolants, when the conflict constraints lie within some suitable fragments of the bit-vector theory, for instance in linear arithmetic modulo [7].

Following work on the application of SMT-solving to intuitionistic propositional reasoning [3, 6], ongoing research also applies the MCSAT approach there, using the worlds of a Kripke model in the assignments of values to variables.

Finally, the connection with quantifier elimination suggests the generalisation of MCSAT to quantified problem. We are currently developing this generalisation, in connection with previous work on quantified satisfaction [1].

References

1. Bjorner, N., Janota, M.: Playing with quantified satisfaction. In: Davis, M., Fehnker, A., McIver, A., Voronkov, A. (eds.) Proceedings of the 20th International Conference on Logic for Programming, Artificial Intelligence, and Reasoning (LPAR-15). LNCS, vol. 9450, pp. 15–27. Springer, November 2015
2. Bonacina, M.P., Graham-Lengrand, S., Shankar, N.: Conflict-driven satisfiability for theory combination: transition system and completeness. J. Autom. Reason. 1–31 (2019, in press)
3. Claessen, K., Rosén, D.: SAT modulo intuitionistic implications. In: Davis, M., Fehnker, A., McIver, A., Voronkov, A.: (eds.) LPAR 2015. LNCS, vol. 9450, pp. 622–637. Springer, Heidelberg (2015). https://doi.org/10.1007/978-3-662-48899-7_43
4. de Moura, L., Jovanović, D.: A model-constructing satisfiability calculus. In: Giacobazzi, R., Berdine, J., Mastroeni, I. (eds.) VMCAI 2013. LNCS, vol. 7737, pp. 1–12. Springer, Heidelberg (2013). https://doi.org/10.1007/978-3-642-35873-9_1
5. Dutertre, B.: Yices 2.2. In: Biere, A., Bloem, R. (eds.) CAV 2014. LNCS, vol. 8559, pp. 737–744. Springer, Cham (2014). https://doi.org/10.1007/978-3-319-08867-9_49
6. Fiorentini, C., Goré, R., Graham-Lengrand, S.: A proof-theoretic perspective on SMT-solving for intuitionistic propositional logic. In: Cerrito, S., Popescu, A. (eds.) Proceedings of the 28th International Conference on Automated Reasoning with Analytic Tableaux and Related Methods (Tableaux'19), September 2019, in press
7. Graham-Lengrand, S., Jovanović, D.: Interpolating bit-vector arithmetic constraints in MCSAT. In: Sharygina, N., Hendrix, J. (eds.) 17th International Work on Satisfiability Modulo Theories (SMT 2019), July 2019
8. Jovanović, D.: Solving nonlinear integer arithmetic with MCSAT. In: Bouajjani, A., Monniaux, D. (eds.) VMCAI 2017. LNCS, vol. 10145, pp. 330–346. Springer, Cham (2017). https://doi.org/10.1007/978-3-319-52234-0_18
9. Jovanović, D., de Moura, L.: Solving non-linear arithmetic. In: Gramlich, B., Miller, D., Sattler, U. (eds.) IJCAR 2012. LNCS, vol 7364, pp. 339–354. Springer, Heidelberg (2012). https://doi.org/10.1007/978-3-642-31365-3_27

Modularity and Automated Reasoning
in Description Logics

Uli Sattler

School of Computer Science, University of Manchester, UK
uli.sattler@manchester.ac.uk

Description Logics [2] are decidable fragments of first order logics closely related to modal logics and the guarded fragment. Through their use as logical underpinning of the Semantic Web Ontology language OWL [5], they are now widely used in a range of areas. As a further consequence, DL reasoners have to deal with logical theories—called ontologies—of increasing size and complexity, and domain experts using DLs ask for increasingly sophisticated tool support. One of the many areas that have been considered in this aspect is *modularity* [4, 8], a concept that has successfully been used to tame complexity and enable separation of concerns in other areas, in particular Software Engineering.

Firstly, we consider the task of extracting, from one ontology, a small/suitable fragment that captures a given topic, usually described in terms of its signature. The question of suitability versus size here is interesting, and has given rise to different notions of modules and their properties and algorithms for their extraction [1, 4, 6, 10–12, 15, 16]. Secondly, it would be extremely useful if we could "modularise" a large ontology into suitable coherent fragments (OWL has an "imports" construct that supports some kind of modular working with/storage of an ontology) [7, 9, 13]. Thirdly, if we have such a nice, modular ontology, the question arises of how a group of domain experts can work independently on these without undesired side effects. Fourth and finally, reasoning over ontologies is often a highly complex task, and a natural question arising is whether/which form of modularity can be used and how to optimise reasoning [3, 14, 18, 19].

References

1. Romero, A.A., Kaminski, M., Cuenca Grau, B., Horrocks, I.: Module extraction in expressive ontology languages via datalog reasoning. J. Artif. Intell. Res. **55**, 499–564 (2016)
2. Baader, F., Calvanese, D., McGuinness, D., Nardi, D., Patel-Schneider, P.F. (eds.) The Description Logic Handbook: Theory, Implementation, and Applications, 2nd edn. Cambridge University Press (2007)
3. Cuenca Grau, B., Halaschek-Wiener, C., Kazakov, Y., Suntisrivaraporn, B.: Incremental classification of description logics ontologies. J. Autom. Reason. **44**(4), 337–369 (2010)
4. Cuenca Grau, B., Horrocks, I., Kazakov, Y., Sattler, U.: Extracting modules from ontologies: a logic-based approach. In: Stuckenschmidt et al. [17], pp. 159–186
5. Cuenca Grau, B., et al.: OWL 2: the next step for OWL. J. Web Seman. **6**(4), 309–322 (2008)

6. Vescovo, C.D., Klinov, P., Parsia, B., Sattler, U., Schneider, T., Tsarkov, D.: Empirical study of logic-based modules: cheap is cheerful. In: Proceedings of the 12th International Semantic Web Conference (ISWC-13) (2013)

7. Vescovo, C.D., Parsia, B., Sattler, U., Schneider, T.: The modular structure of an ontology: atomic decomposition. In: Proceedings of the 22nd International Joint Conference on Artificial Intelligence (IJCAI-11), pp. 2232–2237 (2011)

8. Ghilardi, S., Lutz, C., Wolter, F.: Did I damage my ontology? A case for conservative extensions in description logics. In: Proceedings of the 10th International Conference on the Principles of Knowledge Representation and Reasoning (KR-06), pp. 187–197. AAAI Press/The MIT Press (2006)

9. Konev, B., Lutz, C., Ponomaryov, D., Wolter, F.: Decomposing description logic ontologies. In: Proceedings of the 12th International Conference on the Principles of Knowledge Representation and Reasoning (KR-10), pp. 236–246. AAAI Press/The MIT Press (2010)

10. Konev, B., Lutz, C., Walther, D., Wolter, F.: Logical difference and module extraction with CEX and MEX. In: Proceedings of the 21st International Workshop on Description Logics (DL-08), CEUR, vol. 353 (2008). http://ceur-ws.org/

11. Konev, B., Lutz, C., Walther, D., Wolter, F.: Formal properties of modularisation. In: Stuckenschmidt, H., Parent, C., Spaccapietra, S. (eds.) Modular Ontologies. LNCS, vol. 5445, pp. 25–66. Springer, Heidelberg (2009). https://doi.org/10.1007/978-3-642-01907-4_3

12. Konev, B., Lutz, C., Walther, D., Wolter, F.: Model-theoretic inseparability and modularity of description logic ontologies. Artif. Intell. J. **203**, 66–103 (2013)

13. Martín-Recuerda, F., Walther, D.: Fast modularisation and atomic decomposition of ontologies using axiom dependency hypergraphs. In: Mika, P. et al. (eds.) ISWC 2014. LNCS, vol. 8797, pp. 49–64. Springer, Cham (2014). https://doi.org/10.1007/978-3-319-11915-1_4

14. Matentzoglu, N., Parsia, B., Sattler, U.: OWL reasoning: subsumption test hardness and modularity. J. Autom. Reason. **60**(4), 385–419 (2018)

15. Nortje, R., Britz, K., Meyer, T.: Reachability modules for the description logic $\mathcal{SRIQ}$. In: McMillan, K., Middeldorp, A., Voronkov, A. (eds.) LPAR 2013. LNCS, vol. 8312, pp. 636–652. Springer, Heidelberg (2013). https://doi.org/10.1007/978-3-642-45221-5_42

16. Sattler, U., Schneider, T., Zakharyaschev, M.: Which kind of module should I extract? In: Proceedings of the 22nd International Workshop on Description Logics (DL-09), CEUR, vol. 477 (2009). http://ceur-ws.org/

17. Stuckenschmidt, H., Parent, C., Spaccapietra, S. (eds.) Modular Ontologies: Concepts, Theories and Techniques for Knowledge Modularization. LNCS, vol. 5445, Springer, Heidelberg (2009). https://doi.org/10.1007/978-3-642-01907-4

18. Suntisrivaraporn, B.: Module extraction and incremental classification: a pragmatic approach for $\mathcal{EL}^+$ ontologies. In: Bechhofer, S., Hauswirth, M., Hoffmann, J., Koubarakis, M. (eds.) ESWC 2008. LNCS, vol 5021, pp. 230–244. Springer, Heidelberg (2008). https://doi.org/10.1007/978-3-540-68234-9_19

19. Zhao, H., Sattler, U., Parsia, B.: Avoiding subsumption tests during classification using the atomic decomposition. In: Proceedings of the 25th International Workshop on Description Logics (DL-19), CEUR-WS.org, vol. 2373 (2019)

Contents

Automated Theorem Proving and Model Building

Symmetry Avoidance in MACE-Style Finite Model Finding

Giles Reger[1]([✉]), Martin Riener[1], and Martin Suda[2]

[1] University of Manchester, Manchester, UK
giles.reger@manchester.ac.uk, martin@derivation.org
[2] Czech Technical University, Prague, Czech Republic
martin.suda@cvut.cz

Abstract. This work considers the MACE-style approach to finite model finding for (multi-sorted) first-order logic. This existing approach iteratively assumes increasing domain sizes and encodes the corresponding model existence problem as a SAT problem. The original MACE tool and its successors have considered techniques for avoiding introducing symmetries in the resulting SAT problem, but this has never been the focus of the previous work and has not received concentrated attention. In this work we formalise the symmetry avoiding problem, characterise the notion of a sound symmetry breaking heuristic, propose a number of such heuristics and evaluate them experimentally with an implementation in the Vampire theorem prover. Our results demonstrate that these new heuristics improve performance on a number of benchmarks taken from SMT-LIB and TPTP. Finally, we show that direct symmetry breaking techniques could be used to improve finite model finding, but that their cost means that symmetry avoidance is still the preferable approach.

1 Introduction

Finding finite models of first-order problems can be useful in a number of applications. The most prominent of these being in program verification, where models correspond to bug traces under most common program encodings. This paper considers an existing finite model finding technique and how it can be optimised to handle larger and more complex problems (which correspond to programs in the previous example application).

MACE-style finite model finding (introduced in [13] and extended in [4, 16]) aims to build finite models of first-order problems by reduction to SAT. The general idea behind this approach is as follows. To determine whether a (suitably preprocessed) first-order problem has a model of size n we first instantiate the problem with n fresh constants to produce a ground problem. This ground problem is then translated into a SAT problem such that a model of the SAT

This work was supported by EPSRC Grant EP/P03408X/1. Martin Suda was supported by the ERC Consolidator grant AI4REASON 649043.

A. Herzig and A. Popescu (Eds.): FroCoS 2019, LNAI 11715, pp. 3–21, 2019.
https://doi.org/10.1007/978-3-030-29007-8_1

problem can be translated back to a model of the first-order problem. To find finite models we then iteratively repeat this process for larger values of n. A well known issue with this approach is that the encoding introduces inherent *symmetries* into the SAT problem. That is, if the SAT problem has a model then it actually has $n!$ isomorphic models for the different permutations of fresh constants. This can have a significant impact on the finite model finding process as to find a model of size n in the iterative setting, we must first refute the preceding $n - 1$ cases and this tends to be much harder in the presence of symmetries.

The problem of introducing symmetries in the encoding process is orthogonal to the well-known problem of identifying existing symmetries in the original problem. In the main part of this paper we look at *avoiding* introducing symmetries in our encoding. At the end of the paper we consider existing work on *identifying and breaking* symmetries. The starting point of our work is that the process of processing each produced SAT problem to identify symmetries (many of which we introduce ourselves) is likely to introduce unnecessary overhead. Our experimental analysis finds that, in general, this is true, but there may be something gained on some problems by exploring a close integration of these techniques into the finite model finding process.

Previous work has considered methods for *avoiding* symmetries in the SAT encoding, but the topic has not received concentrated attention. The main approach (also taken here) is to introduce additional constraints that restrict the ways in which elements of the model may be mapped to the fresh constants. The contributions of this paper are

- a characterisation of the symmetry avoidance problem in our context (Sect. 3). This is an extension of restricted functional symmetry from Paradox [4] which was previously stated in a restricted way and without proof;
- a number of heuristic symmetry breaking constraints (Sect. 4);
- an experimental evaluation using the Vampire theorem prover [12] demonstrating their effectiveness at speeding up the finite model finding process (Sect. 5);
- an experimental study examining the use of static symmetry breaking techniques in our process and comparing these to symmetry avoidance (Sect. 6).

Before we present these contributions we briefly revisit the definition of MACE-style finite model finding (Sect. 2).

A Note on Terminology. In this paper we have chosen to call the addition of additional constraints to *avoid* symmetries introduced by our own encoding *symmetry avoidance* as we are avoiding adding symmetries. This is in contrast to the act of symmetry breaking where inherent symmetries are identified and additional constraints added to break them. We note that prior work [4] used the term symmetry breaking for what we call symmetry avoidance.

2   MACE-Style Finite Model Building for First-Order Logic

In this section we describe the finite model finding procedure (in a single-sorted setting), which is a variation of the approach taken by Paradox [4]. Our presentation here follows the one given in our previous work extending this approach to the multi-sorted setting [16]. For simplicity, we only consider the single-sorted setting here (but our later results lift to the multi-sorted setting).

Given a first-order problem S, the general idea is to create, for each integer $n \geq 1$, a SAT problem that is satisfiable if and only if problem S has a finite model of size n. To find a finite model we iterate over the domain sizes $n = 1, 2, 3, \ldots$. Below we introduce the key conceptual details and the previous work [16] provides further examples.

First-Order Logic. We consider first-order logic with equality. A term is either a variable, a constant, or a function symbol applied to terms. A literal is either a propositional symbol, a predicate applied to terms, an equality of two terms, or a negation of either. The set of function and predicate symbols with associated arities defines the signature of a problem (constants are treated as function symbols with arity zero).

We assume all formulas are *clausified* using standard techniques (e.g. [14] and our recent work in [17]). A *clause* is a disjunction of literals where all variables are universally quantified (existentially quantified variables get replaced by Skolem functions during classification). We assume familiarity with the notion of an *interpretation* and *model* of a set of clauses.

DC-Models. Let S be a set of clauses. Let us fix an integer $n \geq 1$. We extend the language by a set of distinct constants $DC = \{d_1, \ldots, d_n\}$ not occurring in S. We will call these *domain constants*. An interpretation is a *DC-interpretation*, if (i) its domain is DC and (ii) it interprets every domain constant as itself. Every model of S that is also a DC-interpretation will be called a *DC-model* of S. If S has a model of size n, then it also has a DC-model. We say that S is n-satisfiable if it has a model of size n.

A *DC-instance* of a clause C is a ground clause obtained by replacing every variable in C by a constant in DC. A clause with k different variables has exactly n^k DC-instances, where n is the current number of domain constants. Let us denote by S^* the set of all DC-instances of the clauses in S.

Theorem 1. *Let I be a DC-interpretation and C a clause. Then C is true in I if and only if all DC-instances of C are true in I.*

Principal Terms. We cannot yet encode the existence of models of size n as a SAT problem, as DC-instances can contain complex terms.[1] By a *principal term*

---

[1] An alternative to encoding the problem into SAT is to target the EUF logic and use an SMT solver instead. This approach has been explored by Vakili and Day [21].

we mean either a constant or an application of a function symbol of arity greater than zero to domain constants. A ground atom is called *principal* if it is either a predicate symbol applied to domain constants or an equality between a principal term and a domain constant. We lift this notion to literals.

Theorem 2. *Let I_1, I_2 be DC-interpretations. If they satisfy the same principal atoms, then I_1 coincides with I_2.*

Theorem 1 reduces n-satisfiability of S to the existence of a DC-interpretation of the set S^* of ground clauses. Theorem 2 shows that DC-interpretations can be identified by the set of principal atoms true in them. Next we introduce a propositional variable for every principal atom and reduce the existence of a DC-model of S^* to satisfiability of a set of clauses using only principal literals.

The SAT Encoding. The main step in the reduction is to transform every C into an equivalent clause C' such that DC-instances of C' consist (almost) only of principal literals (the exceptions are equalities between domain constants, which can be trivially removed). This transformation is known as *flattening* and ensures that all literals are of the form $p(x_1, \ldots, x_m)$, $f(x_1, \ldots, x_m) = y$, or $x = y$ or their negation. Every DC-instance of a flat literal is either a principal literal (for the first two cases), or an equality $d_i = d_j$ between domain constants. We produce the DC-instances of each flattened clause where we immediately remove inconsistent domain constant equalities and omit instances that are tautologous due to equalities between the same constants.

The DC-instances by themselves do not sufficiently constrain the SAT problem as they do not capture what it means to be a function. To do this we add two further kinds of constraints. For each principal term p and distinct domain constants d_i, d_j we produce the *functionality axiom* $p \neq d_i \lor p \neq d_j$. These clauses guarantee that all function symbols are interpreted as (partial) functions. For each principal term p we produce the *totality axiom* $p = d_1 \lor \ldots \lor p = d_n$. These clauses guarantee, together with functionality axioms, that all function symbols are interpreted as total functions.

The following theorem underpins the SAT-based finite model building method:

Theorem 3. *Let S be a set of flat clauses and S' be the set of clauses obtained from S^* as described above. More specifically, S' consists of (1) the non-tautologous DC-instances of the flattened versions of clauses in S^*, (2) the functionality axioms corresponding to the principal terms, and (3) the totality axiom corresponding to them. Then (i) all literals in S' are principal and (ii) S is n-satisfiable if and only if S' is propositionally satisfiable (when understanding principal atoms as propositional variables).*

3   Characterising Symmetry Avoidance

The SAT problem produced above necessarily contains many symmetries. In particular, every permutation of DC applied to a DC-model will give a DC-model, and there are $n!$ such permutations. This gives the SAT solver more work to do when refuting a model size (which it has to do $k - 1$ times if the smallest model is of size k) as every possible interpretation needs to be refuted.

Isomorphic DC-Models. Let M be a DC-interpretation and σ a permutation of DC, i.e. a bijective function from DC to itself. There is always a DC-interpretation M_σ obtained by "relabelling" the domain constants in M according to σ such that σ is an isomorphism between M and M_σ.[2] For example, consider the clauses

$$f(f(x)) = x \qquad a \neq b$$

that have four possible DC-models captured by the following table

	a	b	$f(d_1)$	$f(d_2)$
1	d_1	d_2	d_1	d_2
2	d_1	d_2	d_2	d_1
3	d_2	d_1	d_1	d_2
4	d_2	d_1	d_2	d_1

where the first line captures the model M represented[3] by the set $\{a = d_1, b = d_2, f(d_1) = d_1, f(d_2) = d_2\}$. The last line is then M_σ for $\sigma = \{d_1 \mapsto d_2, d_2 \mapsto d_1\}$. Similarly, the models represented by lines 2 and 3 are isomorphic under σ.

We can now characterise what we want to achieve via symmetry avoidance: the removal of isomorphic interpretations. To appreciate the following definition, recall that no domain constant $d \in DC$ occurs in S (but some may occur in the introduced constraint $\mathcal{C}$).

Definition 1 (Symmetry Avoidance). *A set of clauses $\mathcal{C}$ is said to be a symmetry avoiding constraint (SAC) if*

(i) not every DC-interpretation is a model of $\mathcal{C}$,
(ii) for every set of clauses S and for every DC-model M of S there is a permutation σ of DC such that M_σ is a DC-model of $S \cup \mathcal{C}$.

For the previous example the constraint $a = d_1$ would remove the isomorphic models represented by lines 3 and 4. This constraint satisfies (i) as we have two DC-interpretations that are not models of it, and (ii) if we focus on this particular set of clauses for S we can see that we have already identified the necessary σ.

The question is then what form the constraint $\mathcal{C}$ should take in general. Here we follow the work of Paradox [4]. We begin by assuming a total ordering on domain constants. We then fix a (finite) sequence of principal terms $\mathcal{P}$ and use this sequence to constrain the permissible DC-models. Let $\mathcal{P} = p_1, \ldots, p_m$. We

---

[2] This means that for every function symbol f of arity a we have $M(f)(d_1, \ldots, d_a) = d$ if and only if $M_\sigma(f)(\sigma(d_1), \ldots, \sigma(d_a)) = \sigma(d)$ and for every predicate symbol p of arity b we have $M(p)(d_1, \ldots, d_b)$ if and only if $M_\sigma(p)(\sigma(d_1), \ldots, \sigma(d_b))$.
[3] Recall that a DC-interpretation can be identified by the set of principal atoms true in it.

want to restrict DC-models such that principal terms are assigned to domain constants *in order*, starting with $p_1 = d_1$. As S may imply equalities between principal terms we cannot straightforwardly assign $p_i = d_i$. Instead, we wish to specify that a principal term p_i is only interpreted as one of the first i domain constants, and, moreover, that the principal term p_i should only be interpreted as d_k if there is some principal term p_j such that $j < i$ and p_j is interpreted as d_{k-1}. This naturally leads to the addition of two kinds of clauses. The first kind is

$$p_i = d_1 \vee \ldots \vee p_i = d_i \tag{1}$$

for $i \le \min(m, n)$. Notice that these take a form of strengthened totality constraints for the respective p_i. The second kind translates to

$$p_i \ne d_j \vee p_1 = d_{j-1} \vee \ldots \vee p_{i-1} = d_{j-1} \tag{2}$$

for $1 < i \le m$ and $2 < j \le i$.[4] Together these capture the above notion of order. Let $C_\mathcal{P}$ be the set of all such clauses.

In our previous example, given $\mathcal{P}$ as $p_1 = a, p_2 = b$ we would add the clauses

$$a = d_1, \qquad b = d_1 \vee b = d_2,$$

which would exclude the models represented by lines 3 and 4 in the previous table. Note that in this case we did not need constraints of the second kind (as previously observed).

Previously [4], this concept was introduced for ordering constants and extended to functions in a restricted sense. However, this previous work did not provide a proof that the approach is sound (does not exclude a possible model).

Let us, for the sake of clarity, also first consider the constant-only setting to later explain how it can be generalized.

Theorem 4. *Let $\mathcal{P} = p_1, \ldots, p_m$ be a non-empty sequence of constant symbols from the problem signature. Then $C_\mathcal{P}$ is a symmetry avoiding constraint.*

Proof. We show both parts of Definition 1. For (i), notice that since $\mathcal{P}$ is non-empty, $C_\mathcal{P}$ contains the unit clause $p_1 = d_1$ as an instance of (1) which is not satisfied by those DC-interpretations that do not map p_1 to d_1. For (ii), given a DC-model M of S we construct σ, a permutation of DC, such that the isomorphic model M_σ additionally satisfies $C_\mathcal{P}$. We do this by describing a construction of the inverse mapping σ^{-1}. This is obviously equivalent, but makes the intuition more transparent.

Let us consider $\mathcal{P}_M = \{M(p_i) \,|\, p_i \in \mathcal{P}\}$, the set of domain constants that are interpretation by M of some element of $\mathcal{P}$, and denote its size by $k = |\mathcal{P}_M|$.[5]

---

[4] For $j = 2$ the clauses contain $p_1 = d_1$ which is always true given (1). For $j > i$ the literal $p_i \ne d_j$ and thus the corresponding constraint (2) follow from (1) and the functionality axioms.

[5] We necessarily have $k \le m$ and $k < m$ implies $M(p_i) = M(p_j)$ for some $i \ne j$.

We set $\sigma^{-1}(d_1) = M(p_1)$ and for every $1 < i \leq k$ we pick $\sigma^{-1}(d_i) = M(p_j)$ for the smallest j such that $M(p_j)$ is not among $\{\sigma^{-1}(d_1), \ldots, \sigma^{-1}(d_{i-1})\}$. By construction, this function is injective and we can complete it to a permutation on DC, if necessary (i.e. if $k < n$), by arbitrarily "pairing up" the remaining $\{d_{k+1}, \ldots, d_n\}$ with the remaining values from $DC \setminus \mathcal{P}_M$. This construction implements the intuitive idea of using the smallest "unused" domain constant d_i for interpreting a term p_i unless it is in the model already taking a value of some "used" domain constant. It is easy to verify that M_σ satisfies both the constraints (1) and (2) and $\mathcal{C}_\mathcal{P}$ is therefore a SAC.   □

The intuition for using general principal terms in $\mathcal{P}$ rather than just constants is that they provide another way of denoting domain elements in the model and may thus help us avoid further symmetries. E.g., we may not have enough constants, or the right constants. However, since non-constant principal terms directly refer to domain constants as arguments, we have an extra complication to deal with: while the construction from the proof of Theorem 4 is making sure it satisfies $\mathcal{C}_\mathcal{P}$ in M_σ, it is looking at the original model M to decide what to do with each next p_i. Thus its natural extension to non-constant terms cannot proceed, unless the arguments of p_i have already established value in M via the partially constructed σ^{-1}.

As an example of this complication, consider the one-element sequence $\mathcal{P}$ with $p_1 = f(d_1)$. Until we decide what d_1 from M_σ refers to in M, i.e. until we define $\sigma^{-1}(d_1)$, the construction cannot proceed.[6] Thus we pick $\sigma^{-1}(d_1)$ arbitrarily at which moment it becomes "used". But if f does not happen to map this domain constant to itself in M, i.e. if $M(f)(\sigma^{-1}(d_1)) \neq \sigma^{-1}(d_1)$, the smallest "unused" domain constant for p_1 in M_σ is d_2, i.e. we set $\sigma^{-1}(d_2) = M(f)(\sigma^{-1}(d_1))$. All in all, in this example, we can only restrict the symmetries by adding the following clause of the first kind (1) to $\mathcal{C}_\mathcal{P}$ on behalf of p_1:

$$f(d_1) = d_1 \vee f(d_1) = d_2,$$

but not the stronger $f(d_1) = d_1$. (It is easy to see how this would become unsound by considering an input problem containing the unit clause $f(x) \neq x$.)

Even if we require that in the sequence $\mathcal{P}$ a domain constant d_j does not occur as an argument of a principal term p_i unless $i > j$ (which solves the above complication), it is not generally sound to add clauses of the second kind (2) for non-constant principal terms. To see this, consider the sequence $\mathcal{P}$ with $p_1 = a, p_2 = f(d_1), p_3 = f(d_2)$ and assume that after the straightforward $\sigma^{-1}(d_1) = M(a)$, we learn that $M(f)(\sigma^{-1}(d_1)) = \sigma^{-1}(d_1)$ and thus we do not need to "use" a new domain constant to process p_2. However, similarly to the previous example, we are now forced to define $\sigma^{-1}(d_2)$ before we can proceed to p_3. Moreover, it is easy to imagine a model M in which any choice of such next element results in $M(f)(\sigma^{-1}(d_2)) \notin \{\sigma^{-1}(d_1), \sigma^{-1}(d_2)\}$ and we are forced to define $\sigma^{-1}(d_3) = M(f)(\sigma^{-1}(d_2))$. Thus the new model M_σ will satisfy $f(d_2) = d_3$, but also $f(d_1) \neq d_2$ and $a \neq d_2$.

---

[6] Speculating what this value could be if we proceed anyway is an interesting direction for further research not covered in this paper.

The following theorem reflects these observations and formalises and further generalises the results reported in [4].

Theorem 5. *Let $\mathcal{P} = p_1, \ldots, p_m$ be a non-empty sequence of principal terms such that whenever a domain constant d_j occurs as an argument of a principal term p_i then $j < i$.[7] Moreover, let the domain constants appear in $\mathcal{P}$ "in order", i.e. if d_j for $j > 0$ occurs in p_i then there is $i' \leq i$ such that d_{j-1} occurs in $p_{i'}$. Let $\mathcal{D_P}$ consist of all the clauses of the first kind (1) and of the clauses of the second kind (2) for any $1 < i \leq m$ and $2 < j \leq i$ such that d_{j-1} does not occur in any $p_{i'}$ for $1 \leq i' \leq i$. Then $\mathcal{D_P}$ is a symmetry avoiding constraint.*

Proof. Let us immediately focus on the sole non-trivial point of Definition 1, namely point (ii). As in the proof of Theorem 4 we recursively construct a permutation σ used for relabelling the elements of a given model M such that M_σ additionally satisfies $\mathcal{D_P}$. And as before, we describe the construction of σ^{-1}. Let us by σ_i^{-1} denote the partial permutation obtained after processing the sequence $\mathcal{P}$ up to element p_i and let us initiate the construction with σ_0^{-1} as the empty mapping.

We now consider the i-th step of the construction for some $1 \leq i \leq m$ assuming σ_{i-1}^{-1} is already defined. First, if there is a domain constant d which occurs in p_i that is not in the domain of σ_{i-1}^{-1}, we pick an arbitrary domain constant e not in the range of σ_{i-1}^{-1} and set $\sigma_i'^{-1} = \sigma_{i-1}^{-1} \cup \{\mathsf{d} \mapsto \mathsf{e}\}$. If this happens, we say that d enters the domain of σ^{-1} to *define an argument* of p_i. We may need to repeat this several times until we obtain τ_i^{-1}, an extension of σ_{i-1}^{-1}, whose domain contains all the domain constants occurring in p_i. Let $p_i = f(\mathsf{d}_1, \ldots, \mathsf{d}_a)$ and let $\mathsf{e} = M(f)(\tau_i^{-1}(\mathsf{d}_1), \ldots, \tau_i^{-1}(\mathsf{d}_a))$. If e is in the range of τ_i^{-1} we set $\sigma_i^{-1} = \tau_i^{-1}$. Otherwise, let d be the least domain constant not in the domain of τ_i^{-1} and we set $\sigma_i^{-1} = \tau_i^{-1} \cup \{\mathsf{d} \mapsto \mathsf{e}\}$. In this case we say that d enters the domain of σ^{-1} to *stand for the value* of p_i. As in the proof of Theorem 4, we obtain the final σ^{-1} from σ_m^{-1} by "pairing up" the remaining domain constants "not yet" in the domain of σ_m^{-1} with the remaining domain constants "not yet" in its range arbitrarily. These domain constants are said to enter the domain of σ^{-1} to *finish it up*.

Let us now verify that M_σ satisfies $\mathcal{D_P}$. We first look at clauses of the first kind (1). These are satisfied, because our construction maintains that the domain of σ_i^{-1}, which contains $M_\sigma(p_i)$, is always a subset of $\{d_1, \ldots, d_i\}$. To see this, we proceed by induction. First, the domain σ_0^{-1} is the empty set. Next, assuming that the domain of σ_{i-1}^{-1} is a subset of $\{d_1, \ldots, d_{i-1}\}$ (the induction hypothesis), we check that the domain of τ_i^{-1} is always a subset of $\{d_1, \ldots, d_{i-1}\}$ using the assumption that whenever a domain constant d_j occurs as an argument of a principal term p_i then $j < i$. To finish, we recall that the construction only possibly adds one more element when extending τ_i^{-1} to σ_i^{-1} and this is always the least domain constant "not yet" in the domain of τ_i^{-1}.

---

[7] In particular, p_1 must be a constant.

Finally, we look at the clauses of the second kind (2). Let $1 < i \leq m$ and $2 < j \leq i$ and let

$$C = (p_i \neq d_j \vee p_1 = d_{j-1} \vee \ldots \vee p_{i-1} = d_{j-1})$$

be one such clause. Let us assume that C is false in M_σ. Because $M_\sigma(p_i) = d_j$, neither the domain constant d_j nor d_{j-1} did enter the domain of σ^{-1} to finish it up. Moreover, since $M_\sigma(p_{i'}) \neq d_{j-1}$ for $1 \leq i' < i$ the domain constant d_{j-1} did not enter the domain of σ^{-1} to stand for the value for any of these $p_{i'}$. Thus d_{j-1} must have entered the domain of σ^{-1} to define an argument of some $p_{i'}$ for $1 \leq i' \leq i$. But then d_{j-1} occurs in some $p_{i'}$ for $1 \leq i' \leq i$ and C thus cannot be part of $\mathcal{D}_P$.   □

4   Symmetry Avoidance Heuristics

The previous section characterised the notion of a symmetry breaking constraint determined by a list of principal terms $\mathcal{P}$. In this section we propose a number of heuristics for selecting a good $\mathcal{P}$. The underlying idea is that as we can only add n clauses of the 'first kind' (1) we want to pick the 'best' n principal terms, i.e. those that avoid most symmetries. The best set $\mathcal{P}$ is such that S together with C_P ensures that each element of $\mathcal{P}$ must be interpreted by a distinct domain constant. However, checking this is impractical and therefore we introduce heuristics for this.

To ensure completeness, we optionally enforce the constraints set out in Theorems 4 and 5 from the previous section by limiting the principal terms added to P where they would otherwise break these constraints. Note that the *diagonal* approach below naturally preserves these constraints in all cases and in most cases it is not necessary to restrict P. We preserve the option to run in an incomplete mode where it is no longer possible to report that a model cannot be found.

Ordering Function Symbols. The first heuristic considers how function symbols should be ordered. Consider the problem $S = \{a = b, a = c, a \neq d\}$, selecting $p_1 = a, p_2 = b$ will not be as effective as selecting $p_1 = a, p_2 = d$. In the first case, the equality $a = b$ induces a stronger constraint than the ordering. In the second case, the ordering constraint is stronger than that induced by the inequality $a \neq d$. We consider the following variations:

- *Occurrence.* By default, function symbols are ordered by their order of appearance in the input problem. This may perform poorly if similar functions (those whose interpretations overlap significantly e.g. principal terms are interpreted as the same domain constants) are defined close together in the input file; conversely it may perform well if differing function symbols are defined close together.
- *Input Usage Frequency.* This orders symbols by their frequency in the input.
- *Preprocessed Usage Frequency.* This orders symbols by their frequency in the pre-processed clauses (pre-processing may copy some symbols many times).

- *Arity.* This orders symbols from the smallest to largest arity. The reasoning here is that it is simpler to show that functions with lower arity are distinct.

The hypothesis around using frequency is that the most used symbols are likely to be distinct. In case the opposite is true, in both frequency cases we also add their reverse. We also consider a *randomised* order.

Ordering the Construction of Principal Terms. We consider how complex principal terms are ordered. One approach is to put all principal terms for one function before those for the other. But if the problem contains, e.g. $f(x) = a$, all principal f- terms already have the same interpretation and cannot be strictly ordered. Conversely, we may wish to order by argument value (all those with d_1 before those with d_2). But if the problem contains, e.g. $f(x) = g(x)$ then again the interpretation of the principal f-terms must agree with the succeeding g-term in the sequence $f(d_1), g(d_1), f(d_2), g(d_2), \ldots$ such that their ordering constraint becomes ineffective. Based on these observations we consider the following variations which make use of an ordering $<_f$ on function symbols and the ordering $<_{DC}$ on domain constants.

- *Function First.* Orders principal term by $<_f$ and then $<_{DC}$
- *Argument First.* Orders principal terms by $<_{DC}$ and then $<_f$
- *Diagonal.* Orders principal terms for each function by $<_{DC}$ and then for each function symbol in turn (according to $<_f$) selects the next principal term *starting* with the ith term for the ith function e.g. we may have $f(d_1), g(d_2), h(d_3), f(d_2), \ldots$.

We also consider a *randomised* order.

Restricting Symmetry Avoidance Clauses. This heuristic does not consider the order of $\mathcal{P}$ but the clauses we add for $\mathcal{P}$. Given principal terms $\mathcal{P}$ and a target model size n, we add n clauses of the first kind and $|\mathcal{P}| \times n$ clauses of the second kind. The large number of these second kind of clauses may become too expensive for the SAT solver. Therefore, by default we restrict $\mathcal{P}$ to have at most n elements and we can optionally add a multiplier k (such that $k \leq |\mathcal{P}| \times n$) to this.

5   Experimental Evaluation

In this section we experimentally address a number of research questions, evaluating the effectiveness of the techniques introduced earlier. Vampire relies on a schedule of strategies for attacking a problem and our evaluation reflects our desire to identify options of complementary strengths, as discussed elsewhere [15].

-fmbsso	-fmbswo	-fmbse
occurrence	**function_first**	0 = $\mathcal{P}$ as defined
input_usage	argument_first	1 = empty $\mathcal{P}$
preprocessed_usage	diagonal	2 = $\mathcal{P}$ restricted to constants
random	random	
reverse_input_usage		
reverse_preprocessed_usage		
arity		

Fig. 1. Option values for symmetry avoiding strategies (defaults in bold).

Experimental Setup. We considered problems from the TPTP [20] library (version 7.0) in the FOF or CNF format that were either (counter-)satisfiable or belong to the effectively propositional (Bernays–Schönfinkel) fragment (as this process is complete for this fragment). We removed all problems known to only have infinite models (determined by Infinox [3]). This led to a set of 2790 problems of which 1512 are known to be satisfiable, 969 are known to be unsatisfiable and 23 are open problems.

The techniques described in the previous sections were implemented in the Vampire theorem prover.[8] The version of Vampire used in these experiments can be found online.[9] Experiments were run on the StarExec cluster [19], whose nodes are equipped with Intel Xeon 2.4 GHz processors and 128 GB of memory. For each experiment we will report the number of problems solved with the time limit of 600 s.

The options related to symmetry avoidance covered were the order of symbols (-fmbsso) and the enumeration strategies between functions applied to domain constants only (-fmbswo). Further, we added options to turn off symmetry avoidance altogether (-fmbse 1) and to order only constants (-fmbse 2). We also limited vampire's proof search strategy to MACE style finite model finding (-sa fmb). Figure 1 summarises the options and their values (which correspond directly to those described in Sect. 4).

Summary. We ran 30 experiments with sensible[10] combinations of the above options. Across all experiments we solved 1901 out of 2790 problems. Out of these 1150 were shown to be satisfiable and 734 were shown to be unsatisfiable. The mean solution time for satisfiable problems was 8.3 s and for unsatisfiable problems it was 9.2 s. Table 1 provides some general statistics. On the left we see the best, mean, and worst solving times for problems. This means that the majority of problems are solved quickly by some strategy. But, only 58 problems were solved by all experiments. There were 264 problems that took longer than 10 s to solve where the difference between best and worst experiment was at

---

[8] https://vprover.github.io/.
[9] https://derivation.org/frocos2019.
[10] Some combinations are not sensible. For example, randomising the ordering of principal terms means that any ordering of function symbols will be ignored.

least 5 s. These are interesting problems as they demonstrate real differences in solution times. Within this set, there is considerable variation between the best and worst solving times. Figure 2 illustrates the distribution of the *speedup* between best and worst strategy on this set. Very large speedups are seen where problems are solved in minutes by one strategy and seconds by another.

Table 1. General statistics about problems solved.

| | # problems solved in X time | | | | |
	< 10s	< 30s	< 1m	< 5m	Total
Best	1715	1797	1828	1888	1901
Mean	1673	1773	1817	1885	1901
Worst	1593	1686	1753	1859	1901

| | # problems solved in X experiments | | | | |
	All	< 25	< 20	< 10	< 5	1
Satisfiable	46	1119	21	15	15	10
Unsatisfiable	12	724	63	2	2	0

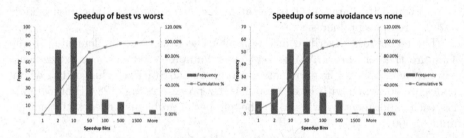

Fig. 2. Histograms of speedups comparing best and worst strategies and no avoidance with best strategy for our 264 interesting problems.

Which Ordering Heuristics Perform Best? Table 2 presents the results for comparing the different ordering heuristics introduced earlier. Since testing all combinations of options would lead to 84 constellations, we always vary one option and leave all others at their respective defaults. In each case we record how many problems that option was the best (fastest) for and what the mean speedup (over the second best) was in the case where the option was the best. Note that each line includes all strategies where that option was selected i.e. more than one experiment. Here we focus explicitly on problems taking >10 s as these are the ones that are, in principle, the harder problems.

Here we can see that the performance of different values is varied. Note that the speedup value addresses the question of how much we gain by adding a single strategy on top of the rest. However, this hides particular outlier cases. For example, the problem HWV052-1.007.004 was solved in 13 s with the diagonal approach, the other principal term orders take at least 535 s, a speedup of a factor of almost 38. Conversely, for NLP077-1.p the diagonal approach took 10% longer.

Table 2. Comparing the different options for ordering heuristics for problems >10 s.

Value	Best	Mean Speedup
occurrence	61	1.04
input_usage	49	1.89
reverse_input_usage	11	1.16
preprocess_usage	44	1.04
reverse_preprocess_usage	13	1.03
arity	12	1.04
random	2	1.01

Value	Best	Mean Speedup
function_first	72	1.06
argument_first	27	1.03
diagonal	36	2.22
random	57	1.03

Of the function ordering options, the reverse frequency options fared worse than the standard frequency options, which supports a hypothesis that it is better to avoid symmetries on common symbols. Interestingly, randomising the order was hardly ever the best approach, suggesting that there is a benefit from our heuristic orderings. We are surprised that the arity option did not fare well. However, this may be attributable to the fact that the majority of functions in problems are typically of low arity anyway.

Of the principal term ordering options, the best approach was the function-first approach. This suggests that problems typically contain functions which are distinct in their arguments. It is interesting to note that the randomisation approach here fared very well. This suggests that there are orderings that perform well outside of our heuristics and we should inspect what elements of these random orders were beneficial and attempt to encode them in new heuristics.

What is the Effect of Limiting Symmetry Avoidance Clauses? Table 3 compares the results of limiting the size of $\mathcal{P}$ as some multiple of n. Here we can see that the number of solved problems increases monotonically. However, the amount of time taken to find solutions varies and in some cases restricting to n provides the best (fastest) solution, whereas including more and more values in

Table 3. Comparing the different values for limiting symmetry avoiding clauses.

Value	Solved	Best	Mean speedup
1	1884	67	5.12
5	1882	127	4.03
10	1883	130	7.71
100	1886	88	4.23
1000	1886	131	9.37

$\mathcal{P}$ can help in other situations. It is interesting to note that for the largest multiplier we see the biggest speedup. This suggests that where a large multiplier can be of use it will make a large difference. We will keep this option and the various values for strategy building.

Does Symmetry Avoidance Always Help? Next we question whether adding symmetry avoidance constraints is always helpful. Overall, there were 96 problems where the fastest solution was to not add symmetry avoiding constraints. On average the next fastest solution was 24% slower. The majority of these were short runs (under 10 s), but in some cases the difference was significant. For example, problem ALG333-1.p was solved in 32 s without symmetry avoiding constraints, but the next best solution solved it in 54 s.

Furthermore, there were many problems only solved using symmetry avoidance. Without symmetry avoidance we only solve 173 of our 264 interesting problems (with 91 unsolved). On these problems, the resulting speedups are given in Fig. 2. Again, we see that symmetry avoidance brings large performance gains. Although there are 12 problems where solving without symmetry avoidance is the best (fastest) strategy.

Our final question is whether restricting symmetry avoiding constraints to constants only has any benefit, or conversely whether there are cases where we need to avoid symmetries on non-constant terms. There were 55 problems where it was better (i.e. the solution was faster) to exclude non-function symbols from symmetry avoiding. This means that ordering principal terms is an interesting research question.

How Does this Compare to Paradox? Finally, we compare our results to Paradox. Overall, Paradox solves 48 problems that we do not solve and we solve 54 problems unsolved by Paradox. All 54 of these problems rely on symmetry avoidance options. Of the interesting problems, roughly half (145) are solved more quickly by Paradox and the rest are solved more quickly by Vampire, out of these 36 problems are solved at least 10 times faster with Vampire.

Discussion. The above experimental results show that the issue of symmetry avoiding is important and that a portfolio solver such as Vampire needs many options available to it. These experiments have allowed us to *prioritise* options within our portfolio and suggest further exploration is required. In particular, we need to explore the correlation between the success of symmetry avoiding heuristics and the structure of properties, especially the number and distribution of function symbols with different arities.

6   Comparing Symmetry Breaking and Symmetry Avoidance

So far we have focussed on avoiding introducing new symmetries into the SAT problem. There also exist tools for identifying symmetries in SAT problems. In the final part of this paper we utilise one such tool to answer the following two questions:

1. Could incorporating static symmetry breaking improve the performance of finite model finding?
2. Are symmetry avoidance and symmetry breaking complementary (i.e. do the avoidance constraints help symmetry breaking) or is avoidance subsumed by breaking?

The Symmetry Breaking Problem. The symmetry breaking problem is similar to the symmetry avoiding one, but in a more general setting. Slightly informally, given a SAT problem S is it possible to produce some constraints C such that

Table 4. Comparing solving with and without breaking. T/O means timeout and BiD means BreakID.

Without Breaking			With Breaking				Gained		Lost		Loss/Gain
Sat	Unsat	T/O	Sat	Unsat	T/O (BiD)	T/O (Sat)	Sat	Unsat	Sat	Unsat	
1,194	12,919	423	954	11,991	1,435	156	3	191	262	1,171	7.39

Table 5. Solving statistics by SAT problem. T/O means timeout and BiD means BreakID.

Options	Total	Without BreakID			With BreakID				Gained		Lost		Loss/Gain
		Sat	Unsat	T/O	Sat	Unsat	T/O (BiD)	T/O (Sat)	Sat	Unsat	Sat	Unsat	
prepro, ff	13,791	1,289	12,242	260	1,067	11,441	1,062	221	4	15	230	831	55.84
occ, ff	13,788	1,272	12,254	262	1,062	11,421	1,063	221	2	15	224	861	63.82

the models of S and $S \cup C$ are the same up to isomorphism, but there are fewer models of $S \cup C$. The problem of symmetries has been studied extensively in the constraint programming, the ASP and the SAT communities [9,10,18]. The main differentiation of the techniques lies between dynamic [2,22,23] and static [1,7] symmetry breaking. The dynamic setting aims to identify and break symmetries during the solving process whilst the static setting updates the problem directly. In this work we focus on one of the best existing static symmetry breaking tools BreakID [7].

Experimental Setup. We select the same 2970 problems as in Sect. 5 and run finite-model finding on each problem for 60 s, recording the SAT problems produced for each model size in the DIMACS format [11]. Note that for each problem where we explore up to model size n we will produce at least $n - 1$ unsatisfiable SAT problems. Therefore, the majority of the SAT problems will be unsatisfiable.

We then run the BreakID static symmetry breaker [7] on each SAT problem for 60 s. BreakID produces a copy of the problem with additional constraints added that break identified symmetries in the problem. This will cover both symmetries in the original problem and any symmetries introduced via our encoding. Finally, we run Minisat [8] on each SAT problem (this is the SAT solver used by Vampire internally).

We repeat the above experiment for different heuristics. To establish a baseline, we start without symmetry avoidance and investigate symbol orders by occurrence and preprocessed_usage that fared well before (see Table 2). In both cases we construct terms by functions first. The system used for the experiments is an Intel Xeon E5520 with 2.27 GHz and 16 GB memory.

6.1   The Effect of Symmetry Breaking

First we look at the effect that static symmetry breaking can have on the finite-model finding process independently of our symmetry avoidance heuristics. Running finite-model finding using the default strategy (without symmetry avoidance) produces 14,536 SAT problems. Table 4 reports the difference between running with and without static symmetry breaking. Overall, more problems are solved without symmetry breaking than with. However, this is mainly due to the timing out of the static symmetry breaking process. There are 194 SAT problems that are solved with static symmetry breaking that were not solved without it. This represents an opportunity for making further progress in the finite model finding process. As expected, this has a far greater effect on the unsatisfiable problems, which will partly be due to the fact that over 80% of problems are unsatisfiable and partly due to the fact that these are fundamentally harder.

In this we spent 60 s on static symmetry breaking and 60 s on SAT solving. The next question to ask is whether the time spent on static symmetry breaking can be justified. In 1,811 experiments the time spent on breaking and solving combined is roughly equivalent to that of solving by itself without breaking. In 1,062 problems the solution was faster without breaking, leaving 56 problems where the combination of breaking and solving performed faster than solving without breaking.

This experiment shows that whilst static symmetry breaking can help on a small number of problems, in general it reduces performance.

6.2 Comparing Breaking and Avoidance

Next we want to see what happens when we combine the symmetry avoiding heuristics with static symmetry breaking. To do this we run the two best symmetry avoiding strategies from the previous section and repeat the above experiment.

Table 5 reports only 13,791 and 13,788 generated files. This is due to the time spent in symmetry avoidance. Compared to the baseline, there are fewer time-outs and solved unsatisfiable problems, but more satisfiable ones. The rate of time-outs (1,062 and 1,063) during symmetry breaking is also similar, which leads to a high number of lost solutions. However, the number of solutions gained by symmetry breaking over avoidance is significantly lower (19 and 17). This suggests that symmetry avoidance was already having a significant impact on solving times.

It is possible that the distinction between solutions gained and lost is too rough. Next we investigate the speed-ups in timing between problems of unsatisfiable solutions for pairs of symmetry-avoidance and symmetry-breaking options. We also restrict the problems to those where the model size is larger than the number of constants. In these cases, not all domain constants can be assigned to input constants which leaves room for the different symmetry orders with regard to functions. Table 6 shows the number of problems that were solved faster and slower. The time for BreakID includes the time taken for static symmetry breaking. Most timings were sufficiently close that jitter effects could tip the balance either way. For this reason all results within 2 s were excluded.

When applying BreakId, about 10% of the SAT problems cannot be processed within the 60 s time limit of the full input problem. This leads to a high ratio of problems lost due to symmetry breaking against the new solutions gained.

Table 6. Pairwise comparison of SAT problems with model size > number of constants

A	B	A slower than B	A faster than B	Too close
baseline	preprocessed, ff	147	16	1,063
baseline	occ, ff	145	16	1,064
preprocessed, ff	occ, ff	0	0	1,640
baseline	baseline+BreakId	56	1,062	1,811
preprocessed, ff	preprocessed, ff+BreakId	13	408	1,139
occ, ff	preprocessed, ff+BreakId	13	405	1,139
baseline+BreakId	preprocessed, ff+BreakId	279	7	877
baseline+BreakId	occ, ff+BreakId	276	7	870
preprocessed, ff+BreakId	occ, ff+BreakId	0	0	1,550

There is also a consistent disparity in the gain/loss ratio between satisfiable and unsatisfiable problems. Two factors could contribute to this phenomenon. First, the separation into symmetry breaking and SAT solving comes with a significant overhead in parsing and duplication of data structures. Moreover, BreakId itself depends on the automorphism library saucy [5,6] which leads to another duplication of data-structures. Second, we need to take the whole sequence of models generated into account. When BreakId times out already for small model sizes the larger model sizes are likely to follow. This artificially amplifies the number of lost unsatisfiable solutions. On the other hand, the satisfiable solutions depend more strongly on the heuristics of the SAT solver which leads to less predictable timings.

As a consequence, we compare the gains and losses between the baseline and the two symmetry orders as well. The baseline loses about 7 times as many problems as gained by symmetry breaking. Both the preprocessed and occurrence symmetry order retain a similar number of lost problems. Also the number of satisfiable problems gained is similar to the baseline. The main improvement of symmetry avoidance lies with the unsatisfiable lost problems where more than 90% of the problems gained versus the baseline can be recovered by the heuristics.

Most results are indistinguishable. Both symmetry avoidance options tend to speed solving up more than slowing it down when compared to the baseline, but they themselves are indistinguishable. Even without time-outs, symmetry breaking tends to be slower than symmetry avoidance. Combining symmetry breaking and symmetry avoidance mostly improves the solving times. Again there is no distinguishable difference between the two avoidance options.

6.3 Discussion

We summarise answers to our two initial research questions. Symmetry breaking can help solve more problems, but in the majority of cases, the cost of static symmetry breaking is higher than symmetry avoidance. When considered alongside symmetry avoidance, the benefits of symmetry breaking are more modest, suggesting that overall the effort of incorporating these techniques directly into the finite model finding process may not be worthwhile.

7 Conclusion and Future Work

In this paper, we have characterised the symmetry avoidance problem for MACE-style finite model finding, suggested a number of sound heuristics for symmetry avoidance, and experimentally evaluated these heuristics. We found that some of these variations can significantly speed up the finite model finding process. Finally, we looked at whether directly identifying and breaking symmetries in the SAT problems would give any further improvements. In further work we would like to explore further heuristics and the correlation between the ordering heuristics and the signature of a problem.

Acknowledgement. We thank the anonymous reviewers for critically reading the paper and suggesting substantial improvements.

References

1. Aloul, F.A., Markov, I.L., Sakallah, K.A.: Shatter: efficient symmetry-breaking for Boolean satisfiability. In: Proceedings of the 40th Design Automation Conference, DAC 2003, Anaheim, CA, USA, 2–6 June 2003, pp. 836–839 (2003)
2. Audemard, G., Henocque, L.: The eXtended least number heuristic. In: Goré, R., Leitsch, A., Nipkow, T. (eds.) IJCAR 2001. LNCS, vol. 2083, pp. 427–442. Springer, Heidelberg (2001). https://doi.org/10.1007/3-540-45744-5_35
3. Claessen, K., Lillieström, A.: Automated inference of finite unsatisfiability. J. Autom. Reason. **47**(2), 111–132 (2011)
4. Claessen, K., Sörensson, N.: New techniques that improve MACE-style model finding. In: CADE-19 Workshop: Model Computation - Principles, Algorithms and Applications (2003)
5. Darga, P.T., Katebi, H., Liffiton, M., Markov, I.L., Sakallah, K.: Saucy. http://vlsicad.eecs.umich.edu/BK/SAUCY
6. Darga, P T., Liffiton, M.H., Sakallah, K.A., Markov, I.L.: Exploiting structure in symmetry detection for CNF. In: Proceedings of the 41st Design Automation Conference, DAC 2004, San Diego, CA, USA, 7–11 June 2004, pp. 530–534. ACM (2004)
7. Devriendt, J., Bogaerts, B., Bruynooghe, M., Denecker, M.: Improved static symmetry breaking for SAT. In: Creignou, N., Le Berre, D. (eds.) SAT 2016. LNCS, vol. 9710, pp. 104–122. Springer, Cham (2016). https://doi.org/10.1007/978-3-319-40970-2_8
8. Eén, N., Sörensson, N.: An extensible SAT-solver. In: Giunchiglia, E., Tacchella, A. (eds.) SAT 2003. LNCS, vol. 2919, pp. 502–518. Springer, Heidelberg (2004). https://doi.org/10.1007/978-3-540-24605-3_37
9. Gebser, M., Kaminski, R., Kaufmann, B., Schaub, T.: Answer set solving in practice. In: Synthesis Lectures on Artificial Intelligence and Machine Learning. Morgan & Claypool Publishers, San Rafael (2012)
10. Gent, I.P., Petrie, K.E., Puget, J.: Symmetry in constraint programming. In: Handbook of Constraint Programming, pp. 329–376 (2006)
11. SAT Competitions: SAT Competition 2009: Benchmark Submission Guidelines. https://www.satcompetition.org/2009/format-benchmarks2009.html

12. Kovács, L., Voronkov, A.: First-order theorem proving and VAMPIRE. In: Sharygina, N., Veith, H. (eds.) CAV 2013. LNCS, vol. 8044, pp. 1–35. Springer, Heidelberg (2013). https://doi.org/10.1007/978-3-642-39799-8_1

13. Mccune, W.: A Davis-Putnam program and its application to finite first-order model search: quasigroup existence problems. Technical report, Argonne National Laboratory (1994)

14. Nonnengart, A., Weidenbach, C.: Computing small clause normal forms. In: Handbook of Automated Reasoning (in 2 volumes), pp. 335–367 (2001)

15. Reger, G., Suda, M., Voronkov, A.: The challenges of evaluating a new feature in vampire. In: Proceedings of the 1st and 2nd Vampire Workshops. EPiC Series in Computing, vol. 38, pp. 70–74. EasyChair (2016)

16. Reger, G., Suda, M., Voronkov, A.: Finding finite models in multi-sorted first-order logic. In: Creignou, N., Le Berre, D. (eds.) SAT 2016. LNCS, vol. 9710, pp. 323–341. Springer, Cham (2016). https://doi.org/10.1007/978-3-319-40970-2_20

17. Reger, G., Suda, M., Voronkov, A.: New techniques in clausal form generation. In: GCAI 2016, 2nd Global Conference on Artificial Intelligence. EPiC Series in Computing, vol. 41, pp. 11–23. EasyChair (2016)

18. Sakallah, K.A.: Symmetry and satisfiability. In: Handbook of Satisfiability, pp. 289–338 (2009)

19. Stump, A., Sutcliffe, G., Tinelli, C.: StarExec, a cross community logic solving service (2012). https://www.starexec.org

20. Sutcliffe, G.: The TPTP problem library and associated infrastructure. J. Autom. Reason. **43**(4), 337–362 (2009)

21. Vakili, A., Day, N.A.: Finite model finding using the logic of equality with uninterpreted functions. In: Fitzgerald, J., Heitmeyer, C., Gnesi, S., Philippou, A. (eds.) FM 2016. LNCS, vol. 9995, pp. 677–693. Springer, Cham (2016). https://doi.org/10.1007/978-3-319-48989-6_41

22. Zhang, J., Zhang, H.: SEM: a system for enumerating models. In: IJCAI 1995, pp. 298–303 (1995)

23. Zhang, J., Zhang, H.: System description generating models by SEM. In: McRobbie, M.A., Slaney, J.K. (eds.) CADE 1996. LNCS, vol. 1104, pp. 308–312. Springer, Heidelberg (1996). https://doi.org/10.1007/3-540-61511-3_96

On the Expressivity and Applicability of Model Representation Formalisms

Andreas Teucke[1,2], Marco Voigt[1,2], and Christoph Weidenbach[1(✉)]

[1] Max Planck Institute for Informatics,
Saarland Informatics Campus E1 4, 66123 Saarbrücken, Germany
andreas.teucke@prostep.de, {mvoigt,weidenbach}@mpi-inf.mpg.de
[2] Graduate School of Computer Science, Saarbrücken, Germany

Abstract. A number of first-order calculi employ an explicit model representation formalism in support of non-redundant inferences and for detecting satisfiability. Many of these formalisms can represent infinite Herbrand models. The first-order fragment of monadic, shallow, linear, Horn (MSLH) clauses, is such a formalism used in the approximation refinement calculus (AR). Our first result is a finite model property for MSLH clause sets. Therefore, MSLH clause sets cannot represent models of clause sets with inherently infinite models. Through a translation to tree automata, we further show that this limitation also applies to the linear fragments of implicit generalizations, which is the formalism used in the model-evolution calculus (ME), to atoms with disequality constraints, the formalisms used in the non-redundant clause learning calculus (NRCL), and to atoms with membership constraints, a formalism used for example in decision procedures for algebraic data types. Although these formalisms cannot represent models of clause sets with inherently infinite models, through an additional approximation step they can. This is our second main result. For clause sets including the definition of an equivalence relation with the help of an additional, novel approximation, called reflexive relation splitting, the approximation refinement calculus can automatically show satisfiability through the MSLH clause set formalism.

1 Introduction

Proving satisfiability of a first-order clause set is more difficult than proving unsatisfiability, in general. Still, for many applications the detection of failing refutations by establishing a counter model is more than desirable. In the past, several methods, calculi and systems have been presented that can detect satisfiability of a clause set, in particular, if there is a finite model that is not too large. The approaches can be separated into the following classes:

(1) the model building is integrated into a first-order calculus or a decision procedure for some fragment, directly operating on the first-order clause set, complete for unsatisfiability, e.g., [1,3,5,6,8,19,23],

A. Herzig and A. Popescu (Eds.): FroCoS 2019, LNAI 11715, pp. 22–39, 2019.
https://doi.org/10.1007/978-3-030-29007-8_2

(2) the model building is integrated into a first-order calculus that operates on the first-order clause set modulo an approximation, complete for unsatisfiability, e.g., [14,16,27],

(3) the model building aims at finding finite models without being complete for unsatisfiability, e.g., [9,17,21],

(4) the model building aims at finding finite and infinite models without being complete for unsatisfiability, e.g., [18],

where superposition [2] does not belong to any of the above classes, because the model building is implicit and reached by a finite saturation of the clause set modulo inferences and the elimination of redundant clauses.

The approaches in classes (1) and (2) select inferences with respect to the explicit (partial) model by identifying a false clause (instance). Therefore, the representation of models needs to be effective, e.g., falsity of a clause (instance) with respect to the model needs to be (efficiently) decidable.

For superposition it is undecidable whether a clause is false with respect to a saturated clause set, in general. This can be seen by a reduction through the Post Correspondence Problem (PCP) [20]. The clause set consisting of $R(\epsilon, \epsilon)$ and clauses $R(x, y) \rightarrow R(t_i[x], s_i[y])$ where the t_i, s_i are terms built over the monadic functions g, h and variables x, y, respectively, is saturated with strictly maximal atoms $R(t_i[x], s_i[y])$ and encodes the words $(w_1, \ldots, w_n)$, $(v_1, \ldots, v_n)$ generated by a PCP over letters g, h. That means words are represented by nestings of monadic functions. The PCP has a solution iff a ground atom $R(g(t), g(t))$ or $R(h(t), h(t))$ is a consequence of the above clause set. This corresponds to testing whether one of the clauses $R(g(x), g(x))$ or $R(h(x), h(x))$ has a false instance with respect to the implicit model of the saturated PCP clause set.

Reasoning with respect to a (partial) model assumption has advantages. The superposition completeness proof shows that an inference with a clause that is false in the current partial model is not redundant [2]. This has meanwhile also been shown for the CDCL [30] and the NRCL [1] calculus. The non-redundant inference property might also hold for other calculi of classes (1) and (2). It requires exhaustive model generation and eager conflict detection.

Our first contribution is showing that the model representation used in [27], monadic shallow linear Horn clauses (MSLH) has the finite model property, Sect. 3. This means that if a finite MSLH clause set has a model, it also has a finite model. Hence, MSLH clause sets cannot be used directly to represent models of clause sets with inherently infinite models. A further consequence is that any calculus in class (1), where the model representation can be represented by an MSLH clause set, cannot terminate on satisfiable clause sets with inherently infinite models. A more detailed discussion of this aspect is contained in Sect. 4.

The fact that MSLH clause sets have the finite model property does not mean that the approximation refinement (AR) calculus presented in [27] cannot be used for finding infinite models of clause sets with inherently infinite models. The reason is that the MSLH model representation in [27] does not directly relate to a model of the original clause set, but via an approximation. For the approximation it is shown in a constructive way that it preserves satisfiability.

This is done modulo the *minimal* Herbrand model of a saturated MSLH clause set. Such Herbrand models become infinite as soon as there are non-constant function symbols. So the question is whether AR can actually terminate on clause sets with inherently infinite models. In Sect. 5, we show that this is the case for certain classes of such clause sets relying on reflexivity of a binary (equivalence) relation. The technique we propose is an additional approximation called *reflexive relation splitting*. A similar relationship between a clause set and its approximation was already observed in [18] where an approximation of a first-order clause set into a class of tree automata is used in order to find finite and infinite models.

Our results concerning the MSLH fragment and the reflexive relation splitting modulo the AR calculus can be demonstrated by the following example. Consider the following three clauses defining a reflexive binary relation R (see [8], page 55 for further discussion of this example).

$$\{R(x,x), \quad R(g(x),g(y)) \to R(x,y), \quad \neg R(g(x),c)\}$$

This set has only infinite models. No resolution inference between $R(x,x)$ and $\neg R(g(x),c)$ is possible. Following the AR approach [27], the MSLH clause set

$$\{T(f_R(x,y)), \quad T(f_R(g(x),g(y))) \to T(f_R(x,y)), \quad \neg T(f_R(g(x),c))\}$$

is generated. We write unit clauses as single literals, and non-unit clauses as implications. The relation R is translated into a binary function f_R over a monadic predicate T. The approximation is the replacement of $R(x,x)$ by $T(f_R(x,y))$, where now the connection between the non-linear occurrences of x is lost. As a consequence, a refutation containing a resolution step between $T(f_R(x,y))$ and $\neg T(f_R(g(x),c))$ with substitution $\{x \mapsto g(v), y \mapsto c\}$ is possible, which cannot be lifted to the original clause set because $g(v)$ and c are not unifiable. The refinement then excludes this particular instance by generating $R(g(x),g(x))$, however, after approximating this clause, the empty clause can be derived again. This time the derivation also uses the second clause, where the substitution instance of the refutation contains one further nesting of g. The approximation refinement approach does not terminate on this example.

If in the approximation the inference between $T(f_R(x,x))$ and $\neg T(f_R(g(x),c))$ can be blocked, saturation will terminate without finding a contradiction. As said, in the original clause set this inference is not possible, because of the non-linear occurrence of x. Now the idea is to split the relation R into its reflexive and irreflexive part, denoted by the two predicates R_{ref} and R_{irr}. The original clause set is satisfiable if and only if the following clause set is satisfiable

$$\{R_{\text{ref}}(x,x), \quad R_{\text{irr}}(g(x),g(y)) \to R_{\text{irr}}(x,y), \quad \neg R_{\text{irr}}(g(x),c)\},$$

details are explained in Sect. 5. After approximation it becomes

$$\{T(f_{R_{\text{ref}}}(x,y))^*, T(f_{R_{\text{irr}}}(g(x),g(y)))^+ \to T(f_{R_{\text{irr}}}(x,y)), \neg T(f_{R_{\text{irr}}}(g(x),c))^*\} \quad (\dagger)$$

where $*$ highlights maximal and $^+$ selected literals of the ordered resolution calculus used to decide MSLH clauses [26,27]. There are no possible inferences generating further clauses, i.e. the set is already saturated.

The infinite minimal Herbrand model is $\mathcal{I} = \{T(f_{R_{\text{ref}}}(g^i(c), g^j(c))) \mid i, j \geq 0\}$ which is also a model for the clause set before approximation [26,27] by simply undoing the shift of R_{irr}, R_{ref} to the function level: $\mathcal{I} = \{R_{\text{ref}}(g^i(c), g^j(c))) \mid i, j \geq 0\}$. Nestings of functions in the Herbrand model representing relations, e.g., $f_{R_{\text{ref}}}$, can be prevented by adding further MSLH clauses. We omit these here for simplicity. This model can then be translated, see the proof of Lemma 9, into the Herbrand model $\mathcal{I} = \{R(g^i(c), g^i(c))) \mid i \geq 0\}$ of the original clause set.

In Sect. 3, we prove a finite model property for saturated, satisfiable MSLH clause sets. For the example, see (†), the thus constructed model has the domain $A := \{a_c, a^{(1)}, a^{(2)}, a^{(3)}, b^{(1)}, b^{(2)}, b^{(3)}\}$. The predicate T is interpreted with the set $\{b^{(1)}, b^{(2)}, b^{(3)}\}$. For the constant c we use the distinguished element a_c. The interpretation of the function $f_{R_{\text{ref}}}$ is given in the following function table:

$$\langle a_c, a_c \rangle \longmapsto b^{(1)}$$
$$\langle a^{(i)}, a^{(i)} \rangle \longmapsto b^{(j)} \quad \text{for every } i \text{ and some } j \neq i$$
$$\langle b^{(i)}, b^{(i)} \rangle \longmapsto b^{(j)} \quad \text{for every } i \text{ and some } j \neq i$$
$$\langle c, d \rangle \longmapsto a^{(j)} \quad \text{for any c, d} \in A \text{ with c} \neq \text{d and}$$
$$\text{some } j \text{ chosen such that for any } i,$$
$$\text{if c or d is equal to } a^{(i)} \text{ or } b^{(i)}, \text{ then } j \neq i$$

For the function $f_{R_{\text{irr}}}$ we get a similar function table in which every pair $\langle c, d \rangle$ is mapped to some $a^{(j)}$, where j is chosen such that c, d $\neq a^{(j)}$. Finally, the interpretation of the function g is given by $g(a_c) = a^{(1)}$, $g(a^{(i)}) = a^{(j)}$ and $g(b^{(i)}) = a^{(j)}$ for every i and some $j \neq i$.

The paper is now organized as follows: after fixing some notions and notations, Sect. 2, the finite model property of MSLH clause sets is shown in Sect. 3. Consequences of this result for other model representation formalisms are discussed in Sect. 4. In Sect. 5 reflexive relation splitting is introduced and its application to AR investigated. The present paper ends with a discussion on the obtained results and future research directions, Sect. 6. Due to space limitations, not all proof details could be included. The interested reader will find the full details in the extended preprint [25].

2 Preliminaries

We consider a standard first-order language without equality where letters $v, w,$ x, y, z denote variables, f, g, h functions, a, b, c constants, s, t terms, and Greek letters σ, τ, ρ are used for substitutions. S, P, Q, R denote predicates, A, B atoms, E, K, L literals, C, D clauses, N clause sets and $\mathcal{V}$ sets of variables. The notation $[\neg]A$ denotes A or its negation. The signature $\Sigma = (\mathcal{F}, \mathcal{P})$ consists of two disjoint, non-empty, in general infinite sets of function and predicate symbols $\mathcal{F}$ and $\mathcal{P}$, respectively. The set of all *terms* over the variables in $\mathcal{V}$ is $\mathcal{T}(\mathcal{F}, \mathcal{V})$. If there are no variables, then terms, literals and clauses are called *ground*, respectively. A *substitution* σ is denoted by pairs $\{x \mapsto t\}$. A substitution σ is a *grounding* substitution for a term, atom, literal, clause if the application of σ yields a ground term, ground atom, ground literal, ground clause, respectively.

The set of *free* variables of an atom A (term t, literal L, clause C) is denoted by $\text{vars}(A)$ ($\text{vars}(t), \text{vars}(L), \text{vars}(C)$). A predicate with exactly one argument is called *monadic*. A term is *complex* if it is not a variable and *shallow* if it is a constant, a variable, or of the form $f(x_1, \ldots, x_n)$. A term, atom is called *linear* if there are no duplicate variable occurrences.

A *clause* is a multiset of literals which we write as an implication $\Gamma \to \Delta$ where the atoms in the multiset Δ (the *succedent*) denote the positive literals and the atoms in the multiset Γ (the *antecedent*) the negative literals. Alternatively, we write a clause also as a disjunction of its literals. We write $\square$ for the empty clause. We abbreviate disjoint set union with sequencing, for example, we write $\Gamma, \Gamma' \to \Delta, L$ instead of $\Gamma \cup \Gamma' \to \Delta \cup \{L\}$. A clause $\Gamma \to \Delta$ is called an *MSLH* clause, if (i) Δ contains at most one atom, i.e., the clause is Horn, (ii) all occurring predicates are monadic, (iii) the argument of any monadic atom in Δ is shallow and linear. The first-order fragment consisting of finite MSLH clause sets we call *MSLH*.

An *atom ordering* $\prec$ is an irreflexive, well-founded, total ordering on ground atoms. It is lifted to literals by defining $A \prec \neg A \prec B$ for any atoms A, B with $A \prec B$. It is lifted to clauses by its multiset extension. The ordering is lifted from the ground level through ground instantiation: for two different atoms A, B containing variables, $A \prec B$ if $A\sigma \prec B\sigma$ for all grounding substitutions σ and the atoms are incomparable otherwise. A literal L is *maximal* (*strictly maximal*) in a clause $C \vee L$ if there is no literal $K \in C$ with $L \prec K$ ($L \preceq K$). The clause ordering is compatible with the atom ordering; if the maximal atom in C is greater than the maximal atom in D then $D \prec C$. We use $\prec$ simultaneously to denote an atom ordering and its multiset, literal, and clause extensions. For a ground clause set N and clause C, the set $N^{\prec C} = \{D \in N \mid D \prec C\}$ denotes the clauses of N smaller than C.

As usual, we interpret atoms, clauses, and clause sets with respect to *structures* $\mathcal{A}$, also called *interpretations*, consisting of a nonempty universe A and interpretations $c^{\mathcal{A}}$, $f^{\mathcal{A}}$, and $P^{\mathcal{A}}$ of all occurring constants, functions, and predicates. We often use a special kind of interpretations, called *Herbrand interpretations*, whose universe is the set of all ground terms. A *Herbrand interpretation* $\mathcal{I}$ is represented by a – possibly infinite – set of ground atoms. A ground atom A is *true* in $\mathcal{I}$ if $A \in \mathcal{I}$ and *false*, otherwise. $\mathcal{I}$ is said to *satisfy* a ground clause $C = \Gamma \to \Delta$, denoted by $\mathcal{I} \vDash C$, if $\Delta \cap \mathcal{I} \neq \emptyset$ or $\Gamma \not\subseteq \mathcal{I}$. A non-ground clause C is satisfied by $\mathcal{I}$ if $\mathcal{I} \vDash C\sigma$ for every grounding substitution σ. An interpretation $\mathcal{I}$ is called a *model* of N, $\mathcal{I} \vDash N$, if $\mathcal{I} \vDash C$ for every $C \in N$. A Herbrand model $\mathcal{I}$ of N is considered *minimal* (with respect to set inclusion) if there is no model $\mathcal{I}'$ with $\mathcal{I}' \subset \mathcal{I}$ and $\mathcal{I}' \vDash N$. A set of clauses N is *satisfiable*, if there exists a model that satisfies N. Otherwise, the set is *unsatisfiable*.

The superposition calculus [2] restricted to first-order logic without equality results in the ordered resolution calculus together with the superposition redundancy criterion and partial model operator, see below. For ordered resolution, a selection function is assumed that may select negative literals in clauses. Then $(C \vee D)\sigma$ is an ordered resolution inference between a clause $C \vee A$ and a clause $D \vee \neg B$, if (i) σ is the mgu between A and B, (ii) $A\sigma$ is strictly maximal in $(C \vee A)\sigma$ and nothing is selected in $C \vee A$, (iii) $\neg B\sigma$ is maximal in $(D \vee \neg B)\sigma$ or selected. The clause $(C \vee A)\sigma$ is an ordered factoring inference on a clause $C \vee A \vee A'$, if (i) σ is the mgu between A and A', (ii) $A\sigma$ is maximal in $(C \vee A)\sigma$ and nothing is selected in $C \vee A \vee A'$. Selection is stable under instantiation, i.e., if $\neg A$ is selected in $\neg A \vee C$ it is also selected in $(\neg A \vee C)\sigma$, for any substitution σ. A clause C is *redundant* with respect to a clause set N, if for all ground instances $C\sigma$ there are ground instances $D_1\sigma_1, \ldots, D_n\sigma_n$, $\{D_1, \ldots, D_n\} \subseteq N$, $D_i\sigma_i \prec C\sigma$ for all i, such that $D_1\sigma_1, \ldots, D_n\sigma_n \models C\sigma$, i.e., $C\sigma$ is implied by smaller ground instances from clauses in N. A clause set N is called *saturated* if all clauses generated by ordered resolution or ordered factoring from clauses in N are either redundant or contained in N. Given a ground clause set N and an ordering $\prec$ we can construct a (partial) Herbrand model $N_\mathcal{I}$ for N by the superposition (partial) model operator inductively as follows:

$$N_C := \bigcup_{D \prec C} \delta_D$$

$$\delta_D := \begin{cases} \{P(t_1, \ldots, t_n)\} & \text{if } D = D' \vee P(t_1, \ldots, t_n), P(t_1, \ldots, t_n) \text{ strictly maxi-} \\ & \text{mal in } D, \text{ no literal selected in } D \text{ and } N_D \not\models D \\ \emptyset & \text{otherwise} \end{cases}$$

$$N_\mathcal{I} := \bigcup_{C \in N} \delta_C$$

Clauses C with $\delta_C \neq \emptyset$ are called *productive*. For a non-ground clause set N we define $N_\mathcal{I} := (\{C\sigma \mid C \in N, \sigma \text{ grounding for } C\})_\mathcal{I}$. The main completeness result of superposition is: for a clause set N let N^* be its (possibly infinite) saturation, then either $\square \in N^*$ and N is unsatisfiable, or $N_\mathcal{I}^* \models N$ [2].

Basically, inferences of the superposition calculus are restricted to maximal, or selected negative literals. If all non-redundant inferences of a clause set are performed, i.e., the clause set is saturated, then the superposition model operator generates an overall model for the clause set.

3   MSLH Model Properties

By definition, Herbrand models for MSLH clause sets with non-constant function symbols have an infinite domain. In what follows we show how to construct non-Herbrand models with finite domains for satisfiable finite MSLH clause sets. The constructed model is a finite representation of the *minimal Herbrand model*.

Consider a satisfiable finite MSLH clause set N. It is known that N can be finitely saturated using superposition (ordered resolution) with an appropriate ordering and selection strategy such that the following property holds for the obtained saturated clause set N^* [29]. Every clause C in N^* that is productive in the sense of the superposition model operator has the form $C = P_1(x_1), \ldots, P_n(x_n) \rightarrow S(f(y_1, \ldots, y_m))$ where $\{x_1, \ldots, x_n\} \subseteq \{y_1, \ldots, y_m\}$,

$f(y_1, \ldots, y_m)$ is linear, and $S(f(y_1, \ldots, y_m))$ is strictly maximal in C. Such a saturation can, e.g., be obtained by choosing for $\prec$ a Knuth-Bendix-Ordering (KBO) with weight one for all function symbols, variables, and a selection strategy that selects a negative literal $P_i(t_i)$ in any clause $P_1(t_1), \ldots, P_n(t_n) \to S(f(y_1, \ldots, y_m))$ if t_i is not a variable, if t_i is a variable that does not occur in $f(y_1, \ldots, y_m)$, or if t_i is a variable in a clause $P_1(x), \ldots, P_n(x) \to S(x)$ [28,29].

Proposition 1 (Entailed by Lemma 4 from [29]). *Consider a satisfiable finite MSLH clause set N. There is a finite MSLH clause set N^* such that $N \subseteq N^*$ and $N \models N^*$ and there is a (minimal) Herbrand model $\mathcal{H} \models N^*$ such that for every ground atom A of the form $S(f(s_1, \ldots, s_m))$ we have $\mathcal{H} \models A$ only if there is some clause C in N^* and a variable assignment β with the following properties (notice that for $m = 0$ f degenerates to a constant symbol):*

(a) *C has the form $P_1(x_1), \ldots, P_n(x_n) \to S(f(y_1, \ldots, y_m))$ where $\{x_1, \ldots, x_n\} \subseteq \{y_1, \ldots, y_m\}$, the $y_1, \ldots, y_m$ are pairwise distinct, and $m, n \geq 0$;*
(b) *we have $\beta(y_i) = s_i$ for every i, $1 \leq i \leq m$; and*
(c) *we have $\mathcal{H}, \beta \models P_j(x_j)$ for every j, $1 \leq j \leq n$.*

Since N^* is satisfiable and all its clauses are Horn, it possesses a unique minimal Herbrand model $\mathcal{H}$ (cf. [12], Chapter XI, Theorem 3.8). The property described in Proposition 1 provides the key to construct a finite model for N and N^* from $\mathcal{H}$. The following example is intended to illustrate the ideas underlying the construction in a simplified form.

Example 2. Consider the following set of MSLH clauses with constants a and b:

$$N := \{P(a), \; Q(b), \quad \neg P(z) \vee \neg Q(z) \vee \neg R(z),$$
$$\neg P(u) \vee \neg P(u') \vee P(f(u, u')), \quad \neg Q(v) \vee \neg Q(v') \vee Q(f(v, v')),$$
$$\neg P(x) \vee R(f(x, y)), \quad \neg P(y) \vee R(f(x, y)),$$
$$\neg Q(x) \vee R(f(x, y)), \quad \neg Q(y) \vee R(f(x, y))\} \; .$$

The set N is satisfied by the minimal Herbrand interpretation $\mathcal{H}$ with

$$P^{\mathcal{H}} := \{a, f(a, a), f(a, f(a, a)), f(f(a, a), a), f(f(a, a), f(a, a)), \ldots\} \, ,$$
$$Q^{\mathcal{H}} := \{b, f(b, b), f(b, f(b, b)), f(f(b, b), b), f(f(b, b), f(b, b)), \ldots\} \, ,$$
$$R^{\mathcal{H}} := \{f(s, t) \mid s \in P^{\mathcal{H}} \text{ or } t \in Q^{\mathcal{H}}\} \, .$$

The interpretation $\mathcal{H}$, together with $N^* := N$, satisfies the conditions of Proposition 1: for every term $f(s, t)$ that belongs to $R^{\mathcal{H}}$ we have that one of the clauses $\neg P(x) \vee R(f(x, y))$ or $\neg P(y) \vee R(f(x, y))$ or $\neg Q(x) \vee R(f(x, y))$ or $\neg Q(y) \vee R(f(x, y))$ enforces $\mathcal{H} \models R(f(s, t))$ because of $\mathcal{H} \models P(s)$ or $\mathcal{H} \models P(t)$ or $\mathcal{H} \models Q(s)$ or $\mathcal{H} \models Q(t)$, respectively. Similarly, the presence of any term $f(\ldots)$ in $P^{\mathcal{H}}$ or $Q^{\mathcal{H}}$ is enforced by one of the clauses $\neg P(u) \vee \neg P(u') \vee P(f(u, u'))$ or $\neg Q(v) \vee \neg Q(v') \vee Q(f(v, v'))$.

These requirements towards the minimality of $\mathcal{H}$ provide us with a certain knowledge about distinct terms $f(s, t)$ and $f(s', t')$. Suppose the terms s and s'

are indistinguishable with respect to their membership in $P^{\mathcal{H}}, Q^{\mathcal{H}}, R^{\mathcal{H}}$. Further suppose that the same holds for the terms t and t'. Then, $f(s,t)$ and $f(s',t')$ are also indistinguishable with respect to their belonging to $P^{\mathcal{H}}, Q^{\mathcal{H}}$, and $R^{\mathcal{H}}$, because the arguments s, t and s', t' trigger the same productive clauses. A formal statement of this property is given in Lemma 3.

Based on this observation, we use $\mathcal{H}$ as a blueprint for a finite model $\mathcal{A}$, which is depicted in Fig. 1. The domain of $\mathcal{A}$ shall be $A := \{a, b, c, d, e\}$, and we set $a^{\mathcal{A}} := a$ and $b^{\mathcal{A}} := b$. The predicate symbols are interpreted by $P^{\mathcal{A}} := \{a, c\}, Q^{\mathcal{A}} := \{b, d\}, R^{\mathcal{A}} := \{c, d, e\}$. Moreover, we define

$$f^{\mathcal{A}}(a, a) := c \qquad f^{\mathcal{A}}(a, c) := c \qquad f^{\mathcal{A}}(c, a) := c \qquad f^{\mathcal{A}}(c, c) := c$$
$$f^{\mathcal{A}}(b, b) := d \qquad f^{\mathcal{A}}(b, d) := d \qquad f^{\mathcal{A}}(d, b) := d \qquad f^{\mathcal{A}}(d, d) := d.$$

For all other inputs, $f^{\mathcal{A}}$ shall yield e as output. Every domain element in A represents one equivalence class of the terms in $\mathcal{H}$'s Herbrand domain with respect to membership in the sets $P^{\mathcal{H}}, Q^{\mathcal{H}}$, and $R^{\mathcal{H}}$. The domain element a represents the class $[a] := \{a\}$ of terms that belong to $P^{\mathcal{H}}$ and to no other set. Similarly, b represents $[b] := \{b\}$ of terms that belong to $Q^{\mathcal{H}}$ and to no other set. The element c represents the class of all terms belonging to $P^{\mathcal{H}} \cap R^{\mathcal{H}}$, i.e. to the class containing $f(a, a), f(a, f(a, a))$ and so on. The class of terms belonging to $Q^{\mathcal{H}} \cap R^{\mathcal{H}}$ is represented by d. Finally, e corresponds to the class of all terms that are member of $R^{\mathcal{H}}$ but of none of the other predicates, e.g. $f(a, b), f(a, f(b, a))$.

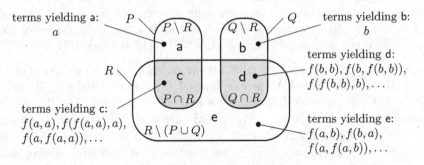

Fig. 1. Illustration of the model $\mathcal{A}$ of N from Example 2.

Next, we describe formally how to construct a finite model for the given satisfiable and finite MSLH clause set N. Let N^* and $\mathcal{H}$ be the objects described in Proposition 1. Then, we have $\mathcal{H} \models N^*$ and $\mathcal{H} \models N$. Let H be the domain of $\mathcal{H}$, i.e. H is the set of all ground terms over the vocabulary underlying N. We aim at constructing a finite model $\mathcal{A} \models N$ starting from $\mathcal{H}$.

Let Π denote the set of all predicates occurring in N, and recall that Π contains only unary predicate symbols. Let $\sim$ be the equivalence relation on H such that $s \sim t$ holds if and only if we have for every $P \in \Pi$ that $\mathcal{H} \models P(s)$ if and only if $\mathcal{H} \models P(t)$.

Lemma 3. *For every non-constant function symbol f in N of arity m and all tuples $\langle s_1, \ldots, s_m \rangle, \langle t_1, \ldots, t_m \rangle \in \mathsf{H}^m$ for which $s_i \sim t_i$ holds for every i we have $f(s_1, \ldots, s_m) \sim f(t_1, \ldots, t_m)$.*

Proof. By Definition of $\mathcal{H}$, $\mathcal{H} \models S(f(s_1, \ldots, s_m))$ entails that there is a clause C of the form $\neg P_1(x_1) \vee \ldots \vee \neg P_n(x_n) \vee S(f(y_1, \ldots, y_m))$ in N^* and a variable assignment β that satisfy Properties (a) to (c) from Proposition 1. Let γ be a variable assignment for which we have $\gamma(y_i) := t_i$ for every i. Notice that such a γ with $\langle \gamma(y_1), \ldots, \gamma(y_m) \rangle = \langle t_1, \ldots, t_m \rangle$ always exists because the $y_1, \ldots, y_m$ are pairwise distinct. Since we assume $s_i \sim t_i$ for every i and because of $\{x_1, \ldots, x_n\} \subseteq \{y_1, \ldots, y_m\}$, Conditions (b) and (c) of Proposition 1 stipulate for every j that $\beta(x_j) \in P_j^{\mathcal{H}}$ and, hence, we also have $\gamma(x_j) \in P_j^{\mathcal{H}}$. Since $\mathcal{H}$ is a model of N^*, we have $\mathcal{H}, \gamma \models C$. This together with $\mathcal{H}, \gamma \models P_j(x_j)$, for every j, entails $\mathcal{H}, \gamma \models S(f(y_1, \ldots, y_m))$. Put differently, we have $\mathcal{H} \models S(f(t_1, \ldots, t_m))$.

Consequently, for every S we observe that $\mathcal{H} \models S(f(s_1, \ldots, s_m))$ entails $\mathcal{H} \models S(f(t_1, \ldots, t_m))$. The converse direction can be shown by a symmetric argument. $\quad\square$

We now construct the finite structure $\mathcal{A}$. The universe of $\mathcal{A}$ shall be $\mathsf{A} := \{[s]_\sim \mid s \in \mathsf{H}\}$, where $[s]_\sim$ denotes the (unique) equivalence class with respect to $\sim$ which contains the term s. For every function symbol f (including constants) we set $f^{\mathcal{A}}([s_1]_\sim, \ldots, [s_m]_\sim) := [f(s_1, \ldots, s_m)]_\sim$ for all ground terms $s_1, \ldots, s_m$. Finally, we define each predicate P under $\mathcal{A}$ by $P^{\mathcal{A}} := \{[s]_\sim \mid \mathcal{H} \models P(s)\}$.

Lemma 4. *Let γ be any variable assignment over $\mathcal{A}$'s domain. Let β be some variable assignment over $\mathcal{H}$'s domain defined such that for every x we have $\gamma(x) = [\beta(x)]_\sim$. By definition of $\mathcal{H}$, such a β must exist. Then, for every term t in N and every predicate P we have $\mathcal{A}, \gamma \models P(t)$ if and only if $\mathcal{H}, \beta \models P(t)$.*

Proof (Sketch). We proceed by case distinction regarding the structure of the term t. If $t = x$ is a variable, then we have $\mathcal{A}, \gamma \models P(x)$ if and only if $\gamma(x) = [\beta(x)]_\sim \in P^{\mathcal{A}}$ if and only if $\beta(x) \in P^{\mathcal{H}}$ if and only if $\mathcal{H}, \beta \models P(x)$. If $t = c$ is a constant, then we have $\mathcal{A}, \gamma \models P(c)$ if and only if $c^{\mathcal{A}} = [c]_\sim \in P^{\mathcal{A}}$ if and only if $c \in P^{\mathcal{H}}$ if and only if $\mathcal{H}, \beta \models P(c)$.

Suppose $t = f(s_1, \ldots, s_m)$ for some function f of arity $m \geq 1$ and terms $s_1, \ldots, s_m$. Let $t_1, \ldots, t_m$ be ground terms such that $\mathcal{A}(\gamma)(s_i) = [t_i]_\sim$. Such terms exist by definition of $\mathcal{H}$. Then, $\mathcal{A}, \gamma \models P(f(s_1, \ldots, s_m))$ if and only if $f^{\mathcal{A}}([t_1]_\sim, \ldots, [t_m]_\sim) = [f(t_1, \ldots, t_m)]_\sim \in P^{\mathcal{A}}$ if and only if $\mathcal{H} \models P(f(t_1, \ldots, t_m))$. A straightforward induction on the structure of the terms s_i yields $t_i \sim \mathcal{H}(\beta)(s_i)$ for every i (see [25] for details), where $\mathcal{H}(\beta)(s_i)$ denotes the value of the term s_i under $\mathcal{H}$ and β. Then, by Lemma 3, we have $\mathcal{H} \models P(f(t_1, \ldots, t_m))$ if and only if $\mathcal{H} \models P(f(\mathcal{H}(\beta)(s_1), \ldots, \mathcal{H}(\beta)(s_m)))$ if and only if $\mathcal{H}, \beta \models P(f(s_1, \ldots, s_m))$. $\quad\square$

For the special case of ground terms, there is a simpler form of Lemma 4:

Corollary 5. *For every ground term t and every predicate symbol P we have $\mathcal{A} \models P(t)$ if and only if $\mathcal{H} \models P(t)$.*

Using Lemma 4, it is easy to show that N is satisfied by the finite structure $\mathcal{A}$ (see [25] for details).

Theorem 6 (Finite Model Property for MSLH). *Every satisfiable finite MSLH clause set N has a finite model whose domain contains at most 2^p elements, where p is the number of predicates occurring in N.*

For a number of fragments enjoying the finite model property, such as the Bernays-Schoenfinkel fragment, the size of minimal models also depends on the number of constants. Ground unit clauses are sufficient to force the growth of models. Ground unit clauses such as the unit clause $T(f(a,b,c))$ are not admitted in MSLH. But they can be encoded. For the example, the unit clauses $S_1(a)$, $S_2(b)$, $S_3(c)$ together with the clause $\neg S_1(x) \vee \neg S_2(y) \vee \neg S_3(z) \vee T(f(x,y,z))$ entail the ground unit clause $T(f(a,b,c))$. Forcing the growth of models via ground unit clauses requires the introduction of additional predicates in MSLH.

4   Model Representation Formalisms

Many known explicit first-order model representation formalisms are built on sequences of literals, often enhanced with constraints, eventually representing Herbrand models, e.g., [1,3,5,6,19], so called constraints atomic representations (CARMs) [8]. A thorough discussion of all known CARM model representation formalisms is beyond the scope of this paper. We concentrate on three basic building blocks of known model representation formalisms: atoms with disequality constraints [8,11] (ADCs), implicit generalizations [13] (IGs) and atoms with membership constraints [8,10] (AMCs). They form the basis for a number of concrete model representation formalisms that actually appear in the above mentioned calculi. For this section we consider a fixed, finite signature $\Sigma = (\mathcal{F}, \mathcal{P})$, e.g., the function and predicate symbols occurring in some finite clause set N. The results in this section for all three model representations will be the same: if terms, literals are linear, the models represented by the respective approaches have the finite model property. We will prove this as follows: (i) we provide an effective linear time translation of atoms with disequality constraints to implicit generalizations; (ii) we provide a linear time translation of implicit generalizations to intersections of tree automata [10] or complements thereof; (iii) we represent an atom with membership constraints by a tree automaton. Then, because tree automata are closed under intersection and complement, potentially causing an exponential blow up in size [10], the atoms generated by ADCs and IGs can also be represented by the accepted language of a single tree automaton. The accepted language of a tree automaton can be represented by a finite MSLH clause set, e.g., see [15]. Thus, by Theorem 6, linear ADCs, linear IGs, and linear AMCs have all the finite model property, i.e., they cannot represent models for clause sets with inherently infinite models.

A *linear* ADC [8,11] has the form $(A: x_1 \neq t_1, \ldots, x_n \neq t_n)$ where the x_i are all different and occur in A, the x_i do not occur in any t_j, the variables of the t_j do not occur in A and A as well as all t_j are linear. The ground atoms generated by such an ADC are all ground atoms $A\sigma$ such that there is no δ with $x_i\sigma = t_i\delta$ for some i. A *linear* IG [13] is an expression $A/\{B_1,\ldots,B_n\}$ where A and the B_i are linear atoms. Every ground instance of A that is not an instance of any B_i is generated by the IG $A/\{B_1,\ldots,B_n\}$. The ground atoms generated by an ADC are exactly the ground atoms generated by the respective linear IG $A/\{A\{x_1 \mapsto t_1\},\ldots,A\{x_n \mapsto t_n\}\}$.

A tree automaton [7,10] consists of a finite set $\mathcal{Q}$ of states, a finite set $\mathcal{O}$ of operators, a subset of accepting states $\mathcal{Q}_A \subseteq \mathcal{Q}$, and a finite set of rules $f(q_1 \ldots, q_n) \mapsto q$ where $q, q_i \in \mathcal{Q}$, $f \in \mathcal{O}$. The accepted language of a tree automaton is inductively defined by $f(t_1,\ldots,t_n) \in q^{\mathcal{A}}$ if there is a rule $f(q_1 \ldots, q_n) \mapsto q$ and $t_i \in q_i^{\mathcal{A}}$ for all i. The overall accepted language is then $\bigcup \{q^{\mathcal{A}} \mid q \in \mathcal{Q}_A\}$.

For example, the ground instances of the linear atom $R(x, g(a, y))$ over signature $\Sigma = (\{g, a, b\}, \{R\})$ is the accepted language of the tree automaton $\mathcal{O} = \{R, g, a, b\}$ with rules $a \mapsto q_1$, $b \mapsto q_1$, $g(q_1, q_1) \mapsto q_1$, hence state q_1 accepts all ground terms, $a \mapsto q_2$, $g(q_2, q_1) \mapsto q_3$, and $R(q_1, q_3) \mapsto q_4$ where q_4 is the only accepting state recognizing all ground instances of $R(x, g(a, y))$.

If ta is a function mapping linear atoms to a tree automata accepting the respective ground instances, then the ground atoms generated by an IG $A/\{B_1,\ldots, B_n\}$ are accepted by the tree automaton $\text{ta}(A) \cap \neg\text{ta}(B_1) \cap \ldots \cap \neg\text{ta}(B_n)$. Recall that tree automata are closed under intersection ($\cap$) and complement ($\neg$), however the above tree automaton may be exponentially larger in size compared to the size of $\text{ta}(A)$ and the $\text{ta}(B_i)$.

A *linear* atom with membership constraint $A\colon x \in S$ is the pair of a linear atom A and a constraint $x \in S$ where x occurs in A and S is represented by a tree automaton. It generates all ground instances $A\sigma$ where $x\sigma$ is accepted by the tree automaton representing S. There is a function $\text{ta}(A\colon x \in S)$ that computes in linear time a tree automaton accepting exactly the generated ground instances of $A\colon x \in S$. Basically, the state(s) representing the instances of x in A in $\text{ta}(A)$ have to be replaced by the accepting states of the tree automaton representing S.

Finally, tree automata can be straight forwardly represented via MSLH clause sets. For example, the tree automaton representing the ground instances of $R(x, g(a, y))$ shown before, can be translated into the MSLH clause set $\to Q_1(a)$; $\to Q_1(b)$; $Q_1(x), Q_1(y) \to Q_1(g(x, y))$; $\to Q_2(a)$; $Q_2(x), Q_1(y) \to Q_3(g(x, y))$; and $Q_1(x), Q_3(y) \to Q_f(f_R(x, y))$. This, together with Theorem 6, eventually proves the following theorem.

Theorem 7. *Linear disequality constraints (ADCs), linear implicit generalizations (IGs) and linear atoms with membership constraints (AMCs) have the finite model property.*

This result can be easily generalized to any "Boolean combination" of linear ADCs, IGs, and AMCs, because tree automata are closed under Boolean operations. Our restriction on linearity does not imply that non-linear ADCs, IGs, and AMCs do *not* have the finite model property. This is an open problem. For example, the non-linear IG $R(x, x)/\{R(g(x), g(x))\}$ over signature

$\Sigma = (\{g, h, a\}, \{R\})$ generates the infinite Herbrand model $\{R(a, a)\} \cup \{R(h(x),$ $h(x))\sigma \mid \sigma \text{ grounding}\}$. However, it also has a finite model over the domain $\mathsf{A} := \{\mathsf{a}, \mathsf{b}\}$ of two elements where a is interpreted by a, g maps constantly to b, h maps constantly to a, and R is the relation $\{(\mathsf{a}, \mathsf{a})\}$.

Non-linear MSH clause sets do not have the finite model property, because they are as expressive as full first-order logic.

5   Model Finding by Approximation Refinement

The AR calculus as it is used here works as follows [27]. Starting from a clause set N it is approximated into a MSLH clause set N' by the following steps: (i) all non monadic relation literals are turned into function terms below of a new monadic predicate T, (ii) all non-linear variable occurrences in positive literals are linearized, (iii) all nested function terms in positive literals are abstracted through the introduction of further monadic predicates, (iv) non Horn clauses are split into Horn clauses after removing variable dependencies between positive literals. Then if N' is satisfiable, so is N. If N' is unsatisfiable, the AR calculus tries to lift the proof to N. This may fail, in particular, because of the variable linearizations. In this case the respective clauses are instantiated and again approximated in order to get rid of the particular proof in N' and the AR calculus continues. If the proofs out of N' are generated in a fair way, the AR calculus is complete [27]. The Horn splitting can be omitted but then a decision procedure for MSL clause sets is needed [28].

The approximation refinement approach [27] cannot show satisfiability of the simple clause set with the two unit clauses

$$R(x, x), \quad \neg R(y, g(y)).$$

The approximated clause set consisting of the three clauses

$$T(f_R(x, y)), \quad \neg S(z) \vee \neg T(f_R(y, z)), \quad S(g(y))$$

immediately yields a refutation. The problem is that $R(x, x)$ cannot be refined in such a way that all instances of the conflict clause $\neg R(y, g(y))$ are excluded. The refinement loop instead ends up enumerating all $R(g^i(x), g^i(x))$ but $R(g^{i+1}(y), g^{i+2}(y))$ will always remain as a conflict clause.

The non-termination can be resolved, if the resolution inference in the abstracted clause set can be blocked. Our suggestion in case of reflexive relations is *reflexive relation splitting*, i.e., we split a reflexive relation into its reflexive part R_{ref} and irreflexive part R_{irr}. For the example, this yields

$$R_{\mathrm{ref}}(x, x), \quad \neg R_{\mathrm{irr}}(y, g(y))$$

and after approximation

$$T(f_{R_{\mathrm{ref}}}(x, y)), \quad \neg S(z) \vee \neg T(f_{R_{\mathrm{irr}}}(y, z)), \quad S(g(y)).$$

Now the approximation is saturated. The operation preserves satisfiability because the two R literals could not be resolved anyway.

In general, for each predicate R with a reflexivity axiom, all occurrences of atoms $R(s,t)$ are replaced with $R_{\text{ref}}(s,t)$ and/or $R_{\text{irr}}(s,t)$. If s and t are not unifiable, $R(s,t)$ is replaced with $R_{\text{irr}}(s,t)$. If there is an mgu σ of s and t, $R(s,t)$ is replaced with both $R_{\text{ref}}(s\sigma, t\sigma)$ and $R_{\text{irr}}(s,t)$. More precisely, any clause $C \vee [\neg]R(s,t)$ is replaced by two clauses: $C \vee [\neg]R_{\text{irr}}(s,t)$ and $C\sigma \vee [\neg]R_{\text{ref}}(s\sigma, t\sigma)$. The process is repeated until all atom occurrences with R have been replaced. In the final result, any clause that contains an atom of the form $R_{\text{irr}}(s,s)$ can be deleted.

More formally, the following transition system replaces a reflexive R by the two new predicates.

Irreflexive $N \uplus \{[\neg]R(s,t) \vee C\} \Rightarrow_{\text{RRS}} N \uplus \{[\neg]R_{\text{irr}}(s,t) \vee C\}$
provided s and t are not unifiable

Reflexive $N \uplus \{[\neg]R(s,t) \vee C\} \Rightarrow_{\text{RRS}} N \uplus \{[\neg]R_{\text{irr}}(s,t) \vee C, [\neg]R_{\text{ref}}(s\sigma, t\sigma) \vee C\sigma\}$
provided s and t are unifiable by an mgu σ

Delete $\quad N \uplus \{[\neg]R_{\text{irr}}(s,s) \vee C\} \Rightarrow_{\text{RRS}} N$

Lemma 8. $\Rightarrow_{RRS}$ *is terminating and confluent.*

Proof (Sketch). Termination is easy to prove. Each application of the rules Irreflexive or Reflexive reduces the multiset of the numbers of R-occurrences in all clauses, and no new occurrences of R are ever introduced when Delete is applied. Each application of the rule Delete reduces the number of occurrences of R_{irr}. Combining these two properties into a well-founded multi-set-based ordering completes the proof of termination. For local confluence, the non-obvious case is a clause $[\neg]R(s,t) \vee [\neg]R(s',t') \vee C$ where $R(s,t)$ and $R(s',t')$ share variables, and without loss of generality, s and t are unifiable by the mgu σ. Applying first the reflexive transformation to the first literal yields the two clauses $[\neg]R_{\text{ref}}(s\sigma, t\sigma) \vee [\neg]R(s'\sigma, t'\sigma) \vee C\sigma$ and $[\neg]R_{\text{irr}}(s,t) \vee [\neg]R(s',t') \vee C$. Now the interesting case is where s', t' are unifiable but $s'\sigma$ and $t'\sigma$ are not. Then we get with the mgu τ of s',t': $[\neg]R_{\text{ref}}(s\sigma, t\sigma) \vee [\neg]R_{\text{irr}}(s'\sigma, t'\sigma) \vee C\sigma$, $[\neg]R_{\text{irr}}(s,t) \vee [\neg]R_{\text{irr}}(s',t') \vee C$, and $[\neg]R_{\text{irr}}(s\tau, t\tau) \vee [\neg]R_{\text{ref}}(s'\tau, t'\tau) \vee C\tau$. This is also exactly the result we get when starting with a translation of $[\neg]R(s',t')$: if $s'\sigma, t'\sigma$ are not unifiable, then $s\tau, t\tau$ are not unifiable as well. For otherwise, $s\tau\tau', t\tau\tau'$ for unifier τ' is an instance of $s\sigma, t\sigma$, so $s'\sigma, t'\sigma$ must be unifiable as well, a contradiction to the above assumption. All other cases are similar to this case. By Newman's Lemma, termination plus local confluence implies confluence. $\square$

Given any finite clause set N, we write $\text{rrs}(N)$ to address the normal form of N after exhaustively applying $\Rightarrow_{\text{RRS}}$. Notice that any clause $D \in \text{rrs}(N)$ is an instance of a clause in N with respect to the renaming of $R_{\text{ref}}, R_{\text{irr}}$ with R. Moreover, we use $\text{rrs}(C)$ as shorthand for $\text{rrs}(\{C\})$ for any clause C.

Lemma 9 (Reflexive Relation Splitting). *Let N be a finite clause set that does not contain the predicates R_{ref} and R_{irr}. N is satisfiable if and only if* rrs(N) *is satisfiable.*

Proof (Sketch). Consider the derivation $N \Rightarrow_{RRS} N_1 \Rightarrow_{RRS} \cdots \Rightarrow_{RRS}$ rrs(N) where we assume that the rule Delete is applied with priority whenever it is applicable. By confluence of $\Rightarrow_{RRS}$, this is not a restriction.

We use an auxiliary result that is not hard to prove (see [25] for details):
Claim: Let M_1, M_2 be clause sets such that $M_1 \Rightarrow_{RRS} M_2$. Moreover, let $\mathcal{I}$ be any Herbrand interpretation such that (1) for every ground term s we have $R_{ref}(s, s) \in \mathcal{I}$ if and only if $R(s, s) \in \mathcal{I}$, (2) for all ground terms s, t and all $R_{ref}(s, t) \in \mathcal{I}$ we have $s = t$, (3) for all ground terms s, t we have $R_{irr}(s, t) \in \mathcal{I}$ if and only if $R(s, t) \in \mathcal{I}$. Then, $\mathcal{I} \models M_1$ if and only if $\mathcal{I} \models M_2$. $\diamondsuit$

Let $\mathcal{I}$ be a Herbrand model of N. Since N does not contain the predicates R_{ref} and R_{irr}, we can bring $\mathcal{I}$ into the shape that meets the conditions of the above claim and still ensure that $\mathcal{I} \models N$. It then follows that $\mathcal{I} \models N, \mathcal{I} \models N_1, \ldots, \mathcal{I} \models$ rrs(N). Symmetrically, let $\mathcal{I}$ be a Herbrand model of rrs(N). Since rrs(N) does not contain the predicate R, we can reshape $\mathcal{I}$ so that the above claim is applicable and $\mathcal{I}$ is still a model of rrs(N). Then, we get $\mathcal{I} \models$ rrs(N), $\ldots, \mathcal{I} \models N$. $\square$

Notice that the above lemma holds independently of the fact whether there is a reflexivity clause in N or not. Such a clause would, of course, also be transformed by $\Rightarrow_{RRS}$.

Let us take a look at an example that is a little bit more involved. Consider an equivalence relation R with the respective axiom clauses.

$$\rightarrow R(x, x)$$
$$R(x, y) \rightarrow R(y, x)$$
$$R(x, y), R(y, z) \rightarrow R(x, z)$$

Applying $\Rightarrow_{RRS}$ exhaustively results in the clause set

$$\rightarrow R_{ref}(x, x)$$
$$R_{irr}(x, y) \rightarrow R_{irr}(y, x)$$
$$R_{ref}(x, x) \rightarrow R_{ref}(x, x)$$
$$R_{irr}(x, y), R_{irr}(y, z) \rightarrow R_{irr}(x, z)$$
$$R_{irr}(x, y), R_{irr}(y, x) \rightarrow R_{ref}(x, x)$$
$$R_{irr}(x, y), R_{ref}(y, y) \rightarrow R_{irr}(x, y)$$
$$R_{ref}(x, x), R_{irr}(x, z) \rightarrow R_{irr}(x, z)$$
$$R_{ref}(x, x), R_{ref}(x, x) \rightarrow R_{ref}(x, x).$$

After removing redundant clauses, we are conveniently left with just

$$\rightarrow R_{ref}(x, x)$$
$$R_{irr}(x, y) \rightarrow R_{irr}(y, x)$$
$$R_{irr}(x, y), R_{irr}(y, z) \rightarrow R_{irr}(x, z)$$

which are no longer trivialized by the linear approximation $T(f_R(x, y))$ of the reflexivity axiom generated by the AR calculus. See also the example in the introduction, Sect. 1, for another application of reflexive relation splitting.

The rule Reflexive replaces a clause by two clauses and can, therefore, cause an exponential blow up in the number of generated clauses. However, this is only the case for a clause with several occurrences $R(s_i, t_i)$ such that the respective term pairs are all simultaneously unifiable. This situation can be detected and then reflexive relation splitting may not be efficiently applicable. However, the above example on the equivalence relation R shows that in the case of variable chains as they occur in the transitivity axiom, all of the eventually generated clauses become redundant, except one: $R_{\mathrm{irr}}(x, y), R_{\mathrm{irr}}(y, z) \to R_{\mathrm{irr}}(x, z)$. We have integrated reflexive relation splitting into SPASS-AR [24, 27] and have run it on the overall TPTP [22]. There is no example in TPTP v.7.2.0 showing the exponential blow up and the set of problems solved by SPASS-AR with reflexive relation splitting is strictly larger than without.

Nevertheless, reflexive relation splitting is, of course, not sufficient to transform all problems with inherently infinite models based on a (ir)reflexive relation into clause sets that can eventually be decided by AR via MSLH clause sets. Consider a strict partial ordering without endpoints:

$$R(x, x) \to$$
$$\to R(x, g(x))$$
$$R(x, y), R(y, z) \to R(x, z).$$

Reflexive relation splitting yields

$$R_{\mathrm{ref}}(x, x) \to$$
$$\to R_{\mathrm{irr}}(x, g(x))$$
$$R_{\mathrm{irr}}(x, y), R_{\mathrm{irr}}(y, z) \to R_{\mathrm{irr}}(x, z)$$
$$R_{\mathrm{irr}}(x, y), R_{\mathrm{irr}}(y, x) \to R_{\mathrm{ref}}(x, x)$$

but after approximation, the abstraction refinement does not terminate on the example. The reason is the approximation of the clause $R_{\mathrm{irr}}(x, g(x))$ into the two clauses $S(g(x))$ and $S(y) \to T(f_{R_{\mathrm{irr}}}(x, y))$ where the property is lost that in any ground instance of $R_{\mathrm{irr}}(x, g(x))$ the first argument has one occurrence of g less than the second. This was resolved in [18] by the use of tuple tree automata.

6   Discussion

We have shown that the MSLH clause fragment has the finite model property and can therefore not represent models of clause sets with inherently infinite models. This applies to the model representation building blocks atoms with disequality constraints, implicit generalizations, and atoms with membership constraints as well, if atoms and terms are linear. For non-linear terms, our finite model property proof breaks, and, in fact, the example from the introduction shows already that non-linear atoms can represent models for clause sets with inherently infinite models.

Unsatisfiability of monadic shallow Horn clause sets is undecidable. One occurrence of a clause $\Gamma \rightarrow S(f(x,x))$ suffices to this end. This can be seen by a respective monadic reformulation of the PCP encoding from the introduction. On the other hand, models represented by ground instances of finite sets of (linear or non-linear) atoms are also restricted in expressivity, because they cannot express any recursive structure. For example, MSLH clause sets and extensions thereof have been successfully used for the analysis of security protocols [4,29] where (counter-) models cannot be expressed by ground instances of finite sets of atoms. In summary, and not surprisingly, there is currently no unique superior model representation formalism.

If models are eventually constructed through the reversal of an approximation, the used representation may have the finite model property and can still show satisfiability of clause sets with inherently infinite models. We obtained this result via reflexive relation splitting. This insight is already a consequence of [18]. There, an approximation into a theory of tuple tree automata is described and it is even complete with respect to models generated out of these automata. We can currently not provide such a completeness result although this would be highly desirable. On the other hand, our techniques are embedded into a refutationally complete procedure, whereas the approach in [18] can only show satisfiability.

Acknowledgments. This work was funded by DFG grant 389792660 as part of TRR 248. We thank our reviewers for their valuable comments.

References

1. Alagi, G., Weidenbach, C.: NRCL – A model building approach to the Bernays-Schönfinkel fragment. In: Lutz, C., Ranise, S. (eds.) FroCoS 2015. LNCS (LNAI), vol. 9322, pp. 69–84. Springer, Cham (2015). https://doi.org/10.1007/978-3-319-24246-0_5
2. Bachmair, L., Ganzinger, H.: Rewrite-based equational theorem proving with selection and simplification. J. Log. Comput. **4**(3), 217–247 (1994)
3. Baumgartner, P., Fuchs, A., Tinelli, C.: Lemma learning in the model evolution calculus. In: Hermann, M., Voronkov, A. (eds.) LPAR 2006. LNCS (LNAI), vol. 4246, pp. 572–586. Springer, Heidelberg (2006). https://doi.org/10.1007/11916277_39
4. Blanchet, B.: Automatic proof of strong secrecy for security protocols. In: 2004 IEEE Symposium on Security and Privacy, pp. 86–100 (2004)
5. Bonacina, M.P., Furbach, U., Sofronie-Stokkermans, V.: On first-order model-based reasoning. In: Martí-Oliet, N., Ölveczky, P.C., Talcott, C. (eds.) Logic, Rewriting, and Concurrency. LNCS, vol. 9200, pp. 181–204. Springer, Cham (2015). https://doi.org/10.1007/978-3-319-23165-5_8
6. Bonacina, M.P., Plaisted, D.A.: Semantically-guided goal-sensitive reasoning: model representation. J. Autom. Reason. **56**(2), 113–141 (2016). Inference System and Completeness in **59**(2), JAR

7. Brainerd, W.S.: The minimalization of tree automata. Inf. Control **13**, 484–491 (1968)
8. Caferra, R., Leitsch, A., Peltier, N.: Automated Model Building. Applied Logic Series, vol. 31. Kluwer, Dordrecht (2004). https://doi.org/10.1007/978-1-4020-2653-9
9. Claessen, K., Soerensson, N.: New techniques that improve mace-style finite model finding. In: Proceedings of the CADE-19 Workshop: Model Computation - Principles, Algorithms, Applications (2003)
10. Comon, H., Dauchet, M., Gilleron, R., Löding, C., Jacquemard, F., Lugiez, D., Tison, S., Tommasi, M.: Tree automata techniques and applications (2007). http://tata.gforge.inria.fr/. Release 12 Oct 2007
11. Comon, H.: Disunification: A survey. In: Computational Logic - Essays in Honor of Alan Robinson, pp. 322–359. The MIT Press, Cambridge (1991)
12. Ebbinghaus, H.-D., Flum, J., Thomas, W.: Mathematical Logic, 2nd edn. Springer, New York (1994). https://doi.org/10.1007/978-1-4757-2355-7
13. Fermüller, C.G., Pichler, R.: Model representation over finite and infinite signatures. J. Log. Comput. **17**(3), 453–477 (2007)
14. Hernandez, J.C.L., Korovin, K.: Towards an abstraction-refinement framework for reasoning with large theories. In: IWIL@LPAR 2017. EasyChair (2017)
15. Jacquemard, F., Meyer, C., Weidenbach, C.: Unification in extensions of shallow equational theories. In: Nipkow, T. (ed.) RTA 1998. LNCS, vol. 1379, pp. 76–90. Springer, Heidelberg (1998). https://doi.org/10.1007/BFb0052362
16. Korovin, K.: Inst-Gen – A modular approach to instantiation-based automated reasoning. In: Voronkov, A., Weidenbach, C. (eds.) Programming Logics. LNCS, vol. 7797, pp. 239–270. Springer, Heidelberg (2013). https://doi.org/10.1007/978-3-642-37651-1_10
17. McCune, W.: Mace4 reference manual and guide. CoRR, cs.SC/0310055 (2003)
18. Peltier, N.: Constructing infinite models represented by tree automata. Ann. Math. Artif. Intell. **56**, 65–85 (2009)
19. Piskac, R., de Moura, L.M., Bjørner, N.: Deciding effectively propositional logic using DPLL and substitution sets. J. Autom. Reason. **44**(4), 401–424 (2010)
20. Post, E.L.: A variant of a recursively unsolvable problem. Bull. Am. Math. Soc. **52**, 264–268 (1946)
21. Slaney, J.: FINDER: Finite domain enumerator system description. In: Bundy, A. (ed.) CADE 1994. LNCS, vol. 814, pp. 798–801. Springer, Heidelberg (1994). https://doi.org/10.1007/3-540-58156-1_63
22. Sutcliffe, G.: The TPTP problem library and associated infrastructure: the FOF and CNF parts, v3.5.0. J. Autom. Reason. **43**(4), 337–362 (2009)
23. Suter, P., Dotta, M., Kuncak, V.: Decision procedures for algebraic data types with abstractions. In: Proceedings of the 37th ACM SIGPLAN-SIGACT Symposium on Principles of Programming Languages, POPL 2010, Madrid, Spain, 17–23 January 2010, pp. 199–210. ACM (2010)
24. Teucke, A.: An approximation and refinement approach to first-order automated reasoning. Doctoral thesis, Saarland University (2018)
25. Teucke, A., Voigt, M., Weidenbach, C.: On the expressivity and applicability of model representation formalisms. arXiv preprint, arXiv:1905.03651 [cs.LO] (2019)
26. Teucke, A., Weidenbach, C.: First-order logic theorem proving and model building via approximation and instantiation. In: Lutz, C., Ranise, S. (eds.) FroCoS 2015. LNCS (LNAI), vol. 9322, pp. 85–100. Springer, Cham (2015). https://doi.org/10.1007/978-3-319-24246-0_6

27. Teucke, A., Weidenbach, C.: Ordered resolution with straight dismatching constraints. In: Fontaine, P., Schulz, S., Urban, J. (eds.) 5th Workshop on Practical Aspects of Automated Reasoning (PAAR@IJCAR 2016) co-located with International Joint Conference on Automated Reasoning (IJCAR) 2016. CEUR Workshop Proceedings, vol. 1635, pp. 95–109. CEUR-WS.org (2016). http://ceur-ws.org/Vol-1635
28. Teucke, A., Weidenbach, C.: Decidability of the monadic shallow linear first-order fragment with straight dismatching constraints. In: de Moura, L. (ed.) CADE 2017. LNCS (LNAI), vol. 10395, pp. 202–219. Springer, Cham (2017). https://doi.org/10.1007/978-3-319-63046-5_13
29. Weidenbach, C.: Towards an automatic analysis of security protocols in first-order logic. CADE 1999. LNCS (LNAI), vol. 1632, pp. 314–328. Springer, Heidelberg (1999). https://doi.org/10.1007/3-540-48660-7_29
30. Weidenbach, C.: Automated reasoning building blocks. In: Meyer, R., Platzer, A., Wehrheim, H. (eds.) Correct System Design. LNCS, vol. 9360, pp. 172–188. Springer, Cham (2015). https://doi.org/10.1007/978-3-319-23506-6_12

A Neurally-Guided, Parallel Theorem Prover

Michael Rawson$^{(\boxtimes)}$ ⓘ and Giles Reger

University of Manchester, Manchester, UK
michael@rawsons.uk, giles.reger@manchester.ac.uk

Abstract. We present a prototype of a neurally-guided automatic theorem prover for first-order logic with equality. The prototype uses a neural network trained on previous proof search attempts to evaluate subgoals based directly on their structure, and hence bias proof search toward success. An existing first-order theorem prover is employed to dispatch easy subgoals and prune branches which cannot be solved. Exploration of the search space is asynchronous with respect to both the evaluation network and the existing prover, allowing for efficient batched neural network execution and for natural parallelism within the prover. Evaluation on the MPTP dataset shows that the prover can improve with learning.

Keywords: ATP · Graph Convolutional Network · Tableaux · MCTS

1 Introduction

Recent advances in neural network systems allow for processing graph-structured data in a neural context. Graphs are a natural representation for logical formulae as found in automatic theorem provers (ATPs), suggesting a new breed of *neural ATP* in which proof search is guided by a neural black-box acting as "mathematician's intuition". However, in practice there are several implementation issues [31] which must be avoided in order for neural systems to integrate with efficient traditional ATPs:

1. Proof state in such systems may be of impractical size, such as in saturation-based provers, leading to training data which is impractical to learn from and slow to evaluate. In a saturation context, the size of the current proof state may be many times the size of the eventual proof: while neural networks are in principle capable of processing large amounts of data, throughput suffers and scalability is a concern.
2. Data structures employed may be very opaque or "unnatural", containing artifice designed for efficiency rather than natural comprehension by a neural network.
3. Systems may be very sensitive to latency, which can result in the introduction of neural guidance systems crippling prover throughput and hence performance.

A. Herzig and A. Popescu (Eds.): FroCoS 2019, LNAI 11715, pp. 40–56, 2019.
https://doi.org/10.1007/978-3-030-29007-8_3

Attempting to solve these issues with a novel prover architecture, and exploring several options to improve overall efficiency, the prototype system LERNA[1] takes an alternative step toward useful neural automatic theorem provers.

2   Background

We assume basic familiarity with first-order logic, theorem proving, and neural networks [13].

2.1   Logic and Theorem Proving

First-Order Logic. LERNA works with formulas in standard first-order logic with equality. Terms t and formulas ϕ are recursively defined as follows

$$t = x \mid f(t_1, \ldots, t_n) \mid c$$
$$\phi = \top \mid \bot \mid t_1 = t_2 \mid p(t_1, \ldots, t_n) \mid \phi_1 \Rightarrow \phi_2 \mid \phi_1 \equiv \phi_2 \mid \neg\phi \mid$$
$$\phi_1 \wedge \ldots \wedge \phi_n \mid \phi_1 \vee \ldots \vee \phi_n \mid \forall x.\phi \mid \exists x.\phi$$

where x is a variable, f is a n-ary function symbol, c is a constant, and p is a n-ary predicate symbol. Their meaning is defined as usual.

Automatic Theorem Provers. An automated theorem prover (ATP) is a system able to automatically establish whether a formula (in first-order logic) is *satisfiable* or *unsatisfiable*; although, given the undecidability of this problem, ATPs may also return *unknown*. Both saturation-based provers (e.g. E [37], iProver [21], Vampire [33]) and SMT solvers (e.g. CVC4 [6] and Z3 [4]) utilise efficient proof calculi combined with highly-configurable search routines in order to explore a large search space efficiently.

2.2   Machine Learning and Theorem Proving

Despite the efficiency of modern ATP systems, they can still spend time exploring areas that a human mathematician would discard, and tuning such systems is, in general, extremely difficult [32]. This has led to the application of machine-learning techniques, with the eventual aim of an "intelligent" theorem prover able to learn from past experience to develop an intuition, discard uninteresting search space, and tune performance in a more principled way.

Previous work has focussed on premise selection [14,23,43,45], static strategy selection [3,24,25], dynamic (run-time) strategy selection [30] and more recently, direct proof guidance [15–17,26,44]. Proof guidance typically involves a form of

---

[1] **L**earning to **R**eason with **N**eural **A**rchitectures. Lerna is also the lair of the mythical many-headed beast HYDRA. Source code available at https://github.com/MichaelRawson/lerna.

machine-learned *heuristic* which biases proof search in some way, allowing the prover to avoid parts of the search space deemed uninteresting by the heuristic.

Work on integrating machine-learned heuristics into automatic theorem provers has relied on hand-engineered features [16,17,44] or other embedding methods [15,20], which have the advantage of simplicity and relative efficiency, but do not fully encode the syntactic structure of proof state and therefore lose information. By contrast, a neural method which takes into account all information (as utilised in this work) should allow for greater precision in proof guidance systems. Deep Network Guided Proof Search (DNGPS) [26] is an example of previous work in this area, which integrated a deep neural guidance system into the saturation-based prover E [37]. DNGPS achieved successful results, but suffered from the latency introduced into the system by the neural heuristic: despite processing only a reduced amount of the available proof state, the reduction in throughput necessitated a two-phase approach in which the prover was neurally-guided in the first phase, before falling back to traditional proof search in the second.

rlCoP. The rlCoP system [17] is a connection-based reinforcement-learning prover which is not presently neurally-guided, but takes a similar approach to that taken in this paper and achieves impressive results.

Neural Networks for Formulae. Neural networks are well-known tools for supervised learning [13], and combined with trainable convolution/pooling operators are suitable for processing large-scale data such as images [22].

Processing structured data such as logical formulae is a relatively new domain for neural networks. Some work attempts to use unstructured representations of such formulae, such as text, or build entirely-new models for a specific logic [7], whereas others attempt to re-use neural techniques for generic structures such as trees [2]. A promising direction in this area is recent research on neural methods working with graphs [5,19,36], which have already been applied to premise selection [45]. Graph neural networks tend to include network layers inspired by convolution operators in image-processing networks, combining information from neighbouring nodes (pixels) [19].

The MPTP Problem Set. For training and evaluation purposes a set of valid propositions exported from the Mizar Mathematical Library [12] by the MPTP [42] system are used. Urban et al. [17] took a subset[2] of the large *M40k* problem set (containing 32,524 problems) and called it *M2k* (containing 2004 problems).

3   Design

In order to achieve the goal of a neural theorem prover without the disadvantages associated with neural approaches, a new design of theorem prover is required.

---

[2] https://github.com/JUrban/deepmath/blob/master/M2k_list.

Popular calculi used in existing ATPs tend to be unfriendly to neural guidance. For such a system, we desire the following from the calculus:

1. *Proof state must be reasonably-sized.* Attempting to evaluate large proof states structurally requires a lot of computation and resources. Saturation-based provers can have very large proof states, for example.
2. *Evaluation of states must be possible in parallel.* Machine-learning algorithms operate more efficiently in batches. Tree-based approaches (tableau *etc.*) lend themselves to this, whereas saturation provers are inherently sequential.
3. *Subgoals must be independent and self-contained.* If the prover has a notion of (sub-)goals which must be dispatched (such as in tableau provers), these should be independent of the rest of the search space, without e.g. unifiers. Otherwise, the learning system is trying to learn while blind to the context of the search.
4. *Subgoals must be intelligible.* Adding "noise" such as clausification obscures the original intuition behind a goal, at least for human observers. While this is not necessarily the case for machine-learning algorithms, it seems likely that removing structure and adding artefacts will reduce model performance.

We therefore implement a refutation prover based on a first-order tableaux calculus without unification, on non-clausal formulae. Each goal in this case is the set of formulae present on the tableau branch. In this context, proof state is small (only the current branch), evaluation of states is possible in parallel, each branch is independent and contains all information required, and all available structure from the original problem is kept.

3.1 Search

In the calculus (see Sect. 4) for this prover, there are two branching factors: each goal has a set of possible inferences, and each inference contains a set of possible sub-goals. To prove a goal, at least one inference must be proved. To prove an inference, all the inferences' sub-goals must be proved (e.g. shown to be unsatisfiable). A simple optimisation is that sub-goals may be shared between inferences, so search becomes a directed acyclic graph, alternating between goals and inferences (illustrated in Fig. 1).

Now the search graph can be explored: in each step, a leaf (goal) node is selected for expansion, and all resulting inferences and sub-goals are added to the graph. If a goal has no possible inferences, it is satisfiable and can be removed from the search space. On the other hand, if a goal is trivial (i.e. contains a contradiction), it is unsatisfiable and can be marked as proven. This idea is lifted to inferences: if an inference contains any satisfiable sub-goal, it too is satisfiable, whereas if an

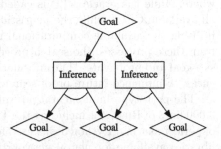

Fig. 1. Search in the LERNA system, showing shared sub-goals.

Fig. 2. Illustrating information-flow in the system.

inference contains all unsatisfiable goals, it is unsatisfiable. Proof search continues until the timeout is reached or the root goal is shown to be (un-)satisfiable. In order to dispatch trivial sub-goals quickly, an existing fast *oracle* ATP is used (see Sect. 5). This may mark goals as (un-)satisfiable, at which point no further exploration is required.

Search is biased by heuristic evaluation. The neural heuristic function (see Sect. 6) evaluates each goal and assigns a score corresponding to whether the network believes that the goal is satisfiable or unsatisfiable. In order to balance exploitation of promising directions and exploration of all parts of the search space, a principled UCT-based search algorithm is used, as in MonteCoP [8]. At each sub-goal g, the prover chooses the inference i with subgoals s according to

$$\max_{i \in g} \left[\underbrace{\min_{s \in i} (\mathsf{score}(s))}_{\text{exploitation}} + c \times \underbrace{\sqrt{\frac{\ln \mathsf{visits}\,(g)}{\mathsf{visits}\,(i)}}}_{\text{exploration}} \right]$$

where score gives the heuristic score, visits gives the total number of visits to that node so far, and c is the exploration parameter (theoretically $\sqrt{2}$). The subgoal with the minimal score is then selected: this prioritises subgoals considered possibly satisfiable by the heuristic, as satisfiable subgoals allow large parts of the search space to be pruned.

3.2   Architecture and Prototype Implementation

The system aims to consume all available CPU and GPU resources as efficiently as possible. To that end, proof search is asynchronous: the search algorithm generates new sub-goals, which are placed on two separate queues: one for the oracle ATP, another for heuristic evaluation. Proof search then continues elsewhere, while the oracle ATP is called in parallel on each sub-goal (consuming all available CPU) while the heuristic consumes batches of subgoals, efficiently utilising the available computational resource. As information flows backwards from these processes, the search process updates its information about a given sub-goal and propagates that information upwards to the sub-goal's parent inferences, to influence future proof search: see Fig. 2.

The prototype implementation (minus the heuristic) is currently just under 3,000 lines of Rust, not including the TPTP format parser or the implementation of perfect sharing. Python 3 was used for the heuristic due to the large number of libraries available for neural network implementation in Python. The heuristic is implemented as a server, communicating with the main prover via a TCP socket. In principle this allows for the heuristic to be a shared resource with a centralised heuristic server, or a load-balanced cluster.

CONTRADICTION $\dfrac{}{\phi, \neg\phi, \Gamma}$

EQUAL $\dfrac{t = s, \phi\,[t/s]\,, \Gamma}{t = s, \phi, \Gamma}$

IMPLIES $\dfrac{\neg\phi, \psi, \Gamma}{\phi \Rightarrow \psi, \Gamma}$

EQUIVALENT $\dfrac{\neg\phi, \neg\psi, \Gamma \qquad \phi, \psi, \Gamma}{\phi \equiv \psi, \Gamma}$

CONJUNCTION $\dfrac{\phi_1, \phi_2, \ldots, \phi_n, \Gamma}{\phi_1 \wedge \phi_2 \wedge \ldots \wedge \phi_n, \Gamma}$

DISJUNCTION $\dfrac{\phi_1, \Gamma \qquad \phi_2, \Gamma \qquad \ldots \qquad \phi_n, \Gamma}{\phi_1 \vee \phi_2 \vee \ldots \vee \phi_n, \Gamma}$

INSTANTIATION $\dfrac{\forall x_1, x_2, \ldots x_n.\phi[f(x_1, x_2, \ldots x_n)/x], \forall x.\phi, \Gamma}{\forall x.\phi, \Gamma}$

NON-EMPTY $\dfrac{\phi[k/x], \Gamma}{\forall x.\phi, \Gamma}$

EXISTS $\dfrac{\phi[k/x], \Gamma}{\exists x.\phi, \Gamma}$

Fig. 3. A complete inference system for LERNA. Rules for negation are as usual and not shown here for brevity. In rule INSTANTIATION, f is a function symbol of arity n in the conclusion's signature and $x_1 \ldots x_n$ are fresh for the conclusion. In rules NON-EMPTY and EXISTS, k is fresh for the conclusion. $\phi[t/s]$ is a capture-avoiding substitution replacing t for s in ϕ.

4   Calculus

The proof calculus used in the above architecture may be extremely general: in fact, any function from goals to a finite set of possible inferences (themselves finite sets of sub-goals) will suffice, as long as each goal remains independent of any other such that the heuristic function can process all available information. If the inference system is complete, there are no additional constraints such as orderings or fairness to ensure the completeness of the prover, as the balanced search algorithm (see Sect. 3) will ensure this.

LERNA presently implements a refutation tableaux calculus [35] without unification. The calculus described is deliberately naïve in order to easily satisfy the design constraints given above, but may be replaced by a stronger calculus in the future. A naïve calculus is not necessarily a problem as the heuristic should select promising areas to explore and ignore uninteresting sub-goals. However, a more efficient calculus would improve performance where the heuristic fails.

Refutation Tableaux. In order to show a conjecture C from a set of axioms A_i, it suffices to negate C and then show that the resulting conjunction $A_1 \wedge A_2 \wedge \ldots \wedge \neg C$ is unsatisfiable. A set of inference rules of the form

$$\frac{\Gamma_1 \qquad \Gamma_2 \qquad \ldots \qquad \Gamma_n}{\Delta}$$

where Γ_i, Δ are sets of formulae and $\neg(\Gamma_1 \wedge \Gamma_2 \wedge \ldots \Gamma_n) \Rightarrow \neg\Delta$ is an unconditional tautology, form a refutation calculus. Proofs in this calculus can be expressed by closed trees of inference rules.

$$\textbf{DOUBLE-NEG} \quad \frac{\phi, \Gamma}{\neg\neg\phi, \Gamma} \qquad \textbf{CONJ-ASSOC} \quad \frac{\phi \wedge \psi \wedge \pi, \Gamma}{\phi \wedge (\psi \wedge \pi)} \qquad \textbf{DISJ-PROP} \quad \frac{\phi, \Gamma}{\phi \vee \bot, \Gamma} \qquad \textbf{REFL} \quad \frac{\top, \Gamma}{t = t, \Gamma} \qquad \textbf{FREE} \quad \frac{\phi, \Gamma}{\forall x.\phi, \Gamma}$$

Fig. 4. Some simplification rules implemented in LERNA. In rule FREE, x is free in ϕ. Several other rules are implemented.

Complete Inferences. The inference rules in Fig. 3 form a complete inference system, by analogy with a first-order tableaux calculus without unification. A difference and point of interest is the rule for instantiating universal quantifiers: instead of instantiating a variable with any possible term t—an infinite space— it is instantiated with one function symbol (or constant) at a time, quantifying over new variables as needed. This allows for instantiating any term over multiple inference rules (effectively enumerating the Herbrand universe for the goal), but without an infinite number of possible inferences at any point. Equality is handled by a rule rewriting classes of equal ground terms. Both of these rules are complete yet inefficient, but both are likely to be used only a few times in order to provide enough of a "hint" to the oracle system for it to find a proof.

Weakening. A weakening rule is an important part of LERNA's calculus, since the INSTANTIATION and EQUAL rule can produce a large number of formulae, some of which must be removed to help the oracle to prove the goal. Each application of the rule removes some amount of information from the goal in order to simplify it—this is sound and corresponds to removing an axiom from proof search. The rule is merely

$$\textbf{WEAKEN} \quad \frac{\Gamma}{\phi, \Gamma}$$

Simplifications. Before each inferred goal is added to proof search, it is simplified, removing tedious inferences such as double-negation elimination and generally reducing the search space. Figure 4 gives example simplification rules.

5   Oracle

One problem with the calculus as described is that proofs can be quite lengthy, even if the goal is relatively trivial. To rectify the situation, new goals generated by ongoing proof search are enqueued for attempted proof by an existing *oracle* ATP system, as described in Sect. 3. In our prototype implementation we use the mature Z3 SMT solver [4], which supports quantified first-order logic via a combination of decision procedures for decidable fragments (such as the Bernays-Schönfinkel class of formulae), and heuristic quantifier instantiation routines [11]. Z3 is attractive for this application due to its low startup times and its ability to produce both satisfiable and unsatisfiable results.

LERNA uses Z3 as an external system (it could be replaced by an alternative ATP), running it with its Model-Based Quantifier Instantiation heuristic for 20 ms. This was chosen as the shortest time in which the oracle can dispatch a reasonable amount of trivial goals (and in fact Z3 is so strong it dispatches some goals immediately: see Sect. 7). Longer oracle runtimes might produce better performance in future, but for this work longer runtimes begin to conflate the performance of the oracle and the performance of the system as a whole. This application is unusual for ATP systems—very short runtimes, and a mix of true and false problem statements.

Acting as a Preprocessor. LERNA might also be seen as an intelligent preprocessor for existing ATPs in this setting: existing theorem provers are known to be sensitive to small changes in their input [40], and generally make little attempt to split their input into smaller sub-goals, for parallelism [41] or otherwise. The system can therefore act as an adapter for any existing ATP, adding parallelism opportunities and "smoothing out" sensitivity to input syntax.

6   Learned Heuristic

A suitable heuristic function for the system must predict a value between 0 and 1 for a given formula F, where 0 represents a satisfiable goal and 1 represents unsatisfiability, based on a set of tagged formulae seen in previous proof search. Although the data is collected by running the system itself and might be considered *reinforcement* learning, for this approach data collection and learning were considered separately and hence forms a classic supervised-learning problem.

6.1   Data Collection

A large dataset of satisfiable and unsatisfiable goals were collected by running the unguided prover on the *M40k* dataset for 10 s. As soon as the prover determines the satisfiability of any sub-goal, the formula it represents and its status is recorded. This resulted in 18,340 unsatisfiable examples and 1,845,267 satisfiable examples, occupying 6 GB of disk space. The dataset is very imbalanced (due to a combination of weakening rules producing a large number of trivially-satisfiable examples, and to immediate prover termination after the goal is shown to be unsatisfiable), at a ratio of around 100:1.

6.2   Translation to Graphs

Wang et al. [45] give a translation from higher-order formulae to directed graphs, and a similar scheme is used here. Constants, function symbols, predicate symbols, and bound variables are given their own node. Applications of functions and predicates to arguments are represented as an "application node" with two children: the symbol node and an "argument list" node representing the list

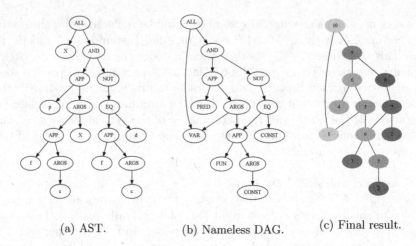

(a) AST.   (b) Nameless DAG.   (c) Final result.

Fig. 5. The translation process for $\forall x.\,[p\,(f(c),x) \wedge \neg\,(f(c) = d)]$ to a graph, as seen by the neural network.

of arguments. Propositional connectives and equality have the obvious representation, while quantifiers have two children: the variable they bind and their sub-formula.

To produce an input graph from a formula F, the formula is first parsed into an abstract syntax tree. Common sub-trees up to α-equivalence [1] are merged, then the resulting directed acyclic graph has any named-symbol nodes replaced with an opaque, nameless label such as "predicate" or "variable"—since distinct symbols remain as distinct nodes under this scheme, no information is lost other than the natural-language semantics of the symbol name. In practice, undirected graphs improved model performance so the graph is made undirected before encoding node labels as one-hot inputs to produce the final input graphs. An example formula's translation is shown in Fig. 5.

6.3   Augmentation

One possible solution [39] to the problem of classification on imbalanced domains is to synthesise new data for under-represented classes—in this case unsatisfiable formulae—from existing data by augmenting it. An example is augmenting image data by cropping, flipping or adding noise to existing images. There are many possible ways to augment formulae graphs. For this prototype, a simple approach is taken in which a small number of nonsense formulae are added to the graph by randomly adding nodes/edges where appropriate. This approach has the advantage of exposing the network to "noise" such as additional axioms which might well occur in practice, but if the network is adequately capable of filtering these then no new formulae are actually seen.

6.4   Neural Architecture

In a typical convolutional network architecture for images [22], there are a series of filtering stages, followed by a densely-connected neural network. Each filtering stage intuitively combines data from local features (via *convolution*), then reduces the dimensions of the image (via *pooling*) for the next stage. Graph neural networks have analogous convolution [19] (combining information from neighbouring nodes) and pooling [10] (merging nodes to reduce the size of the input graph) operators. A brief period of experimentation with these operators yielded the following network architecture, shown in Fig. 6.

1. Input. A graph G consisting of one-hot encoded nodes N and edges E.
2. Embedding. Each node is mapped to an embedding vector of size 64 via a trained dense embedding.
3. Initial Convolution. 4 convolution layers are applied to the graph with rectified linear activations. This yields a graph of the same size, but with information exchanged between nodes.
4. Convolution/Pooling. Similar convolution layers are then passed through *top-k* [10] layers, retaining $k = 60\%$ of the graph's nodes. This is repeated 3 times, reducing the size of the graph considerably.
5. Convolution/Max-Pooling. A final convolution layer feeds into a max-pooling layer, combining all remaining node data into one datum, and dropping the edge data.
6. Fully Connected. A fully-connected hidden layer with rectified linear activation halves the input size.
7. Fully Connected/Softmax. A fully-connected final layer outputs two class labels, with softmax activation.

It is not claimed that this is the optimal configuration, and no grid search has yet taken place to optimise the network architecture or hyper-parameters. To reduce over-fitting, dropout [38] is applied in convolutional and fully-connected layers, $p = 0.1$.

6.5   Implementation and Training

This architecture was implemented with the PyTorch [29] neural network library, combined with a graph-processing ("geometric") extension library, PyTorch Geometric [9], which together provide facilities for automatic differentiation, GPU-accelerated training, pre-programmed layers for graph processing, and various utilities. The dataset is split into a large training set and a smaller test set (200 balanced examples), since unsatisfiable examples were time-consuming to obtain in this setting. The unsatisfiable training data were then augmented as described in Sect. 6.3 to produce a balanced total training set of 3.5 million examples.

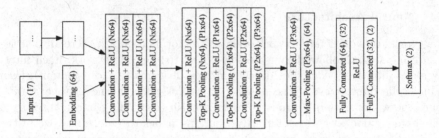

Fig. 6. The neural network architecture. Initially there are N nodes, then after pooling there are P_1, P_2, P_3 nodes. Node-level embedding layers are shown per-node, graph-level convolutional and pooling layers are shown per-graph.

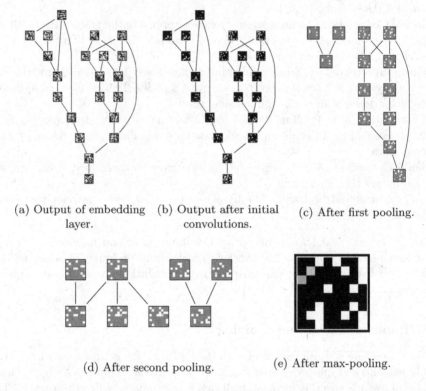

(a) Output of embedding layer.

(b) Output after initial convolutions.

(c) After first pooling.

(d) After second pooling.

(e) After max-pooling.

Fig. 7. Computation in the neural network, showing intermediate values involved in the network (correctly) predicting the satisfiability of an input formula.

The network was trained on commodity desktop hardware with a mid-range GPU[3] for 8 epochs/24 h, optimising a negative log-likelihood loss function.

---

[3] NVIDIA® GeForce® GT 730.

Table 1. Accuracy metrics for the neural heuristic.

Metric	Score	Metric	Score
Accuracy	93.0%	True Positive	99
Precision	0.990	True Negative	87
Recall	0.884	False Positive	13
F_1	0.934	False Negative	1

Table 2. Total successful proof attempts on the *M2k* dataset.

Configuration	Proofs
Z3 (10 s, as baseline)	1216
Z3 (20 ms, as oracle)	711
LERNA, unguided (10 s, with oracle)	969
LERNA, guided (10 s, with oracle)	1023

6.6 Network Evaluation

The network was evaluated on the balanced test set of 200 examples, as described. Various metrics for accuracy are shown in Table 1. While these results are very promising, it should be emphasised that it is unclear how effective a train/test split is in this setting (since similar subgoals may occur in both sets, even with proper data hygiene), and that this network is not attempting to determine the satisfiability of arbitrary formulae, merely those that occur in proof attempts on the *M40k* dataset. The higher precision and lower recall values are likely an artefact of the augmentation process. However, even with these caveats, the network performance is surprising and is practically useful for improving proof search in this dataset.

7 Experimental Results

To show that neural guidance can improve the performance of LERNA the system was run with and without guidance for 10 s on all available CPU cores. All results were collected on commodity desktop hardware[4].

Table 2 shows the total number of theorems proved using various configurations of Z3 and LERNA on the *M2k* dataset. Z3 ran for a full 10 s to establish baseline performance, then as an oracle for 20 ms to determine the number of "trivial" problems. LERNA ran on an identical dataset, first without guidance from the neural heuristic, then with guidance. With neural guidance LERNA was able to solve an additional 54 problems and overall LERNA was shown to be complementary to Z3, proving 114 problems that Z3 was unable to solve on its own, and 40 that neither unguided LERNA nor Z3 could solve. Conversely, Z3

---

[4] Intel® Core™ i7-6700 CPU @ 3.40 GHz, 16 GB RAM.

was able to solve more problems in total, which is unsurprising given the maturity of the tool. These results show that LERNA is able to learn from experience and complement an existing ATP.

8 Future Work

Given the prototype nature of this work, we have included a detailed discussion on future directions. As LERNA is a very new system, there is likely much to be gained by simple engineering and tuning: for example, the UCT exploration parameter c has been left at its theoretical optimum value $\sqrt{2}$, but it is likely that a higher value will account for neural network inaccuracies and hence improve performance. Training on, benchmarking with, and optimising for other datasets (such TPTP or SMT-LIB) is also left as future work.

Proof Search. LERNA is well-suited for long-term proof search attempts in mathematics, such as those employed in the AIM project [18]: search is stable over time and does not produce a combinatorial explosion in the same way that some traditional systems tend to after a short period. Additionally, the amount of information ("confidence") in the system grows over time, as a result of a growing number of oracle invocations and neural network evaluations. Proof search can in principle be manually inspected more easily than in saturation-based provers to examine promising subgoals and remove known falsehoods from the search space. The authors hope to explore applying the system to this interesting domain.

Another future direction for proof search is a principled incomplete mode where branches deemed sufficiently uninteresting by the heuristic are pruned, perhaps in response to resource constraints as in limited resource strategies [34]. This approach, while clearly incomplete, would significantly accelerate proof search in the direction of more promising search within the available resources.

Prover Calculus. The calculus currently employed is deliberately naïve and extensions should be explored. In particular, the simplification routines can be improved to remove more trivial sub-formulae as, while in general the oracles' preprocessing will remove these, they serve as noise for the neural network and might also increase the number of inference steps required to reach a proof. As one possible view of this approach is as an intelligent preprocessor for an existing ATP, more aggressive and/or weakening inferences might be included in the calculus. For instance, *prenexing* (or conversely *miniscoping*) formulae can have a significant effect on proof search for some theorem provers, so including suitable quantifier-manipulation rules might prove to be a useful extension.

Ideas from other refutation-tableaux calculi could well be suitable for this system. The authors are attempting to integrate an adapted connection rule from the non-clausal connection calculus [27], as used in nanoCoP [28], in order to reduce the number of proof steps required to instantiate universal quantifiers. Finally, this prover architecture can support other logics without excessive modification. Given that Z3 is already capable of supporting many *theories*, such as arithmetic or datatypes, a many-sorted first order logic such as those described by SMTLIB or the TFF0 dialect of TPTP seems appropriate.

Oracle. While Z3 is a strong theorem prover in its own right and performs well here, it remains to be seen if it is the best for this application. Other ATPs (or counter-example-finding systems) should be explored. A *portfolio* of several oracle systems working in tandem might also be considered, although of course this will eventually retard proof search linearly in the number of systems present. Reducing the number of oracle invocations is another area for optimisation. Currently, the system calls an oracle for every new sub-goal generated. It seems unlikely that the sub-goal is materially easier to dispatch than its parent (especially in the case of propositional inferences that do not split the goal), so heuristically or probabilistically removing such subgoals from the oracle's queue is a possible area for improvement. LERNA does not currently use any information from the oracle beyond its status: using auxiliary information such as satisfying models or unused formulae could well aid proof search.

Machine-Learned Heuristic. Many other graph-based neural architectures are possible. PyTorch Geometric alone currently includes nearly 40 other graph-specific neural layers pre-programmed from the literature[5]. Neural models specifically for theorem proving are relatively under-studied. To combat this, data used for this paper will be published in the near future so that the machine-learning community can improve upon our simple models. Different approaches to formula-to-graph translation, symbol embeddings, data augmentation, and model integration may also be explored.

9 Conclusions

The introduced prototype LERNA system successfully implements a theorem prover with a neural heuristic processing the entire proof state, structured as a graph. After training on data automatically generated by the prover system, the neural network approach is shown to be practically useful for improving proof search performance. A number of approaches (batching, oracle invocations, parallelism) are employed to improve system efficiency. While the prototype is not yet a successful state-of-the-art ATP, it has some unique desirable properties, among them simplicity, parallelism, parametricity with respect to calculus/oracle/heuristic, and introspection of proof state. The general approach is flexible and presently unexplored.

Acknowledgements. The authors wish to thank Josef Urban and his group in ČVUT, Prague for their help and encouragement with early iterations of this work, and for supplying the Mizar dataset used in this paper.

---

[5] https://rusty1s.github.io/pytorch_geometric/build/html/modules/nn.html.

References

1. Barendregt, H.P., et al.: The Lambda Calculus. North-Holland, Amsterdam (1984)
2. Bowman, S.R., Potts, C., Manning, C.D.: Recursive neural networks can learn logical semantics. arXiv preprint arXiv:1406.1827 (2014)
3. Bridge, J.P., Holden, S.B., Paulson, L.C.: Machine learning for first-order theorem proving. J. Autom. Reason. **53**(2), 141–172 (2014)
4. de Moura, L., Bjørner, N.: Z3: an efficient SMT solver. In: Ramakrishnan, C.R., Rehof, J. (eds.) TACAS 2008. LNCS, vol. 4963, pp. 337–340. Springer, Heidelberg (2008). https://doi.org/10.1007/978-3-540-78800-3_24
5. Defferrard, M., Bresson, X., Vandergheynst, P.: Convolutional neural networks on graphs with fast localized spectral filtering. In: Advances in Neural Information Processing Systems, pp. 3844–3852 (2016)
6. Deters, M., Reynolds, A., King, T., Barrett, C.W., Tinelli, C.: A tour of CVC4: how it works, and how to use it. In: Formal Methods in Computer-Aided Design, FMCAD 2014, Lausanne, Switzerland, 21–24 October 2014, p. 7 (2014)
7. Evans, R., Saxton, D., Amos, D., Kohli, P., Grefenstette, E.: Can neural networks understand logical entailment? arXiv preprint arXiv:1802.08535 (2018)
8. Färber, M., Kaliszyk, C., Urban, J.: Monte Carlo connection prover. arXiv preprint arXiv:1611.05990 (2016)
9. Fey, M., Lenssen, J.E.: Fast graph representation learning with PyTorch geometric. In: ICLR Workshop on Representation Learning on Graphs and Manifolds (2019)
10. Gao, H., Ji, S.: Graph U-Net (2018). Preprint: https://openreview.net/forum?id=HJePRoAct7
11. Ge, Y., de Moura, L.: Complete instantiation for quantified formulas in satisfiabiliby modulo theories. In: Bouajjani, A., Maler, O. (eds.) CAV 2009. LNCS, vol. 5643, pp. 306–320. Springer, Heidelberg (2009). https://doi.org/10.1007/978-3-642-02658-4_25
12. Grabowski, A., Kornilowicz, A., Naumowicz, A.: Mizar in a nutshell. J. Formalized Reason. **3**(2), 153–245 (2010)
13. Haykin, S.: Neural Networks: A Comprehensive Foundation. Prentice Hall PTR, Upper Saddle River (1994)
14. Irving, G., Szegedy, C., Alemi, A.A., Een, N., Chollet, F., Urban, J.: DeepMath – deep sequence models for premise selection. In: Advances in Neural Information Processing Systems, pp. 2235–2243 (2016)
15. Jakubův, J., Urban, J.: ENIGMA: efficient learning-based inference guiding machine. In: Geuvers, H., England, M., Hasan, O., Rabe, F., Teschke, O. (eds.) CICM 2017. LNCS (LNAI), vol. 10383, pp. 292–302. Springer, Cham (2017). https://doi.org/10.1007/978-3-319-62075-6_20
16. Kaliszyk, C., Urban, J.: FEMaLeCoP: fairly efficient machine learning connection prover. In: Davis, M., Fehnker, A., McIver, A., Voronkov, A. (eds.) LPAR 2015. LNCS, vol. 9450, pp. 88–96. Springer, Heidelberg (2015). https://doi.org/10.1007/978-3-662-48899-7_7
17. Kaliszyk, C., Urban, J., Michalewski, H., Olšák, M.: Reinforcement learning of theorem proving. In: Advances in Neural Information Processing Systems, pp. 8822–8833 (2018)
18. Kinyon, M., Veroff, R., Vojtěchovský, P.: Loops with Abelian inner mapping groups: an application of automated deduction. In: Bonacina, M.P., Stickel, M.E. (eds.) Automated Reasoning and Mathematics. LNCS (LNAI), vol. 7788, pp. 151–164. Springer, Heidelberg (2013). https://doi.org/10.1007/978-3-642-36675-8_8

19. Kipf, T.N., Welling, M.: Semi-supervised classification with graph convolutional networks. arXiv preprint arXiv:1609.02907 (2016)
20. Komendantskaya, E., Heras, J.: Proof mining with dependent types. In: Geuvers, H., England, M., Hasan, O., Rabe, F., Teschke, O. (eds.) CICM 2017. LNCS (LNAI), vol. 10383, pp. 303–318. Springer, Cham (2017). https://doi.org/10.1007/978-3-319-62075-6_21
21. Korovin, K.: iProver – an instantiation-based theorem prover for first-order logic (system description). In: Armando, A., Baumgartner, P., Dowek, G. (eds.) IJCAR 2008. LNCS (LNAI), vol. 5195, pp. 292–298. Springer, Heidelberg (2008). https://doi.org/10.1007/978-3-540-71070-7_24
22. Krizhevsky, A., Sutskever, I., Hinton, G.E.: ImageNet classification with deep convolutional neural networks. In: Advances in Neural Information Processing Systems, pp. 1097–1105 (2012)
23. Kühlwein, D., Blanchette, J.C., Kaliszyk, C., Urban, J.: MaSh: machine learning for sledgehammer. In: Blazy, S., Paulin-Mohring, C., Pichardie, D. (eds.) ITP 2013. LNCS, vol. 7998, pp. 35–50. Springer, Heidelberg (2013). https://doi.org/10.1007/978-3-642-39634-2_6
24. Kühlwein, D., Schulz, S., Urban, J.: E-MaLeS 1.1. In: Bonacina, M.P. (ed.) CADE 2013. LNCS (LNAI), vol. 7898, pp. 407–413. Springer, Heidelberg (2013). https://doi.org/10.1007/978-3-642-38574-2_28
25. Kühlwein, D., Urban, J.: MaLeS: a framework for automatic tuning of automated theorem provers. J. Autom. Reason. **55**(2), 91–116 (2015)
26. Loos, S., Irving, G., Szegedy, C., Kaliszyk, C.: Deep network guided proof search. arXiv preprint arXiv:1701.06972 (2017)
27. Otten, J.: A non-clausal connection calculus. In: Brünnler, K., Metcalfe, G. (eds.) TABLEAUX 2011. LNCS (LNAI), vol. 6793, pp. 226–241. Springer, Heidelberg (2011). https://doi.org/10.1007/978-3-642-22119-4_18
28. Otten, J.: nanoCoP: A non-clausal connection prover. In: Olivetti, N., Tiwari, A. (eds.) IJCAR 2016. LNCS (LNAI), vol. 9706, pp. 302–312. Springer, Cham (2016). https://doi.org/10.1007/978-3-319-40229-1_21
29. Paszke, A., et al.: Automatic differentiation in PyTorch (2017)
30. Rawson, M., Reger, G.: Dynamic strategy priority: empower the strong and abandon the weak. In: AITP 2018 (2018)
31. Rawson, M., Reger, G.: Towards an efficient architecture for intelligent theorem provers. In: AITP 2019 (2019)
32. Reger, G., Suda, M., Voronkov, A.: The challenges of evaluating a new feature in Vampire. In: Vampire Workshop, pp. 70–74 (2014)
33. Riazanov, A., Voronkov, A.: The design and implementation of VAMPIRE. AI Commun. **15**(2, 3), 91–110 (2002)
34. Riazanov, A., Voronkov, A.: Limited resource strategy in resolution theorem proving. J. Symb. Comput. **36**(1–2), 101–115 (2003)
35. Robinson, A.J., Voronkov, A.: Handbook of Automated Reasoning, vol. 1. Gulf Professional Publishing, Houston (2001)
36. Schlichtkrull, M., Kipf, T.N., Bloem, P., van den Berg, R., Titov, I., Welling, M.: Modeling relational data with graph convolutional networks. In: Gangemi, A., et al. (eds.) ESWC 2018. LNCS, vol. 10843, pp. 593–607. Springer, Cham (2018). https://doi.org/10.1007/978-3-319-93417-4_38
37. Schulz, S.: E - A brainiac theorem prover. AI Commun. **15**(2, 3), 111–126 (2002)
38. Srivastava, N., Hinton, G., Krizhevsky, A., Sutskever, I., Salakhutdinov, R.: Dropout: a simple way to prevent neural networks from overfitting. J. Mach. Learn. Res. **15**(1), 1929–1958 (2014)

39. Sun, Y., Wong, A.K., Kamel, M.S.: Classification of imbalanced data: a review. Int. J. Pattern Recogn. Artif. Intell. **23**(04), 687–719 (2009)
40. Sutcliffe, G., Melville, S.: The practice of clausification in automatic theorem proving (1996)
41. Suttner, C.B., Schumann, J.: Parallel automated theorem proving. Mach. Intell. Pattern Recogn. **14**, 209–257 (1994). Elsevier
42. Urban, J.: MPTP 0.2: design, implementation, and initial experiments. J. Autom. Reason. **37**(1–2), 21–43 (2006)
43. Urban, J.: MaLARea: a metasystem for automated reasoning in large theories. In: ESARLT, vol. 257 (2007)
44. Urban, J., Vyskočil, J., Štěpánek, P.: MaLeCoP machine learning connection prover. In: Brünnler, K., Metcalfe, G. (eds.) TABLEAUX 2011. LNCS (LNAI), vol. 6793, pp. 263–277. Springer, Heidelberg (2011). https://doi.org/10.1007/978-3-642-22119-4_21
45. Wang, M., Tang, Y., Wang, J., Deng, J.: Premise selection for theorem proving by deep graph embedding. In: Advances in Neural Information Processing Systems, pp. 2786–2796 (2017)

A Language-Independent Framework for Reasoning About Preferences for Declarative Problem Solving

Alireza Ensan$^{(\boxtimes)}$ and Eugenia Ternovska$^{(\boxtimes)}$

Simon Fraser University, Burnaby, Canada
{aensan,ter}@sfu.ca

Abstract. Automated decision making often requires solving difficult and primarily NP-hard problems. In many AI applications (e.g., planning, robotics, recommender systems, etc.), users can assist decision making by specifying their preferences over some domain of interest. To take preferences into account, we take a model-theoretic approach to computationally hard problems with preferences. Computational problems are characterized as Model Expansion, that is, the logical task of expanding an input structure to satisfy a set of specifications. The uniformity of the model-theoretic approach allows us to combine computational problems with preferences regardless of the syntax of their specifications. We introduce a formalism to represent preferences of users associated with computationally hard problems. We introduce Prioritized Model Expansion, which is Model Expansion based on preferences. We investigate properties of Prioritized Model Expansion and conduct a thorough study of the impact of introducing preferences on the computational complexity of Σ_k^P-complete Model Expansion problems. We also discuss how Prioritized Model Expansion is related to other preference-based declarative approaches, such as SAT with preferences and preference-based Logic Programming.

Keywords: Preference · Model Expansion · Computational problems

1 Introduction

Solving computationally hard problems (e.g., NP-hard) is in the core of many AI tasks. Due to the significant progress in the performance of modern solvers, finding solutions to such problems (e.g., planning, travelling salesman, graph colouring, etc.) has become feasible in many applications. We view such hard problems as Model Expansion [25], which is the logical task of expanding a structure (a problem instance) to a solution structure that satisfies a formula (the problem specification) that is written in a certain language. The main declarative approaches in AI, including Satisfiability problems (SAT), Constraint Satisfaction Problems (CSP), and Answer Set Programming (ASP), can be encoded as

© Springer Nature Switzerland AG 2019
A. Herzig and A. Popescu (Eds.): FroCoS 2019, LNAI 11715, pp. 57–73, 2019.
https://doi.org/10.1007/978-3-030-29007-8_4

Model Expansion [25]. By distinguishing between problem instances and problem specifications, Model Expansion provides a robust modelling framework and establishes a connection to Descriptive Complexity [23].

It is common that a decision maker prioritizes the solutions. Since preferences play a key role in AI, a large number of frameworks for handling preferences have been proposed during the last two decades, e.g., [1,5,12,15,29]. As it was discussed in [19], these proposals are often language-dependent because they are added to a host formal language such as ASP [10,12,18] or default logic [11,17].

In real-world applications, search and decision problems often consist of a number of sub-problems that interact with each other. For example, suppose a vacation planner includes a component that generates a vacation package based on the constraints of a travel agency by solving answer set programs and a component that solves integer linear programs to find the best plan based on the needs and priorities of a traveler. The modular nature of many AI tasks necessitates the integrating of preference-based problems regardless of the language of their specifications. We tackle this issue by proposing a preference framework for Model Expansion. Given that Model Expansion underlies all predominant declarative frameworks such as ASP, SAT, and CSP, we show how our language-independent preference-based framework corresponds to these approaches with preferences, such as Answer Set Optimization [12], Logic Programming with Preferences [26], CSP with CP-nets [6], etc. The main motivation for our work is to connect model theory, descriptive complexity, and preference modelling to study computationally hard problems with preferences. To the best of our knowledge, this is the first proposal of this kind in the literature. We propose that preferences are expressed as an ordering relation on ground atoms. The relation among atoms is lifted to a preference ordering relation among structures using a number of different preference semantics (lifting methods). We define the *Dominant Structure* problem, which is the problem of deciding whether a structure is preferred to another structure. We prove that solving the *Dominant Structure* problem is polynomial in the size of the domain of structures. Our framework allows other methods of lifting as long as the *Dominant Structure* problem is polynomial, which makes the following complexity results applicable.

A model-theoretic view on modular systems with preferences was presented in [21]. The authors showed the connection of their proposal to other formalisms such as CP-nets [5]. They used Codd's relational algebra [16] to combine modules with preferences. The combination was static – the authors did not focus on Model Expansion.

Our main contributions are as follows: First, we introduce the notion of Prioritized Model Expansion, a declarative framework for specifying computational problems with preferences. Prioritized Model Expansion extends Model Expansion by modelling preferences of a decision maker. Second, we show that adding preferences even in the simplest formulations leads to a rise of the computational complexity of Σ_k^P-complete Model Expansion problems to Σ_{k+1}^P-complete Model Expansion problems. Third, we study the relations of some preference-based frameworks with Prioritized Model Expansion. We apply the computational complexity result to some associated reasoning tasks to obtain similar results for those frameworks.

2   Background

A τ-structure $\mathcal{A} = (A, R_1^{\mathcal{A}}, ..., R_n^{\mathcal{A}}, C_1^{\mathcal{A}}, ..., C_m^{\mathcal{A}})$ is a tuple where τ is a vocabulary, which is a set of non-logical relation symbols R_i with associated arity k_i where $i \in [1, n]$ and constant symbols C_j where $j \in [1, m]$ and A is a domain. For any $R_i \in \tau$, $R_i^{\mathcal{A}}$ is called the interpretation of R_i and $R_i^{\mathcal{A}} \subseteq A^{k_i}$. Also, for every $C_j \in \tau$, $C_j^{\mathcal{A}} \in Dom$. A structure is called finite if its domain is finite. Throughout this paper, we assume that all structures are finite. For a formula ψ in a logic $\mathcal{L}$, $vocab(\psi)$ denotes the set of vocabulary symbols appearing in ψ. The definition of expansion is standard in logic literature and is defined inductively as follows: Let $\mathcal{A}$ be a σ-structure and $\mathcal{B}$ be a τ-structure where $\sigma \subseteq \tau$. $\mathcal{B}$ expands $\mathcal{A}$ if the domain of $\mathcal{B}$ is the same as the domain of $\mathcal{A}$ and for all $R \in \sigma$, $R^{\mathcal{A}} = R^{\mathcal{B}}$. Model Expansion (MX) is the task of expanding a structure to satisfy a formula in logic $\mathcal{L}$ [25]. The Model Expansion problem is defined as follows:

Definition 1 (Model Expansion Problem $MX_{\sigma, \psi}$).
Given: an arbitrary σ-structure $\mathcal{I}$ over a finite domain Dom, formula ψ in a logic $\mathcal{L}$ where vocabulary $\sigma \subseteq vocab(\psi)$,
Find a τ-structure $\mathcal{A}$ where $\mathcal{A} \models \psi$ and expands $\mathcal{I}$. (The decision version: is there a τ-structure $\mathcal{A}$ such that $\mathcal{A} \models \psi$ and $\mathcal{A}$ expands $\mathcal{I}$?)

We call $\mathcal{A}$ an *expansion structure* of $MX_{\sigma, \psi}$. Each expansion structure $\mathcal{A}$ is a τ-structure with domain Dom. In this paper, we are interested in data complexity (ψ is fixed and the domain of input is variable). For logic $\mathcal{L}$, the data complexity of Model Expansion (MX) is always in-between model checking (MC) and satisfiability (SAT). For example, for first-order logic, MC is AC_0, MX is in NP, and SAT is undecidable. Graph colouring can be characterized as a first-order Model Expansion problem (i.e, the problem specification is in first-order logic) as follows:

Example 1. Let E be a binary relation. Let unary relation symbols R, G, and B denote red, green, and blue, respectively. The following formula specifies three-colouring:

$$\psi = \forall x \; [(R(x) \lor B(x) \lor G(x))$$
$$\land \neg((R(x) \land B(x)) \lor (R(x) \land G(x)) \lor (B(x) \land G(x)))]$$
$$\land \; \forall x \forall y \; [E(x, y) \supset (\neg(R(x) \land R(y))$$
$$\land \neg(B(x) \land B(y)) \land \neg(G(x) \land G(y)))].$$

A graph $\mathcal{G} = (V, E)$ is an instance structure with vocabulary $\sigma = \{E\}$ and domain V, which is the set of vertices. Model Expansion problem $MX_{\{E\}, \psi}$ finds expansion structure $\mathcal{A}$ (i.e., three-colouring of $\mathcal{G}$) that interprets symbols R, B, and G satisfying ψ as follows:

$$\underbrace{(\overbrace{V; E^{\mathcal{G}}}^{\mathcal{G}}, \; R^{\mathcal{A}}, B^{\mathcal{A}}, G^{\mathcal{A}})}_{\mathcal{A}} \models \psi.$$

Computational Complexity, a Review: Let X be a complexity class.

Notation 1. P^X *is the class of languages (complexity class) that can be computed in polynomial time by a deterministic Turing machine with an oracle in* X. *Also,* NP^X *is the class of languages that can be computed in polynomial time by a nondeterministic Turing machine using an oracle in* X.

Notation 2. *co-X is the complexity class of decision problems whose complements are in X.*

The Polynomial Hierarchy (PH) is defined as $\Sigma_0^P = \Pi_0^P = \Delta_0^P = P$, $\Sigma_{k+1}^P = NP^{\Sigma_k^P}$, $\Delta_{k+1}^P = P^{\Delta_k^P}$, and $\Pi_{k+1}^P = \text{coNP}^{\Sigma_k^P}$ for $k > 0$.

3   Model Expansion with Preferences

In this section, we introduce the notion of Prioritized Model Expansion (PMX). We study the computational complexity of solving problems related to the PMX including *Dominant Structure* (i.e., given two structures, whether one is preferred to another), *Optimal Expansion* (i.e., given a structure, whether it is an optimal expansion of a Model Expansion problem), and *Goal-Oriented Optimal Expansion* (i.e., deciding whether there is an optimal expansion satisfying a certain goal).

3.1   Preference Expression

Let Dom be a domain of elements. Consider first-order variables $X = \{x_1, ..., x_r\}$ over Dom, vocabulary τ, and k-ary $R \in \tau$. Let $\nu : X \to Dom$ be an assignment function that assigns a domain element to each variable. For an ordered set of variables $\bar{x} = (x_1, ..., x_k)$, we call $\bar{a} = (a_1, ..., a_k)$ a k-ary tuple when there is an assignment ν such that for $1 \leq i \leq k$, $\nu(x_i) = a_i$. We use the symbol $\bar{a}[x_i]$ to denote value a_i. For k-ary predicate symbol $R \in \tau$, we call $R(\bar{a})$ a ground atom of τ over Dom. We say a structure $\mathcal{A}$ satisfies a ground atom $R(\bar{a})$ (notation $\mathcal{A} \models R(\bar{a})$) if $\bar{a} \in R^{\mathcal{A}}$.

Definition 2 (Preference Expression). *A preference expression P over Dom is defined as a pair $P = (\mathcal{S}_\tau, \sqsupseteq_P)$ where $\mathcal{S}_\tau$ is the set of all ground atoms of vocabulary τ over Dom and $\sqsupseteq_P$ is a preorder on S_τ.*

Let $R(\bar{a})$ and $T(\bar{b})$ be ground atoms where k-ary predicate R and k'-ary predicate T are in τ, k-ary tuple $\bar{a} \in Dom^k$, and k'-ary tuple $\bar{b} \in Dom^{k'}$. The expression $R(\bar{a}) \sqsupseteq_P T(\bar{b})$ is read as $R(\bar{a})$ is preferred to $T(\bar{b})$. Also, $R(\bar{a})$ is called strictly preferred to $T(\bar{b})$ with notation $R(\bar{a}) \sqsupset_P T(\bar{b})$ if $R(\bar{a}) \sqsupseteq_P T(\bar{b})$ is true and $T(\bar{b}) \sqsupseteq_P R(\bar{a})$ does not hold.

We shall introduce a preference ordering $\geq_P^s$ on structures based on a preference expression P and a preference semantics (lifting method) s. Lifting method s specifies how $\geq_P^s$ is constructed from $\sqsupseteq_P$. Comparing two sets with members that are prioritized has been widely studied in different areas, such as in database systems [27], or even beyond the realm of theoretical computer science, such as in economics and decision theory [14]. Inspired by [1,9,13,27], here we introduce three different methods to lift a preference ordering on ground atoms to a preference ordering on structures. In each of the following methods, relation $\geq_P^s$ among τ-structures with the same domain is constructed from $\sqsupseteq_P$.

Definition 3 *(Preference Relations on Structures).*
Given a preference expression $P = (S_\tau, \sqsupseteq_P)$ over domain Dom, let $\mathcal{A}$ and $\mathcal{B}$ be two τ-structures with domain Dom,

- **Weak Pareto (WP).** $\mathcal{A} \geq_P^{wp} \mathcal{B}$ *iff for all $R, S \in \tau$ and for all $\overline{a} \in R^{\mathcal{A}}$ and all $\overline{b} \in S^{\mathcal{B}}$, $R(\overline{a}) \sqsupseteq_P S(\overline{b})$.*
- **Upper Bound Dominance (UBD).** $\mathcal{A} \geq_P^{ubd} \mathcal{B}$ *iff for all $S \in \tau$ and for all $\overline{b} \in S^{\mathcal{B}}$, for some $R \in \tau$, there is $\overline{a}$ such that $\overline{a} \in R^{\mathcal{A}}$ and $R(\overline{a}) \sqsupseteq_P S(\overline{b})$.*
- **Element Dominance (ED).** $\mathcal{A} \geq_P^{ed} \mathcal{B}$ *iff for some $R, S \in \tau$, there is $\overline{b} \in S^{\mathcal{B}}$ and there is $\overline{a} \in R^{\mathcal{A}}$ such that $R(\overline{a}) \sqsupseteq_P S(\overline{b})$ and there is no $\overline{c}$ for some $T \in \tau$ such that $\overline{c} \in T^{\mathcal{B}}$ and $T(\overline{c}) \sqsupseteq_P R(\overline{a})$.*

The Weak Pareto semantic uses the idea of Pareto dominance [28] such that $\mathcal{A}$ is preferred to $\mathcal{B}$ if every ground atom that is satisfied by $\mathcal{A}$ is at least as preferred as any ground atom which $\mathcal{B}$ satisfies. In a stronger version, all ground atoms that are satisfied by $\mathcal{A}$ must be at least as preferred as ground atoms satisfied by $\mathcal{B}$ except one ground atom satisfied by $\mathcal{A}$ that is strictly preferred to a ground atom that $\mathcal{B}$ satisfies. The Upper Bound Dominance approach is a weaker version of the Weak Pareto such that if $\mathcal{A}$ satisfies any ground atom that is at least as preferred as the maximal element (based on preorder $\sqsupseteq_P$) of atoms satisfied by $\mathcal{B}$, then $\mathcal{A}$ is preferred to $\mathcal{B}$. Finally, based on the Element Dominance semantics, there is an adequate reason to drive that $\mathcal{A}$ is preferred to $\mathcal{B}$ if there is a ground atom, say $R(\overline{a})$, that $\mathcal{A}$ satisfies and is preferred to some ground atoms satisfied by $\mathcal{B}$ and no ground atom satisfied by $\mathcal{B}$ is strictly preferred to $R(\overline{a})$.

These semantics (lifting methods) may illustrate similar, or in some cases, different behavior. For example, the computational complexity of reasoning tasks associated with preferred models using each of these semantics is the same. Also, relation $>_P^y$ is transitive when y is the Upper Bound Dominance or the Weak Pareto semantics. However, if y is the Element Dominance semantics, $>_P^y$ is not necessarily transitive. For example, consider the case where the relational vocabulary is $\tau = \{R\}$ and the domain is $Dom = \{1, 2, 3, 4\}$. Assume the preorder over ground atoms is defined as $R(1) \sqsupseteq R(2)$ and $R(3) \sqsupseteq R(4)$. Assume $\mathcal{A}$, $\mathcal{B}$, and $\mathcal{C}$ are τ-structures such that $R^{\mathcal{A}} = \{1\}$, $R^{\mathcal{B}} = \{2, 3\}$, and $R^{\mathcal{C}} = \{4\}$. One can check that for the Element Dominance semantics, $\mathcal{A} >^{ed} \mathcal{B}$, $\mathcal{B} >^{ed} \mathcal{C}$, but $\mathcal{A} >^{ed} \mathcal{C}$ does not hold. However, the transitivity is not a requirement for relation $>_P^y$ in solving *Optimal Expansion* and *Goal-oriented Optimal Expansion* problems. We note that the lifting methods are not limited to what was proposed in Definition 3. Other lifting methods are allowed if the *Dominant structure* problem remains in polynomial time. Defining different preference semantics on the condition that the *Dominant Structure* problem is in polynomial time gives us the alternatives to pick stronger or weaker versions of preference semantics based on a particular application while the complexity of associated reasoning tasks does not vary.

The strict version of $\geq_P^s$ where $s \in \{\text{wp, ubd, ed}\}$ is defined as $\mathcal{A} >_P^s \mathcal{B}$ if $\mathcal{A} \geq_P^s \mathcal{B}$ and $\mathcal{B} \geq_P^s \mathcal{A}$ does not hold. Also, we say $\mathcal{A}$ is *dominant* to $\mathcal{B}$ based on a preference semantics $s \in \{\text{wp, ubd, ed}\}$ whenever $\mathcal{A} >_P^s \mathcal{B}$.

Definition 4 (Dominant Structure Problem).

> **Input:** *a preference expression* $P = (\mathcal{S}_\tau, \sqsupseteq_P)$ *over Dom,* τ*-structures* $\mathcal{A}$ *and* $\mathcal{B}$ *with domain Dom, and a preference semantics* $s \in \{wp, ubd, ed\}$,
> **Question:** *is* $\mathcal{A} >_P^s \mathcal{B}$?

The following result indicates that the problem of deciding whether a structure is dominant to another structure using one of the preference semantics in Definition 3 is solvable in polynomial time in the size of the domain of the structures.

Proposition 1. *The Dominant Structure problem is solvable in polynomial time in the size of Dom.*

Proof. As stated by Definition 3, at most, we compare all tuples in $R^{\mathcal{A}}$ and $R^{\mathcal{B}}$ for all $R \in \tau$. The total possible number of k-ary tuples is $|Dom|^k$ where k is the maximum arity of predicate symbols in τ. Therefore, $\mathcal{O}(|Dom|^{2k})$ comparisons are required for each $R \in \tau$. Thus, deciding whether $\mathcal{A} >_P^s \mathcal{B}$ is in $\mathcal{O}(m \cdot |Dom|^{2k})$ (polynomial in the size of Dom) where m is the number of elements in τ. ∎

We note that vocabulary τ is considered to be fixed and our discussion of computational complexity is focused on the size of the domain of $\mathcal{A}$ and $\mathcal{B}$ in the *Dominant Structure* problem.

3.2 Prioritized Model Expansion

We characterize search and decision problems with preferences as Prioritized Model Expansion (PMX), which is the task of expanding an input structure to the most preferred expansion structures with respect a preference expression.

Definition 5 (Prioritized Model Expansion Problem).

> **Input:** *an arbitrary input* σ*-structure* $\mathcal{I}$*, formula* ψ*, input vocabulary* $\sigma \subseteq vocab(\psi)$*, a preference expression* $P = (\mathcal{S}_\tau, \sqsupseteq_P)$ *over the domain of* $\mathcal{I}$*, and a preference semantics* s
> **Find:** *structure* $\mathcal{A}$ *such that* $\mathcal{A}$ *is an expansion structure of* $MX_{\sigma,\psi}$ *and there is no expansion structure* $\mathcal{B}$ *such that* $\mathcal{B} >_P^s \mathcal{A}$.

Notation 3. $\Pi_{\sigma,\psi} = (MX_{\sigma,\psi}, P)$ *is a Prioritized Model Expansion problem (based on a preference semantics* s*) where* $MX_{\sigma,\psi}$ *is a Model Expansion problem and* $P = (\mathcal{S}_\tau, \sqsupseteq_P)$ *is a preference expression over the domain of the input structure.*

Each solution of a Prioritized Model Expansion problem $\Pi_{\sigma,\psi}$ is called an optimal expansion of $\Pi_{\sigma,\psi}$. It is worth noting that all expansion structures retain the domain of input structure $\mathcal{I}$. Also, ψ and $vocab(\psi)$ are assumed to be fixed. Hereafter, unless it is mentioned otherwise, we only study the data complexity of associated reasoning tasks. The data complexity points to the fact that the domain of input $\mathcal{I}$ (and hence the size of $\mathcal{I}$) varies while the vocabulary of input (i.e., σ) and specifications (and therefore $vocab(\psi) = \tau$) are considered to be fixed.

Example 2. Consider the problem of graph colouring that was described as Model Expansion in Example 1. Let $\mathcal{G} = (V, E)$ be the input graph where $V = \{v_1, v_2, v_3, v_4, v_5\}$ and $E^{\mathcal{G}} = \{(v_1, v_2), (v_2, v_1), (v_1, v_3), (v_1, v_3), (v_3, v_1), (v_2, v_4),$ $(v_4, v_2), (v_4, v_5), (v_5, v_4), (v_3, v_5), (v_5, v_3)\}$. Assume that we prefer red for v_1. Also, a red v_4 is favoured over a red v_5 and a blue v_2 is preferred to a green v_2. These preference statements can be encoded by a preference expression P such that $R(v_1) \sqsupset_P B(v_1)$ and $R(v_1) \sqsupset_P G(v_1)$. Also, $R(v_4) \sqsupset_P R(v_5)$ and $B(v_2) \sqsupset_P G(v_2)$. Prioritized Model Expansion problem $\Pi_{\{E\},\psi} = (MX_{\{E\},\psi}, P)$ where $MX_{\{E\},\psi}$ is the characterization of three-colouring for input graph $\mathcal{G}$ and P is the preference expression. The input graph $\mathcal{G}$ has 18 possible three-colourings. Among these solutions, $\mathcal{A}$ is an optimal expansion of $\mathcal{G}$ (based on the Element Dominance semantics) where $R^{\mathcal{A}} = \{v_1, v_4\}$, $B^{\mathcal{A}} = \{v_2, v_5\}$, and $G^{\mathcal{A}} = \{v_3\}$.

In the rest of this subsection, we discuss some decision problems that are associated with Prioritized Model Expansion.

Definition 6 *(Optimal Expansion Problem).*

> **Input:** *a τ-structure $\mathcal{A}$ and a Prioritized Model Expansion problem $\Pi_{\sigma,\psi} = (MX_{\sigma,\psi}, P)$ based on a preference semantics s where $MX_{\sigma,\psi}$ is a Model Expansion problem with an arbitrary input σ-structure $\mathcal{I}$ such that $\sigma \subseteq \tau = vocab(\psi)$ and $P = (\mathcal{S}_\tau \sqsupset_P)$ is a preference expression over the domain of $\mathcal{I}$,*
> **Question:** *Is $\mathcal{A}$ an optimal expansion of $\Pi_{\sigma,\psi}$?*

Proposition 2. *For a Model Expansion problem $MX_{\sigma,\psi}$, let model checking of ψ (given a structure $\mathcal{A}$, decide if $\mathcal{A} \models \psi$) be in a complexity class Y. The problem of Optimal Expansion is in co-NP^Y.*

Proof. The complementary problem is deciding whether there is an expansion structure $\mathcal{B}$ such that $\mathcal{B} >_P^s \mathcal{A}$. The complementary problem can be solved by a non-deterministic polynomial Turing machine guessing $\mathcal{B}$ with access to an oracle in Y that decides whether $\mathcal{B}$ is an expansion of $MX_{\sigma,\psi}$ (this includes checking if $\mathcal{B}$ expands $\mathcal{I}$ in polynomial time and whether $\mathcal{B} \models \psi$ in complexity Y) and, based on Proposition 1, in polynomial time checks whether $\mathcal{B} >_P^s \mathcal{A}$. Thus, the complementary problem is in NP^Y and the original problem is in co-NP^Y. ∎

To put the impact of defining preferences in perspective, consider that deciding whether a given structure $\mathcal{A}$ is an expansion of $MX_{\sigma,\psi}$ is in complexity Y

because it is required to first check whether $\mathcal{A}$ is an expansion of $\mathcal{I}$ that can be decided in polynomial time and then determine whether $\mathcal{A} \models \psi$ in complexity Y. On the other hand, deciding whether $\mathcal{A}$ is an optimal expansion is in co-NP^Y. In fact, to decide whether a structure is an optimal expansion, not only must it be verified as an expansion, but it must also be compared to all possible expansion structures.

One of the common tasks in many AI applications is to determine if a certain goal is achieved by solutions to a problem, e.g., in automated AI planning [2]. In the context of Prioritized Model Expansion, we ask whether there is an optimal expansion that satisfies a certain formula (goal). The problem is formulated as follows:

Definition 7 *(Goal-Oriented Optimal Expansion Problem).*

> **Input:** $\Pi_{\sigma,\psi} = (MX_{\sigma,\psi}, P)$ *where* $MX_{\sigma,\psi}$ *is a Model Expansion problem with an input* σ*-structure* $\mathcal{I}$ *with a domain* Dom, $\tau = vocab(\psi)$, $P = (\mathcal{S}_\tau, \sqsupseteq_P)$ *is a preference expression over the domain of* $\mathcal{I}$, *and* ϕ *is a formula of the form* $R_i(\overline{a}_j) \wedge ... \wedge R_l(\overline{a}_k)$ *where* $R_i, ..., R_l \in \tau$ *and* $R_i(\overline{a}_j), ..., R_l(\overline{a}_k)$ *are ground atoms over* Dom *where every element of* Dom *is also a constant in vocabulary* τ *that is interpreted as itself by every expansion structure of* $MX_{\sigma,\Psi}$,
> **Question:** *Is there an optimal expansion* $\mathcal{A}$ *of* $\Pi_{\sigma,\psi}$ *such that* $\mathcal{A} \models \phi$?

Proposition 3. *Let solving Optimal Expansion problem* $\Pi_{\sigma,\psi} = (MX_{\sigma,\psi}, P)$ *be in the complexity class* X. *The problem of Goal-Oriented Optimal Expansion is in* NP^X.

Proof. First, we non-deterministically guess a τ-structure $\mathcal{A}$ and in polynomial time check if $\overline{a} \in R^{\mathcal{A}}$, for all ground atoms $R(\overline{a})$ appearing in ϕ, that can be done by means of a non-deterministic polynomial Turing machine. Second, we check whether our guess is an optimal expansion that is in complexity class X by the assumption. Thus, the problem can be solved by a non-deterministic polynomial Turing machine using an oracle in X. Hence, the problem is in NP^X. ∎

A generalization of the *Goal-Oriented Optimal Expansion* problem is to find an optimal expansion satisfying a formula ϕ in a certain logic $\mathcal{L}^*$. In this case, the complexity of model checking in logic $\mathcal{L}^*$ (i.e., given a structure $\mathcal{A}$ if $\mathcal{A} \models \phi$?) is taken into account. However, for the sake of simplicity, in this chapter we consider goal ϕ as a conjunction of ground atoms. Hence, deciding whether a structure $\mathcal{A}$ satisfies ϕ can be verified in polynomial time.

Prioritized Σ_k^P-Complete Model Expansion Problems. In this subsection, we discuss the computational complexity impact of introducing preferences on Σ_k^P-complete Model Expansion problems. As was discussed in [25], any boolean query computable in NP can be expressed as a first-order Model Expansion $MX_{\sigma,\psi}$ where ψ is a first-order formula. Based on Fagin's theorem [22], NP is the class of boolean queries expressible in existential second-order logic ($\exists$SO). This shows that a first-order MX and existential second-order logic have the same expressive power. Similarly, the Polynomial Hierarchy is the set of boolean queries expressible in second-order logic and any query computable in Σ_k^P ($k > 1$) can be encoded as $MX_{\sigma,\psi}$ where ψ is a formula of the form $Q_1, ..., Q_{k-1}\psi^*$ such that for $1 \leq i \leq k$, Q_is are alternating second-order quantifiers (alternation between $\exists$ and $\forall$), $Q_1 = \forall$, Q_{k-1} is $\forall$ if k is even and $\exists$ otherwise, and ψ^* is a first-order formula.

If the decision version of a Model Expansion problem $MX_{\sigma,\psi}$ is in Σ_k^P, then the problem has second-order specification ψ of the form $Q_1, ..., Q_{k-1}\psi^*$. Thus, the complexity of model checking of ψ is in Π_{k-1}^P and, hence, based on Proposition 2, solving the Optimal Expansion problem ($MX_{\sigma,\psi}, P$) is in Σ_k^P. For Σ_1^P-complete Model Expansion problems, we show that the problem of deciding the existence of minimal solutions to an abductive logic program [20] satisfying a goal can be reduced to Goal-Oriented Optimal Expansion similar to [26]. An abductive logic program is defined as $ALP = \langle H, M, \mathcal{P} \rangle$ over a set A of propositional atoms where $\mathcal{P}$ is a logic program, $H \subseteq A$ is called hypothesis and $M \subseteq A \cup \{\neg a | a \in A\}$ is manifestation. A solution of ALP is a set $N \subseteq H$ such that there is a stable model S of $\mathcal{P} \cup N$ and $M \subseteq S$. A solution N is called (H) minimal if there is no solution N' such that $N' \subset N$. For a given hypothesis $h \in H$, deciding whether there is a minimal solution N such that $h \in N$ is Σ_2^P-complete.

For problems in the higher levels of the Polynomial Hierarchy, we consider the following: Σ_k^P-complete problems can be encoded as a combined logic program [4]. $\Pi = (\mathcal{P}_g, \mathcal{P}_t)$ is called a combined logic program where $\mathcal{P}_g$ and $\mathcal{P}_t$ are logic programs over a set of propositional variables G and T respectively. M is a model of Π if it is a stable model of $\mathcal{P}_g$ and there is not a stable model N of $\mathcal{P}_t$ such that $M \cap G = N \cap T$. The decision version of this problem is Σ_2^P-complete. Recursively, the existence of a model of a combined program in depth 2 defined as $\Pi_2 = (\mathcal{P}_{g_2}, (\mathcal{P}_{g_1}, \mathcal{P}_t))$ is Σ_3^P-complete and, similarly, in depth k, the existence of a model of $(\mathcal{P}_{g_{k-1}}, \Pi_{k-2})$ is Σ_k^P-complete. We introduce abductive combined program as $\mathcal{C} = \langle H, M, \Pi \rangle$ where $\Pi = (\mathcal{P}_g, \mathcal{P}_t)$ is a combined logic program. W is a solution of $\mathcal{C}$ if there is a model S of $(\mathcal{P}_g \cup W, \mathcal{P}_t)$ such that $M \subseteq S$. W is minimal if there is not a solution W' such that $W' \subset W$.

Lemma 1. *The problem of deciding whether $\mathcal{C} = \langle H, M, \Pi_k \rangle$ for a given $h \in H$ has a minimal solution containing h is Σ_{k+1}^P-complete.*

Proof. The proof includes a translation from a quantified boolean formula (QBF) to $\mathcal{C}$ for $k = 2$ and then, by induction on k for $k > 2$, the result follows. Let φ be a boolean formula in CNF and $X = \{x_1, ..., x_m\}$, $W = \{w_1, ..., w_m\}$, $X' = \{x_1', ..., x_m'\}$, $Y = \{y_1, ..., y_n\}$, and $Z = \{z_1, ..., z_l\}$ be a set of boolean variables in φ. Let t, h, and f also be boolean variables. Consider $\mathcal{P}_g$ to be a set of rules of the form $\{t \leftarrow x_i, x_i'\}$, $\{w_i \leftarrow x_i\}$, $\{w_i \leftarrow x_i'\}$, $\{t \leftarrow y_1, ...y_n, h\}$, and $\{f \leftarrow l_1, ..., l_r\}$ where $\neg(l_1 \wedge, ..., \wedge l_r) \in \varphi$ similar to [20]. For $X \cup X' \subseteq H$, an H-minimal solution of $\langle H, \{t\} \cup W, \mathcal{P}_g \rangle$ does not contain f and it has either x_i or x_i'. On the other hand, similar to [4], assume $\mathcal{P}_t$ determines the truth value of a set of boolean variables Z. Also, for each clause $C \in \varphi$, suppose that $\mathcal{P}_t$ includes a set of rules of the form $t \leftarrow \neg C$ and $f \leftarrow \neg f, t$ that means t must not be in any stable model of $\mathcal{P}_t$. This implies that the validity of $\exists X \forall Y \exists Z \varphi$ is equivalent to the existence of an H-minimal solution of $\mathcal{C}$ that contains h. So, for $k = 2$, the existence of a minimal solution to an abductive combined logic program containing an atom h is Σ_3^P-complete.   ∎

The following result shows the impact of introducing preferences to Σ_k^P-complete Model Expansion problems.

Theorem 1. *Let the decision version of a Model Expansion problem $MX_{\sigma,\psi}$ be Σ_k^P-complete. The problem of Goal-Oriented Optimal Expansion for $MX_{\sigma,\psi}$ is Σ_{k+1}^P-complete.*

Proof. The membership to Σ_{k+1}^P follows from the results of Propositions 2, 3, and properties of Model Expansion. Since the Model Expansion problem is in Σ_k^P, it has a second-order specification with $k-1$ number of alternations between second-order quantifiers. Therefore, the complexity of model checking of ψ is in Π_{k-1}^P. Thus, based on Proposition 2, the complexity of the Optimal Expansion problem is in co-NP$^{\Sigma_{k-1}^P}$ that is equal to Π_k^P. Also, based on Proposition 3, the Goal-Oriented Optimal Expansion problem is in NP$^{\Pi_k^P}$ or NP$^{\Sigma_k^P}$ that is equal to Σ_{k+1}^P.

For the proof of hardness, we consider an abductive logic program $ALP = \langle H, M, \mathcal{P} \rangle$. Let us define a logic program $\mathcal{P}'$ as a set of rules of the form $r : R(\bar{a}) \leftarrow \neg S(\bar{b})$ for any $R(\bar{a}) \sqsupseteq_P S(\bar{b})$ such that $S(\bar{b}) \in H$. Rule r says that a better conclusion is drawn from not making a less preferred assumption. Define $\mathcal{P}^* = \mathcal{P} \cup \mathcal{P}'$. The problem of deciding the existence of a stable model of a logic program is NP-complete and it can be translated into the decision version of a Model Expansion problem $MX_{\sigma,\psi}$. The program can be represented by an instance structure and the stable model semantics is characterized by ψ (e.g., a first-order Model Expansion characterization of ASP was shown in [25]). The problem of finding out whether there is an H-minimal solution of ALP can be reduced to deciding whether there is an optimal expansion in $(MX_{\sigma,\psi}, P)$ where $\mathcal{P}^*$ is translated into $MX_{\sigma,\psi}$. Assume X_1 and X_2 are two stable models of $\mathcal{P}^*$. If X_1 is preferred to X_2 with respect to one of the preference semantics in Definition 3, then there is $R(\bar{a}) \in X_1$ and $S(\bar{b}) \in X_2$ such that $R(\bar{a}) \sqsupseteq_P S(\bar{b})$. So, we have $X_1 \cap H \subseteq X_2 \cap H$ and therefore, each preferred answer set is H-minimal. Hence, finding a minimal solution for $\langle H, M, \mathcal{P} \rangle$ is reduced to finding an optimal expansion of $\Pi_{\sigma,\psi}$ that satisfies a goal M. Thus, *Goal-Oriented Optimal Expansion* for an NP-complete MX is Σ_2^P-complete. By using the same argument and according to Lemma 1, finding a minimal solution for an abductive combined logic program in level k can be translated into a *Goal-Oriented Optimal Expansion* where the Model Expansion problem is Σ_k^P-complete and hence the result follows.   ∎

Theorem 1 presents an important consequence of adding preferences to a Σ_k^P-complete Model Expansion problem. For the problem of deciding whether there is an expansion that satisfies a goal ϕ, adding preferences leads to a jump in the

Polynomial Hierarchy. So, the preference relation between expansion structures derived from a preference expression can not be translated into axiomatization ψ with polynomial time model checking unless $P = NP$ or the Polynomial Hierarchy collapses.

Example 3. *Deciding whether a graph is Hamiltonian (i.e., whether a graph has a Hamiltonian cycle) is a well-known NP-complete problem. We first characterize the Hamiltonian graph problem as first-order Model Expansion and then examine the Goal-Oriented Prioritized Model Expansion problem for an input graph with some preferences. Consider vocabulary $\tau = \{E, H\}$. For an arbitrary graph $\mathcal{G} = (V, E^{\mathcal{G}})$ (represented as a structure) such that V is the set of vertices of the graph and $E^{\mathcal{G}}$ specifies edges of $\mathcal{G}$, the Hamiltonian graph problem is defined as a Model Expansion problem $MX_{\{E\}, \Psi}$ where $\{E\}$ is the vocabulary of input and $\Psi = \psi_1 \wedge \psi_2 \wedge \psi_3$ such that*

$$\psi_1 = \forall x \forall y (H(x,y) \vee H(y,x))$$
$$\psi_2 = \forall x \forall y \forall z (H(x,y) \wedge H(y,x) \supset H(x,z))$$
$$\psi_3 = \forall x \forall y ((H(x,y) \wedge \neg \exists z [H(x,z) \wedge H(z,y)]) \supset E(x,y))$$

where ψ_1 indicates there is a Hamiltonian path between any arbitrary pair of vertices x and y, ψ_2 stipulates the transitivity property of the path, and, based on ψ_3, if there are two adjacent vertices in the path, they must be connected through an edge of the graph. A τ-structure $\mathcal{A}$ is an expansion structure of $MX_{E,\Psi}$ if $\mathcal{A}$ expands $\mathcal{G}$ and satisfies ψ as follows:

$$\underbrace{(\overbrace{V; E^{\mathcal{G}}}^{\mathcal{G}}, H^{\mathcal{A}})}_{\mathcal{A}} \models \psi$$

Model Expansion problem $MX_{E,\psi}$ asks whether there is a Hamiltonian path (and therefore a Hamiltonian cycle) in the input graph. If the answer is yes, then there is a τ-structure $\mathcal{B}$ such that $H^{\mathcal{B}}$ constitutes a Hamiltonian path. Assume $V = \{v_1, v_2, v_3, v_4\}$ is a set of vertices and $\mathcal{G} = (V, E^{\mathcal{G}})$ is defined $E^{\mathcal{G}} = \{(v_1, v_2), (v_2, v_3), (v_3, v_4), (v_4, v_1), (v_1, v_4), (v_3, v_1), (v_4, v_2)\}$. A preference expression P is defined as $H(v_4, v_2) \sqsupseteq_P H(v_3, v_4)$ which means it is preferred that a Hamiltonian path includes $H(v_4, v_2)$ (i.e., edge $E(v_4, v_2)$ due to specification ψ_3) rather than $H(v_3, v_4)$ (i.e., edge $E(v_4, v_2)$ because of specification ψ_3).

The Prioritized Model Expansion problem $\Pi_{\{E\}, \psi} = (MX_{\{E\}, \psi}, P)$ (in the search version) finds the preferred Hamiltonian paths of $\mathcal{G}$ if there are such paths. Let us define a goal formula $\phi = H(v_3, v_1)$. The Goal-Oriented Model Expansion Problem asks whether there is a preferred expansion structure (i.e., Hamiltonian path) that includes $H(v_3, v_1)$ and hence edge $E(v_3, v_1)$. There are two possible Hamiltonian paths $H^{\mathcal{A}} = \{(v_1, v_2), (v_2, v_3), (v_3, v_4), (v_4, v_1)\}$ and $H^{\mathcal{B}} = \{(v_3, v_1), (v_1, v_4), (v_4, v_2), (v_2, v_3)\}$. Based on Definition 3, $\mathcal{A}$ characterizes a path that is preferred and it is comprised of $H(v_3, v_4)$.

3.3   Conditional Preferences

Preferences of users are often expressed in conditional statements. For example, A is preferred to B if C is true. Contextual preferences are widely studied in the literature. Examples include [5,7,8,24]. Here, we show how the Prioritized Model Expansion framework handles conditional preferences.

Let p be a conditional preference of the form $p : R_q(\overline{a}_u), ..., R_s(\overline{a}_v) \supset S_i(\overline{b}_l) \sqsupseteq_p S_j(\overline{b}_m)$. Conditional preference p is read as $S_i(\overline{b}_l)$ is preferred to $S_j(\overline{b}_m)$ if $R_q(\overline{a}_u) \wedge ... \wedge R_s(\overline{a}_v)$ is true. Intuitively, we aim to construct a partial order $\geq_p$ from p such that for structures $\mathcal{A}$ and $\mathcal{B}$ with the same domain and vocabulary, $\mathcal{A}$ is preferred to $\mathcal{B}$ with respect to p if $\mathcal{A} \models R_q(\overline{a}_u) \wedge ... \wedge R_s(\overline{a}_v) \wedge S_i(\overline{b}_l)$ and $\mathcal{B} \models R_q(\overline{a}_u) \wedge ... \wedge R_s(\overline{a}_v) \wedge S_j(\overline{b}_m)$. We call $R_q(\overline{a}_u) \wedge ... \wedge R_s(\overline{a}_v)$ the body of p with notation $body(p)$.

Definition 8. $\Pi_{\sigma,\psi} = (MX_{\sigma,\psi}, \mathcal{P})$ *is called a General Prioritized Model Expansion Problem where* $\mathcal{P} = \{p_1, ..., p_n\}$ *is a set of conditional preferences.*

A translation of $\Pi_{\sigma,\psi}$ into a standard Prioritized Model Expansion problem $\Pi^*_{\sigma,\psi^*} = (MX_{\sigma,\psi^*}, P^*)$ is as follows: First, we add each element of *Dom* as a constant symbol to τ. We assume that for all $a \in \tau$ such that $a \in Dom$ and for all optimal expansions $\mathcal{A}$, $a^{\mathcal{A}} = a$. For conditional preference p, let us introduce two new (ground) auxiliary atoms T and T'. Consider formulas $\psi_1 :$ $(R_q(\overline{a}_u) \wedge ... \wedge R_s(\overline{a}_v) \wedge S_i(\overline{b}_l)) \supset T$ and $\psi_2 : (R_q(\overline{a}_u) \wedge ... \wedge R_s(\overline{a}_v) \wedge S_j(\overline{b}_m)) \supset T'$. Set $\psi^* = \psi \wedge \psi_1 \wedge \psi_2$, $T \sqsupseteq_{P^*} T'$, and $\tau^* = \tau \cup \{T, T'\}$. It is clear that an expansion τ^*-structure $\mathcal{A}$ is preferred to another expansion τ^*-structure $\mathcal{B}$ with respect to p if $\mathcal{A}$ and $\mathcal{B}$ satisfy $R_q(\overline{a}_u) \wedge ... \wedge R_s(\overline{a}_v)$, $\mathcal{A} \models S_i(\overline{b}_l)$, and $\mathcal{B} \models S_j(\overline{b}_m)$. The binary relation $\geq^s_{P^*}$ is constructed from $\mathcal{P}$ based on the preference semantics *Weak Pareto*, *Upper Bound Dominance*, and *Element Dominance* similarly to before.

Example 4. *For a graph three-colouring problem with conditional preferences* $\Pi_{\{E\},\psi} = (MX_{\{E\},\psi}, \mathcal{P})$, *consider the following conditional preferences: red* v_1 *is preferred to blue* v_2 *if* v_5 *is green which is expressed as* $p : R(v_1) \supset (B(v_2) \sqsupseteq_p G(v_5))$. *We introduce new atoms* T_1 *and* T_2 *such that* $\psi_1 : (R(v_1) \wedge B(v_2)) \supset T_1$ *and* $\psi_2 : (R(v_1) \wedge G(v_5)) \supset T_2$. *Also, we set* $\psi^* = \psi \wedge \psi_1 \wedge \psi_2$ *and* $T_1 \sqsupseteq_p T_2$. *For an input graph* $\mathcal{G} = (V, E^{\mathcal{G}})$ *where* $V = \{v_1, ..., v_5\}$ *and* $E^{\mathcal{G}} = \{(v_1, v_2), (v_2, v_1),$ $(v_1, v_3), (v_1, v_3), (v_3, v_1), (v_2, v_4), (v_4, v_2), (v_4, v_5), (v_5, v_4), (v_3, v_5), (v_5, v_3)\}$, *three-colouring* $\mathcal{A}$ *where* $R^{\mathcal{A}} = \{v_1, v_4\}$, $B^{\mathcal{A}} = \{v_2, v_5\}$, *and* $G^{\mathcal{A}} = \{v_3\}$ *is preferable based on the Week Pareto semantics.*

4   Relation to Other Preference-Based Declarative Approaches

4.1   Preference-Based SAT

3-SAT is a canonical NP-complete problem. Let φ be a Conjunctive Normal Form (CNF) boolean formula and $X = \{x_1, ..., x_n\}$ be the set of boolean variables appearing in φ. A truth assignment $\Im$ is a mapping from X to {true, false}. The problem of deciding whether φ is satisfiable (i.e., there is a truth assignment $\Im$ that satisfies φ) can be converted into a Model Expansion problem $\mathrm{MX}_{\sigma,\psi}$ with an input σ-structure $\mathcal{I}$. The general idea is to represent formula φ by $\mathcal{I}$. The domain of $\mathcal{I}$ is X. Also, the expansion vocabulary (i.e., $\tau \backslash \sigma$) includes unary predicates T and F that specify each boolean variable as true or false. An interpretation of the expansion vocabulary represents a truth assignment to the boolean variables in φ. Formula ψ specifies the notion of satisfying a boolean CNF formula by a truth assignment.

Preference-based SAT, which is related to the problem of max-SAT [3], is the problem of finding truth assignments satisfying a boolean formula when some variables are favourite to be assigned the value true. A preference-based SAT problem for a boolean formula φ and the set X of boolean variables appearing in φ is defined as a pair $(\varphi, (X, \geq))$ where $\geq$ is a preorder on X that specifies a preference over variables in X. Let $\Im$ and $\Im'$ be truth assignments that satisfy φ. We say $\Im$ is preferred to $\Im'$ if all variables assigned the value true by $\Im$ are preferred to all variables that $\Im'$ maps to true.

Theorem 2. *The problem of deciding whether there is a preferred truth assignment $\Im$ satisfying φ that maps all variables in some $Y \subset X$ to true is Σ_2^P-complete.*

Proof. Consider a Prioritized NP-complete Model Expansion problem $\Pi_{\sigma,\psi} = (\mathrm{MX}_{\sigma,\psi}, P)$. All NP-complete problems, obviously, can be reduced to SAT in polynomial time. Also, by considering the Weak Pareto semantics in the Prioritized Model Expansion framework, preference relation $\geq$ in the preference-based SAT framework is matched with $\sqsupseteq_P$. For each relation $R(\overline{a}) \sqsupseteq_P S(\overline{b})$, we consider $x_i \geq x_j$ in the preference-based SAT framework where x_i and x_j are boolean variables representing ground atoms $R(\overline{a})$ and $S(\overline{b})$, respectively. In order to reduce an NP-complete $\mathrm{MX}_{\sigma,\psi}$ problem to SAT, some auxiliary propositional variables are introduced that are considered to be equally preferred with respect to relation $\sqsupseteq_P$. Therefore, Prioritized NP-complete Model Expansion problem $\Pi_{\sigma,\psi}$ is reduced to a preference-based SAT S in polynomial time. Thus, the *Goal-oriented Optimal Expansion* problem for $\Pi_{\sigma,\psi} = (\mathrm{MX}_{\sigma,\psi}, P)$ where $\mathrm{MX}_{\sigma,\psi}$ is an NP-complete problem can be reduced (in polynomial time) to deciding whether there is a preferred truth assignment $\Im$ satisfying φ that maps all variables in some $Y \subset X$ to true, which is, based on Theorem 1, Σ_2^P-complete. ∎

4.2 Logic Programs with Preferences

Logic programming with stable model semantics is one of the main declarative approaches for specifying problems in NP. Let P be a program which is defined as a set of rules of the form $r : c_1, ..., c_l \leftarrow a_1, ..., a_m, \mathrm{not}\ b_1, ..., \mathrm{not}\ b_n$ where a_i for $i \in [1, m]$, b_j for $j \in [1, n]$, and c_k for $k \in [1, l]$ are propositional atoms. Let us define vocabulary symbols $Rule$, $Stable$, $Body^+$, $Body^-$, and $Head$. Symbol $Stable(x)$ denotes that x belongs to a stable model of program P, $Rule(y)$

means that y is a rule of program P, $Body^+(y,x)$ indicates that x is a positive atom in the body of rule y and, similarly, $Body^-(y,x)$ points out that x is an atom in the negative part of the body of y. Also, $Head(y,x)$ means that atom x is in the head of rule y. For $\sigma = \{Rule, Stable, Body^+, Body^-, Head\}$, a σ-structure $\mathcal{P}$ specifies a program by interpreting predicate symbols in σ. A first-order formula ψ characterizes the stable model semantics as $\psi = \forall x \big(\exists y (Rule(y) \land Head(x,y) \land \forall z [Body^+(y,z) \supset Stable(z)] \land \forall w [Body^-(y,w) \supset \neg Stable(w)]) \supset Stable(x) \big) \land \forall x \big(\exists y (Rule(y)) \land Head(x,y) \land \forall z [\neg Body^+(y,z)] \land \forall w [\neg Body^-(y,w)] \supset Stable(x) \big)$.

A stable model of program P is represented by an expansion structure $\mathcal{M}$ that expands input σ-structure $\mathcal{P}$, which represents program P, and satisfies ψ.

Preferred Models

Prioritized logic program (PLP) [26] is one of the impactful frameworks proposed for logic programming with preferences. A PLP program is a pair (Pr, Φ) where Pr is a general extended disjunctive logic program with answer set semantics and Φ is a set of preference relations among propositional atoms of the form $a \succeq b$ that means a is preferred to b. The transitive closure of Φ is denoted by Φ_c. The reflexive transitive binary relation $\sqsupseteq$ among answer sets of Pr is defined as: (1) $X_1 \sqsupseteq X_1$, (2) if there exist $a \in X_1 - X_2$ and $b \in X_2 - X_1$ where $(a \succeq b) \in \Phi_c$ and there is no $d \in X_1 - X_2$ such that $(b \succ d) \in \Phi_c$, then $X_1 \sqsupseteq X_2$, and (3) if $X_1 \sqsupseteq X_2$ and $X_2 \sqsupseteq X_3$, then $X_1 \sqsupseteq X_3$. X is called a preferred answer set if there is no answer set Y such that $Y \sqsupset X$. One could examine conditions 1 and 2 in polynomial time in the size of the input (the number of propositional atoms). However, condition 3 requires possibly an exponential number of comparisons over the answer sets of Pr. The complexity results of the decision problems associated to a PLP program are based on the assumption that deciding whether X is preferable to Y is in polynomial time that is not accurate due to condition 3. The role of condition 3 is to make relation $\sqsupseteq$ transitive. On the other hand, relation $>_P^s$ in the Prioritized Model Expansion framework is not necessarily transitive for some preference semantics (e.g., the Element Dominance semantics).

Theorem 3. *Let* $\Pi_{\sigma,\psi} = (MX_{\sigma,\psi}, P)$ *be a Prioritized Model Expansion problem with an input σ-structure $\mathcal{I}$ and $\Gamma = (Pr, \Phi_c)$ be a PLP program. Assume ψ characterizes the stable model semantics, $\mathcal{I}$ represents Pr, and P specifies Φ_c. If there are expansion structures $\mathcal{A}$ and $\mathcal{B}$, then Pr has answer sets M_1 that is represented by $\mathcal{A}$ and M_2 that is represented by $\mathcal{B}$ such that if $\mathcal{A} >_P^{ed} \mathcal{B}$, then $M_1 \sqsupset M_2$.*

Proof. Φ_c can be viewed as a preference expression in the PMX framework and finding answer sets of generalized extended disjunctive program Pr can be expressed by an $MX_{\sigma,\psi}$ problem. As discussed in the previous subsection, there is a correspondence between the expansion structures of $MX_{\sigma,\psi}$ and the answer sets of Pr. Each expansion structure of $MX_{\sigma,\psi}$ can be one-to-one mapped in polynomial time to an answer set of Pr and vice versa. The relation $>_P^{ed}$ with the Element Dominance semantics is a subset of relation $\sqsupseteq$ in the PLP because it satisfies conditions 1 and 2 in the definition of $\sqsupset$ while it does not guarantee the transitivity of the preference relation among the expansion structures. So, for structures $\mathcal{A}$ and $\mathcal{B}$, Pr has answer sets M_1 and M_2 such that $M_1 \sqsupset M_2$ and M_1 and M_2 are represented by $\mathcal{A}$ and $\mathcal{B}$, respectively. ∎

4.3 Answer Set Optimization

An Answer Set Optimization (ASO) program [12] is a pair (P_g, R) where P_g is a generating normal logic program and R is a set of rules of the form $r : \; C_1 > ... > C_k \leftarrow a_1, ..., a_n, not\ b_1, ..., not\ b_m$. In each rule, a_i and b_i are literals. Also, C_i is defined as a combination of atoms integrated by conjunction, disjunction, default negation (not) and strong negation ($\neg$) that must appear only before atoms. $C_i > C_j \leftarrow body$ means that if $body$ is satisfied, C_i is preferred to C_j. Given a set of l rules $r_1, ..., r_l$, each answer set M of P_g is associated with a satisfaction vector $d(M) = \langle d_1(M), ..., d_l(M) \rangle$ where $d_i(M)$ is called the satisfaction degree of M in r_i. Satisfaction degree denotes the minimum j of C_js in r_i that are satisfied by M whenever M satisfies $body$, and 1 in other case. Let M_1 and M_2 be two answer sets of P_g. M_1 is preferred to M_2 with respect to R (notation $M_1 \succeq M_2$) if for all $i \leq l$, $d_i(M_1) \leq d_i(M_2)$. When in each rule $r \in R$, C_is in the head of r are literals, the relation between ASO and Prioritized Model Expansion is formulated as follows:

Theorem 4. *Let $ASO = (P_g, R)$ be an ASO program where P_g is a normal logic program and R is a set of preference rules. There is a Prioritized Model Expansion problem $\Pi_{\sigma,\psi} = (MX_{\sigma,\psi}, P)$ with an input $\mathcal{I}$ such that each preferred answer set of ASO is represented by an optimal expansion of $\Pi_{\sigma,\psi}$.*

Proof. Let P_g^* be a logic program such that $P_g^* = P_g \cup R^*$ where R^* is a set of r_1^* and r_2^* rules that are constructed as follows: For each rule r in R of the form $C_1 > C_2 \leftarrow \text{body}(r)$, we introduce auxiliary atoms n_1 and n_2 and define r_1^* as $r_1^* : n_1 \leftarrow C_1, \text{body}(r)$ and r_2^* as $r_2^* : n_2 \leftarrow C_2, \text{body}(r)$. Normal logic program P_g^* with stable model semantics can be cast as Model Expansion problem $MX_{\sigma,\psi}$ such that ψ specifies stable model semantics and $\mathcal{I}$ represents P_g^*. Also, let us define preference expression P such that for auxiliary atoms n_1 and n_2, we have $n_2 \sqsupseteq_P n_1$. We consider all other ground atoms in P_g as equally preferred. Let M_1 and M_2 be answer sets of P_g. Assume $\mathcal{A}$ and $\mathcal{B}$ are expansion structures of $MX_{\sigma,\psi}$ that represent M_1, and M_2, respectively. If $M_2 \succ M_1$ in ASO, for each C_i in the head of each rule $r \in R$ such that $M_1 \models C_i$, there is C_j such that $M_2 \models C_j$ and $C_j > C_i$. This is equivalent to say that for each auxiliary atom n_i satisfied by $\mathcal{A}$, there is an auxiliary atom n_j satisfied by $\mathcal{B}$ such that $n_j \sqsupseteq_P n_i$ that is matched with the Upper Bound Dominance semantics. So, $\mathcal{A} >_P^{ubd} \mathcal{B}$ and the result follows. □

We showed that an ASO program can be viewed as a Prioritized Model Expansion. Also every Prioritized NP-complete Model Expansion problem with the Upper Bound Dominance semantics can be encoded as an ASO program. The problem of deciding the existence of a stable model of a normal program is NP-complete and, obviously, an NP-complete problem can be reduced in polynomial time to another NP-complete problem. Preference expression P is encoded by a single rule $r \in R$ of the form $a_1 > a_2.... > a_n \leftarrow$ where a_is are ground atoms and $a_i > a_j$ if $a_i \sqsupseteq_P a_j$.

As a result, *Goal-oriented Prioritized NP-complete Model Expansion* problems can be reduced to deciding whether some answer sets of an ASO satisfy a formula in polynomial time. The existence of an answer set that satisfies a set of ground atoms is NP-complete (i.e., brave reasoning in logic programs with stable model semantics), and determining the existence of a solution of ASO that satisfies a goal formula ϕ is Σ_2^P-complete [12]. Likewise, for an NP-complete $MX_{\sigma,\psi}$, the problem of deciding whether there is an optimal expansion of $\Pi_{\sigma,\psi}$ that satisfies a goal ϕ, based on Theorem 1, is Σ_2^P-complete.

5   Conclusion

We proposed a novel language-independent preference framework for characterizing preference-based computational decision and search problems. We demonstrated that adding preferences raises the computational complexity of deciding the existence of an expansion structure satisfying a goal. Our proposal can also be related to a variety of other preference frameworks, such as CP-nets [5] that model conditional preferences. A CP-net can be approximated by a Prioritized Model Expansion problem such that if an outcome o_1 is preferred to an outcome o_2 in a CP-net, then for associated expansion structures $\mathcal{A}$ and $\mathcal{B}$ in the Prioritized Model Expansion problem, $\mathcal{A}$ is preferred to $\mathcal{B}$. Moreover, finding preferred repairs of a database that violates some integrity constraints [27] can be translated into a Prioritized Model Expansion problem using the Upper Bound Dominance semantics. One possible future direction is to devise an algorithm that solves Prioritized Model Expansion problems using generic solvers empowered by propagators. The solver would provide symbolic explanations for rejecting and accepting models to prune the search space.

References

1. Amgoud, L., Vesic, S.: Repairing preference-based argumentation frameworks. In: IJCAI, pp. 665–670. Citeseer (2009)
2. Baier, J.A., McIlraith, S.A.: Planning with preferences. AI Mag. **29**(4), 25–37 (2008)
3. Biere, A., Heule, M., van Maaren, H.: Handbook of Satisfiability, vol. 185. IOS Press, Amsterdam (2009)
4. Bogaerts, B., Janhunen, T., Tasharrofi, S.: Stable-unstable semantics: beyond np with normal logic programs. Theory Pract. Log. Program. **16**(5–6), 570–586 (2016)
5. Boutilier, C., Brafman, R.I., Domshlak, C., Hoos, H.H., Poole, D.: CP-nets: a tool for representing and reasoning with conditional ceteris paribus preference statements. J. Artif. Intell. Res. (JAIR) **21**, 135–191 (2004)
6. Boutilier, C., Brafman, R.I., Domshlak, C., Hoos, H.H., Poole, D.: Preference-based constrained optimization with CP-nets. Comput. Intell. **20**(2), 137–157 (2004)

7. Brafman, R.I., Domshlak, C.: Introducing variable importance tradeoffs into CP-nets. In: Proceedings of the Eighteenth Conference on Uncertainty in Artificial Intelligence, pp. 69–76. Morgan Kaufmann Publishers Inc. (2002)
8. Brafman, R.I., Domshlak, C., Shimony, S.E.: On graphical modeling of preference and importance. J. Artif. Intell. Res. **25**, 389–424 (2006)
9. Brewka, G.: Logic programming with ordered disjunction. In: AAAI/IAAI, pp. 100–105 (2002)
10. Brewka, G., Eiter, T.: Preferred answer sets for extended logic programs. Artif. Intell. **109**(1), 297–356 (1999)
11. Brewka, G., Eiter, T.: Prioritizing default logic: abridged report. Festschrift on the occasion of Prof. Dr. W. Bibel 60th birthday. Kluwer, Dordrecht (1999)
12. Brewka, G., Niemelä, I., Truszczynski, M.: Answer set optimization. IJCAI **3**, 867–872 (2003)
13. Brewka, G., Truszczynski, M., Woltran, S.: Representing preferences among sets. In: AAAI (2010)
14. Censor, Y.: Pareto optimality in multiobjective problems. Appl. Math. Optim. **4**(1), 41–59 (1977)
15. Chomicki, J.: Preference formulas in relational queries. ACM Trans. Database Syst. (TODS) **28**(4), 427–466 (2003)
16. Codd, E.F.: Extending the database relational model to capture more meaning. ACM Trans. Database Syst. (TODS) **4**(4), 397–434 (1979)
17. Delgrande, J., Schaub, T.: Expressing preferences in default logic. Artif. Intell. **123**(1), 41–87 (2000)
18. Delgrande, J., Schaub, T., Tompits, H.: Logic programs with compiled preferences. arXiv preprint cs/0003028 (2000)
19. Delgrande, J., Schaub, T., Tompits, H., Wang, K.: A classification and survey of preference handling approaches in nonmonotonic reasoning. Comput. Intell. **20**(2), 308–334 (2004)
20. Eiter, T., Gottlob, G., Leone, N.: Abduction from logic programs: semantics and complexity. Theor. Comput. Sci. **189**(1–2), 129–177 (1997)
21. Ensan, A., Ternovska, E.: Modular systems with preferences. In: IJCAI, pp. 2940–2947 (2015)
22. Fagin, R.: Generalized first-order spectra and polynomial-time recognizable sets (1974)
23. Immerman, N.: Descriptive Complexity. Graduate Texts in Computer Science. Springer, Heidelberg (1999). https://doi.org/10.1007/978-1-4612-0539-5
24. Malizia, E., Lukasiewicz, T.: On the complexity of MCP-nets (2016)
25. Mitchell, D.G., Ternovska, E.: A framework for representing and solving NP search problems. In: AAAI, pp. 430–435 (2005)
26. Sakama, C., Inoue, K.: Prioritized logic programming and its application to commonsense reasoning. Artif. Intell. **123**(1), 185–222 (2000)
27. Staworko, S., Chomicki, J., Marcinkowski, J.: Prioritized repairing and consistent query answering in relational databases. Ann. Math. Artif. Intell. **64**(2–3), 209–246 (2012)
28. Voorneveld, M.: Characterization of pareto dominance. Oper. Res. Lett. **31**(1), 7–11 (2003)
29. Wilson, N.: Preference inference based on lexicographic models. In: Proceedings of the Twenty-First European Conference on Artificial Intelligence, pp. 921–926. IOS Press (2014)

Combinations of Systems

Ilinva: Using Abduction to Generate Loop Invariants

Mnacho Echenim, Nicolas Peltier, and Yanis Sellami[✉]

Univ. Grenoble Alpes, CNRS, LIG, 38000 Grenoble, France
{Mnacho.Echenim,Nicolas.Peltier,Yanis.Sellami}@univ-grenoble-alpes.fr

Abstract. We describe a system to prove properties of programs. The key feature of this approach is a method to automatically synthesize inductive invariants of the loops contained in the program. The method is generic, *i.e.*, it applies to a large set of programming languages and application domains; and lazy, in the sense that it only generates invariants that allow one to derive the required properties. It relies on an existing system called GPiD for abductive reasoning modulo theories [14], and on the platform for program verification Why3 [16]. Experiments show evidence of the practical relevance of our approach.

1 Introduction

Hoare logic – together with strongest post-conditions or weakest pre-conditions calculi – allow one to verify properties of programs defined by bounded sequences of instructions [20]. Given a pre-condition ϕ satisfied by the inputs of program P, algorithms exist to compute the strongest formula ψ such that $\phi \{P\} \psi$ holds, meaning that if ϕ holds initially then ψ is satisfied after P is executed, and any formula ψ' that holds after P is executed is such that $\psi \models \psi'$. To check that the final state satisfies some formula ψ', we thus only have to check that ψ' is a logical consequence of ψ. However, in order to handle programs containing loops, it is necessary to associate each loop occurring within the program with an *inductive invariant*. An inductive invariant for a given loop L is a formula that holds every time the program enters L (*i.e.*, it must be a logical consequence of the preconditions of L), and is preserved by the sequence of instructions in L. Testing whether a formula is an inductive invariant is a straightforward task, and the difficulty resides in generating candidate invariants. These can be supplied by the programmer, but this is a rather tedious and time-consuming task; for usability and scalability, it is preferable to generate those formulas automatically when possible. In this paper, we describe a system to generate such invariants in a completely automated way, via abductive reasoning modulo theories, based on the methodology developed in [13]. Roughly speaking, the algorithm works as follows. Given a program P decorated with a set of assertions that are to be established, all loops are first assigned the same candidate invariant ⊤. These invariants are obviously sound: they hold before the loops and are preserved by the sequence of instructions in the loop; however they are usually not strong enough

© Springer Nature Switzerland AG 2019
A. Herzig and A. Popescu (Eds.): FroCoS 2019, LNAI 11715, pp. 77–93, 2019.
https://doi.org/10.1007/978-3-030-29007-8_5

to prove the assertions decorating the program. They are therefore strengthened by adding hypotheses that are sufficient to ensure that the assertions hold; these hypotheses are generated by a tool that performs *abductive inferences*, and the strengthened formulas are *candidate invariants*. Additional strengthening steps are taken to guarantee that these candidates are actual invariants, *i.e.*, that they are preserved by the sequence of instructions in the loop. These steps are iterated until a set of candidate invariants that are indeed inductive is obtained.

We rely on two existing systems to accomplish this task. The first one is Why3 (see, *e.g.*, http://why3.lri.fr/ or [16]), a well-known and widely-used platform for deductive program verification that is used to compute verification conditions and verify assertions. The second system, GPiD, is designed to generate implicants[1] of quantifier-free formulas modulo theories [14]. This system is used as an abductive reasoning procedure, thanks to the following property: if $\phi \not\models \psi$, finding a hypothesis ϕ' such that $\phi \wedge \phi' \models \psi$ is equivalent to finding ϕ' such that $\phi' \models \phi \Rightarrow \psi$. GPiD is generic, since it only relies on the existence of a decision procedure for the considered theory (counter-examples are exploited when available to speed-up the generation of the implicants when available). Both systems are connected in the ILINVA framework.

Related Work. A large number of different techniques have been proposed to generate loop invariants automatically, especially on numeric domains [9,10], but also in more expressive logics, for programs containing arrays or expressible using combination of theories [8,18,22–24,26]. We only briefly review the main ideas of the most popular and successful approaches. Methods based on abstract interpretations (see, *e.g.*, [11,25]) work by executing the program in a symbolic way, on some abstract domain, and try to compute over-estimations of the possible states of the memory after an unbounded number of iterations of the loop. Counter-examples generated from runs can be exploited to refine the considered abstraction [17,19]. The idea is that upon detection of a run for which the assertion is violated, if the run does not correspond to a concrete execution path, then the considered abstraction may be refined to dismiss it.

Candidate invariants can also be inferred by generating formulas of some user-provided patterns and testing them against some particular executions of the program [15]. Those formulas that are violated in any of the runs can be rejected, and the soundness of the remaining candidates can be checked afterwards. Invariants can be computed by using iterative backward algorithms [27], starting from the post-condition and computing weakest pre-conditions until a fixpoint is reached (if any). Other approaches [21] have explored the use of quantifier elimination to refine properties obtained using a representation of all execution paths.

The work that is closest to our approach is [13], which presents an algorithm to compute invariants as boolean combinations of linear constraints over integers. The algorithm is similar to ours, and also uses abduction to strengthen candi-

---

[1] An implicant of a formula ψ is a formula ϕ such that $\phi \models \psi$. It is the dual notion of that of implicates.

date invariant so that verification conditions are satisfied. The algorithms differ by the way the verification conditions and abductive hypotheses are proceeded: in our approach the conditions always propagate forward from an invariant to another along execution paths, and we eagerly ensure that all the loop invariants are inductive. Another difference is that we use a completely different technique to perform abductive reasoning: in [13] is based on model construction and quantifier elimination for Presburger arithmetic, whereas our approach uses a generic algorithm, assuming only the existence of a decision procedure for the underlying theory. This permits to generate invariants expressed in theories that are out of the scope of [13].

Contribution. The main contribution is the implementation of a general framework for the generation of loop invariants, connecting the platform Why3 and GPiD. The evaluation demonstrates that the system permits to generate loop invariants for a wide range of theories, though it suffers from a large search space which may induce a large computation time.

2   Verification Conditions

In what follows, we consider formulas in a base logic expressing properties of the memory and assume that such formulas are closed under the usual boolean connectives. These formulas are interpreted modulo some theory $\mathcal{T}$, where $\models_\mathcal{T}$ denotes logical entailment w.r.t. $\mathcal{T}$. The memory is modified by programs, which are sequences of instructions; they are inductively defined as follows:

$$P = \texttt{empty} \mid I \texttt{ ; } P'$$
$$I = \langle\texttt{base-instruction}\rangle \mid \texttt{assume } \phi \mid \texttt{assert } \phi$$
$$\mid \texttt{if C then } P_1 \texttt{ else } P_2 \mid \texttt{while C do } P_1\{\phi\} \texttt{ end}$$

where P', P_1 and P_2 are programs, C is a condition on the state of the memory, ϕ is a formula and I is an instruction. Assumptions correspond to formulas that are taken as hypotheses, they are mostly useful to specify pre-conditions. Assertions correspond to formulas that are to be proved. Base instructions are left unspecified, they depend on the target language and application domain; they may include, for instance, assignments and pointer redirection. The formula ϕ in the while loop is a *candidate loop invariant*, it is meant to hold every time condition C is tested. In our setting each candidate loop invariant will be set to $\top$ before invoking Ilinva (except when another formula is provided by, *e.g.*, the user), and the program will iteratively update these formulas. We assume that conditions contain no instructions, *i.e.*, that the evaluation of these conditions does not affect the memory. We write $P \sim P'$ if programs P and P' are identical up to the loop candidate invariants.

An example of a program is provided in Fig. 1. It uses assignments on integers and usual constructors and functions on lists as base instructions. It contains one loop with candidate invariant $\top$ (Line 3) and one assertion (Line 6).

```
1  let i ← 1 ;
2  let L ← list(1, nil) ;
3  while unknown() do {⊤}
4  │   i ← i + 1 ;
5  └   L ← list(i, L) ;
6  assert head(L) = length(L) ;
```

Fig. 1. A simple program on lists

It contains one loop for which we will generate an invariant.

A *location* is a finite sequence of natural numbers. The empty location is denoted by ε and the concatenation of two locations ℓ and ℓ' is denoted by $\ell.\ell'$. If ℓ is a location and S is a set of locations then $\ell.S$ denotes the set $\{\ell.\ell' \mid \ell' \in S\}$. The set of locations in a program P or in an instruction I is inductively defined as follows:

- If P is an empty sequence then $loc(P) = \{0\}$.
- If $P = I ; P'$ then $loc(P) = \{0\} \cup 0.loc(I) \cup \{(i+1).p \mid i \in \mathbb{N}, i.p \in loc(P')\}$.
- If I is a base instruction or an assumption/assertion, then $loc(I) = \emptyset$.
- If $I = \texttt{if C then } P_1 \texttt{ else } P_2$ then $loc(I) = 1.loc(P_1) \cup 2.loc(P_2)$.
- If $I = \texttt{while C do } P_1\{\phi\} \texttt{ end}$ then $loc(I) = 1.loc(P_1)$.

For instance, a program $I_1 ; I_2$ where I_1, I_2 denote base instructions has three locations: 0 (beginning of the program), 1 (between I_1 and I_2) and 2 (end of the program). Note that there are no locations within an atomic instruction. The program in Fig. 1 has eight locations, namely 0, 1, 2, 2.1.0, 2.1.1, 2.1.2, 3, 4. We denote by $P|_\ell$ the instruction occurring just after location ℓ in P (if any):

- If $P = I ; P'$ then $P|_0 = I$, $P|_{0.\ell} = I|_\ell$ and $P|_{(i+1).\ell} = P'|_{i.\ell}$.
- If $I = \texttt{if C then } P_1 \texttt{ else } P_2$ then $I|_{1.\ell} = P_1|_\ell$ and $I|_{2.\ell} = P_2|_\ell$.
- If $I = \texttt{while C do } P_1\{\phi\} \texttt{ end}$ then $I|_{1.\ell} = P_1|_\ell$.

Note that $\ell \mapsto P|_\ell$ is a partial function, since locations denoting the end of a sequence do not correspond to an instruction. We denote by $lloc(P)$ the set of locations ℓ in P such that $P|_\ell$ is a loop and by $loops(P) = \{P|_\ell \mid \ell \in lloc(P)\}$ the set of loops occurring in P. For instance, if P denotes the program in Fig. 1, then $P|_1$ is $\textbf{let } L \leftarrow \textbf{list}(1, \textbf{nil})$, and $lloc(P) = \{2\}$.

We denote by $<$ the usual order on locations: $\ell < \ell'$ iff either there exist numbers i, j and locations ℓ_1, ℓ_2, ℓ_3 such that $\ell = \ell_1.i.\ell_2$, $\ell = \ell_1.j.\ell_3$ and $i < j$, or there exists a location ℓ'' such that $\ell' = \ell.\ell''$.

We assume the existence of a procedure VCgen that, given a program P, generates a set of *verification conditions* for P. These verification conditions are formulas of the form $\phi \Rightarrow \psi$, each of which is meant to be valid. Given a program P, the set of conditions VCgen(P) can be decomposed as follows:

1. *Assertion conditions*, which ensure that the assertion formulas hold at the corresponding location in the program. These conditions also include additional properties to prevent memory access errors, *e.g.*, to verify that the index of an array is within the defined valid range of indexes. The set of assertion conditions for program P is denoted by $VCgen_a(P)$.
2. *Propagation conditions*, ensuring that loop invariants do propagate. Given a loop L occurring at position ℓ in program P, we denote by $VCgen_{ind}(P, \ell)$ the set of assertions ensuring that the loop invariant for L propagates.

$$wp(\phi, \texttt{empty}) = \phi$$
$$wp(\phi, \texttt{I} ; \texttt{P}) = wp(wp(\phi, \texttt{P}), \texttt{I})$$
$$wp(\phi, \texttt{assume } \phi') = \phi' \Rightarrow \phi$$
$$wp(\phi, \texttt{assert } \phi') = \phi' \wedge \phi$$
$$wp(\phi, \texttt{if C then P}_1 \texttt{ else P}_2) = \texttt{C} \Rightarrow wp(\phi, \texttt{P}_1) \wedge \neg\texttt{C} \Rightarrow wp(\phi, \texttt{P}_2)$$
$$wp(\phi, \texttt{while C do P}_1\{\psi\} \texttt{ end}) = \psi \wedge \forall \boldsymbol{x}. \ (\psi \Rightarrow wp(\psi, \texttt{P}_1)) \wedge \forall \boldsymbol{x}. \ (\psi \wedge \neg\texttt{C} \Rightarrow \phi)$$

The formula in the last line states that the loop invariant holds when the loop is entered, that it propagates and that it entails the formula ϕ . The vector $\boldsymbol{x}$ denotes the vector of variables occurring in $\texttt{P}_1$.

Fig. 2. A Weakest Precondition Calculus

$$sp(\phi, \texttt{empty}) = \phi$$
$$sp(\phi, \texttt{I} ; \texttt{P}') = sp(sp(\phi, \texttt{I}), \texttt{P}')$$
$$sp(\phi, \texttt{assume } \phi') = \phi \wedge \phi'$$
$$sp(\phi, \texttt{assert } \phi') = \phi$$
$$sp(\phi, \texttt{if C then P}_1 \texttt{ else P}_2) = sp(\phi \wedge \texttt{C}, \texttt{P}_1) \vee sp(\phi \wedge \neg\texttt{C}, \texttt{P}_2)$$
$$sp(\phi, \texttt{while C do P}_1\{\psi\} \texttt{ end}) = \psi \wedge \neg\texttt{C}$$

$sp(\phi, \texttt{P})$ describes the state of the memory after $\texttt{P}$. The conditions corresponding to loops are approximated by using the provided loop invariants (the corresponding verification conditions are not stated).

Fig. 3. A Strongest Postcondition Calculus

3. *Loop pre-conditions*, ensuring that the loop invariants hold when the corresponding loop is entered. Given a loop $\texttt{L}$ occurring at position ℓ in program $\texttt{P}$, we denote by $\mathrm{VCgen}_{\mathrm{init}}(\texttt{P}, \ell)$ the set of assertions ensuring that the loop invariant holds before loop $\texttt{L}$ is entered.

Thus, $\mathrm{VCgen}(\texttt{P}) = \mathrm{VCgen}_{\mathrm{a}}(\texttt{P}) \cup \left(\bigcup_{\ell \in \mathrm{lloc}(\texttt{P})} (\mathrm{VCgen}_{\mathrm{ind}}(\texttt{P}, \ell) \cup \mathrm{VCgen}_{\mathrm{init}}(\texttt{P}, \ell)) \right)$. Such verification conditions are generally defined using standard weakest precondition or strongest post-condition calculi (see, *e.g.*, [12]), where loop invariant are used as under-approximations. Formal definitions are recalled in Figs. 2 and 3 (the definition for the basic instructions depends on the application language and is thus omitted). For the sake of readability, we assume, by a slight abuse of notation, that the condition $\texttt{C}$ is also a formula in the base logic.

This permits to define the goal of the paper in a more formal way: our aim is to define an algorithm that, given a program $\texttt{P}$, constructs a program $\texttt{P}' \sim \texttt{P}$ (*i.e.*, constructs loop invariants for each loop in $\texttt{P}$) such that $\mathrm{VCgen}(\texttt{P}')$ only contains valid formulas. Note that all the loops and invariants must be handled globally since verification conditions depend on one another.

Algorithm 1. GPID($\phi, M, A, \mathcal{P}$)

1 **if** M *unsatisfiable (modulo $\mathcal{T}$)* **or** $\neg \mathcal{P}(M)$ **then**
2 $\quad\rfloor$ **return** $\emptyset$;
3 **if** $M \models \phi$ **then**
4 $\quad\rfloor$ **return** $\{M\}$;
5 **let** $\mathfrak{m}$ *be a model of* $\{\neg\phi\} \cup M$;
6 **let** $\phi = $ SIMPLIFY(ϕ, M);
7 **let** $A = \{l \in A \mid M \cup \neg\phi \not\models_{\mathcal{T}} l, M \not\models_{\mathcal{T}} l^c\}$;
8 **foreach** $l \in A$ *such that* $\mathfrak{m} \not\models l$ **do**
9 $\quad\big\lvert$ **let** $A_l = \{l' \in A \mid l' < l \wedge \mathfrak{m} \models l'\} \cup \{l' \in A \mid l < l'\}$;
10 $\quad\rfloor$ **let** $P_l = $ GPID($\phi, M \cup \{l\}, A_l, \mathcal{P}$);
11 **return** $\bigcup_{l \in A} P_l$;

---

3   Abduction

As mentioned above, abductive reasoning will be performed by generating implicants. Because it would not be efficient to blindly generate all implicants of a formula, this generation is controlled by fixing the literals that can occur in an implicant. We thus consider a set $\mathcal{A}$ of literals in the considered logic, called the *abducible literals*.

Definition 1. *Let ϕ be a formula. An $\mathcal{A}$-implicant of ϕ (modulo $\mathcal{T}$) is a conjunction (or set) of literals $l_1 \wedge \cdots \wedge l_n$ such that $l_i \in \mathcal{A}$, for all $i \in [\![1 .. n]\!]$ and $l_1 \wedge \cdots \wedge l_n \models_{\mathcal{T}} \phi$.*

We use the procedure GPID described in [14] to generate $\mathcal{A}$-implicants. A simplified version of this procedure is presented in Algorithm 1. A call to the procedure GPID($\phi, M, A, \mathcal{P}$) is meant to generate $\mathcal{A}$-implicants of ϕ that: (i) are of the form $M \cup A'$, for some $A' \subseteq A$; (ii) are as general as possible; and (iii) satisfy property $\mathcal{P}$. When M itself is not an $\mathcal{A}$-implicant of ϕ, a subset of relevant literals from A is computed (Line 7), and for each literal in this subset, a recursive call is made to the procedure after augmenting M with this literal and discarding all those that become irrelevant (Lines 9 and 10). In particular, the algorithm is parameterized by an ordering $<$ on abducible literals which is used to ensure that sets of hypotheses are explored in a non-redundant way. The algorithm relies on the existence of a decision procedure for testing satisfiability in $\mathcal{T}$ (Line 1). In practice, this procedure does not need terminating or complete[2], *e.g.*, it may be called with a timeout (any "unknown" result is handled as "satisfiable"). At Line 8, a model of the formula $\{\neg\phi\} \cup M$ is used to prune the search space, by dismissing some abducible literals. In practice, no such model may be available, either because no model building algorithm exists for the considered theory or because of termination issues. In this case, no such pruning is performed. Property $\mathcal{P}$ denotes an abstract property of sets of literals. It is used to control the

---

[2] However, Theorem 2 only holds if the proof procedure is terminating and complete.

form of generated $\mathcal{A}$-implicants, it is for example possible to force the algorithm to only generate $\mathcal{A}$-implicants with a fixed maximal size. For Theorem 2 to hold, it is simply required that $\mathcal{P}$ be *closed under subsets*, *i.e.*, that for all sets of abducible literals B and C, $B \subseteq C \wedge \mathcal{P}(C) \Rightarrow \mathcal{P}(B)$.

Compared to [14], details that are irrelevant for the purpose of the present paper are skipped and the procedure has been adapted to generate $\mathcal{A}$-implicants instead of implicates (implicants and implicates are dual notions).

Theorem 2 [14]. *The call* $\text{GPID}(\phi, \emptyset, \mathcal{A}, \mathcal{P})$ *terminates and returns a set of* $\mathcal{A}$-*implicants of* ϕ *satisfying* $\mathcal{P}$. *Further, if* $\mathcal{P}$ *is closed under subsets, then for every* $\mathcal{A}$-*implicant* I *of* ϕ *satisfying* $\mathcal{P}$, *there exists* $I' \in \text{GPID}(\phi, \emptyset, \mathcal{A}, \mathcal{P})$ *such that* $I \models_\mathcal{T} I'$.

This procedure also comes with generic algorithms for pruning redundant $\mathcal{A}$-implicants *i.e.*, for removing all $\mathcal{A}$-implicants I such that there exist another $\mathcal{A}$-implicant I' such that $I \models_\mathcal{T} I'$, see [14, Sect. 4].

4   Generating Loop Invariants

In this section, we present an algorithm for the generation of loop invariants. As explained in Sect. 2, we distinguish between 3 kinds of verification conditions, which will be handled in different ways: assertion and propagation conditions; and loop pre-conditions. As can be seen from the rules in Fig. 2, loop invariants can occur as antecedents in verification conditions, this is typically the case when a loop occurs just before an assertion in some execution path. In such a situation, we say that the considered condition *depends on* loop L. When a condition depends on a loop, a strengthening of the loop invariant of loop L yields a strengthening of the hypotheses of the verification condition, *i.e.*, makes the condition less general (easier to prove).

This principle is used in Algorithm 2, which we briefly describe before going into details. Starting with a program P in which it is assumed that every loop invariant is inductive, the algorithm attempts to recursively generate invariants that make all assertion conditions in P valid. It begins by selecting a non-valid formula ϕ from $\text{VCgen}_\text{a}(\text{P})$ and a location $\ell \in \text{lloc}(\text{P})$ such that ϕ depends on ℓ, then generates a set of hypotheses that would make ϕ valid (Line 4). For each such hypothesis ξ, a loop location ℓ' such that $\ell' \leq \ell$ is selected, and a formula ξ' that is a weakest precondition at ℓ' causing ξ to hold at location ℓ is computed (Line 7). This formula is added to the invariant of the loop at location ℓ' (Line 8), so that if this invariant was ψ, the new candidate invariant is $\xi' \wedge \psi$. If ξ' does not hold before entering the loop then ξ is discarded (Line 9); otherwise, the program attempts to update the other loop invariants to ensure that ξ' propagates (Line 10). When this succeeds, a recursive call is made with the updated invariants (Line 12) to handle the other non-valid assertion conditions.

Procedure $\text{ABDUCE}(\phi)$ (invoked Line 4 of Algorithm 2) is described in Algorithm 3. It generates formulas ξ that logically entail ϕ; it is used to generate the candidate hypotheses for strengthening. It first extracts a set of abducible

---

Algorithm 2. ILINVA (Program P)

1 **if** *all formulas in* $\mathrm{VCgen_a(P)}$ *are valid* **then**
2 $\quad\lfloor$ **return** P;
3 **let** ϕ be a non valid formula in $\mathrm{VCgen_a(P)}$, depending on a loop at location ℓ;
4 **let** $\Xi \longleftarrow \textsc{Abduce}(\phi, \mathrm{P}, \ell)$;
5 **foreach** $\xi \in \Xi$ **do**
6 $\quad$ **foreach** $\ell' \in \mathrm{lloc(P)}$ such that $\ell' \leq \ell$ **do**
7 $\quad\quad$ **let** $\xi' \longleftarrow bp(\xi, \mathrm{P}, \ell, \ell')$;
8 $\quad\quad$ **let** $\mathrm{P}_\xi \longleftarrow \mathrm{Strengthen}(\mathrm{P}, \ell', \xi')$;
9 $\quad\quad$ **if** $\mathrm{VCgen_{init}}(\mathrm{P}_\xi, \ell')$ *is valid* **then**
10 $\quad\quad\quad$ **let** $\mathrm{P}'_\xi \longleftarrow \textsc{Ind}(\mathrm{P}_\xi, \ell')$;
11 $\quad\quad\quad$ **if** $\mathrm{P}'_\xi \neq$ **fail then**
12 $\quad\quad\quad\quad$ **let** $\mathrm{P}''_\xi \longleftarrow \textsc{Ilinva}(\mathrm{P}'_\xi)$;
13 $\quad\quad\quad\quad$ **if** $\mathrm{P}''_\xi \neq$ **fail then**
14 $\quad\quad\quad\quad\quad\lfloor$ **return** P''_ξ;

15 **return fail** ;

Algorithm 3. ABDUCE(Formula ϕ, Program P, Location ℓ)

1 **let** $\mathcal{A} \longleftarrow \textsc{GetAbducibles}(\phi)$;
2 **let** $\mathcal{A} \longleftarrow \{l \mid l \in \mathcal{A} \wedge \phi \not\models_{\mathcal{T}} l\}$;
3 **let** $\Xi \longleftarrow \mathrm{GPiD}(\phi, \emptyset, \mathcal{A}, \mathcal{P})$;
4 **let** $\Xi' \longleftarrow \{\xi_1 \vee \cdots \vee \xi_n \mid n \in \mathbb{N}, \xi_i \in \Xi\}$;
5 **return** Ξ'

---

literals $\mathcal{A}$ by collecting variables and symbols from the program and/or from the theory $\mathcal{T}$ and combining them to create literals up to a certain depth (procedure GETABDUCIBLES at Line 1). To avoid any redundancy, this task is actually done in two steps: a set of abducible literals for the entire program is initially constructed (this is done once at the beginning of the search), and depending on the considered program location, a subset of these literals is selected. The abducible literals that are logically entailed by ϕ modulo $\mathcal{T}$ are filtered out (Line 2), and procedure GPiD is called to generate $\mathcal{A}$-implicants of ϕ. Finally, $\mathcal{A}$-implicants are combined to form disjunctive formulas. Note that another way of generating disjunction of literals would be to add these disjunction in the initial set of abducible literals, but this solution would greatly increase the search space.

Each of the hypotheses ξ generated by ABDUCE(ϕ) is used to strengthen the invariant of a loop occurring at position $\ell' \leq \ell$ (Line 8 in Algorithm 2). The strengthening formula is computed using the Weakest Precondition Calculus on ξ, on a program obtained from P by ignoring all loops between ℓ' and ℓ, since they have corresponding invariants. To this purpose we define a function $bp(\phi, \mathrm{P}, \ell, \ell')$ which, for positions $\ell' \leq \ell$, back-propagates abductive hypotheses from a location ℓ to ℓ' (see Fig. 4). This is done by extracting the part of the code $path(\mathrm{P}, \ell', \ell)$

$$path(\mathtt{P}, \ell, \ell) = \mathtt{empty}$$
$$path(\mathtt{P}, \ell, \ell'.(i+1)) = path(\mathtt{P}, \ell, \ell'.i) \bullet \mathtt{P}|_{\ell'.i} \quad \text{if } \ell \leq \ell'.i$$
$$path(\mathtt{P}, \ell, \ell'.0) = path(\mathtt{P}, \ell, \ell') \qquad \text{if } \ell \leq \ell'$$
$$path(\mathtt{P}, \ell.i.\ell', \ell.(i+1)) = path(\mathtt{P}, \ell.i.\ell', \ell.i.m) \quad m = \max\{j \mid \ell.i.j \in loc(\mathtt{P})\}$$

$$bp(\phi, \mathtt{P}, \ell, \ell') = wp(\phi, \mathtt{P}') \qquad \text{if } \mathtt{P}' = path(RmLoops(\mathtt{P}), \ell', \ell)$$
$$fp(\phi, \mathtt{P}, \ell, \ell') = sp(\phi, \mathtt{P}') \qquad \text{if } \mathtt{P}' = path(RmLoops(\mathtt{P}), \ell, \ell')$$

$RmLoops(\mathtt{P})$ denotes the program obtained from $\mathtt{P}$ by removing all $\mathtt{while}$ instructions and $\bullet$ denotes the concatenation operator on programs.

Fig. 4. Backward and forward propagation of abductive hypotheses

---

Algorithm 4. IND (Program P, Location ℓ)

1 **if** *all formulas in* $VCgen_{ind}(\mathtt{P}, \ell)$ *are valid* **then**
2   **return** P;
3 **let** ϕ be a non-valid formula in $VCgen_{ind}(\mathtt{P}, \ell)$;
4 **let** $\Xi \longleftarrow$ ABDUCE$(\phi, \mathtt{P}, \ell)$;
5 **foreach** $\xi \in \Xi$ **do**
6   **foreach** $\ell' \in \mathrm{lloc}(\mathtt{P})$ *such that ℓ is a prefix of ℓ' (with possibly $\ell = \ell'$)* **do**
7   **let** $\xi' \longleftarrow fp(\xi, \mathtt{P}, \ell, \ell')$;
8   **let** $\mathtt{P}'_\xi \longleftarrow$ Strengthen$(\mathtt{P}, \ell', \xi')$;
9   **if** $VCgen_{init}(\mathtt{P}'_\xi, \ell')$ *is valid* **then**
10   **let** $\mathtt{P}''_\xi \longleftarrow$ IND$(\mathtt{P}'_\xi, \ell)$;
11   **if** $\mathtt{P}''_\xi \neq$ **fail then**
12   **return** $\mathtt{P}''_\xi$;

13 **return fail** ;

---

between the locations ℓ' and ℓ while ignoring loops, and computing the weakest precondition corresponding to this part of the code and the formula ϕ.

The addition of hypothesis ξ' to the invariant of the loop at position ℓ' ensures that the considered assertion ϕ holds, but it is necessary to ensure that this strengthened invariant is still inductive. This is done as follows. Line 9 of Algorithm 2 filters away all candidates for which the precondition before entering the loop is no longer valid, and Algorithm 4 ensures that the candidate still propagates. This algorithm behaves similarly to Algorithm 2 (testing the verification conditions in $VCgen_{ind}(\mathtt{P}, \ell)$ instead of those in $VCgen_a(\mathtt{P})$), except that it strengthens the invariants that correspond either to the considered loop, or to other loops occurring within it (in the case of nested loops). Note that in this case, properties must be propagated forward, from location ℓ to the actual location of the strengthened invariant, using a Strongest Postcondition Calculus (Function $fp(\phi, \mathtt{P}, \ell, \ell')$ in Fig. 4). This technique avoids considering hypotheses that do not propagate.

When applied on the program in Fig. 1, ILINVA first sets the initial invariant of the loop to $\top$ and considers the assertion $\phi : \textbf{head}(\texttt{L}) = \textbf{length}(\texttt{L})$. As the entailment $\top \models \phi$ does not hold, it will call GPiD to get an implicant of $\top \Rightarrow \phi$. Assume that GPiD returns the (trivial) solution ϕ. As ϕ indeed holds when the loop is entered[3], ILINVA will add ϕ to the invariant of the loop and call IND. Since ϕ does not propagate IND will further strengthen the invariant, yielding, e.g., the correct solution: $\phi \wedge \texttt{i} = \textbf{head}(\texttt{L})$.

The efficiency of Algorithm 2 crucially depends on the order in which candidate hypotheses are processed at Line 5 for the strengthening operation. The heuristic used in our current implementation is to try the simplest hypotheses with the highest priority. Abducible atoms are therefore ordered as follows: first boolean variables, then equations between variables of the same sort, then applications of predicate symbols to variables (of the appropriate sorts) and finally deep literals involving function symbols (up to a certain depth). In every case, negative literals are also considered, with the same priority as the corresponding atom. Similarly, unit $\mathcal{A}$-implicants are tested before non-unit ones, and single $\mathcal{A}$-implicants before disjunctions of $\mathcal{A}$-implicants. In the iteration on line 6 of Algorithm 2, the loops that are closest to the considered assertions are considered first. Due to the number of loops involved, numerous parameters are used to control the application of the procedures, by fixing limits on the number of abducible literals that may be considered and on the maximal size of $\mathcal{A}$-implicants. When a call to ILINVA fails, these parameters are increased, using an iterative deepening search strategy. The parameter controlling the maximal number of $\mathcal{A}$-implicants in the disjunctions (currently either 1 or 2) is fixed outside of the loop as it has a strong impact on the computation cost.

The following theorem states the main properties of the algorithm.

Theorem 3. *Let* P *be a program such that* $\text{VCgen}_{\text{ind}}(\text{P}, \ell)$ *and* $\text{VCgen}_{\text{init}}(\text{P}, \ell)$ *are valid for all* $\ell \in \text{lloc}(\text{P})$. *If* ILINVA *(P) terminates and returns a program* P′ *other than* **fail**, *then* P $\sim$ P′ *and* $\text{VCgen}(\text{P}')$ *is valid modulo* $\mathcal{T}$. *Furthermore, if the considered set of abducible literals is finite (i.e., if there exists a finite set* $\mathcal{A}$ *such that* GETABDUCIBLES$(\phi) \subseteq \mathcal{A}$ *for all formulas* ϕ*), then* ILINVA *(P) terminates.*

Proof. The proof is provided in the extended version[4].

5   Implementation

5.1   Overview

The ILINVA algorithm described in Sect. 4 has been implemented by connecting Why3 with GPiD. A workflow graph of this implementation is detailed in the

---

[3] This can be checked by computing the weakest precondition of ϕ w.r.t. Lines 1, 2. The obtained formula is $\textbf{head}(\textbf{list}(1, \textbf{nil})) = \textbf{length}(\textbf{list}(1, \textbf{nil}))$ which is equivalent to $\top$ (w.r.t. the usual definitions of **list** and **head**).

[4] https://arxiv.org/abs/1906.11033.

extended paper. Note that both systems themselves call external SMT solvers to check the satisfiability of formulas. In particular, the GPiD toolbox is easy to plug to any SMTLib2-compliant SMT solver. The framework is actually generic, in the sense that it could be plugged with other systems, both to generate and verify proof obligations and to strengthen loop invariants. It is also independent of the constructions used for defining the language: other constructions (*e.g.*, for loops) can be considered, provided they are handled by the program verification framework.

Given an input program written in WHYML, Why3 generates a verification condition the validity of which will ensure that all the asserted properties are verified (including additional conditions related to, *e.g.*, memory safety) This initial verification condition is split by Why3 into several subtasks. These conditions are enriched with all appropriate information (*e.g.*, theories, axioms,...) and sent to external SMT solvers to check satisfiability. The conditions we are interested in are those linked to the proofs of the program assertions, as well as those ensuring that the candidate loop invariants are inductive. In our implementation, Why3 is taken as a black box, and we merely recover the files that are passed from Why3 to the SMT solvers, together with additional configuration data for the solvers we can extract from Why3. If the proof obligation fails, then we relate the file to the corresponding assertion in the WHYML program and extract the set of abducible literals as explained in Sect. 4, restricting ourselves to symbols corresponding to WHYML variables, functions and predicates. We then tune the SMTLib2 file to adapt it for computations by GPiD and invoke GPiD with the same SMT-solver as the one used by Why3 to check satisfiability, as the problem is expected to be optimized/configured for it. We also configure GPiD to skip the exploration of subtrees that will produce candidate invariants that do not satisfy the loop preconditions. GPiD returns a stream of solutions to the abductive reasoning problem. We then backward-translate the formulas into the WHYML formalism and use them to strengthen loop invariants. For efficiency, the systems run in parallel: the generation of abductive hypotheses (by GPiD, via the procedure ABDUCE) and their processing in WHYML (via ILINVA) is organized as a pipe-line, where new abduction solutions are computed during the processing of the first ones.

To bridge ILINVA and Why3, we had to devise an interface, which is able to analyze WHYML programs and to identify loop locations and the corresponding invariants. It invokes Why3 to generate and prove the associated verification tasks, and it recovers the failed ones. The library also includes tools to extract and modify loop invariants, to extract variables and reference variables in WHYML files, as well as types, predicates and functions, and wrappers to call the Why3 executable and external tools, and to extract the files sent by WHYML to SMT-solvers.

5.2 Distribution

The ABDULOT framework is available on GITHUB [7]. It contains an revamped interface to the GPiD libraries and algorithm, a generic library of the Ilinva algorithm automatically plugged with GPID, the code interface for Why3 and the related executables. GPID interfaces and related executables are generated for CVC4, Z3 and ALTERGO[5] via their SMTLIB2 interface. Note that the SMT solvers are not provided by our framework, they must be installed separately (all versions with an SMTLIB2-compatible interface are supported). Additional interfaces and executables can be produced using C++ libraries for MINISAT, CVC4 and Z3 if their supported version is available[6].

The framework also provides libraries and toolbox executables to work with abducible files, C++ libraries to handle WHYML files, helpers for the generation of abducible literals out of SMTLIB2 files, and an extensive lisp parser. It also includes a documentation, which explains in particular how to extend it to other solvers and program verification framework. All the tools can be compiled using any C++ 11 compliant compiler. The whole list of dependencies is available in the documentation, as well as a dependency graph for the different parts of the framework.

6 Experiments

We use benchmarks collected from several sources [1–6, 13] (see also [7] for a more detailed view of the benchmark sources), with additional examples corresponding to standard algorithms for division and exponentiation (involving lists, arrays, and non linear arithmetic). Some of these benchmarks have been translated[7] from C or JAVA into WHYML. In all cases, the initial invariant associated with each loop is $\top$. We used Z3 for the benchmarks containing real arithmetic, ALTERGO for lists and arrays and CVC4 in all the other cases. All examples are embedded with the source of the Ilinva tool.

6.1 Results

We ran Ilinva on each example, first without disjunctive invariants (i.e., taking $n = 1$ in Procedure ABDUCE) then with disjunctions of size 2. The results are reported in Fig. 5. For each example, we report whether our tool was able generate invariants allowing Why3 to check the soundness of all program assertions before the timeout, in which case we also report the time Ilinva took to do so (columns T(C) when generating conjunctions only and T(D) when generating implicants containing disjunctions). We also report the number of candidate invariants that have been tried (columns C(D) and C(D)) and the number of abducible literals that were sent to the GPID algorithm (column Abd). Note that the number of candidate invariants does not correspond to the number

---

[5] Those are the three solvers the Why3 documentation recommends to work with as an initial setup. (see also http://why3.lri.fr/@External Provers.).

[6] The ALTERGO interface provided by the tool uses an SMTLIB2 interface that is under heavy development and that, in practice, does not work well with the examples we send it.

[7] The translation was done by hand.

of SMT calls that are made by the system: those made by GPiD to generate these candidates are not taken into account. The timeout is set to 20 min. For some of the examples that we deemed interesting, we allowed the algorithm to run longer. We report those cases by putting the results between parentheses. Light gray cells indicate that the program terminates before the timeout without returning any solution, and dark gray cells indicate that the timeout was reached. Empty cells mean that the tool could not generate any candidate invariant. The last column of both tables report the time Why3 takes to prove all the assertions of an example when correct invariants are provided.

The tests were performed on a computer powered by a dual-core Intel i5 processor running at 1.3 GHz with 4 GB of RAM, under macOS 10.14.3. We used Why3 version 1.2.0 and the SMT solvers ALTERGO (version 2.2.0), CVC4 (prerelease of version 1.7) and Z3 (version 4.7.1).

An essential point concerns the handling of local solver timeouts. Indeed, most calls to the SMT solver in the abductive reasoning procedure will involve satisfiable formulas, and the solvers usually take a lot of time to terminate on such formulas (or in the worst case will not terminate at all if the theory is not decidable, *e.g.*, for problems involving first-order axioms). We thus need to set a timeout after which a call will be considered as satisfiable (see Sect. 3). Obviously, we neither want this timeout to be too high as it can significantly increase computation time, nor too low, since it could make us miss solutions. We decided to set this timeout to 1 second, independently of the solver used, after measuring the computation time of the Why3 verification conditions already satisfied (for which the solver returns unsat) across all benchmarks. We worked under the assumption that the computation time required to prove the other verification conditions when possible would be roughly similar.

6.2 Discussion

As can be observed, ILINVA is able to generate solutions for a wide range of theories, although the execution time is usually high. The number of invariant candidates is relatively high, which has a major impact on the efficiency and scalability of the approach.

When applied to examples involving arithmetic invariants, the program is rather slow, compared to the approach based on minimization and quantifier elimination [13]. This is not surprising, since it is very unlikely that a purely generic approach based on a model-based tree exploration algorithm involving many calls to an SMT solver can possibly compete with a more specific procedure exploiting particular properties of the considered theory. We also wish to emphasize that the fact that our framework is based on an external program verification system (which itself calls external solvers) involves a significant overcost compared to a more integrated approach: for instance, for the Oxy examples (taken from [13]), the time used by Why3 to check the verification conditions once the correct invariants have been generated is often greater than the total time reported in [13] for computing the invariants and checking all properties.

	Abd	T(C)	C(C)	T(D)	C(D)	Why3
001	36	9.68	7	11.89	10	0.26
002	536	3'18.9	66		1126	0.45
004	108	50.47	32	2'31.4	156	0.26
005	266	1'9.07	5	1'3.2	5	0.31
006	390	6'13.6	56	18'5.1	552	0.72
007	594	1'50.1	13	15'40.6	355	0.38
008	210	2'35.5	61	9'35.8	528	0.42
009	390		0		0	0.56
010	90	1'39.54	65	12'56.9	0	0.35
011	180	2'17.7	63		942	0.26
012	782		0		0	0.53
013	296	2'4.5	0		1621	0.30
014	270		0		0	0.34
015	36	32.53	21		888	0.27
016	60	12.54	8	29.72	32	0.26
017	36	40.88	26	2'42.5	134	0.33
018	38	58.49	38	6'53.3	0	0.30
019	60	1'59.5	111		1620	0.31
020	546		380		870	0.49
021	90	0.76	0	0.76	0	0.38
022	270	2'10.1	20	2'11.9	20	0.48
023	36	4.6	5	4.7	5	0.28
025	60	1'23.4	20	2'38.4	44	0.39
026	396	6'23.2	21	7'13.9	66	0.83
028		2'3.9	137	16'22.8	1331	0.31
029	61776		0		0	0.65
030	36	31.43	26	41.66	45	0.26
031	67050		0		0	0.49
032	40	0.865	0	0.833	0	0.50
033	90	1'11.3	12	1'19.9	21	0.45
034	6768	0.798	0	0.79	0	0.44
035	18	18.42	25	2'7.9	200	0.26
036	61778		0		0	1.09
037	36	0.752	0	0.769	0	0.34
038	630		444	3'54.4	0	0.48
039	546		1581		1840	0.40
040	272		0		0	0.84
041			0		0	0.37
042	271	1'50.4	25		605	1.12
043	60	4.27	2	3.67	2	0.29
044		22.481	13	5'7.8	290	0.35
045			0		0	1.50
046			513		813	0.61

	Abd	T(C)	C(C)	T(D)	C(D)	Why3
509	130	(1h50')	(95)		0	0.66
534	172k		8		0	0.62
H04	120	2'54.8	223		1383	0.31
H05	1260		0		0	0.37
list0	60	6'30.4	77		1722	0.40
list1	20	40.82	3	3'26.2	385	0.47
list2	720		40		0	0.40
list3	126	3'35.1	11		930	0.44
list4	816		18		0	
list5	468		22		0	0.44
array0			0		0	0.72
array1			0		0	0.50
array2			0		0	0.50
array3			0		0	0.82
expo0	171	(6h36')	(9)		0	0.40
expo1	2130		0		0	
square	705		62		148	
real0	965		81		213	0.55
real1	965		73		115	0.55
real2	240		9		2	0.40
real00	36	4'9.6	25	5'32.18	40	0.47
realS	66	1'5.3	5	1'0.1	5	0.33
real3	17460		0		0	
BM	1260	3'15.2	74		33	3.35
Scmp			0		0	0.83
Dmd	42		6		0	1'44.9
B00	639k		0		0	0.76
DIV0	560	3'58	35		534	0.83
DIV1	310	14.6	19	14.6	19	0.44
DIVE	42250		0		0	

Fig. 5. Experimental results

Of course, our choice also has clear advantages in terms of genericity, generality and evolvability.

When applied to theories that are harder for SMT solvers, the algorithm can still generate satisfying invariants. However, due to the high number of candidates it tries, combined with the heavy time cost of a verification (which can be several seconds), it may take some time to do so.

The number of abducible literals has a strong impact on the efficiency of the process, leading to timeouts when the considered program contains many variables or function/predicate symbols. It can be observed that the abduction depth is rather low in all examples (1 or 2).

Our prototype has some technical limitations that have a significant impact on the time cost of the execution. For instance, we use SMTLIB2 files for communication between GPID and CVC4 or Z3, instead of using the available APIs. We went back to this solution, which is clearly not optimal for performance, because we experienced many problems coping with the numerous changes in the specifications when updating the solvers to always use the latest versions. The fact that Why3 is taken as a black box also yields some time consumption, first in the (backward and forward) translations (*e.g.*, to associate program variables to their logical counterparts), but also in the verification tasks, which have to be rechecked from the beginning each time an invariant is updated. Our aim in the present paper was not to devise an efficient system, but rather to assess the feasability and usefulness of this approach. Still, the cost of the numerous calls to the SMT solvers and the size of the search tree of the abduction procedure remain the bottleneck of the approach, especially for hard theories (*e.g.*, non-linear arithmetics) for which most calls with satisfiable formulas yield to a local timeout (see Sect. 6.1).

7   Conclusion and Future Work

By combining our generic system GPID for abductive reasoning modulo theories with the Why3 platform to generate verification conditions, we obtained a tool to check properties of WHYML programs, which is able to compute loop invariants in a purely automated way.

The main drawback of our approach is that the set of possible abducible literals is large, yielding a huge search space, especially if disjunctions of $\mathcal{A}$-implicants are considered. Therefore, we believe that our system in its current state is mainly useful when used in an interactive way. For instance, the user could provide the properties of interest for some of the loops and let the system automatically compute suitable invariants by combining these properties, or the program could rely on the user to choose between different solutions to the abduction problem before applying the strengthening. Beside, it is also useful for dealing with theories for which no specific abductive reasoning procedure exists, especially for reasoning in the presence of user-defined symbols or axioms.

In the future, we will focus on the definition of suitable heuristics for automatically selecting abducible literals and ordering them, to reduce the search space and avoid backtracking. The number of occurrences of symbols should be taken into account, as well as properties propagating from previous invariant strengthening. A promising approach is to use dynamic program analysis tools to select relevant abducibles. It would also be interesting to adapt the GPID algorithm to explore the search space width-first, to ensure that simplest solutions are always generated first. Another option is to give ILINVA a more precise control on the GPID algorithm, *e.g.*, to explore some branches more deeply, based on information related to the verification conditions. GPID could also be tuned to generate disjunctions of solutions in a more efficient way.

From a more technical point of view, a tighter integration with the Why3 platform would certainly be beneficial, as explained in Sect. 6.2. The framework could be extended to handle procedures and functions (with pre- and -post conditions).

A current limitation of our tool is that it cannot handle problems in which Why3 relies on a combination of different solvers to check the desired properties. In this case, ILINVA cannot generate the invariants, as the same SMT solver is used for each abduction problem (trying all solvers in parallel on every problem would be possible in theory but this would greatly increase the search space). This problem could be overcome by using heuristic approaches to select the most suited solver for a given problem.

From a theoretical point of view, it would be interesting to investigate the completeness of our approach. It is clear that no general completeness result possibly holds, due to usual theoretical limitations, however, if we assume that a program $P' \sim P$ such that $VCgen(P')$ is valid exists, does the call ILINVA(P) always succeed? This of course would require that the invariants in P' can be constructed from abducibles occurring in the set returned by the procedure GETABDUCIBLES.

References

1. http://toccata.lri.fr/gallery/
2. http://pauillac.inria.fr/~levy//why3/sorting/
3. https://www.lri.fr/~sboldo/research.html
4. Invgen tool. http://pub.ist.ac.at/agupta/invgen/
5. Neclabs NECLA verification benchmarks. http://www.nec-labs.com/research/system/systemsSAV-website/benchmarks.php
6. SATCONV benchmarks
7. Abdulot framework/GPiD-Ilinva tool suite. https://github.com/sellamiy/GPiD-Framework
8. Beyer, D., Henzinger, T.A., Majumdar, R., Rybalchenko, A.: Invariant synthesis for combined theories. In: Proceedings of 8th International Conference on Verification, Model Checking, and Abstract Interpretation, VMCAI 2007, Nice (2007)
9. Bradley, A.R.: IC3 and beyond: incremental, inductive verification. In: Madhusudan, P., Seshia, S.A. (eds.) CAV 2012. LNCS, vol. 7358, pp. 4–4. Springer, Heidelberg (2012). https://doi.org/10.1007/978-3-642-31424-7_4
10. Bradley, A.R., Manna, Z.: Property-directed incremental invariant generation. Formal Asp. Comput. **20**(4–5), 379–405 (2008)
11. Cousot, P., Halbwachs, N.: Automatic discovery of linear restraints among variables of a program. In: Proceedings of the 5th ACM SIGACT-SIGPLAN Symposium on Principles of Programming Languages, POPL 1978. ACM, New York (1978)
12. Dijkstra, E.W.: A Discipline of Programming, 1st edn. Prentice Hall PTR, Upper Saddle River (1997)
13. Dillig, I., Dillig, T., Li, B., McMillan,: Inductive invariant generation via abductive inference. In: Hosking, A.L., Eugster, P.T., Lopes, C.V. (eds.) Proceedings of OOPSLA 2013, Indianapolis, pp. 443–456. ACM (2013)
14. Echenim, M., Peltier, N., Sellami, Y.: A generic framework for implicate generation modulo theories. In: Galmiche, D., Schulz, S., Sebastiani, R. (eds.) IJCAR 2018. LNCS (LNAI), vol. 10900, pp. 279–294. Springer, Cham (2018). https://doi.org/10.1007/978-3-319-94205-6_19

15. Ernst, M.D., Cockrell, J., Griswold, W.G., Notkin, D.: Dynamically discovering likely program invariants to support program evolution. In: Proceedings of the 21st International Conference on Software Engineering, ICSE 1999, pp. 213–224. ACM, New York (1999)

16. Filliâtre, J.-C., Paskevich, A.: Why3 — where programs meet provers. In: Felleisen, M., Gardner, P. (eds.) ESOP 2013. LNCS, vol. 7792, pp. 125–128. Springer, Heidelberg (2013). https://doi.org/10.1007/978-3-642-37036-6_8

17. Flanagan, C., Leino, K.R.M.: Houdini, an annotation assistant for ESC/Java. In: Oliveira, J.N., Zave, P. (eds.) FME 2001. LNCS, vol. 2021, pp. 500–517. Springer, Heidelberg (2001). https://doi.org/10.1007/3-540-45251-6_29. Kindly provide volume number for Ref. [18]

18. Ghilardi, S., Ranise, S.: Backward reachability of array-based systems by SMT solving: termination and invariant synthesis. Logical Methods Comput. Sci. 6(4) (2010)

19. Henzinger, T.A., Jhala, R., Majumdar, R., Sutre, G.: Software verification with BLAST. In: Ball, T., Rajamani, S.K. (eds.) SPIN 2003. LNCS, vol. 2648, pp. 235–239. Springer, Heidelberg (2003). https://doi.org/10.1007/3-540-44829-2_17

20. Hoare, C.A.R.: An axiomatic basis for computer programming. Commun. ACM 12(10), 576–580 (1969)

21. Kapur, D.: A quantifier-elimination based heuristic for automatically generating inductive assertions for programs. J. Syst. Sci. Complex. 19, 307–330 (2006)

22. Karbyshev, A., Bjørner, N., Itzhaky, S., Rinetzky, N., Shoham, S.: Property-directed inference of universal invariants or proving their absence. J. ACM 64(1), 71–733 (2017)

23. Kovács, L., Voronkov, A.: Finding loop invariants for programs over arrays using a theorem prover. In: Proceedings of the 12th International Conference on Fundamental Approaches to Software Engineering, FASE 2009, Held as Part of the Joint European Conferences on Theory and Practice of Software, ETAPS 2009, York, UK, 22–29 March 2009, pp. 470–485 (2009)

24. Kovács, L., Voronkov, A.: Interpolation and symbol elimination. In: Schmidt, R.A. (ed.) CADE 2009. LNCS (LNAI), vol. 5663, pp. 199–213. Springer, Heidelberg (2009). https://doi.org/10.1007/978-3-642-02959-2_17

25. Miné, A.: The octagon abstract domain. Higher Order Symbol. Comput. 19, 31–100 (2006)

26. Padon, O., Immerman, N., Shoham, S., Karbyshev, A., Sagiv, M.: Decidability of inferring inductive invariants. In: Proceedings of the 43rd Annual ACM SIGPLAN-SIGACT Symposium on Principles of Programming Languages, POPL 2016, St. Petersburg, FL, USA, 20–22 January 2016, pp. 217–231 (2016)

27. Suzuki, N., Ishihata, K.: Implementation of an array bound checker (1977)

An Algebra of Modular Systems: Static and Dynamic Perspectives

Eugenia Ternovska[(✉)]

Simon Fraser University, Burnaby, Canada
ter@sfu.ca

Abstract. We introduce static and dynamic algebras for specifying combinations of modules communicating among them via shared second-order variables. In the *static* algebra, atomic modules are classes of structures. They are composed using operations of extended Codd's relational algebra, or, equivalently, first-order logic with least fixed point. The *dynamic* algebra has essentially the same syntax, but with a specification of inputs and outputs in addition. In the dynamic setting, atomic modules are formalized in any framework that allows for the specification of their input-output behaviour by means of model expansion. Algebraic expressions are interpreted by binary relations on structures. We demonstrate connections of the dynamic algebra with a modal temporal logic and deterministic while programs.

1 Introduction

In this paper, we introduce a formalism for specifying and reasoning about modular systems. The goal is to be able to combine reusable components, potentially written in different languages, for solving complex computational tasks.[1] We start with first-order logic with fixpoints. We use an algebraic syntax, similar to Codd's relational algebra, but the idea is the same. We redefine FO(LFP), i.e., first-order logic with the least fixpoint operator, over a vocabulary of *atomic module symbols* that replaces a relational vocabulary. In this static setting, each atomic symbol is interpreted as a set of structures rather than a relational table (set of tuples). That is, by a boolean query, a decision procedure. Thus, while the syntax is first-order, the semantics is second-order because variables range over relations. This gives us the first logic.

The second stage is a dynamic setting where we add information flows. An information flow is a *propagation of information from inputs to outputs*. Formally, it is given by two functions, I and O that partition the relational variables of atomic modules into inputs and outputs. Semantically, modules are *binary relations on structures*. The relations describe how information propagates. This gives us an *algebra of binary relations*, where we can reason about information

---

[1] The heterogeneous components could be web services, knowledge bases, declarative specifications such as Integer Liner Programs, Constraint Satisfaction Problems, Answer Set Programs etc.

© Springer Nature Switzerland AG 2019
A. Herzig and A. Popescu (Eds.): FroCoS 2019, LNAI 11715, pp. 94–111, 2019.
https://doi.org/10.1007/978-3-030-29007-8_6

flows and control the expressive power by means of restricting the algebraic operations and the logics for axiomatizing atomic modules.

Algebras of binary relations have been studied before. Such an algebra was first introduced by De Morgan. It has been extensively developed by Peirce and then Schröder. It was abstracted to relation algebra RA by Jónsson and Tarski in [1]. For a historic perspective please see Pratt's informative historic overview paper [2]. More recently, relation algebras were studied by Fletcher, Van den Bussche, Surinx and their collaborators in a series of paper, see, e.g. [3,4]. The algebras of relations consider various subsets of operations on binary relations as primitive, and other as derivable. In another direction, [5,6] and others study partial functions and their algebraic equational axiomatizations.

When our algebra is interpreted over a pointed Kripke structure, it becomes a modal temporal (dynamic) logic. The logic allows one to specify patterns of execution inside (definable) modalities, similar to Dynamic Logic (see, e.g., [7]) and LDL$_f$ [8]. Just like in PDL and LDL$_f$, the main constructs of imperative programming (e.g., *while* loops) are definable. The main difference of our logic from PDL and LDL$_f$ is that we impose the Law of Inertia for atomic components: the interpretation of the variables not affected by a direct change must remain the same. In this way, the logic is similar to Reiter's situation calculus [9] and Golog [10]. However unlike the first-order successor state axioms of the situation calculus, we allow atomic changes to be non-deterministic, to be specified in a logic with any expressive power where the main computational task can be formalized as the task of Model Expansion, of any complexity. We formulate the main computational task, the Model Expansion task for processes, in the modal setting of our logic as the existence of an information flow that results in a successful computation.

This paper continues the line of research that started at FROCOS 2011 [11] and continued in [12] and then in [13] and [14]. Unlike the previous work, we base our static formalism in classical logic, so the set of our algebraic operations is different. We also develop a novel dynamic perspective, through an algebra of binary relations, and then a modal temporal (dynamic) logic. The development of the dynamic view constitutes most of this paper. Since, in our logic, all the variables that are not constrained by the algebraic expressions are implicitly cylinrified, the closest related work is that on cylindric algebras [15]. These algebras were introduced by Tarski and others as a tool in the algebraization of the first-order predicate calculus.[2] However, a fundamental difference is that, in our logic, unconstrained variables are not only cylindrified, but their interpretation, if not modified, is transferred to the next state by inertia. This property gives us, mathematically, a very different formalism, which is suitable for reasoning about the dynamics of information flows.

The rest of the paper is organized as follows. In Sect. 2, we define the main computational task of Model Expansion in the context of related tasks. Then, in Sect. 3, we introduce the syntax and two different semantics, static and dynamic, of our algebras. The algebra under the dynamic semantics is called a Logic of

---

[2] See [16] for a historic context in applications to Database theory.

Information Flows (LIF). In Sect. 4, we show that, just by adding input and output specifications to classical logic (here, in an algebraic form), we obtain multiple operations that are given as primitive in many algebras of binary relations. In Sect. 5, we show a connection with modal logic. Finally, we conclude, in Sect. 6, with a broader perspective and future research directions.

2   Model Expansion, Related Tasks

Model Expansion [17] is the task of expanding a structure to satisfy a specification (a formula in some logic). It is the central task in declarative programming: in Answer Set Programming, Constraint Satisfaction Problem, Integer Linear Programming, Constraint Programming, etc. In this section, we define Model Expansion and compare it to two other related computational problems.

For a formula ϕ in any logic $\mathcal{L}$ with model-theoretic semantics, we can associate the following three tasks (all three for the same formula), satisfiability (SAT), model checking (MC) and model expansion (MX). We now define them for the case where ϕ has no free object variables.

Definition 1 (Satisfiability (SAT_ϕ)). *Given: Formula ϕ. Find: structure $\mathfrak{B}$ such that $\mathfrak{B} \models \phi$. (The decision version is: Decide: $\exists \mathfrak{B}$ such that $\mathfrak{B} \models \phi$?).*

Definition 2 (Model Checking (MC_ϕ)). *Given: Formula ϕ, structure $\mathfrak{A}$ for $vocab(\phi)$. Decide: $\mathfrak{A} \models \phi$? There is no search counterpart for this task.*

The following task (introduced in [17]) is at the core of this paper. The decision version of it can be seen as being of the form "guess and check", where the "check" part is the model checking task we just defined.

Definition 3 (Model Expansion (MX_ϕ^σ)). *Given: Formula ϕ with designated input vocabulary $\sigma \subseteq vocab(\phi)$ and σ-structure $\mathfrak{A}$. Find: structure $\mathfrak{B}$ such that $\mathfrak{B} \models \phi$ and expands σ-structure $\mathfrak{A}$ to $vocab(\phi)$. (The decision version is: Decide: $\exists \mathfrak{B}$ such that $\mathfrak{B} \models \phi$ and expands σ-structure $\mathfrak{A}$ to $vocab(\phi)$?).*

Any logic that can be interpreted over first-order (Tarski) structures can be used for writing specifications ϕ. In general, vocabulary σ can be empty, in which case the input structure $\mathfrak{A}$ consists of a domain only. When $\sigma = vocab(\phi)$, model expansion collapses to model checking, $\mathsf{MX}_\phi^\sigma = \mathsf{MC}_\phi$. Note that, in general, the domain of the input structure in MC and MX can be infinite. For complexity analysis, in this paper, we focus on finite input structures.

Let ϕ be a sentence, i.e., has no free object variables. Data complexity [18] is measured in terms of the size of the finite active domain. For the decision versions of the problems, data complexity of MX lies in-between model checking (full structure is given) and satisfiability (no part of structure is given):

$$\mathsf{MC}_\phi \leq \mathsf{MX}_\phi^\sigma \leq \mathsf{SAT}_\phi.$$

For example, for FO logic, MC is non-uniform AC^0, MX captures NP (Fagin's theorem), and SAT is undecidable. In SAT, the domain is not given. In MC and

MX, at least, the (active) domain is always given, which significantly reduces the complexity of these tasks compared to SAT. The relative complexity of the three tasks for several logics, including ID-logic of [19] and guarded logics, has been studied in [20].

In this paper, we will view Model Expansion as a (nondeterministic) transduction, i.e., a binary relation from input to outputs, that are τ-structures. We will develop an algebra of such transductions. The following example illustrates what we will consider as an atomic transduction. In the development of our algebra, we will abstract away from what exactly the atomic transductions are. We will become more specific towards the end of the paper, when we restrict our attention to a specific logic and prove a complexity result.

Example 1. Consider the following first-order formula with free relational variables. $\phi_{3\text{Col}}(V, E, R, G, B) :=$

$$
\begin{aligned}
&\forall x \ (V(x) \to [R(x) \lor B(x) \lor G(x)]) \ \land \\
&\forall x \ (V(x) \to \neg[(R(x) \land B(x)) \lor (R(x) \land G(x)) \lor (B(x) \land G(x))]) \\
&\land \quad \forall x \forall y \ [V(x) \land V(y) \land E(x,y) \to \\
&\quad \neg((R(x) \land R(y)) \lor (B(x) \land B(y)) \lor (G(x) \land G(y)))].
\end{aligned}
$$

This formula axiomatizes a class of structures. A class of structures, which is closed under isomorphism, represents a boolean query. In this case, the query specifies all 3-colourable graphs with all their proper clourings. If we identify $I_1 = \{E, V\}$ as the input vocabulary, and $O_1 = \{R, G, B\}$ as the output (solution) vocabulary, then we obtain the classic 3-Colouring computational problem. It can be viewed as a transduction or a binary relation on structures, defined by the binary semantics below. We can also identify $I_2 = \{V, R, G, B\}$ as an input vocabulary, and $O_2 = \{E\}$ as the output, and it will give us a rather different computational problem, with no specific name.

One of the parameters to control the expressive power of the logic is the formalism for the atomic transductions (atomic modules). In the example above, the axiomatization is first-order, and the free second-order variables implicitly make it $\exists$SO. But later in the paper, we consider axiomatizations that are output-monadic non-recursive Datalog programs, which are much less expressive.

3   Algebras: Static and Dynamic

For essentially the same syntax, we produce two algebras, static and dynamic, by giving different interpretations to the algebraic operations and to the elements of the algebras. In the second algebra, atomic modules have a direction of information propagation, which corresponds to solving MX task for those modules. The algebras correspond to classical and modal logics (as we will see later), respectively. We use a version of Codd's relational algebra instead of first-order logic, since we need an algebraic notation, however, the equivalence of the two formalisms is well-known.

Syntax. Assume we have a countable sequence Vars $= (X_1, X_2, \dots)$ of *relational variables* each with an associated finite *arity*. For convenience, we use X, Y, Z, etc. Let ModAt $= \{M_1, M_2, \dots\}$ be a fixed vocabulary of *atomic module symbols*. Each $M_i \in$ ModAt has an associated *variable vocabulary* $vvoc(M_i)$ whose length can depend on M_i. We may write $M_i(X_{i_1}, \dots, X_{i_k})$, (or $M_i(\bar{X})$), to indicate that $vvoc(M) = (X_{i_1}, \dots, X_{i_k})$. Similarly, ModVars $= \{Z_1, Z_2, \dots\}$ is a countable sequence of *module variables*, where each $Z_j \in$ ModVars has its own $vvoc(Z_j)$. Algebraic expressions are built by the grammar:

$$\alpha ::= \mathrm{id} \mid M_i \mid Z_j \mid \alpha \cup \alpha \mid \alpha^- \mid \pi_\delta(\alpha) \mid \sigma_\Theta(\alpha) \mid \mu Z_j.\alpha. \tag{1}$$

Here, M_i is any symbol in ModAt of the form $M_i(\bar{X})$, δ is any finite set of relational variables in Vars, Θ is any expression of the form $X = Y$, for relational variables of equal arity that occur in Vars, Z_j is a module variable in ModVars which must occur positively in the expression α, i.e., under an even number of the complementation ($^-$) operator. By equality symbol '$=$' in Selection condition Θ, we mean the equality of the interpretations. It is a slight abuse of notations, however the definition of the semantics specifies the intended meaning precisely.

Atomic modules can be specified in any formalism with a model-theoretic semantics. For example, we saw an axiomatization of 3Colouring in Example 1. Modules occurring within one algebraic expression can even be axiomatized in different logics, if needed. They can also be viewed as abstract decision procedures. But, as far as the static algebra is concerned,

their only relevant feature is the *classes of structures they induce*.

When the domain is specified, we talk about sets of structures rather than classes.

Static (Unary) Semantics. Fix a finite relational vocabulary τ. Algebraic expressions will be used as "constraints". A *variable assignment s* is a function that assigns, to each relational variable, a symbol in τ of the same arity. We introduce notation $V := s^{-1}(\tau)$. Clearly, $V \subset Vars$. Function s gives us the flexibility to apply the same algebraic expression in multiple contexts, without a priori binding to a specific vocabulary.

Now fix a domain Dom.[3] The domain can be finite or infinite. Let $\mathbf{U}$ be the set of all τ-structures over the domain Dom. The following definition is mathematically necessary in defining the semantics of atomic modules.

Definition 4. *Given a sub-vocabulary γ of τ, a subset $W \subseteq \mathbf{U}$ is determined by γ if it satisfies*

$$\text{for all } \mathfrak{A}, \mathfrak{B} \in \mathbf{U} \text{ such that } \mathfrak{A}|_\gamma = \mathfrak{B}|_\gamma \text{ we have}$$
$$\mathfrak{A} \in W \text{ iff } \mathfrak{B} \in W.$$

---

[3] Usually, in applications, domain Dom is the (active) domain of an input structure for a task of interest such as MX.

Given a well-formed algebraic expression α defined by (1), we say that structure $\mathfrak{A}$ *satisfies* α (or that is a *model* of α) under variable assignment s, notation $\mathfrak{A} \models_s \alpha$, if $\mathfrak{A} \in [\alpha]^s$, where *unary interpretation* $[\,\cdot\,]^s$ is defined as follows. Given a variable assignment s, function $[\,\cdot\,]^s$ assigns a subset $[M_i]^s \subseteq \mathbf{U}$ and a subset $[Z_j]^s \subseteq \mathbf{U}$ to each atomic module symbol $M_i \in \mathrm{ModAt}$ and each module variable $Z_j \in \mathrm{ModVars}$, with the property that $[M_i]^s$ is determined by $s(vvoc(M_i))$ (respectively, $[Z_j]^s$ is determined by $s(vvoc(Z_j))$). The unary interpretation of atomic modules $[\,\cdot\,]^s$ (parameterized with s) can be viewed as a function that provides "oracles" or decision procedures, or answers to boolean queries. In general, these oracles can be of arbitrary computational complexity.

We extend the definition of $[\,\cdot\,]^s$ to all algebraic expressions.

$[\mathrm{id}]^s := \mathbf{U}.$
$[\alpha_1 \cup \alpha_2]^s := [\alpha_1]^s \cup [\alpha_2]^s.$
$[\alpha^-]^s := \mathbf{U} \setminus [\alpha]^s.$
$[\pi_\delta(\alpha)]^s := \{\mathfrak{A} \in \mathbf{U} \mid \exists \mathfrak{B} \ (\mathfrak{B} \in [\alpha]^s \text{ and } \mathfrak{A}|_{s(\delta)} = \mathfrak{B}|_{s(\delta)})\}.$
$[\sigma_{X=Y}(\alpha)]^s := \{\mathfrak{A} \mid \mathfrak{A} \in [\alpha]^s \text{ and } \mathfrak{A}|_{s(X)} = \mathfrak{A}|_{s(Y)}\}.$
$[\mu Z_j.\alpha]^s := \bigcap \{R \subseteq \mathbf{U} \mid [\alpha]^s_{[Z:=\alpha]} \subseteq R\}.$

Here, $[\alpha]^s_{[Z:=\alpha]}$ means an interpretation that is exactly like given by the function $[\,\cdot\,]^s$, except Z is interpreted as α. Note that Projection $\pi_\delta(\alpha)$ is equivalent to cylindrification $C_\gamma(\alpha)$, where $\gamma = V \setminus \delta$.

Free and Bound Variables. These notions are exactly the same as in classical logic. The role of an existentional quantifier is played by Cylinderfication. We define them as follows. $free(M) := vvoc(M)$, $free(\mathrm{id}) := \varnothing$, $free(\alpha \cup \beta) := free(\alpha) \cup free(\alpha)$, $free(\alpha^-) := free(\alpha)$, $free(\pi_\delta(\alpha)) := \delta$, $free(\sigma_{X=Y}(\alpha)) := free(\alpha) \cup \{X, Y\}$, $free(\mu_{\bar{X}, Z}\alpha[\bar{X} : \bar{t}]) := free(\bar{t}) \cup (free(\alpha) \setminus \{\bar{X}, Z\})$. Taking into account that Projection $\pi_\delta(\alpha)$ is equivalent to cylindrification $C_\gamma(\alpha)$, where $\gamma = vvoc(\alpha) \setminus \delta$, we also have: $free(C_\gamma(\alpha)) := free(\alpha) \setminus \gamma$. Bound variables are defined as those that are not free.

Implicit Cylindrification. Algebraic expressions can be viewed as constraints on the free variables. The following proposition shows that everything outside the free variables of α is implicitly cylindrified. Recall that $V := s^{-1}(\tau)$.

Proposition 1. *If α is an atomic module symbol, then* $[\alpha] = [\pi_{free(\alpha)}(\alpha)]$.

Proof. The proposition holds for the atomic case because, by the static semantics of atomic modules, the set of structures $[M_i]^s$ that interprets an atomic module is determined by $s(vvoc(M_i))$, see Definition (4), and $vvoc(M_i) = free(M_i)$.

We now give a binary semantics to the algebra. The algebra under this semantics is called a **Logic of Information Flows (LIF)**.[4]

Dynamic (Binary) Semantics. The Dynamic semantics is produced by adding information flows. Such flows are initiated by Model Expansion task,

---

[4] Please note that the goals of this paper have no connection with information flows in security.

where we provide inputs by giving a part of a structure (say, a graph), and expand to obtain the solution part (say, a possible 3-colouring). Since information propagates from inputs to outputs, we introduce two functions that specify inputs and outputs of atomic module symbols, respectively. As a consequence of specifying inputs and outputs, we transition to generalized binary expressions. Projection now has two cases, for the left and the right parts of the binary relation it applies to, and Selection has three – left, right and mixed.

Let $\text{ModAt}_{I/O}$ denote the set of all atomic module symbols M with all possible *partitions* of $vvoc(M)$ into inputs and outputs, i.e., $I(M) \cup O(M) = vvoc(M)$ and $I(M) \cap O(M) = \varnothing$.[5] This set is larger than the set ModAt (unless both are empty) because the same M can have several different input-output assignments. Similarly, we define $\text{ModVars}_{I/O}$. The well-formed algebraic expression α is defined, again, by (1), except, in the atomic case, we have atomic module symbols (respectively, module variables) from $\text{ModAt}_{I/O}$ (respectively, from $\text{ModVars}_{I/O}$).

While inputs and outputs of atomic modules are always given, the situation with inputs $I(\alpha)$ and outputs $O(\alpha)$ of a general algebraic expression α is much more complicated. The problem is that it is not always possible to syntactically identify the variables whose interpretations are needed as *conditions* for applying algebraic expression α, and those that are the *effects* of α, i.e., can potentially be modified by the expression. A detailed analysis, for a general setting, is a subject of an ongoing collaborative work.

Let s be as above. Given a well-formed α, we say that pair of structures $(\mathfrak{A}, \mathfrak{B})$, *satisfies* α under variable assignment s, notation $(\mathfrak{A}, \mathfrak{B}) \models_s \alpha$, if $(\mathfrak{A}, \mathfrak{B}) \in [\![\alpha]\!]^s$, where *binary interpretation* $[\![\cdot]\!]^s$ is defined by I and II below.

I. Binary Semantics: Atomic Modules and Variables

Definition 5. *For atomic modules in* $\text{ModAt}_{I/O}$, *we have:*

$$[\![M]\!]^s := \big\{ (\mathfrak{A}, \mathfrak{B}) \in \mathbf{U} \times \mathbf{U} \mid \text{ there exists } \mathfrak{C} \in [M]^s \text{ such that}$$

$$\mathfrak{C}|_{s(I(M))} = \mathfrak{A}|_{s(I(M))}, \tag{2}$$
$$\mathfrak{C}|_{s(O(M))} = \mathfrak{B}|_{s(O(M))} \tag{3}$$
$$and \ \ \mathfrak{A}|_{\tau \setminus s(O(M))} = \mathfrak{B}|_{\tau \setminus s(O(M))} \big\}. \tag{4}$$

That is, in each pair of structures in the interpretation of an atomic module, the structure on the left agrees with the unary semantics on the inputs, and the structure on the right agrees with the unary semantics on the outputs. While in the unary semantics, everything that is not explicitly mentioned is implicitly cylindrified, here the situation is different. Intuitively, on states where it is defined, an atomic module produces a replica of the current structure except the interpretation of the output vocabulary changes as specified by the action. This preservation of unmodified information, while intuitively obvious, is an

---

[5] Either one of these sets, $I(M)$, $O(M)$, can be empty.

important technical property. For this reason, we call it, rather ostentatiously, the Law of Inertia. The semantics is defined in a way so that atomic modules impose constraints on the $vvoc(M)$ only. The semantics of module variables $Z \in \mathrm{ModVars}_{I/O}$ is defined in exactly the same way as the semantics for atomic module constants.

Properties of Binary Atomic Modules. Before giving binary semantics to the operations, we clarify the properties of the semantics of atomic modules by the following proposition.[6]

Proposition 2. *For all atomic modules, we have, for all structures* $\mathfrak{A}$, $\mathfrak{B}$:

$$(a)\ (\mathfrak{A}, \mathfrak{B}) \in [\![M]\!]^s \Rightarrow (\mathfrak{B}, \mathfrak{B}) \in [\![M]\!]^s,$$
$$(b)\ (\mathfrak{B}, \mathfrak{B}) \in [\![M]\!]^s \Leftrightarrow \mathfrak{B} \in [M]^s.$$

Proof. (a) Assume, towards a contradiction that (a1) $(\mathfrak{A}, \mathfrak{B}) \in [\![M]\!]^s$, but (a2) $(\mathfrak{B}, \mathfrak{B}) \notin [\![M]\!]^s$. Assumption (a1) implies, by the definition of the binary semantics of atomic modules, that there exists $\mathfrak{C} \in [M]^s$ such that conditions (2)–(4) hold. By (4), which is the Law of Inertia, $\mathfrak{A}|_{s(I(M))} = \mathfrak{B}|_{s(I(M))}$. This is because $s(I(M)) \subseteq \tau \setminus s(O(M))$ since $I(M) \cap O(M) = \varnothing$, so the Law of Inertia applies. Thus, $\mathfrak{C}|_{s(I(M))} = \mathfrak{A}|_{s(I(M))} = \mathfrak{B}|_{s(I(M))}$. Assumption (a2) implies that for all $\mathfrak{C} \in [M]^s$, at least one of the conditions (2)–(4), where $\mathfrak{A} = \mathfrak{B}$, must be violated for all structures $\mathfrak{B}$. Violation of (2) and (3) is impossible by our conclusion from the assumption (1a). Violation of (4) is impossible because $\mathfrak{A}$ is the same as $\mathfrak{B}$ in this case.

(b, $\Rightarrow$) Assume $(\mathfrak{B}, \mathfrak{B}) \in [\![M]\!]^s$. Then, by Definition 5 of the binary semantics for atomic modules, there exists $\mathfrak{C} \in [M]^s$ such that $\mathfrak{C}|_{s(I(M))} = \mathfrak{A}|_{s(I(M))}$ and $\mathfrak{C}|_{s(O(M))} = \mathfrak{B}|_{s(O(M))}$. By Proposition 1, in the case of atomic modules, $[M] = [\pi_{free(M)}(M)]$. Thus, since $free(M) = vvoc(M) = I(M) \cup O(M)$, it does not matter how $\mathfrak{B}$ interprets symbols outside $s(free(M))$, and $\mathfrak{C}$ can be taken to be $\mathfrak{B}$.

(b, $\Leftarrow$) Assume $\mathfrak{B} \in [M]^s$. Then, by the unary semantics, there exists $\mathfrak{C} \in [M]^s$ such that $\mathfrak{C}|_{s(I(M))} = \mathfrak{B}|_{s(I(M))}$ and $\mathfrak{C}|_{s(O(M))} = \mathfrak{B}|_{s(O(M))}$. Take $\mathfrak{C} = \mathfrak{B}$. Obviously, $\mathfrak{B} = \mathfrak{B}$ outside of the outputs of M. Thus, all three conditions of Definition 5 are satisfied and $(\mathfrak{B}, \mathfrak{B}) \in [\![M]\!]^s$.

II. Binary Semantics: the Remaining Cases. We are now ready to extend the binary interpretation $[\![\cdot]\!]^s$ to all algebraic expressions α:

---

[6] Part (b) of this proposition is stated without proof as Theorem 4.1 for *compound expressions* in Shahab Tasharrofi thesis. The language has Projection, Sequential Composition, Union and Feedback. The operations of Projection and Sequential Composition have a different semantics than ours, and we do not have Feedback.

$$[\![id]\!]^s := \{(\mathfrak{A}, \mathfrak{B}) \in \mathbf{U} \times \mathbf{U} \mid \mathfrak{A} = \mathfrak{B}\},$$
$$[\![\alpha_1 \cup \alpha_2]\!]^s := [\![\alpha_1]\!]^s \cup [\![\alpha_2]\!]^s,$$
$$[\![\alpha^-]\!]^s := \mathbf{U} \times \mathbf{U} \setminus [\![\alpha]\!]^s,$$
$$[\![\mu Z_j.\alpha]\!]^s := \bigcap \{R \subseteq \mathbf{U} \times \mathbf{U} \mid [\![\alpha]\!]^s_{[Z:=R]} \subseteq R\},$$
$$[\![\pi^l_\delta(\alpha)]\!]^s := \{(\mathfrak{A}, \mathfrak{B}) \in \mathbf{U} \times \mathbf{U} \mid$$
$$\exists\, (\mathfrak{A}', \mathfrak{B}) \in [\![\alpha]\!]^s \text{ such that } \mathfrak{A}'|_{s(\delta)} = \mathfrak{A}|_{s(\delta)}\},$$
$$[\![\pi^r_\delta(\alpha)]\!]^s := \{(\mathfrak{A}, \mathfrak{B}) \in \mathbf{U} \times \mathbf{U} \mid$$
$$\exists\, (\mathfrak{A}, \mathfrak{B}') \in [\![\alpha]\!]^s \text{ such that } \mathfrak{B}'|_{s(\delta)} = \mathfrak{B}|_{s(\delta)}\},$$
$$[\![\sigma^l_{X=Y}(\alpha)]\!]^s := \{(\mathfrak{A}, \mathfrak{B}) \in [\![\alpha]\!]^s \mid (s(X))^{\mathfrak{A}} = (s(Y))^{\mathfrak{A}}\},$$
$$[\![\sigma^r_{X=Y}(\alpha)]\!]^s := \{(\mathfrak{A}, \mathfrak{B}) \in [\![\alpha]\!]^s \mid (s(X))^{\mathfrak{B}} = (s(Y))^{\mathfrak{B}}\},$$
$$[\![\sigma^{lr}_{X=Y}(\alpha)]\!]^s := \{(\mathfrak{A}, \mathfrak{B}) \in [\![\alpha]\!]^s \mid (s(X))^{\mathfrak{A}} = (s(Y))^{\mathfrak{B}}\}.$$

Operation id is sometimes called the *"nil"* action, or it can be seen as an empty word which is denoted ε in the formal language theory. It is convenient to extend the selection operation to $\Theta \in \{X = Y, X \neq Y, X = R, X \neq R\}$, where R is a relational constant. This extension is done in an obvious way. According to the semantics, Left Projection keeps the interpretation of a subset of the vocabulary in the first element of the binary relation defined by α while cylindrifying everything else on the left. It keeps the second element of the binary relation intact. The semantics of Right Projection is defined symmetrically.[7]

Standard Models: Induction Principle. The semantics of the algebra of binary relations on $\mathbf{U}$ gives us transition systems (Kripke structures) with states that are elements of $\mathbf{U}$ and transition given by the binary semantics. In this paper, we are interested in reachability from the input structure. We need to ensure categoricity of the theories in the logic, to avoid non-standard models that, in particular, do not originate in the input structure. For that purpose, we *semantically* impose the following restriction:

> *only structures reachable from the input structures by means of applying atomic modules are in the allowable Kripke models.*

This semantic constraint can also be imposed axiomatically, although we do not do it in this paper. For example, in Dynamic Logic, which is a fragment of the Logic of Information Flows, it would be expressed by an axiom schema $p \wedge [a^*](p \rightarrow [a]p) \rightarrow [a^*]p$. This schema is a form of an inductive definition. Such a definition always has a construction principle that specifies how to construct a set, and an induction principle that says "nothing else is" in the set being defined. Together, the two principles produce, depending on the logic, an axiom similar to the the second-order induction axiom of Peano Arithmetic or the Dynamic Logic axiom above [21].[8]

---

[7] Equivalently, we could have introduced appropriate Cylindrification operations instead of the two Projections.

[8] The idea of connecting dynamic systems with Peano Arithmetic goes back to Reiter [9]. He introduced second-order Induction axiom to the Basic Action Theory of the situation calculus, which is a formalism for reasoning about actions based on classical first and second-order logic.

In addition to the algebraic operations above, we will also use Sequential Composition $(\alpha; \beta)$. This operation is sometimes also called relative, dynamic, or multiplicative conjunction as its properties are similar to the properties of the logical (additive, static) conjunction $(\alpha \cap \beta)$. The semantics of sequential composition is given as follows.

$$[\![\alpha; \beta]\!] := \{(\mathfrak{A}, \mathfrak{B}) \mid \exists \mathfrak{C}((\mathfrak{A}, \mathfrak{C}) \in [\![\alpha]\!] \text{ and } (\mathfrak{C}, \mathfrak{B}) \in [\![\beta]\!])\}.$$

This operation is definable, under some conditions on inputs and outputs, through the other operations. The full study of the primitivity of this operation is an ongoing collaborative work.

As a decision task, we are interested in checking whether a program α has a successful execution, including a witness for its free relational variables, starting from an input structure $\mathfrak{A}$. This is specified by $\mathfrak{A} \models_s |\alpha\rangle \mathbf{T}$, where $|\alpha\rangle$ is a right-facing possibility modality, and $\mathbf{T}$ represents *true*, that is, all states. We formally introduce and explain this modality in Sect. 5 on Modal Logic. To evaluate α in $\mathfrak{A}$, we use s to match the vocabulary of $\mathfrak{A}$ with the relational input variables of α, while matching the arities as well, and then apply the binary semantics as defined above. We will come back to this decision task in Definition 7.

Static-Dynamic Duality for Atomic Modules. Note that, for a given domain, each atomic module is, simultaneously, (a) a set of structures, according to the unary semantics, and (b) a binary relation, i.e., a set of pairs of structures, according to the binary semantics.

4 Definable Constructs

We now introduce several *definable* operations, and we study some of their properties. All of those constructs are present in algebras of binary relations and partial functions. There are studies on which operations are primitive and which are definable [3]. It turns out that the only thing lacking in classical logic to define most of these constructs is information propagation, i.e., a specification of inputs and outputs. By adding it, we obtain a surprisingly rich logic. In the following, we assume that all structures range over universe $\mathbf{U}$, and all pairs of structures over $\mathbf{U} \times \mathbf{U}$.

Set-Theoretic Operations

$$
\begin{aligned}
\mathrm{di} &:= \mathrm{id}^-, & \text{(diversity)} \\
\top &:= \mathrm{id}^- \cup \mathrm{id}, & \text{(all)} \\
\bot &:= \top^-, & \text{(empty)} \\
\alpha \cap \beta &:= (\alpha^- \cup \beta^-)^-, & \text{(intersection)} \\
\alpha - \beta &:= (\alpha^- \cup \beta)^-, & \text{(difference)} \\
\alpha \sim \beta &:= (\alpha^- \cup \beta) \cap (\beta^- \cup \alpha). & \text{(similar)}
\end{aligned}
$$

In the following, we use $I(\alpha)$ and $O(\alpha)$ as a generalization of inputs and outputs of atomic modules to compound algebraic expressions.[9]

Projection onto the Inputs (Domain). $\text{Dom}(\alpha) := \pi^{l}_{I(\alpha)}(\alpha) \cap \text{id}$. This operation is also called "projection onto the first element of the binary relation". It identifies the states in V where there is an outgoing α-transition. Thus,

$$[\![\text{Dom}(\alpha)]\!] = \{(\mathfrak{B}, \mathfrak{B}) \mid \exists \mathfrak{B}' \; (\mathfrak{B}, \mathfrak{B}') \in [\![\alpha]\!]\}.$$

Projection onto the Outputs (Image). $\text{Img}(\alpha) := \pi^{r}_{O(\alpha)}(\alpha) \cap \text{id}$. This operation can also be called "projection onto the second element of the binary relation". It follows that

$$[\![\text{Img}(\alpha)]\!] = \{(\mathfrak{B}, \mathfrak{B}) \mid \exists \mathfrak{B}' \; (\mathfrak{B}', \mathfrak{B}) \in [\![\alpha]\!]\}.$$

Forward Unary Negation (Anti-domain). Regular complementation includes all possible transitions except α. We introduce a stronger negation which is essentially unary (binary with equal elements in the pair) and excludes states where α originates.

$$\curvearrowright\alpha := (\pi_{I(\alpha)}(\alpha))^{-} \cap \text{id}.$$

It says "there is no outgoing α-transition". By this definition,

$$[\![\curvearrowright\alpha]\!] = \{(\mathfrak{B}, \mathfrak{B}) \mid \forall \mathfrak{B}' \; (\mathfrak{B}, \mathfrak{B}') \notin [\![\alpha]\!]\}.$$

Backwards Unary Negation (Anti-image). We define a similar operation for the opposite direction.

$$\curvearrowleft\alpha := (\pi_{O(\alpha)}(\alpha))^{-} \cap \text{id}.$$

It says "there is no incoming α-transition". We obtain:

$$[\![\curvearrowleft\alpha]\!] = \{(\mathfrak{B}, \mathfrak{B}) \mid \forall \mathfrak{B}' \; (\mathfrak{B}', \mathfrak{B}) \notin [\![\alpha]\!]\}.$$

Each of the unary negations is a restriction of the regular negation (complementation). Unlike regular negation, these operations preserve determinism of the components. In particular, De Morgan's Law does not hold for $\curvearrowright$ and $\curvearrowleft$. We have demonstrated that these connectives have the properties of the Intuitionistic negation. The proofs do not fit into the conference format and will be given in a journal version of this paper.

---

[9] We do not give a formal definition of the more general concept of inputs and outputs here since it is long and an informal understanding is sufficient. The formal definition will be given in another paper (with coauthors).

Iteration (Kleene Star). This operator is the *iteration* operator, also called the Kleene star. The expression α^* means "execute α some nondeterministically chosen finite number of times. We define it as follows: $\alpha^* := \mu Z.(\mathrm{id} \cup Z; \alpha)$. By this definition,

$$[\![\alpha^*]\!] = \{(\mathfrak{A}, \mathfrak{B}) \mid \mathfrak{A} = \mathfrak{B} \text{ or there exists } n < 0$$
$$\text{and } \mathfrak{C}_0, \ldots, \mathfrak{C}_n \in \mathbf{U} \text{ such that}$$
$$\mathfrak{A} = \mathfrak{C}_0, \mathfrak{B} = \mathfrak{C}_n, \text{ and for all } i < n, (\mathfrak{C}_i, \mathfrak{C}_{i+1}) \in [\![\alpha]\!]\}.$$

That is, α^* is a transitive reflexive closure of α.

Converse. This operation is equivalent to switching $I(\alpha)$ and $O(\alpha)$. It changes the direction of information propagation. The semantics is as follows.

$$[\![\alpha^{\smile}]\!] := \{(\mathfrak{A}, \mathfrak{B}) \mid (\mathfrak{B}, \mathfrak{A}) \in \alpha\}.$$

Converse is *implicitly* definable: $\beta = \alpha^{\smile}$ iff $\begin{aligned}\mathrm{Dom}(\alpha) &= \mathrm{Img}(\beta),\\ \mathrm{Dom}(\beta) &= \mathrm{Img}(\alpha).\end{aligned}$

Logical Equivalence (Equality of Algebraic Terms). We say that α and β are *logically equivalent*, notation $\alpha = \beta$ if $\big((\mathfrak{A}, \mathfrak{B}) \models_s \alpha$ iff $(\mathfrak{A}, \mathfrak{B}) \models_s \beta\big)$, for all τ-structures $\mathfrak{A}, \mathfrak{B}$, for any variable assignment s.

The following proposition clarifies semantical connections between the operations.

Proposition 3.

$$\curvearrowright\alpha = \mathrm{Dom}(\alpha)^- \cap \mathrm{id} = \mathrm{Dom}(\alpha^-) - \mathrm{Dom}(\alpha) = \curvearrowright\mathrm{Dom}(\alpha) = \curvearrowleft\mathrm{Dom}(\alpha),$$
$$\curvearrowleft\alpha = \mathrm{Img}(\alpha)^- \cap \mathrm{id} = \mathrm{Img}(\alpha^-) - \mathrm{Img}(\alpha) = \curvearrowright\mathrm{Img}(\alpha) = \curvearrowleft\mathrm{Img}(\alpha),$$

$$\mathrm{Dom}(\alpha) = \curvearrowright\curvearrowright\alpha, \quad \mathrm{id} = \curvearrowright\bot = \curvearrowleft\bot, \qquad\qquad\qquad \curvearrowright\curvearrowright\alpha = \curvearrowright\alpha,$$
$$\mathrm{Img}(\alpha) = \curvearrowleft\curvearrowleft\alpha, \quad \bot = \curvearrowright\mathrm{id} = \curvearrowleft\mathrm{id} = \curvearrowright\top = \curvearrowleft\top, \ \curvearrowleft\curvearrowleft\curvearrowleft\alpha = \curvearrowleft\alpha.$$

Proof. The logical equivalences follow directly from the semantics of the operations.

Notice that $\curvearrowright$ inherits a property of intuitionistic negation: $\curvearrowright\curvearrowright\alpha \neq \alpha$. This is because Anti-domain ($\curvearrowright$), when applied twice, gives us Domain of α, which is clearly different from α itself. But Domain of Anti-domain is Anti-domain, so $\curvearrowright\curvearrowright\curvearrowright\alpha = \mathrm{Dom}(\curvearrowright\alpha) = \curvearrowright\alpha$. It is also possible to show that $\curvearrowright$ and $\curvearrowleft$ distribute over $\cap$ and $\cup$, so De Morgan Law does not hold for them. Also, $\curvearrowright\top = \bot$, but $\curvearrowright\bot \neq \top$. Indeed, $\curvearrowright\bot = \mathrm{id}$.

5 Modal Logic

We now define a modal logic which we call $L\mu\mu$, since it is similar to the mu-calculus $L\mu$, but has two fixed points, unary and binary. The modal logic is used, in particular, to formalize the main computational task, the Model Expansion task for processes in Definition 7.

5.1 Two-Sorted Syntax, $L\mu\mu$

The algebra with information flows can be equivalently represented in a "two-sorted" syntax, with sorts for processes (α) and state formulae (ϕ). This syntax gives us a modal logic, similar to Dynamic Logic. The syntax is given by the grammar:

$$
\begin{aligned}
\alpha &::= \text{id} \mid M_a \mid Z_j \mid \alpha \cup \alpha \mid \alpha^- \mid \pi_\delta(\alpha) \mid \sigma_\Theta(\alpha) \mid \phi? \mid \mu Z_j.\alpha \\
\phi &::= \mathbf{T} \mid M_p \mid X_i \mid \phi \vee \phi \mid \neg\phi \mid |\alpha\rangle\,\phi \mid \langle\alpha|\,\phi \mid \mu X_i.\phi.
\end{aligned}
\tag{5}
$$

The first line defines *process formulae*. It is essentially our original syntax (1). The second line specifies *state formulae*. There, we have two possibility modalities, $|\alpha\rangle$ is a forward "exists execution of α" modality, and $\langle\alpha|$ is its backwards counterpart. We can also introduce their duals, the two necessity modalities: $|\alpha]\,\phi := \neg(\,|\alpha\rangle\,\neg\phi)$ and $[\alpha|\,\phi := \neg(\langle\alpha|\,\neg\phi)$. Symbols M_a stand for modules that are "actions". Symbols M_p stand for modules that are "propositions". Operation $\mathbf{T}$ represents a proposition that is true in every state. It replaces id under unary semantics.[10]

Test ϕ? turns every unary operation in the second line into a binary one by repeating the arguments, such as in e.g. going from $p(x)$ to $p(x,x)$, i.e., they are (partial) identities on $\mathbf{U}$. *Atomic tests* are (a) atomic modules-propositions (MC modules) and (b) expressions of the form $\pi_\delta(\text{id})$ and $\sigma_\Theta(\text{id})$.

We will see that the state formulae "compile out", i.e., are expressible using the operations in the first line. Despite state formulae being redundant, they are useful for expressing properties of processes relative to states, as in other modal temporal logics. In particular, they give an easy way to express quantification over executions (sequences of transitions) by means of modalities.

Semantics of $L\mu\mu$. The modal logic is interpreted over a transition system, where the set of states $\mathbf{U}$ is the set of all τ-structures over the same domain *Dom*.[11]

State Formulae (line 2 of (5)): Atomic modules M_p (modules-propositions) and module variables X_i are interpreted exactly like in the unary semantics. That is, M_p are Model Checking (MC) modules, i.e., those where the expansion (output) vocabulary is empty. The rest of the formulae are interpreted exactly as in the μ-calculus, except we have a backwards modality in addition:

$$
\begin{aligned}
[\mathbf{T}] &:= \mathbf{U}, \\
[\phi_1 \vee \phi_2] &:= [\phi_1] \cup [\phi_2], \\
[\neg\phi] &:= \mathbf{U} \setminus [\phi], \\
[|\alpha\rangle\phi] &:= \{\mathfrak{A} \mid \exists\mathfrak{B}\,(\,(\mathfrak{A},\mathfrak{B}) \in [\![\alpha]\!] \text{ and } \mathfrak{B} \in [\phi]\,)\,\}, \\
[\langle\alpha|\phi] &:= \{\mathfrak{B} \mid \exists\mathfrak{A}\,(\,(\mathfrak{A},\mathfrak{B}) \in [\![\alpha]\!] \text{ and } \mathfrak{A} \in [\phi]\,)\,\}, \\
[\mu Z_j.\phi] &:= \bigcap\{R \subseteq \mathbf{U} : [\phi]^{[Z:=R]} \subseteq R\}.
\end{aligned}
$$

---

[10] Note that $\mathbf{T}$ is unary, as every other state formula in the second line of (5), which makes it different from the binary $\top$ and id.

[11] In the case of solving Model Expansion task, the domain is determined by the domain of the input structure.

Process Formulae (line 1 of (5)): These formulae are interpreted exactly as in the binary semantics. In particular, modules-actions are interpreted as Model Expansion (MX) tasks, since they have inputs and outputs. In addition, tests are interpreted as in Dynamic Logic: $[\![\phi?]\!] := \{(\mathfrak{A}, \mathfrak{A}) \mid \mathfrak{A} \in [\phi] \}$. In particular, $[\![\mathbf{T}?]\!] = [\![\text{id}]\!]$, where id is the relative multiplicative identity (using the terminology introduced for algebras in the style of Tarski and Givant) in the syntax of $L\mu\mu$ (5).

Satisfaction Relation for $L\mu\mu$. We say that state $\mathfrak{A}$, where $\mathfrak{A} \in \mathbf{U}$, *satisfies* ϕ under variable assignment s, notation $\mathfrak{A} \models_s \phi$, if $\mathfrak{A} \in [\phi]$. For process formulae α, the definition of the satisfaction relation is exactly as in the binary semantics.

Structures as Transitions and States. Note that, for each $\alpha \in L\mu\mu$, its model is a Kripke structure where transitions represent MX tasks for all subformulae of α, according to the binary semantics. In that Kripke structure, states are Tarski's structures, and atomic transitions are also Tarski's structures, over the same vocabulary.[12]

5.2   Two-Sorted = One-Sorted Syntax

The two representations of the algebra, one-sorted (1) and two-sorted (5), are equivalent.[13] We show that all operations in the second line of (5) are reducible to the operations in the first line.

Theorem 1. *For every state formula ϕ in two-sorted syntax (5), there is a formula $\hat{\phi}$ in the one-sorted syntax (1) such that $\mathfrak{B} \models_s \phi$ iff $(\mathfrak{B}, \mathfrak{B}) \models_s$ Dom/Img$(\hat{\phi})$. For every process formula α there is an equivalent formula $\hat{\alpha}$ in the one-sorted syntax.*

The notation Dom/Img above means that either of the two operations can be used.

Proof. We need to translate all the state formulae into process formulae. We do it by induction on the structure of the formula. Atomic constant modules and module variables remain unchanged by the transformation, except, monadic variables are now considered as binary. Similarly, $\mathbf{T}$ is translated into binary as $\hat{\mathbf{T}} := \text{id}$.

- If $\phi = \phi_1 \vee \phi_2$, we set $\hat{\phi} := \hat{\phi}_1 \cup \hat{\phi}_2$.
- If $\phi = \neg\phi_1$, we set $\hat{\phi} := \frown(\hat{\phi}_1)$. Equivalently, we can set $\hat{\phi} := \frown(\hat{\phi}_1)$, since state formulae are unary, and the two negations are essentially unary, i.e., are subsets of the Diagonal relation id.
- If $\phi = |\alpha_1\rangle \, \phi_1$, we set $\hat{\phi} := \text{Dom}(\hat{\alpha}_1; \hat{\phi}_1)$.

---

[12] Structures can be viewed as computing devices. They store information and expand an interpretation of an input sub-vocabulary to an output sub-vocabulary to satisfy a specification.

[13] Similar statements have been shown for other logics, e.g. [22].

- If $\phi = \langle \alpha_1 | \phi_1$, we set $\hat{\phi} := \mathrm{Img}(\hat{\phi_1}; \hat{\alpha_1})$.
- If $\phi = \mu X.(\phi_1)$, we set $\hat{\phi} := \mu X.\mathrm{Dom}(\hat{\phi_1})$. Equivalently, we can set $\hat{\phi} := \mu X.\mathrm{Img}(\hat{\phi_1})$, since, again, we are dealing with unary formulae here.

Operations $\curvearrowright$, $\curvearrowleft$, Dom and Img are expressible using the basic operations of the algebra, under the binary semantics. This gives us a transformation for the state formulae.

All process formulae α except test ϕ_1? remain unchanged under this transformation. For test, we have:

- If $\alpha = \phi_1$?, we set $\hat{\alpha} := \mathrm{Dom}(\hat{\phi_1})$. Equivalently, we can set $\hat{\alpha} := \mathrm{Img}(\hat{\phi_1})$.

It is easy to see that, under this transformation, the semantic correspondence holds.

We now comment on a connection of the propositional version of $L\mu\mu$ (i.e., a fragment without projection and selection) with well-known logics. Propositional Dynamic Logic (PDL) [23,24] and Linear Dynamic Logic (LDL$_f$) [8]. Both logics have the same syntax:[14]

$$\alpha ::= \mathrm{id} \mid M_a \mid \alpha; \alpha \mid \alpha \cup \alpha \mid \alpha^* \mid \phi?,$$
$$\phi ::= \mathbf{T} \mid M_p \mid \phi \vee \phi \mid \neg\phi \mid |\alpha\rangle \phi. \tag{6}$$

However, the semantics is different is each case. In particular, LDL$_f$ is interpreted over finite paths. Both logics are fragments of the propositional version (no projection, selection) of the modal logic $L\mu\mu$. To see it, recall that the Kleene star is expressible by $\alpha^* := \mu Z.(\mathrm{id} \cup Z; \alpha)$. Note also that unary negation is implicit in the process line of (6). This is because, in our translation from the two-sorted to one-sorted syntax, if $\phi = \neg\phi_1$, we set $\hat{\phi} := \curvearrowright(\hat{\phi_1})$.

It is known that we can use non-deterministic operations of Union and the Kleene star, which are used in PDL, to define basic imperative constructs called Deterministic Regular programs.[15]

Definition 6. DetRegular (While) programs *are defined by restricting the constructs $\cup$, $*$ and ? to appear only in the following expressions:*

$$\begin{aligned}
\mathbf{skip} &:= \mathbf{T}?, \\
\mathbf{fail} &:= (\neg\mathbf{T})?, \\
\mathbf{if}\ \phi\ \mathbf{then}\ \alpha\ \mathbf{else}\ \beta &:= (\phi?; \alpha) \cup ((\neg\phi)?; \beta), \\
\mathbf{while}\ \phi\ \mathbf{do}\ \alpha &:= (\phi?; \alpha)^*; (\neg\phi)?.
\end{aligned} \tag{7}$$

An unrestricted use of sequential composition is allowed.

While the programs are deterministic, their definition uses non-deterministic operations. For a complexity-theoretic analysis, it is possible to show that some

---

[14] Some description logics have a similar syntax and may include Converse operation.

[15] Please note that Deterministic Regular expressions and the corresponding Glushkov automata are unrelated to what we study here. In those terms, expressions $a; a^*$ are Deterministic Regular, while $a^*; a$ are not. Here, the term Deterministic Regular comes from another name for While programs.

deterministic algebraic operations are sufficient to define the same imperative constructs. We leave such an analysis to future work. As an application, Deterministic Regular programs can be used to specify dynamic behaviour of complex modular systems, in the style of Golog programming language [25].

5.3   The Main Decision Task: Definition

We now present a counterpart of Definition 3 of Model Expansion task for processes. It will be our main task in the rest of the paper. Recall that $\mathfrak{A} \models_s |\alpha\rangle \mathbf{T}$ means that program α has a successful execution starting from an input structure $\mathfrak{A}$. We show now that checking $\mathfrak{A} \models_s |\alpha\rangle \mathbf{T}$ corresponds to the decision version of the MX task for process α. Recall that, by the translation in the proof of Theorem 1, $|\alpha\rangle \mathbf{T} = \text{Dom}(\alpha) = \curvearrowright\curvearrowright \alpha$. Recall also that $\llbracket \text{Dom}(\alpha) \rrbracket^s = \{(\mathfrak{B}, \mathfrak{B}) \mid \exists \mathfrak{B}'\ (\mathfrak{B}, \mathfrak{B}') \in \llbracket \alpha \rrbracket^s\}$. Thus, we have: $\mathfrak{A} \models_s |\alpha\rangle \mathbf{T}$ iff $(\mathfrak{A}, \mathfrak{A}) \in \llbracket \text{Dom}(\alpha) \rrbracket^s$ iff $\exists \mathfrak{B}\ (\mathfrak{A}, \mathfrak{B}) \in \llbracket \alpha \rrbracket^s$ iff $\exists \mathfrak{B}$ over the same vocabulary as $\mathfrak{A}$ such that if $\mathfrak{A}|_{s(I(\alpha))}$ interprets the inputs of α, then $\mathfrak{B}|_{s(O(\alpha))}$ interprets the outputs of α. This is an MX task. Thus, we formulate our problem as follows:

Definition 7 (MX task for Processes (Decision Version)).

Problem: MX task for Processes (Decision Version)
Input: τ-structure $\mathfrak{A}$, formula α with variables $I(\alpha) \cup O(\alpha)$, variable assignment $s : vvoc(\alpha) \to \tau$.
Question: $\mathfrak{A} \models_s |\alpha\rangle \mathbf{T}$?

---

6   Conclusion

Motivated by the need to combine preexisting components for solving complex problems, we developed two algebras, static and dynamic, for combining systems that communicate through common variables. The variables are second-order, i.e., they range over sets. Atomic modules are axiomatized in any formalism where the task of finding solutions can be specified as the task of Model Expansion. The dynamic algebra treats such specifications as "black boxes". We showed that, many operations studied in algebras of binary relations become definable if we add information propagation, i.e., specify inputs and outputs of atomic modules. We also showed that, when interpreted over transition systems, the dynamic algebra is equivalent to a modal temporal (dynamic) logic.

The logic can be viewed as a significant generalization of Reiter's situation calculus and Golog [9,10] in that first-order successor state axioms are replaced with potentially non-deterministic atomic modules that can be of arbitrary expressive power and computational complexity, and can be axiomatized in multiple logics. In place of Golog programs, we have algebraic terms inside the modalities that specify desired patterns of execution. Since our "successor state axioms" – atomic modules – are no longer first-order, a Prolog implementation, as in the case of Golog, is no longer possible. Different solving methods are needed. Some methods for solving modular systems for fragments of the current language have already been developed [26,27]. One method, [26], took inspiration in the CDCL algorithm for SAT solving, where modules are called as oracles during the execution. In the other method, [27], a parallel algebra of propagators has been defined and used for solving Model Expansion task for modular systems. An important research direction is to extend the previous methods to the full algebra, as well as to develop new solving techniques.

Another research direction is to analyze the computational complexity of the main computational task in the Logic of Information Flows, under various assumptions on the expressiveness of atomic modules and allowable algebraic operations. In particular, it is very important to provide guarantees to the user that: (1) all problems in a particular complexity class are expressible in a particular fragment, to guarantee completeness of the fragment with respect to that complexity class; and (2) no more than the problems in that class are expressible, to ensure implementability of the system by a chosen technique. Providing such guarantees is at the core of the Model Expansion project and its connection to Descriptive Complexity [28], and a lot of work is currently under way in this direction.

Acknowledgements. Many thanks to Brett McLean, Jan Van den Bussche, Bart Bogaerts and other colleagues for useful discussions. The research is supported by NSERC.

References

1. Jónsson, B., Tarski, A.: Representation problems for relation algebras. Bull. Amer. Math. Soc. **74**, 127–162 (1952)
2. Pratt, V.R.: Origins of the calculus of binary relations. In: Proceedings of the Seventh Annual Symposium on Logic in Computer Science (LICS 1992), Santa Cruz, California, USA, 22–25 June 1992, pp. 248–254 (1992)
3. Surinx, D., den Bussche, J.V., Gucht, D.V.: The primitivity of operators in the algebra of binary relations under conjunctions of containments. In: LICS 2017 (2017)
4. Fletcher, G., et al.: Relative expressive power of navigational querying on graphs. Inf. Sci. **298**, 390–406 (2015)
5. Jackson, M., Stokes, T.: Modal restriction semigroups: towards an algebra of functions. IJAC **21**(7), 1053–1095 (2011)
6. McLean, B.: Complete representation by partial functions for composition, intersection and anti-domain. J. Log. Comput. **27**(4), 1143–1156 (2017)
7. Harel, D., Kozen, D., Tiuryn, J.: Dynamic Logic (Foundations of Computing) (2000)
8. De Giacomo, G., Vardi, M.Y.: Linear temporal logic and linear dynamic logic on finite traces. In: Proceedings of the 23rd International Joint Conference on Artificial Intelligence, IJCAI 2013, Beijing, China, 3–9 August 2013, pp. 854–860 (2013)
9. Reiter, R.: Knowledge in Action: Logical Foundations for Specifying and Implementing Dynamical Systems. MIT Press, Cambridge (2001)
10. Levesque, H., Reiter, R., Lespérance, Y., Lin, F., Scherl, R.: GOLOG: a logic programming language for dynamic domains. J Log. Program. Spec. Issue Actions **31**(1–3), 59–83 (1997)

11. Tasharrofi, S., Ternovska, E.: A semantic account for modularity in multi-language modelling of search problems. In: Proceedings of the 8th International Symposium on Frontiers of Combining Systems (FroCoS), October 2011, pp. 259–274 (2011)
12. Tasharrofi, S.: Arithmetic and modularity in declarative languages for knowledge representation. Ph.D. dissertation, School of Computing Science, Simon Fraser University, December 2013
13. Ternovska, E.: An algebra of combined constraint solving. In: Global Conference on Artificial Intelligence, GCAI 2015, Tbilisi, Georgia, 16–19 October 2015, pp. 275–295 (2015)
14. Ternovska, E.: Recent progress on the algebra of modular systems. In: Proceedings of the 11th Alberto Mendelzon International Workshop on Foundations of Data Management and the Web, Montevideo, Uruguay, 7–9 June 2017 (2017)
15. Henkin, L., Monk, J., Tarski, A.: Cylindric Algebras Part I. North-Holland, Amsterdam (1971)
16. Bussche, J.: Applications of Alfred Tarski's ideas in database theory. In: Fribourg, L. (ed.) CSL 2001. LNCS, vol. 2142, pp. 20–37. Springer, Heidelberg (2001). https://doi.org/10.1007/3-540-44802-0_2
17. Mitchell, D.G., Ternovska, E.: A framework for representing and solving NP search problems. In: Proceedings of AAAI 2005, pp. 430–435 (2005)
18. Vardi, M.Y.: The complexity of relational query language. In: 14th ACM Symposium Theory of Computing, Springer Verlag (Heidelberg, FRG and NewYork NY, USA)-Verlag, 1982
19. Denecker, M., Ternovska, E.: A logic of non-monotone inductive definitions. ACM Trans. Comput. Log. (TOCL) 9(2), 1–52 (2008)
20. Kolokolova, A., Liu, Y., Mitchell, D., Ternovska, E.: On the complexity of model expansion. In: Fermüller, C.G., Voronkov, A. (eds.) LPAR 2010. LNCS, vol. 6397, pp. 447–458. Springer, Heidelberg (2010). https://doi.org/10.1007/978-3-642-16242-8_32
21. Ternovskaia, E.: Inductive definability and the situation calculus. In: Freitag, B., Decker, H., Kifer, M., Voronkov, A. (eds.) DYNAMICS 1997. LNCS, vol. 1472, pp. 227–248. Springer, Heidelberg (1998). https://doi.org/10.1007/BFb0055501
22. Abu Zaid, F., Grädel, E., Jaax, S.: Bisimulation safe fixed point logic. In: Invited and Contributed Papers from the Tenth Conference on Advances in Modal Logic 10. Advances in Modal Logic. Held in Groningen, The Netherlands, 5–8 August 2014, pp. 1–15 (2014)
23. Pratt, V.R.: Semantical considerations on Floyd-Hoare logic. In: 17th Annual Symposium on Foundations of Computer Science, Houston, Texas, USA, 25–27 October 1976, pp. 109–121 (1976)
24. Fischer, M.J., Ladner, R.E.: Propositional dynamic logic of regular programs. J. Comput. Syst. Sci. 18(2), 194–211 (1979)
25. Levesque, H., Reiter, R., Lespérance, Y., Lin, F., Scherl, R.: GOLOG: a logic programming language for dynamic domains. J. Log. Program. 31, 59–84 (1997)
26. Mitchell, D., Ternovska, E.: Clause-learning for modular systems. In: Calimeri, F., Ianni, G., Truszczynski, M. (eds.) LPNMR 2015. LNCS (LNAI), vol. 9345, pp. 446–452. Springer, Cham (2015). https://doi.org/10.1007/978-3-319-23264-5_37
27. Bogaerts, B., Ternovska, E., Mitchell, D.: Propagators and solvers for the algebra of modular systems. In: Logic for Programming, Artificial Intelligence and Reasoning (LPAR) (2017)
28. Immerman, N.: Descriptive Complexity. Graduate Texts in Computer Science. Springer, Heidelberg (1999). https://doi.org/10.1007/978-1-4612-0539-5

Mechanised Assessment of Complex Natural-Language Arguments Using Expressive Logic Combinations

David Fuenmayor[1(✉)] and Christoph Benzmüller[1,2]

[1] Freie Universität Berlin, Berlin, Germany
david.fuenmayor@fu-berlin.de
[2] University of Luxembourg, Esch-sur-Alzette, Luxembourg

Abstract. We present and illustrate an approach to combining logics based on shallow semantical embeddings, a technique that harnesses the high expressive power of classical higher-order logic (HOL) as a meta-language in order to embed the syntax and semantics of some object logic. This approach allows us to reuse existing (higher-order) automated reasoning infrastructure for seamlessly combining and reasoning with different non-classical logics (modal, deontic, intensional, epistemic, etc.). In particular, the work presented here illustrates the utilisation of the Isabelle proof assistant for the representation and assessment of linguistically complex arguments. We illustratively combine a dyadic deontic logic (also featuring alethic modalities) enhanced with higher-order quantifiers and a 2D-semantics drawing on Kaplan's logic of indexicals.

Keywords: Logic combinations · Higher-order logic · Deontic logic · Argumentation · Higher-order theorem proving · Isabelle

1 Introduction

Our approach to combining logics is based on *shallow semantical embeddings* (SSE). SSEs harness the high expressive power of classical higher-order logic (HOL) as a meta-language in order to embed the syntax and semantics of some object logics [3], thus allowing us to reuse existing (higher-order) automated reasoning infrastructure for seamlessly combining and reasoning with different non-classical logics (modal, deontic, intensional, epistemic, etc.) [1]. A semantical embedding for an object logic corresponds to adding a set of axioms and definitions to the expressive meta-logic (HOL) in such a way as to encode the connectives of the object logic as meta-logical constants. This has interesting practical implications. For example, the semantically embedded object logics (or their combinations) can easily be varied by adding or removing (meta-logical) axioms, which thus enables the rapid prototyping and formal verification of complex object logics and their combinations. Moreover, due to the expressivity of

C. Benzmüller—Supported by VolkswagenStiftung, grant *Consistent, Rational Arguments in Politics (CRAP)*.

A. Herzig and A. Popescu (Eds.): FroCoS 2019, LNAI 11715, pp. 112–128, 2019.
https://doi.org/10.1007/978-3-030-29007-8_7

HOL, it is also possible to directly encode bridge rules, or, as an alternative, their corresponding semantic counterparts.

In this paper, we illustrate how a non-trivial combination of logics can be stepwise developed and assessed. In particular, we demonstrate the utilisation of the SSE approach within the Isabelle proof assistant for the representation and assessment of complex linguistic phenomena in natural-language arguments.[1] The presented examples require the extension and combination of a dyadic deontic logic (DDL) [7] with higher-order quantification and a 2D-Semantics [17] drawing on Kaplan's logic of indexicals [15]. The extended logic DDL is immune to known paradoxes in normative reasoning, in particular to *contrary-to-duty* scenarios [8]. Moreover, conditional obligations in DDL are of a defeasible and paraconsistent nature, and thus lend themselves to reasoning with incomplete and inconsistent knowledge. Kaplan's logic of indexicals aims at modelling the behaviour of certain context-sensitive linguistic expressions known as *indexicals* (such as pronouns, demonstrative pronouns, and some adverbs and adjectives). It is characteristic of an indexical that its content varies with context, i.e. they have a context-sensitive *character*. We have modelled Kaplanian contexts by introducing a new type of object (context) and by modelling sentence meanings as so-called "characters" [15], i.e. functions from contexts to sets of possible worlds (following a Kripke semantics). For simplicity of exposition, we have omitted tenses in our treatment of Kaplan's logical theory.

With our running example we demonstrate that complex natural-language arguments can nowadays be adequately reconstructed and formally verified by higher-order provers when utilising the SSE approach. It is worth mentioning that such a rich and heterogeneous combination of expressive logics as presented here has not been automated before. By allowing higher-order quantification (e.g. as required by the ethical argument in Sect. 4.3) and being immune to *contrary-to-duty* paradoxes, the mechanisation of this particular logic combination also constitutes a significant improvement over related work on automated deontic reasoning (e.g., [6,11,13,16]). In particular, we overcome unintuitive, machine-oriented formula representations and provide means for intuitive user interaction.

2   Semantical Embedding of (augmented) DDL

In this section, we introduce an extension of the work developed by Benzmüller et al. [2], where a (propositional) Dyadic Deontic Logic (DDL) originally presented by Carmo and Jones [7, Sect. 4] has been embedded in classical higher-order logic (HOL). That work features a faithfulness proof, i.e. soundness and completeness of the HOL-embedded logic with respect to Carmo and Jones original semantics, as well as an encoding of this embedding in Isabelle/HOL together with an illustrative example demonstrating how the approach can successfully cope with a well-known *contrary-to-duty* scenario: Chisholm's paradox [8]. In Sect. 4 below, we will exemplarily showcase our embedding work by encoding an extended,

---

[1] The SSE approach has also been illustrated in [1] by formalising the "Wise Men Puzzle" (a riddle in multi-agent epistemic reasoning).

more complex version of Chisholm's paradox. We will often refer the interested reader to Benzmüller et al. [2] for further details.

Part of the embedding work presented here has been made available as a computer-verified data publication in the Archive of Formal Proofs [9]. Relevant portions of that previous work are summarily presented in Sect. 4.3.[2] We have also uploaded the corresponding Isabelle/HOL sources for this paper to motivate the interested reader to experimentally assess and extend our work (see [10]).

As a first measure, we extend the embedding introduced by Benzmüller et al. [2] to a two-dimensional semantics [17] by introducing an additional type c (for Kaplanian contexts, which will be discussed further in Sect. 3). With this new base type, we lift (again) the type used to represent sentence meanings, which were previously lifted from simple *bool* to its corresponding intensions (of type $w{\Rightarrow}bool$), thus representing propositions as sets of worlds. The rest of the embedding remains the same, excepting for the introduction of an additional argument (of type c) for each lambda expression in the embedding of logical and modal operators. We then use the automated tools integrated with the Isabelle proof assistant to formally verify that our extended embedding indeed validates the (double type-lifted) original Carmo and Jones axiom system.

2.1 Definition of Types

The type w corresponds to the original type for possible worlds/situations in DDL (cf. [2]). We draw in this present work upon Kaplan's *logic of indexicals/demonstratives* as originally presented in [15] (and later revisited in [14]). In Kaplan's logical theory, entities of the aforementioned type w would correspond to his so-called "circumstances of evaluation". Moreover, Kaplan introduces an additional dimension c, called "contexts of use", which allows for the modelling of particular context-dependent linguistic expressions, i.e. *indexicals* (see Sect. 3). We additionally introduce some type aliases: wo for propositional contents (intensions), which are identified with their truth sets, i.e. the set of worlds at which the proposition is true, and cwo (aliased m) for sentence meanings (also called "characters" in Kaplan's theory), which are modelled as functions from contexts to intensions. Type e is introduced to enable referencing and quantifying over individuals.

> **typedecl** w   — Type for Kaplanian "circumstances of evaluation"
> **typedecl** c   — Type for Kaplanian "contexts of use"
> **type-synonym** wo = w⇒bool — Type for propositional contents
> **type-synonym** cwo = c⇒wo — Type for sentence meanings ("characters")
> **type-synonym** m = cwo   — Type alias 'm' for characters
> **typedecl** e   — Type for individuals

---

[2] The embedding introduced in [9] was developed with a focus on providing verified and extensible Isabelle/HOL sources enabling the reconstruction of a special argument in normative ethics (Alan Gewirth's argument for the so-called "Principle of Generic Consistency" [12]). In particular, it does not yet embed the operators "dthat" and "actually" (see Sects. 3.3 and 3.4 below). That work can be considered as a complementary resource to this paper and is briefly revisited in Sect. 4.3.

2.2 Semantic Characterisation of the DDL by Carmo and Jones

In this section, for the sake of completeness, we briefly summarise the SSE of the DDL by Carmo and Jones in the Isabelle/HOL logic.[3] A detailed presentation of this work is given in [2]. The aim here is to illustrate our methodology and to highlight the fact that an SSE for an object logic (DDL in this case) 'simply' corresponds to adding a set of concise and intuitive axioms and definitions to the expressive meta-logic (HOL). We thereby make use of some basic set operators in the definitions/abbreviations for the connectives of the object logic. Furthermore, we use automated reasoning tools to formally verify that the embedding validates some intended principles. This includes a verification of the original DDL axioms, which, as expected, become theorems in our SSE.

Set Operators: We introduce some basic set-theoretic operators which are used in the definitions and axioms below:

abbreviation subset::wo$\Rightarrow$wo$\Rightarrow$bool (**infix** $\sqsubseteq$) **where** $\alpha \sqsubseteq \beta \equiv \forall$w. α w $\longrightarrow \beta$ w

abbreviation intersection::wo$\Rightarrow$wo$\Rightarrow$wo (**infixr** $\sqcap$) **where** $\alpha \sqcap \beta \equiv \lambda$x. α x $\wedge \beta$ x

abbreviation union::wo$\Rightarrow$wo$\Rightarrow$wo (**infixr** $\sqcup$) **where** $\alpha \sqcup \beta \equiv \lambda$x. α x $\vee \beta$ x

abbreviation complement::wo$\Rightarrow$wo ($\sim$-) **where** $\sim\alpha \equiv \lambda$x. $\neg\alpha$ x

abbreviation instantiated::wo$\Rightarrow$bool ($\mathcal{I}$-) **where** $\mathcal{I} \varphi \equiv \exists$x. φ x

abbreviation setEq::wo$\Rightarrow$wo$\Rightarrow$bool (**infix** $=_s$) **where** $\alpha =_s \beta \equiv \forall$x. α x $\longleftrightarrow \beta$ x

abbreviation univSet :: wo ($\top$) **where** $\top \equiv \lambda$w. True

abbreviation emptySet :: wo ($\bot$) **where** $\bot \equiv \lambda$w. False

Set-Theoretic Conditions: The semantics of the DDL by Carmo and Jones draws on Kripke semantics for its (normal) alethic modal operators and on a neighbourhood semantics[4] for its (non-normal) deontic operators. To embed those, we introduce the operators av and pv (accessibility relations between worlds), and ob (denoting a neighbourhood function operating on sets of worlds) at the meta-logical level. Axioms are introduced below to properly constrain them. We employ the model finder *Nitpick* [5] to formally verify the consistency of our axiomatisation.[5] We refer the reader to [7] and [2] for further details.

---

[3] Notice that at this level we still do not make use of the additional c type.

[4] Neighbourhood semantics is a generalisation of Kripke semantics, developed independently by Dana Scott and Richard Montague. Whereas a Kripke frame features an accessibility relation $R : W \rightarrow 2^W$ indicating which worlds are alternatives to (or, accessible from) others, a neighbourhood frame $N : W \rightarrow 2^{2^W}$ (or, as in our case, $N : 2^W \rightarrow 2^{2^W}$) features a neighbourhood function assigning to each world (or set of worlds) a set of sets of worlds.

[5] Calls to model finder Nitpick are pre-configured with the flags *user-axioms = true* and *expect = genuine* (which we don't show here for better readability). By finding a *genuine* model satisfying some tautology (e.g. the "True" formula as shown below) while taking into account all given *user axioms*, Nitpick indeed proves the consistency of an axiom system. Similarly, Nitpick can prove, by finding a countermodel, the non-validity of a given formula (in the context of a background axiom system). The models (resp. countermodels) reported by Nitpick were inspected manually by us.

consts
av::w⇒wo   — av(w) are the worlds which are 'open alternatives' of w
pv::w⇒wo   — pv(w) are the worlds which are 'possible alternatives' of w
ob::wo⇒wo⇒bool — ob(p) are the propositions obligatory in the given set of worlds

axiomatization where
sem-3a: ∀w. $\mathcal{I}$(av w) **and** — in every situation there is always an open alternative
sem-4a: ∀w. av w ⊑ pv w **and** — open alternatives are possible alternatives
sem-4b: ∀w. pv w w **and** — every situation is a possible alternative to itself
sem-5a: ∀X. ¬(ob X ⊥) **and** — contradictions cannot be obligatory
sem-5b: ∀X Y Z. (X ⊓ Y) $=_s$ (X ⊓ Z) ⟶ (ob X Y ⟷ ob X Z) **and**
sem-5c: ∀X Y Z. $\mathcal{I}$(X ⊓ Y ⊓ Z) ∧ ob X Y ∧ ob X Z ⟶ ob X (Y ⊓ Z) **and**
sem-5d: ∀X Y Z. (Y ⊑ X ∧ ob X Y ∧ X ⊑ Z) ⟶ ob Z ((Z ⊓ (∼X)) ⊔ Y) **and**
sem-5e: ∀X Y Z. Y ⊑ X ∧ ob X Z ∧ $\mathcal{I}$(Y ⊓ Z) ⟶ ob Y Z

lemma True **nitpick**[satisfy] **oops** — model found: axioms consistent

2.3   Semantical Embedding of DDL

The following abbreviations/definitions realise the SSE of the logical connectives of DDL as lambda expressions of the meta-logic HOL (Isabelle/HOL).

Basic Propositional Connectives: In the SSE presented in [2], and in accordance with [3], the propositional connectives of DDL were identified with truth sets of type $w\Rightarrow bool$ in HOL, where w is the type of possible worlds. In these and various related papers we have called this a "type lifting". In our given context this type lifting is conservatively extended to also cover the additional type c of Kaplanian contexts. In other words, the intuitive boolean type of propositions of our object logic is now "doubly type lifted" in the embedding to type $c\Rightarrow w\Rightarrow bool$ (or simply: m).

abbreviation pand::m⇒m⇒m (**infixr**∧) **where** $\varphi\wedge\psi \equiv \lambda$c w. $(\varphi$ c w)∧$(\psi$ c w)
abbreviation por::m⇒m⇒m (**infixr**∨) **where** $\varphi\vee\psi \equiv \lambda$c w. $(\varphi$ c w)∨$(\psi$ c w)
abbreviation pim::m⇒m⇒m (**infix**→) **where** $\varphi\rightarrow\psi \equiv \lambda$c w. $(\varphi$ c w)⟶$(\psi$ c w)
abbreviation peq::m⇒m⇒m (**infix**↔) **where** $\varphi\leftrightarrow\psi \equiv \lambda$c w. $(\varphi$ c w)⟷$(\psi$ c w)
abbreviation pnot::m⇒m (**¬-**) **where** $\neg\varphi \equiv \lambda$c w. $\neg(\varphi$ c w)

Modal Operators: These correspond to the two alethic modal operators introduced in DDL. As above, their embedding is based on a double type lifting of the intuitive boolean type of propositions to type $(c\Rightarrow w\Rightarrow bool)\Rightarrow(c\Rightarrow w\Rightarrow bool)$. In the definition of these operators we make use of the previously defined av and pv accessibility relations. For a detailed presentation of the SSE of modal logics in HOL we refer the reader to [3].

abbreviation boxa :: m⇒m ($\square_a$-) **where** $\square_a\varphi \equiv \lambda$c w. ∀v. (av w) v ⟶ $(\varphi$ c v)
abbreviation diaa :: m⇒m ($\Diamond_a$-) **where** $\Diamond_a\varphi \equiv \lambda$c w. ∃v. (av w) v ∧ $(\varphi$ c v)
abbreviation boxp :: m⇒m ($\square_p$-) **where** $\square_p\varphi \equiv \lambda$c w. ∀v. (pv w) v ⟶ $(\varphi$ c v)
abbreviation diap :: m⇒m ($\Diamond_p$-) **where** $\Diamond_p\varphi \equiv \lambda$c w. ∃v. (pv w) v ∧ $(\varphi$ c v)
abbreviation taut :: m (⊤) **where** ⊤ $\equiv \lambda$c w. True
abbreviation contr :: m (⊥) **where** ⊥ $\equiv \lambda$c w. False

Deontic Operators: These correspond to the two unary and the dyadic deontic operators introduced in DDL. Their SSE analogously applies the double type lifting idea as illustrated above. For a detailed presentation of the SSE of DDL deontic operators in HOL we refer the reader to [2].

> **abbreviation** cjod :: m⇒m⇒m (**O**⟨-|-⟩) **where** $\mathbf{O}\langle\varphi|\sigma\rangle \equiv \lambda$c w. ob ($\sigma$ c) (φ c)
> **abbreviation** cjos :: m⇒m (**O**⟨-⟩) **where** $\mathbf{O}\langle\varphi\rangle \equiv \mathbf{O}\langle\varphi|\top\rangle$
> **abbreviation** cjoa :: m⇒m (**O**$_a$-) **where**
> $\mathbf{O}_a\varphi \equiv \lambda$c w. (ob (av w)) ($\varphi$ c) $\wedge$ ($\exists$x. (av w) x $\wedge \neg(\varphi$ c x))
> **abbreviation** cjop :: m⇒m (**O**$_i$-) **where**
> $\mathbf{O}_i\varphi \equiv \lambda$c w. (ob (pv w)) ($\varphi$ c) $\wedge$ ($\exists$x. (pv w) x $\wedge \neg(\varphi$ c x))

Logical Validity: The classical notion of validity in modal logic is requiring truth in all worlds. Since we have double lifted our type for propositions to $c{\Rightarrow}w{\Rightarrow}bool$, we introduce here two notions of validity: context-dependent and global validity. The latter corresponds to the former holding in every context. This well illustrates the two-dimensionality aspect of our embedding.

> **abbreviation** modvalidctx :: m⇒c⇒bool ($\lfloor$-$\rfloor^M$) **where** $\lfloor\varphi\rfloor^M \equiv \lambda$c. $\forall$w. φ c w
> **abbreviation** modvalid :: m⇒bool ($\lfloor$-$\rfloor$) **where** $\lfloor\varphi\rfloor \equiv \forall$c. $\lfloor\varphi\rfloor^M$ c

2.4 Verifying the Embedding

Modal Collapse: Our axioms do not validate modal (alethic or deontic) collapse. Nitpick computes intuitive countermodels (which are not displayed here).

> **lemma** $\lfloor$P → $\mathbf{O}_a$P$\rfloor$ **nitpick oops** — countermodel found: no collapse
> **lemma** $\lfloor$P → $\mathbf{O}_i$P$\rfloor$ **nitpick oops** — countermodel found: no collapse
> **lemma** $\lfloor$P → $\square_a$P$\rfloor$ **nitpick oops** — countermodel found: no collapse
> **lemma** $\lfloor$P → $\square_p$P$\rfloor$ **nitpick oops** — countermodel found: no collapse

Necessitation: We verify that the necessitation rule is validated by the axioms.

> **lemma** NecDDLa: $\lfloor$A$\rfloor \implies \lfloor\square_aA\rfloor$ **by** simp
> **lemma** NecDDLp: $\lfloor$A$\rfloor \implies \lfloor\square_pA\rfloor$ **by** simp

Original Axiom System: We have employed the automated reasoning tools integrated with Isabelle to verify that our SSE indeed validates the axiom system presented by Carmo and Jones in their original work (cf. [7, p. 293ff]). In the following, we present an extract of the proven axioms and refer the reader to the corresponding Isabelle/HOL sources [10] and [9] for the rest.[6]

---

[6] Note that the provided axioms are encoded as globally (and classically) valid. They are proved by employing some of the proof tactics supported by Isabelle. Some of the tactics we employed are: *simp* (term rewriting engine), *blast* (tableaux prover), *metis* (resolution and paramodulation prover), *smt* (SMT solver), and *auto* (term rewriting and proof search using different methods). These tactics were automatically suggested and applied by Isabelle's metaprover *Sledgehammer*.

lemma CJ-3: $\lfloor \Box_p A \to \Box_a A \rfloor$ **by** (simp add: sem-4a)
lemma CJ-4: $\lfloor \neg \mathbf{O}\langle\bot|A\rangle \rfloor$ **by** (simp add: sem-5a)
lemma CJ-7: $\lfloor A \leftrightarrow B \rfloor \longrightarrow \lfloor \mathbf{O}\langle C|A\rangle \leftrightarrow \mathbf{O}\langle C|B\rangle \rfloor$ **using** sem-5ab sem-5e **by** blast
lemma CJ-9p: $\lfloor \Diamond_p \mathbf{O}\langle B|A\rangle \to \Box_p \mathbf{O}\langle B|A\rangle \rfloor$ **by** simp
lemma CJ-12p: $\lfloor \Box_p A \to (\neg \mathbf{O}_i A \wedge \neg \mathbf{O}_i(\neg A)) \rfloor$ **using** sem-5ab **by** blast
lemma CJ-13p: $\lfloor \Box_p(A \leftrightarrow B) \to (\mathbf{O}_i A \leftrightarrow \mathbf{O}_i B) \rfloor$ **using** sem-5b **by** metis

An ideal obligation which is actually possible both to fulfil and to violate entails an actual obligation (cf. [7, p.319]).

lemma CJ-Oi-Oa: $\lfloor (\mathbf{O}_i A \wedge \Diamond_a A \wedge \Diamond_a(\neg A)) \to \mathbf{O}_a A \rfloor$
using sem-5e sem-4a **by** blast

The following lemma highlights the relationship between conditional obligations and implications.

lemma CJ-O-O: $\lfloor \mathbf{O}\langle B|A\rangle \to \mathbf{O}\langle A \to B|\top\rangle \rfloor$ **using** sem-5bd4 **by** presburger

The following can be seen as bridge relations between conditional obligations and actual/ideal obligations:

lemma CJ-14p: $\lfloor \mathbf{O}\langle B|A\rangle \wedge \Box_p A \wedge \Diamond_p B \wedge \Diamond_p \neg B \to \mathbf{O}_i B \rfloor$ **using** sem-5e **by** blast
lemma CJ-15p: $\lfloor (\mathbf{O}\langle B|A\rangle \wedge \Diamond_p(A \wedge B) \wedge \Diamond_p(A \wedge \neg B)) \to \mathbf{O}_i(A \to B) \rfloor$
using CJ-O-O sem-5e **by** fastforce

Model finder Nitpick has found counterexamples for two of the axioms initially provided by Carmo and Jones (see axioms 5 and 11 in [7, p. 293]), which proves their non-validity (w.r.t. our semantic embedding in Isabelle/HOL). Quite interestingly, those two axioms have indeed been revisited by Carmo and Jones later in this very same work, where they have been weakened in order to avoid inconsistency of the axiom system (see the discussion in [7, p. 323]). Moreover, we could prove the validity of the new, weakened versions (w.r.t. our semantic embedding) as shown below.

lemma CJ-5: $\lfloor (\mathbf{O}\langle B|A\rangle \wedge \mathbf{O}\langle C|A\rangle) \to \mathbf{O}\langle B\wedge C|A\rangle \rfloor$
nitpick oops — countermodel found by nitpick for this strong variant
lemma CJ-5-weak: $\lfloor \Diamond_p(A \wedge B \wedge C) \wedge (\mathbf{O}\langle B|A\rangle \wedge \mathbf{O}\langle C|A\rangle) \to \mathbf{O}\langle B\wedge C|A\rangle \rfloor$
by (simp add: sem-5c) — however this weaker variant is validated

lemma CJ-11p: $\lfloor (\mathbf{O}_i A \wedge \mathbf{O}_i B) \to \mathbf{O}_i(A \wedge B) \rfloor$
nitpick oops — countermodel found by nitpick for this strong variant
lemma CJ-11p-weak: $\lfloor \Diamond_p(A \wedge B) \wedge (\mathbf{O}_i A \wedge \mathbf{O}_i B) \to \mathbf{O}_i(A \wedge B) \rfloor$
using sem-5c **by** auto — however this weaker variant is validated

3   Extending the Embedding

In the previous section, we have modelled Kaplanian contexts by introducing a new type of object (type c) and modelled sentence meanings as Kaplanian *characters*, i.e. functions from contexts to sets of worlds (type $c \Rightarrow w \Rightarrow bool$). We also made the corresponding adjustments to the semantical embedding of Carmo and Jones DDL presented in [2]. So far we haven't said much about what these Kaplanian contexts are or which effect they should have on the evaluation of logical validity. We restricted ourselves to illustrating that their introduction does not have any influence on the (classical) logical validity of key DDL axioms. Indeed we showed how we can leverage our semantical embedding to prove the validity of DDL axioms using Isabelle's automated tools. In this section, we introduce an alternative notion of logical validity as introduced by Kaplan (cf. [14,15]), which is well-suited for working with context-dependent expressions. This notion is called *indexical validity*.

3.1 Context Features

Kaplan's theory [14,15] aims at modelling the behaviour of certain context-sensitive linguistic expressions such as pronouns ("I", "my", "your"), demonstrative pronouns ("that", "this"), some adverbs ("here", "now", "tomorrow") and adjectives ("actual", "present"). Such expressions are known as *indexicals*, and thus Kaplan's logical system (among others) is usually referred to as a "logic of indexicals". In his seminal work [15], though, Kaplan referred to it as "Logic of Demonstratives" (LD).

It is characteristic of an indexical that its content varies with context, i.e. it has a context-sensitive character. Non-indexicals have a fixed character, i.e. the same content is invoked in all contexts. Kaplan's logical system models context-sensitivity by representing a context as a quadruple of features: $\langle Agent(c), Position(c), World(c), Time(c) \rangle$. The *Agent* and the *Position* of a context c can be seen as the actual speaker and place of the utterance respectively, while the *World* and the *Time* of c stand for the circumstances of evaluation of the expression's content and allow for the interaction of indexicals with alethic and tense modalities respectively. For our present purposes,[7] we can think of a context c as the pair: $\langle Agent(c), World(c) \rangle$. We introduce the concepts of *Agent* and *World* as functional constants.

> **consts** Agent::c⇒e — function retrieving the agent corresponding to context c
> **consts** World::c⇒w — function retrieving the world corresponding to context c

3.2 Logical Validity

Kaplan's notion of (context-dependent) logical truth for a sentence corresponds to its (context-sensitive) formula (of type $c{\Rightarrow}w{\Rightarrow}bool$) being true in the given context and at its corresponding world.

> **abbreviation** ldtruectx::m⇒c⇒bool (⌊-⌋-) **where** $\lfloor\varphi\rfloor_c \equiv \varphi$ c (World c)

Kaplan's notion of context-independent logical validity for a sentence corresponds to its being true in all contexts. This notion is known as *indexical validity*.

> **abbreviation** ldvalid::m⇒bool (⌊-⌋^{D}) **where** $\lfloor\varphi\rfloor^D \equiv \forall$c. $\lfloor\varphi\rfloor_c$

---

[7] Note that we do not consider tenses (as Kaplan does). An extension of our work to operate on context quadruples is possible using the same approach presented here (adding new types and further type-lifting the corresponding formulas).

Isabelle's integrated automated reasoning tools allow us to easily verify that indexical validity is indeed weaker than its classical counterpart (truth at all worlds for all contexts):

> **lemma** $\lfloor A \rfloor \Longrightarrow \lfloor A \rfloor^D$ **by** simp
> **lemma** $\lfloor A \rfloor^D \Longrightarrow \lfloor A \rfloor$ **nitpick oops** — countermodel found

Importantly, we can also easily verify that the interplay between indexical validity and the DDL modal and deontic operators does not result in modal collapse.

> **lemma** $\lfloor P \rightarrow O_a P \rfloor^D$ **nitpick oops** — countermodel found: no collapse
> **lemma** $\lfloor P \rightarrow \Box_a P \rfloor^D$ **nitpick oops** — countermodel found: no collapse

Next we show that the necessitation rule does not work for indexical validity (in contrast to classical modal validity as defined for DDL).

> **lemma** NecLDa: $\lfloor A \rfloor^D \Longrightarrow \lfloor \Box_a A \rfloor^D$ **nitpick oops** — countermodel found
> **lemma** NecLDp: $\lfloor A \rfloor^D \Longrightarrow \lfloor \Box_p A \rfloor^D$ **nitpick oops** — countermodel found

Below we introduce a kind of *a priori necessity* operator (to be contrasted to the more traditional alethic necessity). This operator (quite trivially) satisfies the necessitation rule for indexical validity.[8] In Kaplan's framework, a sentence being logically (i.e. indexically) valid means that it is true *a priori*: it is guaranteed to be true in every possible context in which it is uttered, even though it may express distinct propositional contents (intensions) in different contexts. This correlation between indexical validity and *a prioricity* has also been claimed in other two-dimensional semantic frameworks [17].

> **abbreviation** ldvalidbox :: m$\Rightarrow$m ($\Box^D$-) **where** $\Box^D \varphi \equiv \lambda c$ w. $\lfloor \varphi \rfloor^D$
> **lemma** NecLD: $\lfloor A \rfloor^D \Longrightarrow \lfloor \Box^D A \rfloor^D$ **by** simp — necessitation principle

3.3   Operator "dthat"

Kaplan's operator *dthat* is aimed at modelling a special kind of indexicals: demonstratives (e.g. "this/that", "this/that [description]"). As mentioned before, the referent of a (pure) indexical depends on the context. In the case of demonstratives, the referent depends on the associated demonstration (mostly a definite description). We also extend our embedding by introducing type-lifted descriptions (see operator *the* below) and use these to introduce (as syntactic sugar) a related operator named *Dthat*.

> **type-synonym** cwe = c$\Rightarrow$w$\Rightarrow$e — type alias for indexical individual terms

> **abbreviation** cthe::(c$\Rightarrow$w$\Rightarrow$e$\Rightarrow$bool)$\Rightarrow$cwe (the)
>   **where** the $\varphi \equiv \lambda c$ w. THE x. φ c w x
> **abbreviation** ctheBinder::(c$\Rightarrow$w$\Rightarrow$e$\Rightarrow$bool)$\Rightarrow$cwe (**binder** the)
>   **where** the x. (φ x) $\equiv$ the φ

---

[8] Note that this operator is not part of the original Kaplan's theory. It has been added by us in order to provide an object-logical necessity operator useful to model modal expressions which satisfy the necessitation rule with respect to indexical validity, thus adding more expressiveness to our embedded logic combination.

abbreviation dthat::cwe⇒cwe (dthat[-])
   where dthat[α] ≡ λc w. α c (World c)
abbreviation Dthat::(c⇒w⇒e⇒bool)⇒cwe (Dthat[-])
   where Dthat[α] ≡ dthat[the α]

Below we use Isabelle's automated reasoning tools once more to formally validate some important characteristics of Kaplan's demonstratives. We start by introducing equality for indexical individual terms (of type *cwe* as introduced before). We also introduce the modal operator $\square^{S5}$ to signify that a formula is necessarily true (in all possible worlds) at a given context. Then we show that many equations involving demonstratives are indeed indexically valid while not being classically valid or necessarily true. Details on the theoretical and philosophical rationale behind these results can be found in [15, p. 539 (and also p. 547ff)]. For our present purposes, it is important to note that our results fully coincide with the ones shown by Kaplan in his logical theory.

abbreviation ceq:: cwe⇒cwe⇒m (**infix** ≈) **where** $\alpha{\approx}\beta$ ≡ λc w. α c w = β c w
abbreviation boxS5 :: m⇒m ($\square^{S5}$-) **where** $\square^{S5}\varphi$ ≡ λc w. $\forall$v. φ c v

According to the new notion of indexical validity, demonstratives refer *a priori* (though not necessarily!) to the same objects as their associated demonstrations (resp. descriptions) in all contexts of use. Note that this is not the case for classical validity.

lemma $\lfloor\alpha \approx$ dthat[α]$\rfloor^D$ **by** simp — using indexical validity
lemma $\lfloor\square^{S5}(\alpha \approx$ dthat[α])$\rfloor^D$ **nitpick oops** — counterexample
lemma $\lfloor\alpha \approx$ dthat[α]$\rfloor$ **nitpick oops** — counterexample if using classical validity

Necessary equality in a certain context x does not imply *a priori* equality (i.e. in all contexts).

lemma $\lfloor\square^{S5}($dthat[β] ≈ dthat[α])$\rfloor_x$⟹$\lfloor($dthat[β] ≈ dthat[α])$\rfloor^D$
   nitpick oops — counterexample

The *a priori* (i.e. in all contexts) equality of demonstratives is equivalent to the *a priori* equality of their respective demonstrations/descriptions. Similarly, it holds *a priori* (i.e. indexically valid or true in all contexts of use) that equality of demonstratives is equivalent to equality of their respective demonstrations/descriptions.

lemma $\lfloor$dthat[β] ≈ dthat[α]$\rfloor^D$ ⟷ $\lfloor\beta \approx \alpha\rfloor^D$ **by** simp
lemma $\lfloor$dthat[β] ≈ dthat[α] ↔ ($\beta \approx \alpha$) $\rfloor^D$ **by** simp

3.4 Operator "Actually"

Below we introduce the predicate $\mathcal{A}$ used to model the sentential operator "it is actually the case that". We use this term to indicate that the given sentence is true in the (actual) world of the context in which it is uttered (*World c*), i.e. independently of the world or situation of evaluation. More details can be found in [15, p. 539 (and also p. 547ff)].

abbreviation cactually :: m⇒m ($\mathcal{A}$-) **where** $\mathcal{A}\varphi$ ≡ λc w. φ c (World c)

We again formally validate some important characteristics of this operator.

lemma $\lfloor \varphi \leftrightarrow \mathcal{A}\varphi \rfloor^D$ **by** simp
lemma $\lfloor \square^{S5}(\varphi \leftrightarrow \mathcal{A}\varphi) \rfloor^D$ **nitpick oops** — counterexample
lemma $\lfloor \square^{S5}(\varphi \leftrightarrow \mathcal{A}\varphi) \rfloor$ **nitpick oops** — counterexample
lemma $\lfloor \varphi \rfloor^D \longleftrightarrow \lfloor \mathcal{A}\varphi \rfloor$ **by** simp

3.5 Quantification

By utilising Isabelle/HOL's parameterised types (rank-1 polymorphism), we can easily enrich our logic with (first-order and higher-order) quantifiers.

abbreviation mforall::$(^{\prime}\text{t}{\Rightarrow}\text{m}){\Rightarrow}\text{m}$ ($\forall$) **where** $\forall \Phi \equiv \lambda$c w.$\forall$x. $(\Phi$ x c w)
abbreviation mexists::$(^{\prime}\text{t}{\Rightarrow}\text{m}){\Rightarrow}\text{m}$ ($\exists$) **where** $\exists \Phi \equiv \lambda$c w.$\exists$x. $(\Phi$ x c w)

Additionally, we can add binder syntax (as syntactic sugar) for our quantifiers.

abbreviation mforallBinder::$(^{\prime}\text{t}{\Rightarrow}\text{m}){\Rightarrow}\text{m}$ (**binder**$\forall$) **where** $\forall$x. $(\varphi$ x) $\equiv \forall \varphi$
abbreviation mexistsBinder::$(^{\prime}\text{t}{\Rightarrow}\text{m}){\Rightarrow}\text{m}$ (**binder**$\exists$) **where** $\exists$x. $(\varphi$ x) $\equiv \exists \varphi$

3.6 Some Meta-logical Results

Below we introduce the meta-logical predicates *stable* (content) and *stableCharacter*. The former is employed to indicate that a sentential term has a fixed, stable content (i.e. has the same denotation in all possible worlds) for a given context; the latter is used to indicate that a sentence has a *stable character* (i.e. has the same *stable content* in all contexts) [15].

abbreviation stable::m$\Rightarrow$c$\Rightarrow$bool **where** stable φ c $\equiv \forall$w. φ c w $\longrightarrow \lfloor \varphi \rfloor^M$c
abbreviation stableCharacter::m$\Rightarrow$bool
    where stableCharacter $\varphi \equiv \forall$c. stable φ c

These predicates are used to represent some interesting meta-logical results, some of which we reproduce below (cf. [15, p. 547ff]). In particular, we show that (i) sentences of the form "it is actually the case that ..." are stable. We also show that for any sentence φ with a stable character: (ii) indexical validity implies classical validity and (ii) the principle of (alethic) necessitation holds.

lemma $\forall$c. stable $(\mathcal{A}\varphi)$ c **by** simp — (i)
lemma stableCharacter $\varphi \longrightarrow (\lfloor \varphi \rfloor^D \longrightarrow \lfloor \varphi \rfloor)$ **by** blast — (ii)
lemma stableCharacter $\varphi \longrightarrow (\lfloor \varphi \rfloor^D \longrightarrow \lfloor \square_a \varphi \rfloor^D)$ **by** blast — (iii)
lemma $\lfloor \varphi \rfloor^D \longrightarrow \lfloor \square_a \varphi \rfloor^D$ **nitpick oops** — counterexample for general case

4 Examples

4.1 Chisholm's Paradox (Propositional)

(A1) It ought to be that Jones goes to assist his neighbours
(A2) It ought to be that if Jones goes, then he tells them he is coming
(A3) If Jones doesn't go, then he ought not tell them he is coming
(A4) Jones doesn't go (locally valid statement uttered in context 'C').

We first present and assess a propositional version of Chisholm's paradox [8]. One of the main virtues of Carmo and Jones's DDL [7] is that it allows us to adequately represent (avoiding explosion) the paradoxical set of sentences listed above. As is well known, by using standard (normal) deontic logic (SDL) to model this set of sentences, we can indeed derive a contradiction: John ought [not] to tell his neighbours he is coming. Explosion is the result in SDL, and thus we can infer anything. Chisholm's example is known in the literature as a "contrary-to-duty" scenario [8], since it arises from the fact that an individual (Jones) has not honoured its duties. DDL is a logic purposely designed to be immune to this well-known paradox (among others). Below we present the paradox as originally formalised in [2] using (type-lifted propositional) Carmo and Jones DDL [7]. We use Isabelle's automated reasoning tools to show that the encoded axiom set is consistent and verify its intended consequences (see sources in [10] for details).

consts JonesGo::m — Jones goes to assist his neighbours
consts JonesTell::m — Jones tells his neighbours he is coming
consts C::c — current context of use

axiomatization where
A1: $\lfloor \mathbf{O}\langle \text{JonesGo}\rangle \rfloor$ **and**
A2: $\lfloor \mathbf{O}\langle \text{JonesTell}|\text{JonesGo}\rangle \rfloor$ **and**
A3: $\lfloor \mathbf{O}\langle \neg\text{JonesTell}|\neg\text{JonesGo}\rangle \rfloor$ **and**
A4: $\lfloor \neg(\text{JonesGo})\rfloor_C$

Below we formalise the notion of obligation's violation. In our framework, it corresponds to having an (ideal) obligation to do something and not doing it.[9]

abbreviation violated $\varphi \equiv \mathbf{O}_i(\varphi) \wedge \neg\varphi$

We use model finder Nitpick to show that the encoded axiom set is consistent.

lemma True **nitpick** [satisfy] **oops** — model found

We have employed Isabelle's provided SMT solvers (Z3 and CVC4) to prove that (a subset of) the introduced axioms indeed entails that, while having violated the obligation to go help his neighbours, Jones actually ought to *not* tell them he is coming.

lemma $(\lfloor \Box_a\neg(\text{JonesGo})\rfloor_C \wedge \lfloor \Diamond_p(\text{JonesGo} \wedge \text{JonesTell})\rfloor_C \wedge$
$\lfloor \Diamond_p(\text{JonesGo} \wedge \neg\text{JonesTell})\rfloor_C \wedge \lfloor \neg\text{JonesTell}\rfloor_C \wedge$
$\lfloor \Diamond_a\text{JonesTell}\rfloor_C \wedge \lfloor \Diamond_a(\neg\text{JonesTell})\rfloor_C)$
$\longrightarrow (\lfloor \text{violated JonesGo}\rfloor_C \wedge \lfloor \mathbf{O}_a(\neg\text{JonesTell})\rfloor_C)$
using sem-4a sem-4b sem-5e A1 A3 A4 sem-5b **by** smt

4.2   Chisholm's Paradox (Enhanced)

(B1) It ought to be that I go to assist my neighbours
(B2) It ought to be that if I go, then I tell them I am coming

---

[9] A discussion of the difference between *actual* and *ideal* obligations in the DDL framework is out of the scope of this paper. We refer the interested reader to [7].

(B3) If I don't go, then I ought not tell them I am coming
(B4) I don't go (locally valid statement uttered in context 'C').

We can use our expressive logic combination to represent Chisholm's example from the standpoint of a speaker. We introduce the pronoun I (an indexical), which corresponds to the agent of the context of use: $Agent(c)$. Note that this example can also be formulated using other demonstratives (e.g. Kaplan's "dthat").

> **type-synonym** cwe = c⇒w⇒e — type alias for indexical individual terms
> **abbreviation** I::cwe **where** I ≡ λc w. Agent c

Since this variant is no longer propositional, we need to introduce some predicate constants and type-lifting definitions/abbreviations.

> **consts** goPred::e⇒m — predicate: to go to assist one's neighbours
> **consts** tellPred::e⇒m — predicate: to tell one is coming
> **abbreviation** Go::(c⇒w⇒e)⇒m
>   **where** Go α ≡ λc w. goPred (α c w) c w — type-lifted predicate
> **abbreviation** Tell::(c⇒w⇒e)⇒m
>   **where** Tell α ≡ λc w. tellPred (α c w) c w — type-lifted predicate

> **axiomatization where**
> B1: $\lfloor \mathbf{O}\langle \text{Go(I)}\rangle \rfloor^D$ **and**
> B2: $\lfloor \mathbf{O}\langle \text{Tell(I)}|\text{Go(I)}\rangle \rfloor^D$ **and**
> B3: $\lfloor \mathbf{O}\langle \neg\text{Tell(I)}|\neg\text{Go(I)}\rangle \rfloor^D$ **and**
> B4: $\lfloor \neg(\text{Go(I)})\rfloor_C$

Analogous to above, we use Nitpick to verify consistency and prove that (a subset of) the given axioms indeed entails that, while having violated the obligation to go help my neighbours, I actually ought to *not* tell them I am coming.

> **lemma** True **nitpick** [satisfy] **oops** — model found: axioms consistent
> **lemma** ($\lfloor \Box_a \neg(\text{Go(I)})\rfloor_C \wedge \lfloor \Diamond_p(\text{Go(I)} \wedge \text{Tell(I)})\rfloor_C \wedge$
> $\lfloor \Diamond_p(\text{Go(I)} \wedge \neg(\text{Tell(I)}))\rfloor_C \wedge \lfloor \neg(\text{Tell(I)})\rfloor_C \wedge$
> $\lfloor \Diamond_a(\text{Tell(I)})\rfloor_C \wedge \lfloor \Diamond_a(\neg(\text{Tell(I)}))\rfloor_C)$
> $\longrightarrow (\lfloor \text{violated } (\text{Go(I)})\rfloor_C \wedge \lfloor \mathbf{O}_a(\neg(\text{Tell(I)}))\rfloor_C)$
> **using** sem-4a sem-4b sem-5b sem-5e B1 B3 B4 **by** smt

4.3 Applications in Formal Ethics

Relying on the expressive logic combination presented here, we have previously encoded and mechanised an ethical argument (and background theory) presented by the philosopher Gewirth in [12], which aims at justifying an upper moral principle called the "Principle of Generic Consistency" (PGC) [9]. In a nutshell, according to this principle, any intelligent agent (by virtue of its self-understanding as an agent) is rationally committed to asserting that (i) it has rights to freedom and well-being, and (ii) all other agents have those same rights. The argument used by Gewirth to derive the PGC (presented in detail in [4,12]) is by no means trivial and has stirred much controversy in legal and moral philosophy during the last decades. To get a general idea of Gewirth's argument we take a look at its main steps (taken from [4]):

(1) [Premise] I act voluntarily for some purpose E (i.e. I am a PPA).
(2) E is (subjectively) good (i.e. I value E proactively).
(3) My freedom and well-being (FWB) are generically necessary conditions of my agency (i.e. I need them to achieve any purpose whatsoever).
(4) My FWB are necessary goods (at least for me).
(5) I have (maybe nobody else) a claim right to my FWB.
(13) Every PPA has a claim right to their FWB.

Note how any formalisation of this argument needs to support the modelling of complex linguistic expressions such as alethic and deontic modalities, quantification and indexicals. The expressive logic introduced in this paper is especially appropriate for this kind of purposes. In the following, we present some axioms and definitions used to model key concepts of Gewirth's ethical theory.

Agency: Below we give "purposes" the same type as sentence meanings (type $c{\Rightarrow}w{\Rightarrow}bool$ aliased as m), so that "acting on a purpose" is represented analogously to having a certain propositional attitude (like "desiring that so and so").

> **type-synonym** p = e⇒m — function from individuals to characters
> **consts** ActsOnPurpose:: e⇒m⇒m
> **consts** NeedsForPurpose:: e⇒p⇒m⇒m

In Gewirth's ethical theory, an individual with agency (i.e. capable of purposive action) is said to be a "prospective purposive agent" (PPA). This definition is supplemented with an axiom stating that being a PPA is an essential (i.e. identity-constitutive) property of an individual.

> **definition** PPA:: p **where** — Definition of PPA
> **axiomatization where** essentialPPA: $\lfloor \forall a.\ PPA\ a \to \Box^D(PPA\ a)\rfloor^D$

Goodness: Gewirth's concept of (subjective) goodness applies to purposes and is relative to some agent. It is thus modelled as a binary relation relating an individual (of type e) with a purpose (of type m). The axioms below interrelate the concept of goodness with agency and are given as *indexically valid* sentences. In particular, the axiom *explGood3* represents the intuitive notion of "seeking the good", i.e. necessarily good purposes are not only action motivating, but also entail an instrumental obligation to their realization (but only where possible).

> **consts** Good::e⇒m⇒m
> **axiomatization where**
> explGood1: $\lfloor \forall a\ P.\ ActsOnPurpose\ a\ P \to Good\ a\ P\rfloor^D$
> explGood2: $\lfloor \forall P\ M\ a.\ Good\ a\ P \land NeedsForPurpose\ a\ M\ P \to Good\ a\ (M\ a)\rfloor^D$
> explGood3: $\lfloor \forall \varphi\ a.\ \Diamond_p\varphi \to \mathbf{O}\langle\varphi \mid \Box^D Good\ a\ \varphi\rangle\rfloor^D$

Freedom and Well-Being (FWB): Enjoying FWB is the *contingent* property which is *always* required to be able to act on *any* purpose whatsoever.

consts FWB::p — FWB is a property (has type $e \Rightarrow m$)
axiomatization where
  explicationFWB1: $\lfloor \forall P\ a.\ \text{NeedsForPurpose a FWB P} \rfloor^D$
  explicationFWB2: $\lfloor \forall a.\ \Diamond_p\ \text{FWB a} \rfloor^D$
  explicationFWB3: $\lfloor \forall a.\ \Diamond_p\ \neg \text{FWB a} \rfloor^D$

Obligation and Interference: The so-called *Kant's law* (aka. "ought implies can") plays an important role in Gewirth's argument and is indeed derivable directly in DDL from the definition of the deontic operators. We have noticed the need to slightly amend it in order to render the argument as logically valid. We axiomatise a new variant that reads as: "ought implies *ought to* can".

lemma $\lfloor O_i\varphi \rightarrow \Diamond_p\varphi \rfloor$ **using** sem-5ab **by** simp
axiomatization where OIOAC: $\lfloor O_i\varphi \rightarrow O_i(\Diamond_a\varphi) \rfloor^D$

The existence of an individual b interfering with some state of affairs φ implies that φ cannot possibly be obtained in any of the actually possible situations (and vice versa). This implies that if someone (successfully) interferes with agent a having FWB, then a can no longer possibly enjoy its FWB (and the converse).

consts InterferesWith::e$\Rightarrow$m$\Rightarrow$m
axiomatization where explInterference: $\lfloor (\exists b.\ \text{InterferesWith b } \varphi) \leftrightarrow \neg\Diamond_a\varphi \rfloor$
lemma InterfWithFWB: $\lfloor \forall a.(\exists b.\ \text{InterferesWith b (FWB a))} \leftrightarrow \neg\Diamond_a(\text{FWB a}) \rfloor$
  using explInterference **by** blast

Rights and Other-Directed Obligations: Gewirth ([12, p. 66]) points out the existence of a correlation between an agent's own claim rights and other-referring obligations. A claim right is a right which entails duties or obligations for other agents regarding the right-holder (so-called Hohfeldian claim rights in legal theory). We model this concept in such a way that an individual a has a (claim) right to having some property φ if and only if it is obligatory that every (other) individual b does not interfere with the state of affairs ($\varphi\ a$).

definition RightTo::e$\Rightarrow$(e$\Rightarrow$m)$\Rightarrow$m **where**
  RightTo a $\varphi \equiv O_i(\forall b.\ \neg\text{InterferesWith b } (\varphi\ a))$

We use *Nitpick* to show the consistency of the theory by computing a corresponding model (not shown) having one context, one individual and two worlds.

lemma True **nitpick**[satisfy, card c = 1, card e = 1, card w = 2] **oops**

We paraphrase the following variant of the PGC as: "From every agent's point of view [C], it is true that if it is a PPA, then it has a claim right to FWB".

theorem PGC: **shows** $\forall C.\ \lfloor \text{PPA (Agent C)} \rightarrow (\text{RightTo (Agent C) FWB}) \rfloor_C$

Figure 1 (see appendix) shows an extract of the formal reconstruction of Gewirth's argument in Isabelle/HOL by employing the previously formalised concepts. Unabridged computer-verified sources for that work are available in [9].

5   Conclusion

We have enhanced a dyadic deontic logic with higher-order quantification and a 2D-semantics drawing on Kaplan's logic of indexicals. This logic combination has been implemented in Isabelle/HOL using the shallow semantical embeddings (SSE) technique and its core properties have been formally verified. In particular, we have shown that the combined logic is stable against different versions of Chisholm's paradox as intended. We have also motivated applications of the combined logic, e.g., for the encoding of challenging ethical theories.

Appendix

```
183
184  (**In the following we present a formalised proof for the Principle of Generic Consistency (PGC):
185  "Every PPA has a claim right to its freedom and well-being (FWB)".*)
186  theorem PGC: shows "∀C. ⌊PPA (Agent C) → (RightTo (Agent C) FWB)⌋c"
187  proof - {
188      fix C::c (**'C' is some arbitrarily chosen context (agent's perspective)*)
189      let ?I := "(Agent C)" (**'I' is/am the agent with perspective 'C'*)
190      {
191          fix E::m (**'E' is some arbitrarily chosen purpose*)
192          {
193              assume P1: "⌊ActsOnPurpose ?I E⌋c" (**(1) I act voluntarily on purpose E*)
194              from P1 have P1a: "⌊PPA ?I⌋c" using PPA_def by auto (**(1a) I am a PPA*)
195              from P1 have C2: "⌊Good ?I E⌋c" using explicationGoodness1 essentialPPA by meson
196                  (**(2) purpose E is good for me*)
197              from explicationFWB1 have C3: "⌊∀P. NeedsForPurpose ?I FWB P⌋ᴰ*" by simp
198                  (**(3) I need FWB for any purpose whatsoever*)
199              hence "∃P.⌊Good ?I P ∧ NeedsForPurpose ?I FWB P⌋ᴰ*"
200                  using explicationFWB2 explicationGoodness3 sem_5ab by blast
201              hence "⌊Good ?I (FWB ?I)⌋ᴰ*" using explicationGoodness2 by blast
202                  (**FWB is (a priori) good for me (in a kind of definitional sense)*)
203              hence C4: "⌊□ᴰ(Good ?I (FWB ?I))⌋c" by simp (**(4) FWB is an (a priori) necessary good for me*)
204              have "⌊O(FWB ?I | □ᴰ(Good ?I) (FWB ?I))⌋c" using explicationGoodness3 explicationFWB2 by blast
205                  (**I ought to pursue my FWB on the condition that I consider it to be a necessary good*)
206              hence "⌊O₁(FWB ?I)⌋c" using explicationFWB2 explicationFWB3 C4 CJ_14p by fastforce
207                  (**There is an (other-directed) obligation to my FWB*)
208              hence "⌊O₁(◇ₐ(FWB ?I))⌋c" using OIOAC by simp
209                  (**It must therefore be the case that my FWB is possible*)
210              hence "⌊O₁(∀a. ¬InterferesWith a (FWB ?I))⌋c" using InterferenceWithFWB by simp
211                  (**There is an obligation for others not to interfere with my FWB *)
212              hence C5: "⌊RightTo ?I FWB⌋c" using RightTo_def by simp (**(5) I have a claim right to my FWB*)
213          }
214          hence "⌊ActsOnPurpose ?I E → RightTo ?I FWB⌋c" by (rule impI)
215              (**I have a claim right to my FWB (since I act on some purpose E)*)
216      }
217      hence "⌊∀P. ActsOnPurpose ?I P → RightTo ?I FWB⌋c" by (rule allI)
218          (** 'allI' is a logical generalisation rule: "all-quantifier introduction"*)
219      hence "⌊PPA ?I → RightTo ?I FWB⌋c" using PPA_def by simp
220          (**(seen from my perspective C) I have a claim right to my FWB since I am a PPA*)
221      hence "⌊PPA (Agent C) → RightTo (Agent C) FWB⌋c" by simp
222          (**(seen from the perspective C) C's agent has a claim right to its FWB since it is a PPA*)
223  }
224  thus C13: "∀C. ⌊PPA (Agent C) → (RightTo (Agent C) FWB)⌋c" by (rule allI)
225      (**(13) For every perspective C: C's agent has a claim right to its FWB*)
226  qed
227
```

Fig. 1. A variant of Gewirth's proof in the Isabelle proof assistant (cf. [9]).

References

1. Benzmüller, C.: Universal (meta-)logical reasoning: recent successes. Sci. Comput. Program. **172**, 48–62 (2019)
2. Benzmüller, C., Farjami, A., Parent, X.: A dyadic deontic logic in HOL. In: Broersen, J., Condoravdi, C., Nair, S., Pigozzi, G. (eds.), Proceedings of DEON 2018—Deontic Logic and Normative Systems, pp. 33–50. College Publications (2018)
3. Benzmüller, C., Paulson, L.: Quantified multimodal logics in simple type theory. Log. Univers. (Spec. Issue Multimodal Log.) **7**(1), 7–20 (2013)
4. Beyleveld, D.: The Dialectical Necessity of Morality: An Analysis and Defense of Alan Gewirth's Argument to the Principle of Generic Consistency. UCP, Chicago (1991)
5. Blanchette, J.C., Nipkow, T.: Nitpick: a counterexample generator for higher-order logic based on a relational model finder. In: Kaufmann, M., Paulson, L.C. (eds.) ITP 2010. LNCS, vol. 6172, pp. 131–146. Springer, Heidelberg (2010). https://doi.org/10.1007/978-3-642-14052-5_11
6. Bringsjord, S., Arkoudas, K., Bello, P.: Toward a general logicist methodology for engineering ethically correct robots. IEEE Intell. Syst. **21**(4), 38–44 (2006)
7. Carmo, J., Jones, A.J.I.: Deontic logic and contrary-to-duties. In: Gabbay, D.M., Guenthner, F. (eds.) Handbook of Philosophical Logic, vol. 8, pp. 265–343. Springer, Heidelberg (2002). https://doi.org/10.1007/978-94-010-0387-2_4
8. Chisholm, R.M.: Contrary-to-duty imperatives and deontic logic. Analysis **24**, 33–36 (1963)
9. Fuenmayor, D., Benzmüller, C.: Formalisation and evaluation of Alan Gewirth's proof for the principle of generic consistency in Isabelle/HOL. Archive of Formal Proofs (2018). https://www.isa-afp.org/entries/GewirthPGCProof.html
10. Fuenmayor, D., Benzmüller, C.: Isabelle/HOL sources associated with this paper. Github (2019). https://github.com/davfuenmayor/2DDDL
11. Furbach, U., Schon, C.: Deontic logic for human reasoning. In: Eiter, T., Strass, H., Truszczyński, M., Woltran, S. (eds.) Advances in Knowledge Representation, Logic Programming, and Abstract Argumentation. LNCS (LNAI), vol. 9060, pp. 63–80. Springer, Cham (2015). https://doi.org/10.1007/978-3-319-14726-0_5
12. Gewirth, A.: Reason and Morality. University of Chicago Press, Chicago (1981)
13. Govindarajulu, N.S., Bringsjord, S.: On automating the doctrine of double effect. In: Proceedings of the Twenty-Sixth International Joint Conference on Artificial Intelligence, IJCAI-17, pp. 4722–4730 (2017)
14. Kaplan, D.: Afterthoughts. In: Almog, J., Perry, J., Wettstein, H. (eds.), Themes from Kaplan, pp. 565–614. Oxford University Press (1989)
15. Kaplan, D.: Demonstratives. In: Almog, J., Perry, J., Wettstein, H. (eds.), Themes from Kaplan, pp. 481–563. Oxford University Press (1989)
16. Pereira, L.M., Saptawijaya, A.: Programming Machine Ethics. Springer, Heidelberg (2016). https://doi.org/10.1007/978-3-319-29354-7
17. Schroeter, L.: Two-dimensional semantics. In: Zalta, E.N. (eds.), The Stanford Encyclopedia of Philosophy (2017). Summer 2017 edition

Constraint Solving

A CDCL-Style Calculus for Solving Non-linear Constraints

Franz Brauße[1(✉)], Konstantin Korovin[2], Margarita Korovina[3], and Norbert Müller[1]

[1] Abteilung Informatikwissenschaften, Universität Trier, Trier, Germany
brausse@informatik.uni-trier.de, mueller@uni-trier.de
[2] The University of Manchester, Manchester, UK
konstantin.korovin@manchester.ac.uk
[3] A.P. Ershov Institute of Informatics Systems, Novosibirsk, Russia
rita.korovina@gmail.com

Abstract. In this paper we propose a novel approach for checking satisfiability of non-linear constraints over the reals, called ksmt. The procedure is based on conflict resolution in CDCL-style calculus, using a composition of symbolical and numerical methods. To deal with the non-linear components in case of conflicts we use numerically constructed restricted linearisations. This approach covers a large number of computable non-linear real functions such as polynomials, rational or trigonometrical functions and beyond. A prototypical implementation has been evaluated on several non-linear SMT-LIB examples and the results have been compared with state-of-the-art SMT solvers.

1 Introduction

Continuous constraints occur naturally in many areas of computer science such as verification of safety-critical systems, program analysis and theorem proving. Historically, there have been two major approaches to solving continuous constraints. One of them is the symbolic approach, originated by the Tarski's decision procedure for the real closed fields [31], and developed further in procedures based on cylindrical decomposition (CAD) [5], Gröbner basis [3,14], and virtual substitution [7,20]. Another one is the numerical approach, based on interval computations, where the technique of interval constraint propagations have been explored to deal with continuous constraints on compact intervals, e.g., [1,10–12]. It is well known that both approaches have their strengths and weaknesses concerning completeness, efficiency and expressiveness.

Recently, a number of methods has been developed aimed at merging strengths of symbolical and numerical methods, e.g. [4,9,27,28]. In particular, the approach developed in this paper is motivated by extensions of CDCL-style

The research leading to these results has received funding from the DFG grant WERA MU 1801/5-1 and the DFG/RFBR grant CAVER BE 1267/14-1 and 14-01-91334. ▮ This project has received funding from the European Union's Horizon 2020 research and innovation programme under the Marie Skłodowska-Curie grant agreement No 731143.

© Springer Nature Switzerland AG 2019
A. Herzig and A. Popescu (Eds.): FroCoS 2019, LNAI 11715, pp. 131–148, 2019.
https://doi.org/10.1007/978-3-030-29007-8_8

reasoning into domains beyond propositional logic such as linear [15–17,23] and polynomial constraints [13]. In this paper we develop a conflict-driven framework called ksmt for solving non-linear constraints over large class of functions including polynomial, exponential and trigonometric functions. Our approach combines model guided search for a satisfying solution and constraint learning as the result of failed attempts to extend the candidate solution.

In the nutshell, our ksmt algorithm works as follows. Given a set of non-linear constraints, we first separate the set into linear and non-linear parts. Then we incrementally extend a candidate solution into a solution of the system and when such extension fails we resolve the conflict by generating a lemma that excludes a region which includes the falsifying assignment. There are two types of conflicts: between linear constraints which are resolved in a similar way as in [17] and non-linear conflicts which are resolved by local linearisations developed in this paper. One of the important properties of our algorithm is that all generated lemmas are linear and hence the non-linear part of the problem remains unchanged during the search. In other words, our algorithm can be seen as applying gradual linear approximations of non-linear constraints by local linearisations guided by solution search in the CDCL-style.

The quantifier-free theory of reals with transcendental functions is well known to be undecidable [30] and already problems with few variables pose considerable challenge for automated systems. In this paper we focus on a practical algorithm for solving non-linear constraints applicable to problems with large number of variables rather than on completeness results. Our ksmt algorithm can be used for both finding a solution and proving that no solution exists. In addition to a general framework we discuss how our algorithm works in a number of important cases such as polynomials, transcendental and some discontinuous functions. In this paper we combine solution guided search in the style of conflict resolution, bound propagation and MCSAT [6] with linearisations of real computable functions. The theory of computable functions has been developed in Computable Analysis [32] with implementations provided by exact real arithmetic [24]. Linearisations have been employed in different SMT theories before, including NRA and a recently considered one with transcendental functions [4,21,29], however, not for the broad class we consider here. We define a general class of functions called *functions with decidable rational approximations* to which our approach is applicable. This class includes common transcendental functions, exponentials, logarithms but also some discontinuous functions.

We implemented the ksmt algorithm and evaluated it on SMT benchmarks. Our implementation is at an early stage and lacking many features but already outperforms many state-of-the-art SMT solvers on certain classes of problems.

2   Preliminaries

We consider the reals extended with non-linear functions $\mathbb{R}_{nl} = (\mathbb{R}, \langle \mathcal{F}_{lin} \cup \mathcal{F}_{nl}, \mathcal{P} \rangle)$, where $\mathcal{F}_{lin}$ consists of rational constants, addition and multiplication by rational constants; $\mathcal{F}_{nl}$ consists of a selection of non-linear functions including multiplication, trigonometric, exponential and logarithmic functions; $\mathcal{P} = \{<, \leq, >, \geq\}$ are predicates.

We consider a set of variables V. We will use x, y, z possibly with indexes for variables in V, similar we will use q, a, b, c, d for rationals, f, g for non-linear functions in $\mathcal{F}_{nl}$. Terms, predicates and formulas over X are defined in the standard way. We will also use predicates $\neq, =$, which can be defined using predicates in $\mathcal{P}$. An atomic formula is a formula of the form $t \diamond 0$ where $\diamond \in \mathcal{P}$. A literal is either an atomic formula or its negation. In this paper we consider only quantifier-free formulas in conjunctive normal form. We will use conjunctions and sets of formulas interchangeably.

We assume that terms are suitably normalised. A linear term is a term of the form $q_1 x_1 + \ldots + q_n x_n + q_0$. A linear inequality is an atomic formula of the form $q_1 x_1 + \ldots + q_n x_n + q_0 \diamond 0$. A linear clause is a disjunction of linear inequalities and a formula is in linear CNF if it is a conjunction of linear clauses.

2.1 Separated Linear Form

In this paper we consider the satisfiability problem of quantifier-free formulas in CNF over $\mathbb{R}_{nl}$, where the linear part is separated from the non-linear part which we call separated linear form.

Definition 1. *A formula F is in* separated linear form *if it is of the form $F = \mathcal{L} \cup \mathcal{N}$ where $\mathcal{L}$ is a set of clauses containing predicates only over linear terms and $\mathcal{N}$ is a set of unit-clauses each containing only non-linear literals of the form $x \diamond f(t)$, where $f \in \mathcal{F}_{nl}$, t is a vector of terms and $\diamond \in \mathcal{P}$.*

Lemma 1 (Monotonic flattening). *Any quantifier-free formula F in CNF over $\mathbb{R}_{nl}$ can be transformed into an equi-satisfiable separated linear form in polynomial time.*

Proof. Consider a clause C in F which contains a linear combination of non-linear terms, i.e., is of the form $C = qf(t) + p \diamond 0 \vee D$, where $f \in \mathcal{F}_{nl}$ and $q \neq 0$. Then we introduce a fresh variable x, add $x \diamond' f(t)$ into $\mathcal{N}$ and replace C with $qx + p \diamond 0 \vee D$. Here, $\diamond'$ is $\geq$, if either $q > 0$ and $\diamond \in \{\leq, <\}$ or $q < 0$ and $\diamond \in \{\geq, >\}$; and $\diamond'$ is $\leq$ otherwise. The resulting formula is equi-satisfiable to F. The claim follows by induction on the non-linear monomials.

Let us remark that monotonic flattening avoids introducing equality predicates, which is based on the monotonicity of linear functions. In some cases we need to flatten non-linear terms further (in particular to be able to represent terms as functions in the $\mathcal{F}_{DA}$ class introduced in Sect. 5). In most cases this can be done in the same way as in Lemma 1 based on monotonicity of functions in corresponding arguments, but we may need to introduce linear conditions expressing regions of monotonicity. For simplicity of the exposition we will not consider such cases here.

2.2 Trails and Assignments

Any sequence of single variable assignments $\alpha \in (V \times \mathbb{Q})^*$ such that a variable is assigned at most once is called a *trail*. By ignoring the order of assignments in

α, we will regard α as a (partial) assignment of the real variables in V and use $V(\alpha) \subseteq V$ to denote the set of variables assigned in α. We use the notation $[\![t]\!]^\alpha$ to denote the (partial) application of α to a term t, that is, the term resulting from replacing every free variable x in t such that $x \in V(\alpha)$ by $\alpha(x)$ and evaluating term operations on constants in their domains. We extend $[\![\cdot]\!]^\alpha$ to predicates over terms and to CNF in the usual way. An evaluation of a formula results in true or false, if all variables in the formula are assigned, or else in a partially evaluated formula. A *solution* to a CNF $\mathcal{C}$ is a total assignment α such that each term in $\mathcal{C}$ is defined under α and for each clause $C \in \mathcal{C}$ there is (at least) one literal $l \in C$ with $[\![l]\!]^\alpha = $ true.

Any triple $(\alpha, \mathcal{L}, \mathcal{N})$ when α is a trail, $\mathcal{L}$ is a set of clauses over linear predicates and $\mathcal{N}$ is a set of unit clauses over non-linear predicates is called *state*. A state is called *linearly conflict-free* if $[\![\mathcal{L}]\!]^\alpha \neq $ false. It is called *conflict-free* if it is linearly conflict-free and $[\![\mathcal{N}]\!]^\alpha \neq $ false.

The main problem we consider in this paper is finding a solution to $\mathcal{L} \wedge \mathcal{N}$ or showing that no solution exists.

3   The ksmt Algorithm

Our ksmt algorithm will be based on a CDCL-type calculus [22,25] and is in the spirit of Conflict Resolution [16,17], Bound Propagation [8,18], GDPLL [23], MCSAT [6] and related algorithms.

The ksmt calculus will be presented as a set of transition rules that operate on the states introduced previously. The *initial state* is a state of the form $(\text{nil}, \mathcal{L}, \mathcal{N})$. A final state will be reached when no further ksmt transition rules (defined below) are applicable.

Informally, the ksmt algorithm starts with a formula in separated linear form and the empty trail, and extends the trail until the solution is found or a trivial inconsistency is derived by applying the ksmt transition rules. During the extension process the algorithm may encounter conflicts which are resolved by deriving lemmas which will be linear clauses. These lemmas are either derived by resolution between two linear clauses or by linearisation of non-linear conflicts, which is described in detail in Sect. 3.4. One of the important properties of our calculus is that we only generate linear lemmas during the run of the algorithm and the non-linear part $\mathcal{N}$ remains fixed.

3.1   General Procedure

Let $(\alpha, \mathcal{L}, \mathcal{N})$ be a conflict-free state and $z \in V \setminus V(\alpha)$ be a variable unassigned in α. Assume there is no $q \in \mathbb{Q}$ such that $(\alpha :: z \mapsto q, \mathcal{L}, \mathcal{N})$ is linearly conflict-free. That means that for any potential assignment q there is a clause $D \in \mathcal{L}$ not satisfied under $\alpha :: z \mapsto q$. Another way of viewing this situation, called a *conflict*, is that there are clauses consisting under α only of predicates linear in and only depending on z that contradict each other. Analogously to resolution in propositional logic,

$$\frac{A \vee \ell \quad B \vee \neg \ell}{A \vee B}$$

the following inference rule we call *arithmetical resolution on x* is sound [17,23] on clauses over linear predicates:

$$\frac{A \vee (cx + d \leq 0) \quad B \vee (-c'x + d' \leq 0)}{A \vee B \vee (c'd + cd' \leq 0)}$$

where c, c' are positive rational constants and d, d' are linear terms. Similar rules exist for strict comparisons. We denote by $R_{\alpha,\mathcal{L},z}$ a set of resolvents of clauses in $\mathcal{L}$ upon variable z such that $[\![R_{\alpha,\mathcal{L},z}]\!]^\alpha = \mathsf{false}$. In Sect. 3.3 we discuss how to obtain such a set.

We consider the following rules for transforming states into states under some preconditions, i.e., the binary relation $\Rightarrow$ on states.

Assignment refinement: In order to refine an existing partial assignment α by assigning $z \in V$ to $q \in \mathbb{Q}$ in a state $(\alpha, \mathcal{L}, \mathcal{N})$, the state needs to be linearly conflict-free, that is, no clause over linear predicates in $\mathcal{L}$ must be false under α. Additionally, under this assignment the clauses over linear predicates in $\mathcal{L}$ must be valid under the new assignment, formally: For any state $(\alpha, \mathcal{L}, \mathcal{N})$, $z \in V$ and $q \in \mathbb{Q}$

$$(\alpha, \mathcal{L}, \mathcal{N}) \Rightarrow (\alpha :: z \mapsto q, \mathcal{L}, \mathcal{N}) \tag{A}$$

whenever $[\![\mathcal{L}]\!]^\alpha \neq \mathsf{false}$, $z \notin V(\alpha)$, and $[\![\mathcal{L}]\!]^{\alpha::z \mapsto q} \neq \mathsf{false}$. In the linear setting of [17], this rule exactly corresponds to "assignment refinement".

Conflict resolution: Assume despite state $(\alpha, \mathcal{L}, \mathcal{N})$ being linearly conflict-free and $z \in V$ unassigned in α there is no rational value to assign to z that makes the resulting state linearly conflict-free. This means, that for any $q \in \mathbb{Q}$ there is a *conflict*, i.e., a clause in $\mathcal{L}$ that is false under $\alpha :: z \mapsto q$. In order to progress in determining sat or unsat, the partial assignment α needs to be excluded from the search space. Arithmetical resolution $R_{\alpha,\mathcal{L},z}$ provides exactly that: a set of clauses preventing any $\beta \sqsupseteq \alpha$ from being linearly conflict-free. For any state $(\alpha, \mathcal{L}, \mathcal{N})$ and $z \in V$

$$(\alpha, \mathcal{L}, \mathcal{N}) \Rightarrow (\alpha, \mathcal{L} \cup R_{\alpha,\mathcal{L},z}, \mathcal{N}) \tag{R}$$

whenever $[\![\mathcal{L}]\!]^\alpha \neq \mathsf{false}$, $z \notin V(\alpha)$ and $\forall q \in \mathbb{Q} : [\![\mathcal{L}]\!]^{\alpha::z \mapsto q} = \mathsf{false}$. In the linear setting of [17], this rule corresponds to "conflict resolution".

Backjumping: In case the state $(\alpha, \mathcal{L}, \mathcal{N})$ contains one or more top-level assignments that make it not linearly conflict-free, these assignments are removed. This is commonly known as backjumping. Indeed, when transitioning to applying this rule, the information on the size of the suffix of assignments to remove is already available, as is detailed in Sect. 3.2. Formally, for a state $(\alpha, \mathcal{L}, \mathcal{N})$ such that $[\![\mathcal{L}]\!]^\alpha = \mathsf{false}$, let γ be the maximal prefix of α such that $[\![\mathcal{L}]\!]^\gamma \neq \mathsf{false}$. Then, Backjumping is defined as follows:

$$(\alpha, \mathcal{L}, \mathcal{N}) \Rightarrow (\gamma, \mathcal{L}, \mathcal{N}) \tag{B}$$

Linearisation: The above rules are only concerned with keeping the (partial) assignment linearly conflict-free. This rule extends the calculus to ensure that the non-linear clauses in $\mathcal{N}$ are conflict-free as well. In essence, the variables involved in a non-linear conflict are "lifted" into the linear domain by a linearisation of the conflict local to α. The resulting state will not be linearly conflict-free as is shown in Lemma 4. Formally, if $(\alpha, \mathcal{L}, \mathcal{N})$ is a state and $L_{\alpha,\mathcal{N}}$ a non-empty set of linearisation clauses as detailed in Sect. 3.4, then the rule reads as

$$(\alpha, \mathcal{L}, \mathcal{N}) \Rightarrow (\alpha, \mathcal{L} \cup L_{\alpha,\mathcal{N}}, \mathcal{N}) \qquad \text{(L)}$$

whenever $[\![\mathcal{L}]\!]^\alpha \neq \mathsf{false}$ and $[\![\mathcal{N}]\!]^\alpha = \mathsf{false}$.

Let us note that the set $\mathcal{N}$ remains unchanged over any sequence of states obtained by successive application of the above rules.

Lemma 2 (Soundness). *Let I be an input instance in separated linear form. Let $(S_0, S_1, \ldots, S_n)$ be a sequence of states $S_i = (\alpha_i, \mathcal{L}_i, \mathcal{N})$ where S_0 is the initial state and each S_{i+1} is derived from S_i by application of one of the rules* (A), (R), (B), (L).

1. *For all $i < n$ and total assignments $\alpha : V \to \mathbb{Q}$: $[\![\mathcal{L}_i \wedge \mathcal{N}]\!]^\alpha = [\![\mathcal{L}_{i+1} \wedge \mathcal{N}]\!]^\alpha$.*
2. *If no rule is applicable to S_n then the following are equivalent:*
   - *I is satisfiable,*
   - *α_n is a solution to I,*
   - *S_n is linearly conflict-free,*
   - *the trivial conflict clause $(1 \leq 0)$ is not in $\mathcal{L}_n$.*

Lemma 3 (Progress). *Let $(S_i)_i$ be a sequence of states $S_i = (\alpha_i, \mathcal{L}_i, \mathcal{N})$ produced from initial state S_0 by the* ksmt *rules, n be the number of variables and*

$$\Lambda_i := \{\alpha : \text{(A) cannot be applied to } (\alpha, \mathcal{L}_i, \mathcal{N}) \text{ linearly conflict-free}\}.$$

Then $\Lambda_i \supseteq \Lambda_{i+1}$ and $\Lambda_i \neq \Lambda_{i+n+2}$ hold for all i.

The proofs follow from the following:

1. (A) does not change Λ and can be applied consecutively at most n times,
2. after application of (R) or (L) the set Λ is reduced which follows from the properties of the resolvent, and Corollary 2 respectively, and
3. (B) does not change Λ and can be applied only after (R) or (L).

Corollary 1. *After at most $n + 2$ steps the search space is reduced.*

3.2   Concrete Algorithm

The algorithm transforms the initial state by applying ksmt transition rules exhaustively. The rule applicability graph is shown in Fig. 1. The rule (B) is applicable whenever the linear part is false in the current assignment. This is always the case after applications of either (R) or (L). In order to check applicability of remaining rules (A), (R) and (L) the following conditions need to be checked.

1. Is the state conflict-free? In particular, we need to check whether the non-linear part evaluates to false under the current assignment. Decidability of this problem for the broad class of functions $\mathcal{F}_{DA}$ is shown in Sect. 5.1, along with concrete algorithms for common classes of non-linear functions.
2. If the state is linearly conflict-free and a variable is chosen, can it be assigned in a way that the linear part remains conflict-free? A polynomial-time procedure is described in Sect. 3.3.

These computations determine whether (A), (R) or (L) is applicable next. Item 2 has to be checked after each application of (A) and (B). Note that in case of transitioning to an application of rule (B) the size of the suffix of assignments to revoke is syntactically available in form of the highest position in α of a variable in $R_{\alpha,\mathcal{L},z}$ or the linearisation $L_{\alpha,\mathcal{N}}$, respectively.

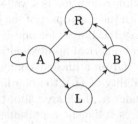

Fig. 1. Transitions between applicability of rules.

Let us note that the calculus allows for flexibility in the choices of:

1. The variable z and value q to assign to z when applying rule (A).
2. Which arithmetical resolutions to perform when applying rule (R).
3. Which linearisations to perform when applying rule (L). We describe the general conditions in Sect. 3.4 and our approach in Sect. 5.2.

Many of the heuristics presented in [8,16] are applicable to items 1 and 2 as well.

3.3 Determining Bounds and Resolvents

In this section we consider the problem of checking whether we can extend the trail of a linearly conflict-free state in such a way that the linear part remains conflict-free after the extension and in this case we apply rule (A), or otherwise there is a conflict which should be resolved by applying rule (R).

Given a linearly conflict-free state $(\alpha, \mathcal{L}, \mathcal{N})$ and a variable z unassigned in α, the problem

$$\exists q \in \mathbb{Q} : [\![\mathcal{L}]\!]^{\alpha::z \mapsto q} \neq \mathsf{false}$$

can be solved efficiently by the following algorithm. Let $\mathcal{L}_{z,\alpha}$ be those partially applied (by α) clauses from $\mathcal{L}$ that only depend on z. The other clauses are either already satisfied or depend on a further unassigned variable. So each $D \in \mathcal{L}_{z,\alpha}$ is 'univariate', i.e. just a set of $z \diamond c_i$. The disjunction of these simple predicates in D is equivalent to a clause of the form (i) $z < a \vee z > b$, perhaps with non-strict inequalities, giving an alternative between a lower and an upper bound or (ii) a unit clause for a lower bound, or (iii) a unit clause for an upper bound, or (iv) an arithmetic tautology. So each clause is equivalent to the union of at most two half-bounded rational intervals. The conjunction of two such clauses corresponds to the intersection of sets of intervals, which is again a set of intervals. This intersection can be computed easily and can also be checked for emptiness. In case the intersection is not empty, it even gives us intervals to choose an assignment q for z with $[\![\mathcal{L}]\!]^{\alpha::z\mapsto q} \neq \mathsf{false}$. If the intersection is empty, we know there is no such q and we can use arithmetical resolution to resolve this conflict to obtain $R_{\alpha,\mathcal{L},z}$.

3.4   Non-linear Predicates

While resolution is a well-established and efficient symbolic technique for dealing with the linear part of the CNF under consideration, there seem to be no similarly easy techniques for non-linear predicates. The approach presented here is based on numerical approximations instead.

Given a linearly conflict-free state $(\alpha, \mathcal{L}, \mathcal{N})$, in order to decide on the applicability of (L), the non-linear unit clauses in $\mathcal{N}$ have to be checked for validity under α. If all are valid, then, by definition, $(\alpha, \mathcal{L}, \mathcal{N})$ is conflict-free. Lemma 5 gives sufficient conditions on the non-linear functions in $\mathcal{F}_{nl}$ in order to make this problem decidable. In this section, we will describe how we deal with the case that some unit clause $\{P\} \in \mathcal{N}$ is false under α, where according to (L) we construct a linearisation of P with respect to α. We will not need the order of variables given in the trail α, so we will only use α as a partial assignment.

Definition 2. *Let P be a non-linear predicate and let α be a partial assignment with $[\![P]\!]^\alpha = \mathsf{false}$. An (α, P)-linearisation is a clause $L_{\alpha,P} = \{L_i : i \in I\}$ consisting of finitely many rational linear predicates $(L_i)_{i\in I}$ with the properties*

1. $\{\beta : [\![P]\!]^\beta = \mathsf{true}\} \subseteq \{\beta : [\![L_{\alpha,P}]\!]^\beta = \mathsf{true}\}$, *and*
2. $[\![L_{\alpha,P}]\!]^\alpha = \mathsf{false}$.

If we let c_α denote the values assigned in α and x the vector of assigned variables, we can reformulate the properties of $L_{\alpha,P}$ as a formula:

$$\left(P \implies \bigvee_{i\in I} L_i\right) \wedge \left(x = c_\alpha \implies \neg \bigvee_{i\in I} L_i\right)$$

This formula will not be added to the system but is just used as a basis for discussions. Later we will use a similar formalism to define linearisation clauses.

A central idea of our approach is to add $L_{\alpha,P}$ as a new clause to the CNF, as well as the predicates L_i. Adding $L_{\alpha,P}$ is sound, as the following lemma shows:

Lemma 4. *Suppose a partial assignment α violates a predicate P with $\{P\} \in \mathcal{N}$, so $[\![P]\!]^\alpha = \mathsf{false}$. Further suppose $L_{\alpha,P}$ is an (α, P)-linearisation.*

1. *Any β, which is a solution for $\mathcal{L} \cup \mathcal{N}$, is also a solution for $\mathcal{L} \cup \{L_{\alpha,P}\} \cup \mathcal{N}$.*
2. *$(\alpha, \mathcal{L} \cup \{L_{\alpha,P}\}, \mathcal{N})$ is not linearly conflict-free.*

Corollary 2. *Whenever (L) is applied, the search space is reduced.*

Hence at least the partial assignment α (and all extensions thereof) are removed from the search space for the linear part of our CNF, at the cost of adding the clause $L_{\alpha,P}$ usually containing several new linear predicates L_i. In

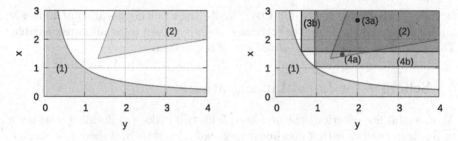

Fig. 2. Initial system and linearisations constructed.

general, our linearisations will not just remove single points but rather polytopes from the search space.

We should emphasise several remarks on the linearisations: There is a high degree of freedom when choosing a linearisation for a given pair (α, P). Techniques for constructing these will be discussed in Sect. 5.2. They will all be based on numerical approximations.

Furthermore we are allowed to add more than one clause in one step, so we can construct several linearisations for different (α, P') as long as $[\![P']\!]^\alpha = \mathsf{false}$, and then add all of them. This has already been formulated in (L) as a *set* of linearisation clauses $L_{\alpha,\mathcal{N}}$ instead of a single clause $L_{\alpha,P}$.

4   Example

As a basic example describing our method we consider the conjunction of the non-linear predicate $P : (x \leq \frac{1}{y})$, and linear constraints $L_1 : (x \geq y/4 + 1)$ and $L_2 : (x \leq 4 \cdot (y-1))$, shown on Fig. 2. We will first detail on how linearisations can be constructed numerically for P. In Sect. 5.2 we will detail on how linearisations can be constructed in general.

Linearisation of P. Assume $[\![P]\!]^\alpha = \mathsf{false}$ under assignment α. By definition, α assigns (x, y) to some values (c_x, c_y) such that $c_x > 1/c_y$, (point (3a), at $(8/3, 2)$). Here we will only discuss the case $c_y > 0$ needed below. The other cases can be dealt with in a similar way. To construct an (α, P)-linearization, first we compute the rational number d such that $1/c_y < d < c_x$. In this example, we take $d := (c_x + 1/c_y)/2$, that is, for this linearisation $19/12 \approx 1.58$. In general, such values are computed by numerical approximations to the function value. Then the clause $L_{\alpha,P} = \{x \leq d, y \leq 1/d\}$ is the required linearisation (which excludes region (3b) containing the conflicting assignment). Indeed, $L_{\alpha,P}$ is implied by P and $[\![L_{\alpha,P}]\!]^\alpha = \mathsf{false}$.

After adding $L_{\alpha,P}$ to the linear constraints, region (3b) is excluded from the search space and backjumping to the empty assignment is performed (since $8/3$ is not a linearly conflict-free assignment to x anymore). The system again is linearly conflict-free. In the next iteration we obtain a solution (4a) roughly at $(1.47, 1.63)$ to the new linear system, linearisation at (4a) results in linear lemma excluding region (4b) where $d \approx 1.04$. Finally, the resulting linear constraints are unsatisfiable and therefore the original system is proven to be also unsatisfiable. This example is based on an actual run of our system.

5   Schemes for Local Linearisations

A successful linearisation scheme has to fulfil two tasks: (a) deciding whether a trail α is in conflict with a non-linear predicate P and then, if there is a conflict, (b) finding reasonable linearisations $L_{\alpha,P}$. We first address task (a).

5.1   Deciding Non-linear Conflicts

By Definition 1, P is of the form $x \diamond f(t)$, where f is a function symbol, t is a vector of terms, and $\diamond \in \{<, \leq, >, \geq\}$. In the following assume that the terms in t use the variables $(y_1, \ldots, y_k) = y \in V^k$. So the semantical interpretation $[\![f(t)]\!]$ of the syntactical term $f(t)$ is a function $g : \mathbb{R}^k \to \mathbb{R}$.

In order to introduce the class $\mathcal{F}_{DA}$ we use the following notion of approximable function.

Definition 3. *We call a partial function $g : \mathbb{R} \to \mathbb{R}$ approximable if the set*

$$\Box_g := \{(p,q,s,t) : g([p,q]) \subset (s,t),\ p,q,s,t \in \mathbb{Q}\}$$

is computably enumerable. Here, $g(I)$ denotes the set-evaluation of g on I, that is, $\{g(x) : x \in I \cap \operatorname{dom} g\}$.

This definition can easily be generalized to the multi-variate case by taking boxes $[p_1,q_1] \times \cdots \times [p_k,q_k]$ with $p,q \in \mathbb{Q}^k$. For total continuous real functions, approximability coincides with the notion of computability known from Computable Analysis (TTE) [2,32].

Given a number $d \in \mathbb{Q}$ and a vector $c \in \mathbb{Q}^k$ with $d \neq g(c)$ we can always decide whether $d \diamond g(c)$ holds if $g : \mathbb{R}^k \to \mathbb{R}$ is a total approximable function. However, in general we cannot decide the premise $d \neq g(c)$. Therefore we restrict our considerations to a general class of functions where this problem is decidable.

Definition 4. *A partial function $g : \mathbb{R}^k \to \mathbb{R}$ is called a function with decidable rational approximations, denoted $g \in \mathcal{F}_{DA}$, if the following holds.*

- *$\operatorname{dom}(g)$ is decidable on $\mathbb{Q}^k$,*
- *graph(g) is decidable on $\mathbb{Q}^k \times \mathbb{Q}$, and*
- *g is approximable.*

The following important classes of functions belong to $\mathcal{F}_{DA}$.

Multivariate Polynomials. For multivariate polynomials g with rational coefficients, rational arguments are mapped to rational results using rational arithmetic and the relations $\diamond$ under consideration are decidable on $\mathbb{Q}^2$.

Selected Elementary Transcendental Functions. Let $g \in \{\exp, \ln, \log_b, \sin, \cos,$ $\tan, \arctan\}$, where in the case of $\log_b$, $b \in \mathbb{Q}$. Let us show that $g \in \mathcal{F}_{\mathrm{DA}}$. Indeed, it is well known that $g : \mathbb{R} \to \mathbb{R}$ is computable [32]. Since emptiness of $[p,q] \backslash \mathrm{dom}\, g$ is decidable, g is also approximable. In addition, $X_g := \mathrm{graph}(g) \cap \mathbb{Q}^2$ either consists of a single point, or in the case of $\log_b$, is of the form $X_g = \{(b^n, n) : n \in \mathbb{Z}\}$ [26] and therefore is decidable, as is the respective domain.

Selected Discontinuous Functions. Additionally, $\mathcal{F}_{\mathrm{DA}}$ includes some discontinuous functions like e.g. the step-functions taking rational values with discontinuities at finitely many rational points and more generally piecewise polynomials defined over intervals with a decidable set of rational endpoints. Multi-variate piecewise defined functions with non-axis-aligned discontinuities are included as well.

Lemma 5. *Let P be a predicate over reals and let α be a trail assigning all variables used in P. If P is linear or $P : (x \diamond f(t))$ with $[\![f(t)]\!] \in \mathcal{F}_{\mathrm{DA}}$ then $[\![P]\!]^\alpha$ is computable.*

Proof. By definition, trails α contain rational assignments. If P is linear, there is nothing to show. Let $P : (x \diamond f(t))$ with $g(y) = [\![f(t)]\!] \in \mathcal{F}_{\mathrm{DA}}$ where y is the vector of free variables in terms t. The cases $[\![y]\!]^\alpha \notin \mathrm{dom}\, g$ and $[\![(y,x)]\!]^\alpha \in \mathrm{graph}(g)$ are decidable by the definition of $\mathcal{F}_{\mathrm{DA}}$. The remaining case is $z := [\![y]\!]^\alpha \in \mathrm{dom}\, g$ and $[\![(y,x)]\!]^\alpha \notin \mathrm{graph}(g)$. Perform a parallel search for (1) $q \in \mathbb{Q}$ with $(z, q) \in \mathrm{graph}(g)$ and for (2) a rational interval box $I \times J$ in $\square_{\tilde{g}}$ with $z \in I$ and $[\![x]\!]^\alpha \notin J$. We now show that this search terminates. Either $g(z) \in \mathbb{Q}$, then $q = g(z)$ can be found in the graph of g, or $g(z) \notin \mathbb{Q}$, then $|[\![x]\!]^\alpha - g(z)| > 0$, thus there is a rational interval box $I \times (s,t) \in \square_g$ with $z \in I$ and $s, t \in \mathbb{Q}$ such that $[\![x]\!]^\alpha \notin (s,t)$. Note that I can be the point-interval $[z]$ since $z \in \mathrm{dom}\, g$.

In particular, if all predicates $P : (x \diamond f(t))$ appearing in a given problem instance are such that the function $[\![f(t)]\!]$ used in this instance are from $\mathcal{F}_{\mathrm{DA}}$, we can decide if a ksmt state is conflict-free as required in Sect. 3.2.

5.2 Linearisations for Functions in $\mathcal{F}_{\mathrm{DA}}$

This section addresses task (b), namely finding reasonable linearisations $L_{\alpha,P}$ in case a trail α is in conflict with a non-linear predicate P, that is, $[\![P]\!]^\alpha = \mathsf{false}$. In order to reduce the number of cases, we assume that the comparison operator $\diamond$ in $P : x \diamond f(t)$ is from $\{<, \leq\}$. The other two cases $\{>, \geq\}$ are symmetric.

Again let $g = [\![f(t)]\!] : \mathbb{R}^k \to \mathbb{R}$ be the function represented by the term $f(t)$. We assume that $g \in \mathcal{F}_{\mathrm{DA}}$. Let $c_x = [\![x]\!]^\alpha \in \mathbb{Q}$ and $c_y = [\![y]\!]^\alpha \in \mathbb{Q}^k$ be the values assigned by α to the free variables y in t, additionally, let $c_y \in \mathrm{dom}\, g$. Furthermore let $c_g = g(c_y) = [\![f(t)]\!]^\alpha \in \mathbb{R}$ be the value resulting from an exact evaluation of g. Note that c_g will only be used in the discussion and will not be added to the constraints, since in general $c_g \notin \mathbb{Q}$. Then our assumption of an existing conflict $[\![P]\!]^\alpha = \mathsf{false}$ can be read as $c_x > c_g$ for $\diamond \in \{\leq\}$, and as $c_x \geq c_g$ for $\diamond \in \{<\}$. Let us note that c_x and c_y are rational, but c_g is a real number and usually irrational. Since $g \in \mathcal{F}_{DA}$ we can compute approximations $\bar{c}_g \in \mathbb{Q}$ to c_g with $|\bar{c}_g - c_g| \leq \varepsilon$ for any rational $\varepsilon > 0$ using Lemma 5.

We now give a list of possible linearisations of g, starting from trivial versions where we exclude just the conflicting point $(c_x, \boldsymbol{c_y})$ to more general linearisations excluding larger regions containing this point.

Point Linearisation: A trivial (α, P)-linearisation excluding the point $(c_x, \boldsymbol{c_y})$ is

$$(\boldsymbol{y} = \boldsymbol{c_y} \implies x \neq c_x)$$

Half-Line Linearisation: An (α, P)-linearisation excluding a closed half-line starting in c_x is

$$(\boldsymbol{y} = \boldsymbol{c_y} \implies x < c_x)$$

In the following we will develop more powerful linearisations with the aim to exclude larger regions of the search space.

For better linearisations, we can exploit additional information about the predicate P and the trail α, especially about the behaviour of g in a region around $\boldsymbol{c_y}$. This information could be obtained by a per-case analysis on $\mathcal{F}_{nl}$, or during run time using external algebra systems or libraries for exact real arithmetic or interval arithmetic on the extended real numbers $\mathbb{R} \cup \{-\infty, +\infty\}$. Our focus, however, is on the numerical and not the symbolical approach.

As we aim at linearisations, the regions should have linear rational boundaries, so we concentrate on finite intersections of half-spaces:

Definition 5. *An (open or closed) rational half-space $H \subseteq \mathbb{R}^k$ is the solution set of a linear predicate $\boldsymbol{a} \cdot \boldsymbol{y} \leq b$ or $\boldsymbol{a} \cdot \boldsymbol{y} < b$ for some $\boldsymbol{a} \in \mathbb{Q}^k$, $b \in \mathbb{Q}$. A rational polytope $R \subseteq \mathbb{R}^k$ is a finite intersection of rational half-spaces.*

Any such polytope R is a convex and possibly unbounded set and can be represented as the conjunction of linear predicates over the variables $\boldsymbol{y}$. Therefore the complement $\mathbb{R}^k \setminus R$ can be represented as a linear clause $\{L_i : i \in I\}$ denoting the predicate $\boldsymbol{y} \notin R$. For the ease of reading, instead of writing clauses like $\bigvee_{i \in I} L_i \vee D$ we will use $\boldsymbol{y} \in R \implies D$ in the following.

Since $g \in \mathcal{F}_{DA}$ and approximable it follows that for any bounded rational polytope $R \subseteq \mathbb{R}^k$ in the domain of g we can find arbitrarily precise rational over-approximations (a, b) such that $g(R) \subset (a, b)$.

Interval Linearisation: Suppose we have $c_x \neq c_g$. By approximating c_g we compute $d \in \mathbb{Q}$ with $c_g < d < c_x$. The proof of Lemma 5 provides an initial rational polytope $R \in \mathbb{R}^k$ with $\boldsymbol{c_y} \in R$ such that $d \notin g(R)$. Then

$$\boldsymbol{y} \in R \implies x \leq d \tag{5.1}$$

is an (α, P)-linearisation. Using specific properties of g, e.g., monotonicity, we can extend the polytope R to an unbounded one.

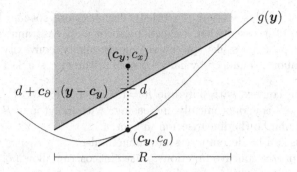

Fig. 3. Tangent Space Linearisation shown for univariate g. The shaded area will be excluded from the search space.

This linearisation excludes the set $\{x : x > d\} \times R$ from the search space which is a polytope, now in $\mathbb{R} \times \mathbb{R}^k$, containing the point $(c_x, \boldsymbol{c_y})$.

Linearisations in Example 4 are of this type, there $c_g = 1/c_y$ and $R = (1/d, \infty)$ defined by $y > 1/d$ which is the negation of $y \leq 1/d$, the second literal in the linear lemma $L_{\alpha,P}$ is the right hand side of the implication (5.1).

The univariate predicate $x \leq d$ corresponds to a very special half-space in $\mathbb{R} \times \mathbb{R}^k$, as it is independent from the variables in $\boldsymbol{y}$. Usually, using partial derivatives gives better linearisations:

Tangent Space Linearisation: Suppose we again have $c_x \neq c_g$. Assume the partial derivatives of g at $\boldsymbol{c_y}$ exist and we are able to compute a vector $\boldsymbol{c_\partial} = (c_1, \ldots, c_k)$ of rational approximations, that is, $c_i \approx \frac{\partial g}{\partial y_i}(\boldsymbol{c_y})$. As before we construct $d \in \mathbb{Q}$ with $c_g < d < c_x$ and search for a rational polytope $R \in \mathbb{R}^k$ with $\boldsymbol{c_y} \in R$. But instead of just $d \notin g(R)$ now R has to fulfil the constraint
$$\forall \boldsymbol{r} \in R : g(\boldsymbol{r}) \leq d + \boldsymbol{c_\partial} \cdot (\boldsymbol{r} - \boldsymbol{c_y})$$
using the dot product of $\boldsymbol{c_\partial}$ and $(\boldsymbol{r} - \boldsymbol{c_y})$. Again, R can be found using interval computation. Then
$$\boldsymbol{y} \in R \implies x \leq d + \boldsymbol{c_\partial} \cdot (\boldsymbol{y} - \boldsymbol{c_y})$$
is an (α, P)-linearisation, since the dot-product is a linear and rational operation. This situation is schematically depicted in Fig. 3.

Using the tangent space, we are able to get a much better 'fit' of $d + \sum c_i y_i$ to g than just using the naive interval evaluations. This allows to choose d closer to c_g for given R, or to choose a bigger polytope R for a given d. Some examples of Tangent Space Linearisations are available.[1]

Lemma 6. *By construction, the above procedures indeed provide linearisations as stated in Definition 2.*

---

[1] http://informatik.uni-trier.de/~brausse/ksmt

For the rest of this section, we briefly discuss more specific linearisations for some important cases when we can perform a by-case analysis on g and exploit further properties like (piecewise) monotonicity, convexity or boundedness, which cannot be deduced by naive interval arithmetic, see Sect. 6 for details.

- $g(y) = y^{2n}$ is convex, with polytope $R = (-\infty, +\infty)$ for $\diamond \in \{>, \geq\}$.
- $g(y) = y^{2n+1}$ is monotonically increasing, with polytopes R of the form $(-\infty, c]$, similar to the linearisation in Sect. 4.
- Polynomials can be decomposed into monomials.
- Piecewise convex/concave functions g like sin, cos, tan allow polytopes covering a convex area in their domain.
- More direct ways of computing linearisations of the elementary transcendental functions can be obtained e.g. by bounding the distance of the image of specific g to algebraic numbers, such bounds are given in [19, Sect. 4.3].

6   Evaluation

We implemented our approach in the ksmt system, which is open source and publicly available (See footnote 1). The ksmt system supports a subset of QF_LRA and QF_NRA logics as defined in the SMT-LIB standard. As with Z3, when no logic is specified in the input script, our extended signature $\mathbb{R}_{nl}$ is the default.

Choices made in the implementation include:

- Selecting a rational value in a non-empty interval as smallest dyadic or by continued fractions.
- The decision which clauses to resolve on conflict is guided by an internal SAT-solver.
- Heuristic about reusing existing constraints when computing polytope R, leading to piecewise linear approximations of g.
- Specialised linearisation algorithms for specific combinations of subclasses of functions $g \in \mathcal{F}_{DA}$ and c_y:
  differentiable: Use Tangent Space Linearisation.
  convex/concave: Derive the polytope R from computability of unique intersections between g and the linear bound on y.
  piecewise: This is a meta-class in the sense that dom g is partitioned into $(P_i)_{i \in I}$ where the P_i are linear or non-linear predicates in y, and for each $i \in I$ there is a linearisation algorithm, then the decision which linearisation to use is based on membership of the exact rational value c_y in one of the P_i.
  rational: Evaluate c_g exactly in order to decide on linearisation to use.
  transcendental: Bound $|c_x - c_g|$ by a rational from below by approximating c_g by the TTE implementation iRRAM[2] [24] in order to compute d.

---

[2] http://irram.uni-trier.de.

Table 1. Benchmarks of $K_{n,d}$ for different n, d.

d	n		ksmt		cvc4		z3		mathsat		yices		dreal		rasat
2	2	s	0.01s	?	0.03s	s	0.01s	s	0.02s	s	0.01s	δ	0.01	s	0.02
	3	s	0.03s	?	0.08s	>	60m	s	0.24s	s	0.03s	δ	0.02	>	8h
	4	>	8h	u	1474.16s	>	60m	u	8.11s	>	17h	δ	0.05	>	8h
	5	u	1.43s	u	0.45s	>	8h	u	0.28s	>	8h	u	3581.96	>	8h
	6	u	5.00s	u	0.75s	>	8h	u	0.40s	>	166m	>	8h	>	8h
3	5	s	0.93s	?	465.45s	>	8h	s	0.12s	s	0.06s	>	8h	>	8h
	6	s	6.02s	>	143m	>	7h	>	8h	>	6h	>	8h	>	8h
4	5	s	0.38s	?	1544.87s	s	2165.78s	s	0.10s	s	7.34s	>	8h	>	8h
	6	s	0.57s	>	91m	>	8h	s	0.23s	s	0.38s	>	8h	>	8h
	7	s	14.27s	>	160m	>	8h	s	0.18s	>	8h	>	8h	>	8h

s: 'sat'
δ: 'δ-sat', δ = 10⁻³
δ = 10^{-3}
u: 'unsat'
?: 'unknown'
>: timeout

Table 2. Benchmarks of C_r for different r.

r		ksmt		cvc4		z3		mathsat		yices		dReal		raSAT
$\sqrt{37}$	u	0.07s	u	0.76s	u	510.67s	u	40.55s	u	0.07s	u	0.01	>	8h
$\sqrt{49}$	u	0.40s	u	2.46s	u	23211.20s	u	6307.18s	u	0.11s	u	0.03	>	8h
$\sqrt{62}$	u	11.61s	u	5.07s	u	210.16s	>	14.5h	u	76.82s	u	2.00	>	8h
$\sqrt{63}$	u	55.84s	?	0.48s	u	3925.65s	>	14.5h	u	0.10s	u	12.38	>	8h
$\sqrt{64}$	s	0.01s	?	0.01s	s	0.00s	>	21.6h	s	0.00s	δ	0.01	>	8h

We evaluated our approach over higher dimensional sphere packing benchmarks which are available at (See footnote 1). Sphere packing is a well known problem which goes back to Kepler's conjecture, and in higher dimensions is also of practical importance e.g., in error correcting codes. The purpose of this evaluation is to exemplify that our approach is viable and can contribute to the current state-of-the-art, extensive evaluation is left for future work.

The solvers[3] were compiled with GCC-8.2 according to their respective documentation (except for mathsat, which is not open-source). Experiments were run on a machine with 32 GiB RAM, 3.6 GHz Core i7 processor and Linux 3.18.

Example 1 (Sphere packing). Let $n, d \in \mathbb{N}$ and let

$$K_{n,d} := \exists \boldsymbol{x}_1, \dots, \boldsymbol{x}_n \in \mathbb{R}^d : \bigwedge_{1 \le i \le n} \|\boldsymbol{x}_i\|_\infty \le 1 \wedge \bigwedge_{1 \le i < j \le n} \|\boldsymbol{x}_i - \boldsymbol{x}_j\|_2 > 2$$

An instance $K_{n,d}$ is sat iff n balls fit into a d-dimensional box of radius 2 without touching each other. In the SMT-Lib language the $\|\cdot\|_\infty$ norms in these instances are formulated using per-component comparisons to the lower and upper endpoints of the range, while the euclidean norms $\|\boldsymbol{s}\|_2 > t$ are expressed by the equivalent squared variant $\sum_i s_i^2 > t^2$. Table 1 provides a comparison of different solvers on instances of this kind.

---

[3] ksmt-0.1.3, cvc4-1.6+gmp, z3-4.7.1+gmp, mathsat-5.5.2, yices-2.6+lpoly-1.7, dreal-v3.16.08.01, rasat-0.3.

Example 2. Let $r \in \mathbb{Q}$, then

$$C_r := \exists x, y \in \mathbb{R}^3 : \|x\|_2^2 \leq r^2 \wedge \|y\|_2^2 \geq 8^2 \wedge \|x - y\|_\infty \leq \tfrac{1}{100}.$$

C_r is `sat` for some $r \in [0, 8]$ iff there is a translation of the center x of the 3-dimensional ball $B_r(x)$ in a box of radius $\frac{1}{100}$ such that it intersects the complement of $B_8(y)$. Since the constraints are expressed as square-root-free expressions, obviously for $r \geq 8 - \frac{1}{100}$, there is a solution. Table 2 list running times for various r of our solver and other solvers of non-linear real arithmetic.

Noteworthy about these benchmarks is the monotonicity of the running times of `ksmt` in contrast to e.g. `yices` in conjunction with unlimited precision, which seems to be what prevents `cvc4` from deciding the instance for $r = \sqrt{63}$ and even $r = \sqrt{64}$.

These experiments show that already in the early stage of the implementation, our system can handle high dimensional non-linear problems which are challenging for most SMT solvers.

7   Conclusions and Future Work

In this paper we presented a new approach for solving non-linear constraints over the reals. Our `ksmt` calculus combines model-guided solution search with targeted linearisations for resolving non-linear conflicts. We implemented our approach in the `ksmt` system, our preliminary evaluation shows promising results demonstrating viability of the proposed approach.

For future work we are developing more precise linearisations for specific trigonometric functions and are analyzing the complexity of deciding conflicts in general. We are working on extending the applicability of our implementation and a more extensive evaluation. We are also investigating theoretical properties of our calculus, such completeness in restricted settings and δ-completeness.

Acknowledgements. We thank the anonymous reviewers and Stefan Ratschan for their helpful comments.

References

1. Benhamou, F., Granvilliers, L.: Continuous and interval constraints. In: Handbook of Constraint Programming, pp. 571–603. Elsevier (2006)
2. Brattka, V., Hertling, P., Weihrauch, K.: A tutorial on computable analysis. In: Cooper, S.B., Löwe, B., Sorbi, A. (eds.) New Computational Paradigms, pp. 425–491. Springer, Heidelberg (2008). https://doi.org/10.1007/978-0-387-68546-5_18
3. Buchberger, B.: A theoretical basis for the reduction of polynomials to canonical forms. ACM SIGSAM Bull. **10**(3), 19–29 (1976)
4. Cimatti, A., Griggio, A., Irfan, A., Roveri, M., Sebastiani, R.: Incremental linearization for satisfiability and verification modulo nonlinear arithmetic and transcendental functions. ACM Trans. Comput. Log. **19**(3), 19:1–19:52 (2018)

5. Collins, G.E.: Quantifier elimination for real closed fields by cylindrical algebraic decompostion. In: Brakhage, H. (ed.) GI-Fachtagung 1975. LNCS, vol. 33, pp. 134–183. Springer, Heidelberg (1975). https://doi.org/10.1007/3-540-07407-4_17
6. de Moura, L., Jovanović, D.: A model-constructing satisfiability calculus. In: Giacobazzi, R., Berdine, J., Mastroeni, I. (eds.) VMCAI 2013. LNCS, vol. 7737, pp. 1–12. Springer, Heidelberg (2013). https://doi.org/10.1007/978-3-642-35873-9_1
7. Dolzmann, A., Sturm, T.: REDLOG: computer algebra meets computer logic. ACM SIGSAM Bull. 31(2), 2–9 (1997)
8. Dragan, I., Korovin, K., Kovács, L., Voronkov, A.: Bound propagation for arithmetic reasoning in Vampire. In: Proceedings SYNASC 2013, pp. 169–176. IEEE (2013)
9. Fontaine, P., Ogawa, M., Sturm, T., To, V.K., Vu, X.T.: Wrapping computer algebra is surprisingly successful for non-linear SMT. In: SC-Square 2018, Oxford, United Kingdom, July 2018
10. Fränzle, M., Herde, C., Teige, T., Ratschan, S., Schubert, T.: Efficient solving of large non-linear arithmetic constraint systems with complex Boolean structure. JSAT 1(3–4), 209–236 (2007)
11. Gao, S., Avigad, J., Clarke, E.M.: δ-complete decision procedures for satisfiability over the reals. In: Gramlich, B., Miller, D., Sattler, U. (eds.) IJCAR 2012. LNCS (LNAI), vol. 7364, pp. 286–300. Springer, Heidelberg (2012). https://doi.org/10.1007/978-3-642-31365-3_23
12. Hladík, M., Ratschan, S.: Efficient solution of a class of quantified constraints with quantifier prefix Exists-Forall. Math. Comput. Sci. 8(3–4), 329–340 (2014)
13. Jovanović, D., de Moura, L.: Solving non-linear arithmetic. In: Gramlich, B., Miller, D., Sattler, U. (eds.) IJCAR 2012. LNCS (LNAI), vol. 7364, pp. 339–354. Springer, Heidelberg (2012). https://doi.org/10.1007/978-3-642-31365-3_27
14. Kapur, D., Sun, Y., Wang, D.: A new algorithm for computing comprehensive Gröbner systems. In: Proceedings ISSAC 2010, pp. 29–36. ACM, New York, USA (2010)
15. Korovin, K., Košta, M., Sturm, T.: Towards conflict-driven learning for virtual substitution. In: Gerdt, V.P., Koepf, W., Seiler, W.M., Vorozhtsov, E.V. (eds.) CASC 2014. LNCS, vol. 8660, pp. 256–270. Springer, Cham (2014). https://doi.org/10.1007/978-3-319-10515-4_19
16. Korovin, K., Tsiskaridze, N., Voronkov, A.: Implementing conflict resolution. In: Clarke, E., Virbitskaite, I., Voronkov, A. (eds.) PSI 2011. LNCS, vol. 7162, pp. 362–376. Springer, Heidelberg (2012). https://doi.org/10.1007/978-3-642-29709-0_31
17. Korovin, K., Tsiskaridze, N., Voronkov, A.: Conflict resolution. In: Gent, I.P. (ed.) CP 2009. LNCS, vol. 5732, pp. 509–523. Springer, Heidelberg (2009). https://doi.org/10.1007/978-3-642-04244-7_41
18. Korovin, K., Voronkov, A.: Solving systems of linear inequalities by bound propagation. In: Bjørner, N., Sofronie-Stokkermans, V. (eds.) CADE 2011. LNCS (LNAI), vol. 6803, pp. 369–383. Springer, Heidelberg (2011). https://doi.org/10.1007/978-3-642-22438-6_28
19. Lefévre, V.: Moyens arithmetiques pour un calcul fiable. PhD thesis, École normale supérieure de Lyon (2000)
20. Loos, R., Weispfenning, V.: Applying linear quantifier elimination. Comput. J. 36(5), 450–462 (1993)

21. Maréchal, A., Fouilhé, A., King, T., Monniaux, D., Périn, M.: Polyhedral approximation of multivariate polynomials using Handelman's theorem. In: Jobstmann, B., Leino, K.R.M. (eds.) VMCAI 2016. LNCS, vol. 9583, pp. 166–184. Springer, Heidelberg (2016). https://doi.org/10.1007/978-3-662-49122-5_8

22. Marques-Silva, J.P., Sakallah, K.A.: GRASP: a search algorithm for propositional satisfiability. IEEE Trans. Comput. **48**(5), 506–521 (1999)

23. McMillan, K.L., Kuehlmann, A., Sagiv, M.: Generalizing DPLL to richer logics. In: Bouajjani, A., Maler, O. (eds.) CAV 2009. LNCS, vol. 5643, pp. 462–476. Springer, Heidelberg (2009). https://doi.org/10.1007/978-3-642-02658-4_35

24. Müller, N.T.: The iRRAM: exact arithmetic in C++. In: Blanck, J., Brattka, V., Hertling, P. (eds.) CCA 2000. LNCS, vol. 2064, pp. 222–252. Springer, Heidelberg (2001). https://doi.org/10.1007/3-540-45335-0_14

25. Nieuwenhuis, R., Oliveras, A., Tinelli, C.: Solving SAT and SAT modulo theories: from an abstract Davis-Putnam-Logemann-Loveland procedure to DPLL(T). J. ACM **53**(6), 937–977 (2006)

26. Niven, I.: Irrational Numbers. Mathematical Association of America, Washington, D.C. (1956)

27. Passmore, G.O., Paulson, L.C., de Moura, L.: Real algebraic strategies for Meti-Tarski proofs. In: Jeuring, J., et al. (eds.) CICM 2012. LNCS (LNAI), vol. 7362, pp. 358–370. Springer, Heidelberg (2012). https://doi.org/10.1007/978-3-642-31374-5_24

28. Reger, G., Bjørner, N., Suda, M., Voronkov, A.: AVATAR modulo theories. In: Benzmüller, C., Sutcliffe, G., Rojas, R. (eds.), 2nd Global Conference on Artificial Intelligence, EPiC Series in Computing, vol. 41, pp. 39–52. EasyChair (2016)

29. Reynolds, A., Tinelli, C., Jovanović, D., Barrett, C.: Designing theory solvers with extensions. In: Dixon, C., Finger, M. (eds.) FroCoS 2017. LNCS (LNAI), vol. 10483, pp. 22–40. Springer, Cham (2017). https://doi.org/10.1007/978-3-319-66167-4_2

30. Richardson, D.: Some undecidable problems involving elementary functions of a real variable. J. Symb. Log. **33**(4), 514–520 (1968)

31. Tarski, A.: A decision method for elementary algebra and geometry. In: 2nd edn. University of California (1951)

32. Weihrauch, K.: Computable Analysis: An Introduction. Springer, Secaucus (2000). https://doi.org/10.1007/978-3-642-56999-9

Restricted Cutting Plane Proofs in Horn Constraint Systems

Hans Kleine Büning[1], Piotr Wojciechowski[2(✉)], R. Chandrasekaran[3], and K. Subramani[2]

[1] Computer Science Institute, University of Paderborn, Paderborn, Germany
kbcsl@uni-paderborn.de
[2] LCSEE, West Virginia University, Morgantown, WV, USA
pwojciec@mix.wvu.edu, k.subramani@mail.wvu.edu
[3] Computer Science and Engineering, The University of Texas at Dallas, Richardson, USA
chandra@utdallas.edu

Abstract. In this paper, we investigate variants of cutting plane proof systems for a class of integer programs called *Horn constraint systems (HCS)*. Briefly a system of linear inequalities $\mathbf{A} \cdot \mathbf{x} \geq \mathbf{b}$ is called a Horn constraint system, if each entry in $\mathbf{A}$ belongs to the set $\{0, 1, -1\}$ and furthermore there is at most one positive entry per row. Our focus is on deriving refutations i.e., proofs of unsatisfiability of such programs in variants of the cutting plane proof system. Horn systems generalize Horn formulas, i.e., CNF formulas with at most one positive literal per clause. A Horn system which results from rewriting a Horn clausal formula is called a Horn clausal constraint system (HClCS). The cutting plane calculus (CP) is a well-known calculus for deciding the unsatisfiability of propositional CNF formulas and integer programs. Usually, CP consists of the addition rule (ADD) and the division rule (DIV). We show that the cutting plane calculus with the addition rule only (CP-ADD) does not require constraints of the form $0 \leq x_i \leq 1$. We also investigate the existence of read-once refutations in Horn clausal constraint systems in the cutting plane proof system. We show that read-once refutations are **incomplete** and furthermore the problem of checking for the existence of a read-once refutation in an arbitrary Horn clausal system is **NP-complete**.

1 Introduction

In this paper, we investigate refutability in Horn constraint systems. Horn constraint systems define a class of polyhedra that find applications in a number of disparate domains [4]. A refutation of an unsatisfiable constraint system (not necessarily Horn) is a negative certificate that attests to the infeasibility of the system. When an algorithm produces a certificate to accompany the output, it is called a certifying algorithm [19]. The literature is replete with certifying algorithms for a number of problems in combinatorial optimization, especially

© Springer Nature Switzerland AG 2019
A. Herzig and A. Popescu (Eds.): FroCoS 2019, LNAI 11715, pp. 149–164, 2019.
https://doi.org/10.1007/978-3-030-29007-8_9

as they relate to graphical structures [5,13,18]. Likewise, there exist a number
of combinatorial algorithms for Horn constraint systems that do not produce
negative certificates [4,22]. This paper discusses negative certificates for Horn
constraint systems in a number of interesting proof systems.

The focus of this paper is on read-once refutations in various proof systems.
In a read-once refutation, each constraint defining the polyhedron can be used at
most *once* in an inference step of the proof system. The advantage of read-once
refutations is that they are short by definition [11]. In general, read-once proof
systems are not complete in that there exist unsatisfiable constraint systems for
which read-once refutations do not exist. A variant of read-once refutation called
input refutation is discussed in [10].

We also utilize cutting plane calculus on Horn constraint systems generated
from Horn formulas. This extends the research in [9] which linked unit resolution
and polyhedral projection.

The principal contributions of this paper are:

1. A proof that the problem of determining if a system of Horn constraints has
   a read-once refutation using only the ADD rule is **NP-complete**.
2. A proof that the problem of determining if a system of Horn constraints has
   a read-once refutation using the ADD and DIV rules is **NP-complete**.
3. A proof that when using only the ADD rule, the constraints $0 \leq x_i \leq 1$
   are redundant when the Horn clausal system is reduced to an integer/linear
   program.
4. A proof that the problem of determining if a system of Horn constraints
   derived from Horn clauses has a read-once refutation using only the ADD
   rule is **NP-complete**.
5. A proof that the problem of determining if a system of Horn constraints
   derived from Horn clauses has a read-once refutation using the ADD and
   DIV rules is **NP-complete**.

The rest of the paper is organized as follows. In Sect. 2, we describe the constraint systems and proof systems under consideration. Section 3 details the problems examined in this paper. In Sect. 4, we discuss the motivation for the problems and describe related work. Section 5 examines systems of Horn constraints.
In Sect. 6, we examine properties of systems of constraints derived from Horn
clausal formulas. Finally, Sect. 7 summarizes our results and describes avenues
for future research.

2   Preliminaries

In this section, we briefly discuss the terms used in this paper.

Definition 1. *A Horn constraint, is a constraint of the form* $\mathbf{a} \cdot \mathbf{x} \geq b$ *where:*

1. *Each element of* $\mathbf{a}$ *belongs to the set* $\{0, 1, -1\}$ *and at most one element of* $\mathbf{a}$
   is 1.
2. *b is an integer.*

Definition 2. *In a Horn constraint* $\mathbf{a} \cdot \mathbf{x} \geq b$, *$b$ is known as the defining constant.*

We can now define a Horn constraint system.

Definition 3. *A conjunction of Horn constraints is known as a Horn Constraint system (HCS). An HCS with m constraints over n variables can be represented in matrix form as* $\mathbf{A} \cdot \mathbf{x} \geq \mathbf{b}$ *where:*

1. *$\mathbf{A}$ is an $m \times n$ matrix.*
2. *The entries in $\mathbf{A}$ belong to the set $\{0, 1, -1\}$.*
3. *Each row of $\mathbf{A}$ contains at most one positive entry.*
4. *$\mathbf{x}$ is an n dimensional vector.*
5. *$\mathbf{b}$ is an integral m dimensional vector.*

There are two main feasibility queries for HCSs depending on how we restrict the domain of $\mathbf{x}$. These are as follows:

Definition 4. *An HCS, $\mathbf{A} \cdot \mathbf{x} \geq \mathbf{b}$ is linear feasible if there exists an $\mathbf{x}^* \in \mathbb{R}^n$ such that $\mathbf{A} \cdot \mathbf{x}^* \geq \mathbf{b}$.*

Definition 5. *An HCS, $\mathbf{A} \cdot \mathbf{x} \geq \mathbf{b}$ is integer feasible if there exists an $\mathbf{x}^* \in \mathbb{Z}^n$ such that $\mathbf{A} \cdot \mathbf{x}^* \geq \mathbf{b}$.*

For both of these queries, we are interested in certificates of infeasibility; in particular, we are interested in restricted cutting-plane refutations. In linear programs (systems of linear inequalities), we use the following rule, which plays the role that resolution does in clausal formulas:

$$\mathbf{ADD}: \frac{\sum_{i=1}^{n} a_i \cdot x_i \geq b_1 \qquad \sum_{i=1}^{n} a_i' \cdot x_i \geq b_2}{\sum_{i=1}^{n}(a_i + a_i') \cdot x_i \geq b_1 + b_2} \tag{1}$$

We refer to Rule (1) as the *ADD* rule. It is easy to see that Rule (1) is sound in that any assignment satisfying the hypotheses **must** satisfy the consequent. Furthermore, the rule is **complete** in that if the original system is linear infeasible (has no real valued solutions), then repeated application of Rule (1) will result in a contradiction of the form: $0 \geq -b$, $b < 0$. The completeness of the ADD rule was established by Farkas [7], in a lemma that is famously known as Farkas' Lemma for systems of linear inequalities [21].

Farkas' lemma along with the fact that linear programs must have basic feasible solutions establishes that the linear programming problem is in the complexity class **NP** $\cap$ **coNP**. Farkas' lemma is one of several lemmata that consider pairs of linear systems in which exactly one element of the pair is feasible. These lemmas are collectively referred to as "Theorems of the Alternative" [20].

Definition 6. *A linear refutation is a sequence of applications of the ADD rule that results in a contradiction of the form $0 \geq b, b > 0$.*

When studying integer feasibility, we typically use an additional rule. This is referred to as the *DIV* rule and is described as follows

$$\textbf{DIV} : \frac{\sum_{i=1}^{n} a_{ij} \cdot x_i \geq b_j \qquad d \in \mathbb{Z}^+ : \frac{a_{ij}}{d} \in \mathbb{Z}, \, i = 1 \ldots n}{\sum_{i=1}^{n} \frac{a_{ij}}{d} \cdot x_i \geq \left\lceil \frac{b_j}{d} \right\rceil} \qquad (2)$$

Rule (2) corresponds to dividing a constraint by a common divisor d of the left-hand coefficients and then rounding the right-hand side. Since each $\frac{a_{ij}}{d}$ is an integer this inference preserves integer solutions but doesn't necessarily preserve linear solutions. However, for systems of Horn constraints the DIV rule preserves linear feasibility, since in Horn polyhedra, linear feasibility implies integer feasibility [4].

Any constraint derived using either the ADD rule or the DIV rule is called a cutting plane. Similarly, a refutation utilizing cutting plane calculus is a refutation utilizing the ADD rule and the DIV rule.

Note that for systems of Horn constraints, an integer refutation still proves linear infeasibility.

We can look at the additional restriction, that each application of the ADD rule must use at least one absolute constraint (a constraint with only one variable). Such a refutation is known as a **unit** refutation. Note that in a unit refutation, at least one coefficient in a non-redundant derived constraint is 1 or -1. Thus, the DIV rule will never be used.

We now formally define the types of refutation discussed in this paper.

Definition 7. *A* **Read-Once** *refutation is a refutation in which each constraint, can be used at most once. This applies to constraints present in the original system and those derived as a result of previous applications of the inference rules.*

Note that this applies to both linear refutations and integer refutations.

We also study constraint systems generated from clausal formulas. We assume that the reader is familiar with elementary propositional logic.

Definition 8. *A* **literal** *is a variable x or its complement $\neg x$. x is termed a positive and $\neg x$ is termed a negative literal.*

Definition 9. *A* **CNF clause** *is a disjunction of literals. The empty clause, which is always false, is denoted as $\sqcup$.*

Using this definition of a clause, we can now define what a CNF formula is.

Definition 10. *A* **CNF formula** *is a conjunction of CNF clauses.*

Definition 11. *A* **Horn** *clause is a CNF clause which contains at most one positive literal.*

From any CNF formula, we can construct a corresponding constraint system. In order to avoid case distinctions we assume that no tautological clause occurs in the formulas.

Definition 12. *Let* $\alpha = \alpha_1, \ldots, \alpha_m$ *be a CNF formula*

1. *For each clause* $\alpha_i = (x_1 \vee \ldots \vee x_n \vee \neg y_1 \vee \ldots \vee \neg y_t)$, *we create the constraint* $(x_1 + \ldots + x_n - y_1 \ldots - y_t) \geq 1 - t$.
   The constraint is denoted as $S(\alpha_i)$. $S(\alpha) := \{S(\alpha_1), \ldots, S(\alpha_m)\}$ *is called the* **standard representation** *of* α.
2. *The* **extended representation** *additionally adds for each variable* x *the constraints* $x \geq 0$ *and* $-x \geq -1$ *to* $S(\alpha)$. *Such a representation is denoted as* $E(\alpha)$.

For each clause α_i in α, we also define the following:

Definition 13.

1. $L(\alpha_i)$ *is the left hand side of the constraint* $S(\alpha_i)$.
2. $R(\alpha_i)$ *is the right hand side of the constraint* $S(\alpha_i)$.
3. $Neg(\alpha_i)$ *is the number of negative literals in* α_i.
4. $Pos(\alpha_i)$ *is the number of positive literals in* α_i.
5. $|\alpha_i|$ *is the number of literals in* α_i.

For a Horn formula α, we refer to the resultant constraint systems ($S(\alpha)$ and $E(\alpha)$) as Horn clausal constraint systems (HClCSs).

3 Statement of Problems

In this section, we define the problems under consideration.
   For systems of Horn constrains, we consider the following problems:

1. ROR(ADD): Does a system of Horn constraints have a read-once refutation using only the ADD rule?
2. ROR(ADD, DIV): Does a system of Horn constraints have a read-once refutation using the ADD and DIV rules?

We also examine constraint systems generated from clausal formulas. As with general systems of constraints, we can consider refutations using only the ADD rule, or both the ADD and DIV rules. This results in the following problems:

1. CP(ADD): Does an HClCS have a refutation using only the ADD rule?
2. CP(ADD, DIV): Does an HClCS have a refutation using the ADD and DIV rules?
3. CP-RO(ADD): Does an HClCS have a read-once refutation using only the ADD rule?
4. CP-RO(ADD, DIV): Does an HClCS have a read-once refutation using the ADD and DIV rules?

It is important to note that both ROR(ADD) and CP-RO(ADD) refer to restricted cutting planes under the read-once proof system; however, the latter applies **only** to Horn clausal systems.

Accordingly, we restate he principal contributions of this paper as follows:

1. A proof that the ROR(ADD) problem for a system of Horn constraints is **NP-complete**.
2. A proof that the ROR(ADD, DIV) problem for a system of Horn constraints is **NP-complete**.
3. A proof that from the perspective of CP(ADD), the constraints $0 \leq x_i \leq 1$ are redundant when the Horn clausal system is reduced to an integer/linear program.
4. A proof that CP-RO(ADD) and CP-RO(ADD, DIV) are **NP-complete** for HClCS.

To obtain several of these results we utilize a reduction from the set packing problem.

Definition 14. *The* **set packing** *problem is the following: Given a set S, m subsets $S_1, \ldots, S_m$ of S, and an integer k, does $\{S_1, \ldots, S_m\}$ contain k mutually disjoint sets.*

This problem is known to be **NP-complete** [14].

4   Motivation and Related Work

Clausal and polyhedral Horn systems have been studied widely in the literature; some of the important applications of the same have been discussed in [4]. Horn clauses are used in logic programming and in particular PROLOG [6]. Horn constraints also arise in program verification [2,17]. Indeed, the HVCS Workshop focuses exclusively on the use of Horn clauses for verification [12]. A linear time algorithm for Horn clauses is discussed in [6].

Horn constraint systems arise in program verification as well [1,8]. Horn constraint systems share an interesting property with difference constraint systems in that the Horn system $\mathbf{A} \cdot \mathbf{x} \geq \mathbf{b}$ has a linear solution if and only if it has an integer solution [4]. Recall that a difference constraint is a linear constraint of the form: $x_i - x_j \geq b_{ij}$. Thus, the techniques discussed in this paper simultaneously provide proofs of both linear and integer infeasibility.

It follows that the length and the structure of proofs (refutations) for Horn constraints are of interest. It is well-known that cutting plane proofs can be exponentially shorter than resolution proofs [3]. Therefore, the comparison of the refutation complexities for various restrictions of CP-systems should be of interest, too.

The current work leads to a better understanding of cutting plane proofs for Horn formulas for various restrictions of cutting plane systems based on the addition and division rule, which can also be compared with resolution based proofs. For example, in favorable circumstances the division rule can be used to reduce the length of CP-proofs compared to proofs using only the addition rule. [15] describes some of our recent work in read-once proofs in Horn clauses. This paper is concerned with Horn constraints.

5 The ROR Problem for Horn Constraint Systems

In this section, we study systems of Horn constraints. Note that not every system of Horn constraints has a read-once refutation.

Example 1. Consider the system of Horn constraints

$$
\begin{aligned}
l_1 &: & x_1 &\geq 1 \\
l_2 &: & -x_1 + x_2 &\geq 1 \\
l_3 &: & -x_1 - x_2 + x_3 &\geq 1 \\
l_4 &: -x_1 - x_2 - x_3 + x_4 &\geq 1 \\
l_5 &: -x_1 - x_2 - x_3 - x_4 &\geq -14
\end{aligned}
$$

The constraint l_5 is necessary for any refutation. To cancel each x_i, $i = 1 \ldots 4$, the constraint l_i, $i = 1 \ldots 4$ must also be used in the refutation. Thus, all five constraints need to be used in any refutation.

However to get a positive number on the right-hand side of the resultant constraint we need to use some of the constraints l_1 through l_4 more than once. Thus, this system does not have a read-once linear refutation.

We now show that ROR(ADD) is **NP-complete** for HCSs. This is done by a reduction from the set packing problem. Note that a read-once refutation is guaranteed to be polynomially sized with respect to the input. Thus, ROR(ADD) is trivially in **NP** for HCSs. All that remains is to show that the problem is **NP-hard**.

Theorem 1. *ROR(ADD) for Horn constraints is* **NP-hard**.

Proof. Let us consider an instance of the set packing problem. We construct the system of Horn constraints **H** as follows.

1. For each $x_i \in S$, create the variable x_i and the constraint $x_i \geq 1$.
2. For $j = 1 \ldots k$, create the variable v_j.
3. For each subset S_l, $l = 1 \ldots m$, and each $j = 1 \ldots k$ create the constraints

$$
v_j - \sum_{x_i \in S_l} x_i \geq 1 - |S_l|.
$$

4. Finally create the constraint $-v_1 - \ldots - v_k \geq 1 - k$.

We now show that **H** is in ROR(ADD) if and only if $\{S_1, \ldots, S_m\}$ contains k mutually disjoint sets.

Suppose that $\{S_1, \ldots, S_m\}$ does contain k mutually disjoint sets. Without loss of generality assume that these are the sets $S_1, \ldots, S_k$.

Let us consider the sets of clauses

$$
\mathbf{H}_j = \{v_j - \sum_{x_i \in S_j} x_i \geq 1 - |S_j|\} \cup \{x_i \geq 1 \mid x_i \in S_j\} \qquad j = 1 \ldots k.
$$

By the construction of $\mathbf{H}$, we have that $\mathbf{H}_j \subseteq \mathbf{H}$ for $j = 1 \ldots k$. Since the sets $S_1, \ldots, S_k$ are mutually disjoint, so are the sets $\mathbf{H}_1, \ldots, \mathbf{H}_k$.

It is easy to see that the constraint $v_j \geq 1$ can be derived by summing all of the constraints in $\mathbf{H}_j$. Since this holds for every $j = 1 \ldots k$ and since the sets $\mathbf{H}_1, \ldots, \mathbf{H}_k$ are mutually disjoint, we have that the set of constraints $\{v_1 \geq 1, \ldots, v_k \geq 1\}$ can be derived from $\mathbf{H}$ by read-once linear resolution.

Together with the constraint $-v_1 - \ldots - v_k \geq 1 - k$, this set of constraints sums together to derive the constraint $0 \geq 1$. It follows that $\mathbf{H}$ has a read-once linear refutation.

Now suppose that $\mathbf{H}$ has a read-once linear refutation $\mathbf{R}$. Note that $\mathbf{H}/\{-v_1 - \ldots - v_k \geq 1 - k\}$ can be satisfied by setting every variable to 1. Thus, $\mathbf{R}$ must use the constraint $-v_1 - \ldots - v_k \geq 1 - k$.

By construction, we must cancel $-v_1, \ldots, -v_k$. Let us consider $-v_j$, $1 \leq j \leq k$. By the construction of $\mathbf{H}$, to cancel this term we must use one of the constraints

$$v_j - \sum_{x_i \in S_l} x_i \geq 1 - |S_l| \qquad l = 1 \ldots m.$$

To cancel the $-x_i$ terms introduced by this constraint, we must use the set of constraints $\mathbf{F}_{l_j} = \{x_i \geq 1 \mid x_i \in S_{l_j}\}$ for some $l_j \leq m$.

Since the refutation is read-once we must have that the sets $\mathbf{F}_{l_j}$ for $j = 1 \ldots k$ are mutually disjoint. Thus, the sets S_{l_j} for $j = 1 \ldots k$ are also mutually disjoint. This means that $\{S_1, \ldots, S_m\}$ contains k mutually disjoint sets.

Thus, $\mathbf{H}$ is in ROR(ADD) if and only if $\{S_1, \ldots, S_m\}$ contains k mutually disjoint sets. As a result of this, the linear ROR problem for systems of Horn constraints is **NP-hard**. $\qquad\square$

6   Horn Clausal Constraint Systems

In this section, we study systems of Horn constraints generated from Horn formulas.

Recall that from a Horn formula α we can define two systems of Horn constraints $S(\alpha)$ and $E(\alpha)$. Note that $E(\alpha)$ adds the restriction that each variable is in the interval $[0, 1]$. We now show that this restriction is unnecessary. First we need to prove the following properties of constraint systems generated from CNF formulas.

Theorem 2. Let α be a CNF formula with m clauses. If $S(\alpha) \in CP(ADD)$, then α contains a unit clause.

Proof. Since $S(\alpha) \in \mathrm{CP}(\mathrm{ADD})$, we have that there exists a refutation R of $S(\alpha)$ using only the ADD rule. For each clause α_i in α, let k_i be the number of times the constraint $S(\alpha_i)$ is used in R. Thus, we have that the constraint

$$\sum_{i=1}^{m} k_i \cdot L(\alpha_i) \geq \sum_{i=1}^{m} k_i \cdot R(\alpha_i)$$

is equivalent the contradiction $0 \geq b$ for some integer $b > 0$. This means that $\sum_{i=1}^{m} k_i \cdot L(\alpha_i) = 0$ and $\sum_{i=1}^{m} k_i \cdot R(\alpha_i) > 0$.

Since $\sum_{i=1}^{m} k_i \cdot L(\alpha_i) = 0$, then, counting repeats, each variable must appear an equal number of times as a positive literal and as a negative literal. Thus, $\sum_{i=1}^{m} k_i \cdot Neg(\alpha_i) = \sum_{i=1}^{m} k_i \cdot Pos(\alpha_i)$.

By definition,

$$\sum_{i=1}^{m} k_i \cdot R(\alpha_i) = \sum_{i=1}^{m} k_i \cdot (1 - Neg(\alpha_i)).$$

Thus,

$$\sum_{i=1}^{m} k_i \cdot (1 - Neg(\alpha_i)) = \sum_{i=1}^{m} k_i \cdot (1 - Pos(\alpha_i)) > 0.$$

This means that

$$\sum_{i=1}^{m} k_i \cdot (2 - |\alpha_i|) = \sum_{i=1}^{m} k_i \cdot (2 - Neg(\alpha_i) - Pos(\alpha_i))$$

$$= \sum_{i=1}^{m} k_i \cdot (1 - Neg(\alpha_i)) + \sum_{i=1}^{m} k_i \cdot (1 - Pos(\alpha_i))$$

$$> 0.$$

Suppose α contains no unit clause. Then for each clause α_i in α, we have $|\alpha_i| \geq 2$. Thus, $\sum_{i=1}^{m} k_i \cdot (2 - |\alpha_i|) \leq 0$. However this contradicts the fact that $\sum_{i=1}^{m} k_i \cdot (2 - |\alpha_i|) > 0$. Thus, α must contain a unit clause. $\square$

Theorem 3. *If $E(\alpha) \in CP(ADD)$, then α contains a unit clause.*

Proof. Suppose there is a formula $\alpha = \{\alpha_1, \ldots, \alpha_m\}$ with no unit clause such that $E(\alpha) \in CP(ADD)$. By Theorem 2, $S(\alpha) \notin CP(ADD)$.

Let R be a refutation of $E(\alpha)$ that uses only the ADD rule. For each clause α_i, $i = 1 \ldots m$, let k_i be the number of times the constraint $S(\alpha_i)$ is used in R. Let l_R the constraint

$$\sum_{1 \leq i \leq m} k_i \cdot L(\alpha_i) \geq \sum_{1 \leq i \leq m} k_i \cdot (1 - Neg(\alpha_i)).$$

Let $P(R)$ be the set of variables that have positive coefficient in the constraint l_R and let $N(R)$ be the set of variables with negative coefficient in l_R. For each variable $x \in P(R)$, let c_x be the coefficient of x in l_R. For each variable $y \in N(R)$, let $-d_y$ be the coefficient of y in l_R. Thus,

$$\sum_{1 \leq i \leq m} k_i \cdot L(\alpha_i) = \sum_{x \in P(R)} c_x \cdot x - \sum_{y \in N(R)} d_y \cdot y.$$

This means that l_R is equivalent to the constraint

$$\sum_{x \in P(R)} c_x \cdot x - \sum_{y \in N(R)} d_y \cdot y \geq \sum_{1 \leq i \leq m} k_i \cdot (1 - Neg(\alpha_i)).$$

The remaining constraints used by R must be from $E(\alpha) \setminus S(\alpha)$. Thus, these constraints must be of the form $x \geq 0$ or $-x \geq -1$ for some variable x. Since R is a refutation, the final constraint derived must be of the form $0 \geq b$ where $b > 0$. Thus the constraints used by R from $E(\alpha) \setminus S(\alpha)$ must cancel c_x copies of each , $x \in P(R)$ and d_y copies of $-y$ for each $y \in N(R)$. Thus, R must have c_x copies of the constraint $-x \geq -1$ for each $x \in P(R)$ and d_y copies of the constraint $y \geq 0$ for each y in $N(R)$. Including these constraints in the summation results in the constraint

$$0 \geq \sum_{1 \leq i \leq m} k_i \cdot (1 - Neg(\alpha_i)) - \sum_{x \in P(R)} c_x.$$

Since R is a refutation, we must have that

$$\sum_{1 \leq i \leq m} k_i \cdot (1 - Neg(\alpha_i)) - \sum_{x \in P(R)} c_x > 0. \tag{3}$$

Let $\beta = \{\beta_1, \ldots, \beta_m\}$ be the CNF formula obtained by negating every variable in $P(R)$.

We have that

$$\sum_{1 \leq i \leq m} k_i \cdot L(\beta_i) = -\sum_{x \in P(R)} c_x \cdot x - \sum_{y \in N(R)} d_y \cdot y.$$

Since only variables with negative coefficients remain in this summation, we have

$$\sum_{i=1}^{m} k_i \cdot Neg(\beta_i) \geq \sum_{i=1}^{m} k_i \cdot Pos(\beta_i).$$

Thus,

$$\sum_{i=1}^{m} k_i \cdot (2 - |\beta_i|) = \sum_{i=1}^{m} k_i \cdot (2 - Pos(\beta_i) - Neg(\beta_i))$$

$$\geq \sum_{i=1}^{m} k_i \cdot (2 - 2 \cdot Neg(\beta_i))$$

$$= 2 \cdot \sum_{i=1}^{m} k_i \cdot (1 - Neg(\beta_i)).$$

Since α, and thus β has no unit clause, we have that for each clause β_i, $|\beta_i| \geq 2$. Thus, $\sum_{i=1}^{m} k_i \cdot (2 - |\beta_i|) \leq 0$ and $\sum_{i=1}^{m} k_i \cdot (1 - Neg(\beta_i)) \leq 0$.

Note the following:

$$\sum_{i=1}^{m} k_i \cdot Neg(\beta_i) - \sum_{i=1}^{m} k_i \cdot Pos(\beta_i) = \sum_{y \in N(R)} d_y + \sum_{x \in P(R)} c_x.$$

$$\sum_{i=1}^{m} k_i \cdot Neg(\alpha_i) - \sum_{i=1}^{m} k_i \cdot Pos(\alpha_i) = \sum_{y \in N(R)} d_y - \sum_{x \in P(R)} c_x.$$

$$\sum_{i=1}^{m} k_i \cdot Neg(\alpha_i) + \sum_{i=1}^{m} k_i \cdot Pos(\alpha_i) = \sum_{i=1}^{m} k_i \cdot Neg(\beta_i) + \sum_{i=1}^{m} k_i \cdot Pos(\beta_i).$$

Thus,

$$\sum_{i=1}^{m} k_i \cdot Neg(\beta_i) = \sum_{i=1}^{m} k_i \cdot Neg(\alpha_i) + \sum_{x \in P(R)} c_x.$$

This means that,

$$0 \geq \sum_{i=1}^{m} k_i \cdot (1 - Neg(\beta_i)) = \sum_{i=1}^{m} k_i \cdot (1 - Neg(\alpha_i)) - \sum_{x \in P(R)} c_x$$

However, this contradicts System (3). Thus, α contains a unit clause. □

We now use these results to show that the addition of the $0 \leq x_i \leq 1$ constraints does not affect the feasibility of the constraint system.

Theorem 4. *For all CNF formulas* α: $S(\alpha) \in CP(ADD)$ *if and only if* $E(\alpha) \in CP(ADD)$.

Proof. If α has a unit clause (x_i), then $S(\alpha)$ contains the constraint $x_i \geq 1$. We can eliminate this constraint from $S(\alpha)$ by summing it with all constraints containing the term $-x_i$. A similar process can be used to eliminate the constraint $-x_i \geq 0$ from $S(\alpha)$ if α contains the unit clause $(\neg x_i)$. We can repeat this process until either we derive a contradiction of the form $0 \geq b$, $b > 0$ or until all constraints corresponding to unit clauses have been eliminated from $S(\alpha)$.

If we derived a contradiction, then this contradiction was derived using only the ADD rule. Thus, $S(\alpha) \in CP(ADD)$. Since $E(\alpha)$ is obtained by adding constraints to $S(\alpha)$, we have that $E(\alpha) \in CP(ADD)$.

If we derive a system with no constraints corresponding to unit clauses, or if α had no unit clauses, then by Theorem 3, $E(\alpha) \notin CP(ADD)$. Since $E(\alpha)$ is obtained by adding constraints to $S(\alpha)$, we have that $S(\alpha) \notin CP(ADD)$. □

Thus, we can assume without loss of generality that the system of constraints generated from the CNF formula α is $S(\alpha)$. It is important to note that the above theorems hold for arbitrary CNF formulas. However, if linear feasibility does not imply integer feasibility of the clausal system, then CP(ADD) is no longer a complete proof system. As shown in the literature, Horn constraint systems in general and Horn clausal systems in particular, have the property that the corresponding constraint system is linear feasible if and only if it is integer feasible [4].

6.1   Addition Rule for Horn Clausal Constraint Systems

First, we study refutations of systems of Horn clause constraints that use only the ADD rule.

We now examine the complexity of determining if an HClCS has a read-once refutation using only the ADD rule.

Lemma 1. *If Φ is an unsatisfiable system of Horn clauses, then the HClCS $S(\Phi) \in CP(ADD)$.*

Proof. We do this by showing that a linear refutation can simulate positive unit resolution. Consider a single resolution step. Let (x) and $(\neg x \vee \neg x_1 \vee \ldots \vee \neg x_s \vee y)$ be two clauses. The resolvent is $(\neg x_1 \vee \ldots \vee \neg x_s \vee y)$.

The constraints corresponding to the original clauses are $x \geq 1$ and $-x - x_1 - \ldots - x_s + y \geq 1 - s$. Summing these inequalities results in $-x_1 - \ldots - x_s + y \geq 1 - (s - 1)$. This is the inequality corresponding to the resolvent. □

Lemma 2. *If Φ has a read-once unit resolution refutation, then the HClCS $S(\Phi) \in CP\text{-}RO(ADD)$. Moreover, $S(\Phi)$ has a read-once unit refutation under the ADD rule.*

This is a direct consequence of Lemma 1.

From [16], we know that determining if a Horn formula has a read-once unit resolution refutation is **NP-complete**. Thus we have the following result.

Corollary 1. *The CP-RO(ADD) problem for HClCSs is* **NP-complete**.

6.2   Division Rule for Horn Clausal Constraint Systems

In this section, we study refutations of systems of Horn clause constraints that use both the ADD rule and the DIV rule.

Example 2. There are CNF formulas α such that $S(\alpha) \in CP\text{-}RO(ADD, DIV)$ which cannot be renamed into Horn formulas. Let α be the formula

$$(x \vee y), (\neg x \vee y), (x \vee \neg y), (\neg x \vee \neg y).$$

$S(\alpha)$ has the following CP-RO(ADD, DIV) refutation:

1. Apply the ADD rule to $x + y \geq 1$ and $-x + y \geq 0$ to obtain $2 \cdot y \geq 1$.
2. Apply the DIV rule to $2 \cdot y \geq 1$ to obtain $y \geq 1$.
3. Apply the ADD rule to $x - y \geq 0$ and $-x - y \geq -1$ to obtain $-2 \cdot y \geq -1$.
4. Apply the DIV rule to $-2 \cdot y \geq -1$ to obtain $-y \geq 0$.
5. Apply the ADD rule to $y \geq 1$ and $-y \geq 0$ to obtain the contradiction $0 \geq 1$.

With the addition of the DIV rule, additional constraint systems have read-once refutations.

Lemma 3. *There is a Horn formula Φ such that $S(\Phi) \in CP\text{-}RO(ADD, DIV)$ and $S(\Phi) \notin CP\text{-}RO(ADD)$.*

Proof. Let $\Phi = (\neg x_1 \vee \neg x_2 \vee x_3) \wedge (\neg x_1 \vee x_2) \wedge (x_1) \wedge (\neg x_1 \vee \neg x_2 \vee \neg x_3)$.
This corresponds to the HClCS

$$l_1 : -x_1 - x_2 + x_3 \geq -1$$
$$l_2 : \qquad -x_1 + x_2 \geq 0$$
$$l_3 : \qquad\qquad x_1 \geq 1$$
$$l_4 : -x_1 - x_2 - x_3 \geq -2$$

This system has the following read-once integer refutation.

First sum the constraints l_1 and l_4 to get the constraint $-2 \cdot x_1 - 2 \cdot x_2 \geq -3$. Then apply the division rule (DIV) with $d = 2$ to get the constraint $-x_1 - x_2 \geq -1$. Now sum this constraint with the constraint l_2. This results in the constraint $-2 \cdot x_1 \geq -1$. Then apply the division rule. with $d = 2$ to get the constraint $-x_1 \geq 0$. Finally, we sum this constraint with constraint l_3 to obtain the contradiction $0 \geq 1$.

However $S(\Phi)$ does not have a read-once refutation using only the ADD rule. The formula is minimal unsatisfiable. Therefore we need to use all four constraints. However summing all four constraints results in the constraint $-2 \cdot x_1 - x_2 \geq -2$. Thus, to derive a contradiction we need to use the constraint l_2 an additional time and the constraint l_3 an additional 3 times.   □

However, not every Horn constraint system has a read-once refutation even with the addition of the DIV rule.

Theorem 5. *There is an unsatisfiable Horn formula Φ such that $S(\Phi) \notin CP\text{-}RO(ADD, DIV)$*

Proof. Let $\Phi = (y_1) \wedge (y_2) \wedge (\neg y_1 \vee x_1) \wedge (\neg y_1 \vee \neg y_2 \vee \neg x_1 \vee x_2) \wedge (\neg y_1 \vee \neg y_2 \vee \neg x_2)$.
This corresponds to the HClCS:

$$l_1 : \quad y_1 \qquad\qquad\qquad \geq 1$$
$$l_2 : \qquad y_2 \qquad\qquad\quad \geq 1$$
$$l_3 : -y_1 \qquad +x_1 \qquad \geq 0$$
$$l_4 : -y_1 - y_2 - x_1 + x_2 \geq -2$$
$$l_5 : -y_1 - y_2 \qquad - x_2 \geq -2$$

Note that $-y_1$ and $-y_2$ each appear in multiple constraints. Thus, the first applications of the ADD rule cannot use either constraint l_1 or l_2. This means that the first application of the ADD rule must be to either constraints l_3 and l_4, constraints l_3 and l_5, or constraints l_4 and l_5.

1. If we apply the ADD rule to constraints l_3 and l_4, then this results in the constraint $-2 \cdot y_1 - y_2 + x_2 \geq -2$. We cannot apply the DIV rule to this constraint. Additionally, $-y_1$ and $-y_2$ still occur in multiple constraints. Thus, l_1 and l_2 cannot be used in the next application of the ADD rule. This means that the next application of the ADD rule involves the new constraint and l_5. This results in the constraint $-3 \cdot y_1 - 2 \cdot y_2 \geq -4$.
2. If we apply the ADD rule to constraints l_3 and l_5, then this results in the constraint $-2 \cdot y_1 - y_2 + x_1 - x_2 \geq -2$. We cannot apply the DIV rule to

this constraint. Additionally, $-y_1$ and $-y_2$ still occur in multiple constraints. Thus, l_1 and l_2 cannot be used in the next application of the ADD rule. This means that the next application of the ADD rule involves the new constraint and l_4. This results in the constraint $-3 \cdot y_1 - 2 \cdot y_2 \geq -4$.

3. If we apply the ADD rule to constraints l_4 and l_5, then this results in the constraint $-2 \cdot y_1 - 2 \cdot y_2 - x_1 \geq -4$. We cannot apply the DIV rule to this constraint. Additionally, $-y_1$ still occurs in multiple constraints and y_2 has a coefficient of 2 in the new constraint. Thus, l_1 and l_2 cannot be used in the next application of the ADD rule. This means that the next application of the ADD rule involves the new constraint and l_3. This results in the constraint $-3 \cdot y_1 - 2 \cdot y_2 \geq -4$.

Note that if the first step is applying the add rule to the constraints l_1 and l_2 the resultant constraint $y_1 + y_2 \geq 2$ encounters the same issues as constraints l_1 and l_2 in the preceding cases.

In all three cases we obtain the constraint $-3 \cdot y_1 - 2 \cdot y_2 \geq -4$. However, we cannot apply the DIV rule to this constraint. Since both $-y_1$ and $-y_2$ have coefficients greater than 1, we cannot use constraints l_1 and l_2 to completely eliminate either of these literals. Thus, the system is not in CP-RO(ADD, DIV).   □

We now show that even with the addition of the DIV rule, the problem of determining if an HClCS has a read-once refutation remains **NP-complete**. This is done by a reduction from the set packing problem.

Theorem 6. *CP-RO(ADD, DIV) is* **NP-complete** *for HClCSs.*

The proof of this theorem can be found in the complete version of the paper. Since HClCSs are a subset of HCSs, we have the following corollary.

Corollary 2. *The ROR(ADD, DIV) problem for HCSs is* **NP-complete**.

7   Conclusion

In this paper, we studied refutability in variants of Horn constraint systems under various proof systems. In particular, the constraint systems we studied include general Horn constraint systems and Horn clausal constraint systems. The proof systems we considered include ADD and ADD, DIV, subject to various restrictions such as Read-once and Unit read-once.

Table 1 summarizes our results.

Table 1. Results for refutations in constraint systems

Constraint system	Proof system	
	ROR(ADD)	ROR(ADD+DIV)
HCS	**NP-complete**	**NP-complete**
HClCS	**NP-complete**	**NP-complete**

Acknowledgments. This work was supported by the Air Force Research Laboratory under US Air Force contract FA8750-16-3-6003. The views expressed are those of the authors and do not reflect the official policy or position of the Department of Defense or the U.S. Government.

This research was made possible by NASA WV EPSCoR Grant # NNX15AK74A and by the AFOSR through grant FA9550-19-1-017.

References

1. Bakhirkin, A., Monniaux, D.: Combining forward and backward abstract interpretation of Horn clauses. In: Ranzato, F. (ed.) SAS 2017. LNCS, vol. 10422, pp. 23–45. Springer, Cham (2017). https://doi.org/10.1007/978-3-319-66706-5_2
2. Bjørner, N., Gurfinkel, A., McMillan, K., Rybalchenko, A.: Horn clause solvers for program verification. In: Beklemishev, L.D., Blass, A., Dershowitz, N., Finkbeiner, B., Schulte, W. (eds.) Fields of Logic and Computation II. LNCS, vol. 9300, pp. 24–51. Springer, Cham (2015). https://doi.org/10.1007/978-3-319-23534-9_2
3. Buss, S.R.: Propositional proof complexity: an introduction. http://www.math.ucsd.edu/~sbuss/ResearchWeb/marktoberdorf97/paper.pdf
4. Chandrasekaran, R., Subramani, K.: A combinatorial algorithm for Horn programs. Discret. Optim. **10**, 85–101 (2013)
5. Dhiflaoui, M., et al.: Certifying and repairing solutions to large LPs how good are LP-solvers? In: SODA, pp. 255–256 (2003)
6. Dowling, W.F., Gallier, J.H.: Linear-time algorithms for testing the satisfiability of propositional Horn formulae. J. Log. Program. **1**(3), 267–284 (1984)
7. Farkas, G.: Über die Theorie der Einfachen Ungleichungen. Journal für die Reine und Angewandte Mathematik **124**(124), 1–27 (1902)
8. Fouilhé, A., Monniaux, D., Périn, M.: Efficient generation of correctness certificates for the abstract domain of polyhedra. In: Logozzo, F., Fähndrich, M. (eds.) SAS 2013. LNCS, vol. 7935, pp. 345–365. Springer, Heidelberg (2013). https://doi.org/10.1007/978-3-642-38856-9_19
9. Hooker, J.N.: Logical inference and polyhedral projection. In: Börger, E., Jäger, G., Kleine Büning, H., Richter, M.M. (eds.) CSL 1991. LNCS, vol. 626, pp. 184–200. Springer, Heidelberg (1992). https://doi.org/10.1007/BFb0023767
10. Hooker, J.N.: Input proofs and rank one cutting planes. INFORMS J. Comput. **1**(3), 137–145 (1989)
11. Iwama, K., Miyano, E.: Intractability of read-once resolution. In: Proceedings of the 10th Annual Conference on Structure in Complexity Theory (SCTC 1995), Los Alamitos, CA, USA, June 1995, pp. 29–36. IEEE Computer Society Press (1995)
12. Kahsai, T., Vidal, G. (eds.): Proceedings 5th Workshop on Horn Clauses for Verification and Synthesis, HCVS 2018, Oxford, UK, 13th July 2018, vol. 278 of EPTCS (2018)
13. Kaplan, H., Nussbaum, Y.: Certifying algorithms for recognizing proper circular-arc graphs and unit circular-arc graphs. Discret. Appl. Math. **157**(15), 3216–3230 (2009)
14. Karp, R.M.: Reducibility among combinatorial problems. In: Miller, R.E., Thatcher, J.W. (eds.), Complexity of Computer Computations, pp. 85–103. Plenum Press, New York (1972)
15. Kleine Büning, H., Wojciechowski, P., Subramani, K.: Read-once resolutions in Horn formulas. In: Chen, Y., Deng, X., Lu, M. (eds.) FAW 2019. LNCS, vol. 11458, pp. 100–110. Springer, Cham (2019). https://doi.org/10.1007/978-3-030-18126-0_9

16. Kleine Büning, H., Zhao, X.: Read-once unit resolution. In: Giunchiglia, E., Tacchella, A. (eds.) SAT 2003. LNCS, vol. 2919, pp. 356–369. Springer, Heidelberg (2004). https://doi.org/10.1007/978-3-540-24605-3_27
17. Komuravelli, A., Bjørner, N., Gurfinkel, A., McMillan, K.L.: Compositional verification of procedural programs using Horn clauses over integers and arrays. In: Formal Methods in Computer-Aided Design, FMCAD 2015, Austin, Texas, USA, 27–30 September 2015, pp. 89–96 (2015)
18. Kratsch, D., McConnell, R.M., Mehlhorn, K., Spinrad, J.: Certifying algorithms for recognizing interval graphs and permutation graphs. In: SODA, pp. 158–167 (2003)
19. McConnell, R.M., Mehlhorn, K., Näher, S., Schweitzer, P.: Certifying algorithms. Comput. Sci. Rev. 5(2), 119–161 (2011)
20. Nemhauser, G.L., Wolsey, L.A.: Integer and Combinatorial Optimization. Wiley, New York (1999)
21. Schrijver, A.: Theory of Linear and Integer Programming. Wiley, New York (1987)
22. Subramani, K., Worthington, J.: Feasibility checking in Horn constraint systems through a reduction based approach. Theor. Comput. Sci. 576, 1–17 (2015)

Description Logics

The Complexity of the Consistency Problem in the Probabilistic Description Logic $\mathcal{ALC}^{\mathsf{ME}}$

Franz Baader[1]($\boxtimes$), Andreas Ecke[1], Gabriele Kern-Isberner[2], and Marco Wilhelm[2]

[1] Department of Computer Science, TU Dresden, Dresden, Germany
franz.baader@tu-dresden.de
[2] Department of Computer Science, TU Dortmund, Dortmund, Germany

Abstract. The probabilistic Description Logic $\mathcal{ALC}^{\mathsf{ME}}$ is an extension of the Description Logic $\mathcal{ALC}$ that allows for uncertain conditional statements of the form "if C holds, then D holds with probability p," together with probabilistic assertions about individuals. In $\mathcal{ALC}^{\mathsf{ME}}$, probabilities are understood as an agent's degree of belief. Probabilistic conditionals are formally interpreted based on the so-called aggregating semantics, which combines a statistical interpretation of probabilities with a subjective one. Knowledge bases of $\mathcal{ALC}^{\mathsf{ME}}$ are interpreted over a fixed finite domain and based on their maximum entropy (ME) model. We prove that checking consistency of such knowledge bases can be done in time polynomial in the cardinality of the domain, and in exponential time in the size of a binary encoding of this cardinality. If the size of the knowledge base is also taken into account, the combined complexity of the consistency problem is NP-complete for unary encoding of the domain cardinality and NExpTime-complete for binary encoding.

1 Introduction

Description Logics (DLs) [2] are a well-investigated family of logic-based knowledge representation languages, which can be used to represent *terminological knowledge* about concepts as well as *assertional knowledge* about individuals. DLs constitute the formal foundation of the Web Ontology Language OWL,[1] and they are frequently used for defining biomedical ontologies [9]. DLs are (usually decidable) fragments of first-order logic, and thus inherit the restrictions of *classical* logic: they cannot be used to represent uncertain knowledge. In many application domains (e.g., medicine), however, knowledge is not necessarily certain. For example, a doctor may not know definitely that a patient has influenza, but only believe that this is the case with a certain probability. This is

---

[1] see https://www.w3.org/TR/owl2-overview/.

This work was supported by the German Research Foundation (DFG) within the Research Unit FOR 1513 "Hybrid Reasoning for Intelligent Systems".

© Springer Nature Switzerland AG 2019
A. Herzig and A. Popescu (Eds.): FroCoS 2019, LNAI 11715, pp. 167–184, 2019.
https://doi.org/10.1007/978-3-030-29007-8_10

an example for a so-called *subjective* probability. From a technical point of view, subjective probabilities are often formalized using probability distributions over possible worlds (i.e., interpretations). To obtain the probability of an assertion like "John has influenza," one then sums up the probabilities of the worlds that satisfy the assertion. Another type of probability, called *statistical*, is needed to treat general statements like "humans have their heart on the left with probability p." In this setting, one wants to compare the number of individuals that are human and have their heart on the left with the number of all humans *within one world*, rather than summing up the probabilities of the worlds where all humans have their heart on the left. Thus, when defining a probabilistic DL, there is a need for treating assertional knowledge using subjective probabilities, and terminological knowledge using a statistical approach. More information on the distinction between statistical and subjective probabilities can be found in [8]. Most probabilistic extensions of DLs handle either subjective probabilities [12] or statistical ones [15], or are essentially classical terminologies over probabilistic databases [4].

The probabilistic DL $\mathcal{ALC}^{ME}$ [23] was designed such that it can accommodate both points of view. In $\mathcal{ALC}^{ME}$, the terminological part of the knowledge base consists of probabilistic conditionals, which are statements of the form $(D|C)[p]$, which can be read as "if C holds for an individual, then D holds for this individual with probability p." Such a probability should be understood as an agent's degree of belief. Formally, the meaning of probabilistic conditionals is defined using the so-called *aggregating semantics* [11]. This semantics generalizes the statistical interpretation of conditional probabilities by combining it with subjective probabilities based on probability distributions over possible worlds. Basically, in a fixed possible world, the conditional $(D|C)$ can be evaluated statistically by the relative fraction of those individuals that belong to both C and D measured against the individuals that belong to C. In the aggregating semantics, this fraction is not built independently for every possible world, but the single numerators and denominators of the fractions are respectively weighted with the probability of the respective possible world, and are summed up thereafter. Hence, the aggregating semantics mimics statistical probabilities from a subjective point of view. Assertions can then be interpreted in a purely subjective way by summing up the probabilities of the worlds in which the respective assertion holds. Due to this combination of statistical and subjective probabilities, the models of $\mathcal{ALC}^{ME}$-knowledge bases are probability distributions over a set of interpretations that serve as possible worlds. These worlds are built over a fixed finite domain, which guarantees that this set of interpretations is also finite and constitutes a well-defined probability space.

The aggregating semantics defines what the models of an $\mathcal{ALC}^{ME}$ knowledge base are. However, reasoning w.r.t. all these models is usually not productive due to the vast number of probabilistic models. For this reason, we choose as a single model of a knowledge base its *maximum entropy* (ME) distribution [14]. From a commonsense point of view, the maximum entropy distribution is a good choice as it fulfills a number of commonsense principles that can be subsumed under the main idea that "essentially similar problems should have essentially similar solutions" [13]. Moreover, the maximum entropy distribution is known to process conditional relationships particularly well according to conditional logic standards [10]. If the knowledge base is *consistent* in the sense that it has an aggregating semantics model, then it also has a unique maximum entropy model [10,14]. Hence, deciding whether an $\mathcal{ALC}^{\mathsf{ME}}$ knowledge base has a maximum entropy model is the same as deciding whether it has a model according to the aggregating semantics. For this reason, we restrict our attention to deciding the latter inference problems. This is relevant also if one wants to use the aggregating semantics without its combination with maximum entropy.

It should be noted that the general approach of using the aggregating semantics in combination with maximum entropy to define the semantics of probabilistic conditionals has been introduced and discussed before [11,20], and is not particular to probabilistic DLs. A detailed discussions of the aggregating semantics (plus ME) and comparisons with related approaches, in particular with approaches by Halpern and colleagues (see, e.g., [7,8]), can be found in [20]. The instantiation of this approach with the DL $\mathcal{ALC}$ was first considered in our previous work [23], and the investigation of the computational properties of the resulting logic $\mathcal{ALC}^{\mathsf{ME}}$ is continued in the present paper. To be more precise, we first show that checking consistency of an $\mathcal{ALC}^{\mathsf{ME}}$ knowledge base is possible in time polynomial in the cardinality of the finite domain used to construct the possible worlds, and in time exponential in the size of the binary encoding of this cardinality. The first of these two complexity results was already shown in [23] for $\mathcal{ALC}^{\mathsf{ME}}$ knowledge bases without assertions. An important tool for proving this result was the use of so-called types, which have also been employed to show complexity results for classical DLs and other logics [16,17]. In order to extend this result to $\mathcal{ALC}^{\mathsf{ME}}$ knowledge bases with probabilistic assertions, we need to modify the notion of types such that it can also accommodate individuals. The second contribution of the present paper is to determine the *combined complexity* of checking consistency in $\mathcal{ALC}^{\mathsf{ME}}$, i.e., the complexity measured w.r.t. the domain size *and* the size of the knowledge base. For unary encoding of the domain cardinality, we show that this problem is in NP, and for binary encoding that it is in NExpTime. Since fixed domain reasoning in classical $\mathcal{ALC}$ is already NP-complete in the unary case [18] and NExpTime-complete in the binary case [6] these complexity bounds are tight. These results show that the complexity of fixed-domain reasoning in $\mathcal{ALC}$ does not increase if probabilistic conditionals and probabilistic assertions with aggregating semantics are added.

The rest of the paper is organized as follows. First, we start with a brief repetition of the classical DL $\mathcal{ALC}$. We extend $\mathcal{ALC}$ with probabilistic conditionals and assertions and introduce the aggregating semantics as a probabilistic interpretation of knowledge bases within the resulting probabilistic DL $\mathcal{ALC}^{\mathsf{ME}}$. Since the consistency problem for $\mathcal{ALC}^{\mathsf{ME}}$ knowledge bases does not depend on the ME distribution, we do not define this distribution formally in the present paper (see [23] for the exact definition), but illustrate its usefulness by an example. After that, we introduce our notion of types, and use it to give an alternative proof of the known ExpTime upper bound for consistency of classical $\mathcal{ALC}$ knowledge bases. Based on the approach used in this proof, we then show our complexity results for consistency in $\mathcal{ALC}^{\mathsf{ME}}$ using a translation into a system of linear equations over the real numbers, whose variables basically correspond to multisets types.

2   The Description Logics $\mathcal{ALC}$ and $\mathcal{ALC}^{\mathsf{ME}}$

We start with a brief introduction of the classical DL $\mathcal{ALC}$, and then introduce its probabilistic variant $\mathcal{ALC}^{\mathsf{ME}}$.

Classical $\mathcal{ALC}$. The basic building blocks of most DLs are the pairwise disjoint sets of concept names N_C, role names N_R, and individual names N_I. From these, the set of $\mathcal{ALC}$ concepts is defined inductively as follows:

- every concept name $A \in N_C$ is an $\mathcal{ALC}$ concept;
- $\top$ (top concept) and $\bot$ (bottom concept) are $\mathcal{ALC}$ concepts;
- if C, D are $\mathcal{ALC}$ concepts and $r \in N_R$ is a role name, then $\neg C$ (negation), $C \sqcap D$ (conjunction), $C \sqcup D$ (disjunction), $\exists r.C$ (existential restriction), and $\forall r.C$ (value restriction) are also $\mathcal{ALC}$ concepts.

An $\mathcal{ALC}$ concept inclusion (GCI) is of the form $C \sqsubseteq D$, where C and D are $\mathcal{ALC}$ concepts. A classical $\mathcal{ALC}$ TBox is a finite set of $\mathcal{ALC}$ concept inclusions. An $\mathcal{ALC}$ assertion is of the form $C(a)$ where C is an $\mathcal{ALC}$ concept and $a \in N_I$, or $r(a, b)$ with $r \in N_R$ and $a, b \in N_I$. A classical $\mathcal{ALC}$ ABox is a finite set of $\mathcal{ALC}$ assertions. Together, TBox and ABox form an $\mathcal{ALC}$ knowledge base (KB).

The semantics of $\mathcal{ALC}$ is based on interpretations. An interpretation $\mathcal{I} = (\Delta^{\mathcal{I}}, \cdot^{\mathcal{I}})$ consists of a non-empty set of elements $\Delta^{\mathcal{I}}$, the domain, and an interpretation function that assigns to each concept name $A \in N_C$ a subset $A^{\mathcal{I}} \subseteq \Delta^{\mathcal{I}}$, to each role name $r \in N_R$ a binary relation $r^{\mathcal{I}} \subseteq \Delta^{\mathcal{I}} \times \Delta^{\mathcal{I}}$, and to each individual name $a \in N_I$ an element $a^{\mathcal{I}} \in \Delta^{\mathcal{I}}$. The interpretation function is extended to $\mathcal{ALC}$ concepts as follows:

$$\top^{\mathcal{I}} = \Delta^{\mathcal{I}}, \qquad\qquad \bot^{\mathcal{I}} = \emptyset, \qquad\qquad (\neg C)^{\mathcal{I}} = \Delta^{\mathcal{I}} \setminus C^{\mathcal{I}},$$
$$(C \sqcap D)^{\mathcal{I}} = C^{\mathcal{I}} \cap D^{\mathcal{I}}, \qquad (C \sqcup D)^{\mathcal{I}} = C^{\mathcal{I}} \cup D^{\mathcal{I}},$$
$$(\exists r.C)^{\mathcal{I}} = \{d \in \Delta^{\mathcal{I}} \mid \exists e \in \Delta^{\mathcal{I}}.(d, e) \in r^{\mathcal{I}} \wedge e \in C^{\mathcal{I}}\},$$
$$(\forall r.C)^{\mathcal{I}} = \{d \in \Delta^{\mathcal{I}} \mid \forall e \in \Delta^{\mathcal{I}}.(d, e) \in r^{\mathcal{I}} \implies e \in C^{\mathcal{I}}\}.$$

An interpretation $\mathcal{I}$ satisfies a concept inclusion $C \sqsubseteq D$ ($\mathcal{I} \models C \sqsubseteq D$) if $C^{\mathcal{I}} \subseteq D^{\mathcal{I}}$. It is a model of a TBox $\mathcal{T}$ if it satisfies all concept inclusions occurring in $\mathcal{T}$. $\mathcal{I}$ satisfies an assertion $C(a)$ ($\mathcal{I} \models C(a)$) if $a^{\mathcal{I}} \in C^{\mathcal{I}}$, and $r(a, b)$ ($\mathcal{I} \models r(a, b)$) if $(a^{\mathcal{I}}, b^{\mathcal{I}}) \in r^{\mathcal{I}}$. It is a model of an ABox $\mathcal{A}$ if it satisfies all assertions in $\mathcal{A}$. A KB $\mathcal{K} = (\mathcal{T}, \mathcal{A})$ is consistent if there exists a model that satisfies both $\mathcal{T}$ and $\mathcal{A}$.

Note that we do *not* employ the unique name assumption (UNA), i.e., we do not assume that different individual names are interpreted by different elements of the interpretation domain.

Probabilistic $\mathcal{ALC}^{\mathsf{ME}}$. In our probabilistic extension $\mathcal{ALC}^{\mathsf{ME}}$ of $\mathcal{ALC}$, we use probabilistic conditionals instead of concept inclusions. A probabilistic $\mathcal{ALC}$ conditional is of the form $(D|C)[p]$, where C and D are $\mathcal{ALC}$ concepts and $p \in [0,1]$. We call a finite set of probabilistic conditionals a CBox. A probabilistic ABox (or pABox) contains assertions labeled with probabilities, i.e., probabilistic assertions of the form $C(a)[p]$ or $r(a,b)[p]$, where again $p \in [0,1]$. A probabilistic knowledge base (pKB) consists of both a CBox and a pABox.[2]

Example 1. Using probabilistic $\mathcal{ALC}^{\mathsf{ME}}$, we can express that every person has at least one friend, on average one in two people are unhappy, and that people with only happy friends are much more likely to be happy themselves in the following CBox:

$$\mathcal{C} = \{(\exists\mathsf{friend}.\mathsf{Person} \mid \mathsf{Person})[1], \quad (\neg\mathsf{Happy} \mid \mathsf{Person})[0.5],$$
$$(\mathsf{Happy} \mid \mathsf{Person} \sqcap \forall\mathsf{friend}.\mathsf{Happy})[0.9]\}.$$

Additionally, let us introduce the persons Emma and Peter, for whom we state that Emma considers Peter a friend, and Peter is quite happy:

$$\mathcal{A} = \{\mathsf{Person}(\mathsf{peter})[1], \quad \mathsf{Person}(\mathsf{emma})[1],$$
$$\mathsf{Happy}(\mathsf{peter})[0.8], \quad \mathsf{friend}(\mathsf{emma}, \mathsf{peter})[0.9]\}.$$

The semantics of probabilistic conditionals and assertions is defined via probabilistic interpretations, which are probability distributions over classical interpretations. For this definition to be well-behaved, we consider a fixed, finite domain Δ and assume that the signature (i.e., the set of concept, role, and individual names) is finite. For the signature, we can simply restrict to those names that actually occur in a given pKB $\mathcal{K}$, i.e., to concept names $\mathsf{sig}_C(\mathcal{K}) = \{A \in N_C \mid A \text{ occurs in } \mathcal{K}\}$, role names $\mathsf{sig}_R(\mathcal{K}) = \{r \in N_R \mid r \text{ occurs in } \mathcal{K}\}$ and individual names $\mathsf{sig}_I(\mathcal{K}) = \{a \in N_I \mid a \text{ occurs in } \mathcal{K}\}$. Then, we denote the set of all interpretations $\mathcal{I} = (\Delta, \mathsf{sig}_C(\mathcal{K}) \to \mathcal{P}(\Delta), \mathsf{sig}_R(\mathcal{K}) \to \mathcal{P}(\Delta \times \Delta), \mathsf{sig}_I(\mathcal{K}) \to \Delta)$ as $\mathcal{I}_{\mathcal{K},\Delta}$. Since Δ and all $\mathsf{sig}_*(\mathcal{K})$ are finite, $\mathcal{I}_{\mathcal{K},\Delta}$ is also finite. Then, a *probabilistic interpretation* is a probability distribution over $\mathcal{I}_{\mathcal{K},\Delta}$, i.e., a function $\mu : \mathcal{I}_{\mathcal{K},\Delta} \to [0,1]$ such that $\sum_{\mathcal{I} \in \mathcal{I}_{\mathcal{K},\Delta}} \mu(\mathcal{I}) = 1$.

The *semantics of probabilistic assertions* is defined as one would expect: a probabilistic interpretation μ satisfies a probabilistic assertion of the form $C(a)[p]$ or the form $r(a,b)[p]$ if

$$\sum_{\substack{\mathcal{I} \in \mathcal{I}_{\mathcal{K},\Delta} \\ s.t.\ a^{\mathcal{I}} \in C^{\mathcal{I}}}} \mu(\mathcal{I}) = p \quad \text{or} \quad \sum_{\substack{\mathcal{I} \in \mathcal{I}_{\mathcal{K},\Delta} \\ s.t.\ (a^{\mathcal{I}}, b^{\mathcal{I}}) \in r^{\mathcal{I}}}} \mu(\mathcal{I}) = p.$$

Defining the *semantics of probabilistic conditionals* is more involved since here we need to consider not only all possible worlds, but also all elements of the

---

[2] We will see later (proof of Corollary 14) that setting all probabilities to 1 in a pKB basically yields a classical KB, and thus $\mathcal{ALC}^{\mathsf{ME}}$ indeed is an extension of $\mathcal{ALC}$.

domain. There are multiple possibilities for how to combine these two dimensions. In this work, we use the aggregating semantics to define the semantics of our probabilistic extension of $\mathcal{ALC}$. Under the aggregating semantics [11], a probabilistic interpretation μ satisfies a probabilistic conditional $(D|C)[p]$, denoted $\mu \models (D|C)[p]$, if

$$\frac{\sum_{\mathcal{I} \in \mathcal{I}_{\mathcal{K},\Delta}} |C^{\mathcal{I}} \cap D^{\mathcal{I}}| \cdot \mu(\mathcal{I})}{\sum_{\mathcal{I} \in \mathcal{I}_{\mathcal{K},\Delta}} |C^{\mathcal{I}}| \cdot \mu(\mathcal{I})} = p. \tag{1}$$

A probabilistic interpretation μ is a *model of a CBox* $\mathcal{C}$ ($\mu \models \mathcal{C}$) if it satisfies all probabilistic conditionals in $\mathcal{C}$, and a *model of a pABox* $\mathcal{A}$ ($\mu \models \mathcal{A}$) if it satisfies all probabilistic assertions in $\mathcal{A}$. It is a *model of a pKB* $\mathcal{K}$ if it is a model of both its CBox and pABox.

Equation (1) formalizes the intuition underlying conditional probabilities by weighting the probabilities $\mu(\mathcal{I})$ with the number of individuals for which the conditional $(D|C)[p]$ is *applicable* ($|C^{\mathcal{I}}|$) or *verified* ($|C^{\mathcal{I}} \cap D^{\mathcal{I}}|$) in $\mathcal{I}$. Hence, the aggregating semantics mimics statistical probabilities from a subjective point of view, and probabilities can be understood as an agent's degrees of belief. If, on the one hand, μ is the distribution that assigns the probability 1 to a single interpretation $\mathcal{I}$, which means that the agent is certain that $\mathcal{I}$ is the real world, then the aggregating semantics boils down to counting relative frequencies in this world. On the other hand, if μ is the uniform distribution on those interpretations that do not contradict facts (conditionals or assertions with 0/1-probability), which means that the agent is minimally confident in her beliefs, then the aggregating semantics means counting relative frequencies spread over all interpretations.

Consistency is the question whether a given pKB has a model (for a given domain size). In previous work [23], we were concerned with the model of a pKB with maximal entropy, as this ME-model has several nice properties. In particular, reasoning with respect to all probabilistic models instead of solely the ME-model leads to monotonic and often uninformative inferences, as demonstrated in the next example.

Example 2. Consider the CBox $\mathcal{C} = \{(\mathsf{Happy}|\mathsf{Wealthy})[0.7], (\mathsf{Happy}|\mathsf{Parent})[0.9]\}$. Then $\mathcal{C}$ has a model in which wealthy parents are happy with probability 0, as well as a model in which wealthy parents are happy with probability 1. This is the case since the marginal probabilities of wealthy persons and of parents, respectively, as stated in $\mathcal{C}$, do not limit the probabilities of wealthy parents. Hence, when reasoning over all probabilistic models of $\mathcal{C}$, it is impossible to make a statement about the happiness of wealthy parents although it is obviously reasonable to assume that wealthy parents are happy with at least probability 0.7.

In the ME-approach, instead, it holds that the maximum entropy probability of wealthy parents being happy is $\mathcal{P}^{\mathsf{ME}}(\mathsf{Happy}|\mathsf{Wealthy} \sqcap \mathsf{Parent}) \approx 0.908$. Note that this holds independently of the domain size $|\Delta| > 0$ (see [22] for details).

However, as mentioned before, if we are only interested in consistency, then this distinction is irrelevant: A pKB has an ME-model iff it has a model at all. For this reason, it is not necessary to introduce the principle of maximum entropy and the definition of the ME-model here.

Example 3. We can now reconsider the pKB in Example 1, and see how its interpretation under aggregation semantics differs from the one under other probabilistic formalisms. For instance, the assertion Happy(peter) [0.8] does not contradict the conditional (Happy | Person) [0.5]. Indeed, the aggregating semantics implies that, on average, people are happy with a probability of 0.5, not that every person needs to have a subjective probability of exactly 0.5 of being happy. Thus, Peter being happy with an above-average probability only means that, for other people, the average probability to be happy will be slightly below 0.5, so that the total average can be 0.5.

Similarly, this pKB is consistent with Emma being unhappy, even if all her friends, like Peter, are happy. Again, the conditional probability of people being happy if all their friends are happy quantifies over all people, so one outlier will not necessarily lead to a contradiction.

3 Checking Consistency Using Types

Types classify individuals into equivalence classes depending on the concepts they satisfy. In this paper, we extend the notion of types for $\mathcal{ALC}$ found in the DL literature (see, e.g., [3,17]) such that named individuals and their relationships with other named individuals, as stated in an ABox, are taken into account. After introducing our notion of types, we will first use it to reprove the ExpTime upper bound for consistency in classical $\mathcal{ALC}$. The constructions and results used for this purpose are important for our treatment of consistency in $\mathcal{ALC}^{\mathsf{ME}}$. Type notions that can deal with individuals have been considered before in the DL literature, but usually in the more complicated setting of DLs that are considerably more expressive than $\mathcal{ALC}$ (see, e.g., [1], where such types are considered in the context of temporal extensions of DLs). Our results for the probabilistic case crucially depend on the exact notion of types introduced in the present paper, and in particular on the model construction employed in the proof of Theorem 7 below.

Types. For the sake of simplicity, we will only consider concepts using the constructors negation, conjunction, and existential restriction. Due to the equivalences $C \sqcup D \equiv \neg(\neg C \sqcap \neg D)$, $\forall r.C \equiv \neg(\exists r.\neg C)$, $\top \equiv A \sqcup \neg A$, and $\bot \equiv A \sqcap \neg A$, any concept can be transformed into an equivalent concept in this restricted form. We also assume that all double negations have been eliminated. For such a concept C, we define the set of its subconcepts as

$$\mathrm{sub}(C) = \{C\} \cup \begin{cases} \mathrm{sub}(C') & \text{if } C = \neg C' \text{ or } C = \exists r.C' \\ \mathrm{sub}(C') \cup \mathrm{sub}(D') & \text{if } C = C' \sqcap D' \end{cases}$$

Similarly, for a pKB $\mathcal{K}$ consisting of a CBox $\mathcal{C}$ and pABox $\mathcal{A}$, the set of all subconcepts is $\mathrm{sub}(\mathcal{K}) = \bigcup_{(D|C)[p] \in \mathcal{C}} \mathrm{sub}(D) \cup \mathrm{sub}(C) \cup \bigcup_{C(a)[p] \in \mathcal{A}} \mathrm{sub}(C)$. The set of subconcepts is defined in an analogous way for a classical $\mathcal{ALC}$ KB $\mathcal{K}$.

For convenience, we also want to include the negation of each concept. Thus, we define the closure of the set of subconcepts under negation as

$$\mathrm{sub}_\neg(\mathcal{K}) = \mathrm{sub}(\mathcal{K}) \cup \{\neg C \mid C \in \mathrm{sub}(\mathcal{K})\},$$

where we again assume that double negation is eliminated. In the presence of assertions, types also need to keep track of individual names and their connections. Basically, we achieve this by employing individuals names from the ABox as nominals [21] within existential restrictions. To be more precises, we use the set of existential restrictions to an individual:

$$\mathrm{EI}_\mathcal{K} = \{\exists r.a, \neg\exists r.a \mid a \in \mathrm{sig}_I(\mathcal{K}), r \in \mathrm{sig}_R(\mathcal{K})\}$$

Then, we can define a type as a set of concepts, existential restrictions to named individuals, and individual names:

Definition 4 (Type). *Given a KB $\mathcal{K}$, a type t for $\mathcal{K}$ is a subset $t \subseteq \mathrm{sub}_\neg(\mathcal{K}) \cup \mathrm{sig}_I(\mathcal{K}) \cup \mathrm{EI}_\mathcal{K}$ such that*

1. *for every $\neg X \in \mathrm{sub}_\neg(\mathcal{K}) \cup \mathrm{EI}_\mathcal{K}$, either X or $\neg X$ belongs to t;*
2. *for every $C \sqcap D \in \mathrm{sub}_\neg(\mathcal{K})$, we have $C \sqcap D \in t$ iff $C \in t$ and $D \in t$.*

We use types to characterize elements of an interpretation. In particular, we want to identify domain elements d of an interpretation $\mathcal{I}$ with the type that contains exactly those concepts the element is an instance of. In addition, we also need to keep track which individual name is interpreted as d, and to which individuals d is related to via a role. This motivates the following definition:

$$\tau(\mathcal{I}, d) := \left\{ C \in \mathrm{sub}_\neg(\mathcal{K}) \mid d \in C^\mathcal{I} \right\} \cup \left\{ a \in \mathrm{sig}_I(\mathcal{K}) \mid a^\mathcal{I} = d \right\}$$
$$\cup \left\{ \exists r.a \mid (d, a^\mathcal{I}) \in r^\mathcal{I} \right\} \cup \left\{ \neg\exists r.a \mid (d, a^\mathcal{I}) \notin r^\mathcal{I} \right\}$$

It is easy to see that the type of an individual is indeed a type in the sense of Definition 4. Due to Definition 4, each type is compatible with the semantics of conjunction and negation. However, the satisfaction of existential restrictions depends on the presence of other types. Given a type t, an existential restriction $\exists r.X \in t$ with X being an individual name or concept, and the set of all negated existential restrictions $\{\neg\exists r.X_1, \ldots, \neg\exists r.X_k\} \subseteq t$ for role r, we say that a *type* t' satisfies $\exists r.X$ in t if $X \in t'$ and $X_i \notin t'$ for $i = 1, \ldots, k$.

Definition 5 (Consistency of a set of types). *A set of types T is consistent if (i) $T \neq \emptyset$, (ii) for every $t \in T$ and every $\exists r.X \in t$ there is a type $t' \in T$ that satisfies $\exists r.X$ in t, and (iii) every $a \in \mathrm{sig}_I(\mathcal{K})$ occurs in exactly one $t \in T$.*

Condition (iii) says that, for every individual, there is exactly one type. Note that we do not require that a type contains at most one individual since we do not impose the UNA.

Consistency in Classical $\mathcal{ALC}$. Before we prove complexity bounds for consistency in $\mathcal{ALC}^{ME}$, we recall how to use types for classical $\mathcal{ALC}$. First, we show that consistent sets of types correspond to $\mathcal{ALC}$ interpretations. On the one hand, for every interpretation $\mathcal{I}$ we can construct a consistent set of types $\tau(\mathcal{I})$ as set of types of its domain elements: $\tau(\mathcal{I}) = \{\tau(\mathcal{I}, d) \mid d \in \Delta^{\mathcal{I}}\}$. On the other hand, given a consistent set of types T, we can build an interpretation $\mathcal{I}_T = (\Delta^{\mathcal{I}_T}, \cdot^{\mathcal{I}_T})$:

$$\Delta^{\mathcal{I}_T} := T,$$
$$A^{\mathcal{I}_T} := \{t \in T \mid A \in t\},$$
$$r^{\mathcal{I}_T} := \{(t, t') \mid \exists X \in \text{sub}_\neg(\mathcal{K}) \cup \text{sig}_I(\mathcal{K}) : t' \text{ satisfies } \exists r.X \text{ in } t\},$$
$$a^{\mathcal{I}_T} \text{ is the unique type } t \in T \text{ with } a \in t.$$

Lemma 6. *Let $\mathcal{K} = (\mathcal{T}, \mathcal{A})$ be a classical $\mathcal{ALC}$ knowledge base consisting of TBox $\mathcal{T}$ and ABox $\mathcal{A}$ and T be a consistent set of types. Then, for every $t \in T$ and $C \in \text{sub}_\neg(\mathcal{K})$ we have $C \in t$ iff $t \in C^{\mathcal{I}_T}$.*

Proof. This can be proved by a simple induction on the structure of C. Here we consider only the most interesting case, which is the case where C is an existential restriction. If $C = \exists r.D$, then $\exists r.D \in t$ implies that there is $t' \in T$ such that t' satisfies $\exists r.D$ in t. This implies that $D \in t'$, and thus by induction $t' \in D^{\mathcal{I}_T}$. By construction of $\mathcal{I}_T$ we also have $(t, t') \in r^{\mathcal{I}_T}$, and thus $t \in (\exists r.D)^{\mathcal{I}_T}$.

Conversely, if $\exists r.D \notin t$, then $\neg \exists r.D \in t$. We need to show that $t \notin (\exists r.D)^{\mathcal{I}_T}$, i.e., if $(t, t') \in r^{\mathcal{I}_T}$, then $t' \notin D^{\mathcal{I}_T}$. However, $(t, t') \in r^{\mathcal{I}_T}$ implies that t' satisfies $\exists r.X$ in t for some X. Since $\neg \exists r.D \in t$, this can only be the case if $D \notin t'$. Induction now yields $t' \notin D^{\mathcal{I}_T}$ as required. □

There is a known correspondence that states that an $\mathcal{ALC}$ TBox $\mathcal{T}$ is consistent iff there exists a consistent set of types T that satisfies all GCIs, i.e., for each $C \sqsubseteq D \in \mathcal{T}$ and each $t \in T$ we have $C \in t$ implies $D \in t$ [3]. We can extend this result to KB consistency as follows:

Theorem 7. *Let $\mathcal{K} = (\mathcal{T}, \mathcal{A})$ be a classical $\mathcal{ALC}$ KB. Then $\mathcal{K}$ is consistent if, and only if, there exists a consistent set of types T such that*

- *for all GCIs $C \sqsubseteq D \in \mathcal{T}$ and types $t \in T$ we have $C \in t$ implies $D \in t$;*
- *for all assertions $C(a) \in \mathcal{A}$ and types $t \in T$ with $a \in t$ we have $C \in t$; and*
- *for all assertions $r(a, b) \in \mathcal{A}$ and types $t \in T$ with $a \in t$ we have $\exists r.b \in t$.*

Proof. If $\mathcal{I}$ is a model of $\mathcal{K}$, then $\tau(\mathcal{I})$ is a consistent set of types, and it is easy to see that this set satisfies the three conditions of the theorem.

For the other direction, assume that T be a consistent set of types that satisfies the three conditions from above. We show that $\mathcal{I}_T$ is a model of $\mathcal{K}$:

- Let $C \sqsubseteq D \in \mathcal{T}$ and assume that $t \in C^{\mathcal{I}_T}$. Then Lemma 6 yields $C \in t$, which implies $D \in t$ by the first condition. Lemma 6 thus yields $t \in D^{\mathcal{I}_T}$, which shows that $\mathcal{I}_T \models C \sqsubseteq D$.

- For every $C(a) \in \mathcal{A}$, we have $C \in t$ for the unique type t that contains a. By the definition of $\mathcal{I}_T$ and Lemma 6, this implies $a^{\mathcal{I}_T} = t \in C^{\mathcal{I}_T}$, and thus $\mathcal{I}_T \models C(a)$.
- For every $r(a, b) \in \mathcal{A}$, we have $\exists r.b \in t$ for the unique type t that contains a. Since T is consistent, there is a type $t' \in T$ that satisfies $\exists r.b$ in t. Consequently, $b \in t'$ and $(t, t') \in r^{\mathcal{I}_T}$. Since $t = a^{\mathcal{I}_T}$ and $t' = b^{\mathcal{I}_T}$; this shows $\mathcal{I}_T \models r(a, b)$.

This completes the proof of the theorem.   □

Based on this theorem, consistency of a classical $\mathcal{ALC}$ KB $\mathcal{K} = (\mathcal{T}, \mathcal{A})$ can be decided using type elimination as follows:

1. Construct the set T of all types $t \subseteq \mathrm{sub}_\neg(\mathcal{K}) \cup \mathrm{EI}_\mathcal{K}$ for $\mathcal{K}$ that do not contain individual names, and for which $C \in t$ implies $D \in t$ for all $C \sqsubseteq D \in \mathcal{T}$.
2. Consider all extensions T' of T with types $t \cup I$ with $t \in T$ and $I \subseteq \mathrm{sig}_I(\mathcal{K})$ such that
   - each individual name $a \in \mathrm{sig}_I(\mathcal{K})$ occurs in exactly one type $t' \in T'$;
   - for all $C(a) \in \mathcal{A}$ and $t' \in T'$, $a \in t'$ implies $C \in t'$; and
   - for all $r(a, b) \in \mathcal{A}$ and $t' \in T'$, $a \in t'$ implies $\exists r.b \in t'$.
3. For each such set T', successively remove all types from T' with unsatisfied existential restrictions until no more such types remain.
4. Return "consistent" if at least one of the sets T' obtained this way is non-empty and contains for each $a \in \mathrm{sig}_I(\mathcal{K})$ a type t with $a \in t$.

Corollary 8. *Consistency of $\mathcal{ALC}$ KBs can be decided in ExpTime.*

Proof. We need to show that the above algorithm is sound and complete, and runs in exponential time. We sketch how to show each claim:

Soundness follows directly from Theorem 7 since it is easy to see that a set T' that leads the algorithm to answer "consistent" is a consistent set of types that satisfies the three conditions of the theorem.

For completeness, assume that $\mathcal{K}$ is consistent, and thus by Theorem 7 a consistent set S of types with the stated properties exists. This consistent set of types S must be a subset of the set T' constructed by the algorithm after step 2 for some guess of the types for each individual name. However, then step 3 will never remove any type of S from T', and thus step 4 of the algorithm will return that $\mathcal{K}$ is indeed consistent.

Regarding runtime, note that the set T constructed in the first step contains at most exponentially many types. In the second step, at most exponentially many extensions T' of T are constructed since this step basically amounts to looking at all possible ways of choosing exactly one type for each of the (linearly many) individuals, and then removing choices that do not satisfy the stated conditions. Since each of the sets T' constructed this way is of at most exponential size, type elimination applied to T' takes at most exponential time.   □

Consistency in $\mathcal{ALC}^{\mathsf{ME}}$. For probabilistic $\mathcal{ALC}$, we need to consider multiple worlds, each corresponding to a classical interpretation. Additionally, the aggregating semantics takes into account how many individuals verify or falsify a conditional, even if those individuals are indistinguishable (i.e., have the same type). Thus, instead of sets of types, we need to consider multisets of types.

Formally, a multiset on a domain X is a function $M : X \to \mathbb{N}$. We denote multisets as mappings, such as $M = \{x_1 \mapsto 3, x_2 \mapsto 1\}$. We say that an element $x \in X$ occurs $M(x)$ times in M, and that it occurs in M if $M(x) > 0$. The cardinality of the multiset M is given by the sum of the number of occurrences of each element, i.e. $|M| = \sum_{x \in X} M(x)$.

As said above, we are interested in multisets of types, and in particular multisets of types with a given cardinality $k = |\Delta|$. These correspond to $\mathcal{ALC}$ interpretations with a domain of size k. We define the (multiset-)type $\tau_M(\mathcal{I})$ of an interpretation $\mathcal{I}$ as follows:

$$\tau_M(\mathcal{I})(t) := |\{d \in \Delta \mid \tau(\mathcal{I}, d) = t\}|.$$

It is easy to see that $|\tau_M(\mathcal{I})| = |\Delta|$.

Consistency of multisets of types is defined analogously to the set case: every existential restriction in every type occurring in the multiset M must be satisfied by some other type occurring in M, and every individual name must occur in exactly one type that occurs exactly once in M. We denote the set of all consistent multisets of types with cardinality k with $\mathcal{M}_{\mathcal{K},k}$.

Similarly to the classical case, we build an interpretation $\mathcal{I}_M = (\Delta^{\mathcal{I}_M}, \cdot^{\mathcal{I}_M})$ from a multiset M of types, except now we take $M(t)$ copies for each element in M, to ensure that the interpretation domain has the same cardinality as M:

$$
\begin{aligned}
\Delta^{\mathcal{I}_M} &:= \{(t,i) \mid 1 \le i \le M(t)\} \\
A^{\mathcal{I}_M} &:= \{(t,i) \in \Delta^{\mathcal{I}_M} \mid A \in t\}, \\
r^{\mathcal{I}_M} &:= \{((t,i),(t',j)) \in \Delta^{\mathcal{I}_M} \times \Delta^{\mathcal{I}_M} \mid \\
&\qquad \exists X \in \mathrm{sub}_\neg(\mathcal{K}) \cup \mathrm{sig}_I(\mathcal{K}) : t' \text{ satisfies } \exists r.X \text{ in } t\}, \\
a^{\mathcal{I}_M} &:= (t,1) \text{ where } t \text{ is the unique type occurring in } M \text{ with } a \in t.
\end{aligned}
\tag{2}
$$

It is easy to show that this construction achieves the same as in the classical case (see Lemma 6):

Lemma 9. *Let $\mathcal{K} = (\mathcal{C}, \mathcal{A})$ be a pKB consisting of a CBox $\mathcal{C}$ and a pABox $\mathcal{A}$, and let $M \in \mathcal{M}_{\mathcal{K},k}$ be a consistent multiset of types. Then $|\Delta^{\mathcal{I}_M}| = k$, and for every $t \in M$, $1 \le i \le M(t)$, and $C \in \mathrm{sub}_\neg(\mathcal{K})$, we have $C \in t$ iff $(t,i) \in C^{\mathcal{I}_M}$.*

In order to use this lemma to obtain a characterization of consistent pKBs, we need to take into account that, in $\mathcal{ALC}^{\mathsf{ME}}$, models are probability distributions over classical interpretations. Consequently, we need to consider probability distributions over the set of all multisets of types of a given cardinality. The aggregating semantics depends on counting instances of concepts. Thus, we need to show that counting instances can be reduced to summing up the number of occurrences of the corresponding types.

Lemma 10. *Let $\mathcal{K}$ be a pKB and $\mathcal{I}$ be an $\mathcal{ALC}$ interpretation with finite domain Δ and $\tau_M(\mathcal{I}) = M$. Then for all $(D|C)[p]$ occurring in $\mathcal{K}$ we have $|C^{\mathcal{I}}| = \sum_{t \in M \text{ s.t. } C \in t} M(t)$ and $|C^{\mathcal{I}} \cap D^{\mathcal{I}}| = \sum_{t \in M \text{ s.t. } \{C,D\} \subseteq t} M(t)$. Additionally, for any $a, b \in \text{sig}_I(\mathcal{K})$, we have $a^{\mathcal{I}} \in C^{\mathcal{I}}$ iff there is $t \in M$ with $\{a, C\} \subseteq t$, and $(a^{\mathcal{I}}, b^{\mathcal{I}}) \in r^{\mathcal{I}}$ iff there is $t \in M$ with $\{a, \exists r.b\} \subseteq t$.*

Proof. $M = \tau_M(\mathcal{I})$ implies that

$$
\begin{aligned}
|C^{\mathcal{I}} \cap D^{\mathcal{I}}| &= \left| \{ d \in \Delta \mid d \in C^{\mathcal{I}} \wedge d \in D^{\mathcal{I}} \} \right| \\
&= \left| \{ d \in \Delta \mid \{C, D\} \subseteq \tau_M(\mathcal{I}, d) \} \right| \\
&= \sum_{t \in M \text{ s.t. } \{C,D\} \subseteq t} M(t).
\end{aligned}
$$

The same argument can be used to show $|C^{\mathcal{I}}| = \sum_{t \in M \text{ s.t. } C \in t} M(t)$.

Let $t \in \tau_M(\mathcal{I})$ be the unique type with $a \in t$. Then $a^{\mathcal{I}} \in C^{\mathcal{I}}$ iff $C \in t$ and thus $\{a, C\} \subseteq t$. If $(a^{\mathcal{I}}, b^{\mathcal{I}}) \in r^{\mathcal{I}}$, then $\exists r.b \in t = \tau(\mathcal{I}, a^{\mathcal{I}})$, and thus $\{a, \exists r.b\} \subseteq t$. Conversely, if $\exists r.b \in t = \tau(\mathcal{I}, a^{\mathcal{I}})$, then $(a^{\mathcal{I}}, b^{\mathcal{I}}) \in r^{\mathcal{I}}$. $\qquad\Box$

Note that Lemma 10 implies that, for interpretations $\mathcal{I}_1$ and $\mathcal{I}_2$ with the same type $\tau_M(\mathcal{I}_1) = \tau_M(\mathcal{I}_2)$, we have $|C^{\mathcal{I}_1}| = |C^{\mathcal{I}_2}|$ and $|C^{\mathcal{I}_1} \cap D^{\mathcal{I}_1}| = |C^{\mathcal{I}_2} \cap D^{\mathcal{I}_2}|$ for all $(D|C)[p]$ occurring in $\mathcal{K}$, as well as $a^{\mathcal{I}_1} \in C^{\mathcal{I}_1}$ iff $a^{\mathcal{I}_2} \in C^{\mathcal{I}_2}$ and $(a^{\mathcal{I}_1}, b^{\mathcal{I}_1}) \in r^{\mathcal{I}_1}$ iff $(a^{\mathcal{I}_2}, b^{\mathcal{I}_2}) \in r^{\mathcal{I}_2}$. This means that the aggregating semantics cannot distinguish between interpretations with the same type. Thus, these types allow us to simplify Eq. (1): instead of summing over all interpretations $\mathcal{I}_{\mathcal{K},\Delta}$, we only have to consider those interpretations with different types. Based on these ideas, the following theorem characterizes consistency of pKBs in $\mathcal{ALC}^{\mathsf{ME}}$.

Theorem 11. *Let $\mathcal{K}$ be a pKB and Δ be a finite domain with $|\Delta| = k$. Then $\mathcal{K}$ is consistent if, and only if, the equation system (3) in Fig. 1 has a non-negative solution $\boldsymbol{p}_M \in \mathbb{R}_{\geq 0}^{\mathcal{M}_{\mathcal{K},k}}$.*

Proof. For each $M \in \mathcal{M}_{\mathcal{K},k}$, let $\mathcal{I}(M) = \{ \mathcal{I} \in \mathcal{I}_{\mathcal{K},\Delta} \mid \tau_M(\mathcal{I}) = M \}$ be the set of interpretations with type M. It is easy to see that, for $M \neq M'$, we have $\mathcal{I}(M) \cap \mathcal{I}(M') = \emptyset$. Using Lemma 10 together with this fact,[3] we can translate between models of $\mathcal{K}$ and solutions of the system of Eqs. 3 as follows.

First, assume that $\mathcal{K}$ is consistent, i.e., there exists a model $\mu : \mathcal{I}_{\mathcal{K},\Delta} \to [0, 1]$ of $\mathcal{K}$. Then it is easy to see that setting $p_M := \sum_{\mathcal{I} \in \mathcal{I}(M)} \mu(\mathcal{I})$ yields a solution of (3).

---

[3] More precisely, this fact is used in the identities marked with $*$ below.

$$\frac{\displaystyle\sum_{\substack{M\in\mathcal{M}_{\mathcal{K},k}}}\sum_{\substack{t\in M\\ \text{s.t. } C\Subset t\wedge D\Subset t}} M(t)\cdot p_M}{\displaystyle\sum_{\substack{M\in\mathcal{M}_{\mathcal{K},k}}}\sum_{\substack{t\in M\\ \text{s.t. } C\Subset t}} M(t)\cdot p_M} = p, \qquad \text{for } (D|C)[p]\in\mathcal{C},$$

$$\sum_{\substack{M\in\mathcal{M}_{\mathcal{K},k}\\ \text{s.t. }\exists t\in M: \{a,C\}\subseteq t}} p_M = p, \qquad \text{for } C(a)[p]\in\mathcal{A}, \tag{3}$$

$$\sum_{\substack{M\in\mathcal{M}_{\mathcal{K},k}\\ \text{s.t. }\exists t\in M: \{a,\exists r.b\}\subseteq t}} p_M = p, \qquad \text{for } r(a,b)[p]\in\mathcal{A},$$

$$\sum_{M\in\mathcal{M}_{\mathcal{K},k}} p_M = 1.$$

Fig. 1. The system of equations that characterizes consistency of pKBs in $\mathcal{ALC}^{\mathsf{ME}}$.

In fact, for $(D|C)[p]\in\mathcal{C}$ we have

$$\frac{\displaystyle\sum_{M\in\mathcal{M}_{\mathcal{K},k}}\sum_{\substack{t\in M\\ \text{s.t. } C\Subset t\wedge D\Subset t}} M(t)\cdot p_M}{\displaystyle\sum_{M\in\mathcal{M}_{\mathcal{K},k}}\sum_{\substack{t\in M\\ \text{s.t. } C\Subset t}} M(t)\cdot p_M} = \frac{\displaystyle\sum_{M\in\mathcal{M}_{\mathcal{K},k}}\sum_{\substack{t\in M\\ \text{s.t. } C\Subset t\wedge D\Subset t}} M(t)\cdot\sum_{\mathcal{I}\in\mathcal{I}_M}\mu(\mathcal{I})}{\displaystyle\sum_{M\in\mathcal{M}_{\mathcal{K},k}}\sum_{\substack{t\in M\\ \text{s.t. } C\Subset t}} M(t)\cdot\sum_{\mathcal{I}\in\mathcal{I}_M}\mu(\mathcal{I})}$$

$$= \frac{\displaystyle\sum_{M\in\mathcal{M}_{\mathcal{K},k}}\sum_{\mathcal{I}\in\mathcal{I}_M}\sum_{\substack{t\in M\\ C\Subset t\wedge D\Subset t}} M(t)\cdot\mu(\mathcal{I})}{\displaystyle\sum_{M\in\mathcal{M}_{\mathcal{K},k}}\sum_{\mathcal{I}\in\mathcal{I}_M}\sum_{\substack{t\in M\\ C\Subset t}} M(t)\cdot\mu(\mathcal{I})}$$

Using Lemma 10 we see that this sum is equal to

$$= \frac{\displaystyle\sum_{M\in\mathcal{M}_{\mathcal{K},k}}\sum_{\mathcal{I}\in\mathcal{I}_M}|C^{\mathcal{I}}\cap D^{\mathcal{I}}|\cdot\mu(\mathcal{I})}{\displaystyle\sum_{M\in\mathcal{M}_{\mathcal{K},k}}\sum_{\mathcal{I}\in\mathcal{I}_M}|C^{\mathcal{I}}|\cdot\mu(\mathcal{I})}$$

$$=^* \frac{\displaystyle\sum_{\mathcal{I}\in\mathcal{I}_{\mathcal{K},\Delta}}|C^{\mathcal{I}}\cap D^{\mathcal{I}}|\cdot\mu(\mathcal{I})}{\displaystyle\sum_{\mathcal{I}\in\mathcal{I}_{\mathcal{K},\Delta}}|C^{\mathcal{I}}|\cdot\mu(\mathcal{I})} = p.$$

For $C(a)[p]\in\mathcal{A}$ we have

$$\sum_{\substack{M\in\mathcal{M}_{\mathcal{K},k}\\ \text{s.t. }\exists t\in M: \{a,C\}\subseteq t}} p_M = \sum_{\substack{M\in\mathcal{M}_{\mathcal{K},k}\\ \text{s.t. }\exists t\in M: \{a,C\}\subseteq t}}\sum_{\mathcal{I}\in\mathcal{I}_M}\mu(\mathcal{I}) =^* \sum_{\substack{\mathcal{I}\in\mathcal{I}_{\mathcal{K},\Delta}\\ a^{\mathcal{I}}\in C^{\mathcal{I}}}}\mu(\mathcal{I}) = p.$$

The assertions $r(a,b)\in\mathcal{A}$ can be treated analogously, and finally we have

$$\sum_{M\in\mathcal{M}_{\mathcal{K},k}} p_M = \sum_{M\in\mathcal{M}_{\mathcal{K},k}}\sum_{\mathcal{I}\in\mathcal{I}_M}\mu(\mathcal{I}) =^* \sum_{\mathcal{I}\in\mathcal{I}_{\mathcal{K},\Delta}}\mu(\mathcal{I}) = 1.$$

For the other direction, let $\boldsymbol{p_M}\in\mathbb{R}_{\geq 0}^{\mathcal{M}_{\mathcal{K},k}}$ be a solution to (3) Then, for every $M\in\mathcal{M}_{\mathcal{K},k}$, $\mathcal{I}(M)$ is not empty since $\tau_M(\mathcal{I}_M) = M$. Thus, we can choose a function $\mu : \mathcal{I}_{\mathcal{K},\Delta} \to [0,1]$ such that $\sum_{\mathcal{I} \in \mathcal{I}_M} \mu(\mathcal{I}) = p_M$ for every $M \in \mathcal{M}_{\mathcal{K},k}$, e.g.,

$$\mu(\mathcal{I}) = \frac{p_{\tau_M}(\mathcal{I})}{|\mathcal{I}_{\tau_M}(\mathcal{I})|}.$$

Then, analogously to the proof above, we can show that μ is indeed a probability distribution and satisfies Eq. (1). □

4   Complexity Bounds for Consistency in $\mathcal{ALC}^{\mathsf{ME}}$

In this section, we use the characterization of consistency given in Theorem 11 to determine the complexity of the consistency problem in $\mathcal{ALC}^{\mathsf{ME}}$. We will start with domain size complexity (where the complexity is measured in terms of the size of the domain Δ only), and then determine the combined complexity (measured in terms of the size of the domain and the knowledge base). In both settings, we will distinguish between unary and binary encoding of the domain size.

Domain Size Complexity. Given a pKB $\mathcal{K}$ and a domain Δ with $|\Delta| = k$, we know that the number n of types can grow exponentially with the size of $\mathcal{K}$, i.e., $n \in \mathcal{O}(2^{|\mathcal{K}|})$. Then, the number of different multisets [19] over those n types of cardinality k is

$$|\mathcal{M}_{\mathcal{K},k}| = \left(\!\!\binom{n}{k}\!\!\right) = \binom{n+k-1}{k} = \frac{(n+k-1)!}{k! \cdot (n-1)!}.$$

Interestingly, this can be simplified to both $|\mathcal{M}_{\mathcal{K},k}| = \frac{(n+k-1)(n+k-2)\cdots n}{k(k-1)\cdots 1} \in \mathcal{O}(n^k)$ and $|\mathcal{M}_{\mathcal{K},k}| = \frac{(n+k-1)(n+k-2)\cdots(k+1)}{(n-1)(n-2)\cdots 1} \in \mathcal{O}(k^n)$.

Since (3) is a linear equation system with $\mathcal{O}(|\mathcal{K}|)$ equations and $|\mathcal{M}_{\mathcal{K},k}|$ variables, and linear equation systems over the real numbers can be solved in polynomial time [5], this yields the following complexities.

Corollary 12 (Domain size complexity). *Let $\mathcal{K}$ be a fixed pKB (which is not part of the input) and Δ be a finite domain with $|\Delta| = k$. Then the consistency of $\mathcal{K}$ w.r.t. Δ can be decided in*

- *P in $|\Delta| = k$ (unary encoding),*
- *ExpTime in $\log(k)$ (binary encoding).*

This result extends an existing P-time result for domain size complexity for unary encoding given in [23] from CBoxes to the case of general probabilistic KBs also including assertional knowledge. It should be noted that the approach used in [23] to show the "in P" result also uses types, but is nevertheless quite different from the one employed here.

Combined Complexity. Both the number of interpretations in Eq. (1) and the number of multisets of types in will usually grow exponentially with the size of the pKB $\mathcal{K}$, and thus will the number of variables. However, the number of linear equations in both systems will always be the number of probabilistic conditionals and probabilistic assertions plus one, i.e., it will at most grow linearly with the size of $\mathcal{K}$. We can exploit this fact using the following "sparse solution lemma" from linear programming:

Lemma 13 ([5], **Theorem 9.3**). *If a system of m linear equations has a non-negative solution in $\mathbb{R}$, then it has a solution with at most m variables positive.*

Thus, we can solve the consistency problem for a given pKB $\mathcal{K}$ with m conditionals and assertions (where $m \in \mathcal{O}(|\mathcal{K}|)$) and a domain Δ non-deterministically, by guessing a set $\mathcal{M}$ of $m + 1$ distinct multisets $M_1, \dots, M_{m+1}$ of types with cardinality $k = |\Delta|$, and checking whether these multisets are consistent and yield a solvable system of equations:

$$
\frac{\displaystyle\sum_{M \in \mathcal{M}} \sum_{\substack{t \in M \\ \text{s.t.}\, C \in t \land D \in t}} M(t) \cdot p_M}{\displaystyle\sum_{M \in \mathcal{M}} \sum_{\substack{t \in M \\ \text{s.t.}\, C \in t}} M(t) \cdot p_M} = p, \qquad \text{for } (D|C)[p] \in \mathcal{C},
$$

$$
\sum_{\substack{M \in \mathcal{M} \\ \text{s.t.}\, \exists t \in M: \{a,C\} \subseteq t}} p_M = p, \qquad \text{for } C(a)[p] \in \mathcal{A},
$$

$$
\sum_{\substack{M \in \mathcal{M} \\ \text{s.t.}\, \exists t \in M: \{a, \exists r.b\} \subseteq t}} p_M = p, \qquad \text{for } r(a,b)[p] \in \mathcal{A},
$$

$$
\sum_{M \in \mathcal{M}} p_M = 1.
$$

(4)

This provides us with the following complexity results:

Corollary 14 (Combined Complexity). *Let $\mathcal{K}$ be a pKB and Δ be a finite domain with $|\Delta| = k$. Then consistency of $\mathcal{K}$ w.r.t. Δ is*

- *NP-complete in $|\mathcal{K}| + k$ (unary encoding of k),*
- *NExpTime-complete in $|\mathcal{K}| + \log(k)$ (binary encoding of k).*

Proof Guessing a multiset of size k can be done by guessing k types (of size at most quadratic in $|\mathcal{K}|$). Thus, in total guessing can be done in non-deterministic time $\mathcal{O}(m \cdot k \cdot |\mathcal{K}|^2) = \mathcal{O}(|\mathcal{K}|^3 \cdot k)$. Evaluating the corresponding linear equation system (4) (of size polynomial in $|\mathcal{K}|$) can then be done in polynomial time. The complexity upper bounds follow directly from this observation.

According to [6,18], fixed-domain reasoning in classical $\mathcal{ALC}$ is already NP-complete for unary encoding of the domain size, and NExpTime-complete for binary encoding of the domain size. There is an easy reduction from fixed-domain consistency in classical $\mathcal{ALC}$ to $\mathcal{ALC}^{\mathsf{ME}}$ consistency: Simply exchange GCIs $C \sqsubseteq D$ with conditionals $(D|C)[1]$ and add probability 1 to all assertions. It is easy to see that each model $\mathcal{I}$ of the original KB can be translated into a model of the new pKB by setting the probability of $\mathcal{I}$ to 1, and of all other interpretations to 0. Similarly, for each model of the pKB all interpretations with non-zero probability must also be models of the original KB. Thus, the original classical KB has a model with domain Δ iff the constructed pKB is consistent w.r.t. Δ, which transfers the hardness results for fixed-domain consistency in classical $\mathcal{ALC}$ to consistency in $\mathcal{ALC}^{\mathsf{ME}}$.   □

Note that the results for combined complexity cannot be shown using the approach employed in [23]. There, the constructed equation system not only has exponentially many variables, but also exponentially many equations. Thus, the sparse solution lemma cannot be used to reduce the complexity.

5   Conclusion

In this paper, we have determined the complexity of the consistency problem in the probabilistic Description Logic $\mathcal{ALC}^{\mathsf{ME}}$, considering both domain size and combined complexity and distinguishing between unary and binary encoding of the domain size. Our results are based on the notion of types, but to use this notion in a setting with assertions, we had to extend it such that it also takes named individuals and their relationships into account. Basically, these results show that probabilities do not increase the complexity of the consistency problem since we obtain the same results as for fixed domain reasoning in $\mathcal{ALC}$. Note that our results can be transferred easily to a variant of $\mathcal{ALC}^{\mathsf{ME}}$ in which probabilistic conditionals are provided with interval probabilities instead of point probabilities.

In future work, we want to extend our complexity results to other reasoning tasks and to DLs other than $\mathcal{ALC}$. In [23] we have already considered drawing inferences, but have only investigated the domain size complexity. More challenging is to go from fixed domain reasoning to finite domain reasoning, i.e., checking whether there is some finite domain Δ such that the pKB is consistent w.r.t. Δ. Finally, if a pKB is consistent, then we know that it has a unique ME-model, but the complexity of computing (an approximation of) this distribution is unclear, though [23] contains some preliminary results in this direction, but again restricted to domain size complexity.

References

1. Baader, F., Borgwardt, S., Koopmann, P., Ozaki, A., Thost, V.: Metric temporal description logics with interval-rigid names. In: Dixon, C., Finger, M. (eds.) FroCoS 2017. LNCS (LNAI), vol. 10483, pp. 60–76. Springer, Cham (2017). https://doi.org/10.1007/978-3-319-66167-4_4
2. Baader, F., Calvanese, D., McGuinness, D.L., Nardi, D., Patel-Schneider, P.F. (eds.): The Description Logic Handbook: Theory, Implementation, and Applications. Cambridge University Press, Cambridge (2003)

3. Baader, F., Horrocks, I., Lutz, C., Sattler, U.: An Introduction to Description Logic. Cambridge University Press, Cambridge (2017). https://doi.org/10.1017/9781139025355

4. Baader, F., Koopmann, P., Turhan, A.-Y.: Using ontologies to query probabilistic numerical data. In: Dixon, C., Finger, M. (eds.) FroCoS 2017. LNCS (LNAI), vol. 10483, pp. 77–94. Springer, Cham (2017). https://doi.org/10.1007/978-3-319-66167-4_5

5. Chvatal, V.: Linear Programming. W.H Freeman (1983)

6. Gaggl, S.A., Rudolph, S., Schweizer, L.: Fixed-domain reasoning for description logics. In: Proceedings of the ECAI 2016, pp. 819–827. IOS Press (2016)

7. Grove, A., Halpern, J., Koller, D.: Random worlds and maximum entropy. J. Artif. Intell. Res. **2**, 33–88 (1994)

8. Halpern, J.Y.: An analysis of first-order logics of probability. Artif. Intell. **46**(3), 311–350 (1990)

9. Hoehndorf, R., Schofield, P.N., Gkoutos, G.V.: The role of ontologies in biological and biomedical research: a functional perspective. Brief. Bioinform. **16**(6), 1069–1080 (2015)

10. Kern-Isberner, G. (ed.): Conditionals in Nonmonotonic Reasoning and Belief Revision. LNCS (LNAI), vol. 2087. Springer, Heidelberg (2001). https://doi.org/10.1007/3-540-44600-1

11. Kern-Isberner, G., Thimm, M.: Novel semantical approaches to relational probabilistic conditionals. In: Proceedings of the KR 2010, pp. 382–392. AAAI Press (2010)

12. Lutz, C., Schröder, L.: Probabilistic description logics for subjective uncertainty. In: Proceedings of the KR 2010, pp. 393–403. AAAI Press (2010)

13. Paris, J.B.: Common sense and maximum entropy. Synthese **117**(1), 75–93 (1999)

14. Paris, J.B.: The Uncertain Reasoner's Companion: A Mathematical Perspective. Cambridge University Press, Cambridge (2006)

15. Peñaloza, R., Potyka, N.: Towards statistical reasoning in description logics over finite domains. In: Moral, S., Pivert, O., Sánchez, D., Marín, N. (eds.) SUM 2017. LNCS (LNAI), vol. 10564, pp. 280–294. Springer, Cham (2017). https://doi.org/10.1007/978-3-319-67582-4_20

16. Pratt, V.R.: Models of program logics. In: Proceedings of the FOCS 1979, pp. 115–122. IEEE Computer Society (1979)

17. Rudolph, S., Krötzsch, M., Hitzler, P.: Type-elimination-based reasoning for the description logic SHIQbs using decision diagrams and disjunctive datalog. Logical Methods in Computer Science **8**(1), 38 p. (2012)

18. Rudolph, S., Schweizer, L.: Not too big, not too small... complexities of fixed-domain reasoning in first-order and description logics. In: Oliveira, E., Gama, J., Vale, Z., Lopes Cardoso, H. (eds.) EPIA 2017. LNCS (LNAI), vol. 10423, pp. 695–708. Springer, Cham (2017). https://doi.org/10.1007/978-3-319-65340-2_57

19. Stanley, R.: Enumerative Combinatorics: Cambridge Studies in Advanced Mathematics. Cambridge University Press, Cambridge (1997)

20. Thimm, M., Kern-Isberner, G.: On probabilistic inference in relationalconditional logics. Logic J. IGPL **20**(5), 872–908 (2012)

21. Tobies, S.: The complexity of reasoning with cardinality restrictions and nominals in expressive description logics. J. Artif. Intell. Res. **12**, 199–217 (2000)

22. Wilhelm, M., Kern-Isberner, G., Ecke, A.: Basic independence results for maximum entropy reasoning based on relational conditionals. In: Proceedings of the GCAI 2017, EPiC Series in Computing, vol. 50, pp. 36–50. EasyChair (2017)
23. Wilhelm, M., Kern-Isberner, G., Ecke, A., Baader, F.: Counting strategies for the probabilistic description logic $\mathcal{ALC}^{ME}$ under the principle of maximum entropy. In: Calimeri, F., Leone, N., Manna, M. (eds.) JELIA 2019. LNCS (LNAI), vol. 11468, pp. 434–449. Springer, Cham (2019). https://doi.org/10.1007/978-3-030-19570-0_28

Extending Forgetting-Based Abduction Using Nominals

Warren Del-Pinto(✉) and Renate A. Schmidt

School of Computer Science, University of Manchester,
Oxford Road, Manchester M13 9PL, UK
warren.del-pinto@manchester.ac.uk

Abstract. Abductive reasoning produces hypotheses to explain new observations with respect to some background knowledge. This paper focuses on ABox abduction in ontologies, where knowledge is expressed in description logics and both the observations and hypotheses are ground statements. The input is expressed in the description logic $\mathcal{ALC}$ and the observation can contain any set of $\mathcal{ALC}$ concept or role assertions. The proposed approach uses forgetting to produce hypotheses in the form of a disjunctive set of axioms, where each disjunct is an independent explanation for the observation and the overall hypothesis is semantically minimal, i.e., makes the least assumptions required. Previous work on forgetting-based abduction is combined with the semantic forgetting method of the system FAME. The hypotheses produced are expressed in an extension of $\mathcal{ALC}$ which uses nominals, role inverses and fixpoints: $\mathcal{ALCOI}\mu(\nabla)$. This combination overcomes the inability of the existing forgetting-based approach to allow role assertions in observations and hypotheses, and enables the computation of other previously unreachable hypotheses. An experimental evaluation is performed using a prototype implementation of the method on a corpus of real world ontologies.

1 Introduction

Abduction was first identified as a form of reasoning by C.S. Peirce, who likened it to a "flash of insight". Like induction, and unlike deduction, abduction is ampliative: the conclusion of the reasoning process extends beyond what already follows from existing background knowledge. Abduction is often seen as the process of hypothesis generation, while induction can be seen as the process of hypothesis evaluation or generalisation. The use cases for abduction have led to a diverse range of investigations into the topic. These include complexity studies [10], applications in natural language interpretation [16], inductive and abductive logic programming [26,29], statistical relational AI [28] and studies of the interaction between abduction and induction [12].

This paper focuses on abductive reasoning in description logics (DLs), which are fragments of first-order logic. In this setting, background knowledge is expressed in an ontology, which contains information regarding concepts and

© Springer Nature Switzerland AG 2019
A. Herzig and A. Popescu (Eds.): FroCoS 2019, LNAI 11715, pp. 185–202, 2019.
https://doi.org/10.1007/978-3-030-29007-8_11

relations between entities. Ontologies are used in a wide variety of fields including bioinformatics, robotics and finance. Benefits of using ontologies include the ability to clearly model, reuse, share and reason about existing knowledge. Most existing reasoning systems in ontologies are deductive. They can be used to derive consequences of the existing ontology that are not explicitly represented. However, they cannot be used directly to explain new observations that do not follow from the existing knowledge, which is required for tasks such as hypothesis generation, diagnostics and belief expansion. The importance of abduction in DLs has been recognised [11] and a variety of work exists on the topic, including complexity studies [3], applications to repair and query explanation [5,21] and methods for different forms of TBox and ABox abduction [8,9,15,17,27].

One approach to performing abductive reasoning in DL ontologies uses *forgetting*. Forgetting aims to eliminate specified symbols in an ontology while preserving all entailments that can be represented in the restricted signature. The dual task is called *uniform interpolation*. Both of these are related to second-order quantifier elimination [13], which translates logical formulae expressed in second-order logic into equivalent formulae in first-order logic by eliminating existentially quantified predicate symbols. The use of second-order quantifier elimination for abduction has been proposed for relatively small theories expressed in propositional or classical logics [7,13,30], while forgetting has been proposed for TBox abduction in DLs [20]. More recently, a method for performing ABox abduction in the DL $\mathcal{ALC}$ was developed [6], which utilises contrapositive reasoning and the resolution-based forgetting system LETHE [19]. This approach produces hypotheses that consist of a disjunctive set of ABox assertions. Each disjunct is an independent explanation [18], resulting in a space of possible explanations. The method has been shown to be practical over large ontologies. However, a limitation to the method is the absence of role assertions in observations and hypotheses, which restricts its use of existing information contained within the ABox. Given an ABox observation, the approach cannot use relationships between individuals to provide a more specific explanation. These explanations would be useful in many applications, such as those involving the use of large knowledge graphs which have seen increasing interest in recent years.

The primary aim of this work is to overcome this limitation by combining the method in [6] with another forgetting system: FAME [32,33]. The key characteristic of FAME is its ability to perform forgetting in $\mathcal{ALCOI}\mu(\nabla)$, which includes nominals. As suggested in [6], nominals can be used to overcome the limitations of the abduction method. This is explored and confirmed in this paper.

2   Problem Definition

In this work, knowledge is expressed in the description logic $\mathcal{ALC}$ [2]. The signature of $\mathcal{ALC}$ is defined by disjoint sets N_c, N_r and N_I containing atomic concept names, role names and individual names respectively. Concepts in $\mathcal{ALC}$ can take the following forms: $\bot \mid \top \mid A \mid \neg C \mid C \sqcup D \mid C \sqcap D \mid \exists r.C \mid \forall r.C$, where A is any atomic concept name, C and D are any $\mathcal{ALC}$ concepts and r is a role name.

An ontology $\mathcal{O}$ expressed in $\mathcal{ALC}$ takes the form $\mathcal{O} = \mathcal{T} \cup \mathcal{A}$, where $\mathcal{T}$ is a *TBox* and $\mathcal{A}$ is an ABox. The TBox contains information about concepts represented as general concept inclusions (GCIs) of the form $C \sqsubseteq D$ or equivalence axioms of the form $C \equiv D$, which can also be expressed as the two GCIs $C \sqsubseteq D$ and $D \sqsubseteq C$. The ABox contains (ground) assertions about specific individuals of the form $C(a)$ or $r(a, b)$ where a, b are arbitrary individual names.

The semantics of $\mathcal{ALC}$ is defined in terms of an interpretation $\mathcal{I}$ as a pair $\mathcal{I} = \langle \Delta^{\mathcal{I}}, \cdot^{\mathcal{I}} \rangle$, where $\Delta^{\mathcal{I}}$ is a non-empty set called the *domain* and $\cdot^{\mathcal{I}}$ is an *interpretation function* mapping each individual $a \in N_I$ to a single element $a^{\mathcal{I}} \in \Delta^{\mathcal{I}}$, each concept to a subset of $\Delta^{\mathcal{I}}$ and each role to a subset of $\Delta^{\mathcal{I}} \times \Delta^{\mathcal{I}}$. This is extended to $\mathcal{ALC}$ concepts as follows:

$$\bot^{\mathcal{I}} = \emptyset \qquad \top^{\mathcal{I}} = \Delta^{\mathcal{I}} \qquad \neg C = \Delta^{\mathcal{I}} \setminus C^{\mathcal{I}}$$
$$(C \sqcap D)^{\mathcal{I}} = C^{\mathcal{I}} \cap D^{\mathcal{I}} \qquad (C \sqcup D)^{\mathcal{I}} = C^{\mathcal{I}} \cup D^{\mathcal{I}}$$
$$(\exists r.C)^{\mathcal{I}} = \{x \in \Delta^{\mathcal{I}} \mid \exists y.(x, y) \in r^{\mathcal{I}} \wedge y \in C^{\mathcal{I}}\}$$
$$(\forall r.C)^{\mathcal{I}} = \{x \in \Delta^{\mathcal{I}} \mid \forall y.(x, y) \in r^{\mathcal{I}} \rightarrow y \in C^{\mathcal{I}}\}$$

For TBox axioms, the GCI $C \sqsubseteq D$ is true in $\mathcal{I}$ iff $C^{\mathcal{I}} \subseteq D^{\mathcal{I}}$ holds. A model of a TBox is an interpretation for which all axioms in the TBox are true, and if a TBox has a model then it is *satisfiable*.

For this paper, it is also necessary to consider the DL $\mathcal{ALCOI}\mu(\nabla)$, which extends $\mathcal{ALC}$ with *nominals*, *role inverses*, the *top role* and in some cases *fixpoints*. For each individual $a \in N_I$, the corresponding nominal $\{a\}$ is interpreted as a concept containing only a. Using nominals, ABox assertions can be expressed as equivalent TBox axioms, i.e., $C(a)$ and $r(a, b)$ can be expressed as $\{a\} \sqsubseteq C$ and $\{a\} \sqsubseteq \exists r.\{b\}$ respectively. The role inverse of a role r is denoted by r^-, and the top role is denoted by ∇. The semantics of these are defined as follows: $(r^-)^{\mathcal{I}} = \{(y, x) \in \Delta^{\mathcal{I}} \times \Delta^{\mathcal{I}} \mid (x, y) \in r\}$ and $\nabla^{\mathcal{I}} = \Delta^{\mathcal{I}} \times \Delta^{\mathcal{I}}$. In some specific cases, described later in this paper, fixpoints may be used to represent cyclic results. We refer to [4] for a full description and the semantics of fixpoints.

Here the focus is on ABox abduction over $\mathcal{ALC}$ ontologies. Our aim is to produce hypotheses that satisfy the following:

Definition 1. *Let $\mathcal{O}$ be an ontology and ψ be a set of ABox assertions, both expressed in $\mathcal{ALC}$, where $\mathcal{O}, \psi \not\models \bot$ and $\mathcal{O} \not\models \psi$. Let $\mathcal{S}_A$ be a set of abducible symbols, containing any subset of the symbols in the signature of $\mathcal{O}, \psi$. The ABox abduction problem is to find a hypothesis $\mathcal{H}$ as a disjunction of ABox assertions, containing only the symbols in $\mathcal{S}_A$, which satisfies the following conditions:*

(i) $\mathcal{O}, \mathcal{H} \not\models \bot$, (ii) $\mathcal{O}, \mathcal{H} \models \psi$

(iii) Each disjunct α_i in $\mathcal{H}$ is an independent explanation for ψ: i.e. for every α_i in $\mathcal{H}$, $\mathcal{O}, \alpha_i \not\models \alpha_1 \sqcup ... \sqcup \alpha_{i-1} \sqcup \alpha_{i+1} \sqcup ... \sqcup \alpha_n$.

(iv) If there exists a $\mathcal{H}'$ which satisfies conditions (i)—(iii), such that $\mathcal{H}'$ contains only symbols in $\mathcal{S}_A$ and $\mathcal{O}, \mathcal{H} \models \mathcal{O}, \mathcal{H}'$, then $\mathcal{O}, \mathcal{H}' \models \mathcal{O}, \mathcal{H}$.

Conditions (i), *consistency*, and (ii), *explanation*, are standard conditions on abductive hypotheses, requiring that the hypothesis computed explains the observation using the information in $\mathcal{O}$ without contradicting it. Condition (iii) requires that there are no redundant disjuncts in the hypothesis $\mathcal{H}$. A redundant disjunct is one that contradicts the information in $\mathcal{O}$, or provides an explanation that is simply stronger than one that is already contained within the rest of the hypothesis $\mathcal{H}$. From this, it can be seen that condition (i) is a consequence of condition (iii). However, condition (i) is still included here for clarity as it is a key requirement. Condition (iv) requires that the overall hypothesis computed is the one that makes the least assumptions required to entail the observation, and is referred to as semantic minimality [15]. As noted in [6], in settings where the hypothesis can contain disjunctions it is necessary to consider the redundancy of individual disjuncts prior to checking for semantic minimality.

The above definition extends the problem defined in [6] by lifting the restrictions on ψ, $\mathcal{S}_A$ and $\mathcal{H}$. Specifically, both ψ and $\mathcal{H}$ may contain any combination of $\mathcal{ALC}$ ABox assertions, including role assertions, and the set of abducibles $\mathcal{S}_A$ is no longer required to contain all role symbols in $\mathcal{O}, \psi$.

In addition, in this work the produced hypothesis consists of a disjunction of $\mathcal{ALCOI}\mu(\nabla)$ axioms. Thus, certain hypotheses that can only be expressed using nominals and inverse roles are also reachable using this extended approach. The exact form of these are discussed alongside the proposed method.

3   Forgetting-Based Abduction

Forgetting eliminates symbols, i.e., concept and role names from an ontology while preserving the entailments that are representable in the restricted signature. The symbols to eliminate are specified by a forgetting signature $\mathcal{F}$, where $\mathcal{F}$ can contain any subset of symbols in the signature of the ontology.

Forgetting can be utilised for abduction via contraposition: $\mathcal{O}, \mathcal{H} \models \psi$ if and only if $\mathcal{O}, \neg\psi \models \neg\mathcal{H}$. For an ontology $\mathcal{O}$ and observation ψ, both expressed in $\mathcal{ALC}$, the steps in forgetting-based abduction are given in Fig. 1.

---

1. Eliminate a specified set of symbols $\mathcal{F}$ from $(\mathcal{O}, \neg\psi)$. The result of this step is a new ontology, $\mathcal{V} = \{\beta_1, ..., \beta_n\}$, which is called the *forgetting solution* of $(\mathcal{O}, \neg\psi)$ with respect to $\mathcal{F}$.
2. Extract a *reduced forgetting solution* $\mathcal{V}^*$ from $\mathcal{V}$. This is done by eliminating all axioms in $\mathcal{V}$ that violate the dual of Definition 1(iii), i.e., those $\beta_i \in \mathcal{V}$ such that $\mathcal{O}, \beta_1, ..., \beta_{i-1}, \beta_{i+1}, ..., \beta_n \models \beta_i$.
3. Negate $\mathcal{V}^*$ to obtain a hypothesis $\mathcal{H}$, in the form of a disjunctive set of axioms, which satisfies Definition 1.

Fig. 1. Steps in forgetting-based abduction [6].

There are several important features of forgetting that make forgetting-based abduction promising [6]. (1) Given that forgetting preserves all remaining entailments, the forgetting solutions can be seen as strongest necessary conditions of an input ontology in the restricted signature. This means that the forgetting solution $\mathcal{V}$ is the strongest necessary condition [22] of $(\mathcal{O}, \neg\psi)$ in the signature $\mathcal{S}_A$. As a result, the negation of $\mathcal{V}$ is a weakest sufficient condition, as strongest necessary and weakest sufficient conditions are dual notions. Weakest sufficient conditions correspond to a weakest abduction result [7,22], i.e., a semantically minimal hypothesis. When combined with the negation step 3 in Fig. 1, this results in a hypothesis $\mathcal{H}$ that satisfies both conditions (iii) and (iv). (2) The use of a forgetting signature $\mathcal{F}$ provides a goal-oriented method for specifying the abducible symbols $\mathcal{S}_A$: for an ontology $\mathcal{O}$ and an observation ψ, $\mathcal{S}_A = sig(\mathcal{O} \cup \{\psi\}) \setminus \mathcal{F}$. It may be the case that a user does not have sufficient information to manually choose the abducibles from a large set of available symbols. In this case, by inspecting the signature of the observation ψ, $\mathcal{F}$ can be defined by simply setting it equal to a subset of the symbols in ψ. This guarantees that inferences are made between $\mathcal{O}$ and ψ in order to eliminate the symbols in $\mathcal{F}$, in turn guaranteeing that a non-trivial hypothesis $\mathcal{H} \neq \psi$ is obtained. (3) Forgetting can be applied iteratively. For example, eliminating a set of symbols $\mathcal{F}_1$ from an ontology $\mathcal{O}$ results in a forgetting result $\mathcal{V}_1$. If a second set of symbols $\mathcal{F}_2$ is then eliminated from $\mathcal{V}_1$, the result obtained will be the same as eliminating all of the symbols in $\mathcal{F}_1 \cup \mathcal{F}_2$ from $\mathcal{O}$. This provides a method for hypothesis refinement: the steps in Fig. 1 can be repeated by eliminating symbols that occur in the current hypothesis to obtain a stronger hypothesis, perhaps based on heuristics or external data. (4) There exist several forgetting systems that have been shown to be efficient across large real-world ontologies, for example [19,23,33].

The abduction method proposed in [6] utilises the resolution-based forgetting approach implemented in the system LETHE [19], which performs forgetting over $\mathcal{ALC}$ ontologies with ABoxes. LETHE adopts the *uniform interpolation* perspective on forgetting [24], meaning that it preserves all consequences of the input ontology in the restricted signature. Thus, the forgetting solution $\mathcal{V}$ computed by LETHE is called a *uniform interpolant*.

By using LETHE for the forgetting step 1 in Fig. 1, the abduction approach in [6] can compute hypotheses which satisfy a restricted form of Definition 1, and has been shown to be sound and complete for this problem. The first main restriction, however, is that the set of abducibles $\mathcal{S}_A$ must contain all role symbols in $(\mathcal{O}, \neg\psi)$. This is due to the fact that the form of role forgetting currently implemented in LETHE is not complete for the abduction problem. This was noted in [6] and an example was provided. Here is another example:

Example 1. Consider the following ontology: $\mathcal{O} = \{B \sqsubseteq \exists r.B\}$. Let the observation be $\psi = \exists r.B(a)$. The expected hypothesis given $\mathcal{S}_A = \{B\}$ is $\mathcal{H} = B(a)$.

The result of applying LETHE's calculus [19] to forget r is an empty uniform interpolant. While this is sufficient for the uniform interpolation problem, for abduction the expected hypothesis $B(a)$ is not computed.

The second restriction is that the observations and hypotheses cannot contain role assertions. Consider the following example:

Example 2. Consider the following ontology $\mathcal{O} = \{\exists r.B \sqsubseteq A, B(b)\}$. Let the observation be $\psi = A(a)$. Case 1: given a set of abducibles $\mathcal{S}_A = \{B, r\}$, the hypothesis satisfying Definition 1 would be $\mathcal{H}_1 = \exists r.B(a)$. Case 2: given $\mathcal{S}_A = \{r\}$, the hypothesis would instead be $\mathcal{H}_2 = r(a, b)$.

The first hypothesis $\mathcal{H}_1$ is reachable using LETHE. However, the second hypothesis $\mathcal{H}_2$ is not. This is due to the fact that LETHE's calculus does not support deriving negated role assertions of the form $\neg r(a, b)$, as it is designed to preserve all entailments of the input that are expressible in $\mathcal{ALC}$ and $\neg r(a, b)$ is not expressible in $\mathcal{ALC}$. Thus, these are not obtained in the reduced forgetting solution $\mathcal{V}^*$ and role assertions will be absent from the hypothesis when $\mathcal{V}^*$ is negated in step 3. This restriction means that the system is not able to utilise existing relationships between individuals in the observation and those in the ABox of the background ontology when generating hypotheses. Thus, many of the more specific hypotheses such as $\mathcal{H}_2$ in the example above are not reachable.

In summary, the existing forgetting-based abduction approach in [6] takes as **input** an $\mathcal{ALC}$ ontology $\mathcal{O}$, an observation of the form $\psi = \{C_1(a_1), ..., C_k(a_k)\}$ where each C_i is an $\mathcal{ALC}$ concept and each a_i is an individual, and a set of abducibles $\mathcal{S}_A$ containing all role symbols in $(\mathcal{O}, \neg\psi)$. The negation of the observation takes the form $\neg\psi = \neg C_1(a_1) \sqcup ... \sqcup \neg C_k(a_k)$. The final hypothesis produced via steps 1–3 in Fig. 1 takes the form $\mathcal{H} = \alpha_1(a_1) \sqcup ... \sqcup \alpha_n(a_n)$ where each α_i is an $\mathcal{ALC}$ concept. It turns out the final output may need to be expressed in $\mathcal{ALC}$ extended with disjunctive ABox assertions $\mathcal{ALCV}$.

4   Extending the System

In this work, the forgetting-based approach is extended via the use of nominals. However, producing hypotheses with nominals requires the use of a forgetting method that can compute forgetting solutions for ontologies expressed in $\mathcal{ALCO}$.

For this purpose, the abduction approach above is combined with the forgetting system FAME [32, 33]. As opposed to the uniform interpolation perspective taken by LETHE, FAME frames the problem of forgetting in terms of *semantic forgetting* [32, 33]. This view is closely related to second-order quantifier elimination [7, 13], where the forgetting result must be equivalent to the original formula in second-order logic. From the viewpoint of abduction, while the steps taken in the approach are conceptually the same when utilising FAME, each step must be extended in several ways compared to the previous approach.

First it is helpful to consider how FAME handles the forgetting process [33]. Any ABox assertions in the input are translated to equivalent TBox axioms involving nominals. Then, the ontology is transformed into a set of clauses $\mathcal{N}$. Before the process of eliminating the symbols in the forgetting signature $\mathcal{F}$ can take place, the set $\mathcal{N}$ must be transformed into the appropriate reduced forms.

For role forgetting, $\mathcal{N}$ is transformed into *r-reduced* form. Given a role symbol to be forgotten r, every clause in $\mathcal{N}$ that contains r must be of the form $C \sqcup \forall r.D$ or $C \sqcup \neg \forall r.D$ where C and D are possibly complex concepts that do not contain r.

During this transformation, definer symbols may need to be introduced. These are fresh symbols that do not appear in the input ontology and are used to incrementally replace the concept symbols C and D in clauses such as the one above, until neither of them contain r. For example, given a forgetting signature $\mathcal{F} = \{r\}$ and a clause $\forall r.A \sqcup \forall r.B$, a definer is introduced to replace $\forall r.A$. This results in the two clauses $D_1 \sqcup \forall r.B$ and $\neg D_1 \sqcup \forall r.A$ respectively.

For concept forgetting, the reduced form is the A-*reduced* form. To forget a concept A, every clause must be of the form $A \sqcup C$ where C is a possibly complex concept which does not contain A or contains only negative occurrences of A. For example, the clauses $A \sqcup B$ and $A \sqcup \forall r.\neg A$ are in A-reduced form.

When forgetting the symbols in $\mathcal{F}$, role symbols are eliminated first followed by concept symbols. In both cases, the set $\mathcal{N}$ is first transformed into r-*reduced* and A-*reduced* forms respectively [33]. Once the appropriate reduced form is obtained, rules based around Ackermann's Lemma [1] are used to forget the symbols in $\mathcal{F}$. Given a symbol A to be eliminated, the essence of Ackermann's lemma is to construct a definition of A, which does not contain it, from the existing clauses in which it occurs. This definition can then be used to replace every instance of A, thereby eliminating it from the original ontology. The Ackermann^R and Purify^R rules are used to eliminate role symbols, while the Ackermann^C and Purify^C rules, shown in Fig. 2, are used to eliminate concept symbols [33]. Finally any definer symbols are eliminated, via the use of the Ackermann^C and Purify^C rules, resulting in the forgetting solution $\mathcal{V}$.

Full details of this process, including the rules for obtaining the reduced forms and the forgetting rules, can be found in the relevant papers [32,33]. The concept forgetting rules have been included for reference in Fig. 2, since these are utilised in illustrative examples throughout this paper.

An important aspect of FAME for this work is the fact that it is sound for forgetting in $\mathcal{ALCOI}\mu(\nabla)$, as expressed in this theorem.

Theorem 1. *For any $\mathcal{ALCOI}\mu(\nabla)$ ontology $\mathcal{O}$ and any signature $\mathcal{F} \subseteq sig(\mathcal{O})$, where sig($\mathcal{O}$) is the set of concept and role symbols in $\mathcal{O}$, FAME always terminates and returns a set $\mathcal{V}$ of clauses. If $\mathcal{V}$ does not contain any symbols in $\mathcal{F}$, then the symbols in $\mathcal{F}$ were successfully forgotten and the set $\mathcal{V}$ is a solution of forgetting the symbols in $\mathcal{F}$ from $\mathcal{O}$.*

This theorem is a weaker form of the theorem in [33], specifically focussed on the description logic $\mathcal{ALCOI}\mu(\nabla)$, as this is the language required in the setting of this paper. The original theorem holds for the logic $\mathcal{ALCOIH}\mu^+(\nabla, \sqcup)$, which also includes role hierarchies of the form $r \sqsubseteq s$ and role conjunction. However, here all inputs are expressed in $\mathcal{ALCO}(\nabla)$. For this setting, role hierarchies are excluded. Role conjunctions are also excluded since they are only needed in the solution when the input is expressed in $\mathcal{ALCOIH}$ [31].

One limitation of using FAME to compute the forgetting result is that FAME is not complete. However, it is worth noting that LETHE is not complete for role forgetting in the context of abduction either [6]. Thus, the incompleteness drawback of FAME is offset by the fact that additional hypotheses can be reached. This is illustrated by Examples 4, 5 and 7 later in this paper.

Non-cyclic Ackermann^C: $\dfrac{\mathcal{N}, C_1 \sqcup A, ..., C_n \sqcup A}{\mathcal{N}^A_{\neg C_1 \sqcup ... \sqcup \neg C_n}}$ *where (i) A does not occur in any C_i (ii) $\mathcal{N}$ is negative with respect to A*
Cyclic Ackermann^C: $\dfrac{\mathcal{N}, C_1[A] \sqcup A, ..., C_n[A] \sqcup A}{\mathcal{N}^A_{\mu X.(\neg C_1 \sqcup ... \sqcup \neg C_n)[X]}}$ *where (i) each C_i is negative with respect to A, (ii) $\mathcal{N}$ is negative w.r.t A*
Purify^C: $\dfrac{\mathcal{N}}{\mathcal{N}^A_{(\neg)\top}}$ *where $\mathcal{N}$ is positive with respect to A*

Fig. 2. Rules used in the forgetting system FAME to forget a concept A, where $\mathcal{N}^A_C$ is the set of clauses obtained from $\mathcal{N}$ by replacing every occurrence of A with C [33].

Via the use of FAME, the forgetting step 1 of the abduction method can now take any ontology $\mathcal{O}$ and observation ψ for which the combination $(\mathcal{O}, \psi)$ is expressible in $\mathcal{ALCO}$, where the signature of abducibles $\mathcal{S}_A$ can be any set of concept or role symbols occurring in $(\mathcal{O}, \psi)$. Note, the set of abducibles $\mathcal{S}_A$ includes all nominals, since no form of nominal forgetting is utilised in this work.

However, it is first necessary to decide how to represent the negation of the observation ψ and the form of the hypothesis $\mathcal{H}$, since FAME operates on and produces $\mathcal{ALCO}$ TBoxes rather than ABox assertions. To illustrate this, as well as the procedure for concept forgetting in FAME, recall Example 2:

Example 3. The $\mathcal{ALCO}$ reformulation of the ontology considered in Example 2 is: $\mathcal{O} = \{\exists r.B \sqsubseteq A, \{b\} \sqsubseteq B\}$ and the observation is $\psi = \{a\} \sqsubseteq A$, where $\{a\}$ and $\{b\}$ are nominals. Given a set of abducibles $\mathcal{S}_A = \{B, r\}$, the hypothesis obtained using FAME in step 1 of Fig. 1 is $\mathcal{H}_1 = \{a\} \sqsubseteq \exists r.B$. If instead $\mathcal{S}_A = \{r\}$, the hypothesis is $\mathcal{H}_2 = \{a\} \sqsubseteq \exists r.\{b\}$. Both $\mathcal{H}_1$ and $\mathcal{H}_2$ satisfy Definition 1.

However, in cases where either the observation or the hypothesis take the form of a conjunction or disjunction of ABox assertions, the reformulation is less obvious. In this case, it is possible to take advantage of the fact that FAME can perform forgetting in the presence of the top role ∇.

Example 4. Consider the following ontology $\mathcal{O} = \{\exists r.B \sqsubseteq A, C \sqsubseteq D, \{b\} \sqsubseteq B\}$ and the observation $\psi = A(a) \sqcap D(c)$. Let $\mathcal{S}_A = \{r, C\}$. The expected hypothesis under Definition 1 should be equivalent to $\mathcal{H} = r(a,b) \sqcap C(c)$. The negation of ψ can be represented as: $\neg\psi = \top \sqsubseteq \forall\nabla.(\neg\{a\} \sqcup \neg A) \sqcup \forall\nabla.(\neg\{c\} \sqcup \neg D)$. Following the steps in Fig. 1 using FAME, in step 1, where $\mathcal{F} = \{A, B, D\}$, the hypothesis obtained can be represented as: $\mathcal{H} = \top \sqsubseteq \exists\nabla.(\neg\{a\} \sqcup \exists r.\{b\}) \sqcup \exists\nabla.(\neg\{c\} \sqcup C)$. This is equivalent to the expected hypothesis $r(a,b) \sqcap C(c)$.

This leads to the general form used for the negated observations and the hypotheses produced. These are shown below:

$$\neg\psi = \top \sqsubseteq \forall\nabla.(\neg\{a_1\} \sqcup \neg C_1) \sqcup ... \sqcup \forall\nabla.(\neg\{a_k\} \sqcup \neg C_k) \tag{1}$$

$$\mathcal{H}_F = \top \sqsubseteq \exists\nabla.D_1 \sqcup ... \sqcup \exists\nabla.D_n \tag{2}$$

where each C_i is an $\mathcal{ALCO}$ concept and each D_i is an $\mathcal{ALCOI}\mu(\nabla)$ concept. From here $\mathcal{H}_F$ is used to denote the hypothesis obtained using FAME in step 1 in Fig. 1 and $\mathcal{H}_L$ is used to refer to the one obtained using LETHE.

The following lemma relates $\mathcal{H}_F$ to the disjunctive form in Definition 1:

Lemma 1. *The hypothesis $\mathcal{H}_F$ is expressed as $\mathcal{H}_F = \alpha_1 \sqcup ... \sqcup \alpha_n$ where each disjunct α_i is of the form $\top \sqsubseteq \exists\nabla.D_i$ and each D_i is an $\mathcal{ALCOI}\mu(\nabla)$ concept.*

It is still possible to satisfy conditions (iii) and (iv) of Definition 1 using this representation. However, it is first necessary to adapt the filtering method of step 2 in Fig. 1 to obtain the reduced forgetting solution $\mathcal{V}^*$, as this is an important part of the feasibility of the approach in practice [6].

An annotation concept ℓ is used to efficiently trace any dependencies on the negated observation $\neg\psi$ in the forgetting result $\mathcal{V}$. Any axioms which do not contain the concept ℓ are removed from $\mathcal{V}$, thereby removing the majority of the axioms that are redundant with respect to Definition 1. Fortunately, extending this approach to the current setting is straightforward. Here, the negated observation provided in step 1 of Fig. 1 is annotated as follows:

$$\neg\psi = \top \sqsubseteq \forall\nabla.(\neg\{a_1\} \sqcup \neg C_1 \sqcup \ell) \sqcup ... \sqcup \forall\nabla.(\neg\{a_k\} \sqcup \neg C_k \sqcup \ell)$$

where as before, ℓ is a fresh concept symbol that does not occur in $(\mathcal{O}, \psi)$, nor in the signature $\mathcal{F}$. The soundness of this filtering approach is expressed below.

Theorem 2. *Let $\mathcal{O}$ be an $\mathcal{ALCOI}\mu(\nabla)$ ontology, ψ an observation as a set of axioms, $\mathcal{F}$ a forgetting signature and ℓ an annotator concept appended disjunctively to each disjunct in $\neg\psi$, where $\ell \notin sig(\mathcal{O})$ and $\ell \notin \mathcal{F}$. For each axiom β in the forgetting result $\mathcal{V}$ obtained by forgetting all symbols in $\mathcal{F}$, if $\ell \notin sig(\beta)$ then β is redundant under the dual of Definition 1(iii), and should be removed in the extraction of the reduced forgetting result $\mathcal{V}^*$.*

Proof sketch: The proof is by induction over the construction of a derivation using the calculus of FAME [33], and takes the same form as the proof in [6]. The annotation concept ℓ does not appear in the signature $\mathcal{F}$. Thus, ℓ is not eliminated and if a clause in the normal form of $(\mathcal{O}, \neg\psi)$ contains the annotation concept ℓ, then any clause derived via inferences on this clause under FAME's forgetting calculus will also contain ℓ. Therefore, any axiom β in the forgetting result $\mathcal{V}$ that does not contain ℓ was derived purely using axioms in the background ontology $\mathcal{O}$, i.e., $\mathcal{O} \models \beta$. Since under Definition 1, $\mathcal{O} \not\models \psi$, such a β will not contribute to the explanation of ψ required by abduction, and should be omitted from $\mathcal{H}_F$ to satisfy Definition 1(iii).

As proposed in [6], the filtering step 3 in Fig. 1 can be performed in an *approximate* or *full* manner. The approximate filtering utilises the annotation-based method to inexpensively remove all redundancies that can be captured using this approach. The result is an approximation of the reduced forgetting result $\mathcal{V}^*$, denoted by $\mathcal{V}^*_{app}$. This can be negated in step 3 to return an approximate hypothesis. Alternatively, the full filtering setting further performs the dual entailment check of Definition 1(iii) over each axiom in $\mathcal{V}^*_{app}$ using an external reasoner. This eliminates any remaining redundancies that cannot be captured using annotations, an example of which appears in [6]. The result is then $\mathcal{V}^*$, which is negated to return a hypothesis satisfying Definition 1.

It is worth noting that, for fixpoints to occur in the hypothesis, a cycle would need to occur both over the symbols in $\mathcal{F}$ and also not be redundant under Theorem 2. As found in [6] this is rare in practice.

Example 5. To illustrate the full procedure, for the ontology $\mathcal{O}$ and the observation ψ from Example 4, the input given to FAME is:

$$\exists r.B \sqsubseteq A \qquad C \sqsubseteq D$$
$$\{b\} \sqsubseteq B \qquad \top \sqsubseteq \forall \nabla.(\neg\{a\} \sqcup A \sqcup \ell) \sqcup \forall \nabla.(\neg\{c\} \sqcup D \sqcup \ell).$$

The set of abducibles is $\mathcal{S}_A = \{C, r\}$ and thus the forgetting signature is $\mathcal{F} = \{A, B, D\}$. In step 1, $(\mathcal{O}, \neg\psi)$ is first transformed into A-reduced form:

$$\forall r.\neg B \sqcup A \qquad \neg C \sqcup D$$
$$\neg\{b\} \sqcup B \qquad \forall \nabla.(\neg\{a\} \sqcup \neg A \sqcup \ell) \sqcup \forall \nabla.(\neg\{c\} \sqcup \neg D \sqcup \ell)$$

This is also in D-reduced form. Forgetting the concepts A and D results in:

$$\neg\{b\} \sqcup B \qquad \forall \nabla.(\neg\{a\} \sqcup \forall r.\neg B \sqcup \ell) \sqcup \forall \nabla.(\neg\{c\} \sqcup \neg C \sqcup \ell)$$

Forgetting the concept B then produces:

$$\forall \nabla.(\neg\{a\} \sqcup \forall r.\neg\{b\} \sqcup \ell) \sqcup \forall \nabla.(\neg\{c\} \sqcup \neg C \sqcup \ell),$$

which is the forgetting result $\mathcal{V}$. In the filtering step 3 of Fig. 1, the axiom is retained and the annotation concept ℓ is set to $\bot$. Neither disjunct in this hypothesis is redundant with respect to the dual of Definition 1(iii) and thus both are retained in the reduced forgetting result $\mathcal{V}^*$, which is then negated in step 3 to produce the hypothesis: $\mathcal{H}_F = \top \sqsubseteq \exists \nabla.(\{a\} \sqcap \exists r.\{b\}) \sqcup \exists \nabla.(\{c\} \sqcap C)$. This is equivalent to the suggested hypothesis $\mathcal{H} = r(a, b) \sqcap C(c)$.

5   Comparing Hypotheses

Since the main aim of abductive reasoning is to produce an *explanation*, the form taken by the hypotheses is important. This is in contrast to the problem of forgetting, where restricting the original ontology while preserving all representable entailments [19] or obtaining an equivalent set of formulae [32] is the main goal. Thus, the readability of the forgetting result has so far received little attention.

For abduction, aside from the conditions in Definition 1, the readability of the hypotheses should be considered to provide insight into unseen observations.

Therefore, it is useful to compare the hypotheses produced by both approaches to forgetting-based abduction: the first using the resolution-based approach of LETHE, and the second using the Ackermann approach of FAME. Consider the following example:

Example 6. Let the background ontology $\mathcal{O}$ contain the following axioms:

$Pogona \sqsubseteq \exists livesIn.(Arid \sqcap Woodlands)$ $Woodlands \sqsubseteq Habitat$
$EucalyptForest \sqsubseteq Woodlands$ $EucalpytForest(SpringbrookPark)$

and consider the observation $\psi = \exists livesIn.Woodlands(Gary)$. Case (1): let $\mathcal{S}_A$ include all symbols in $\mathcal{O}$ except Woodlands, i.e. $\mathcal{F} = \{Woodlands\}$. The hypotheses obtained using LETHE and FAME respectively are:

$$\mathcal{H}_L = Pogona \sqcup \exists livesIn.EucalyptForest(Gary)$$
$$\mathcal{H}_F = \top \sqsubseteq \exists\nabla.(Pogona \sqcap \forall livesIn.(\neg Arid \sqcup \neg Habitat \sqcup \exists livesIn^-.\{Gary\})$$
$$\sqcup \exists\nabla.(\{Gary\} \sqcap \exists livesIn.EucalyptForest),$$

where $livesIn^-$ denotes the inverse of the role $livesIn$.

Example 6 illustrates a potential drawback of utilising a more expressive forgetting approach: the hypothesis produced can be more difficult to interpret, as seen by the additional syntactic redundancy in the first disjunct of $\mathcal{H}_F$. Despite this, the extra expressivity in the target language of FAME can be useful. Since FAME's solution preserves additional entailments compared to LETHE's, it may lead to additional explanations (disjuncts) in the final hypothesis. In Example 6, if $\mathcal{F}$ is extended to $\mathcal{F} = \{Woodlands, EucalyptForest\}$, then $\mathcal{H}_L = Pogona(Gary)$, whereas $\mathcal{H}_F = \top \sqsubseteq \exists\nabla.(Pogona \sqcap \forall livesIn.(\neg Arid \sqcup \neg Habitat \sqcup \exists livesIn^-.\{Gary\}) \sqcup \exists\nabla.(\{Gary\} \sqcap \exists livesIn.\{SpringbrookPark\})$. The second disjunct in $\mathcal{H}_F$ is equivalent to $livesIn(Gary, SpringbrookPark)$, an explanation that is absent from $\mathcal{H}_L$.

In Example 6, the following relations hold: $\mathcal{O}, \mathcal{H}_L \models \mathcal{H}_F$ and $\mathcal{O}, \mathcal{H}_F \not\models \mathcal{H}_L$. This indicates that the hypotheses obtained by using FAME in the forgetting step 1 in Fig. 1 can be weaker than those obtained using LETHE. This is to be expected, since the forgetting solution computed by FAME can be stronger than the uniform interpolant produced by LETHE due to the extended language of FAME's solution. Thus, $\mathcal{H}_F$ can be weaker than $\mathcal{H}_L$ under the background ontology, since these are obtained by negating the reduced forgetting solutions.

6   Experimental Evaluation

To perform a preliminary evaluation of the new forgetting-based abduction method, a prototype was implemented in Java using the OWL-API[1]. Since one of the primary aims of this work is to assess the benefit of utilising FAME for abduction rather than LETHE, the forgetting module in the abduction method utilises either of the two tools: LETHE[2] or FAME [32,33].

Table 1. Characteristics of the experimental corpus.

Ontology name	DL	TBox size	ABox size	Num. concepts	Num. roles
BFO	$\mathcal{EL}$	52	0	35	0
LUBM	$\mathcal{EL}$	87	0	44	24
HOM	$\mathcal{EL}$	83	0	66	0
DOID	$\mathcal{EL}$	7892	0	11663	15
SYN	$\mathcal{EL}$	15352	0	14462	0
ICF	$\mathcal{ALC}$	1910	6597	1597	41
Semintec	$\mathcal{ALC}$	199	65189	61	16
OBI	$\mathcal{ALC}$	28888	196	3691	67
NATPRO	$\mathcal{ALC}$	68565	42763	9464	12

Since no benchmarks exist for abduction problems in DLs, a challenging aspect of experimentally evaluating tools for abduction is the generation of appropriate observations. These observations should not violate the conditions in Definition 1, i.e. they should be consistent with the corresponding background ontology, but should also not be entailed by it. However, it is also necessary to consider the forms the observations take. While it is not possible to know exactly what forms the observations may take outside of case studies, it is important to try to emulate information that may be seen in practice. To do this, in this work the observations were generated randomly using existing information in each background ontology, as in [6]. Specifically, to generate a set of candidate observations for a background ontology, the concepts occurring in the axioms of the ontology were scanned and stored. These were selected at random and combined with $\mathcal{ALC}$ operators, also at random, to encourage variety. Each candidate observation was checked using HermiT to determine if it satisfied the conditions in Definition 1. If it did not, it was discarded. This process was repeated until the required number of observations was obtained.

For the first experiment, the aim was to compare the performance of the abduction method using LETHE and FAME in terms of time and the hypotheses obtained. The set of observations was restricted to those that can be handled by the abduction system using LETHE as in [6]. These included any $\mathcal{ALC}$ concept assertion, with at least one concept symbol that is not $\top$ or $\bot$, over a single individual. For ontologies with an ABox, each individual in the observations was an existing individual, while for those without an ABox the individual was a fresh one. The restriction to one individual was performed because in the OWL

---

[2] http://www.cs.man.ac.uk/koopmanp/lethe/index.html.

API disjunctive assertions cannot be expressed for $\mathcal{ALC}$. For each observation, the forgetting signature $\mathcal{F}$ was set to one random concept symbol in the observation ψ. In this way, the results are indicative of a single step of the abduction procedure, assuming that the user has no additional information that would lead them to further restrict the set of abducibles $\mathcal{S}_A$. Thus, the hypothesis obtained is one of the weakest possible hypotheses (least assumptions). It is assumed that the user would proceed to further refine the hypothesis by forgetting symbols from the hypotheses obtained. The time limit in this experiment was 300s for both the forgetting and filtering steps respectively.

The corpus used in experiment 1 is the same as the one used in [6], which consists of ontologies taken from NCBO Bioportal[3], OBO Foundry[4], the LUBM benchmark [14] and the Semintec[5] financial ontology. The choice of corpus is detailed in [6]. The statistics of this corpus are shown in Table 1.

The aim of the second experiment was to assess the performance of FAME with the approximate and full filtering settings of the abduction approach in the less restrictive setting of this paper. The corpus was extracted from a snapshot of NCBO Bioportal [25]. The observations were generated in the same way as in experiment 1, but without the restrictions which excluded role assertions. The forgetting signature in each case included at least one symbol from the observation, including role symbols. Again the assumption is that, unlike for forgetting, the aim is not to restrict a background ontology to a portion of the original, but to produce a space of independent explanations that does not make too many assumptions without sufficient prior knowledge about the observation. Thus, the forgetting signature was set to small portions of the symbols in the ontology. The timeout for the method was set to 1000 s in total. The success rates reported include cases for which FAME failed to forget at least one symbol, or one of these two steps exceeded the time limit.

Table 2. Characteristics of the experimental corpus used in experiment 2.

Number of	Mean	Median	90th Percentile	Maximum
TBox Axioms	1374	328	3830	8535
ABox Assertions	1014	26	2472	10889
Concepts	783	221	2232	6446
Roles	54	21	76	1043
Individuals	558	23	1605	8220

The requirements for the ontologies in the extracted corpus were as follows. (1) They should be parsable by the OWLAPI, FAME and HermiT. This excludes

---

[3] https://bioportal.bioontology.org/.
[4] http://www.obofoundry.org/.
[5] http://www.cs.put.poznan.pl/alawrynowicz/semintec.htm.

cases for which there were errors in loading the ontology into any of these systems. For this reason, the ontologies were also restricted to those containing at most 100,000 axioms. (2) The observation generation method should succeed after 2,000 attempts. This was done to exclude ontologies for which it is not possible to generate a sufficient number of non-entailed, consistent observations for the given ontology. (3) The ontology should contain an ABox, since the main benefit of this less restrictive setting is that information in the ABox can be used to produce hypotheses that utilise local information about an individual and its relationships with other individuals in the ABox. The final corpus contained 50 ontologies, the statistics of which are summarised in Table 2.

All ontologies were preprocessed into their $\mathcal{ALC}$ fragments, since this is the setting of this work. To do this, axioms not representable in $\mathcal{ALC}$ were removed. Others that were representable in $\mathcal{ALC}$ were translated using simple conversions.

Since fixpoint operators are not utilised in the implementation of FAME, these were not present in the results. Thus, cases requiring fixpoints are deemed to be a failure case and count against the reported success rates. However, these are unlikely to have a significant impact as they are rare in practice [6].

Both experiments were performed on a machine using a 2.8 GHz Intel Core i7-7700HQ CPU and 12 GB of RAM.

Table 3. Results for the first experiment. $\mathcal{H}_L$ ($\mathcal{H}_F$) indicates results for the abduction system using LETHE (FAME). The time limit for forgetting and filtering was 300 s each. For the equivalence check, only cases where both LETHE and FAME computed a hypothesis were compared. For the success rate, failures took into account both times exceeding the timeout and, in the case of FAME, results for which the concept could not be forgotten and results containing definer symbols.

Ont. name	Mean time/s		Max time/s		Mean disjuncts		$\mathcal{O}, \mathcal{H}_L \equiv \mathcal{O}, \mathcal{H}_F$	Success %	
	$\mathcal{H}_L$	$\mathcal{H}_F$	$\mathcal{H}_L$	$\mathcal{H}_F$	$\mathcal{H}_L$	$\mathcal{H}_F$	%	$\mathcal{H}_L$	$\mathcal{H}_F$
BFO	0.05	0.04	0.64	0.26	1.73	1.73	100.0	100.0	100.0
LUBM	0.08	0.06	0.67	0.30	2.53	2.96	60.8	100.0	86.7
HOM	0.06	0.05	0.65	0.26	2.5	2.5	100.0	100.0	100.0
DOID	3.35	3.07	9.97	10.26	4.77	4.77	100.0	100.0	100.0
SYN	6.18	2.84	16.12	13.92	5.6	5.6	100.0	100.0	100.0
ICF	0.96	0.67	3.56	2.16	1.93	1.93	100.0	100.0	100.0
Sem	2.89	3.09	6.70	6.39	1.10	1.63	58.3	96.7	100.0
OBI	34.47	32.97	120.05	108.85	43.45	42.2	91.3	96.7	100.0
NAT	46.04	138.24	301.27	688.87	10.61	4.17	62.5	76.7	76.7

The results for experiment 1 are shown in Table 3. Over most ontologies, utilising FAME resulted in a shorter mean runtime. Two exceptions were the Semintec and NATPRO ontologies. The maximum runtime was longer when using FAME in a few cases, most noticeably over NATPRO, for which it was over double that obtained using LETHE. These differences could be due to the computation of additional explanations requiring the expressivity of FAME's solution, which would necessitate additional entailment checks during the filtering step. Also, for ontologies with large ABoxes, a significant number of axioms need to be transformed to TBox axioms using nominals, which may increase the time taken. In most cases, the success rate when using LETHE was 100%. The same is true using FAME. In LETHE's case, failures occurred over the larger and more expressive ontologies, Semintec, OBI and NATPRO. These are due to timeouts, indicating that LETHE took longer than 300 s to produce a solution. For FAME, failures can occur due to the incompleteness of FAME's calculus: all of the failures over the LUBM ontology were due to this characteristic. For the NATPRO ontology, all of the failures observed using FAME were instead due to timeouts. In most cases, the hypotheses $\mathcal{H}_L$ and $\mathcal{H}_F$ were equivalent under the corresponding ontology. This indicates that it should often be possible to express $\mathcal{H}_F$ in $\mathcal{ALC}$, which may help to improve the readability issue discussed in Example 6 in these cases. Over the LUBM, Semintec, OBI and NATPRO ontologies, a number of the hypotheses produced using FAME were weaker than those returned using LETHE. This is expected: the forgetting result returned by FAME may be stronger than the uniform interpolant produced by LETHE, and in some cases there may be hypotheses that cannot be expressed without the extra expressivity of FAME's result. The following is an example taken from the LUBM experiments, demonstrating the benefit of this in practice.

Example 7. For the observation $\psi = \neg Organization(a)$, where a is a fresh individual, the key axioms in the LUBM ontology were:

$$Person \sqcap \exists worksFor.Organization \sqsubseteq Employee \quad College \sqsubseteq Organization$$
$$Employee \sqsubseteq Person \sqcap \exists worksFor.Organization$$

For the forgetting signature $\mathcal{F} = \{Organization\}$, the hypothesis was:

$$\mathcal{H}_F = \top \sqsubseteq \forall \nabla.(\neg\{a\} \sqcup \exists worksFor^-.(\neg Employee \sqcap Person))$$

Other explanations, such as those equivalent to $\neg College(a)$, are redundant with respect to Definition 1(iii) and are removed by the filtering in step 3 of Fig. 1. Using LETHE, no hypothesis was produced as the above hypothesis requires the use of the inverse role $worksFor^-$, which cannot be produced by LETHE.

The results for experiment 2 are shown in Table 4. As expected, the approximate filtering took less time than the full filtering across all cases, as it does not perform the additional, expensive entailment checks. The maximum time for the approximate filtering for an $\mathcal{F}$ size of 1 is particularly high. It is likely that for this single case the forgetting solution was particularly large, indicating that the forgotten symbol occurred frequently in the given ontology. The mean number of redundant axioms removed from the forgetting results by the approximate filtering was 2444.6, 2510.4 and 2873.3 for $\mathcal{F}$ sizes of 1, 5% and 10% respectively. The mean additional redundancies removed by the full filtering setting was 11.7, 11.3 and 9.7 axioms respectively. This indicates that in many cases the approximate filtering may be sufficient to obtain a space of explanations that is largely free of redundancies. The success rates indicate that the full filtering setting caused a number of additional timeouts for each size of $\mathcal{F}$. However, the majority of failures were the result of FAME failing to forget at least one symbol in $\mathcal{F}$. For the approximate filtering cases, 100%, 100% and 99.5% of failures occurred due to the forgetting step for $\mathcal{F}$ sizes 1, 5% and 10% respectively. For the full filtering cases, the corresponding values were 88.8%, 94.8% and 94.8% respectively. FAME's failure rates for these abduction experiments are higher than those reported for forgetting experiments [31,33]. This may be due to the frequency of role symbols occurring in ABox observations for abduction, many of which included role assertions or complex concepts involving roles.

Table 4. Results for experiment 2. Percentages for $\mathcal{F}$ are relative to $sig(\mathcal{O}, \psi)$. All times are in seconds.

$\mathcal{F}$ size	Forgetting time		Approx. filter time		Full filter time		Successes %	
	Mean	Max	Mean	Max	Mean	Max	Approx.	Full
1	0.05	1.02	0.74	869.63	7.40	880.11	90.3	89.3
5%	0.13	11.15	0.09	28.25	8.29	878.05	81.7	80.9
10%	1.04	75.09	0.06	5.52	6.45	975.24	70.9	70.6

7   Conclusion and Future Work

In this paper the expressivity of forgetting-based abduction was extended using the forgetting system FAME. Role symbols can now be excluded from the abducibles, and observations and hypotheses can now contain role assertions, including conjunctions and disjunctions of these. Hypotheses requiring role inverses can also now be computed. These extensions are useful in practice, as data in the ABox of an ontology can be used to compute more specific hypotheses.

One limitation of the approach is the lack of completeness, due to the fact that FAME uses semantic forgetting, which is not complete. A possible solution is to combine the use of FAME and LETHE, enabling LETHE to forget definer or forgetting symbols in FAME's result. Future work will also include further, fine-grained experimental evaluation and applications such as concept learning. These will benefit significantly from the enhanced expressivity of the approach.

References

1. Ackermann, W.: Untersuchungen über das Eliminationsproblem der mathematischen Logik. Math. Ann. **110**, 330–413 (1935)
2. Baader, F., McGuinness, D.L., Nardi, D., Patel-Schneider, P.F.: The Description Logic Handbook. Cambridge University Press, Cambridge (2003)
3. Bienvenu, M.: Complexity of abduction in the $\mathcal{EL}$ family of lightweight description logics. In: Proceedings of KR 2008, pp. 220–230. AAAI Press (2008)
4. Calvanese, D., De Giacomo, G., Lenzerini, M.: Reasoning in expressive description logics with fixpoints based on automata on finite trees. In: Proceedings of IJCAI 1999, pp. 84–89. AAAI Press (1999)
5. Calvanese, D., Ortiz, M., Simkus, M., Stefanoni, G.: Reasoning about explanations for negative query answers in DL-Lite. J. Artif. Intell. Res. **48**, 635–669 (2013)
6. Del-Pinto, W., Schmidt, R.A.: ABox abduction via forgetting in $\mathcal{ALC}$. In: Proceedings of AAAI 2019. AAAI Press (2019)
7. Doherty, P., Łukaszewicz, W., Szałas, A.: Computing strongest necessary and weakest sufficient conditions of first-order formulas. Artif. Intell. **128**, 143–159 (2001)
8. Du, J., Qi, G., Shen, Y., Pan, J.Z.: Towards practical ABox abduction in large OWL DL ontologies. In: Proceedings of AAAI 2011, pp. 1160–1165. AAAI Press (2011)
9. Du, J., Wan, H., Ma, H.: Practical TBox abduction based on justification patterns. In: Proceedings of AAAI 2017, pp. 1100–1106. AAAI Press (2017)
10. Eiter, T., Gottlob, G.: The complexity of logic-based abduction. J. ACM **42**, 3–42 (1995)
11. Elsenbroich, C., Kutz, O., Sattler, U.: A case for abductive reasoning over ontologies. In: Proceedings of OWL: Experiences and Directions. CEUR Workshop Proceedings, vol. 216. CEUR-WS.org (2006)
12. Flach, P.A., Kakas, A.C.: On the relation between abduction and inductive learning. In: Handbook of Defeasible Reasoning and Uncertainty Management Systems, vol. 4, pp. 155–196 (2000)
13. Gabbay, D.M., Schmidt, R.A., Szałas, A.: Second-Order Quantifier Elimination: Foundations. Computational Aspects and Applications. College Publications, London (2008)
14. Guo, Y., Pan, Z., Heflin, J.: LUBM: a benchmark for OWL knowledge base systems. J. Web Semant. **3**, 158–182 (2005)
15. Halland, K., Britz, K.: ABox abduction in $\mathcal{ALC}$ using a DL tableau. In: Proceedings of SAICSIT 2012, pp. 51–58. ACM (2012)
16. Hobbs, J.R., Stickel, M., Martin, P., Edwards, D.: Interpretation as abduction. Artif. Intell. **63**, 69–142 (1993)
17. Klarman, S., Endriss, U., Schlobach, S.: ABox abduction in the description logic $\mathcal{ALC}$. J. Autom. Reason. **46**, 43–80 (2011)
18. Konolige, K.: Abduction versus closure in causal theories. Artif. Intell. **53**, 255–272 (1992)
19. Koopmann, P., Schmidt, R.A.: Uniform interpolation and forgetting for $\mathcal{ALC}$ ontologies with ABoxes. In: Proceedings of AAAI 2015, pp. 175–181. AAAI Press (2015)
20. Koopmann, P., Schmidt, R.A.: LETHE: saturation based reasoning for nonstandard reasoning tasks. In: Proceedings of ORE 2015. CEUR Workshop Proceedings, vol. 1387, pp. 23–30. CEUR-WS.org (2015)

21. Lambrix, P., Dragisic, Z., Ivanova, V.: Get my pizza right: repairing missing is-a relations in $\mathcal{ALC}$ ontologies. In: Takeda, H., Qu, Y., Mizoguchi, R., Kitamura, Y. (eds.) JIST 2012. LNCS, vol. 7774, pp. 17–32. Springer, Heidelberg (2013). https://doi.org/10.1007/978-3-642-37996-3_2

22. Lin, F.: On strongest necessary and weakest sufficient conditions. Artif. Intell. **128**, 143–159 (2001)

23. Ludwig, M., Konev, B.: Practical uniform interpolation and forgetting for ALC TBoxes with applications to logical difference. In: Proceedings of KR 2014, pp. 318–327. AAAI Press (2014)

24. Lutz, C., Wolter, F.: Foundations for uniform interpolation and forgetting in expressive description logics. In: Proceedings of IJCAI 2011, pp. 989–995. AAAI Press (2011)

25. Matentzoglu, N., Parsia, B.: Bioportal snapshot 30.03.2017 [data set] (2017). Zenodo: https://doi.org/10.5281/zenodo.439510

26. Muggleton, S.H., Bryant, C.H.: Theory completion using inverse entailment. In: Cussens, J., Frisch, A. (eds.) ILP 2000. LNCS (LNAI), vol. 1866, pp. 130–146. Springer, Heidelberg (2000). https://doi.org/10.1007/3-540-44960-4_8

27. Pukancová, J., Homola, M.: Tableau-based ABox abduction for the $\mathcal{ALCHO}$ description logic. In: Proceedings of DL 2017. CEUR Workshop Proceedings, vol. 1879. CEUR-WS.org (2017)

28. Raghavan, S., Mooney, R.: Bayesian abductive logic programs. In: AAAI 2010 Workshop on Statistical Relational AI, pp. 82–87. AAAI Press (2010)

29. Ray, O.: Nonmonotonic abductive inductive learning. J. Appl. Log. **7**, 329–340 (2009)

30. Wernhard, C.: Abduction in logic programming as second-order quantifier elimination. In: Fontaine, P., Ringeissen, C., Schmidt, R.A. (eds.) FroCoS 2013. LNCS (LNAI), vol. 8152, pp. 103–119. Springer, Heidelberg (2013). https://doi.org/10.1007/978-3-642-40885-4_8

31. Zhao, Y.: Automated semantic forgetting for expressive description logics. Ph.D. thesis, The University of Manchester, UK (2018)

32. Zhao, Y., Schmidt, R.A.: Concept forgetting in $\mathcal{ALCOI}$-ontologies using an Ackermann approach. In: Arenas, M., et al. (eds.) ISWC 2015. LNCS, vol. 9366, pp. 587–602. Springer, Cham (2015). https://doi.org/10.1007/978-3-319-25007-6_34

33. Zhao, Y., Schmidt, R.A.: Forgetting concept and role symbols in $\mathcal{ALCOIH}\mu^+(\nabla,\sqcap)$-ontologies. In: Proceedigs of IJCAI 2016, pp. 1345–1352. AAAI Press (2016)

On the Expressive Power of Description Logics with Cardinality Constraints on Finite and Infinite Sets

Franz Baader and Filippo De Bortoli$^{(\boxtimes)}$

Theoretical Computer Science, TU Dresden, Dresden, Germany
{franz.baader,filippo.de_bortoli}@tu-dresden.de

Abstract. In recent work we have extended the description logic (DL) $\mathcal{ALCQ}$ by means of more expressive number restrictions using numerical and set constraints stated in the quantifier-free fragment of Boolean Algebra with Presburger Arithmetic (QFBAPA). It has been shown that reasoning in the resulting DL, called $\mathcal{ALCSCC}$, is PSpace-complete without a TBox and ExpTime-complete w.r.t. a general TBox. The semantics of $\mathcal{ALCSCC}$ is defined in terms of finitely branching interpretations, that is, interpretations where every element has only finitely many role successors. This condition was needed since QFBAPA considers only finite sets. In this paper, we first introduce a variant of $\mathcal{ALCSCC}$, called $\mathcal{ALCSCC}^\infty$, in which we lift this requirement (inexpressible in first-order logic) and show that the complexity results for $\mathcal{ALCSCC}$ mentioned above are preserved. Nevertheless, like $\mathcal{ALCSCC}$, $\mathcal{ALCSCC}^\infty$ is not a fragment of first-order logic. The main contribution of this paper is to give a characterization of the first-order fragment of $\mathcal{ALCSCC}^\infty$. The most important tool used in the proof of this result is a notion of bisimulation that characterizes this fragment.

1 Introduction

Description Logics (DLs) [4] are a well-investigated family of logic-based knowledge representation languages, which are frequently used to formalize ontologies for application domains such as biology and medicine [8]. To define the important notions of such an application domain as formal concepts, DLs state necessary and sufficient conditions for an individual to belong to a concept. These conditions can be Boolean combinations of atomic properties required for the individual (expressed by concept names) or properties that refer to relationships with other individuals and their properties (expressed as role restrictions). For example, the concept of a man that has a son and a daughter can be formalized in the DL $\mathcal{ALC}$ [17] as $Male \sqcap Human \sqcap \exists child.Male \sqcap \exists child.Female$. Number restrictions allow us to formulate numerical constraints on the role successors of the elements of a concept. For example, in the DL $\mathcal{ALCQ}$ [9], the concept

---

Partially supported by the German Research Foundation (DFG) within the Research Unit 1513 (Hybris) and the Research Training Group 1763 (QuantLA).

A. Herzig and A. Popescu (Eds.): FroCoS 2019, LNAI 11715, pp. 203–219, 2019.
https://doi.org/10.1007/978-3-030-29007-8_12

Female ⊓ *Human* ⊓ (≥ 5 *child* . *Female*) ⊓ (≤ 1 *child* . *Male*) describes women that have at least five daughters and at most one son.

In recent work [2], we have extended the DL $\mathcal{ALCQ}$ by means of more expressive number restrictions using numerical and set constraints stated in the quantifier-free fragment of Boolean Algebra with Presburger Arithmetic (QFBAPA) [11]. For example, in the resulting DL $\mathcal{ALCSCC}$, one can describe individuals that have twice as many sons as daughter using the role successor constraint $succ(|child \cap Male| = 2 \cdot |child \cap Female|)$. It has been shown in [2] that reasoning in $\mathcal{ALCSCC}$ has the same complexity as reasoning in its sub-logic $\mathcal{ALCQ}$ [18,19], i.e., PSpace-complete without a TBox and ExpTime-complete in the presence of a TBox.

The semantics of $\mathcal{ALCSCC}$ is defined in terms of finitely branching interpretations, i.e., interpretations where every element has only finitely many role successors. This condition was needed since QFBAPA considers only finite sets. The disadvantage of this meta-condition is that it is not expressible in first-order logic, and thus makes the comparison of the expressive power of $\mathcal{ALCSCC}$ with that of other DLs, which are usually fragments of first-order logic, problematic. Strictly speaking, no $\mathcal{ALCSCC}$ concept is expressible in first-order logic due to this implicit constraint. To overcome this problem, we introduce a variant of $\mathcal{ALCSCC}$, called $\mathcal{ALCSCC}^\infty$, in which we lift the "finite branching" requirement. This is achieved by introducing a variant of QFBAPA, called QFBAPA$^\infty$, in which not just finite, but also infinite sets are considered. We prove that satisfiability in QFBAPA$^\infty$ has the same complexity (NP-complete) as satisfiability in QFBAPA. Based on this, we can show that the complexity results for $\mathcal{ALCSCC}$ mentioned above also hold for $\mathcal{ALCSCC}^\infty$. Alternatively, we could have also used the variant QFBAPA$_\infty$ of QFBAPA with possibly infinite sets introduced in [10], whose satisfiability problem is also NP-complete.

Despite the removal of the "finite branching" requirement—a constraint that destroys expressibility in first-order logic of $\mathcal{ALCSCC}$—$\mathcal{ALCSCC}^\infty$ is still not a fragment of first-order logic. The main contribution of this paper is to give a characterization of the first-order fragment of $\mathcal{ALCSCC}^\infty$. For this purpose, we introduce the fragment $\mathcal{ALCCQU}$ of $\mathcal{ALCSCC}^\infty$, which uses constraints of the logic CQU (counting quantifiers over unary predicates) [7] in place of QFBAPA constraints, and show that $\mathcal{ALCCQU}$ concepts are first-order definable. Basically, in $\mathcal{ALCCQU}$ we can compare the cardinality of successors sets with a constant, but not with the cardinality of another successor set. For example, the $\mathcal{ALCCQU}$ role successor constraint $succ(|friend \cap livesWith \cap Female| \geq 2)$ describes individuals that live together with at least two female friends. To get a handle on the expressive power of $\mathcal{ALCCQU}$, we define a notion of bisimulation that characterizes $\mathcal{ALCCQU}$, in the sense that a first-order formula is invariant under this kind of bisimulation iff it is equivalent to an $\mathcal{ALCCQU}$ concept. This notion of bisimulation is very similar to the counting bisimulation introduced in [13] for $\mathcal{ALCQ}$. Surprisingly, all $\mathcal{ALCSCC}^\infty$ concepts are also invariant under $\mathcal{ALCCQU}$-bisimulation, which allows us to conclude that $\mathcal{ALCCQU}$ consists of exactly the first-order definable concepts of $\mathcal{ALCSCC}^\infty$.

When formulating complexity results for logics that use numbers in their syntax (such as QFBAPA, CQU, $\mathcal{ALCCQU}$, and $\mathcal{ALCSCC}^{\infty}$), it is important to make clear how the input size of the numbers is defined. In this paper, we assume *binary coding* of numbers (e.g., the number 1024 has size 10 rather than size 1024), which makes the complexity upper bounds stronger.

2   The Logics QFBAPA$^{\infty}$ and CQU

In this section, we first introduce the logic QFBAPA$^{\infty}$, whose main difference to the well-known logic QFBAPA [11] is that it allows for solutions involving not just finite, but also infinite sets. Then, we demonstrate that two important results shown in [11] for QFBAPA also hold for QFBAPA$^{\infty}$. Finally, we define the fragment CQU of QFBAPA$^{\infty}$, for which a decision procedure based on column generation was described in [7].

The logic QFBAPA$^{\infty}$. In this logic one can build *set terms* by applying Boolean operations (intersection $\cap$, union $\cup$, and complement $\cdot^c$) to set variables as well as the constants $\emptyset$ and $\mathcal{U}$. Set terms s, t can then be used to state inclusion and equality constraints ($s = t, s \subseteq t$) between sets. *Presburger Arithmetic (PA) expressions* are built from non-negative integer constants, PA variables, and set cardinalities $|s|$ using addition as well as multiplication with a non-negative integer constant. They can be used to form numerical constraints of the form $k = \ell$ and $k < \ell$, where k, ℓ are PA expressions. A QFBAPA$^{\infty}$ *formula* is a Boolean combination of set and numerical constraints.

The semantics of set terms and set constraints is defined using *substitutions* σ that assign a set $\sigma(\mathcal{U})$ to $\mathcal{U}$ and subsets of $\sigma(\mathcal{U})$ to set variables. The evaluation of set terms and set constraints by such a substitution is defined in the obvious way, using the standard notions of intersection, union, complement,[1] inclusion, and equality for sets. PA expressions are evaluated over $\mathbb{N}^{\infty} = \mathbb{N} \cup \{\infty\}$, i.e., the non-negative integers extended with a symbol for infinity. Thus, substitutions additionally assign elements of $\mathbb{N}^{\infty}$ to PA variables. The cardinality expression $|s|$ is evaluated under σ as the cardinality of $\sigma(s)$ if this set is finite, and as ∞ if $\sigma(s)$ is not finite.[2] When evaluating PA expressions w.r.t. a substitution σ, we employ the usual way of adding, multiplying, and comparing integers, extended to $\mathbb{N}^{\infty}$ by the following rules ranging over $N \in \mathbb{N}$:

1. $\infty + N = N + \infty = \infty = \infty + \infty$,
2. if $N \neq 0$ then $N \cdot \infty = \infty = \infty \cdot N$, else $0 \cdot \infty = 0 = \infty \cdot 0$,
3. $N < \infty$ and $\infty \not< N$, as well as $\infty = \infty$ and $\infty \not< \infty$.

A *solution* σ of a QFBAPA$^{\infty}$ formula ϕ is a substitution that evaluates ϕ to true, using the above rules for evaluating set and numerical constraints and the usual interpretation of the Boolean operators occurring in ϕ. The formula ϕ is *satisfiable* if it has a solution.

---

[1] The complement is defined w.r.t. $\sigma(\mathcal{U})$, i.e., $\sigma(s^c) = \sigma(\mathcal{U}) \setminus \sigma(s)$.

[2] Note that we do not distinguish between different infinite cardinalities, such as countably infinite, uncountably infinite, etc.

Note that, in QFBAPA$^\infty$, we can enforce infinity of a set although we do not allow the use of ∞ as a constant. For instance, $|s| = \infty$ is not an admissible numerical constraint, but it is easy to see that the constraint $|s| + 1 = |s|$ can only be satisfied by a substitution that assigns an infinite set to the set term s.

Comparison with QFBAPA and QFBAPA$_\infty$. The logic QFBAPA, as introduced in [11], differs from QFBAPA$^\infty$ as defined above, both syntactically and semantically. From the syntactic point of view, the main difference is that, in QFBAPA$^\infty$, we disallow negative integer constants as well as divisibility by a fixed integer constant. Dispensing with negative constants is not really a restriction since we can always write the numerical constraints of QFBAPA in a way that does not use negative integer constants (by bringing negative summands to the other side of a constraint). Disallowing divisibility may be a real restriction, but in the presence of ∞ it is not clear how to interpret divisibility constraints (Is ∞ even or odd?). In addition, in the context of using the logic within a DL, there does not appear to be an urgent need for such constraints. From a syntactic point of view, the logic QFBAPA$_\infty$ [10] has more general atomic constraints than our logic QFBAPA$^\infty$ (e.g., it allows for the use of rational constants and the explicit statement that a set is infinite), but these constraints can be expressed also in QFBAPA$^\infty$.

From the semantic point of view, the main difference of QFBAPA$^\infty$ and QFBAPA$_\infty$ to QFBAPA is, of course, that the semantics of QFBAPA requires us to interpret $\mathcal{U}$, and thus all set variables, as finite sets. In addition, PA variables are interpreted in QFBAPA$^\infty$ as non-negative integers, but this was already the case for the variant of QFBAPA used in the definition of $\mathcal{ALCSCC}$ in [2] since in that context only set cardinalities (which are non-negative) are used. In QFBAPA$_\infty$, PA variables can also be interpreted as real numbers, but there is a constraint available that allow to state that a PA term must be interpreted by an integer. Since PA variables are not used in the context of $\mathcal{ALCSCC}$ and $\mathcal{ALCSCC}^\infty$, this difference is not relevant here.

Satisfiability in QFBAPA, QFBAPA$^\infty$, and QFBAPA$_\infty$. In [11] it is shown that the satisfiability problem for QFBAPA formulae is NP-complete. Since NP-hardness is clear due to the use of Boolean operations on the formula level, the main task in [11] was to show the "in NP" result. The main tool used in [11] is a "sparse solution" lemma (see Fact 1 in [11] and Lemma 3 in [2]), which was also important for showing the complexity upper bounds for reasoning in $\mathcal{ALCSCC}$ in [2]. We show below that this "sparse solution" lemma also holds for QFBAPA$^\infty$, which implies that satisfiability of QFBAPA$^\infty$ formulae is also in NP.

The "sparse solution" lemma is based on the notion of a Venn region. Assume that ϕ is a QFBAPA formula containing the set variables $X_1, \ldots, X_k$. A *Venn region* for ϕ is of the form

$$X_1^{c_1} \cap \ldots \cap X_k^{c_k},$$

where c_i is either empty or c for $i = 1, \ldots, k$. Venn regions are interesting since every set term s occurring in ϕ can be expressed as the disjoint union of Venn regions, and thus its cardinality is the sum of the cardinalities of these Venn regions. The problem is that there may be exponentially many Venn regions in the size of ϕ. The "sparse solution" lemma basically says that it is possible to restrict the attention to a polynomial number of Venn regions.

To be more precise, it is shown in [11] that a given QFBAPA formula ϕ can be transformed in polynomial time into an equisatisfiable QFBAPA formula $G \wedge F$ where G is a Boolean combination of numerical constraints not containing sets, and F is a conjunction of linearly many expressions $|b_i| = k_i$ $(i = 1, \ldots, m)$, where b_i is a set term and k_i is a PA variable (standing for the cardinality of the set b_i). Using the fact that each b_i is a disjoint union of Venn regions, F can be expressed as a system of linear equations

$$A \cdot x = k, \tag{1}$$

which must be solved over the non-negative integers. Here the ith row of the matrix A is a 0/1 vector that expresses which Venn regions participate in generating the set b_i. The vector x contains a variable x_v for every Venn region v at the position corresponding to the occurrence of this region in A. Intuitively, the value of x_v in a solution of the equation stands for the cardinality of the Venn region. Finally, k is the vector of the variables k_i, and thus the value of k_i stands for the cardinality of the set b_i.

For example, consider the QFBAPA formula

$$\phi = |X_1 \cup X_2| \geq |X_1| + |X_2|.$$

In this case, G is $k_1 \geq k_2 + k_3$ and F is $|X_1 \cup X_2| = k_1 \wedge |X_1| = k_2 \wedge |X_2| = k_3$, and thus $m = 3$ is the number of rows in the matrix A. There are four Venn regions in this example: $v_1 = X_1 \cap X_2$, $v_2 = X_1 \cap X_2^c$, $v_3 = X_1^c \cap X_2$, $v_4 = X_1^c \cap X_2^c$. The system (1) thus has four variables in the vector x, and looks as follows:

$$\begin{pmatrix} 1 & 1 & 1 & 0 \\ 1 & 1 & 0 & 0 \\ 1 & 0 & 1 & 0 \end{pmatrix} \cdot \begin{pmatrix} x_{v_1} \\ x_{v_2} \\ x_{v_3} \\ x_{v_4} \end{pmatrix} = \begin{pmatrix} k_1 \\ k_2 \\ k_3 \end{pmatrix} \tag{2}$$

The first row of A in (2) is explained by the fact that $X_1 \cup X_2 = v_1 \cup v_2 \cup v_3$, and similarly for the other rows. If we take the solution $k_1 = 3, k_2 = 1, k_3 = 1$ of G, then the linear system obtained from (2) by applying this replacement is actually not solvable. In contrast, if we take $k_1 = 2, k_2 = 1, k_3 = 1$, then setting $x_{v_1} = 0$, $x_{v_2} = 1$, $x_{v_3} = 1$, $x_{v_4} = 5$ is a solution of the resulting system (where the value for x_{v_4} is actually irrelevant). Note that $x_{v_1} = 0$ means that the Venn region $v_1 = X_1 \cap X_2$ is empty, which corresponds to the fact that we can only have $|X_1 \cup X_2| \geq |X_1| + |X_2|$ if X_1 and X_2 are interpreted by disjoint sets.

The problem with the system (1) is that it contains exponentially many variables. Using a result by Eisenbrand and Shmonin [6] (called Fact 1 in [11]), it is shown in [11] that there is a bound $N = 2m \log(4m)$ such that, for any solution of G, the system obtained from (1) by applying this solution to the variables k_i has a solution in which at most N of the variables x_v in (1) are non-zero, if it has a solution at all. Note that the value of N is clearly polynomial in the size of ϕ since m is bounded by the number of set terms occurring in ϕ.

On the one hand, this implies that, by guessing (in non-deterministic polynomial time) N Venn regions v whose associated variables in (1) are supposed to be non-zero, we obtain a polynomial-sized system $A' \cdot x' = k$, in which only the variables x_v for the guessed Venn regions and their associated columns remain. The formula G is a Boolean combination of linear (in)equations. After guessing which of them are to be true and which not, we overall obtain a polynomially large system of linear (in)equations, whose solvability in the non-negative integers $\mathbb{N}$ can then be tested by an NP procedure [14]. Note that this NP procedure is not used as an NP oracle, but rather as an extension of the search tree for a solution that has already been built by the guessing done before.

Proposition 1 ([11]). *Satisfiability of QFBAPA formulae is in NP.*

On the other hand, since $x_v = 0$ means that the Venn region v is empty, the above argument also shows that a solvable QFBAPA formula always has a solution in which at most N Venn regions are non-empty. In [2] this result was actually strengthened as follows.

Lemma 1 ([2]). *For every QFBAPA formula ϕ, one can compute in polynomial time a number N whose value is polynomial in the size of ϕ such that the following holds for every solution σ of ϕ: there is a solution σ' of ϕ such that*

(i) $|\{v$ Venn region $\mid \sigma'(v) \neq \emptyset\}| \leq N$, and
(ii) $\{v$ Venn region $\mid \sigma'(v) \neq \emptyset\} \subseteq \{v$ Venn region $\mid \sigma(v) \neq \emptyset\}$.

In the corresponding result shown in [11], the property (ii) is missing. The main idea underlying the proof of our stronger result is that, for a given solution σ of ϕ, one applies the "sparse solution" lemma of [6] not to (1) directly, but to the system obtained from it by removing the variables x_v and the corresponding columns in A for those Venn regions v that satisfy $\sigma(v) = \emptyset$.

Our goal is now to show that Proposition 1 and Lemma 1 also hold if we replace QFBAPA with QFBAPA$^\infty$. For this purpose, let us assume that σ is a solution of G in $\mathbb{N}^\infty$, and consider the system

$$A \cdot x = \sigma(k), \tag{3}$$

where the variables k_i are replaced by $\sigma(k_i) \in \mathbb{N}^\infty$. Then the following lemma is an easy consequence of the way we defined operations involving ∞.

Lemma 2. *The following holds for any solution θ of (3): if $\sigma(k_i) = \infty$, then there is a Venn region v such that $\theta(x_v) = \infty$ and*

1. *the column in A corresponding to v contains 1 at position position i, and*
2. *for all j with $\sigma(k_j) < \infty$, the column in A corresponding to v contains 0 at position j.*

Based on this lemma, we can now extend the "sparse solution" lemma of [6] to the setting where ∞ may occur on the right-hand side of the system and in the solution.

Lemma 3. *If the linear system (3) has a solution in* $\mathbb{N}^\infty$, *then it has a solution in* $\mathbb{N}^\infty$ *where at most* $M = 2m \log(4m) + m$ *of the variables in the vector* x *are non-zero.*

Proof. Assume that (3) has a solution θ in $\mathbb{N}^\infty$. Then the system $B \cdot x = b$ obtained from (3) by removing the rows i for which $\sigma(k_i) = \infty$ also has a solution in $\mathbb{N}^\infty$. In addition, since the vector b does not contain ∞, it is easy to see that $B \cdot x = b$ also has a solution in $\mathbb{N}$. The "sparse solution" lemma of [6] then yields a solution γ of $B \cdot x = b$ such that at most $N = 2m \log(4m)$ of the variables x_v in x are such that $\gamma(x_v) \neq 0$.

We modify γ to obtain a solution γ' of (3) using Lemma 2. Since (3) has the solution θ, we know the following: for every i such that $\sigma(k_i) = \infty$, there is a Venn region v such that 1. and 2. stated in that lemma are satisfied. We now select for each such i one Venn region v with these properties, and set $\gamma'(x_v) := \infty$. For Venn regions u not selected in this way, we set $\gamma'(x_u) := \gamma(x_u)$. In the worst-case, this modification changes m zeros to ∞, and thus γ' satisfies the bound M on the number of non-zero variables. It remains to show that γ' solves (3). Thus, consider the ith equation in this system. If $\sigma(k_i) = \infty$, then there is a v such that $\gamma'(x_v) = \infty$ and 1. in Lemma 2 is satisfied. This implies that γ' solves the ith equation. If $\sigma(k_i) = b_i < \infty$, then 2. in Lemma 2 implies that the modifications made to obtain γ' from γ have no effect on this equation since the modified values are multiplied with 0, and thus removed. Hence, we have shown that γ' solves (3) and it satisfies the required bound on the number of non-zero variables. $\square$

This lemma allows us to extend Proposition 1 and Lemma 1 to QFBAPA$^\infty$.

Theorem 1. *Satisfiability of QFBAPA$^\infty$ formulae is in NP. Moreover, for every QFBAPA$^\infty$ formula* ϕ, *one can compute in polynomial time a number* N *whose value is polynomial in the size of* ϕ *such that the following holds for every solution* σ *of* ϕ: *there is a solution* σ' *of* ϕ *such that*

(i) $|\{v \text{ Venn region} \mid \sigma'(v) \neq \emptyset\}| \leq N$, *and*
(ii) $\{v \text{ Venn region} \mid \sigma'(v) \neq \emptyset\} \subseteq \{v \text{ Venn region} \mid \sigma(v) \neq \emptyset\}$.

Proof. Using Lemma 3, the proof of Lemma 1 can easily be adapted to QFBAPA$^\infty$.

Regarding decidability in NP, Lemma 3 shows that it is sufficient to prove that solvability in $\mathbb{N}^\infty$ of G together with a polynomially large system $A' \cdot x' = k$ can be decided by an NP procedure. In a first step, we guess which of the PA variables in G and k are to be replaced by ∞. For the linear (in)equations in G containing at least one such variable, the truth value is determined by this choice. For example, if we have $x_1 + 2x_2 > x_3$, and x_1 is guessed to be ∞, then this inequation becomes true if x_3 is not guessed to be ∞, and false otherwise. By replacing such (in)equations by the respective truth values, G can be modified to G', which now needs to be solved in $\mathbb{N}$. Regarding the system $A' \cdot x' = k$, we check whether, for each i such that k_i was guessed to be ∞, there is a Venn region v such that 1 and 2 of Lemma 2 are satisfied, where "$\sigma(k_j) < \infty$" is replaced with "k_j is not guessed to be ∞." If this is not the case, than we return the answer "unsolvable." Otherwise, we modify $A' \cdot x' = k$ to the system $A'' \cdot x' = k'$ by removing the rows i for which k_i was guessed to be ∞. We then check whether G' together with this new system is solvable in $\mathbb{N}$. Using Lemma 2 and the construction employed in the proof of Lemma 3, it is not hard to show that this yields a correct NP procedure. □

In [10], similar results are shown for QFBAPA$_\infty$, but again without the property (ii). From a technical point of view, the proof in [10] is quite different from ours, though it is based on similar ideas.

The Logic CQU. This logic is obtained from QFBAPA$^\infty$ by restricting numerical constraints to be of the form $k = N$ and $k < N$, i.e., a CQU formula is a Boolean combination of set constraints and numerical constraints of this restricted form. Since CQU is a fragment of QFBAPA$^\infty$, its satisfiability problem is clearly also in NP, and NP hardness is, on the one hand, due to the Boolean operations on the formula level. Other reasons for NP-hardness are the Boolean operations on the set level, and the fact that numerical constraints can be used to express the knapsack problem [14].

It should be noted that the logic CQU as introduced here is actually the *Boolean closure* of the logic called CQU in [7]. In fact, in [7] only conjunctions of set constraints and numerical constraints of the form $k \leq N$ and $k \geq N$ for set cardinalities k are allowed. When using CQU to define our extension $\mathcal{ALCCQU}$ of $\mathcal{ALCQ}$, this difference is irrelevant since the Boolean operations are available anyway on the DL level. In addition, sums in the PA expressions k in $k = N$ and $k < N$ can be reduced away using disjunction (see the next section). It is actually not hard to see that the logic CQU as defined here has the same expressivity as $\mathcal{C}^1$, the one-variable fragment of first-order logic with counting (see, e.g., [15]).

3   The DLs $\mathcal{ALCSCC}^\infty$, $\mathcal{ALCCQU}$, and $\mathcal{ALCQt}$

In this section, we define the variant $\mathcal{ALCSCC}^\infty$ of the logic $\mathcal{ALCSCC}$ introduced in [2], and its fragments $\mathcal{ALCCQU}$ and $\mathcal{ALCQt}$. First, we argue why the complexity results for $\mathcal{ALCSCC}$ proved in [2] also hold for $\mathcal{ALCSCC}^\infty$. Then, we show that $\mathcal{ALCCQU}$ has the same expressivity as its fragment $\mathcal{ALCQt}$, and that both are expressible in first-order logic.

The DL $\mathcal{ALCSCC}^\infty$. Basically, $\mathcal{ALCSCC}^\infty$ provides us with Boolean operations on concepts and constraints on role successors, which are expressed in QFBAPA$^\infty$. In these constraints, role names and concept descriptions can be used as set variables, and there are no PA variables allowed. The syntax of $\mathcal{ALCSCC}^\infty$ is identical to the one of $\mathcal{ALCSCC}$.

Definition 1 (Syntax of $\mathcal{ALCSCC}^\infty$). *Given finite, disjoint sets N_C of concept names and N_R of role names, the set of $\mathcal{ALCSCC}$ concept descriptions over the signature (N_C, N_R) is inductively defined as follows:*

- *every concept name in N_C is an $\mathcal{ALCSCC}$ concept description over (N_C, N_R);*
- *if C, D are $\mathcal{ALCSCC}$ concept descriptions over (N_C, N_R), then so are $C \sqcap D$, $C \sqcup D$, and $\neg C$;*
- *if Con is a set or numerical constraint of $QFBAPA^\infty$ using role names and already defined $\mathcal{ALCSCC}$ concept descriptions over (N_C, N_R) as (set) variables, then $succ(Con)$ is an $\mathcal{ALCSCC}$ concept description over (N_C, N_R).*

An $\mathcal{ALCSCC}$ TBox over (N_C, N_R) is a finite set of concept inclusions of the form $C \sqsubseteq D$, where C, D are $\mathcal{ALCSCC}$ concept descriptions over (N_C, N_R).

For example, the $\mathcal{ALCSCC}^\infty$ concept description *Female* $\sqcap$ *succ*($|child \cap$ *Female*$| = |child \cap Male|$) describes all female individuals that have exactly as many sons as daughters. Of course, successor constraints can also be nested, as in the $\mathcal{ALCSCC}^\infty$ concept description *succ*($|child \cap succ(child \subseteq Female)| = |child \cap succ(child \subseteq Male)|$), which describes all individuals having as many children that have only daughters as they have children having only sons. As usual in DL, the semantics of $\mathcal{ALCSCC}^\infty$ is defined using the notion of an interpretation.[3]

Definition 2 (Semantics of $\mathcal{ALCSCC}^\infty$). *Given finite, disjoint sets N_C and N_R of concept and role names, respectively, an interpretation of N_C and N_R consists of a non-empty set $\Delta^{\mathcal{I}}$ and a mapping $\cdot^{\mathcal{I}}$ that maps every concept name $A \in N_C$ to a subset $A^{\mathcal{I}}$ of $\Delta^{\mathcal{I}}$ and every role name $r \in N_R$ to a binary relation $r^{\mathcal{I}}$ over $\Delta^{\mathcal{I}}$. Given an individual $d \in \Delta^{\mathcal{I}}$ and a role name $r \in N_R$, we define $r^{\mathcal{I}}(d) := \{e \in \Delta^{\mathcal{I}} \mid (d, e) \in r^{\mathcal{I}}\}$ (r-successors) and $ars^{\mathcal{I}}(d) := \bigcup_{r \in N_R} r^{\mathcal{I}}(d)$ (all role successors).*

The interpretation function $\cdot^{\mathcal{I}}$ is inductively extended to $\mathcal{ALCSCC}^\infty$ concept descriptions over (N_C, N_R) by interpreting $\sqcap$, $\sqcup$, and $\neg$ respectively as intersection, union and complement. Successor constraints are evaluated according to the semantics of $QFBAPA^\infty$: to determine whether $d \in succ(Con)^{\mathcal{I}}$ or not, $\mathcal{U}$ is evaluated as $ars^{\mathcal{I}}(d)$ (i.e., the set of all role successors of d), $\emptyset$ as the empty set, roles r occurring in Con as $r^{\mathcal{I}}(d)$ (i.e., the set of r-successors of d) and concept descriptions D as $D^{\mathcal{I}} \cap ars^{\mathcal{I}}(d)$ (i.e., the set of role successors of d that belong to D).[4] Then $d \in succ(Con)^{\mathcal{I}}$ iff the substitution obtained this way is a solution of the $QFBAPA^\infty$ formula Con.

The interpretation $\mathcal{I}$ is a model *of the TBox $\mathcal{T}$ if $C^{\mathcal{I}} \subseteq D^{\mathcal{I}}$ holds for all $C \sqsubseteq D \in \mathcal{T}$. The $\mathcal{ALCSCC}^\infty$ concept description C is* satisfiable *if there is an interpretation $\mathcal{I}$ such that $C^{\mathcal{I}} \neq \emptyset$, and it is* satisfiable w.r.t. the TBox $\mathcal{T}$ *if there is a model $\mathcal{I}$ of $\mathcal{T}$ such that $C^{\mathcal{I}} \neq \emptyset$. The $\mathcal{ALCSCC}^\infty$ concept descriptions C, D are* equivalent *(written $C \equiv D$) if $C^{\mathcal{I}} = D^{\mathcal{I}}$ for all interpretations $\mathcal{I}$.*

---

[3] A more detailed definition of the semantics can be found in [5].
[4] Note that, by induction, the sets $D^{\mathcal{I}}$ are well-defined.

This semantics differs from the one given in [2] for $\mathcal{ALCSCC}$ as follows. In [2], interpretations are restricted to being finitely branching in the sense that, for any $d \in \Delta^{\mathcal{I}}$, the set $ars^{\mathcal{I}}(d)$ of all role successors of d must be finite. This ensures that, in the evaluation of successor constraints, only finite sets are considered, and thus this evaluation can be done using QFBAPA. Here, we do not make this assumption, and thus QFBAPA$^\infty$ needs to be used to evaluate successor constraints. Note that in $\mathcal{ALCSCC}^\infty$ we can actually force the existence of elements with infinitely many role successors. For example, the successor constraint $succ(|r| + 1 = |r|)$ is unsatisfiable in $\mathcal{ALCSCC}$, but satisfiable in $\mathcal{ALCSCC}^\infty$ in an interpretation that contains an element that has infinitely many r-successors.

The main results shown in [2] are that the satisfiability problem in $\mathcal{ALCSCC}$ is PSpace-complete for the case without a TBox and ExpTime-complete in the presence of a TBox. The hardness results trivially follow from well-known hardness results for $\mathcal{ALC}$ [16,17]. The main tools used in the proof of the complexity upper bounds are Lemma 1 (and in particular property (ii)) and Proposition 1. Since, by Theorem 1, these two results also hold for QFBAPA$^\infty$, we can basically reuse the proofs from [2]. The only places where explicit adaptations are required are the proofs of soundness of the algorithms, where one now must consider infinite sets. Since these adaptations are quite easy, we dispense with spelling them out here.

Theorem 2. *Satisfiability in $\mathcal{ALCSCC}^\infty$ is PSpace-complete without a TBox and ExpTime-complete in the presence of a TBox.*

The DLs $\mathcal{ALCCQU}$ and $\mathcal{ALCQt}$. Fragments of $\mathcal{ALCSCC}^\infty$ can be obtained by restricting the constraints that can be used in successor constraints to fragments of QFBAPA$^\infty$.

Definition 3 ($\mathcal{ALCCQU}$). *The DL $\mathcal{ALCCQU}$ is defined like $\mathcal{ALCSCC}^\infty$, but in successor constraints only constraints of CQU can be used.*

Thus, the concept description

$$succ(|child \cap livesWith^c \cap Female| = 1), \tag{4}$$

which describes individuals that have exactly one daughter that does not live with them, is an $\mathcal{ALCCQU}$ concept description, but $succ(|child \cap livesWith^c \cap Female| = |child \cap livesWith^c \cap Male|)$ is not. In the definition of CQU given in the previous section, we have introduced as atomic constraints only constraints of the form $k = N$ and $k < N$. In $\mathcal{ALCCQU}$, we can also allow the use of constraints of the form $k \leq N$, $k > N$, $k \geq N$, and $k \neq N$ since successor constraints using them can be expressed. For example, $succ(k \geq N) \equiv \neg succ(k < N)$.

Before we can introduce the fragment $\mathcal{ALCQt}$ of $\mathcal{ALCCQU}$ we must define the notion of a safe role type. A role *literal* is a role name r or its complement r^c. Given a finite set of role names N_R, a *role type* for N_R is an intersection τ of role literals such that every role name in N_R occurs exactly once in this conjunction. The role type τ is *safe* if at least one role occurs non-negated. For example, if

$N_R = \{r, s, t\}$, then $r \cap s \cap t^c$ and $r^c \cap s^c \cap t^c$ are role types, but the latter is not safe. The intersections $r \cap s$ and $r \cap s \cap t^c \cap r^c$ are not role types.

Definition 4 ($\mathcal{ALCQ}t$). *The DL $\mathcal{ALCQ}t$ is defined like $\mathcal{ALCSCC}^\infty$, but in successor constraints occurring in $\mathcal{ALCQ}t$ concept descriptions over (N_C, N_R), no set constraints can be used, and numerical constraints are restricted to the form $|\tau \cap C| \bowtie N$, where τ is a safe role type for N_R, C is an $\mathcal{ALCQ}t$ concept description over (N_C, N_R), and $\bowtie \in \{<, \leq, \geq, >, =, \neq\}$.*

The $\mathcal{ALCCQU}$ concept description (4) is actually an $\mathcal{ALCQ}t$ concept description over (N_C, N_R) if N_R contains only the two roles used in this description.

Adopting the syntax usually employed to denote qualified number restrictions in DLs [1], we can write $\mathcal{ALCQ}t$ successor constraints $succ(|\tau \cap C| \bowtie N)$ as $(\bowtie N \tau . C)$ with τ a safe role type. The semantics given by Definition 2 to the successor constraint $succ(|\tau \cap C| \bowtie N)$ indeed coincides with the usual semantics for qualified number restrictions if intersection and complement in τ are respectively interpreted as role intersection and role complement. It should be noted, however, that this is only true since τ is assumed to be safe. In fact, in Definition 2, complement is performed w.r.t. the role successors of the individual under consideration, whereas general role negation is performed w.r.t. all elements of the interpretation domain. But safety of τ ensures that only role successors of the given individual can be τ-successors of this individual. A similar safety requirement for role expressions has been employed by Tobies (see [19], Chapter 4.4), but he considers arbitrary Boolean combinations of roles, and not just role types, and also allows for inverse roles.

Obviously, $\mathcal{ALCQ}t$ is a sub-logic of $\mathcal{ALCCQU}$ since the successor constraints available in $\mathcal{ALCQ}t$ can clearly be expressed in $\mathcal{ALCCQU}$. From a syntactic point of view, $\mathcal{ALCCQU}$ has successor constraints that are not available in $\mathcal{ALCQ}t$. However, we can show that nevertheless all of them can be expressed in $\mathcal{ALCQ}t$.

Theorem 3. *The DLs $\mathcal{ALCCQU}$ and $\mathcal{ALCQ}t$ have the same expressivity.*

Proof. We need to show that the successor constraints of $\mathcal{ALCCQU}$ can be expressed in $\mathcal{ALCQ}t$. Because of space restrictions, we refer the reader to [5] for a detailed proof, and only give a sketch here.

First note that set constraints, which can be used in $\mathcal{ALCCQU}$, but not in $\mathcal{ALCQ}t$, can be expressed as numerical constraints. Indeed, we have $succ(s \subseteq t) \equiv succ(|s \cap t^c| = 0)$. Second, numerical constraints in $\mathcal{ALCCQU}$ may contain linear combinations of set cardinalities, whereas addition and multiplication with a constant are not allowed to be used in numerical constraints of $\mathcal{ALCQ}t$. However, they can be eliminated using Boolean operations. In fact, multiplication with a non-negative integer constant can be expressed by iterated addition, and addition can be eliminated as follows: $succ(|s_1| + \ldots + |s_\ell| \bowtie N)$ for $\bowtie \in \{\leq, =, \geq\}$ is equivalent to the disjunction

$$\bigsqcup_{N_1 + \ldots + N_\ell = N} succ(|s_1| \bowtie N_1) \sqcap \ldots \sqcap succ(|s_\ell| \bowtie N_\ell),$$

where $N_1, \ldots, N_\ell$ range over the non-negative integers. Since N is a fixed non-negative integer, this disjunction is clearly finite. For $\bowtie \in \{<, >\}$, this equivalence would not hold, but we can clearly express $>$ and $<$ using the other comparison operators. For example, $succ(k > N) \equiv \neg succ(k \leq N)$.

Finally, consider successor constraints of the form $succ(|s| \bowtie N)$ where s is a set term built using role names and concept descriptions, and $\bowtie \in \{\leq, =, \geq\}$. The semantics of $\mathcal{ALCSCC}^\infty$ ensures that $succ(|s| \bowtie N)$ is equivalent to $succ(|s \cap (r_1 \cup \ldots \cup r_n)| \bowtie N)$ where $N_R = \{r_1, \ldots, r_n\}$. Using distributivity of set intersection over set union, we can now transform the set term $s \cap (r_1 \cup \ldots \cup r_n)$ into "disjunctive normal form," which yields an equivalent set term of the form $(s_1 \cap C_1) \cup \ldots \cup (s_p \cap C_p)$, where each s_i is a conjunction of role literals containing at least one role positively, and the C_i are concept descriptions. Obviously, each s_i can then be expressed as a union of safe role types. Using the fact that $(\tau \cap C_1) \cup (\tau \cap C_2)$ is equivalent to $(\tau \cap (C_1 \sqcup C_2))$, we thus obtain that $s \cap (r_1 \cup \ldots \cup r_n)$ can be expressed in the form

$$(\tau_1 \cap D_1) \cup \ldots \cup (\tau_q \cap D_q),$$

where $\tau_1, \ldots, \tau_q$ are distinct safe role types and $D_1, \ldots, D_q$ are concept descriptions. Since distinct role types are interpreted as disjoint sets, we thus have

$$succ(|s| \bowtie N) \equiv succ(|(\tau_1 \cap D_1)| + \ldots + |(\tau_q \cap D_q)| \bowtie N)$$
$$\equiv \bigsqcup_{N_1 + \ldots + N_q = N} succ(|\tau_1 \cap D_1| \bowtie N_1) \sqcap \ldots \sqcap succ(|\tau_q \cap D_q| \bowtie N_q).$$

Since the last expression is clearly an $\mathcal{ALCQt}$ concept description, this completes the proof of the theorem. □

It should be noted that the constructions employed in the above proof can lead to an exponential blow-up for several reasons. One example is building the disjunctive normal form in the third part of the proof, and another is expressing addition using disjunction. Thus, it would not be a good idea to use these constructions for the purpose of reducing reasoning in $\mathcal{ALCCQU}$ to reasoning in $\mathcal{ALCQt}$. At the moment, it is not clear to us whether the exponential blow-up can be avoided, but we conjecture that $\mathcal{ALCCQU}$ is exponentially more succinct than $\mathcal{ALCQt}$.

By using the standard translation of $\mathcal{ALCQ}$ and of Boolean operations on roles into first-order logic [4], it can easily be shown that $\mathcal{ALCQt}$, and thus also $\mathcal{ALCCQU}$, can be expressed in first-order logic.

Corollary 1. *The DL $\mathcal{ALCCQU}$ can be expressed in first-order logic, i.e., for every $\mathcal{ALCCQU}$ concept description C there is an equivalent first-order formula, i.e, a first-order formula $\phi_C(x)$ with one free variable x such that $C^\mathcal{I} = \{d \in \Delta^\mathcal{I} \mid \mathcal{I} \models \phi_C(d)\}$ holds for every interpretation $\mathcal{I}$.*

4   Expressive Power

To prove that the concepts of one DL can be expressed in another DL, one usually shows how to construct, for a given concept of the former DL, an equivalent one of the latter, as we have, e.g., done in the proof of Theorem 3. Showing inexpressibility results is usually more involved. An important tool often used in this context is the notion of a bisimulation [12,13], inherited from modal logics [20]. In the following, we first recall the definition of a bisimulation relation tailored towards the DL $\mathcal{ALCQ}$ [13], and use this to show that $\mathcal{ALCCQU}$ is strictly more expressive than $\mathcal{ALCQ}$. Then, we adapt this definition to obtain a bisimulation relation tailored towards $\mathcal{ALCQ}t$. Surprisingly, this relation cannot be used to separate $\mathcal{ALCQ}t$, and thus $\mathcal{ALCCQU}$, from $\mathcal{ALCSCC}^\infty$. In fact, we can show that not only all $\mathcal{ALCCQU}$ concepts are invariant under this notion of bisimulation, but also all $\mathcal{ALCSCC}^\infty$ concepts. As a consequence, we obtain that $\mathcal{ALCCQU}$ is exactly the first-order fragment of $\mathcal{ALCSCC}^\infty$. Finally, we show that $\mathcal{ALCSCC}^\infty$ indeed contains concepts that are not expressible in first-order logic.

$\mathcal{ALCQ}$ Bisimulation. In the context of the present paper, $\mathcal{ALCQ}$ can be defined as the fragment of $\mathcal{ALCCQU}$ where only successor constraints of the form $succ(|r \cap C| \bowtie N)$ can be used, where $r \in N_R$, C is an $\mathcal{ALCQ}$ concept description, $\bowtie \in \{<, \leq, \geq, >, =, \neq\}$, and N is a non-negative integer.

Definition 5 ([13]). *Let $\mathcal{I}_1$ and $\mathcal{I}_2$ be interpretations. The relation $\rho \subseteq \Delta^{\mathcal{I}_1} \times \Delta^{\mathcal{I}_2}$ is an $\mathcal{ALCQ}$ bisimulation between $\mathcal{I}_1$ and $\mathcal{I}_2$ if*

1. *$d_1 \rho d_2$ implies $d_1 \in A^{\mathcal{I}_1}$ iff $d_2 \in A^{\mathcal{I}_2}$, for all $d_1 \in \Delta^{\mathcal{I}_1}$, $d_2 \in \Delta^{\mathcal{I}_2}$, $A \in N_C$;*
2. *if $d_1 \rho d_2$ and $D_1 \subseteq r^{\mathcal{I}_1}(d_1)$ is finite for $r \in N_R$, then there is a set $D_2 \subseteq r^{\mathcal{I}_2}(d_2)$ such that ρ contains a bijection between D_1 and D_2;*
3. *if $d_1 \rho d_2$ and $D_2 \subseteq r^{\mathcal{I}_2}(d_2)$ is finite for $r \in N_R$, then there is a set $D_1 \subseteq r^{\mathcal{I}_1}(d_1)$ such that ρ contains a bijection between D_1 and D_2.*

The individuals $d_1 \in \Delta^{\mathcal{I}_1}$, $d_2 \in \Delta^{\mathcal{I}_2}$ are $\mathcal{ALCQ}$ bisimilar (written $(\mathcal{I}_1, d_1) \sim_{\mathcal{ALCQ}} (\mathcal{I}_2, d_2)$) if there is an $\mathcal{ALCQ}$ bisimulation ρ between $\mathcal{I}_1$ and $\mathcal{I}_2$ such that $d_1 \rho d_2$, and $\mathcal{ALCQ}$-equivalent (written $(\mathcal{I}_1, d_1) \equiv_{\mathcal{ALCQ}} (\mathcal{I}_2, d_2)$) if for all $\mathcal{ALCQ}$ concept descriptions C we have $d_1 \in C^{\mathcal{I}_1}$ iff $d_2 \in C^{\mathcal{I}_2}$.

The following theorem shows that $\mathcal{ALCQ}$ is exactly the fragment of first-order logic that is invariant under this notion of bisimulation. We say that a first-order formula $\phi(x)$ with one free variable x is *invariant under* $\sim_{\mathcal{ALCQ}}$ if $(\mathcal{I}_1, d_1) \sim_{\mathcal{ALCQ}} (\mathcal{I}_2, d_2)$ implies $\mathcal{I}_1 \models \phi(d_1)$ iff $\mathcal{I}_2 \models \phi(d_2)$.

Theorem 4 ([13]). *Let $\phi(x)$ be a first-order formula with one free variable x. Then the following are equivalent:*

1. *there is an $\mathcal{ALCQ}$ concept description C such that C is equivalent to $\phi(x)$;*
2. *$\phi(x)$ is invariant under $\sim_{\mathcal{ALCQ}}$.*

Since $\mathcal{ALCQ}$ is expressible in first-order logic, this theorem in particular implies that $\mathcal{ALCQ}$ bisimilar elements of interpretations are also $\mathcal{ALCQ}$-equivalent. We can use this fact to show that $\mathcal{ALCCQU}$ is strictly more expressive than $\mathcal{ALCQ}$.

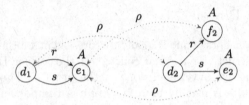

Fig. 1. Two interpretations $\mathcal{I}_1$ and $\mathcal{I}_2$ and an $\mathcal{ALCQ}$ bisimulation ρ.

Corollary 2. *There is no $\mathcal{ALCQ}$ concept description C such that C is equivalent to the $\mathcal{ALCCQU}$ concept description $succ(|r \cap s| > 0)$.*

Proof. Assume that C is an $\mathcal{ALCQ}$ concept description such that $C \equiv succ(|r \cap s| > 0)$, and consider the interpretations $\mathcal{I}_1, \mathcal{I}_2$ and the $\mathcal{ALCQ}$ bisimulation ρ depicted in Fig. 1. Then we have $d_1 \in succ(|r \cap s| > 0)^{\mathcal{I}_1} = C^{\mathcal{I}_1}$, and thus $(\mathcal{I}_1, d_1) \sim_{\mathcal{ALCQ}} (\mathcal{I}_2, d_2)$ implies $d_2 \in C^{\mathcal{I}_2}$. This contradicts our assumption that $C \equiv succ(|r \cap s| > 0)$ since $d_2 \notin succ(|r \cap s| > 0)$. □

$\mathcal{ALCQt}$ Bisimulation. The definition of a bisimulation can be adapted to $\mathcal{ALCQt}$ by replacing role names r with safe role types τ. To be more precise, let τ be a safe role type, $r_1, \ldots, r_k$ the role names occurring positively in τ, and $s_1, \ldots, s_\ell$ the role names occurring negatively, i.e., $\tau = r_1 \cap \ldots \cap r_k \cap s_1^c \cap \ldots \cap s_\ell^c$. For a given interpretation $\mathcal{I}$ and element $d \in \Delta^{\mathcal{I}}$ we then define

$$\tau^{\mathcal{I}}(d) := (r_1^{\mathcal{I}}(d) \cap \ldots \cap r_k^{\mathcal{I}}(d)) \setminus (s_1^{\mathcal{I}}(d) \cup \ldots \cup s_\ell^{\mathcal{I}}(d)).$$

Since τ is safe, we have $k \geq 1$, and thus $\tau^{\mathcal{I}}(d) \subseteq r_1^{\mathcal{I}}(d) \subseteq ars^{\mathcal{I}}(d)$.

$\mathcal{ALCQt}$ *bisimulation*, $\mathcal{ALCQt}$ *bisimilar*, $\mathcal{ALCQt}$ *equivalent*, and *invariance under $\mathcal{ALCQt}$ bisimulation* are now defined as for $\mathcal{ALCQ}$ (Definition 5), but with $\mathcal{ALCQt}$ replacing $\mathcal{ALCQ}$ and safe role types τ for N_R replacing role names $r \in N_R$ (see [5] for a more detailed definition).

Theorem 5. *Let $\phi(x)$ be a first-order formula with one free variable x. Then the following are equivalent:*

1. *there is an $\mathcal{ALCQt}$ concept description C such that C is equivalent to $\phi(x)$;*
2. *$\phi(x)$ is invariant under $\sim_{\mathcal{ALCQt}}$.*

Since the proof of this theorem is very similar to the proof of Theorem 4 given in [13], we omit it here. An explicit proof for the case of $\mathcal{ALCQt}$, which is more detailed than the one in [13], can be found in [5].

The Expressivity of $\mathcal{ALCSCC}^{\infty}$ Relative to $\mathcal{ALCCQU}$. Our original expectation was that we could use Theorem 5 to show that $\mathcal{ALCSCC}^{\infty}$ is strictly more expressive than $\mathcal{ALCQt}$, and thus also $\mathcal{ALCCQU}$. The following proposition implies that this is not possible.

Proposition 2. *If* $(\mathcal{I}_1, d_1) \sim_{\mathcal{ALCQ}t} (\mathcal{I}_2, d_2)$ *then* $(\mathcal{I}_1, d_1) \equiv_{\mathcal{ALCSCC}^\infty} (\mathcal{I}_2, d_2)$.

A detailed proof of this proposition can be found in [5]. Here, we only explain the main ideas underlying this proof. Basically, we must show that, given a PA expression k occurring in an $\mathcal{ALCSCC}^\infty$ concept description, the assumption that $(\mathcal{I}_1, d_1) \sim_{\mathcal{ALCQ}t} (\mathcal{I}_2, d_2)$ implies that evaluating k on the role successors of d_1 yields the same result (i.e., element of $\mathbb{N}^\infty$) as evaluating k on the role successors of d_2. To this purpose, we first observe that k can be written as

$$k = \sum_{i=1}^{\ell} N_i \cdot |\tau_i \cap C_i|,$$

where (for $i = 1, \ldots, \ell$) we have that N_i is a non-negative integer, τ_i is a safe role type, and C_i is an $\mathcal{ALCSCC}^\infty$ concept description. This can be shown by a simple adaptation of the arguments used in the proof of Theorem 3. Consequently, it is sufficient to show the claim for the summands $|\tau_i \cap C_i|$. First, assume that, on the role successors of d_1, this expression evaluates to the non-negative integer N. Then we have $d_1 \in succ(|\tau_i \cap C_i| = N)^{\mathcal{I}_1}$, and since $succ(|\tau_i \cap C_i| = N)$ is an $\mathcal{ALCQ}t$ concept description, Theorem 5 yields $d_2 \in succ(|\tau_i \cap C_i| = N)^{\mathcal{I}_2}$. Consequently, $|\tau_i \cap C_i|$ also evaluates to N on the role successors of d_2. If $|\tau_i \cap C_i|$ evaluates to ∞ on the role successors of d_1, then we have $d_1 \in succ(|\tau_i \cap C_i| > N)^{\mathcal{I}_1}$ for all non-negative integers N, and we can conclude that $d_2 \in succ(|\tau_i \cap C_i| > N)^{\mathcal{I}_2}$ for all non-negative integers N. This shows that $|\tau_i \cap C_i|$ also evaluates to ∞ on the role successors of d_2, which concludes our proof sketch.

Together with Theorem 5, this proposition yields a characterization of $\mathcal{ALCCQU}$ as the first-order fragment of $\mathcal{ALCSCC}^\infty$.

Theorem 6. *Let C be an $\mathcal{ALCSCC}^\infty$ concept description. Then the following are equivalent:*

1. *there is a first-order formula $\phi(x)$ with one free variable x such that C is equivalent to $\phi(x)$;*
2. *C is equivalent to an $\mathcal{ALCCQU}$ concept description.*

Proof. $(2 \Rightarrow 1)$ is an immediate consequence of Corollary 1. Now, assume that 1. holds. Since $\phi(x)$ is equivalent to an $\mathcal{ALCSCC}^\infty$ concept description, it is invariant under $\mathcal{ALCQ}t$ bisimulation by Proposition 2, and thus equivalent to an $\mathcal{ALCQ}t$ concept description by Theorem 5. Since $\mathcal{ALCQ}t$ is a sub-logic of $\mathcal{ALCCQU}$, this yields 2. □

It remains to show that $\mathcal{ALCSCC}^\infty$ itself is not a fragment of first-order logic.

Theorem 7. *The $\mathcal{ALCSCC}^\infty$ concept description $succ(|r \cap A| = |r \cap \neg A|)$ cannot be expressed in first-order logic.*

To prove this theorem, it is sufficient to show that the above concept description cannot be expressed in $\mathcal{ALCCQU}$. The proof of this fact is similar to the one given in [2] to show that $\mathcal{ALCSCC}$ is more expressive than $\mathcal{ALCQ}$, but more involved since $\mathcal{ALCCQU}$ is more expressive that $\mathcal{ALCQ}$.

5 Conclusion

In this paper, we have introduced the variant $\mathcal{ALCSCC}^\infty$ of the DL $\mathcal{ALCSCC}$ investigated in [2], in which the restriction to finitely branching interpretations is lifted. We have shown that this modification does not change the complexity of reasoning. As an auxiliary result we have shown that reasoning in QFBAPA$^\infty$, a variant of QFBAPA in which also infinite sets are allowed, has the same complexity as in QFBAPA. The main result of this paper is the proof that the DL $\mathcal{ALCCQU}$ is exactly the first-order fragment of $\mathcal{ALCSCC}^\infty$.

Regarding future work, it should be noted that we have only investigated the expressive power of the *concept descriptions* of $\mathcal{ALCSCC}^\infty$ and $\mathcal{ALCCQU}$. In [13], the expressivity of *TBoxes* is considered as well. It would be interesting to see whether we can extend our results to TBoxes (or even cardinality constraints on concepts [3]) of $\mathcal{ALCSCC}^\infty$ and $\mathcal{ALCCQU}$. In [5] we have shown how the satisfiability procedure for CQU presented in [7], which is based on column generation, can be extended to a satisfiability procedure for $\mathcal{ALCCQU}$, but it remains to implement and test this procedure. In addition, it would be interesting to see whether this approach can be extended to $\mathcal{ALCSCC}$ and $\mathcal{ALCSCC}^\infty$. It would also be interesting to see what impact the addition of inverse roles to $\mathcal{ALCSCC}$ and $\mathcal{ALCSCC}^\infty$ has on the complexity of reasoning.

Acknowledgment. The authors would like to thank Ulrike Baumann for helpful discussions regarding QFBAPA$^\infty$. We should also like to point out that we have learned about the results regarding QFBAPA$_\infty$ in [10] only a couple of days before the submission of the final version of this paper.

References

1. Baader, F.: Description logic terminology. In: [4], pp. 485–495 (2003)
2. Baader, F.: A new description logic with set constraints and cardinality constraints on role successors. In: Dixon, C., Finger, M. (eds.) FroCoS 2017. LNCS (LNAI), vol. 10483, pp. 43–59. Springer, Cham (2017). https://doi.org/10.1007/978-3-319-66167-4_3
3. Baader, F.: Expressive cardinality constraints on $\mathcal{ALCSCC}$ concepts. In: Proceedings of the 34th Annual ACM Symposium on Applied Computing (SAC 2019), pp. 1123–1131. ACM (2019)
4. Baader, F., Calvanese, D., McGuinness, D., Nardi, D., Patel-Schneider, P.F. (eds.): The Description Logic Handbook: Theory, Implementation, and Applications. Cambridge University Press, Cambridge (2003)
5. De Bortoli, F.: Integrating reasoning services for description logics with cardinality constraints with numerical optimization techniques. EMCL Master's thesis, Chair for Automata Theory, Faculty of Computer Science, TU Dresden (2019). https://tu-dresden.de/inf/lat/theses#DeBo-Mas-19
6. Eisenbrand, F., Shmonin, G.: Carathéodory bounds for integer cones. Oper. Res. Lett. **34**(5), 564–568 (2006)
7. Finger, M., De Bona, G.: Algorithms for deciding counting quantifiers over unary predicates. In: Proceedings of the Thirty-First AAAI Conference on Artificial Intelligence (AAAI 2017), pp. 3878–3884. AAAI Press (2017)

8. Hoehndorf, R., Schofield, P.N., Gkoutos, G.V.: The role of ontologies in biological and biomedical research: a functional perspective. Brief. Bioinform. **16**(6), 1069–1080 (2015)

9. Hollunder, B., Baader, F.: Qualifying number restrictions in concept languages. In: Proceedings of the 2nd International Conference on the Principles of Knowledge Representation and Reasoning (KR 1991), pp. 335–346 (1991)

10. Kuncak, V., Piskac, R., Suter, P.: Ordered sets in the calculus of data structures. In: Dawar, A., Veith, H. (eds.) CSL 2010. LNCS, vol. 6247, pp. 34–48. Springer, Heidelberg (2010). https://doi.org/10.1007/978-3-642-15205-4_5

11. Kuncak, V., Rinard, M.: Towards efficient satisfiability checking for Boolean algebra with Presburger arithmetic. In: Pfenning, F. (ed.) CADE 2007. LNCS (LNAI), vol. 4603, pp. 215–230. Springer, Heidelberg (2007). https://doi.org/10.1007/978-3-540-73595-3_15

12. Kurtonina, N., de Rijke, M.: Expressiveness of concept expressions in first-order description logics. Artif. Intell. **107**(2), 303–333 (1999)

13. Lutz, C., Piro, R., Wolter, F.: Description logic TBoxes: model-theoretic characterizations and rewritability. In: Proceedings of the 22nd International Joint Conference on Artificial Intelligence (IJCAI 2011), IJCAI/AAAI, pp. 983–988 (2011)

14. Papadimitriou, C.H.: On the complexity of integer programming. J. ACM **28**(4), 765–768 (1981)

15. Pratt-Hartmann, I.: On the computational complexity of the numerically definite syllogistic and related logics. Bull. Symb. Logic **14**(1), 1–28 (2008)

16. Schild, K. A correspondence theory for terminological logics: preliminary report. In: Proceedings of the 12th International Joint Conference on Artificial Intelligence (IJCAI 1991), pp. 466–471 (1991)

17. Schmidt-Schauß, M., Smolka, G.: Attributive concept descriptions with complements. Artif. Intell. **48**(1), 1–26 (1991)

18. Tobies, S.: A PSpace algorithm for graded modal logic. In: Ganzinger, H. (ed.) CADE 1999. LNCS (LNAI), vol. 1632, pp. 52–66. Springer, Heidelberg (1999). https://doi.org/10.1007/3-540-48660-7_4

19. Tobies, S.: Complexity results and practical algorithms for logics in knowledge representation. PhD thesis, LuFG Theoretical Computer Science, RWTH-Aachen, Germany (2001). http://tu-dresden.de/inf/lat/theses/#Tobies-PhD-2001

20. van Benthem, J.: Modal Logic and Classical Logic. Bibliopolis, Napoli (1983)

Interactive Theorem Proving

Verifying an Incremental Theory Solver for Linear Arithmetic in Isabelle/HOL

Ralph Bottesch, Max W. Haslbeck[ID], and René Thiemann[✉][ID]

University of Innsbruck, Innsbruck, Austria
rene.thiemann@uibk.ac.at

Abstract. Dutertre and de Moura developed a simplex-based solver for linear rational arithmetic that has an incremental interface and provides unsatisfiable cores. We present a verification of their algorithm in Isabelle/HOL that significantly extends previous work by Spasić and Marić. Based on the simplex algorithm we further formalize Farkas' Lemma. With this result we verify that linear rational constraints are satisfiable over $\mathbb{Q}$ if and only they are satisfiable over $\mathbb{R}$. Hence, our verified simplex algorithm is also able to decide satisfiability in linear real arithmetic.

Keywords: DPLL(T) · Farkas' Lemma · Simplex algorithm · SMT solving

1 Introduction

CeTA [7] is a verified certifier for checking untrusted safety and termination proofs from external tools such as AProVE [12] and T2 [6]. To this end, CeTA also contains a verified SAT-modulo-theories (SMT) solver, since these untrusted proofs contain claims of validity of formulas. It is formalized as a deep embedding and is generated via code generation.

The ultimate aim of this work is the optimization of the existing verified SMT solver, as it is quite basic: The current solver takes as input a quantifier free formula in the theory of linear rational arithmetic, translates it into disjunctive normal form (DNF), and then tries to prove unsatisfiability for each conjunction of literals with the verified simplex implementation of Spasić and Marić [16]. This basic solver has at least two limitations: It only works on small formulas, since the conversion to DNF often leads to an exponential blowup in the formula size; and the procedure is restricted to linear *rational* arithmetic, i.e., the existing formalization only contain results on satisfiability over $\mathbb{Q}$, but not over $\mathbb{R}$.

Clearly, instead of the expensive DNF conversion, the better approach is to verify an SMT solver that is based on DPLL(T) or similar algorithms [4,11].

This research was supported by the Austrian Science Fund (FWF) project Y757. The authors are listed in alphabetical order regardless of individual contributions or seniority.

A. Herzig and A. Popescu (Eds.): FroCoS 2019, LNAI 11715, pp. 223–239, 2019.
https://doi.org/10.1007/978-3-030-29007-8_13

Although there has been recent success in verifying a DPLL-based SAT solver [2], for DPLL(T), a core component is missing, namely a powerful theory solver.

Therefore, in this paper we will extend the formalization of the simplex algorithm due to Spasić and Marić [16]. This will be an important milestone on the way to obtain a fully verified DPLL(T)-based SMT solver. To this end, we change the verified implementation and the existing soundness proofs in such a way that *minimal unsatisfiable cores* are computed instead of the algorithm merely indicating unsatisfiability. Moreover, we provide an *incremental interface* to the simplex method, as required by a DPLL(T) solver, which permits the incremental assertion of constraints, backtracking, etc. Finally, we formalize *Farkas' Lemma*, an important result that is related to duality in linear programming. In our setting, we utilize this lemma to formally verify that unsatisfiability of linear rational constraints over $\mathbb{Q}$ implies unsatisfiability over $\mathbb{R}$. In total, we provide a verified simplex implementation with an incremental interface, that generates minimal unsatisfiable cores over $\mathbb{Q}$ and $\mathbb{R}$.

We base our formalization entirely on the incremental simplex algorithm described by Dutertre and de Moura [10]. This paper was also the basis of the existing implementation by Spasić and Marić, of which the correctness has been formalized in Isabelle/HOL [14].

Although the sizes of the existing simplex formalization and of our new one differ only by a relatively small amount (8143 versus 11167 lines), the amount of modifications is quite significant: 2940 lines have been replaced by 5964 new ones. The verification of Farkas' Lemma and derived lemmas required another 1647 lines. It mainly utilizes facts that are proved in the existing simplex formalization, but it does not require significant modifications thereof.

The remainder of our paper is structured as follows. In Sect. 2 we describe the key parts of the simplex algorithm of Dutertre and de Moura and its formalization by Spasić and Marić. We present the development of the extended simplex algorithm with minimal unsatisfiable cores and incremental interfaces in Sect. 3. We formalize Farkas' Lemma and related results in Sect. 4. Finally, we conclude with Sect. 5.

Our formalization is available in the Archive of Formal Proofs (AFP) for Isabelle 2019 under the entries `Simplex` [13] and `Farkas` [5]. The `Simplex` entry contains the formalization of Spasić and Marić with our modifications and extensions. Our Isabelle formalization can be accessed by downloading the AFP, or by following the hyperlink at the beginning of each Isabelle code listing in Sects. 3 and 4.

Related Work. Allamigeon and Katz [1] formalized and verified an implementation of the simplex algorithm in Coq. Since their goal was to verify theoretical results about convex polyhedra, their formalization is considerably different from ours, as we aim at obtaining a practically efficient algorithm. For instance, we also integrate and verify an optimization of the simplex algorithm, namely the elimination of unused variables, cf. Dutertre and de Moura [10, end of Section 3]. This optimization also has not been covered by Spasić and Marić.

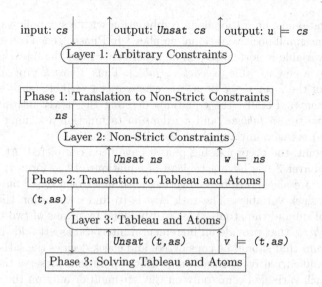

input: cs output: $Unsat$ cs output: $u \models cs$

Layer 1: Arbitrary Constraints

Phase 1: Translation to Non-Strict Constraints

ns

Layer 2: Non-Strict Constraints

$Unsat$ ns $w \models ns$

Phase 2: Translation to Tableau and Atoms

(t, as)

Layer 3: Tableau and Atoms

$Unsat$ (t, as) $v \models (t, as)$

Phase 3: Solving Tableau and Atoms

Fig. 1. The layers and phases of the simplex algorithm

Chaieb and Nipkow verified quantifier elimination procedures (QEP) for dense linear orders and integer arithmetic [9], which are more widely applicable than the simplex algorithm. Spasić and Marić compared the QEPs with their implementation on a set of random quantifier-free formulas [16]. In these tests, their (and therefore our) simplex implementation outperforms the QEPs significantly. Hence, neither of the formalizations subsumes the other.

There is also work on verified certification of SMT proofs, where an untrusted SMT solver outputs a certificate that is checked by a verified certifier. This is an alternative to the development of a verified SMT prover, but the corresponding Isabelle implementation of Böhme and Weber [3] is not usable in our setting, as it relies on internal Isabelle tactics, such as linarith, which are not accessible in Isabelle-generated code such as CeTA.

2   The Simplex Algorithm and the Existing Formalization

The simplex algorithm as described by Dutertre and de Moura is a decision procedure for the question whether a set of linear constraints is satisfiable over $\mathbb{Q}$. We briefly recall the main steps.

For the sake of the formalization, it is useful to divide the work of the algorithm into *phases*, and to think of the data available at the beginning and end of each phase as a *layer* (see Fig. 1). Thus, Layer 1 consists of the set of input constraints, which are (in)equalities of the form $p \sim c$, for some linear polynomial p, constant $c \in \mathbb{Q}$, and $\sim \in \{<, \leq, =, \geq, >\}$. Phase 1, the first preprocessing phase, transforms all constraints of Layer 1 into non-strict inequalities involving δ-rationals, i.e. rationals in combination with a symbolic value δ, representing some small positive rational number.[1] In Phase 2, each constraint with exactly one variable is normalized; in all other constraints the linear polynomial is replaced by a new variable (a *slack variable*). Thus, Phase 2 produces a set of inequalities of the form $x \le c$ or $x \ge c$, where x is a variable (such constraints are called *atoms*). Finally, the equations defining the newly introduced slack variables constitute a *tableau*, and a *valuation* (a function assigning a value to each variable) is taken initially to be the all-zero function.

At this point, the preprocessing phases have been completed. At the end of Phase 2, on Layer 3, we have a tableau of equations of the form $s_j = \sum a_i x_i$, where the s_j are slack variables, together with a set of atoms bounding both original and slack variables. The task now is to find a valuation that satisfies both the tableau and the atoms. This will be done by means of two operations, *assert* and *check*, that provide an incremental interface: assert adds an atom to the set of atoms that should be considered, and check decides the satisfiability of the tableau and currently asserted atoms. Both operations preserve the following invariant: Each variable occurs only on the left-hand or only on the right-hand side of tableau equations, and the valuation satisfies the tableau and the asserted atoms whose variables occur on the right-hand side of tableau equations.

In order to satisfy the invariant, the assert operation has to update the valuation whenever an atom is added whose variable is the right-hand side of the tableau. If this update conflicts with previously asserted atoms in an easily detectable way, assert itself can detect unsatisfiability at this point. Otherwise, it additionally recomputes the valuation of the left-hand side variables according to the equations in the tableau.

The main operation of Phase 3 is check, where the algorithm repeatedly modifies the tableau and valuation, aiming to satisfy all asserted atoms or detect unsatisfiability. The procedure by which the algorithm actually manipulates the tableau and valuation is called *pivoting*, and works as follows: First, it finds a tableau equation where the current valuation does not satisfy an asserted atom, A, involving the left-hand side variable, x. If no such x can be found, the current valuation satisfies the tableau and all asserted atoms. Otherwise, the procedure looks, in the same equation, for a right-hand side variable y for which the valuation can be modified so that the resulting value of x, as given by the equation, exactly matches the bound in A. If no such y can be found, the pivoting procedure concludes unsatisfiability. Otherwise, it updates the valuation for both x and y, and flips the sides of the two variables in the equation, resulting in an equation that defines y. The right-hand side of the new equation replaces all appearances of y on the right-hand side of other equations, ensuring that the invariant is maintained. Since y's updated value may no longer satisfy the asserted atoms involving y, it is not at all clear that repeated applications of pivoting eventually terminate. However, if the choice of variables during pivoting is done correctly, it can be shown that this is indeed the case.

---

[1] Arithmetic on δ-rationals is defined pointwise, e.g., $(a + b\delta) + (c + d\delta) := (a + c) + (b + d)\delta$, and $a + b\delta < c + d\delta := a < c \lor (a = c \land b < d)$ for any $a, b, c, d \in \mathbb{Q}$.

Step	Layer	A	B	C	D	Tableau	Val.
1	1	$x > 5$	$2x + y \leq 12$	$2y \geq 6$	$x - 3y \leq 2$	$-$	$-$
2	2	$x \geq 5 + \delta$	$2x + y \leq 12$	$2y \geq 6$	$x - 3y \leq 2$	$-$	$-$
3	3	$x \geq 5 + \delta$	$s \leq 12$	$y \geq 3$	$t \leq 2$	$\{s = 2x + y, t = x - 3y\}$	v_0
4	3	$\mathbf{x \geq 5 + \delta}$	$\mathbf{s \leq 12}$	$y \geq 3$	$\mathbf{t \leq 2}$	$\{s = 2x + y, t = x - 3y\}$	v_1
5	3	$\mathbf{x \geq 5 + \delta}$	$\mathbf{s \leq 12}$	$y \geq 3$	$\mathbf{t \leq 2}$	$\{s = \frac{7x - t}{3}, y = \frac{x - t}{3}\}$	v_2
6	3	$\mathbf{x \geq 5 + \delta}$	$\mathbf{s \leq 12}$	$\mathbf{y \geq 3}$	$\mathbf{t \leq 2}$	$\{s = \frac{7x - t}{3}, y = \frac{x - t}{3}\}$	v_2
7	3	$\mathbf{x \geq 5 + \delta}$	$\mathbf{s \leq 12}$	$\mathbf{y \geq 3}$	$\mathbf{t \leq 2}$	$\{t = \frac{s - 7y}{2}, x = \frac{s - y}{2}\}$	v_3

Valuation v	$v(x)$	$v(y)$	$v(s)$	$v(t)$
v_0	0	0	0	0
v_1	$5 + \delta$	0	$10 + 2\delta$	$5 + \delta$
v_2	$5 + \delta$	$1 + \frac{1}{3}\delta$	$11 + \frac{7}{3}\delta$	2
v_3	$\frac{9}{2}$	3	12	$-\frac{9}{2}$

Fig. 2. Example run of the simplex algorithm

Consider the example in Fig. 2. The input constraints A–D are given in step 1 and converted into non-strict inequalities with δ-rationals in the step 2. In step 3, the constraint $2y \geq 6$ is normalized to the atom $y \geq 3$, two slack variables $s = 2x + y$ and $t = x - 3y$ are created, and the constraints $2x + y \leq 12$ and $x - 3y \leq 2$ are simplified accordingly. The equations defining s and t then form the initial tableau, and the initial valuation v_0 is the all-zero function. In step 4, the three atoms A, B and D are asserted (indicated by boldface font) and the valuation is updated accordingly. Next, the algorithm invokes check and performs pivoting to find the valuation v_2 that satisfies A, B, D and the tableau. This valuation on Layer 3 assigns δ-rationals to all variables x, y, s, t and can then be translated to a satisfying valuation over $\mathbb{Q}$ for constraints A, B, D on Layer 1. If the incremental interface is then used to also assert the atom C (step 6), unsatisfiability is detected via check after two further pivoting operations (step 7). Hence, the constraints A–D on Layer 1 are also unsatisfiable.

Spasić and Marić use Isabelle/HOL for the formalization, as do we for the extension. Isabelle/HOL is an interactive theorem prover for higher-order logic. Its syntax conforms to mathematical notation, and Isabelle supports keywords such as `fixes`, `assumes` and `shows`, allowing us to state theorems in Isabelle in a way which is close to mathematical language. Furthermore, all terms in Isabelle have a well-defined type, specified with a double-colon: `term` `::` α. We use Greek letters for arbitrary types. Isabelle has built-in support for the types of rational numbers (`rat`) and real numbers (`real`). The type of a function `f` from type α to type β is specified as `f` `::` $\alpha \Rightarrow \beta$. There is a set type (α `set`), a list type (α `list`), an option type (α `option` with constructors `Some` `::` $\alpha \Rightarrow \alpha$ `option` and `None` `::` α `option`) and a sum type ($\alpha + \beta$ with constructors `Inl` `::` $\alpha \Rightarrow \alpha + \beta$ and `Inr` `::` $\beta \Rightarrow \alpha + \beta$). The syntax for function application is `f` `arg1` `arg2`. In this paper we use the terms Isabelle and Isabelle/HOL interchangeably.

Spasić and Marić proved the following main theorem about their simplex implementation `simplex :: rat constraint list ⇒ rat valuation option`.

```
lemma simplex_spasic_maric:
  shows simplex cs = None ⟶ ∄ v :: rat valuation. v ⊨ cs
  shows simplex cs = Some v ⟶ v ⊨ cs
```

The lemma states that if `simplex` returns no valuation, then the constraints `cs` are unsatisfiable. If `simplex` returns a valuation `Some v`, then `v` satisfies `cs`.

To prove the correctness of their algorithm they used a modular approach: Each subalgorithm (e.g. pivoting, incremental assertions) and its properties were specified in a *locale*, a special feature of Isabelle. Locales parameterize definitions and theorems over operations and assumptions. The overall algorithm is then implemented by combining several locales and their verified implementations. Soundness of the whole algorithm is then easily obtained via the locale structure. The modular structure of the formalization allows us to reuse, adapt and extend several parts of their formalization.

3 The New Simplex Formalization

In the following we describe our extension of the formalization of Spasić and Marić through the integration of minimal unsatisfiable cores (Sect. 3.1), the integration of an optimization during Phase 2 (Sect. 3.2) and the development of an incremental interface to the simplex algorithm (Sect. 3.3).

3.1 Minimal Unsatisfiable Cores

Our first extension is the integration of the functionality for producing unsatisfiable cores, i.e., given a set of unsatisfiable constraints, we seek a subset of the constraints which is still unsatisfiable. Small unsatisfiable cores are crucial for a DPLL(T)-based SMT solver in order to derive small conflict clauses, hence it is desirable to obtain *minimal* unsatisfiable cores, of which each proper subset is satisfiable. For example, in Fig. 2, $\{A, B, C\}$ is a minimal unsatisfiable core. We will refer to this example throughout this section.

Internally, the formalized simplex algorithm represents the data available on Layer 3 in a data structure called a *state*, which contains the current tableau, valuation, the set of asserted atoms,[2] and an unsatisfiability flag. Unsatisfiability is detected by the check operation in Phase 3, namely if the current valuation of a state does not satisfy the atoms, and pivoting is not possible.[3] For instance, in step 7 unsatisfiability is detected as follows: The valuation v_3 does not satisfy

---

[2] In the simplex algorithm [10] and the formalization, the asserted atoms are stored via *bounds*, but this additional data structure is omitted in the presentation here.

[3] Asserting an atom can also detect unsatisfiability, but this gives rise to trivial unsatisfiable cores of the form $\{x \leq c, x \geq d\}$ for constants $d > c$.

the atom $x \geq 5 + \delta$ since $v_3(x) = \frac{9}{2}$. The pivoting procedure looks at the tableau equation for x,

$$x = \frac{1}{2}s - \frac{1}{2}y, \tag{1}$$

and checks whether it is possible to increase the value of x. This is only possible if the valuation of s in increased (since s occurs with positive coefficient in (1)), or if y is decreased (since y occurs with a negative coefficient). Neither is possible, because $v_3(s)$ is already at its maximum ($s \leq 12$) and $v_3(y)$ at its minimum ($y \geq 3$). Hence, in order prove unsatisfiability on Layer 3, it suffices to consider the tableau and the atoms $\{x \geq 5 + \delta, s \leq 12, y \geq 3\}$.

We formally verify that this kind of reasoning works in general: Given the fact that some valuation v of a state does not satisfy an atom $x \geq c$ for some left-hand side variable x, we can obtain the corresponding equation $x = p$ of the tableau T, and take the unsatisfiable core as the set of atoms formed of: $x \geq c$, all atoms $y \geq v(y)$ for variables y of p with coefficient < 0, and all atoms $s \leq v(s)$ for variables s of p with coefficient > 0. The symmetric case $x \leq c$ is handled similarly by flipping signs.

We further prove that the generated cores are minimal w.r.t. the subset relation: Let A be a proper subset of an unsatisfiable core. There are two cases. If A does not contain the atom of the left-hand side variable x, then all atoms in A only contain right-hand side variables. Then by the invariant of the simplex algorithm, the current valuation satisfies both the tableau T and A. In the other case, some atom with a variable z of p is dropped. But then it is possible to apply pivoting for x and z. Let T' be the new tableau and v be the new valuation after pivoting. At this point we use the formalized fact that pivoting maintains the invariant. In particular, $v \models T'$ and $v \models A$, where the latter follows from the fact that A only contains right-hand side variables of the new tableau T' (note that x and z switched sides in the equation following pivoting). Since T and T' are equivalent, we conclude that v satisfies both T and A.

In the formalization, the corresponding lemma looks as follows:

```
lemma check_minimal_unsat_state_core: assumes ⊨nolhs s and ◊ s and ...
   shows ¬ U s ⟶ U (check s) ⟶ minimal_unsat_state_core (check s)
```

The assumptions in the lemma express precisely the invariant of the simplex algorithm, and the lemma states that whenever the check operation sets the unsatisfiability flag $\mathcal{U}$, then indeed a minimal unsatisfiable core is stored in the new state `check s`. Whereas the assumptions have been taken unmodified from the existing simplex formalization, we needed to modify the formalized definition of the check operation and the datatype of states, so that `check` can compute and store the unsatisfiable core in the resulting state.

At this point, we have assembled a verified simplex algorithm for Layer 3 that will either return satisfying valuations or minimal unsatisfiable cores. The next task is to propagate the minimal unsatisfiable cores upwards to Layer 2 and 1, since, initially, the unsatisfiable cores are defined in terms of the data available at Layer 3, which is not meaningful when speaking about the first two layers.

A question that arises here is how to represent unsatisfiable cores. Taking the constraints literally is usually not a desirable solution, as then we would have to convert the atoms $\{x \geq 5 + \delta, s \leq 12, y \geq 3\}$ back to the non-strict constraints $\{x \geq 5 + \delta, 2x + y \leq 12, 2y \geq 6\}$ and further into $\{x > 5, 2x + y \leq 12, 2y \geq 6\}$, i.e., we would have to compute the inverses of the transformations in Phases 2 and 1. A far more efficient and simple solution is to use indexed constraints in the same way, as they already occur in the running example. Hence, the unsatisfiable core is just a set of indices ($\{A, B, C\}$ in our example). These indices are then valid for all layers and do not need any conversion.

Since the formalization of Spasić and Marić does not contain indices at all, we modify large parts of the source code so that it now refers to indexed constraints, i.e., we integrate indices into algorithms, data structures, definitions, locales, properties and proofs. For instance, indexed constraints *ics* are just sets of pairs, where each pair consists of an index and a constraint, and satisfiability of indexed constraints is defined as

$$(I, v) \models ics \qquad \text{if and only if} \qquad v \models \{c \mid (i, c) \in ics \wedge i \in I\},$$

where I is an arbitrary set of indices.

In order to be able to lift the unsatisfiable core from Layer 3 to the upper layers, we have to prove that the two transformations (elimination of strict inequalities and introduction of slack variables) maintain minimal unsatisfiable cores. To this end, we modify existing proofs for these transformation, since they are not general enough initially. For instance, the soundness statement for the introduction of slack variables in Phase 2 states that if the transformation on non-strict constraints N produces the tableau T and atoms A, then N and the combination of T and A are equisatisfiable, i.e.,

$$(\exists v.\ v \models N) \longleftrightarrow (\exists v.\ v \models T \wedge v \models A).$$

However, for lifting minimal unsatisfiable cores we need a stronger property, namely that the transformation is also sound for arbitrary indexed subsets I:[4]

$$(\exists v.\ (I, v) \models N) \longleftrightarrow (\exists v.\ v \models T \wedge (I, v) \models A). \tag{2}$$

Here, the indexed subsets in (2) are needed for both directions: given a minimal unsatisfiable core I of T and A, by the left-to-right implication of (2) we conclude that I is an unsatisfiable core of N, and it is minimal because of the right-to-left implication of (2). Note that tableau satisfiability ($v \models T$) is not indexed, since the tableau equations are global.

Our formalization therefore contains several new generalizations, e.g., the following lemma is the formal analogue to (2), where preprocess is the function that introduces slack variables. In addition to the tableau t and the indexed atoms ias, it also provides a computable function trans_v to convert satisfying valuations for t and ias into satisfying valuations for ics.

---

[4] This stronger property is also required, if the preprocessing is performed on the global formula, i.e., including the Boolean structure. The reason is that also there one needs soundness of the preprocessing for arbitrary subsets of the constraints.

```
lemma preprocess: assumes preprocess ics = (t, ias, trans_v)
   shows (I,v) ⊨ ias ⟶ v ⊨ t ⟶ (I, trans_v v) ⊨ ics
   shows (∃ v. (I,v) ⊨ ics) ⟶ (∃ v. (I,v) ⊨ ias ∧ v ⊨ t)
```

After all these modifications we obtain a simplex implementation that indeed provides minimal unsatisfiable cores. The corresponding function `simplex_index` returns a sum type, which is either a satisfying valuation or an unsatisfiable core represented by a set of indices.

```
lemma simplex_index:
   shows simplex_index ics = Inr v ⟶ v ⊨ {c | (i,c) ∈ ics}
   shows simplex_index ics = Inl I ⟶ ∄ v. (I,v) ⊨ ics
   shows simplex_index ics = Inl I ⟶ J ⊂ I ⟶
      distinct_indices ics ⟶ ∃ v. (J,v) ⊨ ics
```

Here, the minimality of the unsatisfiable cores can only be ensured if the indices in the input constraints are distinct. That distinctness is essential can easily be seen: Consider the following indexed constraints $\{(E, x \leq 3), (F, x \leq 5),$ $(F, x \geq 10)\}$ where index F refers to two different constraints. If we invoke the verified simplex algorithm on these constraints, it detects that $x \leq 3$ is in conflict with $x \geq 10$ and hence produces $\{E, F\}$ as an unsatisfiable core. This core is clearly not minimal, however, since $\{F\}$ by itself is already unsatisfiable.

Some technical problems arise, regarding distinctness in combination with constraints involving equality. For example, the Layer 1-constraint $(G, p = c)$ will be translated into the two constraints $(G, p \geq c)$ and $(G, p \leq c)$ on Layer 2,[5] violating distinctness. These problems are solved by weakening the notion of distinct constraints on Layers 2 and 3, and strengthening the notion of a minimal unsatisfiable core for these layers: For each proper subset J of the unsatisfiable subset, each inequality has to be satisfied as if it were an equality, i.e., whenever there is some constraint $(j, p \leq c)$ or $(j, p \geq c)$ with $j \in J$, the satisfying valuation must fulfill $p = c$.

3.2   Elimination of Unused Variables in Phase 2

Directly after creating the tableau and the set of atoms from non-strict constraints in Phase 2, it can happen that there are *unused variables*, i.e., variables in the tableau for which no atoms exist.

Dutertre and de Moura propose to eliminate unused variables by Gaussian elimination [10, end of Section 3] in order to reduce the size of the tableau. We integrate this elimination of variables into our formalization. However, instead of using Gaussian elimination, we implement the elimination via pivoting. To be more precise, for each unused variable x we perform the following steps.

---

[5] Note that it is not possible to directly add equality constraints on Layer 1 to the tableau: First, this would invalidate the incremental interface, since the tableau constraints are global; second, the tableau forms a homogeneous system of equations, so it does not permit equations such as $x - y = 1$ which have a non-zero constant.

– If x is not already a left-hand side variable of the tableau, find any equation $y = p$ in the tableau that contains x, and perform pivoting of x and y, so that afterwards x is a left-hand side variable of the tableau.
– Drop the unique equation from the tableau that has x on its left-hand side, but remember the equation for reconstructing satisfying valuations.

Example 1. Consider the non-strict constraints $\{x + y \geq 5, x + 2y \leq 7, y \geq 2\}$ on Layer 2. These are translated to the atoms $\{s \geq 5, t \leq 7, y \geq 2\}$ in combination with the tableau $\{s = x + y, t = x + 2y\}$, so x becomes an unused variable. Since x is not a left-hand side variable, we perform pivoting of x and s and obtain the new tableau $\{x = s - y, t = s + y\}$. Then we drop the equation $x = s - y$ resulting in the smaller tableau $\{t = s + y\}$. Moreover, any satisfying valuation v for the variables $\{y, s, t\}$ will be extended to $\{x, y, s, t\}$ by defining $v(x) := v(s) - v(y)$.

In the formalization, the elimination has been integrated into the `preprocess` function of Sect. 3.1. In fact, `preprocess` just executes both preprocessing steps sequentially: first, the conversion of non-strict constraints into tableau and atoms, and afterwards the elimination of unused variables as described in this section. Interestingly, we had to modify the locale-structure of Spasić and Marić at this point, since preprocessing now depends on pivoting.

3.3 Incremental Simplex

The previous specifications of the simplex algorithm are monolithic: even if two (consecutive) inputs differ only in a single constraint, the functions `simplex` (in Sect. 2) and `simplex_index` (in Sect. 3.1) will start the computation from scratch. Hence, they do not specify an incremental simplex algorithm, despite the fact that an incremental interface is provided on Layer 3 via assert and check.

Since the incrementality of a theory solver is a crucial requirement for developing a DPLL(T)-based SMT solver, we will provide a formalization of the simplex algorithm that provides an incremental interface at each layer. Our design closely follows Dutertre and de Moura, who propose the following operations.

– Initialize the solver by providing the set of all possible constraints. This will return a state where none of these constraints have been asserted.
– Assert a constraint. This invokes a computationally inexpensive deduction algorithm and returns an unsatisfiable core or a new state.
– Check a state. Performs an expensive computation that decides satisfiability of the set of asserted constraints; returns an unsat core or a checked state.
– Extract a solution of a checked state.
– Compute some checkpoint information for a checked state.
– Backtrack to a state with the help of some checkpoint information.

Since a DPLL(T)-based SMT solver basically performs an exhaustive search, its performance can be improved considerably by having it keep track of checked states from which the search can be restarted in a different direction. This is why the checkpointing and backtracking functionality is necessary.

In Isabelle/HOL we specify this informal interface for each layer as a locale, which fixes the operations and the properties of that layer. For instance, the locale `Incremental_Simplex_Ops` is for Layer 1, where the type-variable σ represents the internal state for the layer, and γ is the checkpoint information.

```
locale Incremental_Simplex_Ops =
fixes init :: (ι × constraint) list ⇒ σ
  and assert :: ι ⇒ σ ⇒ ι list + σ
  and check :: σ ⇒ ι list + σ
  and solution :: σ ⇒ rat valuation
  and checkpoint :: σ ⇒ γ
  and backtrack :: γ ⇒ σ ⇒ σ
  and invariant :: (ι × constraint) list ⇒ ι set ⇒ σ ⇒ bool
  and checked :: (ι × constraint) list ⇒ ι set ⇒ σ ⇒ bool
assumes checked cs {} (init cs)
  and checked cs J s ⟶ invariant cs J s
  and invariant cs J s ⟶ assert j s = Inr s' ⟶
    invariant cs ({j} ∪ J) s'
  and invariant cs J s ⟶ assert j s = Inl I ⟶
    I ⊆ {j} ∪ J ∧ minimal_unsat_core I cs
  and invariant cs J s ⟶ check s = Inr s' ⟶ checked cs J s'
  and invariant cs J s ⟶ check s = Inl I ⟶
    I ⊆ J ∧ minimal_unsat_core I cs
  and checked cs J s ⟶ solution s = v ⟶ (J, v) ⊨ cs
  and checked cs J s ⟶ checkpoint s = c ⟶ invariant cs K s' ⟶
      backtrack c s' = s'' ⟶ J ⊆ K ⟶ invariant cs J s''
```

The interface consists of the six operations `init`, ..., `backtrack` to invoke the algorithm, and the two invariants `invariant` and `checked`, the latter of which entails the former.

Both invariants `invariant` and `checked` take the three arguments cs, J and s. Here, cs is the global set of indexed constraints that is encoded in the state s. It can only be set by invoking `init` cs and is kept constant otherwise. J indicates the set of all constraints that have been asserted in the state s.

We briefly explain the specification of `assert` and `backtrack` and leave the usage of the remaining functionality to the reader.

For the `assert` operation there are two possible outcomes. If the assertion of index j was successful, it returns a new state s' which satisfies the same invariant as s, and whose set of indices of asserted constraints contains j, and is otherwise the same as the corresponding set in s. Otherwise, the operation returns a set of indices I, which is a subset of the set of indices of asserted constraints (including j), such that the set of all I-indexed constraints is a minimal unsatisfiable core.

The backtracking facility works as follows. Assume that one has computed the checkpoint information c in a state s, which is only permitted if s satisfies the stronger invariant for some set of indices J. Afterwards, one may have performed arbitrary operations and transitioned to a state s' corresponding to a superset of indices $K \supseteq J$. Then, solely from s' and c, one can compute via backtrack a new state s'' that corresponds to the old set of indices J. Of course, the implementation should be done in such a way that the size of c is small in comparison to the size of s; in particular, c should not be s itself. And, indeed, our implementation behaves in the same way as the informally described algorithm by Dutertre and de Moura: for a checkpoint c of state s we store the asserted atoms of the state s, but neither the valuation nor the tableau. These are taken from the state s' when invoking backtrack c s'.

In order to implement the incremental interface, we take the same modular approach as Spasić and Marić, namely that for each layer and its corresponding Isabelle locale, we rely upon the existing functionality of the various phases, together with the interface of the lower layers, to implement the locale.

In our case, a significant part of the work has already been done via the results described in Sect. 3.1: most of the generalizations that have been performed in order to support indexed constraints, play a role in proving the soundness of the incremental simplex implementation. In particular, the generalizations for Phases 1 and 2 are vital. For instance, the set of indices I in lemma preprocess on page 9 can not only be interpreted as an unsatisfiable core, but also as the set of currently asserted constraints. Therefore, trans_v allows us to convert a satisfying valuation on Layer 2 into a satisfying valuation on Layer 1 for the currently asserted constraints that are indexed by I. Consequently, the internal state of the simplex algorithm on Layer 1 not only stores the state of Layer 3 as it is described at the beginning of Sect. 3.1, but additionally stores the function trans_v, in order to compute satisfying valuations on Layer 1.

We further integrate and prove the correctness of the functionality of checkpointing and backtracking on all layers, since these features have not been formalized by Spasić and Marić. For instance, when invoking backtrack c s' on Layer 3 with check_point $s = c$, we obtain a new state that contains the tableau t' and valuation v' of state s', but the asserted atoms as of state s. Hence, we need to show that v' satisfies those asserted atoms of as that correspond to right-hand side variables of t'. To this end, we define the invariant on Layer 3 in a way that permits us to conclude that the tableaux t and t' are equivalent. Using this equivalence, we then formalize the desired result for Layer 3. Checkpointing and backtracking on the other layers is just propagated to the next-lower layers, i.e., no further checkpointing information is required on Layers 1 and 2.

Finally, we combine the implementations of all phases and layers to obtain a fully verified implementation of the simplex algorithm w.r.t. the specification defined in the locale Incremental_Simplex_Ops.

Note that the incremental interface does not provide a function to assert constraints negatively. However, this limitation is easily circumvented by passing both the positive and the negative constraint with different indices to the init function. For example, instead of using $(A, x > 5)$ as in Fig. 2, one can use the two constraints $(+A, x > 5)$ and $(-A, x \leq 5)$. Then one can assert both the original and the negated constraint via indices $+A$ and $-A$, respectively.

Only the negation of equations is not possible in this way, since this would lead to disjunctions. However, each equation can easily be translated into the conjunction of two inequalities on the formula-level, i.e., they can be eliminated within a preprocessing step of the SMT-solver.

4 A Formalized Proof of Farkas' Lemma

Farkas' Lemma states that a system of linear constraints is unsatisfiable if and only if there is a linear combination of the constraints that evaluates to a trivially unsatisfiable inequality (e.g. $0 \leq d$ for a constant $d < 0$). The non-zero coefficients in such a linear combination are referred to as *Farkas coefficients*, and can be thought of as an easy-to-check certificate for the unsatisfiability of a set of linear constraints (given the coefficients, one can simply evaluate the corresponding linear combination and check that the result is indeed unsatisfiable.)

One way to prove Farkas' Lemma is by using the Fundamental Theorem of Linear Inequalities; this theorem can in turn be proved in the same way as the fact that the simplex algorithm terminates (see [15, Chapter 7]). Although Spasić and Marić have formalized a proof of termination for their simplex implementation [16], this is not sufficient to immediately prove Farkas' Lemma. Instead, our formalization of the result begins at the point where the simplex algorithm detects unsatisfiability in Phase 3, because this is the only point in the execution of the algorithm where Farkas coefficients can be computed directly from the available data.[6] Then, these coefficients need to be transferred up to Layer 1. In the following we illustrate how Farkas coefficients are computed and propagated through the various phases of the algorithm, by giving examples and explaining, informally, intermediate statements that have been formalized.

To illustrate how Farkas coefficients are determined at the point where the check-operation detects unsatisfiability in Phase 3, let us return once more to the example in Fig. 2. In step 7, the algorithm detects unsatisfiability via the equation $x = \frac{s-y}{2}$, and generates the unsatisfiable core based on this equation. This equality can also be used to obtain Farkas coefficients. To this end, we rewrite the equation as $-x + \frac{1}{2}s - \frac{1}{2}y = 0$, and use the coefficients in this equation (-1 for x, $\frac{1}{2}$ for s, and $-\frac{1}{2}$ for y) to form a linear combination of the corresponding atoms involving the variables:

$$- (x \geq 5 + \delta) + \frac{1}{2}(s \leq 12) - \frac{1}{2}(y \geq 3) \tag{FC3}$$

$$= (-x \leq -5 - \delta) + \left(\frac{1}{2}s \leq 6\right) + \left(-\frac{1}{2}y \leq -\frac{3}{2}\right)$$

$$= \underbrace{\left(-x + \frac{1}{2}s - \frac{1}{2}y\right)}_{p} \leq \underbrace{\left(-\delta - \frac{1}{2}\right)}_{d},$$

---

[6] Again, we here consider only the check operation, since obtaining Farkas coefficients for a conflict detected by assert is trivial, cf. footnote 3.

where $p = 0$ is a reformulation of an equation of the tableau and d is a negative constant. Consequently, we show in the formalization that whenever unsatisfiability is detected for a given tableau T and set of atoms A, there exist Farkas coefficients r_i, i.e., that there is a linear combination $(\sum r_i a_i) = (p \leq d)$, where $d < 0$, $a_i \in A$ for all i, each $r_i a_i$ is a $\leq$-inequality, and $T \models p = 0$. The second-to-last condition ensures that only inequalities are added which are oriented in the same direction, so that the summation is well-defined. The condition $T \models p = 0$ means that for every valuation that satisfies T, p evaluates to 0.

Recall that before detecting unsatisfiability, several pivoting steps may have been applied, e.g., when going from step 3 to step 7. Hence, it is important to verify that Farkas coefficients are preserved by pivoting. This is easily achieved by using our notion of Farkas coefficients: Spasić and Marić formally proved that pivoting changes the tableau T' into an equivalent tableau T, and, hence, the condition $T \models p = 0$ immediately implies $T' \models p = 0$. In the example, we conclude that $T' \models -x + \frac{1}{2}s - \frac{1}{2}y = 0$ for any tableau T' in steps 3–7. Thus, (FC3) provides Farkas coefficients for the atoms and tableau mentioned in any of these steps.

Layer 2 requires a new definition of Farkas coefficients, since there is no tableau T and set of atoms A at this point, but a set N of non-strict constraints. The new definition is similar to the one on Layer 3, except that the condition $T \models p = 0$ is dropped, and instead we require that $p = 0$. To be precise, r_i are Farkas coefficients for N if there is a linear combination $(\sum r_i c_i) = (0 \leq d)$ where $d < 0$, $c_i \in N$ for all i, and each $r_i c_i$ is a $\leq$-inequality.

We prove that the preprocessing done in Phase 2 allows for the transformation of Farkas coefficients for Layer 3 to Farkas coefficients for Layer 2. In essence, the same coefficients r_i can be used, one just has to replace each atom a_i by the corresponding constraint c_i. The only exception is that if a constraint c_i has been normalized, then one has to multiply the corresponding r_i by the same factor. However, this will not change the constant d, and we formally verify that the polynomial resulting from the summation will indeed be 0.

In the example, we would obtain (FC2) for Layer 2. Here, the third coefficient has been changed from $-\frac{1}{2}$ to $-\frac{1}{2} \cdot \frac{1}{2} = -\frac{1}{4}$, where the latter $\frac{1}{2}$ is the factor used when normalizing the constraint $2y \geq 6$ to obtain the atom $y \geq 3$.

$$-(x \geq 5 + \delta) + \frac{1}{2}(2x + y \leq 12) - \frac{1}{4}(2y \geq 6) = \left(0 \leq -\delta - \frac{1}{2}\right) \quad \text{(FC2)}$$

Finally, for Layer 1 the notion of Farkas coefficients must once again be redefined so as to work with a more general constraint type that also allows strict constraints. In particular, we have that either the sum of inequalities is strict and the constant d is non-positive, or the sum of inequalities is non-strict and d is negative. In the example we obtain (again with the same coefficients, but using the original, possibly strict inequalities in the linear combination):

$$-(x > 5) + \frac{1}{2}(2x + y \leq 12) - \frac{1}{4}(2y \geq 6) = \left(0 < -\frac{1}{2}\right). \quad \text{(FC1)}$$

Farkas coefficients r_i on Layer 2 are easily translated to Layer 1, since no change is required, i.e., the same coefficients r_i can be used. We just prove that whenever the resulting inequality in Layer 2 is $0 \leq d$ for $d = a + b\delta$ with $a, b \in \mathbb{Q}$, then the sum of inequalities on Layer 1 will be $0 \leq a$ (and $b = 0$), or it will be $0 < a$. In both cases we use the property that $a + b\delta = d$ is negative, to show that the r_i are Farkas coefficients for Layer 1.

We illustrate the results of our formalization of Farkas coefficients by providing the formal statements for two layers. In both lemmas, cs is a set of linear constraints of the form $p \sim d$ for a linear polynomial p, constant d and $\sim \in \{\leq, <\}$. Here, the first theorem is an Isabelle statement of [8, Lemma 2], i.e., Farkas' Lemma over δ-rationals. The second theorem is a more general version of Farkas' Lemma which also permits strict inequalities, i.e., our statement on Layer 1. It is known as Motzkin's Transposition Theorem [15, Cor. 7.1k] or the Kuhn–Fourier Theorem [17, Thm. 1.1.9].

```
lemma Farkas'_Lemma_Delta_Rationals: assumes finite cs
    and ∀ c ∈ cs. ∃ p d. c = (p ≤ d)          (* only ≤-constraints *)
    shows (∄ v :: QDelta valuation. v ⊨ cs) ⟷
    (∃ C d. d < 0 ∧ (∀ (r, c) ∈ C. r > 0 ∧ c ∈ cs)
    ∧ (Σ(r,c) ← C. r · c) = (0 ≤ d))

theorem Motzkin's_transposition_theorem: assumes finite cs
    shows (∄ v :: rat valuation. v ⊨ cs) ⟷
    (∃ C ineq d. (∀ (r, c) ∈ C. r > 0 ∧ c ∈ cs)
    ∧ (Σ (r,c) ← C. r · c) = ineq
    ∧ ((ineq = (0 ≤ d) ∧ d < 0) ∨ (ineq = (0 < d) ∧ d ≤ 0)))
```

The existence of Farkas coefficients not only implies unsatisfiability over $\mathbb{Q}$, but also unsatisfiability over $\mathbb{R}$: lifting the summation of linear inequalities from $\mathbb{Q}$ to $\mathbb{R}$ yields the same conflict $0 \leq d$, with d negative, over the reals. Hence, we formalize the property that satisfiability of linear rational constraints over $\mathbb{Q}$ and over $\mathbb{R}$ are the same. Consequently, the (incremental) simplex algorithm is also able to prove unsatisfiability over $\mathbb{R}$.

```
lemma rat_real_conversion: assumes finite (cs :: rat constraint set)
    shows (∃ v :: rat valuation. v ⊨ cs)
    ⟷ (∃ v :: real valuation. v ⊨ cs)
```

Note that the finiteness condition of the set of constraints in the previous three statements mainly arose from the usage of the simplex algorithm for doing the underlying proofs, since the simplex algorithm only takes finite sets of constraints as input. However, the finiteness of the constraint set is actually a necessary condition, regardless of how the statements are proved: none of the three properties hold for infinite sets of constraints. For instance, the constraint set $\{x \geq c \mid c \in \mathbb{N}\}$ is unsatisfiable over $\mathbb{Q}$, but there are no Farkas coefficients for these constraints. Moreover, the rational constraints $\{x \geq c \mid c \leq \pi, c \in \mathbb{Q}\} \cup \{x \leq c \mid c \geq \pi, c \in \mathbb{Q}\}$ have precisely one real solution, $v(x) = \pi$, but there is no rational solution since $\pi \notin \mathbb{Q}$.

5 Conclusion

We have presented our development of an Isabelle/HOL formalization of a simplex algorithm with minimal unsatisfiable core generation and an incremental interface. Furthermore, we gave a verified proof of Farkas' Lemma, one of the central results in the theory of linear inequalities. Both of these contributions are related to the simplex formalization of Spasić and Marić [16]: the incremental simplex formalization is an extension built on top of their work, and the formal proof of Farkas' Lemma follows their simplex implementation through the phases of the algorithm.

In our formalization we use locales as the main structuring technique for obtaining modular proofs – as was done by Spasić and Marić. Our formal proofs were mainly written interactively, with frequent use of find_theorems rather than sledgehammer (which only provided a few externally generated proofs).

Both of our contributions form a crucial stepping stone towards our initial goal, the development of a verified SMT solver that is based on the DPLL(T) approach and supports linear arithmetic over $\mathbb{Q}$ and $\mathbb{R}$. The connection of the theory solver and the verified DPLL-based SAT solver [2] remains as future work. Here, we already got in contact with Mathias Fleury to initiate some collaboration. However, he immediately informed us that the connection itself will be a non-trivial task on its own. One issue is that his SAT solver is expressed in the imperative monad, but in our use case we need to apply it outside this monad, i.e., it should have a purely functional type such as formula $\Rightarrow$ bool.

Acknowledgments. We thank the reviewers and Mathias Fleury for constructive feedback.

References

1. Allamigeon, X., Katz, R.D.: A formalization of convex polyhedra based on the simplex method. In: Ayala-Rincón, M., Muñoz, C.A. (eds.) ITP 2017. LNCS, vol. 10499, pp. 28–45. Springer, Cham (2017). https://doi.org/10.1007/978-3-319-66107-0_3

2. Blanchette, J.C., Fleury, M., Lammich, P., Weidenbach, C.: A verified SATsolver framework with learn, forget, restart, and incrementality. J. Autom. Reasoning **61**(1–4), 333–365 (2018). https://doi.org/10.1007/s10817-018-9455-7

3. Böhme, S., Weber, T.: Fast LCF-style proof reconstruction for Z3. In: Kaufmann, M., Paulson, L.C. (eds.) ITP 2010. LNCS, vol. 6172, pp. 179–194. Springer, Heidelberg (2010). https://doi.org/10.1007/978-3-642-14052-5_14

4. Bonacina, M.P., Graham-Lengrand, S., Shankar, N.: Proofs in conflict-driven theory combination. In: 7th ACM SIGPLAN International Conference Certified Programs and Proofs, CPP 2018, pp. 186–200. ACM (2018). https://doi.org/10.1145/3167096

5. Bottesch, R., Haslbeck, M.W., Thiemann, R.: Farkas' Lemma and Motzkin's Transposition Theorem. Archive of Formal Proofs, January 2019. http://isa-afp.org/entries/Farkas.html. Formal proof development

6. Brockschmidt, M., Cook, B., Ishtiaq, S., Khlaaf, H., Piterman, N.: T2: temporal property verification. In: Chechik, M., Raskin, J.-F. (eds.) TACAS 2016. LNCS, vol. 9636, pp. 387–393. Springer, Heidelberg (2016). https://doi.org/10.1007/978-3-662-49674-9_22

7. Brockschmidt, M., Joosten, S.J.C., Thiemann, R., Yamada, A.: Certifying safety and termination proofs for integer transition systems. In: de Moura, L. (ed.) CADE 2017. LNCS (LNAI), vol. 10395, pp. 454–471. Springer, Cham (2017). https://doi.org/10.1007/978-3-319-63046-5_28

8. Bromberger, M., Weidenbach, C.: New techniques for linear arithmetic: cubes and equalities. Formal Methods Syst. Des. **51**(3), 433–461 (2017). https://doi.org/10.1007/s10703-017-0278-7

9. Chaieb, A., Nipkow, T.: Proof synthesis and reflection for linear arithmetic. J. Autom. Reasoning **41**(1), 33 (2008). https://doi.org/10.1007/s10817-008-9101-x

10. Dutertre, B., de Moura, L.: A fast linear-arithmetic solver for DPLL(T). In: Ball, T., Jones, R.B. (eds.) CAV 2006. LNCS, vol. 4144, pp. 81–94. Springer, Heidelberg (2006). https://doi.org/10.1007/11817963_11

11. Ganzinger, H., Hagen, G., Nieuwenhuis, R., Oliveras, A., Tinelli, C.: DPLL(T): fast decision procedures. In: Alur, R., Peled, D.A. (eds.) CAV 2004. LNCS, vol. 3114, pp. 175–188. Springer, Heidelberg (2004). https://doi.org/10.1007/978-3-540-27813-9_14

12. Giesl, J., et al.: Analyzing program termination and complexity automatically with AProVE. J. Autom. Reasoning **58**, 3–31 (2017). https://doi.org/10.1007/s10817-016-9388-y

13. Marić, F., Spasić, M., Thiemann, R.: An incremental simplex algorithm with unsatisfiable core generation. Archive of Formal Proofs, August 2018. http://isa-afp.org/entries/Simplex.html. Formal proof development

14. Nipkow, T., Wenzel, M., Paulson, L.C. (eds.): Isabelle/HOL. LNCS, vol. 2283. Springer, Heidelberg (2002). https://doi.org/10.1007/3-540-45949-9

15. Schrijver, A.: Theory of Linear and Integer Programming. Wiley, Hoboken (1999)

16. Spasić, M., Marić, F.: Formalization of incremental simplex algorithm by stepwise refinement. In: Giannakopoulou, D., Méry, D. (eds.) FM 2012. LNCS, vol. 7436, pp. 434–449. Springer, Heidelberg (2012). https://doi.org/10.1007/978-3-642-32759-9_35

17. Stoer, J., Witzgall, C.: Convexity and Optimization in Finite Dimensions I. Die Grundlehren der mathematischen Wissenschaften, vol. 163 (1970). https://www.springer.com/gp/book/9783642462184

Verifying Randomised Social Choice

Manuel Eberl[(✉)] [iD]

Technische Universität Mänchen, 85748 Garching bei München, Germany
manuel.eberl@tum.de

Abstract. This work describes the formalisation of a recent result from Randomised Social Choice Theory in Isabelle/HOL. The original result had been obtained through the use of linear programming, an unverified Java program, and SMT solvers; at the time that the formalisation effort began, no human-readable proof was available. Thus, the formalisation with Isabelle eventually served as both independent rigorous confirmation of the original result and led to human-readable proofs both in Isabelle and on paper.

This presentation focuses on the process of the formalisation itself, the domain-specific tooling that was developed for it in Isabelle, and how the structured human-readable proof was constructed from the SMT proof. It also briefly discusses how the formalisation uncovered a serious flaw in a second peer-reviewed publication.

1 Introduction

First of all, it must be stressed that this presentation is not intended as an introduction to Social Choice Theory, nor will it repeat the detailed explanation of the proof of the main result in Brandl et al. [1] (of which I am also a co-author). I must also stress that my contribution consists *only* of the formalisation and the human-readable proof for that result, and the purpose of this paper is to present more details of this formalisation process and the technology behind it.

All the background theory of Social Choice Theory that I will mention later on is either folklore or comes from the work of Brandl et al.; again, see their presentation [1] for more details on this background. For the sake of self-containedness, the result and the necessary definitions from Social Choice Theory will nevertheless be sketched here very briefly, but without any deeper explanation or motivation. For this, the reader should consult the original presentation by Brandl et al.

I will attempt to strike a balance between readability and technical details. In particular, I attempt to stay close to the Isabelle definitions, but mostly without actually using Isabelle syntax except in cases where there is real benefit in doing so. The full formal Isabelle proof developments can be found in the *Archive of Formal Proofs* [2,3].

© Springer Nature Switzerland AG 2019
A. Herzig and A. Popescu (Eds.): FroCoS 2019, LNAI 11715, pp. 240–256, 2019.
https://doi.org/10.1007/978-3-030-29007-8_14

2   The Main Result

The main result that was formalised is a typical impossibility result from Social Choice Theory: these are of the form

'There exists no voting scheme for at least m voters and n alternatives that simultaneously has the following properties:'

A large variety of results like this exists for many different types of voting schemes and many different choices for the properties that they should have; two famous ones are Arrow's Theorem [4] and Gibbard's Theorem [5].

The setting that we shall focus on is that of *Social Decision Schemes* (SDSs): We fix some finite set $N = \{1, \ldots, m\}$ of *agents* (or *voters*) and a finite set of alternatives A with $|A| = n$. Each agent i has a *preference relation* $\succeq_i$ over the alternatives. In our setting, these preferences are total preorders, i. e. reflexive, transitive, and total relations. The vector $R = (\succeq_1, \ldots, \succeq_m)$ is called a *preference profile*. An SDS is then a function that, given such a preference profile, returns a *lottery*: a probability distribution of winning alternatives.

The theorem that was formalised is the following:

Theorem 1. *If $m \geq 4$ and $n \geq 4$, there exists no SDS that has the following properties:*[1]

Anonymity: Invariance under renaming of agents
Neutrality: Invariance under renaming of alternatives
SD-Efficiency: If the SDS returns some lottery, it is optimal in the sense that there is no other lottery that all agents prefer to it.
SD-Strategyproofness: No one agent can, by themselves, obtain a better result by lying about their preferences (i. e. strategic voting is not possible).

As we will see later, it is enough to prove the theorem for $m = n = 4$ because any SDS $f(R)$ with the above properties for $m \geq 4$ agents and $n \geq 4$ alternatives would give rise to another SDS (denoted as $f{\downarrow}(R)$) with the same properties for exactly 4 agents and alternatives (see Sect. 3 for details on this). The difficult part is therefore the case of exactly 4 agents and alternatives.

In a nutshell, the strategy Brandl *et al.* pursued to find a proof for this case was the following: Consider the set of all preference profiles for our 4 agents and alternatives. For each profile R (or pair of profiles R_1, R_2), there are certain conditions on the probabilities of the lottery $f(R)$ (resp. the lotteries $f(R_1)$ and $f(R_2)$) resulting from the four conditions (anonymity, neutrality, etc.) It happens that all these conditions can be written as formulæ in quantifier-free linear real arithmetic (QF-LRA), which is a decidable logic that SMT solvers can typically handle fairly efficiently.

Unfortunately, there are 31,640,625 profiles for $m = n = 4$ (or 471,956 modulo anonymity and neutrality), which results in far too many QF-LRA formulæ

---

[1] The meaning of these concepts will be made more precise later – in particular, what it *means* for an agent to prefer one lottery over another.

to compute and check. However, if there really is no SDS with these four properties, these conditions must be inconsistent. When this is the case, there is often a much smaller subset of conditions (or, equivalently, a smaller set of profiles) that is already inconsistent – an *unsatisfiable core*. If one could guess a small set of profiles that already leads to inconsistent conditions, one could pass only these to an SMT solver and obtain a proof of the contradiction more quickly.

Brandl *et al.* used search heuristics to find such a set of profiles, which they then narrowed down to only 47. The search for profile sets likely to lead to a contradiction and the translation to QF-LRA formulæ in the SMT-LIB format was performed by an unverified Java program.

However, there are various problems with this. Computer proofs are notoriously controversial in the mathematical community and even in high-profile computer proofs such as the Kepler conjecture [6] or the Lorenz Attractor [7,8], problems with the computer code were later found (although they turned out to be repairable). In our case, some possible points of criticism are:

- One must trust the SMT solver.
- One must trust the Java program that computes the conditions arising from the profiles and encodes them into the SMT-LIB format.
- The proof cannot realistically be inspected or verified by a human.

The first problem is not too serious, since one can use several different independent SMT solvers to check the result. Some of them can produce proof objects that can be verified by simple independent checkers.

The second problem could be solved by inspecting the generated SMT-LIB file by hand and checking that the generated inequalities are indeed the ones that follow from the 47 preference profiles – a very tedious task, but feasible.

The last problem, however, is difficult to address. While solvers like Z3 can print out unsatisfiability proofs, these proofs are typically fairly large and dense and provide little insight.

To address these concerns, Brandl *et al.* sought out my collaboration to formalise some version of this proof in Isabelle. Since Isabelle can replay SMT proof objects through its own kernel, we were confident that it should be possible to obtain *some* kind of proof of Theorem 1 in Isabelle. It was, however, completely unclear how to achieve the ultimate goal of finding a more structured and human-readable proof and whether such a proof even exists.

3   Definitions

First of all, I will define the basic notions that are required to state and prove the main result. For the Isabelle definitions, I followed the philosophy to keep definitions as simple and as close to the textbook definitions as possible – including syntax – or to at least prove more textbook-style versions as alternative definitions later on. In particular, I also placed great importance on proving various different views on more complex notions (e. g. Stochastic Dominance, SD-Efficiency, and Strategyproofness). This makes working with them more convenient as one can pick whichever form is most suitable in any given situation; it also increases the confidence that the definitions really *are* faithful to the textbook definitions.

I aim to present every notion precisely as it is defined in Isabelle, but for the sake of brevity and readability, I will mostly refrain from using actual Isabelle notation.

Most of the notions discussed here (such as *family of preorders*, *Social Decision Scheme*, *SD-efficient SDS*) are defined as *locales* [9]. These are a kind of named context supporting multiple inheritance that facilitates modular reasoning.

In the remainder of this section, I will list the most relevant definitions for Theorem 1.

Agents and Alternatives. In the Isabelle formalisation, agents and alternatives are opaque: We simply assume that we have finite non-empty sets N of some type ν *set* (agents) and A of some type γ *set* (alternatives).[2] For convenience, I invented the name *election* (with a locale of the same name) to describe a setting with a fixed set of agents and alternatives.

Preferences. Each agent i has their own *preference relation* $\succeq$, which is a *total preorder* (reflexive, transitive, and total – i.e. $x \succeq y \lor y \succeq x$ for all x, y). The collection of the preferences of all the agents forms a vector $(\succeq_1, \ldots, \succeq_m)$; this is called a *preference profile*.

In Isabelle, the preference relations are modelled as functions $\gamma \to \gamma \to$ bool. Preference profiles are a modelled as functions $\nu \to \gamma \to \gamma \to$ bool. By convention, any preference relation must return *false* if one of its inputs is not in A and any preference profile must return an empty relation if its input is not in N. This ensures extensionality in the sense that e. g. two preference relations are logically equal if they agree on all alternatives in A.

Lotteries. A *lottery* is a probability distribution of alternatives. Since there are only finitely many alternatives, the most convenient representation of this is as a *Probability Mass Function* (PMF). In Isabelle/HOL, the type γ *pmf* is defined as the type of all functions $f : \gamma \to \mathbb{R}$ such that $\forall x.\ f(x) \geq 0$ and $\sum_x f(x) = 1$. Various probability- and measure-theoretic concepts are defined for this type so that one can work with it in a fairly idiomatic way. We can simply define the set of *lotteries* as the set of values of type γ *pmf* whose support is a subset of A.

Anonymity and Neutrality. An SDS is *anonymous* if renaming the agents does not change the outcome, i. e. for any permutation π of N, we have $f(R \circ \pi) = f(R)$.

For neutrality, we first need to define what it means to rename an alternative. Let σ be a permutation of A. Then, if $\succeq$ is a preference relation, the relation

---

[2] Readers who are used to systems like Coq or Lean might wonder why one does not simply use the entire types ν and γ. The reason for this is that we sometimes want to decrease or increase the number of agents and alternatives. Doing this without explicit carrier sets can be problematic in Isabelle.

$\succeq^\sigma$ obtained by renaming the alternatives with σ can be defined as $x \succeq^\sigma y \longleftrightarrow$ $\sigma^{-1}(x) \succeq \sigma^{-1}(y)$. By renaming all preferences in a profile R like this, we obtain a profile R^σ. Additionally, we also have to take into account that the elements in the lottery returned by f must also be renamed. This can be accomplished with the function *map_pmf*, which is the *push-forward measure*, i. e. the covariant map function for PMFs. All in all, we obtain the condition

$$f(R^\sigma) = \text{map\_pmf } \sigma \ (f(R)) \ .$$

Pareto Preorder. A family (i. e. a vector) $R = (\succeq_1, \ldots, \succeq_n)$ of preorders gives rise to the *Pareto preorder* of that family, which is simply defined as the intersection of all the $\succeq_i$:

$$x \preceq_{\text{Par}(R)} y \Longleftrightarrow \forall i. \ x \preceq_i y$$

Note that here, the $\succeq_i$ are not assumed to be total, since we will use Par for non-total relations later on. Even if the $\succeq$ *are* total, Par(R) typically is not.

We call x a *Pareto loser* w. r. t. R if there is y such that $x \prec_{\text{Par}(R)} y$; in other words, there exists another alternative y that makes all agents at least as happy as x, and one of them strictly more happy.

Stochastic Dominance. As was mentioned before, we need a notion of when an agent prefers one lottery to another, i. e. to lift a preference relation $\succeq$ on alternatives to one on lotteries. Such a notion is called a *lottery extension*. In general, the resulting relations on lotteries are *not* total. Lottery extensions are typically justified by making some reasonable assumption about the behaviour of agents and then concluding under what circumstances they *must* prefer one lottery over another. An extreme example to illustrate this would be that any agent should be expected to prefer the singleton lottery where their favourite alternative wins with probability 1 over any other lottery.

The lottery extension we shall use is *Stochastic Dominance*. The definition is somewhat technical, namely

$$p \preceq_{SD(\succeq)} q \Longleftrightarrow \forall x \in A. \ P_p[\{y \mid y \succeq x\}] \leq P_q[\{y \mid y \succeq x\}] \ ,$$

i. e. for any alternative x, the probability of getting something at least as good as x in the lottery q is at least as big as that in p.

Another equivalent, but perhaps more intuitive definition is

$$p \preceq_{SD(\succeq)} q \Longleftrightarrow \forall u \in \text{vnM}(\succeq). \ E_p[u] \leq E_q[u],$$

i. e. for all *von Neumann–Morgenstern utility functions* $u : A \to \mathbb{R}$ that are compatible with the preference relation $\succeq$, the lottery q must yield at least as much expected utility as p.

The idea behind SD is that agents are assumed to have a utility function and want to maximise their expected utility. We only know the agent's preference relation, but not the underlying utility function. However, if a lottery q yields at least as much expected utility as p for *all* utility functions that fit the agent's preferences, we expect the agent to consider q at least as good as p – and that is precisely what SD is.

Efficiency. Efficiency of an SDS, in general, means that the SDS never returns a lottery that can be improved upon in a way that satisfies all agents. One basic notion of Efficiency is *ex-post*-Efficiency, which states that for any profile R, the resulting lottery $f(R)$ must not contain a Pareto loser w. r. t. R.

SD-Efficiency, which is used in Theorem 1, is a stronger notion. Using the concepts defined above, we can define it very concisely: a lottery is called *SD-inefficient* w. r. t. a profile R if it is a Pareto loser w. r. t. $SD \circ R$, i. e. there is another profile R' that is weakly *SD*-preferred by all agents and strictly *SD*-preferred by at least one agent.

An SDS is called *SD-efficient* if it never returns an *SD*-inefficient lottery.

Strategyproofness. Strategyproofness captures the intuitive idea that agents should have no benefit from voting strategically. There are various notions of Strategyproofness; for our purposes, we only need (weak) *SD*-Strategyproofness. An SDS f is called *(weakly) SD-strategyproof* if, for any agent $i \in N$, any preference profile $R = (\succeq_1, \ldots, \succeq_m)$, and any preference relation $\succeq_i'$ we have:

$$f(R(i := \succeq_i')) \not\succ_{SD(\succeq_i)} f(R)$$

Intuitively, this means that no single agent can benefit from lying about their preferences. If they submit false preferences $\succeq_i'$ instead of their true preferences $\succeq_i$ (while all other preferences remain the same), the result can never be better (w. r. t. $SD(\succeq_i)$) than if they had submitted their true preferences.

Lifting. As was mentioned before, the impossibility result can be 'lifted' from m agents and n alternatives to m' agents and n' alternatives with $m' \geq m$, $n' \geq n$. The general idea is this: Given a preference profile R for m agents and n alternatives, we can extend this profile to n' alternatives by adding $n' - n$ new 'dummy' alternatives that are all equally good, but strictly worse than all the existing n alternatives. Then, we can extend the profile to m' agents by adding $m' - m$ new 'dummy' agents that are fully indifferent between all n' alternatives. We denote this 'lifted' version of R as $R\uparrow$.

Using this, we can 'lower' any SDS f for m' agents and n' alternatives to an SDS $f\downarrow$ on m agents and n alternatives by defining $f\downarrow(R) := f(R\uparrow)$. In order for $f\downarrow$ to be well-defined, however, it must never return any of the dummy alternatives. Since the dummy alternatives are all Pareto losers, one way to ensure this is if f is *ex-post*-efficient. In this case, $f\downarrow$ is also *ex-post*-efficient.

Notably, if f is *ex-post*-efficient, this construction also preserves anonymity, neutrality, *SD*-Efficiency, and *SD*-Strategyproofness. This way, any impossibility result involving *ex-post*-Efficiency (or something stronger) and any combination of the above-mentioned properties can be lifted to a higher number of agents and alternatives.

Random (Serial) Dictatorship. Let us now turn to two interesting examples of concrete SDSs that I also formalised in Isabelle as an exercise to myself and to the library I developed: *Random Dictatorship* (*RD*) and *Random Serial Dictatorship* (*RSD*).

The former is normally only defined for the subset of preference profiles where each agent has a unique favourite alternative. In this case, *RD* picks an agent uniformly at random and returns that agent's favourite alternative as the winner. Since the present formalisation only allows SDSs over the *full* set of preference relations, I chose the obvious generalisation where one first picks an agent uniformly at random and then returns one of that agent's favourites uniformly at random if there are more than one. The Isabelle definition of *RD* is

$$\text{RD } R = \textbf{do } \{i \leftarrow \text{pmf\_of\_set } N; \ \text{pmf\_of\_set } (\text{Max\_wrt\_among } (R\ i)\ A)\}$$

where *pmf_of_set* X describes the uniform distribution over the set X and *Max_wrt_among* returns the maximal elements among the given set w. r. t. the given preference relation. For details on the monadic **do** notation, see e. g. Eberl *et al.* [10]. The SDS thus defined can then easily be proven to satisfy anonymity, neutrality, and *SD*-Strategyproofness (a stronger version of the latter than the one defined above even). It is, however, not *ex-post*-efficient.

Random Serial Dictatorship is another generalisation of RD to the full set of preference profiles which additionally fulfils *ex-post*-Efficiency. Here, one first chooses a random permutation $i_1, \ldots, i_m$ of the agents and then lets each agent, in that order, delete all those among the remaining alternatives that they 'do not want' (i. e. keep only those that they prefer most among the remaining ones). Then, one returns one of the remaining alternatives (among which all agents are indifferent) uniformly at random. One possible Isabelle definition is

$$\text{RSD } N\ A\ R = \textbf{do } is \leftarrow \text{pmf\_of\_set } (\text{permutations\_of\_set } N)$$
$$\text{pmf\_of\_set } (\text{foldr } (\lambda i\ A'.\ \text{Max\_wrt\_among } (R\ i)\ A')\ is\ A)$$

where *permutations_of_set* N returns the set of all lists that contain each element of N exactly once. An alternative recursive definition is

$$\text{RSD } N\ A\ R = \textbf{if } N = \emptyset \textbf{ then } \text{pmf\_of\_set } A$$
$$\textbf{else do } i \leftarrow \text{pmf\_of\_set } N$$
$$\text{RSD } (N \backslash \{i\})\ (\text{Max\_wrt\_among } (R\ i)\ A)\ R$$

The actual definition in Isabelle uses the generic combinator *fold_ random_ permutation* from the Isabelle library that allows traversing a set in random order. This directly yields the above two definitions as corollaries and allows the user to use whichever form is more convenient.

RSD can then be proven to be anonymous, neutral, strongly *SD*-strategyproof, and *ex-post*-efficient. The proofs of the first two are fairly simple; the other two are somewhat more involved. Writing these non-trivial proofs about a *concrete* SDS like *RSD* served as a good first 'stress test' of the Social Choice library and increased the confidence that the formal definitions were as intended. This is likely the first formalisation of *RD* and *RSD* and their properties.

4 Gathering Consequences from Profiles

Having established the necessary definitions, we can now approach the proof of the main result (Theorem 1). First of all, let us explore how to take the four conditions – anonymity, neutrality, SD-Efficiency, SD-Strategyproofness – and derive all of the arising conditions for a fixed set of profiles, from which we can then hopefully derive a contradiction. Suppose we have an SDS f for some fixed set of m agents and n alternatives. As mentioned before, these four conditions can be fully characterised by QF-LRA formulæ. The variables in these formulæ are the probabilities returned by f for each profile R. We denote these variables as $p_{R,x}$ (the probability that $f(R)$ returns the winner x).

Let us now go through the different types of conditions. Again, I will only sketch the precise constructions here; for more details, see Brandl *et al.* [1].

Anonymity and Neutrality. Anonymity can be handled implicitly by simply considering all preference profiles that differ only by a renaming of agents as equal. An alternative view is to look at a preference profile as a *multiset* of preference relations instead of as a *vector*.

For neutrality, one can similarly consider all profiles equal that differ only by a renaming of alternatives. Here, the only way to implement this in practice seems to be to choose an arbitrary representative among the $n!$ candidates, e. g. the one with the lexicographically smallest representation.

Orbit Conditions. The above does not completely capture anonymity and neutrality; what is still missing are the so-called *orbit conditions* that arise from profile automorphisms: If a permutation σ of alternatives maps a profile R to itself (modulo anonymity), it is clear that by neutrality, all alternatives in an orbit of σ must receive the same probability (e. g. if $\sigma = (a\ b\ c)(d)$, we have $p_{R,a} = p_{R,b} = p_{R,c}$). These orbit conditions tend to arise when R has rich symmetries. Together with the efficiency conditions, they will be extremely useful in the proof later since they greatly restrict the possible values for f.

SD-Strategyproofness. This is easy to capture in QF-LRA: For any pair of profiles $R, \bar{R}$ we must check if $\bar{R}$ differs from R only by the preferences of one agent i. If that is the case, let $\succeq_i$ resp. $\bar{\succeq}_i$ denote the preference relation of agent i in R resp. $\bar{R}$. We must then have $\neg f(\bar{R}) \succ_{SD(\succeq_i)} f(R)$ and $\neg f(R) \succ_{SD(\bar{\succeq}_i)} f(\bar{R})$. When the definition of Stochastic Dominance is unfolded, these conditions simply reduce to a combination of equations and inequalities in the $p_{R,x}$ and $p_{\bar{R},x}$.

Of course, equality must be seen modulo anonymity and neutrality here, and if a renaming of alternatives was necessary for the manipulation, this renaming must also be taken into account.

SD-Efficiency. This is the most difficult condition to handle. Here, the key insight by Brandl *et al.* is that if a lottery is SD-efficient w. r. t. a profile R, then all other lotteries with the same support or a smaller support (w. r. t. inclusion) are *also* SD-efficient. We can therefore define the notion of an SD-efficient support: A set $X \subseteq A$ is called an *SD-efficient support* if the lotteries that have support

X are SD-efficient. Whether such a set X is an SD-efficient support can simply be encoded as a linear programming problem.

Therefore, we only need to find all the inclusion-minimal SD-inefficient supports $X_1, X_2, \ldots$ (of which there are $< 2^m$). The condition that some lottery p be SD-efficient w.r.t. R then reduces to its support not being a superset of any of these minimal SD-inefficient supports, i.e. $\forall k.\ \exists x \in X_k.\ p_{R,x} = 0$. This is a conjunction of disjunctions, and thus a QF-LRA formula. Of course, this support-set characterisation of SD-Efficiency is also fully verified in the system.

Another interesting fact is that a singleton support $\{x\}$ is SD-inefficient iff x is a Pareto loser. This directly implies that SD-Efficiency is stronger than *ex-post*-Efficiency, and it means that we do not have to employ linear programming for singleton sets; we can simply check if the element is a Pareto loser.

Lottery Conditions. Lastly, we still need to take into account that the $p_{R,x}$ are not independent real variables: since they represent probabilities, they are subject to the conditions $p_{R,x} \geq 0$ and $\sum_{x \in A} p_{R,x} = 1$.

5   Tooling

5.1   External Tools and Trusted Code Base

I will now give a brief overview of the two external tools that were used in this project. Neither of them are trusted, i.e. the correctness of the final result does not depend on them. First, however, I would like to clarify what exactly the trusted code base of the result is.

Isabelle is based on a simple intuitionistic logic known as Isabelle/Pure, on top of which the *object logic* HOL is then axiomatised. The basic inference rules of *Pure* are provided as ML functions by the Isabelle kernel, which is the only part of Isabelle that can actually produce theorems[3]. All other parts of Isabelle (e.g. all of its various proof automation tools) can only prove theorems by interfacing with this kernel, so that the trusted code base is effectively only the kernel (and the code for parsing and pretty-printing). A bug in any other part of Isabelle or in my own ML code should therefore, in principle, never lead to an inconsistency. To reiterate: all proofs in this work go through the kernel. There is no use of computational reflection, there are no external computations, and no trusted external tools.

Now, let me clarify what the two external tools *were* used for and in what form.

Z3. This is a well-known SMT solver. It is bundled with the Isabelle distribution and integrated via the *smt* proof method [11], which translates Isabelle/HOL goals into the SMT-LIB format, calls Z3, and attempts to reconstruct an Isabelle proof from the Z3 proof. Here, *Isabelle proof* does not mean Isabelle proof text. *smt* does not produce Isabelle code; it rather constructs Isabelle theorems by

---

[3] Except for *oracles*, which I do not use here.

emulating the Z3 proof rules with basic logical inference. A replayed Z3 proof therefore appears as a single opaque invocation of the *smt* method in Isabelle proof text. Like the Z3 proofs, these reconstructed proofs are very large and low-level and therefore not human-readable. They are, however, just as trustworthy as any other Isabelle proof since the *smt* method has to go through Isabelle's kernel in order to create theorems.

As will be explained in Sect. 6, this *smt* method was very helpful in deriving the 'human-readable' version of the proof of Theorem 1; however the final proof does not contain any invocations of it anymore.

QSOpt_ex. This software is a Linear Programming solver written in C that uses exact rational arithmetic [12,13], i.e. it outputs the exact optimal solutions as rational numbers without any rounding errors. It was developed by Applegate *et al.* using their non-exact solver QSopt as a basis and uses a combination of fast, non-exact floating point operations and exact rational computations based on GMP arbitrary-precision rational numbers. This is important because we want to use the solution returned by the solver to construct witness lotteries, and even a small rounding error would lead Isabelle to reject such a witness.

However, I do not use this version of QSopt_ex since I was unable to compile the code. Fortunately, there is a fork by Steffenson [14] that provides a number of improvements, particularly to the build system. I created rudimentary bindings to interface with this version of QSopt_ex from Isabelle/ML by writing the problems into a problem description file in the LP format, invoking QSopt_ex on it, and parsing the result file.

For our purposes, we only need to *compute* the optimal solutions, but we do not have to *prove* that they are optimal. QSopt_ex is used to check if a support is *SD*-inefficient and – when it is – to compute a witness for this inefficiency (i.e. another lottery that is strictly better w.r.t. Pareto-*SD*). If there were a bug in QSopt_ex, this would either lead to an unprovable goal when trying to use the witness or it would cause us to miss some inefficient supports and therefore give us less information about the consequences of *SD*-Efficiency. It can, by construction, never lead to any inconsistency.

Note that we do not need to show the optimality of the solutions found by QSopt_ex in Isabelle; it is only required on a meta level for the completeness of the approach. We do need to prove the correctness of the solutions, however, and this can easily be done by Isabelle's general-purpose automation.

5.2   Automation in Isabelle/HOL

While all of the many facts following from our four properties for the given set of preference profiles could easily be derived and proven in Isabelle by a human, this would have resulted in a considerable amount of work and boiler-plate proofs. Moreover, this work would have to be re-done for a new proof of a related statement or even if the underlying preference profiles changed slightly, which discourages experimentation. The goal was therefore to develop specialised automation for this in Isabelle that is capable of replacing the unverified Java program by Brandl *et al.*, thereby turning Isabelle into a capable IDE for randomised Social Choice proofs of this kind.

Isabelle itself is written in Standard ML and contains a sophisticated ML system based on Poly/ML that allows compiling and adding new code at runtime. Users can add custom proof methods written in ML to automate proof steps and commands to automatically define constants, derive facts, etc. I developed a number of such Isabelle commands to automate the fact gathering described before:

preference_profiles defines preference profiles and automatically proves their well-definedness. The notation is similar to that found in textbooks: to specify e. g. the preference relation $1 \succ \{2,3\} \succ 4$ (1 is better than 2 or 3 and 2 and 3 are equally good and better than 4) one would write $1, [2,3], 4$.

derive_orbit_equations computes the orbit conditions for a set of given preference profiles and proves them automatically. . For each orbit, a canonical representative x is chosen and the orbit conditions have the form $f(R)(y) = f(R)(x)$, where $y \neq x$ is some other element on the orbit. This makes it possible to use the orbit conditions directly as rewrite rules for Isabelle's simplifier, since the equations are normalising.

find_inefficient_supports computes Pareto losers and *SD*-inefficient supports and automatically proves the corresponding conditions for *ex-post*- and *SD*-efficient SDSs. In order to find *SD*-inefficient supports and prove their inefficiency, the ML code invokes the external Linear Programming solver *QSOpt_ex*.

prove_inefficient_supports takes a list of *ex-post*- and *SD*-inefficient supports where each *SD*-inefficient support is annotated with a witness lottery (i. e. a lottery that is strictly *SD*-preferred to the uniform distribution on the inefficient support). This witness lottery can be read directly from the solution of the corresponding linear program.

The idea is to compute the inefficient supports and their witnesses once with *find_inefficient_supports*, which outputs a hyperlink that can be clicked to automatically insert a corresponding invocation of *prove_inefficient_supports* with all the witnesses filled in as needed. This makes the final proof document completely independent from the external LP solver.

derive_strategyproofness_conditions takes a list of preference profiles and computes all possible manipulations of all profiles in this list that yield another profile in the list. It then derives and proves all the conditions that arise from these manipulations for a (weakly) strategyproof SDS. The user can specify an optional distance threshold to restrict the search to small manipulations (measured as the cardinality of the symmetric difference of the relations). For our purposes, a distance of 2 is sufficient.

Note again that this ML code is *untrusted*: I did not verify it and – as explained in Sect. 5.1 – there is, in fact, no need to verify it.

All of this automation is available in the *Archive of Formal Proofs* entry on randomised Social Choice [2]. The automation also provides ML interfaces so

that for future similar projects, one could easily implement the entire pipeline
of candidate set generation, derivation of all the QF-LRA conditions, and the
invocation of the SMT solver inside Isabelle, turning it into a convenient and
extensible IDE for randomised Social Choice.

6   The Formal Proof of Theorem 1

The formal proof of the main result begins with a definition of the setting: I
define a locale called *sds_impossibility* for the setting of an anonymous, neutral,
SD-efficient and *SD*-strategyproof SDS for $m \geq 4$ agents I and $n \geq 4$ alternatives
N. Building on this, I then define a sublocale called *sds_impossibility_4_4* that
additionally assumes that $I = \{A, B, C, D\}$ and $N = \{a, b, c, d\}$ where the four
agents and alternatives are distinct. Our goal is to prove *False* in the context of
the latter locale and then use the lifting machinery described in Sect. 3 to derive
False in the first locale.

For illustration purposes, I will track the total number of *degrees of freedom*
in our problem, i.e. the number of real variables $p_{R,x}$ that are not constrained
by an equation. In the beginning, we have 141 degrees of freedom (4 for each
profile, minus 1 eliminated since the probabilities must sum to 1).

The Automatic Part. In the context of the locale *sds_impossibility_4_4*, the
machinery described in Sect. 5.2 is invoked: The 47 preference profiles listed in
the proof by Brandl *et al.* are defined using the *preference_profiles* command. The
orbit and strategyproofness conditions are derived fully automatically – we only
have to supply the list of profiles that we are interested in to the corresponding
commands. For the efficiency conditions, we need to run *find_inefficient_supports*
once; for the full set of profiles, this takes about 7 s. The final proof document
only contains the invocation of *prove_inefficient_supports* generated by it.

This automatic part is fairly quick: The proofs of the well-definedness of
the profiles and all the other conditions take about 20 s altogether. The result
returned by these commands is:

- 12 equations of the form $p_{R,x} = p_{R,y}$ from orbit conditions
- 24 equations of the form $p_{R,x} = 0$ from Pareto losers
- 9 conditions of the form $p_{R,x} = 0 \lor p_{R,y} = 0$ from *SD*-inefficient supports
- 256 conditions from Strategyproofness (of which we will use only 85)

Each orbit and Pareto-loser condition immediately eliminates one degree, and 5
of the *SD*-Efficiency conditions also each eliminate one degree immediately due
to orbit conditions. This leaves us with 100 degrees of freedom. Using the *smt*
method mentioned in Sect. 5.1, we can then already prove *False* in Isabelle from
all these conditions fully automatically within about 8 s.

Deriving A Human-Readable Proof. As mentioned before, one of the goals of
the project was to obtain a *structured* proof that a human can follow and, in

principle, check every step. I will now describe how I proceeded to find such a proof.

As a first step, the 5 support conditions mentioned above that eliminate a degree have to be identified by hand. They happen to have the form $p_{R,x} = 0 \vee p_{R,y} = 0$ where we know $p_{R,x} = p_{R,y}$ from an orbit condition, so that we can conclude $p_{R,x} = p_{R,y} = 0$. Naturally, this process could also be automated, but seeing as there are only 5 conditions like this, it is hardly worth the effort.

I then naïvely tried to reason 'forward' from the conditions by combining various Strategyproofness conditions and the 4 remaining unused support conditions. It seemed particularly desirable to me to find exact values for variables (e. g. $p_{R_{39},b} = 0$ or $p_{R_{36},a} = 1/2$) since this immediately greatly simplifies all Strategyproofness conditions in which that variable appears. Any value thus determined can be added to Isabelle's simplifier so that one can easily see what remains of any given condition after all the values that were already determined have been plugged in.

My general approach to derive these new equalities was then initially to pick two corresponding Strategyproofness conditions (i. e. two profiles R_1 and R_2 that differ only by one agent's manipulation modulo a renaming of alternatives). Then I hand these – together with lottery conditions and possibly support conditions – to Isabelle's auto method. In some cases, the assumptions are then automatically simplified to some useful equation like $p_{R_{36},b} = 0$ or $p_{R_{18},c} = p_{R_9,c}$ or at least an inequality like $p_{R_5,d} \geq 1/2$. This worked for quite a while, but eventually, I was unable to find any new information like this.

I then turned towards the SMT solver for guidance. The situation at this point is that there are some structured proofs of facts and we hand these facts (along with many Strategyproofness conditions) to the SMT solver to derive *False*. The way forward was to attempt to *pull out* facts from the set of facts given to the SMT solver. To do this, I conjectured values of variables (e. g. $p_{R_{42},a} = 0$) that seemed likely to be useful (e. g. because they would simplify many other conditions). Of course, since the conditions are inconsistent, *any* conjecture like this is provable in our context, but a 'good' conjecture can be derived from a small subset of the conditions.

I therefore used the *smt* method to check how many conditions suffice to prove my conjecture. When this set was sufficiently small, I proved the conjecture using the *smt* method, added it to the set of facts given to *smt* in the final proof of *False*, and removed as many of its preconditions as possible from that set in order to determine whether the conjecture was indeed a useful one – the goal, after all, is to make the final 'monolithic' proof step smaller.

With this approach, I was able to easily shrink the final proof step until it disappeared completely. I then proceeded to 'flesh out' all the small facts proven with the *smt* method into structured Isabelle proofs, which was fairly easy since they were all relatively small and Isabelle has good automation for linear arithmetic. The end result was a very linear proof without any 'big' case distinctions, which is remarkable considering that there are over 60 disjunctions in the conditions altogether. At this stage, the proof was clear and detailed enough to derive a rigorous and human-readable (albeit rather lengthy) pen-and-paper proof, which is printed in the appendix of the paper by Brandl *et al.* [1].

7 A Mistake in a Related Result

A previous paper by Brandl *et al.* contained a proof of a weaker version of Theorem 1. The difference is that this weaker theorem additionally assumes that the SDS in question must also be an extension of Random Dictatorship in the sense that it returns the same result as RD if each agent has a unique favourite alternative (i. e. whenever RD is defined).

Corollary 1. *If $m \geq 4$ and $n \geq 4$, there exists no SDS that is an extension of RD and has the following properties: Anonymity, Neutrality, SD-Efficiency, SD-Strategyproofness.*

For the motivation behind this result, see the original presentation by Brandl *et al.* [15]. For our purposes, it should only be said that the proof for this theorem was relatively short and human-readable (it involves only 13 profiles). It was therefore decided to first formalise this weaker theorem in Isabelle (in the hope that it would be considerably easier) and then move on to the proof of Theorem 1.

Like their later proof of Theorem 1, the main part here is also the base case $m = n = 4$ and then employs the lifting argument described in Sect. 3. I was able to formalise the base case of $m = n = 4$ quickly and without any problems, although it already became apparent that tool support such as that described in Sect. 5.1 would be very useful.

However, once I attempted to formalise the lifting step (which Brandl *et al.* only described very roughly in a single paragraph since it is usually not very interesting), it became apparent that the lifting argument breaks down in this case: What Brandl *et al.* missed is that unlike the other four properties, the property 'f is an extension of RD' does not 'survive' the lifting, i. e. if f is an RD-extension, it is possible that $f\downarrow$ is *not* an RD-extension anymore.

Brandl *et al.* acknowledged this mistake and published a corrigendum [16] in which they suggest to add the additional requirement that f must ignore fully indifferent agents. The result and its problems were superseded by the later correct proof of Theorem 1 anyway. Nevertheless, I find it notable that the formalisation process found a previously undiscovered mistake in a peer-reviewed published work – in particular, a mistake that could only be repaired by introducing additional assumptions.

8 Related Work

Brandl *et al.* [1,15] already give a good overview of work related to Theorem 1 in Social Choice Theory. Geist & Peters [17] give an overview of computer-aided methods in Social Choice Theory in general. I shall therefore restrict this section to formalisations of results from broader Social Choice Theory in theorem provers.

Nipkow [18,19] formalised Arrow's theorem and the Gibbard–Satterthwaite theorem. Gammie [20,21] formalised some more results such as Arrow's theorem, May's theorem, Sen's liberal paradox, and stable matchings. All of these use Isabelle/HOL. The only formalisation of Social Choice Theory outside of Isabelle that I am aware of is one of Arrow's theorem in Mizar by Wiedijk [22].

Brandt *et al.* [23,24] recently built upon my work to formalise another, simpler impossibility result in Isabelle/HOL: that there is no Social Choice Function (SCF) for at least 3 agents / alternatives that fulfils Anonymity, Fishburn-Strategyproofness, and Pareto-Efficiency. The main differences to this work are:

- SCFs return a *set* of winners, not a lottery. The problem can thus be encoded into SAT and SMT is not needed.
- The proof involves only 21 preference profiles instead of 47 and only 33 Strategyproofness conditions instead of 85.
- They do not attempt to construct a human-readable proof and instead use Isabelle's built-in SAT solver to obtain the contradiction in the end.

Due to the different setting of SCFs, most of the specialised automation developed for SDSs could unfortunately not be reused. The *preference_profiles* command and the substantial amount of library material on preferences, however, could be reused. The general structure of the proof (locales, definitions of various notions related to SDSs/SCFs, lifting) was also sufficiently similar that a considerable amount of material on SDSs could easily be adapted. Due to the much smaller size of the proof, the derivation of the SAT conditions from the preference profiles was done by hand since it would have been significantly more work to adapt the automation to SCFs.

It is worth noting that, in contrast to my work here, all examples listed in this section were only concerned with *non-probabilistic* Social Choice Theory. The present work is therefore probably the first published formalisation concerning *randomised* Social Choice Theory.

9   Conclusion

Based on work by Brandl *et al.* [15,25], I have written a fully machine-checked proof of the incompatibility of SD-Strategyproofness and SD-Efficiency using the Isabelle/HOL theorem prover and, based on this, a 'human-readable' proof. In the process, I have also developed a high-level formalisation of basic concepts of randomised Social Choice Theory and proof automation that automatically defines and derives facts from given preference profiles. Both of these can be used for similar future projects.

This work was also an interesting case study in how interactive theorem provers (like Isabelle) and powerful automated theorem provers (like Z3 and other SMT solvers) can be used not only to formally verify existing mathematical theorems, but also to find completely new and – more or less – human-readable proofs for conjectures. For human mathematicians, simplifying large terms and combining large numbers of complicated linear equations and inequalities is tedious and error-prone, but specialised computer programs (such as SMT solvers or Isabelle's decision procedures for linear arithmetic) excel at it. Using an interactive proof system such as Isabelle has the great advantage that

- it is virtually impossible to make a mistake in a proof,
- one receives immediate feedback on everything, and
- it is easy to check whether an idea works out or not.

The last two points are, in my opinion, often not stressed enough when talking about interactive theorem proving. With a paper proof, changing parts of the proof (e. g. simplifying the presentation or removing unnecessary assumptions) is usually a tedious and error-prone process. With the support of an interactive theorem prover, the consequences of any change become visible immediately, which can make experimentation and 'proof prototyping' much more appealing.

I also believe that this work shows that there is an opportunity for fruitful collaboration between domain experts and interactive proof experts. Together, even brand-new research-level mathematical results can – at least sometimes – be formalised. This can improve the confidence in the correctness of the result tremendously, and, more importantly, it is an excellent way to find and rectify mistakes (as was the case here).

Acknowledgments. I would like to thank Florian Brandl, Felix Brandt, and Christian Geist for bringing the field of randomised Social Choice to my attention as a target for formalisation, and for their continued assistance. I also thank Florian Brandl and Felix Brandt for commenting on a draft of this document. I also thank the anonymous reviewers for their comments.

References

1. Brandl, F., Brandt, F., Eberl, M., Geist, C.: Proving the incompatibility of efficiency and strategyproofness via SMT solving. J. ACM **65**(2), 6:1–6:28 (2018)
2. Eberl, M.: Randomised social choice theory. Archive of Formal Proofs, formal proof development, May 2016
3. Eberl, M.: The incompatibility of SD-efficiency and SD-strategy-proofness. Archive of Formal Proofs, formal proof development, May 2016
4. Arrow, K.J.: A difficulty in the concept of social welfare. J. Polit. Econ. **58**(4), 328–346 (1950)
5. Gibbard, A.: Manipulation of schemes that mix voting with chance. Econometrica **45**(02), 665–681 (1977)
6. Hales, T.C., et al.: A formal proof of the Kepler conjecture. arXiv:1501.0215 (2015)
7. Tucker, W.: The Lorenz attractor exists. Ph.D. thesis, Uppsala universitet (1999). Accessed 10 March 1999
8. Viana, M.: What's new on Lorenz strange attractors? Math. Intell. **22**(3), 6–19 (2000)
9. Ballarin, C.: Locales: a module system for mathematical theories. J. Autom. Reasoning **52**(2), 123–153 (2014)

10. Eberl, M., Hölzl, J., Nipkow, T.: A verified compiler for probability density functions. In: Vitek, J. (ed.) ESOP 2015. LNCS, vol. 9032, pp. 80–104. Springer, Heidelberg (2015). https://doi.org/10.1007/978-3-662-46669-8_4
11. Böhme, S.: Proof reconstruction for Z3 in Isabelle/HOL. In: 7th International Workshop on Satisfiability Modulo Theories (SMT 2009) (2009)
12. Espinoza, D.G.: On Linear Programming, Integer Programming and Cutting Planes. Ph.D. thesis, Georgia Institute of Technology (2006)
13. Applegate, D.L., Cook, W., Dash, S., Espinoza, D.G.: Exact solutions to linear programming problems. Oper. Res. Lett. **35**(6), 693–699 (2007)
14. Steffensen, J.L.: QSopt_ex - an exact linear programming solver (2014)
15. Brandl, F., Brandt, F., Suksompong, W.: The impossibility of extending random dictatorship to weak preferences. Econ. Lett. **141**, 44–47 (2016)
16. Brandl, F., Brandt, F., Suksompong, W.: Corrigendum to the impossibility of extending random dictatorship to weak preferences. Econ. Lett. **141**, 44–47 (2016)
17. Geist, C., Peters, D.: Computer-aided methods for social choice theory. In: Endriss, U. (ed.) Trends in Computational Social Choice, pp. 249–267, AI Access (2017)
18. Nipkow, T.: Arrow and Gibbard-Satterthwaite. Archive of formal proofs formal proof development, September 2008. http://isa-afp.org/entries/ArrowImpossibilityGS.html
19. Nipkow, T.: Social choice theory in HOL. J. Autom. Reasoning **43**(3), 289–304 (2009)
20. Gammie, P.: Some classical results in social choice theory. Archive of Formal Proofs, formal proof development, November 2008. http://isa-afp.org/entries/SenSocialChoice.html
21. Gammie, P.: Stable matching. Archive of Formal Proofs, formal proof development, October 2016. http://isa-afp.org/entries/Stable_Matching.html
22. Wiedijk, F.: Formalizing arrow's theorem. Sadhana **34**(1), 193–220 (2009)
23. Brandt, F., Saile, C., Stricker, C.: Voting with ties: strong impossibilities via sat solving. In: Proceedings of the 17th International Conference on Autonomous Agents and MultiAgent Systems, AAMAS 2018, Richland, SC, International Foundation for Autonomous Agents and Multiagent Systems, pp. 1285–1293 (2018)
24. Brandt, F., Eberl, M., Saile, C., Stricker, C.: The incompatibility of Fishburn-strategyproofness and Pareto-efficiency. Archive of Formal Proofs, formal proof development, March 2018. http://isa-afp.org/entries/Fishburn_Impossibility.html
25. Brandl, F., Brandt, F., Geist, C.: Proving the incompatibility of efficiency and strategyproofness via SMT solving. In: Proceedings of the 25th International Joint Conference on Artificial Intelligence (IJCAI) (2016)

Modal and Epistemic Logics

Epistemic Reasoning
with Byzantine-Faulty Agents

Roman Kuznets[1]([✉]), Laurent Prosperi[2], Ulrich Schmid[1], and Krisztina Fruzsa[1]

[1] TU Wien, Vienna, Austria
{rkuznets,s,kfruzsa}@ecs.tuwien.ac.at
[2] ENS Paris-Saclay, Cachan, France
laurent.prosperi@ens-cachan.fr

> ...By our remembrances of days foregone
> Such were our faults, or then we thought
> them none.

———————————————

W. Shakespeare,
All's Well That Ends Well

Abstract. We introduce a novel comprehensive framework for epistemic reasoning in multi-agent systems where agents may behave asynchronously and may be byzantine faulty. Extending Fagin et al.'s classic runs-and-systems framework to agents who may arbitrarily deviate from their protocols, it combines epistemic and temporal logic and incorporates fine-grained mechanisms for specifying distributed protocols and their behaviors. Besides our framework's ability to express any type of faulty behavior, from fully byzantine to fully benign, it allows to specify arbitrary timing and synchronization properties. As a consequence, it can be adapted to any message-passing distributed computing model we are aware of, including synchronous processes and communication, (un-) reliable uni-/multi-/broadcast communication, and even coordinated action. The utility of our framework is demonstrated by formalizing the *brain-in-a-vat* scenario, which exposes the substantial limitations of what can be known by asynchronous agents in fault-tolerant distributed systems. Given the knowledge of preconditions principle, this restricts preconditions that error-prone agents can use in their protocols. In particular, it is usually necessary to relativize preconditions with respect to the correctness of the acting agent.

1 Introduction

At least since the groundbreaking work by Halpern and Moses [12], the knowledge-based approach [6] is known as a powerful tool for analyzing distributed systems. In a nutshell, it combines epistemic logic [14] and temporal

———————————————

R. Kuznets—Supported by the Austrian Science Fund (FWF) project RiSE/SHiNE (S11405) and ADynNet (P28182).
K. Fruzsa—PhD student in the FWF doctoral program LogiCS (W1255).

A. Herzig and A. Popescu (Eds.): FroCoS 2019, LNAI 11715, pp. 259–276, 2019.
https://doi.org/10.1007/978-3-030-29007-8_15

logic to reason about knowledge and belief in *multi-agent systems* (MAS). Standard epistemic logic relies on Kripke models $\mathcal{M}$ that describe possible global states s of the system, where atomic propositions, e.g., "$x_i = 0$ for a local variable of agent i" or "i has witnessed an external event e," hold true or not, along with an indistinguishability relation $s \sim_i s'$ that tells that i cannot distinguish state s from s' based on its local information. Knowledge of a statement φ about the system in global state s is represented by a modal *knowledge operator* K_i, written $(\mathcal{M}, s) \models K_i\varphi$. Agent i knows φ at global state s iff φ holds in every global state s' that i cannot distinguish from s.

In the *interpreted runs-and-systems* framework for reasoning about distributed and other multi-agent systems [6,12], the semantics of Kripke models is combined with a complex machinery representing runs of distributed MAS, thus, obtaining an additional temporal structure. For the set of all possible runs r of a system $\mathcal{I}$, all possible global states $r(t)$ in all runs $r \in \mathcal{I}$ over discrete time $t \in \mathbb{T} = \mathbb{N}$ are considered. The accessibility relation is also dictated by the distributed component: two global states $r(t)$ and $r'(t')$ are indistinguishable for agent i iff i has the same local state in both, formally, $r_i(t) = r'_i(t')$. Therefore, i knows φ at time t in run $r \in \mathcal{I}$, formally, $(\mathcal{I}, r, t) \models K_i\varphi$ iff $(\mathcal{I}, r', t') \models \varphi$ in every $r' \in \mathcal{I}$ and for every t' with $r_i(t) = r'_i(t')$. Here φ can be a formula containing arbitrary atomic propositions, as well as other knowledge operators and temporal modalities such as $\Diamond$ (eventually) and $\Box$ (always), combined by standard logical operators $\neg, \wedge, \vee, \rightarrow$. Note that agents do not generally know the global time.

Related Work. Whereas the knowledge-based approach has been used successfully for distributed computing problems in systems with uncertainty but no failures [1,2,10], few papers apply epistemic reasoning to byzantine agents that can disseminate false information. Agents suffering from crash and from send omission failures were studied in [24], primarily in the context of agreement problems, which require standard [4] or continual [13] common knowledge. More recent results are unbeatable consensus algorithms in synchronous systems with crash failures [3] and the discovery of the importance of *silent choirs* [11] for message-optimal protocols in crash-resilient systems. Still, to the best of our knowledge, the only attempt to extend epistemic reasoning to systems with some byzantine[1] faults [18] was made in Michel's PhD thesis published as [21], where faulty agents may deviate from their protocols by sending wrong messages. Even there erroneous behavior is restricted to actions that could have also been observed in some correct execution, meaning that Michel's faulty agents may not behave truly arbitrarily.

---

[1] The term "byzantine" originated from [18]. Leslie Lamport chose a defunct country to avoid offending anyone living and also as a pun [26, p. 39] because generals from Byzantium could, in fact, be expected to behave in a byzantine (i.e., devious or treacherous) fashion. Unfortunately, this pun might be responsible for the ensuing unnecessary ([27]) capitalization of the word even for faults unrelated to Byzantium proper.

To some extent, fault-tolerance has also been considered for general multi-agent systems. For non-fault-tolerant MAS, temporal-epistemic languages like CTLK [6] and even model checkers like MCMAS [19] exist, which can be used for specification and automatic verification of temporal-epistemic properties. For MAS that may suffer from faults, replication-based fault-tolerance techniques [8], diagnosis-based approaches [15], lying agents [28], and even fault-injection based model mutation and model checking [5] have been considered. However, to the best of our knowledge, a comprehensive epistemic reasoning framework that also allows byzantine agents did not exist so far.

Contributions and Paper Organization. In Sects. 2 and 3, we present the cornerstones of our comprehensive modeling and analysis framework for epistemic reasoning about fault-tolerant distributed message-passing systems, the full version of which is available as a comprehensive technical report [17]. We demonstrate its utility in Sect. 5, by deriving generic results about what asynchronous agents can(not) know in the presence of byzantine faults. In order to achieve this, we first introduce in Sect. 4 a general method of *run modifications*: to show that agent i cannot know some fact φ, it is sufficient to construct a modified run, imperceptible to agent i, that makes φ false. This way, we obtain our central result, the "brain-in-a-vat lemma" (with the proof relegated to Appendix A) stating that, no matter what it observed, an agent can never rule out the possibility of these observations being wholly fictitious results of its malfunction [25]. Our findings imply that the knowledge of preconditions principle [22] (any precondition for action must be known to the acting agent) severely restricts the kinds of preconditions acceptable in such systems. Thus, we introduce epistemic modalities that convert a desired property, e.g., an occurrence of an event, to a knowable precondition in Sect. 6. Finally, Sect. 7 contains some conclusions and directions of future work.

2 Runs and Systems with Byzantine Faults

We introduce our version of the runs-and-systems framework enhanced with active byzantine agents, which provides the basis for epistemic reasoning in this setting. To prevent the waste of space by multiple definition environments, we give the following series of formal definitions as ordinary text marking the defined objects by italics; consult [17] for all the details.

We consider a non-empty finite set $\mathcal{A} = \{1, \ldots, n\}$ of *agents*, representing individuals and/or computing units. Agent i can perform *actions* from $Actions_i$, e.g., send *messages*, and can witness *events* from $Events_i$, e.g., message delivery. We group all actions and events, collectively termed *haps*[2], taking place after *timestamp* t and no later than $t + 1$ into a *round*, denoted $t + \frac{1}{2}$, and treat all haps of the round as happening simultaneously. Global system timestamps taken from $\mathbb{T} = \mathbb{N}$ are not accessible to our *asynchronous agents*, who need to

---

[2] Cf. "And whatsoever else shall *hap* to-night, Give it an understanding but no tongue." W. Shakespeare, *Hamlet*, Act I, Scene 2.

be woken up during a round to record the passage of time. A *local state* $r_i(t +$ 1), referred to as *(process-time) node* $(i, t+1)$, describes the local view of the system by agent $i \in \mathcal{A}$ after round $t + \frac{1}{2}$. Nodes $(i, 0)$ correspond to *initial local states* $r_i(0)$, taken from a set Σ_i. The set of all possible tuples of initial local states is $\mathcal{G}(0) := \prod_{i \in \mathcal{A}} \Sigma_i$. We assume $r_i(t)$ to be a list of all haps as observed by i in rounds it was *active* in, grouped by round, i.e., if agent i is *awoken* in round $t + \frac{1}{2}$, then $r_i(t+1) = X : r_i(t)$,[3] where $X \subseteq Haps_i := Actions_i \sqcup Events_i$ is the set of all *internal actions* and *external events* as perceived by i in round $t + \frac{1}{2}$. Agents *passive* in the round have no record of it: $r_i(t+1) = r_i(t)$. We denote $Actions := \bigcup_{i \in \mathcal{A}} Actions_i$, $Events := \bigcup_{i \in \mathcal{A}} Events_i$, and $Haps := Actions \sqcup Events$ to be sets of all actions, events, and haps respectively. Each agent has a *protocol* dictating its actions (more details below). Actions prompted by the protocol are deemed *correct*, whereas actions imposed by the environment in circumvention of the protocol are *byzantine* (even when they mirror correct protocol actions). In addition to acting outside its protocol, a *byzantine agent* i may incorrectly record its actions and/or witnessed events. Events recorded correctly (incorrectly) are *correct* (*byzantine*). Thus, $r_i(t)$ may not match reality. Still agents possess *perfect recall*: though imperfect, their memories never change. The set of all local states of i is denoted $\mathscr{L}_i$.

An accurate record $r_\epsilon(t+1)$ of the system after round $t + \frac{1}{2}$ is possessed only by the *environment* $\epsilon \notin \mathcal{A}$ that controls everything but agents' protocols: it determines which agents wake up and which become faulty; it fully controls all byzantine haps (including faulty actions by the agents); it enforces physical and causal laws; and it is the source of indeterminacy (of the type involved in throwing dice). The environment is also responsible for message passing, the details of which can be found in [17] but are largely irrelevant for the results presented in this paper. The crucial features are: messages are agent-to-agent; correctly sending (resp. receiving) a message is an action (resp. event); each sent message, correct or byzantine alike, is supplied with a unique *global message identifier*, or *GMI*, inaccessible for agents and used by ϵ to ensure the causality of message delivery, i.e., that an unsent message cannot be correctly received. The *global state* $r(t+1) := (r_\epsilon(t+1), r_1(t+1), \ldots, r_n(t+1))$ after round $t + \frac{1}{2}$ consists of all local states $r_i(t+1)$, as well as $r_\epsilon(t+1)$. The set of all global states is denoted $\mathcal{G}$.

To distinguish $o \in Haps_i$ from the same o observed by another agent $j \neq i$ and to facilitate message delivery, ϵ transforms each action $a \in Actions_i$ initiated by i's protocol (and, hence, correct) into an extended format $global(i, t, a) \in GActions_i$, e.g., incorporating a unique time-based GMI for each sent message. The main requirement is that $global$ be one-to-one (see [17] for details). Haps in $r_\epsilon(t)$ are recorded in this $global$, or *environment's*, view. The sets of globally recorded correct actions/events/haps are denoted by adding G to the notations above, e.g., $\overline{GEvents_i}$ are pairwise disjoint sets of all i's correct events in global notation.

---

[3] ':' stands for concatenation.

The duality between the local and global views is also crucial for allowing agents to have false memories. Every correct event $E = global(i, t, e)$ for $e \in Events_i$ has a faulty counterpart $fake(i, E)$ representing i being mistaken about witnessing e, with both E and $fake(i, E)$ recorded as e in $r_i(t+1)$. Further, a faulty agent may misinterpret its own actions, by mistakenly believing to have performed $A' = global(i, t, a')$ despite actually performing $A = global(i, t, a)$, where $a, a' \in Actions_i$. This is coded as a byzantine event $fake(i, A \mapsto A')$ resulting in a' recorded in $r_i(t + 1)$ but the causal effects on the whole system being those of A. The case of $A = A'$ corresponds to a correctly recorded byzantine action. In addition, either of A or A' can be a special byzantine action **noop** representing the absence of actions. If $A = $ **noop**, the agent believes to have performed a' without doing anything. If $A' = $ **noop**, the agent performs A without leaving a local record. Finally, $fail(i) := fake(i, $ **noop** $\mapsto$ **noop**$)$ represents the byzantine inaction and leaves no local record for i. The set of all i's byzantine events, whether mimicking correct events or correct actions, is denoted $BEvents_i$, with $BEvents := \bigsqcup_{i \in A} BEvents_i$.

Apart from correct $\overline{GEvents_i}$ and byzantine $BEvents_i$, the environment issues at most one of the *system events* $SysEvents_i = \{go(i), sleep(i), hibernate(i)\}$ per agent i per round. The correct event $go(i)$ activates i's protocol (see below) for the round. Events $sleep(i)$ and $hibernate(i)$ represent i failing to implement its protocol, with $sleep(i)$ enforcing a local record of the round, whereas $r_i(t+1) = r_i(t)$ is possible for $hibernate(i)$. Thus, $GEvents_i := \overline{GEvents_i} \sqcup BEvents_i \sqcup SysEvents_i$ with $GEvents := \bigsqcup_{i \in A} GEvents_i$ and $GHaps := GEvents \sqcup GActions$. The first event from $BEvents_i$, or $sleep(i)$, or $hibernate(i)$ in a run turns i into *byzantine*. Overall, $r_\epsilon(t+1) := X : r_\epsilon(t)$ for the set $X \subseteq GHaps$ of all haps from round $t + \frac{1}{2}$.

As in this definition of $GEvents_i$, throughout the paper horizontal bars signify the correct subsets of phenomena in question, i.e., $\overline{GEvents_i} \subseteq GEvents_i$, $\overline{GHaps} \subseteq GHaps$, etc. Later, this would also apply to formulas, e.g., $\overline{occurred_i}(o)$ is a correctly recorded occurrence of $o \in Haps_i$ whereas $occurred_i(o)$ is any recorded occurrence. Note that this distinction is only made in the global format because locally agents do not distinguish correct haps from byzantine.

Each agent's *protocol* $P_i : \mathcal{L}_i \to \wp(\wp(Actions_i)) \setminus \{\varnothing\}$ is designed to choose a set of actions based on i's current local state in order to achieve some collective goal. At least one set of actions is always available. In case of multiple options, the choice is up to the *adversary* part of the environment. For asynchronous agents, the global timestamp cannot be inferred from their local state.

The environment governs all events, correct, byzantine, and system, via an environment protocol $P_\epsilon : \mathbb{T} \to \wp(\wp(GEvents)) \setminus \{\varnothing\}$, which *can* depend on a timestamp $t \in \mathbb{T}$ but should not depend on the current state because the environment is assumed to be an impartial physical medium. Both the environment's and agents' protocols are non-deterministic, with the choice among the possible options arbitrarily made by the *adversary* part of the environment. It is also required that all events of round $t + \frac{1}{2}$ be mutually compatible (for time t). The complete list of these *coherency* conditions can be found in [17], of which the following are relevant for this paper: (a) at most one event from $SysEvents_i$ at a time is issued per agent; (b) a correct event observed as e by agent i is never accompanied by a byzantine event that i would also register as e, i.e., an agent cannot be mistaken about observing an event that did happen.[4]

Both the global run $r: \mathbb{T} \to \mathcal{G}$ and its local parts $r_i: \mathbb{T} \to \mathcal{L}_i$ provide a sequence of snapshots of system states. Given the *joint protocol* $P := (P_1, \dots, P_n)$ and the environment's protocol P_ϵ, we focus on $\tau_{f,P_\epsilon,P}$-*transitional runs* r that result from following these protocols and are built according to a *transition relation* $\tau_{f,P_\epsilon,P} \subseteq \mathcal{G} \times \mathcal{G}$ for asynchronous agents at most $f \geq 0$ of which may turn byzantine per run. Each such transitional run progresses by ensuring that $r(t) \, \tau_{f,P_\epsilon,P} \, r(t+1)$, i.e., $(r(t), r(t+1)) \in \tau_{f,P_\epsilon,P}$, for each timestamp $t \in \mathbb{T}$.

Figure 1 represents one round of an asynchronous system governed by $\tau_{f,P_\epsilon,P}$, which consists of the following five consecutive phases:

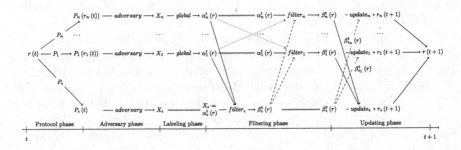

Fig. 1. Details of round $t + \frac{1}{2}$ of a $\tau_{f,P_\epsilon,P}$-transitional run r.

1. Protocol Phase. A non-empty range $P_\epsilon(t) \subseteq \wp(GEvents)$ of possible coherent sets of events is determined by the environment's protocol P_ϵ; for each $i \in \mathcal{A}$, a non-empty range $P_i(r_i(t)) \subseteq \wp(Actions_i)$ of possible sets of i's actions is determined by the agents' joint protocol P.

2. Adversary Phase. The adversary non-deterministically picks one (coherent) set $X_\epsilon \in P_\epsilon(t)$ and one set $X_i \in P_i(r_i(t))$ for each $i \in \mathcal{A}$ from their ranges.

3. Labeling Phase. Locally represented actions in each X_i are translated into the global format: $\alpha_i^t(r) := \{global(i,t,a) \mid a \in X_i\} \subseteq \overline{GActions_i}$.

4. Filtering Phase. Functions $filter_\epsilon$ and $filter_i$ for each $i \in \mathcal{A}$ remove all attempted events from $\alpha_\epsilon^t(r) := X_\epsilon$ and actions from $\alpha_i^t(r)$ that would violate causality. More precisely, the filtering phase is performed in two stages:
1. $filter_\epsilon$ filters out causally impossible events based (a) on the current global state $r(t)$, which could not have been accounted for by P_ϵ, (b) on $\alpha_\epsilon^t(r)$, and (c) on all $\alpha_i^t(r)$, which are not accessible to P_ϵ either. Specifically, two kinds of events are causally impossible and, accordingly, removed by $filter_\epsilon$: (1) each

---
[4] Prohibition (b) does not extend to *actions*, which need not be correctly recorded.

correct receive event that has no matching send either in the global history $r(t)$ or in the current round[5] and (2) all byzantine events if they would have resulted in more than f agents becoming faulty (cf. [17] for details). The resulting set of events to actually occur in round $t + \frac{1}{2}$ is denoted

$$\beta_\epsilon^t (r) := filter_\epsilon \left(r(t), \quad \alpha_\epsilon^t (r), \quad \alpha_1^t (r), \quad \ldots, \quad \alpha_n^t (r) \right).$$

2. For each agent i, $filter_i$ either removes all actions whenever $go(i) \notin \beta_\epsilon^t (r)$ or leaves $\alpha_i^t (r)$ unchanged otherwise. The resulting sets of actions to be actually performed by agents in round $t + \frac{1}{2}$ are denoted

$$\beta_i^t (r) := filter_i \left(\alpha_1^t (r), \quad \ldots, \quad \alpha_n^t (r), \quad \beta_\epsilon^t (r) \right).^6$$

Note that $\beta_i^t (r) \subseteq \alpha_i^t (r) \subseteq \overline{GActions_i}$ and $\beta_\epsilon^t (r) \subseteq \alpha_\epsilon^t (r) \subseteq GEvents$.

5. Updating Phase. The resulting mutually causally consistent events $\beta_\epsilon^t (r)$ and actions $\beta_i^t (r)$ are appended to the global history $r(t)$; for each $i \in \mathcal{A}$, all non-system events from $\beta_{\epsilon_i}^t (r) := \beta_\epsilon^t (r) \cap GEvents_i$ and all actions $\beta_i^t (r)$ are appended in the local form to the local history $r_i(t)$, which may remain unchanged if no action or event triggers an update or be appended with the empty set if an update is triggered only by a system event $go(i)$ or $sleep(i)$:

$$r_\epsilon (t + 1) := update_\epsilon \left(r_\epsilon (t), \quad \beta_\epsilon^t (r), \quad \beta_1^t (r), \quad \ldots, \quad \beta_n^t (r) \right);$$
$$r_i (t + 1) := update_i \left(r_i (t), \quad \beta_i^t (r), \quad \beta_\epsilon^t (r) \right).^7$$

Since only the protocol phase depends on the specific protocols P and P_ϵ, the operations in the remaining phases 2–5 can be grouped into a *transition template* τ_f that produces a transition relation $\tau_{f,P_\epsilon,P}$ given P and P_ϵ.

Properties of runs that cannot be implemented on a round-by-round basis, e.g., *liveness properties* requiring certain things to happen in a run *eventually*, are enforced by restricting the set of allowable runs by *admissibility conditions* Ψ defined as subsets of the set R of all transitional runs. For example, no goal can be achieved unless agents are guaranteed to act from time to time. Thus, it is standard to impose the *Fair Schedule* (*FS*) admissibility condition, which ensures that each *correct* agent is eventually given a possibility to follow its protocol: $FS := \{ r \mid (\forall i \in \mathcal{A}) (\forall t \in \mathbb{T}) (\exists t' \geq t) \beta_\epsilon^{t'} (r) \cap SysEvents_i \neq \varnothing \}$. In scheduling terms, *FS* demands that the environment either provide or wrongfully deny CPU time for every processor infinitely many times. Thus, a process is always given an opportunity to act, unless its faults $sleep(i)$ and/or $hibernate(i)$ persist infinitely often.

Definition 1. *A context* $\gamma = (P_\epsilon, \mathscr{G}(0), \tau_f, \Psi)$ *consists of the environment's protocol* P_ϵ, *a set of global initial states* $\mathscr{G}(0)$, *a transition template* τ_f *for* $f \geq 0$,

---

[5] In $\alpha_\epsilon^t (r)$ for byzantine sends or in $\alpha_i^t (r)$ for correct ones that will be actually performed (see filtering stage 2).

[6] Arguments $\alpha_j^t (r)$ for $j \neq i$ are redundant here but will be used in future extensions.

[7] Full definitions of $update_\epsilon$ and $update_i$ are presented in Appendix in Definition 16.

and an admissibility condition Ψ. For a joint protocol P, we call $\chi = (\gamma, P)$ an agent-context. A run $r \in R$ is called weakly χ-consistent *if $r(0) \in \mathscr{G}(0)$ and the run is $\tau_{f, P_\epsilon, P}$-transitional. A weakly χ-consistent run r is called* (strongly) χ-consistent *if $r \in \Psi$. The set of all χ-consistent runs is denoted R^χ. Agent-context χ is called* non-excluding *if any finite prefix of a weakly χ-consistent run can be extended to a strongly χ-consistent run.*

We distinguish types of agents depending on their expected malfunctions. Let $FEvents_i := BEvents_i \sqcup \{sleep\,(i), hibernate\,(i)\}$ be all faulty events for agent i.

Definition 2. *Environment's protocol P_ϵ makes an agent $i \in \mathcal{A}$:*

  (i) fallible *if $X \in P_\epsilon(t)$ implies $\{fail\,(i)\} \cup X \in P_\epsilon(t)$;*
  (ii) delayable *if $X \in P_\epsilon(t)$ implies $X \setminus GEvents_i \in P_\epsilon(t)$;*
  (iii) error-prone *if $X \in P_\epsilon(t)$ implies that any coherent set $Y \sqcup (X \setminus FEvents_i) \in P_\epsilon(t)$ for $Y \subseteq FEvents_i$;*
  (iv) gullible *if $X \in P_\epsilon(t)$ implies that any coherent set $Y \sqcup (X \setminus GEvents_i) \in P_\epsilon(t)$ for $Y \subseteq FEvents_i$;*
  (v) fully byzantine *if it is error-prone and gullible.*

Thus, fallible agents can always be faulty with the same behavior; delayable agents can be prevented from waking up; error-prone (gullible) agents can exhibit any faults in addition to (without) correct events, thus, implying fallibility (delayability); fully byzantine agents exhibit the widest range of faults.

3   Epistemic Modeling of Byzantine Faults

The runs-and-systems framework is traditionally used as a basis for interpreted systems, a special kind of Kripke models for multi-agent distributed environments [6]. For an agent-context χ, we consider pairs (r, t') of a run $r \in R^\chi$ and timestamp $t' \in \mathbb{T}$. A *valuation function* $\pi \colon Prop \to \wp(R^\chi \times \mathbb{T})$ determines where an atomic proposition from $Prop$ is true. The determination is arbitrary except for a small set of *designated atomic propositions* (and more complex formulas built from them) whose truth value is fully determined by r and t'. More specifically, for $i \in \mathcal{A}$, $o \in Haps_i$, and $t \in \mathbb{T}$ such that $t \le t'$,

- $correct_{(i,t)}$ is true at (r, t') iff no faulty event happened to i by timestamp t, i.e., no event from $FEvents_i$ appears in the $r_\epsilon(t)$ prefix of the $r_\epsilon(t')$ part of $r(t')$;
- $correct_i$ is true at (r, t') iff no faulty event happened to i yet, i.e., no event from $FEvents_i$ appears in $r_\epsilon(t')$ (this is the formal definition of what it means for an agent i to be *correct*; the agent is *faulty* or *byzantine* iff it is not correct);
- $fake_{(i,t)}(o)$ is true at (r, t') iff i has a *faulty* reason to believe that $o \in Haps_i$ occurred in round $t - \frac{1}{2}$, i.e., $o \in r_i(t)$ because (at least in part) of some $O \in BEvents_i \cap \beta_\epsilon^{t-1}(r)$;
- $\overline{occurred}_{(i,t)}(o)$ is true at (r, t') iff i has a *correct* reason to believe that $o \in Haps_i$ occurred in round $t - \frac{1}{2}$, i.e., $o \in r_i(t)$ because (at least in part) of some $O \in (\overline{GEvents_i} \cap \beta_\epsilon^{t-1}(r)) \sqcup \beta_i^{t-1}(r)$;

- $\overline{occurred}_i(o)$ is true at (r, t') iff at least one of $\overline{occurred}_{(i,m)}(o)$ for $1 \leq m \leq t'$ is; also $\overline{occurred}(o) := \bigvee_{i \in \mathcal{A}} \overline{occurred}_i(o)$;
- $occurred_i(o)$ is true at (r, t') iff either $\overline{occurred}_i(o)$ is or at least one of $fake_{(i,m)}(o)$ for $1 \leq m \leq t'$ is.

An *interpreted system* is a pair $\mathcal{I} = (R^\chi, \pi)$. We combine the standard epistemic language with the standard temporal language $\varphi ::= p \mid \neg\varphi \mid (\varphi \wedge \varphi) \mid K_i\varphi \mid \Box\varphi$ for $p \in Prop$ and $i \in \mathcal{A}$, with other Boolean connectives defined in the usual way and $\Diamond\varphi := \neg\Box\neg\varphi$. Truth for these *formulas* is defined in the standard way, in particular, for a run $r \in R^\chi$, timestamp $t \in \mathbb{T}$, atomic proposition $p \in Prop$, agent $i \in \mathcal{A}$, and formula φ we have $(\mathcal{I}, r, t) \models p$ iff $(r, t) \in \pi(p)$; $(\mathcal{I}, r, t) \models K_i\varphi$ iff $(\mathcal{I}, r', t') \models \varphi$ for any $r' \in R^\chi$ and $t' \in \mathbb{T}$ such that $r_i(t) = r'_i(t')$; and $(\mathcal{I}, r, t) \models \Box\varphi$ iff $(\mathcal{I}, r, t') \models \varphi$ for all $t' \geq t$ in the same run r. A formula φ is valid in $\mathcal{I}$, written $\mathcal{I} \models \varphi$, iff $(\mathcal{I}, r, t) \models \varphi$ for all $r \in R^\chi$ and $t \in \mathbb{T}$.

Due to the coherency of protocol P_ϵ, an agent cannot be both right and wrong about an occurrence of an event, i.e., $\mathcal{I} \models \neg(\overline{occurred}_{(i,t)}(e) \wedge fake_{(i,t)}(e))$ for any $i \in \mathcal{A}$, event $e \in Events_i$, and $t \in \mathbb{T}$. Note that for actions this *can* happen.

Following the concept from [7] of global events that are local for an agent, we define conditions under which formulas can be treated as such local events. A formula φ is called *localized for i within an agent-context χ* iff $r_i(t) = r'_i(t')$ implies $(\mathcal{I}, r, t) \models \varphi \Longleftrightarrow (\mathcal{I}, r', t') \models \varphi$ for any $\mathcal{I} = (R^\chi, \pi)$, runs $r, r' \in R^\chi$, and $t, t' \in \mathbb{T}$. By these definitions, we immediately obtain:

Lemma 3. *The following statements are valid for any formula φ localized for an agent $i \in \mathcal{A}$ within an agent-context χ and any interpreted system $\mathcal{I} = (R^\chi, \pi)$:*

$$\mathcal{I} \models \varphi \leftrightarrow K_i\varphi \qquad and \qquad \mathcal{I} \models \neg\varphi \leftrightarrow K_i\neg\varphi.$$

The knowledge of preconditions principle [22] postulates that in order to act on a precondition an agent must be able to infer it from its local state. Thus, the preceding lemma shows that formulas localized for i can *always* be used as preconditions. Our first observation is that the agent's *perceptions* of a run are one example of such epistemically acceptable (though not necessarily reliable) preconditions:

Lemma 4. *For any agent-context χ, agent $i \in \mathcal{A}$, and local hap $o \in Haps_i$, the formula $occurred_i(o)$ is localized for i within χ.*

4 Run Modifications

By contrast, as we will demonstrate, correctness of these perceptions is not localized for i and, hence, cannot be the basis for actions. In fact, correctness can never be established by an agent. Such impossibility results are proved by means of controlled *run modifications*.

Definition 5. *A function $\rho \colon R^\chi \longrightarrow \wp(\overline{GActions}_i) \times \wp(GEvents_i)$ is called an i-intervention for an agent-context χ and agent $i \in \mathcal{A}$. A joint intervention*

$B = (\rho_1, \ldots, \rho_n)$ *consists of i-interventions ρ_i for each agent $i \in \mathcal{A}$. An adjustment $[B_t; \ldots; B_0]$ is a sequence of joint interventions $B_0 \ldots, B_t$ to be performed at rounds from ½ to $t + ½$ for some timestamp $t \in \mathbb{T}$.*

An i-intervention $\rho(r) = (X, X_\epsilon)$ applied to a round $t + ½$ of a given run r can be seen as a meta-action modifying the results of this round for i in such a way that $\beta_i^t(r') = X$ and $\beta_{\epsilon_i}^t(r') = \beta_\epsilon^t(r') \cap GEvents_i = X_\epsilon$ in the artificially constructed new run r'. We denote $\mathfrak{a}\rho(r) := X$ and $\mathfrak{e}\rho(r) := X_\epsilon$. Accordingly, a joint intervention $(\rho_1, \ldots, \rho_n)$ prescribes actions $\beta_i^t(r') = \mathfrak{a}\rho_i(r)$ for each agent i and events $\beta_\epsilon^t(r') = \bigsqcup_{i \in \mathcal{A}} \mathfrak{e}\rho_i(r)$ for the round in question. Thus, an adjustment $[B_t; \ldots; B_0]$ fully determines actions and events in the initial $t + 1$ rounds of run r':

Definition 6. *Let $adj = [B_t; \ldots; B_0]$ be an adjustment where $B_m = (\rho_1^m, \ldots, \rho_n^m)$ for each $0 \leq m \leq t$ and each ρ_i^m is an i-intervention for an agent-context $\chi = ((P_\epsilon, \mathscr{G}(0), \tau_f, \Psi), P)$. A run r' is obtained from $r \in R^\chi$ by adjustment adj iff for all $t' \leq t$, all $T > t$, and all $i \in \mathcal{A}$,*

1. $r'(0) := r(0)$,
2. $r_i'(t' + 1) := update_i(r_i'(t'), \mathfrak{a}\rho_i^{t'}(r), \bigsqcup_{i \in \mathcal{A}} \mathfrak{e}\rho_i^{t'}(r))$,
3. $r_\epsilon'(t' + 1) := update_\epsilon(r_\epsilon'(t'), \bigsqcup_{i \in \mathcal{A}} \mathfrak{e}\rho_i^{t'}(r), \mathfrak{a}\rho_1^{t'}(r), \ldots, \mathfrak{a}\rho_n^{t'}(r))$,
4. $r'(T) \tau_{f,P_\epsilon,P} r'(T + 1)$.

We denote by $R(\tau_{f,P_\epsilon,P}, r, adj)$ the set of all runs obtained from r by adj.

Note that generally not all adjusted runs are $\tau_{f,P_\epsilon,P}$-transitional, i.e., obey Prop. 4 also for $t' \leq t$. Thus, special care is required to produce $\tau_{f,P_\epsilon,P}$-transitional adjustments with required properties. To demonstrate the impossibility of establishing knowledge of correctness, we use several adjustment types to formalize the infamous *brain in a vat* scenario[8], where one agent, the "brain," is to experience a fabricated, i.e., faulty, version of its local history from a given run, whereas all other agents are to remain in their initial states (and made faulty or not at will). This is achieved by using interventions (a) *Fake$_i$* for brain i and (b) *CFreeze* (resp. *BFreeze$_j$*) for other agents j that are to be correct (resp. byzantine).

Definition 7. *For an agent-context χ, agent $i \in \mathcal{A}$, and run $r \in R^\chi$, we define i-interventions $CFreeze(r) := (\varnothing, \varnothing)$, and $BFreeze_i(r) := (\varnothing, \{fail(i)\})$, and*

$$Fake_i^t(r) := (\varnothing,$$

$$\{fail(i)\} \quad \cup \quad (\beta_\epsilon^t(r) \cap BEvents_i) \quad \cup \quad \{fake(i, E) \mid E \in \beta_\epsilon^t(r) \cap \overline{GEvents_i}\} \quad \cup$$

$$\{fake(i, \mathbf{noop} \mapsto A) \mid A \in \beta_i^t(r)\} \quad \sqcup \quad \{sleep(i) \mid r_i(t+1) \neq r_i(t)\}). \quad (1)$$

The following Brain-in-a-Vat Lemma 8, whose proof can be found in the appendix, constructs the desired modified transitional run:

---

[8] For connections to the semantic externalism and a survey of philosophical literature on the subject, see [25].

Lemma 8 (Brain in a Vat). *For an agent $i \in \mathcal{A}$, for an agent-context $\chi = ((P_\epsilon, \mathcal{G}(0), \tau_f, \Psi), P)$ such that P_ϵ makes i gullible and every $j \neq i$ delayable and fallible, for a set $Byz \subseteq \mathcal{A} \setminus \{i\}$ such that $|Byz| + 1 \leq f$, for a run $r \in R^\chi$, and for a timestamp $t > 0$, we consider an adjustment $adj = [B_{t-1}; \ldots; B_0]$ such that $B_m = (\rho_1^m, \ldots, \rho_n^m)$ with $\rho_i^m = Fake_i^m$, with $\rho_j^m = BFreeze_j$ for $j \in Byz$, and with $\rho_j^m = CFreeze$ for $j \notin \{i\} \sqcup Byz$ for all $0 \leq m \leq t - 1$. Then each run $r' \in R(\tau_{f,P_\epsilon,P}, r, adj)$ satisfies the following properties:*

1. *r' is weakly χ-consistent; if $r' \in \Psi$, then $r' \in R^\chi$;*
2. *$(\forall m \leq t)\, r_i'(m) = r_i(m)$;*
3. *$(\forall m \leq t)(\forall j \neq i)\, r_j'(m) = r_j'(0)$.*
4. *agents from $\mathcal{A} \setminus (\{i\} \sqcup Byz)$ remain correct until t.*
5. *i and all agents from Byz become faulty already in round ½;*
6. *$(\forall m < t)(\forall j \neq i)\, \beta_{\epsilon_j}^m(r') \subseteq \{fail(j)\}$. More precisely,*
   $\beta_{\epsilon_j}^m(r') = \varnothing$ iff $\rho_j^m = CFreeze$ and $\beta_{\epsilon_j}^m(r') = \{fail(j)\}$ iff $\rho_j^m = BFreeze_j$;
7. *$(\forall m < t)\, \beta_{\epsilon_i}^m(r') \setminus FEvents_i = \varnothing$;*
8. *$(\forall m < t)(\forall j \in \mathcal{A})\, \beta_j^m(r') = \varnothing$.*

Corollary 9. *If χ is non-excluding, for $t \in \mathbb{T}$ there is a run $r' \in R^\chi$ constructed according to Lemma 8, such that for any $\mathcal{I} = (R^\chi, \pi)$, $o \in Haps$, $j \in \{i\} \sqcup Byz$, and $k \notin \{i\} \sqcup Byz$,*

$$(\mathcal{I}, r', t) \not\models \overline{occurred}(o), \qquad (\mathcal{I}, r', t) \not\models correct_j, \qquad (\mathcal{I}, r', t) \models correct_k. \quad (2)$$

5 Byzantine Limitations of Certainty

The ability to construct a Brain-in-a-Vat run r' in Lemma 8 and its properties in Corollary 9 spell doom for the strategy of asynchronous agents waiting for a definitive proof of correctness before acting. More precisely, agents can never learn a particular event actually happened, nor that they are not byzantine.

Throughout this section, $\chi = ((P_\epsilon, \mathcal{G}(0), \tau_f, \Psi), P)$ is a non-excluding agent-context such that P_ϵ makes agent $i \in \mathcal{A}$ gullible and every other agent $k \neq i$ delayable and fallible (in particular, this covers the case of fully byzantine agents), $\mathcal{I} = (R^\chi, \pi)$ is an interpreted system, and $o \in Haps$.

Theorem 10. *If $f \geq 1$, then for $k \neq i$ the following statements are valid in $\mathcal{I}$:*

$$\mathcal{I} \models \neg K_i \overline{occurred}(o), \qquad \mathcal{I} \models \neg K_i correct_i, \qquad \mathcal{I} \models \neg K_i \neg correct_k. \quad (3)$$

Proof. For any $r \in R^\chi$ and $t \in \mathbb{T}$, by Lemma 8 with $Byz = \varnothing$ and non-exclusiveness of χ, there is $r' \in R^\chi$ such that (2) for $j = i$ and $k \neq i$ holds by Corollary 9. $(\mathcal{I}, r, t) \models \neg K_i \overline{occurred}(o) \wedge \neg K_i correct_i \wedge \neg K_i \neg correct_k$ follows from $r_i(t) = r_i'(t)$ by Lemma 8.2. $\square$

Remark 11. While agent i can never learn that it is correct or that another agent k is faulty, agent i might be able to detect its own faults, for instance, by comparing actions prescribed by its protocol against actions recorded in its local history.

The case of $f = 0$ corresponds to a system without byzantine faults, where correctness of all actions, events, and agents is common knowledge. When $f = 1$, in view of Remark 11, the agent may be able to conclude that all other agents are correct. By reusing the proof of Theorem 10 with $Byz = \{k\}$, we can establish that for $f \geq 2$ this determination is not possible either:

Theorem 12. *If $f \geq 2$ and $k \neq i$, the validity $\mathcal{I} \models \neg K_i \, correct_k$ holds.*

6   Epistemes for Distributed Analysis and Design

The results of Sect. 5 clearly show that most desired properties, such as trigger events, cannot be used as preconditions in asynchronous byzantine settings. The knowledge of a precondition φ requirement stated in [22], i.e., that an agent only act on φ when the agent is sure φ is not false, would typically lead for such simple preconditions to no actions being taken at all: even when an asynchronous agent is correct, it can never discount the scenario of being a brain in a vat. This is, in fact, a "human condition", as philosophy and science have yet to provide a definitive way of discounting each of us being a brain in a vat (see [20] for discussion). It then stands to reason that the human response to act as if everything is fine could also be applied in distributed scenarios. This led to the soft or *defeasible* knowledge $B_i\varphi := K_i(correct_i \rightarrow \varphi)$ considered, e.g., in [23]. In other words, the agent only considers situations where it has not been compromised and, while φ is the desired property, the agent acts on the precondition $correct_i \rightarrow \varphi$ relativized to its correctness.

We believe that this formulation can be improved in at least two directions. Firstly, a typical specification for a fault-tolerant system does not impose any restrictions on byzantine agents. For instance, in distributed consensus, all correct agents must agree on a common value, whereas faulty agents are exempted. Consequently, in a correctness proof for a particular protocol, it is common to verify $B_i\varphi$ only for correct agents. In effect, the condition being verified in such correctness analyses is $H_i\varphi := correct_i \rightarrow K_i(correct_i \rightarrow \varphi)$, which we call the *hope* modality. Note that H_i is not localized for i because, by Theorem 10, the agent itself can never ascertain its own correctness. On the other hand, per Remark 11, the agent can in some cases learn its own faultiness. Assuming the agent is malfunctioning rather than malicious, this information can be used to implement self-correcting protocols or, at least, to minimize the effects of detected faults on the system as a whole. Therefore, exploiting negative introspection and factivity of K_i, we consider the modality *credence* defined by $Cr_i\varphi := \neg K_i\neg correct_i \wedge K_i(correct_i \rightarrow \varphi)$, which is always localized, for protocol design.

Further, Definition 2 shows that our framework easily models agents whose faultiness is restricted in a particular way. For instance, the *send omissions failures* from [24], where an agent may fail to send some of the required messages, arbitrary *receiving failures*, where an agent may receive incorrect messages (or not receive correct ones), and the well-studied *crash failures* can easily be defined. It suffices to introduce restricted propositions such as $crashcorrect_i$, $sendcorrect_i$,

$receivecorrect_i$ and define high-level logical descriptions of the appropriate type of errors on top of it. E.g., replacing $K_i(correct_i \rightarrow \varphi)$ with $K_i(receivecorrect_i \rightarrow \varphi)$ if the truth of φ relies solely on correct communication shrinks the pool of situations ignored by the protocol to only those faults that do impede the agent's ability to ascertain φ.

The following basic relationships among the proposed modalities describing various preconditions immediately follow from the standard S5 properties of K_i:

Lemma 13. *For any formula φ, any agent i, the following formulas are valid in every interpreted system:*

$$\models K_i\varphi \rightarrow B_i\varphi \qquad\qquad \models Cr_i\varphi \rightarrow B_i\varphi \qquad \models B_i\varphi \rightarrow H_i\varphi$$
$$\models correct_i \rightarrow (H_i\varphi \rightarrow Cr_i\varphi) \qquad\qquad\qquad \models \neg correct_i \rightarrow H_i\varphi$$
$$\models K_i\varphi \rightarrow \varphi \qquad\qquad\qquad\qquad\qquad \models correct_i \rightarrow (B_i\varphi \rightarrow \varphi)$$
$$\models correct_i \rightarrow (Cr_i\varphi \rightarrow \varphi) \qquad\qquad \models correct_i \rightarrow (H_i\varphi \rightarrow \varphi)$$
$$\models B_i\varphi \rightarrow K_i B_i\varphi \qquad\qquad\qquad\qquad \models Cr_i\varphi \rightarrow K_i Cr_i\varphi$$
$$\models K_i correct_i \rightarrow (H_i\varphi \rightarrow K_i\varphi)$$

As follows from the preceding lemma, credence is stronger than belief, which is stronger than hope, with knowledge also being stronger than belief. However, for a correct agent, credence, belief, and hope all become equivalent, while knowledge generally remains stronger; for fault-free systems, this hierarchy collapses to the standard notion of knowledge. A faulty agent, however, automatically hopes for everything, making it unnecessary to check preconditions for faulty agents while verifying system correctness. At the same time, all four modalities are factive for correct agents (knowledge is factive for all agents), making them acceptable as precondition criteria modulo correctness. Finally, belief and credence satisfy the self-awareness condition that one should know one's own convictions (cf., e.g., [16]). On the other hand, hope, which represents an external view, does not generally satisfy $H_i\varphi \rightarrow K_i H_i\varphi$. A complete axiomatization of the hope modality, obtained by adding to K45 the axioms $correct_i \rightarrow (H_i\varphi \rightarrow \varphi)$, $\neg correct_i \rightarrow H_i\varphi$, and $H_i correct_i$, can be found in [9].

7   Conclusions and Future Work

We presented a general framework for reasoning about knowledge in multi-agent message-passing systems with byzantine agents. Thanks to its modularity, it allows to model any timing and synchrony properties of agents and messages. We demonstrated the utility of our framework by successfully modeling the brain-in-a-vat scenario in a system of asynchronous agents, some of which are byzantine. Since this result implies that the knowledge of preconditions principle puts severe restrictions on allowable preconditions, we introduced weaker modalities, credence and hope, for the design and analysis of protocols respectively, which translate desired properties into actionable preconditions.

Part of our current work is devoted to further exploring these modalities, as well as their mutual relationships, and to the study of causality in fault-tolerant distributed systems, with the view of obtaining necessary conditions for iterated, coordinated, and simultaneous actions. Future work will be devoted to also incorporate protocols, which are currently specified outside our combined temporal–epistemic logic, into the logic itself, e.g., by using a suitably adaptation of dynamic epistemic logic.

A   Appendix

This section is dedicated to proving the Brain-in-a-Vat Lemma. Before engaging with the proof, we flesh out necessary details of how our framework operates.

For a function $f\colon \Sigma \to \Theta$ and a set $X \subseteq \Sigma$ we use the following notation: $f(X) := \{f(x) \mid x \in X\} \subseteq \Theta$. For functions with multiple arguments, we allow ourselves to mix and match elements with sets of elements, e.g., $global(i, \mathbb{T}, Actions_i) := \{global(i, t, a) \mid t \in \mathbb{T}, a \in Actions_i\}$. As stated in Sect. 2, the function $global\colon \bigsqcup_{i \in \mathcal{A}} (\{i\} \times \mathbb{T} \times Actions_i) \longrightarrow \overline{GActions}$ must be total and satisfy the following properties: for arbitrary $i, j \in \mathcal{A}$, and $t, t' \in \mathbb{T}$, and $a \in Actions_i$, and $b \in Actions_j$,

1. $global(i, \mathbb{T}, Actions_i) = \overline{GActions_i}$;
2. $global(i, t, a) \neq global(j, t', b)$ whenever $(i, t, a) \neq (j, t', b)$.

Thus, it is possible to define an inverse function on $\overline{GHaps} := \overline{GEvents} \sqcup \overline{GActions}$:

Definition 14. *We use a function* $local\colon \overline{GHaps} \longrightarrow Haps$ *converting correct haps from the global format into the local ones for the respective agents in such a way that, for any $i \in \mathcal{A}$, $t \in \mathbb{T}$, and $a \in Actions_i$, (1) $local(\overline{GActions_i}) = Actions_i$; (2) $local(\overline{GEvents_i}) = Events_i$; (3) $local(global(i, t, a)) = a$.*

Recall that $\overline{GEvents_i} \cap \overline{GEvents_j} = \varnothing$ for $i \neq j$,

$$BEvents_i := \{fake(i, E) \mid E \in \overline{GEvents_i}\} \quad \sqcup$$
$$\{fake(i, A \mapsto A') \mid A, A' \in \{\mathbf{noop}\} \sqcup \overline{GActions_i}\},$$

and $SysEvents_i := \{go(i), sleep(i), hibernate(i)\}$. While for correct haps, *local* provides a translation to local format on a hap-by-hap basis, the same cannot be extended to all haps because system events from $SysEvents_i$ and byzantine actions $fake(i, A \mapsto \mathbf{noop})$ do not correspond to any local hap, to be recorded in i's history. Thus, the *localization function* σ is defined on sets of global haps:

Definition 15. *We define a localization function* $\sigma\colon \wp(GHaps) \longrightarrow \wp(Haps)$:

$$\sigma(X) := local\Big((X \cap \overline{GHaps}) \quad \cup \quad \{E \mid (\exists i)\, fake(i, E) \in X\} \quad \cup$$
$$\{A' \neq \mathbf{noop} \mid (\exists i)(\exists A)\, fake(i, A \mapsto A') \in X\}\Big).$$

Thus, as intended, for any $E \in \overline{GEvents}_i$, the local record left by $fake\,(i, E)$ for agent i is the same as the record of E, whereas for any $A' \in \overline{GActions}_i$ and any $A \in \{\mathbf{noop}\} \sqcup \overline{GActions}_i$, the local record of $fake\,(i, A \mapsto A')$ for i is the same as that of A', whichever action A was taken in reality.

Definition 16. *We abbreviate $X := X_\epsilon, X_1, \ldots, X_n$ and $X_{\epsilon_i} := X_\epsilon \cap GEvents_i$ for a tuple of performed events $X_\epsilon \subseteq GEvents$ and actions $X_i \subseteq \overline{GActions}_i$ for each $i \in \mathcal{A}$. Given a global state $r\,(t) = (r_\epsilon\,(t), r_1\,(t), \ldots, r_n\,(t)) \in \mathcal{G}$, we define agent i's update function $update_i: \mathcal{L}_i \times \wp(\overline{GActions}_i) \times \wp(GEvents) \to \mathcal{L}_i$ that outputs a new local state from $\mathcal{L}_i$ based on i's actions X_i and events X_ϵ:*

$$update_i\,(r_i\,(t), X_i, X_\epsilon) := \begin{cases} r_i\,(t) & \text{if } \sigma(X_{\epsilon_i}) = \varnothing \text{ and} \\ & X_\epsilon \cap \{go(i), sleep(i)\} = \varnothing \\ \left[\sigma\big(X_{\epsilon_i} \sqcup X_i\big)\right] : r_i\,(t) & \text{otherwise.} \end{cases}$$

(note that, in transitional runs, $update_i$ is always used after the action $filter_i$; thus, in the absence of $go(i)$, it is always the case that $X_i = \varnothing$). Similarly, the environment's state update function

$$update_\epsilon: \mathcal{L}_\epsilon \times \wp\,(GEvents) \times \wp\left(\overline{GActions}_1\right) \times \cdots \times \wp\left(\overline{GActions}_n\right) \to \mathcal{L}_\epsilon$$

outputs a new state of the environment based on events X_ϵ and all actions X_i: $update_\epsilon\,(r_\epsilon\,(t), X) := (X_\epsilon \sqcup X_1 \sqcup \cdots \sqcup X_n): r_\epsilon\,(t)$. Summarizing,

$$update\,(r\,(t), X) :=$$
$$\left(update_\epsilon\,(r_\epsilon\,(t), X), update_1\,(r_1\,(t), X_1, X_\epsilon), \ldots, update_n\,(r_n\,(t), X_n, X_\epsilon)\right).$$

The following properties directly follow from Definition 7 of the i-intervention $Fake_i^t$:

Lemma 17. *Let $t \in \mathbb{T}$ and r be an arbitrary run. Then*
1. $aFake_i^t\,(r) = \varnothing$, *i.e., $Fake_i^t$ removes all actions.*
2. $go(i) \notin eFake_i^t\,(r)$, *i.e., $Fake_i^t$ never lets agent i act.*
3. $\sigma\left(aFake_i^t\,(r) \sqcup eFake_i^t\,(r)\right) = \sigma\left(eFake_i^t\,(r)\right) = \sigma\left(\beta_i^t\,(r) \sqcup \beta_{\epsilon_i}^t\,(r)\right)$.
4. $r_i(t+1) \neq r_i(t)$ *iff* $eFake_i^t\,(r) \cap \{go(i), sleep(i)\} \neq \varnothing$.

The last two properties mean that from i's local perspective, the intervention is imperceptible (also when agent i was unaware of the passing round in the given run).

*Proof (of **Brain-in-a-Vat Lemma** 8).* Let $r' \in R\,(\tau_{f,P_\epsilon},P,r,adj)$. Prop. 6 follows from the definitions of $CFreeze$ and $BFreeze_j$. Prop. 7 follows from (1). Prop. 8 follows from Lemma 17.1 for i and from the definitions of $CFreeze$ and $BFreeze_j$ for $j \neq i$. Prop. 5 follows from (1) for i and from the definition of $BFreeze_j$ for $j \in Byz$. Prop. 2–4 depend solely on rounds from $\frac{1}{2}$ to $t - \frac{1}{2}$ of r', whereas the transitionality of r' for Prop. 1 from round $t + \frac{1}{2}$ onward directly follows from Definition 6. We now show Prop. 1–4 for $m \leq t$ by induction on m.

R. Kuznets et al.
274

Base: $m = 0$. Prop. 3–4 and transitionality for Prop. 1 are trivial. Prop. 2 follows from Definition 6.

Step from m to $m + 1$. We prove Prop. 1 based on the gullibility of i and delayability (and fallibility) of all other $j \neq i$. In order to show that $r(m) \; \tau_{f,P_\epsilon,P} \; r(m+1)$, we need to demonstrate that the β-sets prescribed by adj can be obtained in a regular round. Since the adversary's choice of actions $\alpha_j^m(r)$ for all $j \in \mathcal{A}$ is immaterial due to the absence of $go(j)$ (by Prop. 7 for i and Prop. 6 for other $j \neq i$), we concentrate on ensuring the adversary can choose suitable α-sets of events. Consider $\alpha_\epsilon^m(r) \in P_\epsilon(m)$ from the original run r. The set $\alpha_\epsilon^m(r)$ is coherent because r is transitional. By the delayability of all $j \neq i$, $\alpha_{\epsilon_i}^m(r) := \alpha_\epsilon^m(r) \cap GEvents_i = \alpha_\epsilon^m(r) \setminus \bigsqcup_{j \neq i} GEvents_j \in P_\epsilon(m)$. Note that for any $Z \subseteq FEvents_i$, $(\alpha_{\epsilon_i}^m(r) \setminus GEvents_i) \sqcup Z = \varnothing \sqcup Z = Z$ because $\alpha_{\epsilon_i}^m(r) \subseteq GEvents_i$. Thus, by the gullibility of i,

$$\alpha_{\epsilon_i}^m(r') := \{fail(i)\} \quad \cup \quad (\beta_\epsilon^m(r) \cap BEvents_i) \quad \cup$$
$$\{fake(i, E) \mid E \in \beta_\epsilon^m(r) \cap \overline{GEvents_i}\} \quad \cup$$
$$\{fake(i, \mathbf{noop} \mapsto A) \mid A \in \beta_i^m(r)\} \quad \sqcup \quad \{sleep(i) \mid r_i(t+1) \neq r_i(t)\} \in P_\epsilon(m)$$

(note that this set is coherent because it contains no correct events and neither $go(i)$ nor $hibernate(i)$). Finally, by the fallibility of all agents $j \in Byz$, $\alpha_\epsilon^m(r') := \alpha_{\epsilon_i}^m(r') \sqcup \{fail(j) \mid j \in Byz\} \in P_\epsilon(m)$. This $\alpha_\epsilon^m(r')$ is coherent and unaffected by filtering (there are no correct receives in $\alpha_\epsilon^m(r')$ to be filtered out, and only at most f agents from $\{i\} \sqcup Byz$ become byzantine).

It remains to show that filtering turns these sets $\alpha_\epsilon^m(r'), \alpha_1^m(r'), \ldots, \alpha_n^m(r')$ into the exact β-sets prescribed by the adjustment adj. Let us abbreviate:

$$\Upsilon := filter_\epsilon\big(r'(m), \quad \alpha_\epsilon^m(r'), \quad \alpha_1^m(r'), \quad \ldots, \quad \alpha_n^m(r')\big) = \alpha_\epsilon^m(r'),$$
$$\Xi_j := filter_j\big(\alpha_1^m(r'), \quad \ldots, \quad \alpha_n^m(r'), \quad \Upsilon\big).$$

Our goal is to show that $\Upsilon_j := \Upsilon \cap GEvents_j = \beta_{\epsilon_j}^m(r')$ and $\Xi_j = \beta_j^m(r')$ for each $j \in \mathcal{A}$. After the filtering phase, for our i and $j \neq i$, we have the following:

$$\Upsilon_i = \alpha_\epsilon^m(r') \cap GEvents_i = \alpha_{\epsilon_i}^m(r') = \beta_{\epsilon_i}^m(r'),$$

$$\Upsilon_j = \alpha_\epsilon^m(r') \cap GEvents_j = \begin{cases} \varnothing & \text{if } \rho_j^m = CFreeze, \\ \{fail(j)\} & \text{if } \rho_j^m = BFreeze_j, \end{cases}$$

the latter being exactly $\beta_{\epsilon_j}^m(r')$. Since $go(j) \notin \Upsilon$ for any $j \in \mathcal{A}$, we also have that $\Xi_j = \varnothing = \beta_j^m(r')$ for all $j \in \mathcal{A}$. This completes the induction step for Prop. 1.

For Prop. 2, the induction step follows from Lemma 17.3–4. We have:

- if $\sigma\big(\beta_{\epsilon_i}^m(r)\big) \neq \varnothing$, then $r_i(m+1) = \sigma\big(\beta_i^m(r) \sqcup \beta_{\epsilon_i}^m(r)\big) \colon r_i(m) = \sigma\big(\beta_i^m(r) \sqcup \beta_\epsilon^m(r)\big) \colon r_i'(m)$ by IH. It remains to use Lemma 17.3 to see that the last expression is the same as $\sigma\big(\beta_i^m(r') \sqcup \beta_\epsilon^m(r')\big) \colon r_i'(m) = r_i'(m+1)$.

- if $\sigma\big(\beta_{\epsilon_i}^m(r)\big) = \varnothing$ but $r_i(m+1) \neq r_i(m)$, then $r_i(m+1) = \sigma\big(\beta_i^m(r) \sqcup \beta_{\epsilon_i}^m(r)\big) \colon r_i(m) = \sigma(\beta_i^m(r)) \colon r_i(m) = \sigma(\beta_i^m(r)) \colon r_i'(m)$ by IH. By Lemma 17.4, we also have $r_i'(m+1) \neq r_i'(m)$. Thus, this case can be concluded by using Lemma 17.3 as it was done in the previous case.

- if $\sigma\left(\beta_{\epsilon_i}^m(r)\right) = \varnothing$ and $r_i(m+1) = r_i(m)$, then $r_i'(m+1) = r_i'(m)$ by Lemma 17.3–4 (note that $go(i) \notin \beta_\epsilon^m(r)$, meaning that $\beta_i^m(r) = \varnothing$). Using IH, we now immediately get, $r_i'(m+1) = r_i'(m) = r_i(m) = r_i(m+1)$.

This completes the proof of the induction step for Prop. 2.

For Prop. 3–4, the induction step is even simpler. Since, for any $j \neq i$, $\beta_{\epsilon_j}^m(r') \subseteq \{fail(j)\}$ by Prop. 6, it follows that $r_j'(m+1) = r_j'(m) = r_j'(0)$ by IH. Similarly, $\beta_{\epsilon_j}^m(r') = \varnothing$ by Prop. 6 for $j \notin \{i\} \sqcup Byz$. Thus, being correct at m by IH, such agents j remain correct after round $m + \frac{1}{2}$.   □

Acknowledgments. We are grateful to Hans van Ditmarsch and Yoram Moses for extensive helpful comments on earlier versions of this paper. We also thank the anonymous reviewers for their comments and suggestions on related research.

References

1. Ben-Zvi, I., Moses, Y.: Agent-time epistemics and coordination. In: Lodaya, K. (ed.) ICLA 2013. LNCS, vol. 7750, pp. 97–108. Springer, Heidelberg (2013). https://doi.org/10.1007/978-3-642-36039-8_9

2. Ben-Zvi, I., Moses, Y.: Beyond Lamport's *happened-before*: On time bounds and the ordering of events in distributed systems. J. ACM **61**(2), 13 (2014). https://doi.org/10.1145/2542181

3. Castañeda, A., Gonczarowski, Y.A., Moses, Y.: Unbeatable consensus. In: Kuhn, F. (ed.) DISC 2014. LNCS, vol. 8784, pp. 91–106. Springer, Heidelberg (2014). https://doi.org/10.1007/978-3-662-45174-8_7

4. Dwork, C., Moses, Y.: Knowledge and common knowledge in a Byzantine environment: Crash failures. Inf. Comput. **88**(2), 156–186 (1990). https://doi.org/10.1016/0890-5401(90)90014-9

5. Ezekiel, J., Lomuscio, A.: Combining fault injection and model checking to verify fault tolerance, recoverability, and diagnosability in multi-agent systems. Inf. Comput. **254**(2), 167–194 (2017). https://doi.org/10.1016/j.ic.2016.10.007

6. Fagin, R., Halpern, J.Y., Moses, Y., Vardi, M.Y.: Reasoning About Knowledge. MIT Press, Cambridge (1995)

7. Fagin, R., Halpern, J.Y., Moses, Y., Vardi, M.Y.: Common knowledge revisited. Ann. Pure Appl. Logic **96**, 89–105 (1999). https://doi.org/10.1016/S0168-0072(98)00033-5

8. Fedoruk, A., Deters, R.: Improving fault-tolerance by replicating agents. In: AAMAS 2002, pp. 737–744. ACM (2002). https://doi.org/10.1145/544862.544917

9. Fruzsa, K.: Hope for epistemic reasoning with faulty agents! In: Proceedings of ESSLLI 2019 Student Session (2019, to appear)

10. Gonczarowski, Y.A., Moses, Y.: Timely common knowledge: Characterising asymmetric distributed coordination via vectorial fixed points. In: Schipper, B.C. (ed.) TARK XIV, pp. 79–93 (2013). https://arxiv.org/pdf/1310.6414.pdf

11. Goren, G., Moses, Y.: Silence. In: PODC 2018, pp. 285–294. ACM (2018). https://doi.org/10.1145/3212734.3212768

12. Halpern, J.Y., Moses, Y.: Knowledge and common knowledge in a distributed environment. J. ACM **37**(3), 549–587 (1990). https://doi.org/10.1145/79147.79161

13. Halpern, J.Y., Moses, Y., Waarts, O.: A characterization of eventual Byzantine agreement. SIAM J. Comput. **31**(3), 838–865 (2001). https://doi.org/10.1137/S0097539798340217

14. Hintikka, J.: Knowledge and Belief: An Introduction to the Logic of the Two Notions. Cornell University Press, Ithaca (1962)

15. Kalech, M., Kaminka, G.A.: On the design of coordination diagnosis algorithms for teams of situated agents. Artif. Intell. **171**(8–9), 491–513 (2007). https://doi.org/10.1016/j.artint.2007.03.005

16. Kraus, S., Lehmann, D.: Knowledge, belief and time. Theor. Comput. Sci. **58**, 155–174 (1988). https://doi.org/10.1016/0304-3975(88)90024-2

17. Kuznets, R., Prosperi, L., Schmid, U., Fruzsa, K., Gréaux, L.: Knowledge in Byzantine message-passing systems I: Framework and the causal cone. Technical report TUW-260549, TU Wien (2019). https://publik.tuwien.ac.at/files/publik_260549.pdf

18. Lamport, L., Shostak, R., Pease, M.: The Byzantine Generals Problem. ACM Trans. Program. Lang. Syst. **4**(3), 382–401 (1982). https://doi.org/10.1145/357172.357176

19. Lomuscio, A., Qu, H., Raimondi, F.: MCMAS: A model checker for the verification of multi-agent systems. In: Bouajjani, A., Maler, O. (eds.) CAV 2009. LNCS, vol. 5643, pp. 682–688. Springer, Heidelberg (2009). https://doi.org/10.1007/978-3-642-02658-4_55

20. McKinsey, M.: Skepticism and content externalism. In: Stanford Encyclopedia of Philosophy (2018). https://plato.stanford.edu/entries/skepticism-content-externalism/

21. Michel, R.: A categorical approach to distributed systems, expressibility and knowledge. In: Rudnicki, P. (ed.) PODS 1989, pp. 129–143. ACM (1989). https://doi.org/10.1145/72981.72990

22. Moses, Y.: Relating knowledge and coordinated action: The knowledge of preconditions principle. In: Ramanujam, R. (ed.) TARK 2015, pp. 231–245 (2015). https://doi.org/10.4204/EPTCS.215.17

23. Moses, Y., Shoham, Y.: Belief as defeasible knowledge. Artif. Intell. **64**(2), 299–321 (1993). https://doi.org/10.1016/0004-3702(93)90107-M

24. Moses, Y., Tuttle, M.R.: Programming simultaneous actions using common knowledge. Algorithmica **3**, 121–169 (1988). https://doi.org/10.1007/BF01762112

25. Pessin, A., Goldberg, S. (eds.): The Twin Earth Chronicles: Twenty Years of Reflection on Hilary Putnam's the "Meaning of Meaning". M. E. Sharpe (1996)

26. Taubenfeld, G.: Distributed Computing Pearls. Morgan & Claypool Publishers (2018). https://doi.org/10.2200/S00845ED1V01Y201804DCT014

27. Trask, R.L.: Mind the Gaffe: The Penguin Guide to Common Errors in English. Penguin Books (2001)

28. van Ditmarsch, H.: Dynamics of lying. Synthese **191**(5), 745–777 (2014). https://doi.org/10.1007/s11229-013-0275-3

Two Is Enough – Bisequent Calculus for S5

Andrzej Indrzejczak[(✉)]

Department of Logic, University of Łódź, Lindleya 3/5, 90–131 Łódź, Poland
andrzej.indrzejczak@filozof.uni.lodz.pl

Abstract. We present a generalised sequent calculus based on the use of pairs of ordinary sequents called bisequents. It may be treated as the weakest kind of system in the rich family of systems operating on items being some collections of ordinary sequents. This family covers hypersequent and nested sequent calculi introduced for several non-classical logics. It seems that for many such logics, including some many-valued and modal ones, a reasonably modest generalization of standard sequents is sufficient. In this paper we provide a proof theoretic examination of **S5** in the framework of bisequent calculus. Two versions of cut-free calculus are provided. The first version is more flexible for proof search but admits only indirect proof of cut elimination. The second version is syntactically more constrained but admits constructive proof of cut elimination. This result is extended to several versions of first-order **S5**.

Keywords: Bisequent calculus · Modal logic · Cut elimination

1 Introduction

During the last five decades researchers trying to apply sequent calculi (SC) to several non-classical logics faced many serious problems. In order to overcome the difficulties they provided a lot of ingenious solutions, mainly based on the changes in the notion of basic items on which rules are defined. Sometimes the machinery involved in the construction of such generalised forms of SC is quite complicated and in special cases may be reduced. The aim of this paper is to provide the simplest cut-free generalised SC which has strictly syntactical character, i.e. no labels or other external devices are required. Of course the assumption that there is a clear-cut distinction between purely syntactic and semantic-based calculi may be questioned. After all, there are results showing that some of the approaches may be seen as notational variants simply[1] and, on the other hand, a labelled SC of Negri [36] admits purely syntactical methods

---

[1] For example, Fitting [16] results concerning the correspondence between prefixed tableaux and nested sequents, or Baaz, Fermüller and Zach [5] concerning n-sided sequents and labelled tableaux for many-valued logics.

The results reported in this paper are supported by the National Science Centre, Poland (grant number: DEC-2017/25/B/HS1/01268).

A. Herzig and A. Popescu (Eds.): FroCoS 2019, LNAI 11715, pp. 277–294, 2019.
https://doi.org/10.1007/978-3-030-29007-8_16

of proving admissibility of cut and other structural rules. Also the notion of simplicity is rather vague; in Introduction to [24] different, sometimes opposing, criteria are discussed. Below we will try to explain in what sense the proposed solution may be seen as the simplest, at least in one, but quite rich and important group of generalised SC of similar character.

Let us propose a name many-sequent calculi for the class of systems which is under inspection here. This class covers a variety of systems using collections of sequents as the basic items – in particular, two families of calculi operating on hyper- or nested sequents. Moreover, many other approaches, e.g. using structured notion of a sequent (e.g. Sato [41]) or multiple kinds of sequents (e.g. Indrzejczak [21]) may be reduced to this group by suitable translation.

Let us recall that hypersequents are structures of the form $\Gamma_1 \Rightarrow \Delta_1 \mid ... \mid \Gamma_i \Rightarrow \Delta_i$ which are usually conceived as sets or multisets of their components[2]. It is commonly believed that hypersequent calculus (HC) was originally introduced by Pottinger [39]. However, this information should be revised since a similar idea was earlier introduced by Mints in [32] and [33] to formalize **S5**. Unfortunately, these papers were written in Russian and unknown to wider community. Even much later, when English translation of [33] was presented in Mints [34] he did not care to underline his priority in this respect. But it was Avron [1] who not only independently introduced such kind of SC but developed its theory, first for relevant, then for many other non-classical logics (see e.g. [2]). Since then, HC was applied widely in many fields (see e.g. [12] or [31]).

Nested sequents are more complicated structures where, in addition to formulae, the elements of a sequent may be other sequents, containing other sequents. This approach in general form was initiated by Došen [14] where one is dealing with a hierarchy of sequents of order $n + 1$ with arguments being finite sets of sequents of order n. In particular, sequents of order 2 consist of finite sets of ordinary sequents (of order 1) on both sides, where elements of the antecedent are treated conjunctively, and elements of the succedent disjunctively. Independently of Došen's general frame (not well known either) similar ideas were extensively applied, under different names (deep inference calculi, tree-hypersequent calculi), in the field of modal and temporal logics (e.g. Bull [11], Kashima [27], Stouppa [43], Brünnler [10], Poggiolesi [38]).

In fact, HC may be seen as a special, simplified case of Došen's general framework. In this perspective hypersequents are just sequents of order 2 with empty antecedents. This shows a deep relationship between these approaches. In particular, if hypersequents are defined not as sets or multisets of sequents, but rather as their sequences, then HC may be interpreted as a restricted version of nested sequent calculi, called by Lellmann [30] linear nested SC and by Indrzejczak [26] non-commutative HC.

In particular, if we use just structures which consist of two sequents only, we obtain a limiting case of either HC or nested SC which we call bisequent calculi (BSC). Hence our proposal may be seen as providing the simplest and most

---

[2] In fact other kinds of components, for example expressing clusters, were also proposed recently, see e.g. Baelde, Lick and Schmitz [6].

restrictive form of all aforementioned systems captured by the general frame of Došen in the sense of simplicity of the basic syntactic structures. Is such restricted calculus of any use? HC already may be seen as quite restrictive form of generalised SC, yet it was shown to be useful in many fields. BSC is even more restrictive but preliminary work on its application is promising. For example, one may apply bisequents successfully to a variety of three- and four-valued logics which may be characterised in terms of Hähnle [19] approach with labels as sets of values (work in progress). In this paper we focus on construction of BSC for modal logic **S5**. It is an open question if this approach may be extended to other modal logics containing axiom 5 or B. But in case of **S5** we obtain an elegant solution which is simple also in the sense of simple modal rules allowing for easy proof search and establishing decidability (in propositional case).

S5 is chosen not only because of its philosophical importance. It is important also for proof theory since it had a remarkable impact on the development of different generalised SC. This well-known and important modal logic was very early recognized as a troublesome case for construction of well-behaving SC (Matsumoto and Ohnishi [37]). It was in the strong contrast with nice semantic, algebraic and many other features of **S5**. Although it is possible to devise a standard cut-free SC it requires global restrictions on the application of modal rules which make it rather complicated in practical proof search (see e.g. Serebriannikov [42] or Braüner [9]). Several proposals for solving the problem were connected not only with aforementied kinds of generalised SC but also with other approaches based on the application of structured sequents (Sato [41]) or variety of sequents (Indrzejczak [21]) or labels (Fitting [15]), to mention just a few proposed solutions. In nested SC there are systems of Stouppa [43], Brünnler [10] and Poggiolesi [38]. In case of HC the number of different formalizations of **S5** is particularly impressive: Mints [32], Pottinger [39], Avron [2], Restall [40], Poggiolesi [38], Lahav [29], Kurokawa [28], Bednarska and Indrzejczak [7].

When we compare different generalised SC for **S5** we can observe that although in standard SC this logic is troublesome, in other approaches it often needs the minimum of what is at hand. For example, in labelled approach formalization of **S5** requires the most simple solution – labels being natural numbers; no necessity for structured prefixes (Fitting [15]) or relational formulae (Negri [36]). Similarly in the approach based on the use of variety of different sequents (Indrzejczak [22]), **S5** requires only two different ones. In what follows we want to show that also in many-sequent approach the overall machinery may be significantly reduced to very simple BSC. One may look at this attempt as a kind of the application of the principle of Ockham's Razor to generalised SC of some sort. It may also be compared with the principle of shallow formalization proposed by Quine. HC in itself may be seen already as a quite simple form of many-sequent calculi, but sometimes we can go further.

In Sect. 2 we describe the basic propositional system called BSC1 and compare it with some approaches represented in HC. In Sect. 3 we will show that its cut-free version is complete. It is shown indirectly by translation from cut-free proofs in double sequent calculus DSC for **S5** which is briefly characterised first. In Sect. 4 we introduce restricted form of BSC1 called BSC2. Although it is less flexible in practical applications we can prove a constructive cut elimination theorem for it. Usually different approaches are restricted to propositional level only, here the last section discusses extensions of BSC to quantified versions with identity. Three variants of modal first-order logics are discussed, one based on classical logic and two on free logic. Surprisingly enough, the first one although unproblematic in the setting of BSC1, cannot be accomodated in BSC2 without addition of axiomatic sequents which destroy full cut elimination. On the other hand, for two variants based on free logic we can still obtain cut elimination theorem in nonrestricted version.

2 The System

We will use standard monomodal language with ordinary boolean connectives and two modal operators of necessity $\Box$ and possibility $\Diamond$. Let us recall that one can axiomatize propositional **S5** by adding to Hilbert system for classical propositional logic **CPL** the following schemata of axioms:

K $\Box(\varphi \to \psi) \to (\Box\varphi \to \Box\psi)$
T $\Box\varphi \to \varphi$
4 $\Box\varphi \to \Box\Box\varphi$
5 $\neg\Box\varphi \to \Box\neg\Box\varphi$ or $\Diamond\varphi \to \Box\Diamond\varphi$
Pos $\Diamond\varphi \leftrightarrow \neg\Box\neg\varphi$

Instead of 5 one can use B ($\neg\varphi \to \Box\neg\Box\varphi$ or $\varphi \to \Box\Diamond\varphi$) and dispense with 4 since it is provable from 5 and T. The only primitive rules are modus ponens MP and Gödel's rule GR. $\Gamma \vdash_{S5} \varphi$ denotes a provability of φ from Γ where applications of GR is restricted to theses only. Since only syntactic proofs will be presented below we do not recall semantic characterisation of **S5**.

The basic system which we call BSC1 is essentially a bisequent counterpart of Gentzen's LK for **CPL** enriched with special modal rules. Bisequents in BSC1 are simply (unordered) pairs of sequents $\Gamma \Rightarrow \Delta \mid \Pi \Rightarrow \Sigma$, where $\Gamma, \Delta, \Pi, \Sigma$ are finite (possibly empty) multisets of formulae. In case when one component of a bisequent is empty (i.e. both arguments of $\Rightarrow$ are empty multisets) we can omit it and a bisequent with single nonempty sequent is just a standard sequent. Most of the rules have active formulae (i.e. side and principal formulae) in one sequent only and this sequent is called active, whereas the second is non-active (for this instance of rule application). For both components of a bisequent we have the same set of rules hence for simplicity in schemata of rules we will state active component always on the left but in the course of the proof respective inferences are allowed in both sequents. As axioms we count all bisequents of the form $\varphi \Rightarrow \varphi \mid S$, where S is any sequent, possibly empty. For classical basis we just take LK (but with all two-premiss rules in multiplicative form):

$(W \Rightarrow) \quad \dfrac{\Gamma \Rightarrow \Delta \mid S}{\varphi, \Gamma \Rightarrow \Delta \mid S} \qquad (\Rightarrow W) \quad \dfrac{\Gamma \Rightarrow \Delta \mid S}{\Gamma \Rightarrow \Delta, \varphi \mid S}$

$(C \Rightarrow) \quad \dfrac{\varphi, \varphi, \Gamma \Rightarrow \Delta \mid S}{\varphi, \Gamma \Rightarrow \Delta \mid S} \qquad (\Rightarrow C) \quad \dfrac{\Gamma \Rightarrow \Delta, \varphi, \varphi \mid S}{\Gamma \Rightarrow \Delta, \varphi \mid S}$

$(\neg \Rightarrow) \quad \dfrac{\Gamma \Rightarrow \Delta, \varphi \mid S}{\neg \varphi, \Gamma \Rightarrow \Delta \mid S} \qquad (\Rightarrow \neg) \quad \dfrac{\varphi, \Gamma \Rightarrow \Delta \mid S}{\Gamma \Rightarrow \Delta, \neg \varphi \mid S}$

$(\wedge \Rightarrow) \quad \dfrac{\varphi, \psi, \Gamma \Rightarrow \Delta \mid S}{\varphi \wedge \psi, \Gamma \Rightarrow \Delta \mid S} \qquad (\Rightarrow \wedge) \quad \dfrac{\Gamma \Rightarrow \Delta, \varphi \mid S \qquad \Pi \Rightarrow \Sigma, \psi \mid S}{\Gamma, \Pi \Rightarrow \Delta, \Sigma, \varphi \wedge \psi \mid S}$

$(\Rightarrow \vee) \quad \dfrac{\Gamma \Rightarrow \Delta, \varphi, \psi \mid S}{\Gamma \Rightarrow \Delta, \varphi \vee \psi \mid S} \qquad (\vee \Rightarrow) \quad \dfrac{\varphi, \Gamma \Rightarrow \Delta \mid S \qquad \psi, \Pi \Rightarrow \Sigma \mid S}{\varphi \vee \psi, \Gamma, \Pi \Rightarrow \Delta, \Sigma \mid S}$

$(\Rightarrow \rightarrow) \quad \dfrac{\varphi, \Gamma \Rightarrow \Delta, \psi \mid S}{\Gamma \Rightarrow \Delta, \varphi \rightarrow \psi \mid S} \qquad (\rightarrow \Rightarrow) \quad \dfrac{\Gamma \Rightarrow \Delta, \varphi \mid S \qquad \psi, \Pi \Rightarrow \Sigma \mid S}{\varphi \rightarrow \psi, \Gamma, \Pi \Rightarrow \Delta, \Sigma \mid S}$

$(Cut) \quad \dfrac{\Gamma \Rightarrow \Delta, \varphi \mid \Lambda \Rightarrow \Theta \qquad \varphi, \Pi \Rightarrow \Sigma \mid \Xi \Rightarrow \Omega}{\Gamma, \Pi \Rightarrow \Delta, \Sigma \mid \Lambda, \Xi \Rightarrow \Theta, \Omega}$

Note that although in case of logical two-premiss rules we keep the second, non-active component, the same in both premisses, for cut we admit different sequents which are mixed in the conclusion. It simplifies a constructive proof of cut elimination which will be stated in Sect. 4.

Now rules for modal operators:

$(\Box \Rightarrow) \quad \dfrac{\varphi, \Gamma \Rightarrow \Delta \mid \Pi \Rightarrow \Sigma}{\Box \varphi, \Gamma \Rightarrow \Delta \mid \Pi \Rightarrow \Sigma} \qquad (\Rightarrow \Box) \quad \dfrac{\Rightarrow \varphi \mid \Gamma \Rightarrow \Delta}{\Rightarrow \Box \varphi \mid \Gamma \Rightarrow \Delta}$

$(\Rightarrow \Diamond) \quad \dfrac{\Gamma \Rightarrow \Delta, \varphi \mid \Pi \Rightarrow \Sigma}{\Gamma \Rightarrow \Delta, \Diamond \varphi \mid \Pi \Rightarrow \Sigma} \qquad (\Diamond \Rightarrow) \quad \dfrac{\varphi \Rightarrow \mid \Gamma \Rightarrow \Delta}{\Diamond \varphi \Rightarrow \mid \Gamma \Rightarrow \Delta}$

As we can see all logical modal rules are symmetric, explicit and separate in the sense defined by Wansing [44]. Moreover, they allow for easy proofs of interdefinability of $\Box$ and $\Diamond$ hence they satisfy most of the desiderata stated for well behaved logical rules. Only $(\Rightarrow \Box)$ and $(\Diamond \Rightarrow)$ are not pure in the sense of Avron. Note also that all rules stated so far are static in the sense that there is no transition of any formula from one sequent to another. In addition to ordinary structural rules W and C we have eight transitional quasi-structural rules:

$(TR \Rightarrow \mid) \quad \dfrac{M\varphi, \Gamma \Rightarrow \Delta \mid \Pi \Rightarrow \Sigma}{\Gamma \Rightarrow \Delta \mid M\varphi, \Pi \Rightarrow \Sigma} \qquad (\Rightarrow TR \mid) \quad \dfrac{\Gamma \Rightarrow \Delta, M\varphi \mid \Pi \Rightarrow \Sigma}{\Gamma \Rightarrow \Delta \mid \Pi \Rightarrow \Sigma, M\varphi}$

$(\mid TR \Rightarrow) \quad \dfrac{\Gamma \Rightarrow \Delta \mid M\varphi, \Pi \Rightarrow \Sigma}{M\varphi, \Gamma \Rightarrow \Delta \mid \Pi \Rightarrow \Sigma} \qquad (\mid \Rightarrow TR) \quad \dfrac{\Gamma \Rightarrow \Delta \mid \Pi \Rightarrow \Sigma, M\varphi}{\Gamma \Rightarrow \Delta, M\varphi \mid \Pi \Rightarrow \Sigma}$

where M is either $\Box$ or $\Diamond$ uniformly in the premiss and the conclusion. These rules are called quasi-structural since no constant is introduced but it is anyway displayed in the schemata of rules.

A proof is defined in the standard way as a tree of bisequents. As an example we provide a proof of B:

$$
\begin{array}{l}
(\Box \Rightarrow) \dfrac{p \Rightarrow p}{\Box p \Rightarrow p} \\
(TR \Rightarrow|) \dfrac{}{\Rightarrow p \mid \Box p \Rightarrow} \\
(\neg \Rightarrow) \dfrac{}{\neg p \Rightarrow \mid \Box p \Rightarrow} \\
(\Rightarrow \neg) \dfrac{}{\neg p \Rightarrow \mid \Rightarrow \neg \Box p} \\
(\Rightarrow \Box) \dfrac{}{\neg p \Rightarrow \mid \Rightarrow \Box \neg \Box p} \\
(\mid \Rightarrow TR) \dfrac{}{\neg p \Rightarrow \Box \neg \Box p} \\
(\Rightarrow \rightarrow) \dfrac{}{\Rightarrow \neg p \rightarrow \Box \neg \Box p}
\end{array}
$$

One can easily prove other axioms of **S5** whereas MP and GR are simulated by cut and $(\Rightarrow \Box)$. In the other direction we can use some translation functions which were developed in general form for nested and hypersequent calculi. Let $\wedge\Gamma, \vee\Gamma$ denote conjunctions and disjunctions of elements of Γ and in case Γ is empty they are interpreted as $\top$ and $\bot$ respectively. Consider the following translation for bisequents: $\Im(\Gamma \Rightarrow \Delta \mid \Pi \Rightarrow \Sigma) := (\wedge\Gamma \rightarrow \vee\Delta) \vee \Box(\wedge\Pi \rightarrow \vee\Sigma)$. This is a (restricted) form of the translation applied to nested sequents. Alternatively, we may use a translation applied to hypersequents, i.e., $\Im(\Gamma \Rightarrow \Delta \mid \Pi \Rightarrow \Sigma) := \Box(\wedge\Gamma \rightarrow \vee\Delta) \vee \Box(\wedge\Pi \rightarrow \vee\Sigma)$. The former is a bit simpler but has a disadvantage that in fact bisequents are treated here as ordered pairs whereas it was not required for BSC1 (although it will be required for BSC2). The fact that both can be used provides one more evidence that provided calculi may be seen as a limit case of both hypersequent and nested sequent calculi. We left to the reader the task of proving that all rules of BSC1 are admissible in **S5** under any of these translations. Alternatively, one may demostrate validity-preservation of translation of rules thereby proving soundness. In consequence we have:

Theorem 1. $\Gamma \vdash_{S5} \varphi$ iff $BSC1 \vdash \Gamma \Rightarrow \varphi$

Before we go to more satisfactory solutions (i.e. cut-free) it is interesting to compare modal rules of BSC1 with several kind of hypersequent rules which were provided so far. Mints [32] is using HLK for **CPL** with addition of the following rules for $\Box$:

$$
(\Rightarrow\Box^K) \dfrac{\Gamma \Rightarrow \Delta \mid \Rightarrow \varphi \mid G}{\Gamma \Rightarrow \Delta, \Box\varphi \mid G} \qquad (\Rightarrow\Box^G) \dfrac{\Rightarrow \varphi \mid G}{\Rightarrow \Box\varphi \mid G}
$$

$$
(\Box\Rightarrow^T) \dfrac{\varphi, \Gamma \Rightarrow \Delta \mid G}{\Box\varphi, \Gamma \Rightarrow \Delta \mid G} \qquad (\Box\Rightarrow^5) \dfrac{\Gamma \Rightarrow \Delta \mid \varphi, \Sigma \Rightarrow \Theta \mid G}{\Box\varphi, \Gamma \Rightarrow \Delta \mid \Sigma \Rightarrow \Theta \mid G}
$$

where G denotes a collection of sequents. Two of them, namely $(\Box \Rightarrow^T)$ and $(\Rightarrow \Box^G)$ are just our rules for $\Box$. The remaining rules are transitional but logical, not quasi-structural like in our system. The only rule which is specific for **S5** is $(\Box \Rightarrow^5)$. This set of rules is in fact redundant and later approaches, of Restall [40] and Poggiolesi [38], were more economical but also partly static, partly transitional on the side of logical modal rules. Approaches of Avron [2], Kurokawa [28] and Lahav [29] were based rather on special quasi-structural rules. One can find a comparison of all these systems in Bednarska and Indrzejczak [7]. Solutions provided for **S5** in the framework of nested calculi are of similar character. What is important is the fact that all proposed rules may be easily simulated in BSC1, if we just take G in the schemata of rules to represent just one sequent, possibly empty. Moreover, the proposed solution seems to be more elegant since all logical rules are static and the only transitional ones are quasi-structural.

3   Cut-Free BSC1

What with cut elimination? Let us call BSC1 without cut BSC1$^-$. It is possible to prove completeness for such cut-free system semantically[3] but to save space we will show it indirectly by translation from proofs in some other kind of generalised cut-free SC for **S5** which is known to be complete. We finished the previous section with the claim that BSC1 can simulate modal rules from several cut-free hypersequent calculi. But devising a direct translation is harder since hypersequents may have more components than two. There are some other generalised SC where such translation is more straightforward; moreover it shows how bisequents can simulate other kind of systems in addition to hypersequent or nested sequent calculi.

One such possibility is connected with SC operating on structured sequents i.e., having additional components in the antecedent or succedent like in Blamey and Humberstone [8] or Heuerding, Seyfried and Zimmermann [20]. In particular, all rules of Sato [41] from cut-free system for **S5** may be simulated in BSC1 under translation $\Im(\Gamma \ [\Sigma] \Rightarrow [\Pi] \ \Delta) := \Gamma \Rightarrow \Delta \mid \Sigma \Rightarrow \Pi$. Another possibility is to refer to multisequent calculi in which only one sequent is used at a time but different kinds of sequents are generally applied in the system. In particular, a cut-free system for **S5** uses only two kinds of sequents. It is called double SC (DSC) since in addition to ordinary sequents there are modal ones of the form $\Gamma \ \Box \Rightarrow \Delta$. The latter appear only in proofs but what is proved are only standard sequents. If it is inessential whether standard or modal sequent is applied both kinds are denoted as $\Gamma \ (\Box) \Rightarrow \Delta$. The idea of using special kind of sequents is due to Curry [13] and it was also used by Zeman [46]. In both cases additional sequent was introduced to express modal character of suitable operations. In fact, its introduction in Curry's formulation of **S4** is not necessary; in Zeman it is essential for obtaining a modal rule characterising **S4.2**. Two kinds of sequents were applied also in Avron, Honsell, Miculan and Paravano [3] but in totally different

---

[3] For example, the method applied in Indrzejczak [25] and based on suitably defined downward saturation and loop check can be adapted to BSC1 as well. Moreover it yields decidability in propositional case.

character. In their system two kinds of sequents correspond to two different deducibility relation – global and local one. Indrzejczak introduced a general construction where several types of modal [22] and temporal sequents [23] were applied in one SC but in case of **S5** a considerable reduction is possible to the effect that only one type of modal sequent is required. Below we briefly describe this system; in addition to [21] one may find a fuller account and comparison with other approaches in Poggiolesi [38] and Wansing [45].

In addition to modal sequents, a language is enriched with a special structural operation of transition (from one argument of a sequent to another). It is unary like negation but cannot be iterated; it is allowed only to add it in front of a formula or to delete it. We will use a sign '$-$' for it, so any formula φ may be transformed into $-\varphi$. In the schemata we will use a convention φ^* in the sense that for ordinary formula φ, $\varphi^* = -\varphi$ and $(-\varphi)^* = \varphi$. Also $\Gamma^* = \{\varphi^* : \varphi \in \Gamma\}$.

Most rules are standard and work the same way on both kinds of sequents. However in order to block uncontrolled transition from one side of a sequent to the other for negation and implication we have symmetric variants:

$$(\neg\Rightarrow) \ \frac{-\varphi, \Gamma(\square)\Rightarrow \Delta}{\neg\varphi, \Gamma(\square)\Rightarrow \Delta} \qquad (\Rightarrow\neg) \ \frac{\Gamma(\square)\Rightarrow \Delta, -\varphi}{\Gamma(\square)\Rightarrow \Delta, \neg\varphi}$$

$$(\Rightarrow\rightarrow) \ \frac{\Gamma(\square)\Rightarrow \Delta, -\varphi, \psi}{\Gamma(\square)\Rightarrow \Delta, \varphi \rightarrow \psi} \ (\rightarrow\Rightarrow) \ \frac{-\varphi, \Gamma(\square)\Rightarrow \Delta \quad \psi, \Gamma(\square)\Rightarrow \Delta}{\varphi \rightarrow \psi, \Gamma(\square)\Rightarrow \Delta}$$

Clearly, Γ and Δ may contain ordinary formulae as well as formulae with $-$; the same remark applies to further rules. We need special rules for transition of the form:

$$(\Rightarrow *) \ \frac{\varphi, \Gamma \Rightarrow \Delta}{\Gamma \Rightarrow \Delta, \varphi^*} \qquad (* \Rightarrow) \ \frac{\Gamma \Rightarrow \Delta, \varphi}{\varphi^*, \Gamma \Rightarrow \Delta} \qquad (TR) \ \frac{\Gamma \square \Rightarrow \Delta}{\Delta^* \square \Rightarrow \Gamma^*}$$

and modal rules:

$$(\square \Rightarrow) \ \frac{\varphi, \Gamma(\square)\Rightarrow \Delta}{\square\varphi, \Gamma(\square)\Rightarrow \Delta} \qquad (\Rightarrow\square) \ \frac{\Gamma \square \Rightarrow M\Delta, \varphi}{\Gamma \Rightarrow M\Delta, \square\varphi} \qquad (NC) \ \frac{\Gamma \Rightarrow \Delta}{\Gamma \square \Rightarrow \Delta}$$

where $M\Delta$ contains only formulae of the form $\square\psi, -\square\psi$ and in (NC) one of the Γ, Δ is either empty or contains only such modal formulae. If we admit $\Diamond$ as a primitive operator, we have dual rules for it and the notion of modal formula is extended to include $\Diamond\psi, -\Diamond\psi$.

It is easy to prove soundness under syntactic translation where standard sequents are dealt with as Gentzen transforms with the addition that formulae preceded with $-$ are translated as negations. Modal sequents are translated as $\wedge\Gamma \rightarrow \square(\vee\Delta)$ with the same proviso for formulae with $-$.

This system is cut-free and has generalised subformula property in the sense that the only formulae which must occur in any proof of $\Gamma \Rightarrow \Delta$ are of the form $\varphi, -\varphi$ for every $\varphi \in SF(\Gamma \cup \Delta)$. Completeness and decidability is proved by Hintikka-style argument in [21].

The obvious translation of modal sequents is: $\Im(\Gamma, -\Delta \,\Box\Rightarrow -\Pi, \Sigma) := \Gamma \Rightarrow \Delta \mid \Pi \Rightarrow \Sigma$; ordinary sequents are treated as bisequents with one component empty.

Theorem 2. *If* $\vdash_{DSC} \Gamma \Rightarrow \Delta$, *then* $BSC1^- \vdash \Im(\Gamma \Rightarrow \Delta)$.

Proof. It goes by induction on the height of a proof in DSC. We must provide stepwise simulation of all rules of DSC under the translation. For most of the rules it is obvious so we consider only the case of $(\Rightarrow \Box)$ and (NC). In case of the former by the induction hypothesis we have provable a bisequent in which one component has φ in the succedent and the remaining formulae are modal. By transitional rules we move all modal formulae to the next component and then apply $(\Rightarrow \Box)$ (from BSC1) to φ. The application of $(\mid\Rightarrow TR)$ to $\Box\varphi$ completes the proof. For (NC) one of Γ, Δ is modal or empty. In the first case a series of application of transitional rules leads to translation of the conclusion; in the second there is nothing to do. $\Box$

This theorem implies completeness of cut-free version of BSC1, that is of BSC1$^-$. It yields, by subformula property, decidability and also admissibility of cut by a simple argument. Since if both premisses of cut are provable, then by soundness they are valid. But cut is validity-preserving, hence the conclusion must be valid either and, by completeness, it is also provable. But we may do even better and prove this result constructively. However, not for a calculus in this shape. Consider the following application of cut:

$$
\begin{array}{c}
(\Rightarrow \Box)\;\dfrac{\Rightarrow \varphi \mid \Gamma \Rightarrow \Delta, \neg\psi}{\Rightarrow \Box\varphi \mid \Gamma \Rightarrow \Delta, \neg\psi} \quad \dfrac{\Lambda \Rightarrow \Theta \mid \Pi \Rightarrow \Sigma, \psi}{\Lambda \Rightarrow \Theta \mid \neg\psi, \Pi \Rightarrow \Sigma}\;(\neg \Rightarrow) \\[2pt]
(Cut)\;\rule{0pt}{1pt}\overline{\qquad\qquad \Lambda \Rightarrow \Theta, \Box\varphi \mid \Gamma, \Pi \Rightarrow \Delta, \Sigma \qquad\qquad}
\end{array}
$$

If we now push cut up to reduce the height of a proof we obtain $\Lambda \Rightarrow \Theta, \varphi \mid \Gamma, \Pi \Rightarrow \Delta, \Sigma$ and in general there is no chance to apply $(\Rightarrow \Box)$ to this bisequent. Therefore, for the aim of constructive proof of cut elimination we must modify slightly a calculus to obtain its variant BSC2.

4   Modified System BSC2

First of all let us restrict the application of all static rules to left sequents only. So what in BSC1 was only a convention applied in the schemata of rules, now is a rigid requirement to the effect that in BSC2 bisequents are ordered pairs. Note that in consequence of this restriction the right sequent is either empty or modal and plays only auxiliary role, similarly like in the sequent calculus of Heuerding, Seyfried and Zimmermann [20] for **S4**; it serves for storing modal data. To simplify things we restrict language to $\Box$ only but the proof works also in the presence of $\Diamond$. We also introduce (Mix) instead of (Cut) to deal with C. It looks like this:

$$(Mix) \quad \frac{\Gamma \Rightarrow \Delta, \varphi^i \mid \Lambda \Rightarrow \Theta \qquad \varphi^k, \Pi \Rightarrow \Sigma \mid \Xi \Rightarrow \Omega}{\Gamma, \Pi \Rightarrow \Delta, \Sigma \mid \Lambda, \Xi \Rightarrow \Theta, \Omega}$$

where $i, k > 0$ and all occurrences of φ are displayed. It is obvious that a system with mix is equivalent to the system with cut by exactly the same argument as stated by Gentzen for LK.

However, to deal with transitional rules we must add the second form of mix. Let $(MMix)$ denote the following rule devised for boxed cut formulae:

$$(MMix) \quad \frac{\Gamma \Rightarrow \Delta, \Box\varphi^i \mid \Lambda \Rightarrow \Theta, \Box\varphi^j \qquad \Box\varphi^k, \Pi \Rightarrow \Sigma \mid \Box\varphi^n, \Xi \Rightarrow \Omega}{\Gamma, \Pi \Rightarrow \Delta, \Sigma \mid \Lambda, \Xi \Rightarrow \Theta, \Omega}$$

with $i + j \geq 1$ and $k + n \geq 1$.,

Note that $(MMix)$ similarly like TR-rules works also on the right sequents, even if $i = k = 0$. Moreover, we require that (Mix) is restricted only to nonmodal cut formulae and denote it by (Mix'). Nothing is lost since if $j = n = 0$, then $(MMix)$ works like (Mix). This is the solution similar to applied by Avron [2] in his cut elimination proof for hypersequent calculus for **S5**. Details of such proof are specified in Bednarska and Indrzejczak [7].

Let us call the system with these two variants of mix BSC2'. One may easily prove that:

Lemma 1. $BSC2 \vdash \Gamma \Rightarrow \Delta$ iff $BSC2' \vdash \Gamma \Rightarrow \Delta$

Proof. From left to right it is enough to show that the application of (Mix) on modal formula is derivable by $(MMix)$. If $j = n = 0$ it is the same. Otherwise, after the application of $(MMix)$ we must introduce the lacking number of occurences of cut formula by W to the left sequent and then by TR move them to the right sequent to restore its full shape.

From right to left it is enough to show that $(MMix)$ is derivable by (Mix) in BSC2. Again only the case with $j \geq 1$ or $n \geq 1$ must be considered. We apply (TR) to such occurrences of cut formula to move them to the left sequent in both premises, then we apply (Mix) so all these occurrences are deleted from resulting bisequent. □

Before we prove elimination of cut for BSC2 one important thing should be noted. Clearly, in the presence of cut BSC1 and BSC2 are equivalent. It is also easy to observe that without cut everything provable in BSC2 must be provable in BSC1 since the former is just restricted form of the latter. But is BSC2 without cut equivalent to BSC1? An examination of a proof of B in BSC1 shows that rules were applied in both sequents. But in BSC2 the application of static rules in the right sequent is forbidden and without cut we are not able to prove B. If we restrict our interest to the system which is only weakly complete, i.e. where all valid formulae are provable, we can apply the approach of Fitting [15] based on the observation that in **S5** it holds that $\vdash \varphi$ iff $\vdash \Box\varphi$. Therefore, at the expense of reducing the problem to weak completeness only we can change slightly a definition of a proof demanding that what we are proving are sequents of the form $\Rightarrow \Box\varphi$. In fact, due to the application of bisequents we may provide more specific formulation. Note first that:

Lemma 2. *In BSC2 (without cut)* $\vdash \Rightarrow \Box\varphi$ *iff* $\vdash \Rightarrow \varphi \mid \Rightarrow \Box\varphi$

Proof. From left to right we just apply $(\Rightarrow TR \mid)$ and $(\Rightarrow W)$; conversely we apply $(\Rightarrow \Box)$, then $(\mid \Rightarrow TR)$ (but to the right sequent) and $(\Rightarrow C)$. $\Box$

For illustration sake let us consider again a problem of proving B in so modified BSC2 (without cut). Here is a proof of $\Rightarrow \neg p \to \Box\neg\Box p \mid \Rightarrow \Box(\neg p \to \Box\neg\Box p)$

$$
\begin{array}{ll}
 & \dfrac{p \Rightarrow p}{} \\[2pt]
(\Box \Rightarrow) & \dfrac{\Box p \Rightarrow p}{} \\[2pt]
(TR \Rightarrow\mid) & \dfrac{\Rightarrow p \mid \Box p \Rightarrow}{} \\[2pt]
(\neg \Rightarrow) & \dfrac{\neg p \Rightarrow \mid \Box p \Rightarrow}{} \\[2pt]
(\Rightarrow W) & \dfrac{\neg p \Rightarrow \Box\neg\Box p \mid \Box p \Rightarrow}{} \\[2pt]
(\Rightarrow\to) & \dfrac{\Rightarrow \neg p \to \Box\neg\Box p \mid \Box p \Rightarrow}{} \\[2pt]
(\Rightarrow \Box) & \dfrac{\Rightarrow \Box(\neg p \to \Box\neg\Box p) \mid \Box p \Rightarrow}{} \\[2pt]
(\mid TR \Rightarrow) & \dfrac{\Box p \Rightarrow \Box(\neg p \to \Box\neg\Box p) \mid \Rightarrow}{} \\[2pt]
(\Rightarrow TR \mid) & \dfrac{\Box p \Rightarrow \mid \Rightarrow \Box(\neg p \to \Box\neg\Box p)}{} \\[2pt]
(\Rightarrow \neg) & \dfrac{\Rightarrow \neg\Box p \mid \Rightarrow \Box(\neg p \to \Box\neg\Box p)}{} \\[2pt]
(\Rightarrow \Box) & \dfrac{\Rightarrow \Box\neg\Box p \mid \Rightarrow \Box(\neg p \to \Box\neg\Box p)}{} \\[2pt]
(W \Rightarrow) & \dfrac{\neg p \Rightarrow \Box\neg\Box p \mid \Rightarrow \Box(\neg p \to \Box\neg\Box p)}{} \\[2pt]
(\Rightarrow\to) & \dfrac{\Rightarrow \neg p \to \Box\neg\Box p \mid \Rightarrow \Box(\neg p \to \Box\neg\Box p)}{}
\end{array}
$$

Now we can prove:

Theorem 3. *If BSC2* $\vdash \Rightarrow \varphi \mid \Rightarrow \Box\varphi$, *then BSC2$^-$* $\vdash \Rightarrow \varphi \mid \Rightarrow \Box\varphi$

Proof. We will use the method of Girard [18] based on the application of cross-cuts. But we apply Gentzen's overall strategy, i.e., we will prove the result for the case where both premisses of (Mix') or $(MMix)$ are cut-free.

The cases where one premiss, say the left one, is axiomatic are simple; we show it only for $(MMix)$:

$$
(MMix)\quad \dfrac{\Box\varphi \Rightarrow \Box\varphi \qquad \Box\varphi^i, \Gamma \Rightarrow \Delta \mid \Box\varphi^j, \Pi \Rightarrow \Sigma}{\Box\varphi, \Gamma \Rightarrow \Delta \mid \Pi \Rightarrow \Sigma}
$$

is replaced by:

$$
\begin{array}{ll}
(\mid TR \Rightarrow) & \dfrac{\Box\varphi^i, \Gamma \Rightarrow \Delta \mid \Box\varphi^j, \Pi \Rightarrow \Sigma}{\Box\varphi^{i+j}, \Gamma \Rightarrow \Delta \mid \Pi \Rightarrow \Sigma} \\[6pt]
(C \Rightarrow) & \dfrac{}{\Box\varphi, \Gamma \Rightarrow \Delta \mid \Pi \Rightarrow \Sigma}
\end{array}
$$

The cases where one cut-formula in one premiss is parametric in all occurrences are similar to reductions in standard LK. For illustration we consider the case of $(MMix)$ when the left premiss is obtained by $(\rightarrow\Rightarrow)$:

$$(MMix) \dfrac{\dfrac{\Gamma \Rightarrow \Delta, \varphi, \Box\chi^i \mid \Pi \Rightarrow \Sigma, \Box\chi^j \quad \psi, \Gamma \Rightarrow \Delta, \Box\chi^i \mid \Pi \Rightarrow \Sigma, \Box\chi^j}{\varphi \rightarrow \psi, \Gamma \Rightarrow \Delta, \Box\chi^i \mid \Pi \Rightarrow \Sigma, \Box\chi^j} \quad \Box\chi^k, \Lambda \Rightarrow \Theta \mid \Box\chi^n, \Xi \Rightarrow \Upsilon}{\varphi \rightarrow \psi, \Gamma, \Lambda \Rightarrow \Delta, \Theta \mid \Pi, \Xi \Rightarrow \Sigma, \Upsilon}$$

is transformed into:

$$(MMix) \dfrac{\Gamma \Rightarrow \Delta, \varphi, \Box\chi^i \mid \Pi \Rightarrow \Sigma, \Box\chi^j \quad \Box\chi^k, \Lambda \Rightarrow \Theta \mid \Box\chi^n, \Xi \Rightarrow \Upsilon}{(\rightarrow\Rightarrow)\dfrac{\Gamma, \Lambda \Rightarrow \Delta, \Theta, \varphi \mid \Pi, \Xi \Rightarrow \Sigma, \Upsilon \qquad\qquad D}{\varphi \rightarrow \psi, \Gamma, \Lambda \Rightarrow \Delta, \Theta \mid \Pi, \Xi \Rightarrow \Sigma, \Upsilon}}$$

where D replaces:

$$\dfrac{\psi, \Gamma \Rightarrow \Delta, \Box\chi^i \mid \Pi \Rightarrow \Sigma, \Box\chi^j \quad \Box\chi^k, \Lambda \Rightarrow \Theta \mid \Box\chi^n, \Xi \Rightarrow \Upsilon}{\psi, \Gamma, \Lambda \Rightarrow \Delta, \Theta \mid \Pi, \Xi \Rightarrow \Sigma, \Upsilon} \ (MMix)$$

Note that in case $\varphi = \Box\chi$ we must additionally restore φ by $(\Rightarrow W)$ to be able to derive the last sequent by $(\rightarrow\Rightarrow)$. If in this case also some $\Box\chi$ were deleted in the right component we restore them by W in the left component and TR. It should be noted that when TR is performed we can always reduce the height even if left sequents are non-active.

The most troublesome cases are with cut formulae being principal in both premisses. Let us consider the case of $\Box\varphi$:

$$(MMix) \dfrac{(\Rightarrow\Box)\dfrac{\Rightarrow\varphi \mid \Gamma \Rightarrow \Delta, \Box\varphi^i}{\Rightarrow\Box\varphi \mid \Gamma \Rightarrow \Delta, \Box\varphi^i} \quad \dfrac{\Box\varphi^j, \varphi, \Lambda \Rightarrow \Theta \mid \Box\varphi^k, \Pi \Rightarrow \Sigma}{\Box\varphi^{j+1}, \Lambda \Rightarrow \Theta \mid \Box\varphi^k, \Pi \Rightarrow \Sigma}(\Box\Rightarrow)}{\Lambda \Rightarrow \Theta \mid \Gamma, \Pi \Rightarrow \Delta, \Sigma}$$

if $i = j = k = 0$ it is enough to perform (Mix') on φ and then possibly restore by $(W \Rightarrow)$ some occurences of φ in Λ. Moreover, if $\varphi = \Box\psi$ and there are some occurrences of it in Δ or Π we actually perform $(MMix)$ and must restore by W also deleted occurrences in these multisets. In case some of $i, j, k \geq 0$ we must first make cross-cuts to delete occurrences of $\Box\varphi$. Of course the most difficult situation is when all of $i, j, k \geq 1$; we perform two cross-cuts:

$$(MMix) \dfrac{\Rightarrow\varphi \mid \Gamma \Rightarrow \Delta, \Box\varphi^i \quad \Box\varphi^{j+1}, \Lambda \Rightarrow \Theta \mid \Box\varphi^k, \Pi \Rightarrow \Sigma}{\Lambda \Rightarrow \Theta, \varphi \mid \Gamma, \Pi \Rightarrow \Delta, \Sigma}$$

$$\dfrac{\Rightarrow\Box\varphi \mid \Gamma \Rightarrow \Delta, \Box\varphi^i \quad \Box\varphi^j, \varphi, \Lambda \Rightarrow \Theta \mid \Box\varphi^k, \Pi \Rightarrow \Sigma}{\varphi, \Lambda \Rightarrow \Theta \mid \Gamma, \Pi \Rightarrow \Delta, \Sigma} \ (MMix)$$

where both applications of $(MMix)$ have lower height and next:

$$\frac{\Lambda \Rightarrow \Theta, \varphi \mid \Gamma, \Pi \Rightarrow \Delta, \Sigma \qquad \varphi, \Lambda \Rightarrow \Theta \mid \Gamma, \Pi \Rightarrow \Delta, \Sigma}{\frac{\Lambda, \Lambda' \Rightarrow \Theta', \Theta \mid \Gamma, \Gamma, \Pi, \Pi \Rightarrow \Delta, \Delta, \Sigma, \Sigma}{\Lambda, \Rightarrow \Theta \mid \Gamma, \Pi \Rightarrow \Delta, \Sigma} (C, TR)} (Mix')$$

where the application of (Mix') is of lower complexity. Λ', Θ' are like Λ, Θ but with deleted occurrences of φ (if any). Again, if $\varphi = \Box\psi$ and there are some occurrences of it in $\Delta, \Sigma, \Gamma, \Pi$ we perform rather $(MMix)$. The last step signed with double line should be explained. No rule is to be applied on the right component, including contraction. However, all formulae are modal so we can perform enough transitions to the left component, make required contractions and move these formulae again to the right component.   □

5   Extensions

Recently Avron and Lahav [4] noticed that all HC for **S5** are restricted to propositional part. In fact, Mints [32] proposed systems for some first-order version of **S5** but, as we mentioned, this work came unnoticed. In general, most of the proposals indeed are restricted to propositional level. However, once we have at our disposal a calculus for which a syntactic cut elimination holds it is possible to extend it to cover at least some first-order versions of **S5**. We will use a version of first-order language commonly applied in proof theoretic research with denumerable set of bound individual variables $x, y, z, \ldots$ and free individual variables (or parameters) $a, b, c, \ldots$. Both sorts of variables are rigid but we additionally admit also nonrigid terms $f_1, f_2, f_3, \ldots$.

Let us consider axiomatic formulations of systems Q1, Q1R and QS as stated by Garson [17], all with **S5** modalities (hence the last is just QS5 since S is just a label for chosen modality). The first and the second are adequate wrt to semantics with all terms rigid whereas QS5 admits also nonrigid terms being individual concepts in the sense of Carnap. Q1 is the logic of constant domain for all states in models whereas the other two admit varying domains. We do not go deeper into semantical matters here since what is of interest for us is their axiomatic characterization. Q1 is based on standard classical first-order logic **CFL** hence to obtain its BSC2-counterpart we may use standard rules for quantifiers:

$$(\forall\Rightarrow) \quad \frac{\varphi[x/t], \Gamma \Rightarrow \Delta \mid S}{\forall x\varphi, \Gamma \Rightarrow \Delta \mid S} \qquad\qquad (\Rightarrow\forall) \quad \frac{\Gamma \Rightarrow \Delta, \varphi[x/a] \mid S}{\Gamma \Rightarrow \Delta, \forall x\varphi \mid S}$$

$$(\exists\Rightarrow) \quad \frac{\varphi[x/a], \Gamma \Rightarrow \Delta \mid S}{\exists x\varphi, \Gamma \Rightarrow \Delta \mid S} \qquad\qquad (\Rightarrow\exists) \quad \frac{\Gamma \Rightarrow \Delta, \varphi[x/t] \mid S}{\Gamma \Rightarrow \Delta, \exists x\varphi \mid S}$$

where t is any (rigid) term but a is not in Γ, Δ and φ.

Note that Barcan Formula $\forall x\Box\varphi \rightarrow \Box\forall x\varphi$ is provable in axiomatic **CFL** with S5-modalities hence it need not be added as a separate axiom as in case of weaker modal logics. Unfortunatelly it is not provable in BSC2$^-$ although it is easily provable in BSC1$^-$:

$$(\Box \Rightarrow) \frac{\varphi[x/a] \Rightarrow \varphi[x/a]}{\Box\varphi[x/a] \Rightarrow \varphi[x/a]}$$

$$(\mid TR \Rightarrow) \frac{\Box\varphi[x/a] \Rightarrow \varphi[x/a]}{\Box\varphi[x/a] \Rightarrow \mid \Rightarrow \varphi[x/a]}$$

$$(\forall \Rightarrow) \frac{\Box\varphi[x/a] \Rightarrow \mid \Rightarrow \varphi[x/a]}{\forall x\Box\varphi \Rightarrow \mid \Rightarrow \varphi[x/a]}$$

$$(\Rightarrow \forall) \frac{\forall x\Box\varphi \Rightarrow \mid \Rightarrow \varphi[x/a]}{\forall x\Box\varphi \Rightarrow \mid \Rightarrow \forall x\varphi}$$

$$(\Rightarrow \Box) \frac{\forall x\Box\varphi \Rightarrow \mid \Rightarrow \forall x\varphi}{\forall x\Box\varphi \Rightarrow \mid \Rightarrow \Box\forall x\varphi}$$

$$(\mid \Rightarrow TR) \frac{\forall x\Box\varphi \Rightarrow \mid \Rightarrow \Box\forall x\varphi}{\forall x\Box\varphi \Rightarrow \Box\forall x\varphi}$$

$$(\Rightarrow \rightarrow) \frac{\forall x\Box\varphi \Rightarrow \Box\forall x\varphi}{\Rightarrow \forall x\Box\varphi \rightarrow \Box\forall x\varphi}$$

We conjecture that BSC1$^-$ is complete but it needs separate semantic proof since constructive cut elimination theorem does not hold for this calculus. As for BSC2$^-$ to save equivalence with Q1 we must add axiomatic sequents $\forall x\Box\varphi \Rightarrow \Box\forall x\varphi$. This formalization is easily proven to be equivalent to standard axiomatic one under the translation stated for propositional case but note that cuts with additional axioms as one of the premises are not eliminable.

In case of Q1R and QS5 the situation is clearer. Since both are based on positive free logic **FL** we must change quantifier rules for their free versions:

$$(\forall\Rightarrow) \frac{\Gamma \Rightarrow \Delta, Et \mid S \quad \varphi[x/t], \Pi \Rightarrow \Sigma \mid S}{\forall x\varphi, \Gamma, \Pi \Rightarrow \Delta, \Sigma \mid S} \qquad (\Rightarrow\forall) \frac{Ea, \Gamma \Rightarrow \Delta, \varphi[x/a] \mid S}{\Gamma \Rightarrow \Delta, \forall x\varphi \mid S}$$

$$(\exists\Rightarrow) \frac{Ea, \varphi[x/a], \Gamma \Rightarrow \Delta \mid S}{\exists x\varphi, \Gamma \Rightarrow \Delta \mid S} \qquad (\Rightarrow\exists) \frac{\Gamma \Rightarrow \Delta, Et \mid S \quad \Pi \Rightarrow \Sigma, \varphi[x/t] \mid S}{\Gamma, \Pi \Rightarrow \Delta, \Sigma, \exists x\varphi \mid S}$$

with the same stipulations concerning instantiated terms but in case of QS5 they may be nonrigid as well. 'E' is an existence predicate. Again proving equivalence with axiomatic formulation of (positive) free logic is unproblematic.

To accomodate identity one may add the following rules to Q1 and QR1:

$$(=\Rightarrow) \frac{t = t, \Gamma \Rightarrow \Delta \mid S}{\Gamma \Rightarrow \Delta \mid S} \qquad (\Rightarrow=) \frac{\Gamma \Rightarrow \Delta, t_1 = t_2 \mid S \quad \Pi \Rightarrow \Sigma, \varphi[x/t_1] \mid S}{\Gamma, \Pi \Rightarrow \Delta, \Sigma, \varphi[x/t_2] \mid S}$$

$$(\Rightarrow = \Box) \frac{\Gamma \Rightarrow \Delta, t_1 = t_2 \mid S}{\Gamma \Rightarrow \Delta, \Box t_1 = t_2 \mid S} \qquad (\Rightarrow \neq \Box) \frac{t_1 = t_2, \Gamma \Rightarrow \Delta \mid S}{\Gamma \Rightarrow \Delta, \Box\neg t_1 = t_2 \mid S}$$

where φ is atomic in $(\Rightarrow=)$. For QS5 only the first two rules are needed since nonrigid terms are admitted. But it should be noted that Et is not counted as atomic formula in case of QS5.

One may in a standard way (see e.g. Negri and von Plato [35]) prove that:

Lemma 3 (Substitution). *If $\vdash \Gamma \Rightarrow \Delta$, then $\vdash (\Gamma \Rightarrow \Delta)[a/t]$ in the height-preserving manner.*

It is then routine to extend our cut elimination to BSC2 counterparts of all these six axiomatic systems (with or without rules for identity) but in case of Q1 in restricted form (see the remarks above concerning Barcan Formula). Reduction of the height in case all occurrences of mix-formula are parametric in one premiss goes as in propositional case. The cases where in both premisses one occurrence of mix formula is principal are also unproblematic. However one should remeber that in case of Q1 and QR1 MMix also takes place when the left premiss is deduced by $(\Rightarrow = \Box)$ or $(\Rightarrow \neq \Box)$ and the right one by $(\Box \Rightarrow)$ or some transitional rule. For the sake of illustration we display one such case:

$$
\begin{array}{c}
(\Rightarrow \neq \Box) \\
(MMix)
\end{array}
\dfrac{
\dfrac{a = b, \Gamma \Rightarrow \Delta, \Box\neg a = b^i \mid \Pi \Rightarrow \Sigma, \Box\neg a = b^j}{\Gamma \Rightarrow \Delta, \Box\neg a = b^{i+1} \mid \Pi \Rightarrow \Sigma, \Box\neg a = b^j}
\quad
\dfrac{\Box\neg a = b^k, \neg a = b, \Lambda \Rightarrow \Theta \mid \Box\neg a = b^n, \Xi \Rightarrow \Omega}{\Box\neg a = b^{k+1}, \Lambda \Rightarrow \Theta \mid \Box\neg a = b^n, \Xi \Rightarrow \Omega} \; (\Box \Rightarrow)
}{
\Gamma, \Lambda \Rightarrow \Delta, \Theta \mid \Pi, \Xi \Rightarrow \Sigma, \Omega
}
$$

by two cross-cuts of lesser height we obtain:

$$
\begin{array}{c}
(\Rightarrow \neq \Box) \\
(MMix)
\end{array}
\dfrac{
\dfrac{a = b, \Gamma \Rightarrow \Delta, \Box\neg a = b^i \mid \Pi \Rightarrow \Sigma, \Box\neg a = b^j}{\Gamma \Rightarrow \Delta, \Box\neg a = b^{i+1} \mid \Pi \Rightarrow \Sigma, \Box\neg a = b^j}
\quad
\Box\neg a = b^k, \neg a = b, \Lambda \Rightarrow \Theta \mid \Box\neg a = b^n, \Xi \Rightarrow \Omega
}{
\neg a = b, \Gamma, \Lambda \Rightarrow \Delta, \Theta \mid \Pi, \Xi \Rightarrow \Sigma, \Omega
}
$$

and

$$
\dfrac{
a = b, \Gamma \Rightarrow \Delta, \Box\neg a = b^i \mid \Pi \Rightarrow \Sigma, \Box\neg a = b^j
\quad
\dfrac{\Box\neg a = b^k, \neg a = b, \Lambda \Rightarrow \Theta \mid \Box\neg a = b^n, \Xi \Rightarrow \Omega}{\Box\neg a = b^{k+1}, \Lambda \Rightarrow \Theta \mid \Box\neg a = b^n, \Xi \Rightarrow \Omega} \; (\Box \Rightarrow)
}{
a = b, \Gamma, \Lambda \Rightarrow \Delta, \Theta \mid \Pi, \Xi \Rightarrow \Sigma, \Omega
} \; (MMix)
$$

and finally:

$$
\begin{array}{c}
(\Rightarrow \neg) \\
(Mix')
\end{array}
\dfrac{
\dfrac{a = b, \Gamma, \Lambda \Rightarrow \Delta, \Theta \mid \Pi, \Xi \Rightarrow \Sigma, \Omega}{\Gamma, \Lambda \Rightarrow \Delta, \Theta, \neg a = b \mid \Pi, \Xi \Rightarrow \Sigma, \Omega}
\quad
\neg a = b, \Gamma, \Lambda \Rightarrow \Delta, \Theta \mid \Pi, \Xi \Rightarrow \Sigma, \Omega
}{
\dfrac{\Gamma, \Gamma', \Lambda, \Lambda' \Rightarrow \Delta', \Delta, \Theta', \Theta \mid \Pi, \Pi, \Xi, \Xi \Rightarrow \Sigma, \Sigma, \Omega, \Omega}{\Gamma, \Lambda \Rightarrow \Delta, \Theta \mid \Pi, \Xi \Rightarrow \Sigma, \Omega} \; C, TR
}
$$

where mix-formula is of lesser complexity and the compact last step is obtained by the series of transitions, contractions and transitions again.
We consider also the case of $\forall x \varphi(x)$:

$$
\dfrac{
\dfrac{Ea, \Gamma \Rightarrow \Delta, \forall x\varphi(x)^k, \varphi(a) \mid \Lambda \Rightarrow \Theta}{\Gamma \Rightarrow \Delta, \forall x\varphi(x)^{k+1} \mid \Lambda \Rightarrow \Theta}
\quad
\dfrac{\forall x\varphi(x)^i, \Pi \Rightarrow \Sigma, Eb \mid \Xi \Rightarrow \Omega \quad \varphi(b), \forall x\varphi(x)^j, \Pi' \Rightarrow \Sigma' \mid \Xi \Rightarrow \Omega}{\forall x\varphi(x)^{i+j}, \Pi, \Pi' \Rightarrow \Sigma, \Sigma' \mid \Xi \Rightarrow \Omega}
}{
\Gamma, \Pi, \Pi' \Rightarrow \Delta, \Sigma, \Sigma' \mid \Lambda, \Xi \Rightarrow \Theta, \Omega
}
$$

where a is fresh, hence by Substitution Lemma we have a proof of the same height of:

$$
Eb, \Gamma \Rightarrow \Delta, \forall x\varphi(x)^k, \varphi(b) \mid \Lambda \Rightarrow \Theta
$$

Now we perform three cross-cuts of lesser height:

$$
\dfrac{
Eb, \Gamma \Rightarrow \Delta, \forall x\varphi(x)^k, \varphi(b) \mid \Lambda \Rightarrow \Theta
\quad
\forall x\varphi(x)^{i+j}, \Pi, \Pi' \Rightarrow \Sigma, \Sigma' \mid \Xi \Rightarrow \Omega
}{
Eb, \Gamma, \Pi, \Pi' \Rightarrow \Delta, \Sigma, \Sigma', \varphi(b) \mid \Lambda, \Xi \Rightarrow \Theta, \Omega
}
$$

$$
\dfrac{
\Gamma \Rightarrow \Delta, \forall x\varphi(x)^{k+1} \mid \Lambda \Rightarrow \Theta
\quad
\forall x\varphi(x)^i, \Pi \Rightarrow \Sigma, Eb \mid \Xi \Rightarrow \Omega
}{
\Gamma, \Pi \Rightarrow \Delta, \Sigma, Eb \mid \Lambda, \Xi \Rightarrow \Theta, \Omega
}
$$

$$\frac{\Gamma \Rightarrow \Delta, \forall x \varphi(x)^{k+1} \mid \Lambda \Rightarrow \Theta \qquad \varphi(b), \forall x \varphi(x)^{j}, \Pi' \Rightarrow \Sigma' \mid \Xi \Rightarrow \Omega}{\varphi(b), \Gamma, \Pi' \Rightarrow \Delta, \Sigma' \mid \Lambda, \Xi \Rightarrow \Theta, \Omega}$$

Two mixes on Eb and $\varphi(b)$ respectively, both of lesser complexity, lead to the required sequent after some contractions. Note that in case $\varphi(b)$ is modal we must apply $(MMix)$ and some applications of transitional rules may be also required. □

Let us conclude with a brief comparison of BSC1 and BSC2. The former is more flexible as far as we want to use it for actual proof search. It is also strongly complete (even without cut) whereas BSC2 without cut is only weakly complete. However, in BSC2 we can keep better control over the structure of proofs and it allows for obtaining a constructive proof of cut elimination which is always seen as an advantage over calculi which can be only semantically shown to be cut-free. In particular, we have made use of it in this section. We restrict our investigation here to the problem of cut elimination but further features and applications of both versions seem to be worth exploring.

References

1. Avron, A.: A constructive analysis of RM. J. Symb. Log. **52**, 939–951 (1987)
2. Avron, A.: The method of hypersequents in the proof theory of propositional non-classical logics. In: Hodges, W., et al. (eds.) Logic: From Foundations to Applications, pp. 1–32. Oxford Science Publication, Oxford (1996)
3. Avron, A., Honsell, F., Miculan, M., Paravano, C.: Encoding modal logics in logical frameworks. Stud. Log. **60**, 161–202 (1998)
4. Avron, A., Lahav, O.: A simple cut-free system of paraconsistent logic equivalent to S5. In: Bezhanishvili, G., et al. (eds.) Advances in Modal Logic, vol. 12, pp. 29–42. College Publications (2018)
5. Baaz, M., Fermüller, C.G., Zach, R.: Dual systems of sequents and tableaux for many-valued logics. Technical report TUW-E185.2-BFZ, 2–92 (1992)
6. Baelde, D., Lick, A., Schmitz, S.: A hypersequent calculus with clusters for linear frames. In: Bezhanishvili, G., et al. (eds.) Advances in Modal Logic, vol. 12, pp. 43–62. College Publications (2018)
7. Bednarska, K., Indrzejczak, A.: Hypersequent calculi for S5 - the methods of cut-elimination. Log. Log. Philos. **24**(3), 277–311 (2015)
8. Blamey, S., Humberstone, L.: A perspective on modal sequent logic. Publications of the Research Institute for Mathematical Sciences, Kyoto University **27**, 763–782 (1991)
9. Braüner, T.: Hybrid Logic and its Proof-Theory. Springer, Roskilde (2009). https://doi.org/10.1007/978-94-007-0002-4
10. Brünnler, K.: Deep sequent systems for modal logic. Arch. Math. Log. **48**(6), 551–571 (2009)
11. Bull, R.A.: Cut elimination for propositional dynamic logic without star. Z. für Math. Log. Und Grundl. Math. **38**, 85–100 (1992)
12. Ciabattoni, A., Ramanayake, R., Wansing, H.: Hypersequent and display calculi - a unified perspective. Stud. Log. **102**(6), 1245–1294 (2014)
13. Curry, H.B.: A Theory of Formal Deducibility. University of Notre Dame Press, Notre Dame (1950)

14. Došen, K.: Sequent-systems for modal logic. J. Symb. Log. **50**, 149–159 (1985)
15. Fitting, M.: Proof Methods for Modal and Intuitionistic Logics. Reidel, Dordrecht (1983)
16. Fitting, M.: Prefixed tableaus and nested sequents. Ann. Pure Appl. Log. **163**, 291–313 (2012)
17. Garson, J.W.: Quantification in modal logic. In: Gabbay, D., Guenther, F. (eds.) Handbook of Philosophical Logic, vol. II, pp. 249–308. Kluwer, Dordrecht (1984)
18. Girard, J.Y.: Proof Theory and Logical Complexity. Bibliopolis, Napoli (1987)
19. Hähnle, R.: Automated Deduction in Multiple-Valued Logics. Oxford University Press, Oxford (1994)
20. Heuerding, A., Seyfried, M., Zimmermann, H.: Efficient loop-check for backward proof search in some non-classical propositional logics. In: Miglioli, P., Moscato, U., Mundici, D., Ornaghi, M. (eds.) TABLEAUX 1996. LNCS, vol. 1071, pp. 210–225. Springer, Heidelberg (1996). https://doi.org/10.1007/3-540-61208-4_14
21. Indrzejczak, A.: Cut-free double sequent calculus for S5. Log. J. IGPL **6**(3), 505–516 (1998)
22. Indrzejczak, A.: Generalised sequent calculus for propositional modal logics. Log. Trianguli **1**, 15–31 (1997)
23. Indrzejczak, A.: Multiple Sequent Calculus for Tense Logics. Abstracts of AiML and ICTL 2000, Leipzig, pp. 93–104 (2000)
24. Indrzejczak, A.: Natural Deduction, Hybrid Systems and Modal Logics. Springer, Heidelberg (2010). https://doi.org/10.1007/978-90-481-8785-0
25. Indrzejczak, A.: Simple decision procedure for S5 in standard cut-free sequent calculus. Bull. Sect. Log. **45**(2), 125–140 (2016)
26. Indrzejczak, A.: Linear time in hypersequent framework. Bull. Symb. Log. **22**(1), 121–144 (2016)
27. Kashima, R.: Cut-free sequent calculi for some tense logics. Stud. Log. **53**, 119–135 (1994)
28. Kurokawa, H.: Hypersequent calculi for modal logics extending S4. In: Nakano, Y., Satoh, K., Bekki, D. (eds.) JSAI-isAI 2013. LNCS (LNAI), vol. 8417, pp. 51–68. Springer, Cham (2014). https://doi.org/10.1007/978-3-319-10061-6_4
29. Lahav O.: From frame properties to hypersequent rules in modal logics. In: Proceedings of LICS, pp. 408–417. Springer (2013)
30. Lellmann, B.: Linear nested sequents, 2-sequents and hypersequents. In: De Nivelle, H. (ed.) TABLEAUX 2015. LNCS (LNAI), vol. 9323, pp. 135–150. Springer, Cham (2015). https://doi.org/10.1007/978-3-319-24312-2_10
31. Metcalfe, G., Olivetti, N., Gabbay, D.: Proof Theory for Fuzzy Logics. Springer, Heidelberg (2008). https://doi.org/10.1007/978-1-4020-9409-5
32. Mints, G.: Some calculi of modal logic [in Russian]. Trudy Mat. Inst. Steklov. **98**, 88–111 (1968)
33. Mints G.: Systems of Lewis and system T' [in Russian], Supplement to Russian edition. In: Feys, R. (ed.) Modal Logic, Nauka, pp. 422–509 (1974)
34. Mints, G.: Selected Papers in Proof Theory. North-Holland, Amsterdam (1992)
35. Negri, S., von Plato, J.: Structural Proof Theory. Cambridge University Press, Cambridge (2001)
36. Negri, S.: Proof analysis in modal logic. J. Philos. Log. **34**, 507–544 (2005)
37. Ohnishi, M., Matsumoto, K.: Gentzen method in modal calculi I. Osaka Math. J. **9**, 113–130 (1957)
38. Poggiolesi, F.: Gentzen Calculi for Modal Propositional Logic. Springer, Heidelberg (2011)

39. Pottinger, G.: Uniform cut-free formulations of T, S4 and S5 (abstract). J. Symb. Log. **48**, 900 (1983)
40. Restall, G.: Proofnets for S5: sequents and circuits for modal logic. Lect. Notes Log. **28**, 151–172 (2007)
41. Sato, M.: A study of kripke-type models for some modal logics by Gentzen's sequential method. Publ. Res. Inst. Math. Sci. Kyoto Univ. **13**, 381–468 (1977)
42. Serebriannikov, O.: Gentzen's Hauptsatz for modal logic with quantifiers. In: Niniluoto, I., Saarinen, E. (eds.) Intensional Logic: Theory and Applications; Acta Philosophica Fennica, vol. 35, pp. 79–88 (1982)
43. Stouppa, P.: A deep inference system for the modal logic S5. Stud. Log. **85**, 199–214 (2007)
44. Wansing, H.: Displaying Modal Logics. Kluwer Academic Publishers, Dordrecht (1999)
45. Wansing, H.: Sequent systems for modal logics. In: Gabbay, D., Guenthner, F. (eds.) Handbook of Philosophical Logic, vol. IV, pp. 89–133. Reidel Publishing Company, Dordrecht (2002)
46. Zeman, J.: Modal Logic. Oxford University Press, Oxford (1973)

Rewriting and Unification

On Asymmetric Unification for the Theory of XOR with a Homomorphism

Christopher Lynch[1], Andrew M. Marshall[2], Catherine Meadows[3], Paliath Narendran[4], and Veena Ravishankar[2(✉)]

[1] Clarkson University, Potsdam, NY, USA
clynch@clarkson.edu
[2] University of Mary Washington, Fredericksburg, VA, USA
{marshall,vravisha}@umw.edu
[3] Naval Research Laboratory, Washington, D.C., USA
catherine.meadows@nrl.navy.mil
[4] University at Albany-SUNY, Albany, NY, USA
pnarendran@albany.edu

Abstract. Asymmetric unification, or unification with irreducibility constraints, is a newly developed paradigm that arose out of the automated analysis of cryptographic protocols. However, there are still relatively few asymmetric unification algorithms. In this paper we address this lack by exploring the application of automata-based unification methods. We examine the theory of xor with a homomorphism, ACUNh, from the point of view of asymmetric unification, and develop a new automata-based decision procedure. Then, we adapt a recently developed asymmetric combination procedure to produce a general asymmetric-ACUNh decision procedure. Finally, we present a new approach for obtaining a solution-generating asymmetric-ACUNh unification automaton. We also compare our approach to the most commonly used form of asymmetric unification available today, variant unification.

1 Introduction

We examine the newly developed paradigm of asymmetric unification in the theory of *xor* with a homomorphism. Asymmetric unification is motivated by requirements arising from symbolic cryptographic protocol analysis [6]. These symbolic analysis methods require unification-based exploration of a space in which the states obey rich equational theories that can be expressed as a decomposition $R \uplus \Delta$, where R is a set of rewrite rules that is confluent, terminating, and coherent modulo Δ. However, in order to apply state space reduction techniques, it is usually necessary for at least part of this state to be in normal form, and to remain in normal form even after unification is performed. This requirement can be expressed as an *asymmetric* unification problem $\{s_1 =_\downarrow t_1, \ldots, s_n =_\downarrow t_n\}$ where the $=_\downarrow$ denotes a unification problem with the restriction that any unifier leaves the right-hand side of each equation irreducible.

At this point there are relatively few such algorithms. Thus in most cases when asymmetric unification is needed, an algorithm based on *variant unification* [8] is used.

© Springer Nature Switzerland AG 2019
A. Herzig and A. Popescu (Eds.): FroCoS 2019, LNAI 11715, pp. 297–312, 2019.
https://doi.org/10.1007/978-3-030-29007-8_17

Variant unification turns an $R \uplus \Delta$-problem into a set of Δ-problems. Application of variant unification requires that a number of conditions on the decomposition be satisfied. In particular, the set of Δ-problems produced must always be finite (this is equivalent to the *finite variant property* [4]) and Δ-unification must be decidable and finitary. Unfortunately, there is a class of theories commonly occurring in cryptographic protocols that do not have decompositions satisfying these necessary conditions: theories including an operator h that is homomorphic over an Abelian group operator $+$, that is AGh. There are a number of cryptosystems that include an operation that is homomorphic over an Abelian group operator, and a number of constructions that rely on this homomorphic property. These include for example RSA [13], whose homomorphic property is used in Chaum's blind signatures [3], and Pallier cryptosystems [12], used in electronic voting and digital cash protocols. Thus an alternative approach is called for.

In this paper we concentrate on asymmetric unification for a special case of AGh: the theory of *xor* with homomorphism, or $ACUNh$. We first develop an automata-based $ACUNh$-asymmetric decision procedure. We then apply a recently developed combination procedure for asymmetric unification algorithms to obtain a general asymmetric decision procedure allowing for free function symbols. This requires a non-trivial adaptation of the combination procedure, which originally required that the algorithms combined were not only decision procedures but produced complete sets of unifiers. In addition, the decomposition of $ACUNh$ we use is $\Delta = ACh$. It is known that unification modulo ACh is undecidable [11], so our result also yields the first asymmetric decision procedure for which Δ does not have a decidable finitary unification algorithm.

We then consider the problem of producing complete sets of asymmetric unifiers for $ACUNh$. We show how the decision procedure developed in this paper can be adapted to produce an automaton that generates a (possibly infinite) complete set of solutions. We then show, via an example, that asymmetric unification modulo $ACUNh$ is not finitary.

1.1 Outline

Section 2 provides a brief description of preliminaries. Section 3 develops an automaton based decision procedure for the $ACUNh$-theory. In Sect. 4 an automaton approach that produces substitutions is outlined. Section 5 develops the modified combination method needed to obtain general asymmetric algorithms. In Sect. 6 we conclude the paper and discuss further work.

2   Preliminaries

We use the standard notation of equational unification [1] and term rewriting systems [1]. Σ-terms, denoted by $T(\Sigma, \mathcal{X})$, are built over the signature Σ and the (countably infinite) set of variables $\mathcal{X}$. The terms $t|_p$ and $t[u]_p$ denote respectively the subterm of t at the position p, and the term t having u as subterm at position p. The symbol of t occurring at the position p (resp. the top symbol of t) is written $t(p)$ (resp. $t(\varepsilon)$). The set of positions of a term t is denoted by $Pos(t)$, the set of non variable positions for a term t over a signature Σ is denoted by $Pos(t)_\Sigma$. A Σ-*rooted* term is a term whose top symbol is in Σ. The set of variables of a term t is denoted by $Var(t)$. A term is *ground* if it contains no variables.

Definition 2.1. *Let Γ be an E-unification problem, let $\mathscr{X}$ denote the set of variables occurring in Γ and $\mathscr{C}$ the set of free constants occurring in Γ. For a given linear ordering $<$ on $\mathscr{X} \cup \mathscr{C}$, and for each $c \in \mathscr{C}$ define the set V_c as $\{x \mid x$ is a variable with $x < c\}$. An E*-unification problem with linear constant restriction *(LCR) is an E*-unification problem with constants, Γ, where each constant c in Γ is equipped with a set V_c of variables. A solution of the problem is an E-unifier σ of Γ such that for all c,x with $x \in V_c$, the constant c does not occur in $x\sigma$. We call σ an E*-unifier with LCR.*

A *rewrite rule* is an ordered pair $l \rightarrow r$ such that $l, r \in T(\Sigma, \mathscr{X})$ and $l \notin \mathscr{X}$. We use R to denote a term rewrite system which is defined as a set of rewrite rules. The rewrite relation on $T(\Sigma, \mathscr{X})$, written $t \rightarrow_R s$, hold between t and s iff there exists a non-variable $p \in Pos_\Sigma(t)$, $l \rightarrow r \in R$ and a substitution σ, such that $t|_p = l\sigma$ and $s = t[r\sigma]_p$. The relation $\rightarrow_{R/E}$ on $T(\Sigma, \mathscr{X})$ is $=_E \circ \rightarrow_R \circ =_E$. The relation $\rightarrow_{R,E}$ on $T(\Sigma, \mathscr{X})$ is defined as: $t \rightarrow_{R,E} t'$ if there exists a position $p \in Pos_\Sigma(t)$, a rule $l \rightarrow r \in R$ and a substitution σ such that $t|_p =_E l\sigma$ and $t' = t[r\sigma]_p$. The transitive (resp. transitive and reflexive) closure of $\rightarrow_{R,E}$ is denoted by $\rightarrow_{R,E}^+$ (resp. $\rightarrow_{R,E}^*$). A term t is $\rightarrow_{R,E}$ *irreducible* (or in R, E-*normal form*) if there is no term t' such that $t \rightarrow_{R,E} t'$. If $\rightarrow_{R,E}$ is confluent and terminating we denote the irreducible version of a term, t, by $t \downarrow_{R,E}$.

Definition 2.2. *We call (Σ, E, R) a* weak decomposition *of an equational theory Δ over a signature Σ if $\Delta = R \uplus E$ and R and E satisfy the following conditions:*

1. *Matching modulo E is decidable.*
2. *R is terminating modulo E, i.e., the relation $\rightarrow_{R/E}$ is terminating.*
3. *The relation $\rightarrow_{R,E}$ is confluent and E-coherent, i.e., $\forall t_1, t_2, t_3$ if $t_1 \rightarrow_{R,E} t_2$ and $t_1 =_E t_3$ then $\exists t_4, t_5$ such that $t_2 \rightarrow_{R,E}^* t_4$, $t_3 \rightarrow_{R,E}^+ t_5$, and $t_4 =_E t_5$.*

This definition is a modification of the definition in [6]. where asymmetric unification and the corresponding theory decomposition are first defined. The last restrictions ensure that $s \rightarrow_{R/E}^! t$ iff $s \rightarrow_{R,E}^! t$ (see [6,8]).

Definition 2.3 (Asymmetric Unification). *Given a weak decomposition (Σ, E, R) of an equational theory, a substitution σ is an* asymmetric R, E-unifier *of a set $\mathscr{S}$ of asymmetric equations $\{s_1 =_\downarrow t_1, \ldots, s_n =_\downarrow t_n\}$ iff for each asymmetric equations $s_i =_\downarrow t_i$, σ is an $(E \cup R)$-unifier of the equation $s_i =^? t_i$ and $(t_i \downarrow_{R,E})\sigma$ is in R, E-normal form. A set of substitutions Ω is a* complete set of asymmetric R, E-unifiers *of $\mathscr{S}$ (denoted $CSAU_{R \cup E}(\mathscr{S})$ or just $CSAU(\mathscr{S})$ if the background theory is clear) iff: (i) every member of Ω is an asymmetric R, E-unifier of $\mathscr{S}$, and (ii) for every asymmetric R, E-unifier θ of $\mathscr{S}$ there exists a $\sigma \in \Omega$ such that $\sigma \leq_E^{Var(\mathscr{S})} \theta$.*

Example 2.1. Let $R = \{x \oplus 0 \rightarrow x, x \oplus x \rightarrow 0, x \oplus x \oplus y \rightarrow y\}$ and E be the AC theory for $\oplus$. Consider the equation $y \oplus x =_\downarrow x \oplus a$, the substitution $\sigma_1 = \{y \mapsto a\}$ is an asymmetric solution but, $\sigma_2 = \{x \mapsto 0, y \mapsto a\}$ is not.

Definition 2.4 (Asymmetric Unification with Linear Constant Restriction). *Let $\mathscr{S}$ be a set of asymmetric equations with some LCR. A substitution σ is an* asymmetric R, E-unifier *of $\mathscr{S}$ with LCR iff σ is an asymmetric solution to $\mathscr{S}$ and σ satisfies the LCR.*

Definition 2.5. *Let R be a term rewriting system and E be a set of identities. We say* (R, E) *is* R, E*-convergent if and only if*

(a) $\to_{R,E}$ *is terminating, and*
(b) for all terms s, t, if $s \approx_{R \cup E} t$*, there exist terms* s'*,* t' *such that* $s \to^!_{R,E} s'$*,* $t \to^!_{R,E}$
     t'*, and* $s' \approx_E t'$

Definition 2.6. *A term t is an* R, Δ*-normal form of a term s if and only if* $s \to^!_{R,\Delta} t$*. This is often represented as* $t = s\!\downarrow_{R,\Delta}$*.*

3   An Asymmetric *ACUNh*-Unification Decision Procedure via an Automata Approach

In this section we develop a new asymmetric unification algorithm for the theory *ACUNh*. The theory *ACUNh* consists of the following identities: $x + x \approx 0$, $x + 0 \approx x$, $h(x + y) \approx h(x) + h(y)$, $h(0) \approx 0$, $(x + y) + z \approx x + (y + z)$, $x + y \approx y + x$
Following the definition of asymmetric unification, we first decompose the theory into a set of rewrite rules, R, modulo a set of equations, Δ. Actually, there are two such decompositions possible. The first decomposition keeps *associativity* and *commutativity* as identities Δ and the rest as rewrite rules. This decomposition has the following *AC*-convergent term rewriting system R_1: $x + x \to 0$, $x + 0 \to x$, $x + (y + x) \to y$, $h(x + y) \to h(x) + h(y)$, $h(0) \to 0$, as well as R'_1: $x + x \to 0$, $x + 0 \to x$, $x + (y + x) \to y$, $h(x) + h(y) \to h(x + y)$, $h(0) \to 0$ (when $+$ is given a higher precedence over h).

The second decomposition has *associativity*, *commutativity* and the distributive homomorphism identity as Δ^1, i.e., $\Delta = ACh$. Our goal here is to prove that the following term rewriting system R_2: $x + x \to 0$, $x + 0 \to x$, $x + (y + x) \to y$, $h(0) \to 0$ is *ACh*-convergent. The proof for convergence of $\to_{R_2, ACh}$ is provided in our tech report [10].

Decidability of asymmetric unification for the theory R_2, *ACh* can be shown by automata-theoretic methods analogous to the method used for deciding the Weak Second Order Theory of One successor (WS1S) [2,5]. In WS1S we consider quantification over finite sets of natural numbers, along with one successor function. All equations or formulas are transformed into finite-state automata which accepts the strings that correspond to a model of the formula [9,14]. This automata-based approach is key to showing decidability of WS1S, since the satisfiability of WS1S formulas reduces to the automata intersection-emptiness problem. We follow the same approach here.

To be precise, what we show here is that *ground* solvability of asymmetric unification, for a given set of constants, is decidable. We explain at the end of this section why this is equivalent to solvability in general, in Lemmas 3.1 and 3.2.

Problems with One Constant. For ease of exposition, let us consider the case where there is only one constant a. Thus every ground term can be represented as a set of natural numbers. The homomorphism h is treated as a successor function. Just as in WS1S, the input to the automata are column vectors of bits. The length of each column vector

---

[1] This is the background theory.

is the number of variables in the problem. $\Sigma = \left\{ \begin{pmatrix} 0 \\ 0 \\ \vdots \\ 0 \end{pmatrix}, \dots, \begin{pmatrix} 1 \\ 1 \\ \vdots \\ 1 \end{pmatrix} \right\}$. The deterministic finite automata (DFA) are illustrated here. The $+$ operator behaves like the *symmetric set difference* operator.

We illustrate how an automaton is constructed for each equation in standard form. In order to avoid cluttering up the diagrams the dead state has been included only for the first automaton. The missing transitions lead to the dead state by default for the others. Recall that we are considering the case of one constant a.

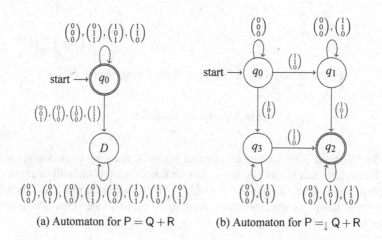

(a) Automaton for $P = Q + R$ (b) Automaton for $P =_{\downarrow} Q + R$

Fig. 1. Automata construction

Figure 1a: Let P_i, Q_i and R_i denote the ith bits of P, Q and R *respectively*. P_i has a value 1, when either Q_i or R_i has a value 1. We need 3-bit alphabet symbols for this equation. The input for this automaton are column vectors of 3-bits each, i.e., $\Sigma = \left\{ \begin{pmatrix} 0 \\ 0 \\ 0 \end{pmatrix}, \dots, \begin{pmatrix} 1 \\ 1 \\ 1 \end{pmatrix} \right\}$. For example, if $R_2 = 0$, $Q_2 = 1$, then $P_2 = 1$. The corresponding alphabet symbol is $\begin{pmatrix} P_2 \\ Q_2 \\ R_2 \end{pmatrix} = \begin{pmatrix} 1 \\ 1 \\ 0 \end{pmatrix}$. Hence, only strings with the alphabet symbols $\left\{ \begin{pmatrix} 0 \\ 0 \\ 0 \end{pmatrix}, \begin{pmatrix} 0 \\ 1 \\ 1 \end{pmatrix}, \begin{pmatrix} 1 \\ 0 \\ 1 \end{pmatrix}, \begin{pmatrix} 1 \\ 1 \\ 0 \end{pmatrix} \right\}$ are accepted by this automaton. The rest of the input symbols $\left\{ \begin{pmatrix} 0 \\ 0 \\ 1 \end{pmatrix}, \begin{pmatrix} 1 \\ 1 \\ 1 \end{pmatrix}, \begin{pmatrix} 0 \\ 1 \\ 0 \end{pmatrix}, \begin{pmatrix} 1 \\ 0 \\ 0 \end{pmatrix} \right\}$ go to the dead state D, as they violate the XOR property. Note that the string $\begin{pmatrix} 1 \\ 0 \\ 1 \end{pmatrix} \begin{pmatrix} 1 \\ 1 \\ 0 \end{pmatrix}$ is accepted by this automaton. This corresponds to $P = a + h(a)$, $Q = h(a)$ and $R = a$.

Figure 1b: To preserve asymmetry on the right-hand side of this equation, $Q + R$ should be irreducible. If either Q or R is empty, or if they have any term in common, then a reduction will occur. For example, if $Q = h(a)$ and $R = h(a) + a$, there is a reduction, whereas if R = h(a) and Q = a, irreducibility is preserved, since there is no common term and neither one is empty. Since neither Q nor R can be empty, any accepted string should have one occurrence of $\binom{1}{0}$ and one occurrence of $\binom{1}{1}$.

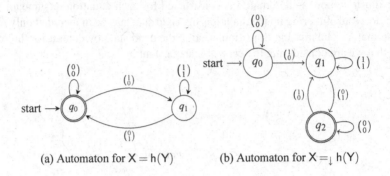

(a) Automaton for $X = h(Y)$ (b) Automaton for $X =_\downarrow h(Y)$

Fig. 2. Automata construction

Figure 2a: We need 2-bit vectors as alphabet symbols since we have two unknowns X and Y. Remember that h acts like the successor function. q_0 is the only accepting state. A state transition occurs with bit vectors $\binom{1}{0}, \binom{0}{1}$. If Y=1 in current state, then X=1 in the next state, hence a transition occurs from q_0 to q_1, and vice versa. The ordering of variables is $\binom{Y}{X}$.

Figure 2b: In this equation, h(Y) should be in normal form. So Y cannot be 0, but can contain terms of the form $u + v$. $\binom{Y}{X}$ is the ordering of variables. Therefore the bit vector $\binom{1}{0}$ should be succeeded by $\binom{0}{1}$, with possible occurrences of the bit vector $\binom{1}{1}$ in between. Thus the string either ends with $\binom{0}{1}$ or $\binom{0}{0}$. For example, if Y = h(a) + a, then $X = h^2(a) + h(a)$, which results in the string $\binom{1}{0} \binom{1}{1} \binom{0}{1}$ is accepted by this automaton. Figure 3a: This automaton represents the disequality $X^a \neq Y^a$. In general, if there are two or more constants, we have to guess which components are not equal. This enables us to handle the disequality constraints mentioned in the next section.

Figure 3b: This automaton represents the disequality $X \neq a$, where a is a constant.

Example 3.1. Let $\left\{ U =_\downarrow V + Y,\ W = h(V),\ Y =_\downarrow h(W) \right\}$ be an asymmetric unification problem. We need 4-bit vectors and 3 automata since we have 4 unknowns in 3 equations, with bit-vectors represented in this ordering of set variables: $\begin{pmatrix} V \\ W \\ Y \\ U \end{pmatrix}$. We include the × ("don't-care") symbol in state transitions to indicate that the values can be either 0 or 1. This is done to avoid cluttering the diagrams. Note that here this × symbol is a placeholder for the variables which do not have any significance in a given automaton. The automata constructed for this example are indicated in Figs. 4a, b and 5a. The

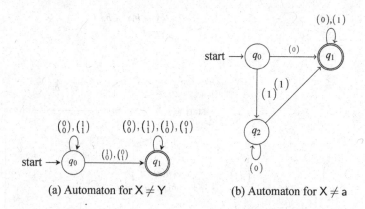

(a) Automaton for X ≠ Y   (b) Automaton for X ≠ a

Fig. 3. Automata construction

string $\begin{pmatrix}1\\0\\0\\1\end{pmatrix}\begin{pmatrix}0\\1\\0\\0\end{pmatrix}\begin{pmatrix}0\\0\\1\\1\end{pmatrix}\begin{pmatrix}0\\0\\0\\0\end{pmatrix}$ is accepted by all the three automata. The corresponding asymmetric unifier is $\{V \mapsto a, W \mapsto h(a), Y \mapsto h^2(a), U \mapsto (h^2(a) + a)\}$.

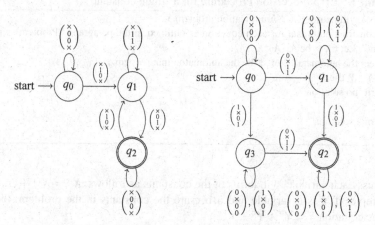

(a) Automata for Example 3.1, Part 1   (b) Automata for Example 3.1, Part 2

Fig. 4. Automata example

Once we have automata constructed for all the formulas, we take the intersection and check if there exists a string accepted by all the automata. If the intersection is not empty, then we have a solution or an asymmetric unifier for the given problem.

Problems with more than One Constant. This technique can be extended to the case where we have more than one constant. Suppose we have k constants, say $c_1, \ldots, c_k$.

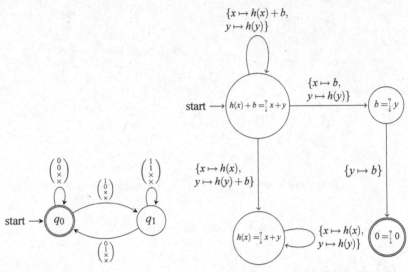

(a) Automata for Example 3.1, Part 3   (b) Substitution producing automaton

Fig. 5. Automata example

Algorithm 1. *ACUNh*-decision Procedure for a single constant

---

Require: Asymmetric *ACUNh*-unification problem S.

For S construct automata for each equation as outlined in the paragraph "Problems with one constant". Let these be $A_1, A_2, \ldots, A_n$.

"Intersect the automata": Let $\mathscr{A}$ be the automaton that recognizes $\bigcap_{i=1}^{n} L(A_i)$.

if $L(\mathscr{A}) = \emptyset$ **then**

    return 'no solution.'

else

    return a solution.

end if

We express each variable X in terms of the constants as follows: $X = X^{c_1} + \ldots + X^{c_k}$. For example, if Y is a variable and a, b, c are the constants in the problem, then we create the equation $Y = Y^a + Y^b + Y^c$.

If we have an equation $X = h(Y)$ with constants a, b, c, then we have equations $X^a = h(Y^a)$, $X^b = h(Y^b)$ and $X^c = h(Y^c)$. However, if it is an asymmetric equation $X =_{\downarrow} h(Y)$ all Y^a, Y^b and Y^c cannot be zeros simultaneously.

Similarly, if the equation to be solved is $X = W + Z$, with a, b, c as constants, we form the equations $X^a = W^a + Z^a$, $X^b = W^b + Z^b$ and $X^c = W^c + Z^c$ and solve the equations. But if it is an asymmetric equation $X =_{\downarrow} W + Z$ then we cannot have W^a, W^b, W^c to be all zero simultaneously, and similarly with Z^a, Z^b, Z^c.

Our approach is to design a nondeterministic algorithm by guessing which constant component in each variable has to be 0, i.e., for each variable Y and each constant b, we "flip a coin" as to whether Y^b will be set equal to 0 by the target solution[2]. Now for the case $X =_\downarrow W + Z$, we do the following:

> for all constants a do:
>> if $X^a = W^a = Z^a = 0$ then skip
>> else if $W^a = 0$ then set $X^a = Z^a$
>>> if $Z^a = 0$ then set $X^a = W^a$
>>> if both W^a and Z^a are non-zero then set $X^a =_\downarrow W^a + Z^a$

Similarly, for the case $X =_\downarrow h(Y)$ we follow these steps:

> for all constants a do:
>> if $X^a = Y^a = 0$ then skip
>> else set $X^a =_\downarrow h(Y^a)$

This is summarized in Algorithm 2. Thus, it follows that

Algorithm 2. Nondeterministic Algorithm when we have more than one constant

---

if there are m variables and k constants **then**
represent each variable in terms of its k constant components.
Guess which constant components have to be 0.
Form symmetric and asymmetric equations for each constant.
Solve each set of equations by the Deterministic Finite Automata (DFA) construction as outlined in Algorithm 1.
end if

Theorem 3.1. *Algorithm 2 is a decision procedure for ground asymmetric unification modulo* (R_2, ACh).

Proof. This holds by construction, as outlined in "Problems with only one constant" and "Problems with more than one constant".

We now show that general asymmetric unification modulo $ACUNh$, where the solutions need not be ground solutions over the current set of constants, is decidable by showing that a general solution exists if and only if there is a *ground* solution in the extended signature where we add an extra constant.

We represent each term as a sum of terms of the form $h^i(\alpha)$ where α is either a constant or variable. The superscript (power) i is referred to as the *degree* of the simple term $h^i(\alpha)$. The degree of a term is the maximum degree of its summands.

Lemma 3.1. *Let t be an irreducible term and d be its degree. Let $\mathcal{V}ar(t) = \{X_1, X_2, \dots, X_n\}$. Suppose c is a constant that does not appear in t. Then for any $D > d$, $t\theta$ is irreducible, where $\theta = \{X_1 \mapsto c, X_2 \mapsto h^D(c), X_3 \mapsto h^{2D}(c), \dots, X_n \mapsto h^{(n-1)(D)}(c)\}$.*

---

[2] The linear constant restrictions in Sect. 5 can also be handled this way: a constant restriction of the form $a \notin X$ can be taken care of by setting $X^a = 0$.

Lemma 3.2. *Let* $\Gamma = \{s_1 \approx^?_\downarrow t_1, \ldots, s_n \approx^?_\downarrow t_n\}$ *be an asymmetric unification problem. Let* β *be an asymmetric unifier of* Γ *and* $V = \mathcal{VRan}(\beta) = \{X_1, \ldots X_m\}$. *Let* $D = 1 + \max\limits_{1 \leq i \leq n} degree(s_i\beta, t_i\beta)$, *and* c *be a constant that does not appear in* Γ. *Then* $\theta = \{X_1 \mapsto c, X_2 \mapsto h^D(c), \ldots, X_m \mapsto h^{(n-1)D}(c)\}$ *is an asymmetric unifier of* Γ.

General solutions *over variables*, without this extra constant c, can be enumerated by back-substituting (abstracting) terms of the form $h^j(c)$ and checking whether the obtained substitutions are indeed solutions to the problem.
The exact complexity of this problem is open.

4   Automaton to Find a Complete Set of Unifiers

In this section we create automata to find all solutions of an ACUNh asymmetric unification problem with constants. We also have linear constant restrictions and disequalities for combination. Our terms will be built from elements in the set described below.

Definition 4.1. *Let* C *be a set of constants and* X *be a set of variables. Define* $H(X, C)$ *as the set* $\{h^i(t) \mid t \in X \cup C\}$. *We also define* $H_n(X, C)$ *as* $\{h^i(t) \mid t \in X \cup C, i \leq n\}$. *For any object* t *we define* $Const(t)$ *to be the set of constants in* t, *except for 0. For an object* t, *define* $H(t) = H(Var(t), Const(t))$ *and* $H_n(t) = H_n(Var(t), Const(t))$.

Terms are sums. We often need to talk about the multiset of terms in a sum.

Definition 4.2. *Let* t *be a term whose* R_h *normal form is* $t_1 + \cdots + t_n$. *Then we define* $mset(t) = \{t_1, \cdots, t_n\}$. *Inversely, if* $T = \{t_1, \cdots, t_n\}$ *then* $\Sigma T = t_1 + \cdots + t_n$.

A term in normal form modulo R_1 can be described as a sum in the following way.

Theorem 4.1. *Let* t *be a term in* R_1 *normal form. Then there exists an* $H \subseteq H(t)$ *such that* $t = \Sigma H$.

Proof. Since t is reduced by $h(x + y) \rightarrow h(x) + h(y)$, it cannot have an h symbol above a $+$ symbol. So it must be a sum of terms of the form $h^i(s)$ where $i \geq 0$ and s is a constant. Since t is also reduced by R_2, there can be no duplicates in the sum.

We show that every substitution θ that is irreducible with respect to R_1, can be represented as a sequence of smaller substitutions, which we will later use to construct an automaton.

Definition 4.3. *Let* ζ *be a substitution and* X *be a set of variables. Then* ζ *is a* zero substitution *on* X *if* $Dom(\zeta) \subseteq X$ *and* $x\zeta = 0$ *for all* $x \in Dom(\zeta)$.

Theorem 4.2. *Let* t *be an object and* θ *be a ground substitution in* R_1 *normal form, such that* $Dom(\theta) = Var(t)$. *Let* m *be the maximum degree in* $mset(Ran(\theta))$. *Then there are substitutions* $\zeta, \theta_0, \cdots, \theta_m$ *such that*

1. ζ *is a zero substitution on* $Dom(\theta)$,
2. $\zeta\theta_0 \cdots \theta_m = \theta$,

3. $Dom(\theta_i) = Var(t\zeta\theta_0 \cdots \theta_{i-i})$
4. for all i and all variables x in $Dom(\theta_i)$, $x\theta_i = \Sigma T$ for some nonempty $T \subseteq Const(Ran(\theta)) \cup \{h(x)\}$.

Proof. By the previous theorem, we know that each $x\theta$ is a sum of h-terms or is 0. Then ζ and θ_i can be defined as follows, where $S^x = mset(x\theta)$ and S_i^x is the set of terms in S with degree i:

– If $x\theta = 0$ then $x\zeta = 0$ else $x\zeta = x$.
– For all $x \in Dom(\theta_i)$
  • If the maximum degree of S^x is i then $x\theta_i = \Sigma S_i^x$.
  • If no terms in S^x have degree i then $x\theta_i = h(x)$.
  • If S^x has terms of degree i and also terms of degree greater than i then $x\theta_i = h(x) + \Sigma S_i^x$.

In the rest of this section we will be considering the ACUNh asymmetric equation $u =_{\downarrow}^? v$, where u and v are in R_1 normal form, and we will build an automaton to represent all the solutions of $u =_{\downarrow}^? v$. We will need the following definitions.

Definition 4.4. *Let t be an object. Define* $loseh(t) = \Sigma\{h^i(t) \mid h^{i+1}(t) \in mset(t \downarrow_{R_h})\}$.

In the next four automata definitions we will use the following notation: Let P be a set of ACUNh asymmetric equations. Let m be the maximum degree of terms in P. Let Θ be the set of all substitutions θ such that $Dom(\theta) \subseteq Var(P)$ and for all $x \in Dom(\theta)$, $x\theta = \Sigma T$ where T is a nonempty subset of $Const(P) \cup \{h(x)\}$. Let $u =_{\downarrow}^? v$ be an ACUNh asymmetric equation.

First we define an automaton to solve the *ACUNh* asymmetric unification problem with constants.

Definition 4.5. *The automaton $M(u =_{\downarrow}^? v, P)$ consists of the quintuple $(Q, q_{u=_{\downarrow}^? v}, F, \Theta, \delta)$, where Q is the set of states, $q_{u=_{\downarrow}^? v}$ is the start state, F is the set of accepting states, Θ is the alphabet, and δ is the transition function, defined as follows:*

– Q is a set of states of the form $q_{s=_{\downarrow}^? t}$, where $s = \Sigma S$ and $t = \Sigma T$, for some S and T subsets of $H_m(P)$.
– $F = \{q_{s=_{\downarrow}^? t} \in Q \mid mset(s) = mset(t)\}$
– $\delta : Q \times \Theta \longrightarrow Q$ such that $\delta(q_{s=_{\downarrow}^? t}, \theta) = q_{loseh(s\theta)\downarrow_{R_1} =_{\downarrow}^? loseh(t\theta)}$ if $Dom(\theta_i) = Var$ $(s =_{\downarrow}^? t)$, $mset((s\theta) \downarrow_{R_1}) \cap H_0(P) = mset(t\theta) \cap H_0(P)$, and $mset(t\theta)$ contains no duplicates.

Next we define an automaton to solve linear constant restrictions.

Definition 4.6. *Let R be a set of linear constant restrictions of the form (x, c). $M_{LCR}(R, P) = (\{q_0\}, q_0, \{q_0\}, \Theta, \delta_{LCR})$ where $\delta_{LCR}(q_0, \theta) = q_0$ if for all variables x and all $(x, c) \in R$, $c \notin Const(x\theta)$.*

Next we define an automaton to solve disequalities between a variable and a constant.

Definition 4.7. *Let D be a set of disequalities of the form $x \neq c$ where x is a variable and c is a constant. $M_{VC}(D,P) = (\{q_0,q_1\}, q_0, \{q_0,q_1\}, \Theta, \delta_{VC})$ where $\delta_{VC}(q_0, \theta) = q_1$ if for all variables x and all $x \neq c \in D$, $x\theta \neq c$. Also $\delta_{VC}(q_1, \theta) = q_1$.*

Finally we define automata for solving disequalities between variables

Definition 4.8. *Let x and y be variables. Then $M_{VV}(x \neq y, P) = (\{q_0,q_1\}, q_0, \{q_1\}, \Theta, \delta_{x \neq y})$ where $\delta_{x \neq y}(q_0, \theta) = q_0$ if $mset(x\theta) = T \cup \{h(x)\}$ and $mset(y\theta) = T \cup \{h(y)\}$ for some T. Also $\delta_{x \neq y}(q_0, \theta) = q_1$ if $mset(x\theta) \neq mset(y\theta)$ and $mset(x\theta)[x \mapsto y] \neq mset(y\theta)$.*

These are all valid automata. In particular, the first automaton described has a finite number of states, and each transition yields a state in the automaton. Now we show that these automata can be used to find all asymmetric ACUNh unifiers.

We need a few properties before we show our main theorem, that the constructed automaton finds all solutions.

Lemma 4.1. *Let t be an object and θ be a substitution, such that, for all $x \in Var(t)$, $mset(x\theta)$ does not contain a variable. Then $mset(t\theta)$ does not contain a variable.*

Proof. Consider $s \in mset(t)$. If s is not a variable then $s\theta$ is not a variable. If s is a variable, then, by our hypothesis, $s\theta$ is not a variable.

Lemma 4.2. *Let $s =^?_{\downarrow} t$ be an ACUNh asymmetric unification equation in P, where $mset(s)$ and $mset(t)$ contain no variables and $mset(s \downarrow_{R_1}) \cap H_0(P) \neq mset(t) \cap H_0(P)$. Then for all substitutions σ, $s\sigma$ and $t\sigma$ are not unifiable.*

Proof. s and t are not unifiable, because, wlog, the multiplicity of some constant in $mset(s \downarrow_{R_1})$ is not in $mset(t \downarrow_{R_1})$. When we apply a substitution, that same constant will appear in $mset((s\sigma) \downarrow_{R_1})$ but not $mset((t\sigma) \downarrow_{R_1})$, since $mset(s)$ and $mset(t)$ contain no variables. So $s\sigma$ and $t\sigma$ are not unifiable.

Lemma 4.3. *Let t be such that $mset(t)$ contains a duplicate. Then $\forall \sigma$, $t\sigma$ is reducible by R_2.*

Proof. We know t is reducible by R_2 because $mset(t)$ contains a duplicate. But then $t\sigma$ also contains a duplicate.

Lemma 4.4. *Let $s =^?_{\downarrow} t$ be an ACUNh asymmetric unification equation in P, such that $mset(s)$ and $mset(t)$ contain no variables. Suppose also that $mset(s \downarrow_{R_1}) \cap H_0(P) = mset(t) \cap H_0(P))$ and $mset(t)$ contains no duplicates. Then σ is an ACUNh asymmetric unifier of $s =^?_{\downarrow} t$ if and only if σ is an ACUNh asymmetric unifier of $loseh(s \downarrow_{R_1}) =^?_{\downarrow} loseh(t)$.*

Proof. Let $s' = loseh(s \downarrow_{R_1})$ and $t' = loseh(t)$. If $mset(s')$ and $mset(t')$ contain no constants, then $s =^?_{\downarrow} t$ and $s' =^?_{\downarrow} t'$ have the same solutions. Since $mset(s)$ and $mset(t)$ contain no variables, the multiset of constants in s is the same as the multiset of constants in $s\sigma$. Similarly for t and $t\sigma$. Therefore $s =^?_{\downarrow} t$ has the same solutions as $s' =^?_{\downarrow} t'$.

Theorem 4.3. *Let P be a set of asymmetric ACUNh equations, such that all terms in P are reduced by R_1. Let θ be a substitution which is reduced by R_1. Let R be a set of linear constant restrictions. Let D be a set of variable/constant disequalities. Let D' be a set of variable/variable disequalities.*

Then θ is a solution to P if and only if there exists a zero substitution ζ on P where all right hand sides in P are irreducible, and a sequence of substitutions $\theta_0, \cdots, \theta_m$ such that $\theta \leq \zeta\theta_0\cdots\theta_m$ and

1. *The string $\theta_0\cdots\theta_m$ is accepted by $M((u =_{\downarrow}^? v)\zeta) \downarrow_{R_1}, P'\zeta)$ for all $u =_{\downarrow}^? v \in P$.*
2. *The string $\theta_0\cdots\theta_m$ is accepted by $M_{LCR}(R, P'\zeta)$.*
3. *The string $\theta_0\cdots\theta_m$ is accepted by $M_{VC}(D, P'\zeta)$.*
4. *The string $\theta_0\cdots\theta_m$ is accepted by $M_{VV}(x \neq y, P'\zeta)$ for all $x \neq y \in D'$.*

where $P' = P \cup \{c =_{\downarrow}^? c\}$ for a fresh constant c.

Proof. First we show that Item 1 holds for a ground substitution θ reduced by R_1. By the previous theorem, θ can be represented as $\zeta\theta_0\cdots\theta_m$.

We show by induction that, for all i, if $\theta = \zeta\theta_0\cdots\theta_i$ and $\delta(q_{(u=_{\downarrow}^? v)\zeta}, \theta_0\cdots\theta_i) = q_{s=_{\downarrow}^? t}$ then $\theta\sigma$ is an asymmetric ACUNh unifier of $u =_{\downarrow}^? v$ if and only if σ is an asymmetric ACUNh unifier of $s =_{\downarrow}^? t$. In the base case, $\theta = \zeta$ and $(s =_{\downarrow}^? t) = (u =_{\downarrow}^? v)\zeta$, so it is true.

For the inductive step, we assume the statement is true for i and prove it for $i+1$. Then let σ' be an arbitrary substitution, and instantiate σ $\theta\sigma'$ in the inductive assumption, where $\theta = \zeta\theta_0\cdots\theta_i$. Our assumption implies that $\theta\theta_{i+1}\sigma$ is an asymmetric ACUNh unifier of $u =_{\downarrow}^? v$ if and only if $\theta_i\sigma$ is an asymmetric ACUNh unifier of $s =_{\downarrow}^? t$ (i.e., σ is an asymmetric ACUNh unifier of $(s =_{\downarrow}^? t)\theta_{i+1}$). If we can now show that σ is an asymmetric ACUNh unifier of $(s =_{\downarrow}^? t)\theta_{i+1}$ if and only if σ is an ACUNh unifier of $loseh(s\theta_{i+1}) =_{\downarrow}^? loseh(t\theta_{i+1})$. and $mset(s\theta_{i+1} \cap H_0(P') = mset(t\theta_{i+1}) \cap H_0(P')$ and $mset(t\theta_{i+1})$ contains no duplicates, then we are done. By Lemma 4.1, we know that $mset(s =_{\downarrow}^? t)\theta_{i+1}$ contains no variables. Then we apply Lemma 4.4 to prove the induction step.

This proves our inductive statement. If θ is not an asymmetric ACUNh unifier of $u =_{\downarrow}^? v$, then Lemmas 4.2 and 4.3 imply that the transition function will not be applicable at some point. Our inductive statement shows that θ is an asymmetric ACUNh unifier of $u =_{\downarrow}^? v$ if and only if there is a final state with id as an asymmetric ACUNh unifier, which will be an accepting state.

This concludes the case for a ground substitution θ. It θ is not ground, then the fact that P' contains a fresh constant c means that we create substitutions with an additional constant. We have already shown in this paper that nonground solutions are generalizations of solutions involving one additional constant.

It is straightforward to see that the other automata only accept valid solutions of linear constant restrictions and disequations.

If desired, we could intersect all the automata, yielding an automaton representing all the solutions of the problem (think of the results after applying ζ as a set of initial states). This shows that the set of solutions can be represented by a regular language, with or without *LCRs* and disequalities. If we only want to decide asymmetric unification, we just check if there is an accepting state reachable from an initial state. We could enumerate all the solutions by finding all accepting states reachable in 1 step, 2 steps, etc. If there is a cycle on a path to an accepting state, then there are an infinite number of solutions, otherwise there are only a finite number of solutions. This will find all the ground substitutions. To find all solutions, we generalize the solutions we find and check them. Indeed, the only terms that need to be generalized are those containing c. This is decidable because there are only a finite number of generalizations.

In Fig. (5b), we show the automaton created for the problem $h(x) + b =_?^? x + y$, without linear constant restrictions and disequality constraints. In this example, the only zero substitution that works is the identity. Notice that c never appears in the domain of a substitution, because no such substitution satisfies the conditions for the transition function. This leads to the following theorem.

Theorem 4.4. *Asymmetric ACUNh unification with constants is not finitary.*

Proof. The automaton constructed for $h(x) + b =_?^? x + y$ has a cycle on a path to an accepting state. Therefore there are an infinite number of solutions. Since there is no c in the range of the solution, all the solutions are ground. So no solution can be more general than another one, which means this infinite set of solutions is also a minimal complete set of solutions.

5   Combining Automata Based Asymmetric Algorithms with the Free Theory

In order to obtain a general asymmetric ACUNh-unification decision procedure we need to add free function symbols. We can do this by using disjoint combination. The problem of asymmetric unification in the combination of disjoint theories was studied in [7] where an algorithm is developed for the problem. However, the algorithm of [7] does not immediately apply to the two methods developed in this paper. This is due to the nature of the two automata based approaches. More formally, let Δ_1 and Δ_2 denote two equational theories with disjoint signatures Σ_1 and Σ_2. Let Δ be the combination, $\Delta = \Delta_1 \cup \Delta_2$, of the two theories having signature $\Sigma_1 \cup \Sigma_2$. The algorithm of [7] solves the asymmetric Δ-unification problem. It assumes that there exists a finitary complete asymmetric Δ_i-unification algorithm with linear constant restrictions, A_i. Based on this assumption the algorithm is able to check solutions produced by the A_1 and A_2 algorithms for theory-preserving and injective properties, discarding those that are not. A substitution σ_i is *injective* modulo Δ_i if $x\sigma_i =_{\Delta_i} y\sigma_i$ iff $x = y$, and σ_i is *theory preserving* if for any variable x of index i, $x\sigma_i$ is not a variable of index $j \neq i$. For the automaton it is not always possible to check solutions, however, it is possible to build constraints into the automaton that enforce these conditions. Algorithm 3 (outlined in our tech report [10]) is a modification of the algorithm from [7] with the following properties:

- $\Delta_1 = ACUNh$ and $\Delta_2 = F_\Omega$, for some free theory F_Ω with symbols Ω.
- For each Δ_1-pure problem, partition, and theory index, an automaton is constructed enforcing the injective and theory preserving restrictions. Since these restrictions are

built into the automata, the only Δ_1 solutions produced will be both theory preserving and injective.
- The solution produced by the F_Ω algorithm is checked as in the original algorithm. If the solution is found not to be injective or theory preserving it is discarded.

The new modified version is presented in Algorithm 3 (included in the appendix due to space). Given the decision procedure of Sect. 3 we obtain the following.

Theorem 5.1. *Assume there exists an asymmetric ACUNh decision procedure that enforces linear constant restrictions, theory indexes, and injectivity. Then Algorithm 3 is a general asymmetric ACUNh decision procedure.*

Proof. The result follows directly from the proof contained in [7]. There it is shown that Algorithm 3 is both sound and complete. The only modification is that in [7] the combination algorithm checks the Δ_1 solutions for the properties of being injective and theory preserving, while in Algorithm 3 it is assumed that the algorithm A_1 itself will enforce these restrictions.

If instead of a decision procedure we want to obtain a general asymmetric *ACUNh* unification algorithm we can use the automata based algorithm from Sect. 4 and again a modification of the asymmetric combination algorithm of [7]. Here, the modification to the combination algorithm is even smaller. We just remove the check on injective and theory preserving substitutions. Again these restrictions are enforced by the automata. The solutions to the *ACUNh* and the free theory are combined as is done in [7] since they obey the same linear constant restrictions. Since asymmetric *ACUNh* unification with constants is not finitary (Theorem 4.4), the general asymmetric *ACUNh* unification algorithm will not in general produce a finite set of solutions. However, based on the algorithm of Sect. 4 we easily obtain the following result.

Theorem 5.2. *Assume there exists an asymmetric ACUNh algorithm that enforces linear constant restrictions, theory indexes and injectivity, and produces a complete set of unifiers. Then there exists a general asymmetric ACUNh algorithm producing a complete set of unifiers.*

6   Conclusion

We have provided a decision procedure and an algorithm for asymmetric unification modulo *ACUNh* using a decomposition $R \uplus ACh$. This is the first example of an asymmetric unification algorithm for a theory in which unification modulo the set Δ of axioms is undecidable. It also has some practical advantages: it is possible to tell by inspection of the automaton used to construct unifiers whether or not a problem has a finitary solution. Moreover, the construction of the automaton gives us a natural way of enumerating solutions; simply traverse one of the loops one more time to get the next unifier.

There are a number of ways in which we could extend this work. For example, the logical next step is to consider the decidability of asymmetric unification of *AGh* with a $\Delta = ACh$. If the methods we used for *ACUNh* extend to *AGh*, then we have an asymmetric unification algorithm for AGh, although with $\Delta = ACh$ instead of AC. On the other hand, if we can prove undecidability of asymmetric unification for AGh with $\Delta = ACh$ as well as with $\Delta = AC$, this could give us new understanding of the problem that might allow us to obtain more general results. Either way, we expect the results to give increased understanding of asymmetric unification when homomorphic encryption is involved.

References

1. Baader, F., Snyder, W.: Unification theory. Handb. Autom. Reasoning **1**, 445–532 (2001)
2. Büchi, J.R.: Weak second-order arithmetic and finite automata. Math. Logic Quart. **6**(1–6), 66–92 (1960)
3. Chaum, D.: Blind signature system. In: Chaum, D. (ed.) Advances in Cryptology, p. 153. Springer, Boston (1984). https://doi.org/10.1007/978-1-4684-4730-9_14
4. Comon-Lundh, H., Delaune, S.: The finite variant property: how to get rid of some algebraic properties. In: Giesl, J. (ed.) RTA 2005. LNCS, vol. 3467, pp. 294–307. Springer, Heidelberg (2005). https://doi.org/10.1007/978-3-540-32033-3_22
5. Elgot, C.C.: Decision problems of finite automata design and related arithmetics. Trans. Am. Math. Soc. **98**(1), 21–51 (1961)
6. Erbatur, S., et al.: Asymmetric unification: a new unification paradigm for cryptographic protocol analysis. In: Bonacina, M.P. (ed.) CADE 2013. LNCS (LNAI), vol. 7898, pp. 231–248. Springer, Heidelberg (2013). https://doi.org/10.1007/978-3-642-38574-2_16
7. Erbatur, S., Kapur, D., Marshall, A.M., Meadows, C., Narendran, P., Ringeissen, C.: On asymmetric unification and the combination problem in disjoint theories. In: Muscholl, A. (ed.) FoSSaCS 2014. LNCS, vol. 8412, pp. 274–288. Springer, Heidelberg (2014). https://doi.org/10.1007/978-3-642-54830-7_18
8. Escobar, S., Meseguer, J., Sasse, R.: Variant narrowing and equational unification. Electr. Notes Theor. Comput. Sci. **238**(3), 103–119 (2009)
9. Klaedtke, F., Ruess, H.: Parikh automata and monadic second-order logics with linear cardinality constraints, Technical report 177, Universität Freiburg (2002)
10. Lynch, C., Marshall, A.M., Meadows, C.A., Narendran, P., Ravishankar, V.: On asymmetric unification for the theory of xor with a homomorphism. Technical report, Clarkson University, University of Mary Washington, Naval Research Laboratory, University at Albany-SUNY (2019). https://www.marshallandrew.net/ach-asymmetric.pdf
11. Narendran, P.: Solving linear equations over polynomial semirings. In: Proceedings, 11th Annual IEEE Symposium on Logic in Computer Science, New Brunswick, New Jersey, USA, 27–30 July 1996, pp. 466–472. IEEE Computer Society (1996)
12. Paillier, P.: Public-key cryptosystems based on composite degree residuosity classes. In: Stern, J. (ed.) EUROCRYPT 1999. LNCS, vol. 1592, pp. 223–238. Springer, Heidelberg (1999). https://doi.org/10.1007/3-540-48910-X_16
13. Rivest, R.L., Shamir, A., Adleman, L.M.: A method for obtaining digital signatures and public-key cryptosystems. Commun. ACM **21**(2), 120–126 (1978)
14. Vardi, M.Y., Wilke, T.: Automata: from logics to algorithms. Logic Automata **2**, 629–736 (2008)

Reviving Basic Narrowing Modulo

Dohan Kim[1], Christopher Lynch[1(✉)], and Paliath Narendran[2]

[1] Clarkson University, Potsdam, USA
{dohkim,clynch}@clarkson.edu
[2] University at Albany, SUNY, Albany, USA
pnarendran@albany.edu

Abstract. We define an inference rule called the Parallel rule. Given a rewrite system R and an equational theory E, where R is E-convergent modulo, we show that if R is saturated under the Parallel rule then Basic Narrowing modulo E is complete for R. If R is finitely saturated under both Parallel and Forward Overlap then Basic Narrowing, with right hand side abstracted, is complete and terminates, and thus it is a decision procedure for unification modulo $R \cup E$. We give examples, such as the theory of XOR, the theory of abelian groups and Associativity with a unit element. We also show that R has the finite variant property modulo E if and only if R can be finitely saturated under Parallel and Forward Overlap, provided that E unification is finitary.

Keywords: Basic Narrowing · E-unification · Finite Variant Property

1 Introduction

If an equational theory can be represented as a convergent rewrite system R, then rewriting with R decides the word problem. However, some equations cannot be oriented into rewrite rules, such as Associativity and Commutativity. Then we may be able to split the equational theory into a rewrite system R and a set of equations E where R is E-convergent, which also decides the word problem.

Narrowing lifts rewriting to solve unification problems. Narrowing with R modulo E produces a complete set of unifiers for the $R \cup E$ unification problem if R is E-convergent [10]. This is useful for applications such as Cryptographic Protocol Analysis [7,8]. Unfortunately, Narrowing modulo E rarely halts, so it is not practical to use. Basic Narrowing is a modification of Narrowing, where unification problems are stored as constraints, rather than solving them immediately. Narrowing may not take place inside a constraint, so Basic Narrowing is more likely to halt. Unfortunately, Basic Narrowing modulo E is non-terminating for many equational theories, and, even worse, it is not complete, i.e., it may not produce a complete set of unifiers [5]. Because of these flaws it has been mostly abandoned, in favor of other Narrowing methods such as Variant Narrowing [9].

This paper is our attempt to revive Basic Narrowing modulo. We create a new inference rule, called the Parallel rule. If R is saturated by the Parallel rule, we

© Springer Nature Switzerland AG 2019
A. Herzig and A. Popescu (Eds.): FroCoS 2019, LNAI 11715, pp. 313–329, 2019.
https://doi.org/10.1007/978-3-030-29007-8_18

show that Basic Narrowing modulo E is complete. We show that if R is finitely saturated under both Parallel and Forward Overlap then Basic Narrowing with Right Hand Side Abstracted (meaning that right hand sides of rewrite rules are assumed to be reduced) is both complete and terminating, which is necessary for applications. This gives a decision procedure for unification. These inference rules are practical, as we illustrate with examples such as the theory of Exclusive OR and the theory of Abelian groups, where the saturation under these inference rules produces very few additional rewrite rules. In fact we show that a rewrite system R can be finitely saturated by Parallel and Forward Overlap w.r.t. a finitary E if and only if R has the Finite Variant Property modulo E (see also [4] for a similar result in the empty theory).

Basic Narrowing modulo was shown to be incomplete [5] for the following AC-convergent rewrite system R_1:

1. $x + 0 \rightarrow x$ 3. $b + b \rightarrow 0$ 5. $b + b + x \rightarrow x$
2. $a + a \rightarrow 0$ 4. $a + a + x \rightarrow x$

where $+$ is an AC symbol with an identity element 0, x is a variable, and a and b are constants. The $R_1 \cup AC$-unification problem $y + z \approx^?_{R_1 \cup AC} 0$ has a solution $\{y \mapsto a+b, z \mapsto a+b\}$, which cannot be found with Basic Narrowing. A Basic Narrowing step with the fourth rule gives $x \approx^?_{R_1 \cup AC} 0$, with a constraint of $y + z \approx_{AC} a + a + x$. One solution of this constraint is $x \mapsto u + v, y \mapsto a + u, z \mapsto a + v$. If we could Narrow into the constraint, corresponding to a Narrowing step at the variable position x, with $b + b \rightarrow 0$ then this problem would be solved, but Basic Narrowing does not allow that, and there is no other way to solve this problem. To solve this problem in this paper, we define an inference rule called Parallel (or E-Parallel and more specifically AC-Parallel). It combines the parallel steps from rules 4 and 3 into one rewrite rule $a + a + b + b \rightarrow 0$. It also creates the extension of this rule $a + a + b + b + x \rightarrow x$. (We sometimes leave out parentheses for AC formulas, when they are not important.) After adding these two additional rules, Basic Narrowing is complete.

To motivate the Forward Overlap rule, let $R_2 = \{h(x) * h(y) \rightarrow h(x * y)\}$. For the purposes of this example, it doesn't matter whether the $*$ and $+$ symbol are free or are associative and commutative. The forward Overlap rule combines two rewrite steps into one. An application of Forward Overlap gives a new rewrite rule $h(h(x)) * h(h(y)) \rightarrow h(h(x * y))$. This process can be repeated an infinite number of times in this particular example.

The Forward Overlap rule is not applicable for R_1. So a form of Narrowing called Basic Narrowing with Right Hand Side Abstracted (BNR) is complete for R_1. In R_1 it was only necessary to add two rewrite rules to make it complete for BNR. In other examples, such as R_2 it takes infinitely many new rewrite rules. But there are many practical examples like R_1 where very few rewrite rules are needed.

We give examples to show that saturation under Parallel and Forward Overlap can often be accomplished by adding just a few rules, in theories such as Exclusive OR and Abelian group theory. We also show that a theory can be finitely saturated by Parallel and Forward Overlap if and only if that theory has the Finite Variant Property, provided that the E unification problem is finitary.

In particular, we show that a rewrite system is saturated by Parallel if and only if every innermost redex can be reduced with an instance of a rule mapping all variables in the right hand side to terms in normal form (IRR). This implies that Basic Narrowing is complete. We also show that a rewrite system is saturated by Parallel and Forward Overlap if and only if every innermost redex can be reduced to normal form in one step (IR1). This implies that Basic Narrowing with Right Hand Side Abstracted is complete, which in turn implies a property we call the Finite Constraint Property, which is a generalization of the Finite Variant Property, to also handle equational theories with an infinitary unification problem, such as the theory of Associativity. If the unification problem is finitary, this is equivalent to the Finite Variant Property (FVP), which in turn implies IR1.

2   Preliminaries

We use standard notation of term rewriting [1,3,6,11] and equational unification [2]. We use the usual definition of substitution. If σ is a substitution and V is a set of variables, then $\sigma|_V$ is the restriction of σ to the variables of V. We say a substitution θ *extends* a substitution σ if $\theta|_{Dom(\sigma)} = \sigma$, where $Dom(\sigma) = \{x \mid x\sigma \neq x\}$. A *complete set of E-unifiers* of an E-unification problem Γ is a set of substitutions, denoted by $CSU_E(\Gamma)$, such that each element of $CSU_E(\Gamma)$ is an E-unifier of Γ and for each E-unifier θ of Γ, there exists some $\sigma \in CSU_E(\Gamma)$ such that $\sigma \leq^V_E \theta$, where V is the set of variables of Γ. An ordering has the *subterm property* no term t is greater than a proper subterm of t. A reduction ordering $>$ is E-compatible if $s' \approx_E s > t \approx_E t'$ implies $s' > t'$ for all s, s', t and t'.

Given a rewrite system R and a set of equations E, denoted by (R, E), the relation $\to_{R,E}$ on $T(\Sigma, V)$ is defined by $s \to_{R,E} t$ (or more specifically $s \xrightarrow{p}_{R,E} t$) iff there is a non-variable position $p \in \mathcal{FP}os(s)$, a rewrite rule $l \to r \in R$, and a substitution σ such that $s|_p \approx_E l\sigma$ and $t = s[r\sigma]_p$. The relation $\to_{R,E}$ is decidable whenever E-matching is decidable. The transitive and reflexive closure of $\to_{R,E}$ is denoted by $\xrightarrow{*}_{R,E}$. We say that a term t is R, E-*irreducible* (or in R, E-normal form) if there is no term t' such that $t \to_{R,E} t'$. If $s \xrightarrow{*}_{R,E} t$ and t is R, E-irreducible, we say that t is a *reduced form* of s (or a *normal form* of s), denoted by $t = s\downarrow_{R,E}$. E is *regular* if $Var(s) = Var(t)$ for all $s \approx t$ in E.

A substitution σ is called R, E-*reduced* if $x\sigma$ is R, E-irreducible for all $x \in V$. We say that a term t is an *innermost redex* of R, E iff t is R, E-reducible only at the top position. Let $s \to t$ be a rewrite rule. Let θ be a substitution. The instance $s\theta \to t\theta$ is a *right-reduced instance* if $x\theta$ is in normal form for all variables x in t. Note that $t\theta$ may or may not be reduced.

The rewrite system (R, E) is *Church-Rosser modulo E* if for all terms s and t with $s =_E t$, there are terms u and v such that $s \xrightarrow{*}_{R,E} u =_E v \xleftarrow{*}_{R,E} t$.

The rewrite system (R, E) is *convergent modulo E* if (R, E) is Church-Rosser modulo E and $\leftrightarrow_E \circ \to_R \circ \leftrightarrow_E$ is well-founded. In this paper, we simply say that the rewrite system R is *R, E-convergent* (or *E-convergent*) if the rewrite system (R, E) is *convergent modulo E*.

3 Inference Rules on the Rewrite System

Throughout the paper, we assume E is a regular equational theory, and R is an E-convergent rewrite theory, under an E-compatible reduction ordering with the subterm property, so we will not explicitly state this in the theorems.

We give an inference rule called Parallel (or E-Parallel) which is a key contribution of this paper. This is the rule that needs to be added to make Basic Narrowing complete modulo an equational theory. It can be viewed as a non-critical overlap below a variable position, but only in very specific cases. The example in the introduction gives an idea where the name comes from. The purpose of the rule is to ensure that every innermost redex can be reduced by an instance of a rewrite rule where substitutions to variables on the right hand side are reduced.

E-Parallel

$$\frac{s \to t \qquad l \to r \qquad v \approx u[l']}{v\sigma \to v'}$$

where

1. $s \to t \in R$
2. $l \to r \in R$
3. $v \approx u[l'] \in E$
4. l' is a strict subterm of u and is not a variable
5. $\sigma \in CSU_E(l \approx^?_E l',\ u \approx^?_E s)$
6. v' is some normal form of $v\sigma$
7. t contains a variable x, where $l'\sigma$ is E-equivalent to a subterm of $x\sigma$

Definition 1. The above Parallel inference rule is *redundant* if either

1. for all s' such that $s' \approx_E s\sigma$, a strict subterm of s' is R, E-reducible, or
2. $s\sigma$ is R, E-reducible by a right-reduced instance of a rule.

In the next section we will define Basic Narrowing, and later show that if R is saturated under Parallel, then Basic Narrowing is complete.

Next we define the Forward Overlap rule, which is like the Critical Pair rule, except it reduces an instance of the right side of a rule instead of the left side. It ensures that all innermost redexes can be reduced to normal form in one step.

ForwardOverlap

$$\frac{u \to v[s'] \qquad s \to t}{(u \to v[t])\theta}$$

where

1. $u \to v[s'] \in R$
2. $s \to t \in R$
3. s' is not a variable
4. $\theta \in CSU_E(s = s')$

Definition 2. The above Forward Overlap inference rule is *redundant* if, for all $u' \approx_E u\theta$, u' is R, E reducible by a right-reduced instance of a rule $l \to r$, with matching substitution σ, and either

1. $l\sigma < u\theta$ or
2. $l\sigma \approx_E u\theta$ and $r\sigma < v[s']\theta$.

The notions of redundancy in this section are slightly different than the standard notions of redundancy. Instead of just requiring that redundant rules are implied by smaller instances of rules, this requires that redundant rules are implied by smaller instances of rules, where all substitutions to variables on the right hand sides of the rules are reduced. This will be necessary to make Basic Narrowing complete.

In the next section we will define Basic Narrowing with Right Hand Side Abstracted, and show that if R is saturated under the Parallel Rule and Forward Overlap then Basic Narrowing with Right Hand Side Abstracted is complete. Since we will see that Basic Narrowing with Right Hand Side Abstracted always terminates, this gives a decision procedure for unification.

We now give an example to illustrate the inference rules. There are also many interesting examples toward the end of the paper.

Example 1. $R_0 = \{f(x_1) \to g(x_1), k(x_2) \to q(x_2), b \to c\}$. Let $E = \{f(h(k(x))) \approx p(x), h(q(a)) \approx b\}$. There is a Parallel inference between $f(x_1) \to g(x_1)$ and $k(x_2) \to q(x_2)$ involving the equation $f(h(k(x))) \approx p(x)$. This is because $f(x_1)$ unifies with $f(h(k(x)))$, and $k(x_2)$ unifies with $k(x)$. Let $\sigma \in CSU_E(f(x_1) \approx^?_E f(h(k(x))), k(x_2) \approx^?_E k(x))$. So $\sigma = \{x_1 \mapsto h(k(x)), x_2 \mapsto x\}$. Since $k(x)$ is a subterm of $x_1\sigma$, the Parallel rule can be applied. The result is $p(x) \to g(h(q(x)))$. Let $R_1 = R_0 \cup \{p(x) \to g(h(q(x)))\}$. R_1 is saturated by Parallel, but it is not saturated by Forward Overlap. There is a Forward Overlap inference between $p(x) \to g(h(q(x)))$ and $b \to c$, because $h(q(x))$ is unifiable with b using the substitution $x \mapsto a$. The result of applying the Forward Overlap rule is $p(a) \to g(c)$. Let $R_2 = R_1 \cup \{p(a) \to g(c)\}$. Now R_2 is saturated by Parallel and Forward Overlap rule.

We define a set of inference rules to be *saturated* if all inferences are redundant, according to the definition of redundancy we give in each rule. An E-convergent rewrite system could be constructively saturated by applying the inferences exhaustively and adding new rewrite rules. The set of rewrite rules will still be E-convergent.

4   Inference Rules for Solving the Unification Problem

We introduce constrained terms, of the form $t|\varphi$, where t is a term and φ is a set of unification problems. Solutions and instances of constraints are defined as:

Definition 3. Let E be an equational theory. Let $t|\varphi$ be a constrained term. The *solutions of* φ are $Sol(\varphi) = \{\sigma \mid u\sigma \approx_E v\sigma \text{ for all } u\approx_E^? v \in \varphi\}$. The *irreducible instances of* $t|\varphi$ are $IInst(t|\varphi) = \{t\sigma \mid \sigma \in Sol(\varphi) \text{ and } x\sigma \text{ is in normal form for all } x \in Var(t)\}$.

Narrowing is a relation on constrained terms, with notation $t_1|\varphi_1 \rightsquigarrow t_2|\varphi_2$. Completeness is defined as follows:

Definition 4. A narrowing inference system is *complete* if given a term s and a reduced substitution σ, there is a sequence of narrowing steps $s \mid \top \overset{*}{\rightsquigarrow} t \mid \varphi$ and a substitution θ such that

1. σ can be extended to θ,
2. θ is a solution of φ, and
3. $t\theta$ is a normal form of $s\sigma$.

In this section we present two Narrowing rules. BN stands for Basic Narrowing, and BNR stands for Basic Narrowing with Right Hand Side Abstracted.

BN

$$\frac{u[s'] \mid \varphi \qquad s \to t}{u[t] \mid \varphi, s \approx_E^? s'}$$

where

1. $s \to t \in R$
2. s' is not a variable

Example 2. Consider the rewrite system R_0 from Example 1, and apply BN to $p(x)|\top$. The only reduction is with $f(x) \to g(x)$, which gives $g(x') \mid f(x')\approx_E^? p(x)$. (Note that $p(x) \approx_E f(h(k(x)))$.) All further BN steps have unsatisfiable constraints, but there are instances that are not reduced. This shows that BN is not complete for R_0. However, it can be checked that BN is complete for R_1.

Next we introduce the BNR inference rule, where the right hand side of the rewrite rule used for narrowing gets extracted into the constraint.

BNR

$$\frac{u[s']|\varphi \qquad s \to t}{u[x] \mid \varphi, s \approx_E^? s', x\approx_E^? t}$$

where

1. $s \to t \in R$
2. s' is not a variable
3. x is a fresh variable

Example 3. In Example 1, BNR is not complete for R_1. The term $p(a)$ cannot be reduced to its normal form $g(c)$ in one step. So, for example, a BNR from $p(a)$, using $p(x) \to g(h(q(x)))$ gives $y \mid p(a) \approx^?_E p(x), y \approx^?_E g(h(q(x)))$, which cannot be reduced further. It can be checked that BNR is complete for R_2.

BN and BNR are used, as usual, to find normal forms of every instance of a term. They can also be used to solve equational unification in $R \cup E$, in combination with an E-unification inference rule.

5   Optional Inference Rules

In this section we give some inference rules to augment the Basic Narrowing rules. These rules are not necessary for any of the results in this paper. But they are rules that are useful for designing an implementation that is efficient in practice. In these inference rules, as opposed to the earlier rules in the paper, the hypothesis is replaced by the conclusion.

The Concretization rule says that we can remove a constraint completely or partially remove a constraint, and apply a substitution satisfying the constraint directly to the unification problem.

Concretization

$$\frac{u|\varphi}{u\sigma|\varphi}$$

where σ is the most general unifier of φ.

The Split rule allows us to split a unification problem into two if the instances remain the same. Suppose a constraint has a finite number of solutions. We could split up a unification problem into one for each solution, and then apply Concretization to apply the substitutions.

Split

$$\frac{u|\varphi}{u|\varphi_1 \quad u|\varphi_2}$$

where $IInst(u|\varphi) = IInst(u|\varphi_1) \cup IInst(u|\varphi_2)$.

Simplify is an important rule. Suppose a unification problem simplifies using a rewrite rule, then we are allowed to directly simplify it, without the nondeterminism that would come with a Basic Narrowing rule.

Simplify

$$\frac{u[s']|\varphi}{u[t\sigma]|\varphi}$$

where $s \to t \in R$ and $s\sigma \approx_E s'$.

A unification problem can be removed if all solutions of its constraint are reducible. This reduces the search space for narrowing.

ReducibleSubstitution

$$\frac{u|\varphi}{}$$

where σ is reducible over the variables of u for all $\sigma \in Sol(\varphi)$.

6   Completeness Proofs

In this section we prove the main completeness results of the paper. We show that if a set of rewrite rules R is saturated under our inference rules, then any minimal sequence of R, E rewrite steps, under an ordering we give below, can be lifted to a sequence of Basic Narrowing steps. This is a generalization of what can be done for Basic Narrowing in the empty theory, where any innermost sequence of R rewrite steps can be lifted to a Basic Narrowing sequence.

We first need an ordering to compare rewrite steps. We prefer smaller rewrite steps under this ordering. This means we prefer to use right-reduced instances of rules, because of the subterm property of our ordering. Our next preference is rules with smaller left hand sides, i.e., innermost reductions. Our last preference is rules with smaller right hand sides, i.e., to get to the normal form faster.

Definition 5. Let $s \to t$ and $u \to v$ be rewrite rules. Let θ_1 and θ_2 be substitutions. We define a relation on pairs of rewrite rules and substitutions.

- We say $(s \to t, \theta_1) \leq_N (u \to v, \theta_2)$ if $s\theta_1 \to t\theta_1$ is a right-reduced instance, or $u\theta_2 \to v\theta_2$ is not.
- We say $(s \to t, \theta_1) \leq_L (u \to v, \theta_2)$ if $s\theta_1 \leq u\theta_2$.
- We say $(s \to t, \theta_1) \leq_R (u \to v, \theta_2)$ if $t\theta_1 \leq v\theta_2$.
- Then define $\leq_B$ to be the lexicographic combination $(\leq_N, \leq_L, \leq_R)$.

We will show that saturation under Parallel is equivalent to the ability to reduce every innermost redex with a right-reduced instance of a rule, and closure under Parallel and Forward Overlap is equivalent to the ability to reduce every innermost redex to normal form in one step.

Definition 6. We say that R is IRR if every innermost redex is reducible by a right-reduced instance of R. We say that R is $IR1$ if every innermost redex is reducible to normal form in one step.

Theorem 1. *R is saturated by Parallel if and only if R is IRR.*

Proof. First the forward direction. Assume R is saturated by Parallel. Given an innermost redex s' and a reduction of s', let rule $s \rightarrow t$ and substitution θ be the smallest reduction of s' wrt $\leq_B$. We show that if $s\theta \rightarrow t\theta$ is not a right-reduced instance, then there is another reduction of s' which is smaller than $(s \rightarrow t, \theta)$.

Since $s\theta \rightarrow t\theta$ is not a right-reduced instance, there is a rewrite rule $l \rightarrow r$, a variable x in t and therefore also in s, and a substitution θ_1, extending θ, such that $l\theta_1$ is E-equivalent to a subterm of $x\theta$. Since s' is an innermost redex, we know that $l\theta_1$ is not a subterm of s'. Therefore, $s\theta$ is E-equivalent to s' but not identical. Therefore there must be some equation $u[l'] \approx v$ in E, and some substitution θ_2, extending θ_1 such that $l'\theta_2 \approx_E l\theta_1$, and l' is not a variable. Also, there must be some substitution θ_3, extending θ_2, such that $s\theta$ is E-equivalent to $u\theta_3$. θ_3 must be a unifier of $l \approx^? l'$ and $u \approx^? s$.

Therefore, the conditions of the Parallel rule are applicable. Let $\sigma \in CSU_E(l \approx_E^? l', u \approx_E^? s)$ such that $\sigma \leq_E \theta_3$ over the variables of the problem. The result of applying the Parallel rule is $v\sigma \rightarrow (v\sigma) \downarrow$. This rewrite rule can be used to reduce s'. The first component of the $\leq_B$ ordering either stays the same or gets smaller, since the right hand side was originally not a right-reduced instance. The second component stays the same, but the third one is smaller. Therefore the new rewrite step is smaller with respect to $\leq_B$.

This inference might be redundant. Suppose it is redundant because a strict subterm of every term E-equivalent to $s\sigma$ is reducible. Then there is a rewrite rule reducing a strict subterm of s', which is smaller in the $\leq_B$ ordering. Suppose that this inference is redundant because $s\sigma$ is reducible by a right-reduced instance of a rule. Then s' is also reducible by a right-reduced instance of a rule. A contradiction with the assumption has been obtained.

Now the reverse direction. Assume R is IRR. We need to show that all Parallel inferences are redundant. This is trivially true, because one one condition of the definition of redundancy for Parallel rules is that all innermost redexes can be reduced by a right-reduced instance of a rule. $\square$

Theorem 2. *R is saturated by Parallel and Forward Overlap iff R is IR1.*

Proof. First the forward direction. Assume R is saturated by the Parallel and Forward Overlap rules. Once again we assume the smallest reduction to obtain a contradiction. Given an innermost redex s' and a reduction using rule $s \rightarrow t$ and substitution θ, we show that if $t\theta$ is not in normal form, then there is another reduction of s' which is smaller than $(s \rightarrow t, \theta)$ with respect to $\leq_B$.

Since $t\theta$ is not in normal form, there is a rewrite rule $l \rightarrow r$ and a substitution θ_1, extending θ, such that $l\theta_1$ is E-equivalent to a subterm of $t\theta$. By the previous theorem, and the fact that R is saturated by Parallel, we can assume that $s\theta \rightarrow t\theta$ is a right-reduced instance, therefore $l\theta_1$ is E-equivalent to a subterm of $t\theta$ at a non-variable position of t. Let l' be that subterm of t.

Therefore, the conditions of the Forward Overlap rule are applicable. There is a Forward Overlap among $s \rightarrow t[l']$ and $l \rightarrow r$. The result is $s\sigma \rightarrow t[r]\sigma$ for some $\sigma \in CSU_E(l \approx^? l')$. Then $s\sigma \rightarrow t[r]\sigma$ can reduce s'. It is smaller in the $\leq_B$ ordering, because it must be a right-reduced instance, the left hand sides are the same, and $t[r]\sigma\theta_1$ is smaller than $t[l]\theta_1$.

It is also possible that this inference is redundant because $s\sigma$ is reducible by a right-reduced instance of a rule smaller than $s\sigma \to t[l]\sigma$. This must be smaller with respect to $\leq_B$.

Now the reverse direction. Assume R is $IR1$. We need to show that all Parallel and Forward Overlap inferences are redundant. We have already showed that all Parallel rules are redundant in the last theorem. In order to show all Forward Overlap rules are redundant, consider a Forward Overlap of $u \to v[s']$ and $s \to t$, resulting in $u\theta \to v[t]\theta$. If $u\theta$ does not have an innermost redex, then this inference is redundant, because all equivalents of $u\theta$ have a reduction below the top. The smallest such reduction must be a right reduced instance. If $u\theta$ has an innermost redex, then there must be another rule reducing $u\theta$ to normal form in one step because R is $IR1$, and this rule must be a right reduced instance, so this inference is redundant.   □

BN and BNR are clearly sound. We show that BN is complete for IRR theories, and BNR is complete for $IR1$ theories, with or without the optional rules. Since BNR halts, as long as Split is only applied finitely many times, BNR gives a decision procedure for unification in $IR1$ theories, and BN gives a complete procedure for unification in IRR theories.

Theorem 3. *If R is IRR then BN (with or without optional rules) is complete.*

Proof. We show that if $s\theta \in IInst(s \mid \varphi)$ and there exists t such that $s\theta \to t$ then there is a constrained term $t' \mid \varphi'$ and a sequence of one or more inference steps from $s \mid \varphi$ to $t' \mid \varphi'$ with $t \in IInst(t'|\varphi')$. That will show by induction that some rewrite sequence from $w\sigma$ to its normal form, where w is a term and σ is a reduced substitution, can be lifted to a narrowing sequence from $w \mid \top$.

Note that for Concretization, if $s\theta \in IInst(u \mid \varphi)$ then $s\theta \in IInst(u\sigma \mid \varphi)$. For Split, if $s\theta \in IInst(u \mid \varphi)$ then $s\theta \in IInst(u \mid \varphi_1)$ or $s\theta \in IInst(u \mid \varphi_2)$. So any sequence of those optional rules will preserve irreducibility. Also note that the ReducibleSubstitution rule is not applicable to $s \mid \varphi$. For Simplify, the conclusion $u[t\sigma] \mid \varphi$ has the same constraint and a subset of the variables of the hypothesis $u[s'] \mid \varphi$, so $u[t\sigma]\theta \in IInst(u[t\sigma] \mid \varphi)$ if $u[s']\theta \in IInst(u[s'] \mid \varphi)$.

If Simplify is not applied, and s is reducible, then, because R is IRR, s must be of the form $s[l']$ and there is some rule $l \to r$ such that $l'\theta =_E l\theta$ and $\theta|_{Var(r)}$ is irreducible. There is then a BN application from $s[l'] \mid \varphi$ to $s[r] \mid \varphi, l\approx_E^? l'$. Let $x \in Var(s[r])$. Then either $x \in Var(s[l'])$ or $x \in Var(r)$, and in both cases $x\theta$ is irreducible. So $s[r]\theta \in IInst(s[r] \mid \varphi, l\approx_E^? l')$.   □

Theorem 4. *If R is $IR1$ then BNR, with or without optional rules, is complete.*

Proof. The proof is the same as the previous. Just redo the case where Simplify is not applied, and s is reducible, then, because R is $IR1$, s must be of the form $s[l']$ and there is some rule $l \to r$ such that $l'\theta\approx_E l\theta$ and $r\theta$ is irreducible. There is then a BNR application from $s[l'] \mid \varphi$ to $s[y] \mid \varphi, l\approx_E^? l', y\approx_E^? r$. Let $x \in Var(s[y])$. Then either $x \in Var(s[l'])$, in which case $x\theta$ is irreducible, or $x = y$, in which case again $x\theta$ is irreducible. So $s[r]\theta \in IInst(s[r] \mid \varphi, l\approx_E^? l', x\approx_E^? r)$.   □

These theorems imply completeness of $R \cup E$ unification. We can decide the $R \cup E$ unification problem, and also find a complete set of $R \cup E$ unifiers if E unification is finitary. In the case of BNR it gives a complexity bound, since BNR narrowing branches nondeterministically but the length of a BNR sequence is at most linear in the size of the term. The size of the terms and constraints are linear in the size of the term. If E-unification is NP or better, then the complexity bound is NP. If E-unification is PSPACE or worse, then the complexity bound is the same as the complexity bound for unification modulo E.

We now give the definition of Finite Variant Property for rewrite systems R modulo E. We define R, E to have the FVP if a finite number of substitutions can be constructed, representing all normal forms of a given term. This requires that the E-unification problem is finitary. We generalize this to a Finite Constraint Property, which is also applicable to infinitary theories. R, E has the FCP if a finite number of constraints can be constructed, representing all normal forms of a given term. For finitary theories, this is the same as the Finite Variant Property. We show that if BNR is complete then R, E has the FCP. In the reverse direction, we show that if R, E has the FVP then R is $IR1$.

Definition 7. A term-substitution pair (t, θ) is an R, E variant of a term s if θ is normalized and $s\theta \approx_{R \cup E} t$. A complete set of R, E variants of s, denoted $[[s]]$, is a set of R, E variants of s such that:

1. for all $(t, \theta) \in [[s]]$, $s\theta \xrightarrow{*} t$ with t in normal form, and
2. For all reduced substitutions σ and reduced terms s' such that $s\sigma \xrightarrow{*} s'$, there exists a pair $(t, \theta) \in [[s]]$ and a substitution ρ such that $t\rho \approx_E s'$ and $\theta\rho \approx_E \sigma$.

R, E has the *Finite Variant Property (FVP)* if a finite $[[s]]$ can be constructed for all s.

Definition 8. A term/constraint pair (t, φ) is an R, E *constraint variant* of term s if $s\theta \approx_{R \cup E} t$ for all solutions θ of φ. A complete set of R, E constraint variants of s, denoted $[[s]]_c$, is a set of R, E constraint variants of s such that:

1. for all $(t, \varphi) \in [[s]]_c$ and $\theta \in Sol(\varphi)$, $s\theta \xrightarrow{*} t$ with t in normal form, and
2. For all reduced substitutions σ and reduced terms s' such that $s\sigma \xrightarrow{*} s'$, there exists a pair $(t, \varphi) \in [[s]]_c$ and a substitution $\theta \in Sol(\varphi)$ such that σ can be extended to θ and $t\theta \approx_E s'$.

R, E has the *Finite Constraint Property (FCP)* if a finite $[[s]]_c$ can be constructed for all s.

Theorem 5. *If BNR is complete for R then R, E has the FCP.*

Proof. Saturate a term s under BNR. Then $[[s]]_c$ is the set of all pairs $(t \mid \varphi)$ such that BNR produces $t \mid \varphi$. □

The inverse of the above theorem is not necessarily true. But the inverse of the below corollary is true, as shown by the results of this paper.

Corollary 1. *Let R be a finite rewrite system. If BNR is complete for R, and unification modulo E is finitary, then R, E has the FVP.*

Theorem 6. *Let R be a finite equational rewrite system. If R, E has the FVP then R has a finite saturation under Parallel and Forward Overlap.*

Proof. We definite a rewrite system V_R as follows:

$$V_R = \{s\theta \to s' \mid s \to t \in R, (s', \theta) \in [[s]] \text{ and } s\theta \text{ is an innermost redex}\}$$

Since R, E has the finite variant property, V_R is finite.

Let R^* be a (possibly infinite) saturation of R. Then R^* is $IR1$. This means that every innermost redex can be reduced to normal form in one step in R^*. Consider some $s\theta \to s'$ in V_R. Then $s\theta$ is reducible to its normal form s' in one step in R^*. So there is a $u \to v \in R^*$ and a substitution ρ such that $u\rho \approx_E s\theta$ and $v\rho \approx_E s'$. This means there is a finite set $V_R' \subseteq R^*$ such that all members of V_R are subsumed by some member of V_R', and therefore every innermost redex can be rewritten to normal form in one step by a member of V_R'. So V_R' is $IR1$. By definition, terms have the same normal form in V_R' as they do in R.

Since V_R' is finite, all rules from V_R' will appear in finite time in the saturation of R. At that time, the set of rules will be $IR1$, so saturated under Parallel and Forward Overlap.   □

7   Examples of Equational Theories

In this section, we consider a few examples of equational theories, and show how the E-Parallel rule is adapted for those theories.

First, consider the empty theory. Since the E-Parallel rule requires an equational axiom, it does not apply to the empty theory. Therefore, if R is convergent modulo E then BN is complete for R, and BNR is complete for R if R is saturated under Forward Overlap.

Now we consider AC, the theory of Associativity and Commutativity. When we instantiate the E-Parallel rule to AC, we get the following inference rule.

AC-Parallel

$$\frac{u_2 + x \to w \qquad p + s \to r}{(u_2 + x)\sigma \to (w\sigma)\downarrow}$$

where

1. $u_2 + x \to w$ or $x + u_2 \to w$ is in R
2. $p + s \to r \in R$
3. x is a variable which appears in w
4. $\sigma = [x \mapsto p + s]$ or $[x \mapsto p + s + y]$ for a fresh variable y

We show that this inference rule is correct.

Theorem 7. *AC-Parallel is an instance of E-Parallel for AC.*

Proof. Using the notation of the E-Parallel rule, we know that since l appears on the left hand side of a rewrite rule, it cannot be a variable. So it must be the sum of two terms, since it must unify with a nonvariable position of one side of an equation from AC. This justifies $p + s \rightarrow r$ as the right premise of the AC-Parallel inference rule. Since $p + s$ must unify with a strict subterm of an AC equation, we can assume wlog that $p + s$ unifies with $x_1 + y_1$ of the equation $(x_1 + y_1) + z_1 \approx x_1 + (y_1 + z_1)$.

The left hand side of the left premise of the inference rule must be of the form $u_2 + x$ since it is not a variable, it is unifiable with one side of an equation from AC, and it must contain the variable x, since t and therefore s contains the variable x. So $u_2 + x$ unifies with $(x_1 + y_1) + z_1$. Let $\sigma \in CSU_{AC}(p + s \approx^?_{AC} x_1 + y_1, u_2 + x \approx^?_{AC} (x_1 + y_1) + z_1)$.

$(p + s)\sigma$ must be AC-equivalent to a subterm of $x\sigma$ by Condition 6 of the E-Parallel rule. If $(p + s)\sigma$ is AC-equivalent to a strict subterm of $x\sigma$ then $x\sigma = (p + s + y)\sigma$ for some fresh variable y. Since $(p + s)\sigma \approx_{AC} (x_1 + y_1)\sigma$, this implies that $u_2\sigma + y\sigma = z_1\sigma$. Then $(u_2 + x)\sigma \approx_{AC} ((x_1 + y_1) + z_1)\sigma \approx_{AC} ((p + s)\sigma + u_2\sigma + y\sigma)$.

A similar, but slightly simpler argument holds if $x\sigma =_{AC} (p + s)\sigma$. $\square$

In practice, AC-Parallel inferences are usually redundant if u_2 is not a sum. We now give an A-Parallel rule for the theory of Associativity.

A-Parallel

$$\frac{u_1 + x + u_2 \rightarrow w \qquad p + s \rightarrow r}{(u_1 + x + u_2)\sigma \rightarrow (w\sigma)\downarrow}$$

where

1. $u_1 + x + u_2 \rightarrow w \in R$
2. $p + s \rightarrow r \in R$
3. x is a variable which appears in w
4. $\sigma = [x \mapsto p + s]$ or $[x \mapsto p + s + y]$ for a fresh variable y

Theorem 8. *A-Parallel is an instance of E-Parallel for Associativity.*

Proof. As in the AC case, using the notation from the E-Parallel rule, we know that since l appears on the left hand side of a rewrite rule, it cannot be a variable. So it must be the sum of two terms, since it must unify with a a nonvariable position of one side of an equation from A. This justifies $p + s \rightarrow r$ as the right premise of the A-Parallel inference rule. Since $p + s$ must unify with a strict subterm of an A equation, we can assume that $p + s$ either unifies with $y_1 + z_1$ of the equation $x_1 + (y_1 + z_1) \approx (x_1 + y_1) + z_1$.

Let $s \rightarrow t$ be the left premise of if the inference rule. s is not a variable but must contain a variable x, and it is unifiable with one side of an equation from A. So s unifies with $x_1 + (y_1 + z_1)$. Let $\sigma \in CSU_A(p + s \approx^?_A y_1 + z_1, s \approx^?_A x_1 + (y_1 + z_1))$.

Suppose s is of the form $u_2 + x$. $(p+s)\sigma$ must be A-equivalent to a subterm of $x\sigma$. Suppose that $x\sigma =_A (p+s)\sigma$. Since $(p+s)\sigma \approx_A (y_1 + z_1)\sigma$, then $u_2\sigma = x_1\sigma$. Then $(u_2 + x)\sigma \approx_A (x_1 + (y_1 + z_1))\sigma \approx_A u_2\sigma + (p+s)\sigma$, which is of the form $t_1 + t_2$. If t_2 contains $p\sigma + s\sigma$ as part of its sum, then t_2 is reducible, and $t_1 + t_2$ is reducible below the root. Suppose t_2 does not contain $p\sigma + s\sigma$. Then t_1 must contain $u_2\sigma$. But since R is convergent modulo A, $p\sigma + s\sigma + t_3$ must be reducible for any term t_3. Therefore t_1 is reducible and $t_1 + t_2$ is again reducible below the root. In either case, the inference is redundant. If $(p+s)\sigma$ is A-equivalent to a strict subterm of $x\sigma$, the argument is identical. It is also an identical argument if s is of the form $x + u_2$.

Now suppose s is of the form $u_1 + x + u_2$. The argument here is the same as the argument for the AC case. $\qquad\qquad\qquad\qquad\qquad\qquad\qquad\qquad\qquad\qquad$ □

8   Examples of Rewrite Systems

In this section we apply our results to some rewrite systems that are convergent modulo AC or A or modulo two AC operators.

Example 4. Consider the example from the introduction. If we apply Parallel to this theory, we create two new rules: $a + a + b + b \to 0$ and $a + a + b + b + x \to x$. All other Parallel inferences are redundant, and Forward Overlap cannot be applied. So this rewrite system is now saturated by Parallel and Forward Overlap, and BNR is complete and terminating.

Example 5. Let $R = \{a + b \to c, a + b + x \to c + x\}$ where $+$ is AC. This cannot be finitely saturated under Parallel. It creates all possible rules of the following forms: $\{a^n + b^n \to c^n, a^n + b^n + x \to c^n + x\}$. We use a^n as an abbreviation for a sum of n occurrences of a.

None of these rules are redundant. Since this rewrite system cannot be finitely saturated under Parallel, it does not have the Finite Variant Property. It is interesting that such simple rewrite systems do not have the finite variant property, but much more complicated rewrite systems sometimes do.

Example 6. The theory of Exclusive OR satisfies Associativity, Commutativity, Unit and Nilpotence. It consists of the following rewrite rules, modulo AC of $+$.

1. $x + x \to 0$ $\qquad\qquad\qquad$ 2. $x + 0 \to x$ $\qquad\qquad\qquad$ 3. $x + x + y \to y$

Every application of Parallel is redundant in this theory. For example, a Parallel inference between Rule 3 and Rule 2 gives $x + x + x' + 0 \to x'$. Every AC-equivalent of $x + x + x' + 0$ is reducible below the root. A Parallel inference between Rule 3 and Rule 1 results in $x + x + x' + x' \to 0$. Every AC-equivalent of $x + x + x' + x'$ is reducible below the root, except for $(x + x') + (x + x')$, which is reducible at the root by a right reducible instance of $x + x \to 0$. Similarly for all applications of Parallel. There are no instances of Forward Overlap.

Example 7. Consider the rewrite presentation of Abelian Groups from Lankford, given in the Comon/Delaune paper [5], where $*$ is an AC operator.

1. $x * 1 \rightarrow x$
2. $(x^{-1})^{-1} \rightarrow x$
3. $1^{-1} \rightarrow 1$
4. $(x^{-1} * y)^{-1} \rightarrow y^{-1} * x$
5. $x * x^{-1} \rightarrow 1$

6. $x * (x^{-1} * y) \rightarrow y$
7. $x^{-1} * y^{-1} \rightarrow (x * y)^{-1}$
8. $x^{-1} * (y^{-1} * z) \rightarrow (y * x)^{-1} * z$
9. $(x * y)^{-1} * x \rightarrow y^{-1}$
10. $(x * y)^{-1} * (y * z) \rightarrow x^{-1} * z$

All applications of Parallel are redundant and there are two applications of Forward Overlap that are not redundant. A Forward Overlap between Rule 10 and Rule 7 gives $(x * y)^{-1} * (y * z^{-1}) \rightarrow (z * x)^{-1}$. A Forward Overlap between Rule 10 and Rule 8 gives $(x * y)^{-1} * (y * z^{-1}) * w \rightarrow (z * x)^{-1} * w$.

It can be checked that when these two new rules are added, the rewrite system is saturated under Parallel and Forward Overlap.

Example 8. Here we consider a homomorphism from an *AC* operator to another *AC* operator. Notice this is not an endomorphism as is often considered, because the binary operator on the left hand side is not the same as the binary operator on the right hand side. Let $R = \{h(x) * h(y) \rightarrow h(x+y), h(x) * h(y) * z \rightarrow h(x+y) * z\}$ where $+$ and $*$ are both *AC* symbols.

There are many applications of Parallel, and Forward Overlap. One of the applications of Parallel gives $h(x) * h(y) * h(u) * h(v) \rightarrow h(x + y + u + v)$. Every equivalent instance can be rewritten below the root. Similarly, the other applications of Parallel and the applications of Forward Overlap derive rules where all equivalent instances of the left hand side can be rewritten below the root. So all Parallel and Forward Overlap rules are redundant. Therefore the two rules above are saturated under Parallel and Forward Overlap.

Example 9. Consider the homomorphism theory over *AC*, where the binary operator is the same on both sides. Let $R = \{h(x) * h(y) \rightarrow h(x * y), h(x) * h(y) * z \rightarrow h(x * y) * z\}$. R is saturated under Parallel, for the same reason as the other homomorphism theory. But it cannot be finitely saturated under Forward Overlap. Therefore, BN is complete for this theory, but BNR cannot be made complete.

We could flip the order of the rules in this example. We would get $R = \{h(x * y) \rightarrow h(x) * h(y)\}$. Since the top symbol on the left hand side is not *AC*, there are no extensions or Parallel inferences. So BN is complete. But this theory also cannot be saturated by Forward Overlap.

Even though Associative Unification is infinitary, we can still represent them with a constraint. Even when we cannot list out all the unifiers we can still give a constraint representing them. Associative constraints are decidable, so we can decide unification in theories that are closed under Parallel and Forward Overlap. This is an advantage over the Finite Variant Property, which does not allow infinitary theories, so it does not cover Associativity.

Example 10. Consider the theory *AU* of an associative operator with a unit, as given by $R = \{x + 0 \rightarrow x, 0 + x \rightarrow x\}$. There are no applications of Parallel and Forward Overlap. So it is saturated under Parallel and Forward Overlap.

9   Conclusion

Basic Narrowing modulo an equational theory is known to be incomplete for E-convergent rewrite systems R [5]. We defined an inference rule called Parallel, and showed that if R is saturated by Parallel then Basic Narrowing is complete. If R is also saturated by Forward Overlap, then BNR, a restricted form of Basic Narrowing, is complete. Since BNR always terminates, this gives a decision procedure for $R \cup E$ unification, which runs in NP time if E-unification is decidable in NP. If E-unification is finitary, we can also produce a complete set of unifiers.

Since Basic Narrowing was shown to be incomplete, recent research on narrowing modulo E has focused on Variant Narrowing [9], which works if R, E has the Finite Variant Property. We show that R has the Finite Variant Property modulo E if and only if R can be finitely saturated by Parallel and Forward Overlap wrt E, and the finite saturation of R makes BNR complete modulo E.

The work on the Finite Variant Property may deal with many sorted/order sorted theories [12]. We see no issues in extending our work to cover order sorted theories, but that is left for future work. On the other hand, we allow theories where E-unification is infinitary such as Associativity, while the Finite Variant Property does not cover that. We have generalized the Finite Variant Property to something called the Finite Constraint Property, which we believe would also allow Variant Narrowing to deal with infinitary equational theories. If E is infinitary, it may not be possible to saturate R; but it can be saturated in cases that do not require infinitary unification. We give the example of Associativity with a unit in this paper.

For future work, we will extend BNR to handle sorts. We also think there would not be a problem to extend our results to unfailing completion and full first order theorem proving. We have given some examples in this paper, like Exclusive OR and Abelian groups. We would like to find other interesting and practical theories where BNR gives a decision procedure.

References

1. Baader, F., Nipkow, T.: Term Rewriting and All That. Cambridge University Press, Cambridge (1998)
2. Baader, F., Snyder, W.: Unification theory. In: Robinson, A., Voronkov, A. (eds.) Handbook of Automated Reasoning, chap. 8, vol. 1, pp. 445–532. Elsevier Science, Amsterdam (2001)
3. Bachmair, L., Dershowitz, N.: Completion for rewriting modulo a congruence. Theor. Comput. Sci. **67**(2), 173–201 (1989)
4. Bouchard, C., Gero, K.A., Lynch, C., Narendran, P.: On forward closure and the finite variant property. In: Fontaine, P., Ringeissen, C., Schmidt, R.A. (eds.) FroCoS 2013. LNCS (LNAI), vol. 8152, pp. 327–342. Springer, Heidelberg (2013). https://doi.org/10.1007/978-3-642-40885-4_23
5. Comon-Lundh, H., Delaune, S.: The finite variant property: how to get rid of some algebraic properties. In: Giesl, J. (ed.) RTA 2005. LNCS, vol. 3467, pp. 294–307. Springer, Heidelberg (2005). https://doi.org/10.1007/978-3-540-32033-3_22

6. Dershowitz, N., Plaisted, D.A.: Rewriting. In: Robinson, A., Voronkov, A. (eds.) Handbook of Automated Reasoning, chap. 9, vol. 1, pp. 535–610. Elsevier Science, Amsterdam (2001)
7. Erbatur, S., et al.: Effective symbolic protocol analysis via equational irreducibility conditions. In: Foresti, S., Yung, M., Martinelli, F. (eds.) ESORICS 2012. LNCS, vol. 7459, pp. 73–90. Springer, Heidelberg (2012). https://doi.org/10.1007/978-3-642-33167-1_5
8. Escobar, S., Meadows, C., Meseguer, J.: Maude-NPA: cryptographic protocol analysis modulo equational properties. In: Aldini, A., Barthe, G., Gorrieri, R. (eds.) FOSAD 2007-2009. LNCS, vol. 5705, pp. 1–50. Springer, Heidelberg (2009). https://doi.org/10.1007/978-3-642-03829-7_1
9. Escobar, S., Sasse, R., Meseguer, J.: Folding variant narrowing and optimal variant termination. J. Logic Algebraic Program. **81**(7), 898–928 (2012)
10. Hullot, J.-M.: Canonical forms and unification. In: Bibel, W., Kowalski, R. (eds.) CADE 1980. LNCS, vol. 87, pp. 318–334. Springer, Heidelberg (1980). https://doi.org/10.1007/3-540-10009-1_25
11. Kirchner, H.: Some extensions of rewriting. In: Comon, H., Jounnaud, J.-P. (eds.) TCS School 1993. LNCS, vol. 909, pp. 54–73. Springer, Heidelberg (1995). https://doi.org/10.1007/3-540-59340-3_5
12. Meseguer, J.: Strict coherence of conditional rewriting modulo axioms. Theor. Comput. Sci. **672**, 1–35 (2017). https://doi.org/10.1016/j.tcs.2016.12.026

Automated Proofs of Unique Normal Forms w.r.t. Conversion for Term Rewriting Systems

Takahito Aoto[1][(✉)] and Yoshihito Toyama[2]

[1] School of Natural Sciences, Niigata University, Niigata, Japan
aoto@ie.niigata-u.ac.jp
[2] RIEC, Tohoku University, Sendai, Japan
toyama@riec.tohoku.ac.jp

Abstract. The notion of normal forms is ubiquitous in various equivalent transformations. Confluence (CR), one of the central properties of term rewriting systems (TRSs), concerns uniqueness of normal forms. Yet another such property, which is weaker than confluence, is the property of unique normal forms w.r.t. conversion (UNC). Recently, automated confluence proof of TRSs has caught attentions; some powerful confluence tools integrating multiple methods for (dis)proving the CR property of TRSs have been developed. In contrast, there have been little efforts on (dis)proving the UNC property automatically yet. In this paper, we report on a UNC prover combining several methods for (dis)proving the UNC property. We present an equivalent transformation of TRSs preserving UNC, as well as some new criteria for (dis)proving UNC.

1 Introduction

The notion of normal forms is ubiquitous in various equivalent transformations—normal forms are objects that cannot be transformed further. A crucial issue around the notion of normal forms is that whether they are unique so that normal forms (if exist) can represent the equivalence classes of objects. For this, the notion of confluence (CR), namely that $s \xleftarrow{*} \circ \xrightarrow{*} t$ implies $s \xrightarrow{*} \circ \xleftarrow{*} t$ for all objects s and t, is most well-studied. Here, $\xrightarrow{*}$ is the reflexive transitive closure of the equivalent transformation $\rightarrow$, and $\circ$ stands for the composition. In term rewriting, various methods for proving confluence of term rewriting systems (TRSs) have been studied (see e.g. slides of [20] for a survey). Yet another such a property is the property of unique normal forms w.r.t. conversion (UNC)[1], namely that two convertible normal forms are identical, i.e. $s \xleftrightarrow{*} t$ with normal forms s, t implies $s = t$. In term rewriting, famous examples that are UNC but not

---

[1] The uniqueness of normal forms w.r.t. conversion is also often abbreviated as UN in the literature; here, we prefer UNC to distinguish it from a similar but different notion of unique normal forms w.r.t. reduction (UNR), following the convention employed in CoCo (Confluence Competition).

© Springer Nature Switzerland AG 2019
A. Herzig and A. Popescu (Eds.): FroCoS 2019, LNAI 11715, pp. 330–347, 2019.
https://doi.org/10.1007/978-3-030-29007-8_19

CR include TRSs consisting of S,K,I-rules for combinatory logic supplemented with various pairing rules [13,22], whose non-CR have been shown in [12].

It is undecidable whether $\mathcal{R}$ is UNC for a given TRS $\mathcal{R}$ in general. However, it is known that the UNC property is decidable for left-linear right-ground TRSs [6] and for shallow TRSs [17]. Another class for which the UNC property is decidable is terminating TRSs, for which the CR property and the UNC property coincide (e.g. [7]). Some classes of TRSs having the UNC property are also known: non-ω-overlapping TRSs [10] and non-duplicating weight-decreasing joinable TRSs [21]. Another important topic on the UNC property is modularity. It is known that the UNC property is modular for persistent decomposition [2] and layer-preserving decomposition [1]. These results allow us to use the divide-and-conquer approach for (dis)proving the UNC property. Compared to the CR property, however, not much has been studied on the UNC property in the field of term rewriting.

Recently, automated confluence proof of TRSs has caught attentions leading to investigations of automatable methods for (dis)proving the CR property of TRSs; some powerful confluence tools have been developed as well, such as ACP [3], CSI [14], Saigawa [11] for TRSs, and also tools for other frameworks such as conditional TRSs and higher-order TRSs. This leads to the emergence of the Confluence Competition (CoCo)[2], yearly efforts since 2012. In contrast, there have been little efforts on (dis)proving the UNC property automatically. Indeed, there are few tools that are capable of (dis)proving the UNC property; furthermore, only few UNC criteria have been elaborated in these tools.

In this paper, we report on a UNC prover comprising multiple methods for (dis)proving the UNC property and integrating them in a modular way. We present new automated methods to prove or disprove the UNC property; these methods enabled our tool to win the UNC category of CoCo 2018.

The rest of the paper is organized as follows. After introducing necessary notions and notations in Sect. 2, we first revisit the conditional linearization technique for proving UNC, and obtain new UNC criteria based on this approach in Sect. 3. In Sect. 4, we present a slightly generalized version of the critical pair criterion presented in the paper [21], and report an automation of the criterion. In Sect. 5, we present a new method for proving or disproving UNC. We show an experiment of the presented methods in Sect. 6. In Sect. 7, we report our prover ACP which supports the presented methods and integrates them based on the modularity results. Section 8 concludes.

2 Preliminaries

We now fix notions and notations used in the paper. We assume familiarity with basic notions in term rewriting (e.g. [4]).

We use $\sqcup$ to denote the multiset union and $\mathbb{N}$ the set of natural numbers. A sequence of objects $a_1, \ldots, a_n$ is written as $\boldsymbol{a}$. Negation of a predicate P is denoted by $\neg P$. The composition of relation R and S is denoted by $R \circ S$.

---

[2] http://project-coco.uibk.ac.at/.

Let $\rightarrow$ be a relation on a set A. The reflexive transitive (reflexive, symmetric, equivalent) closure of the relation $\rightarrow$ is denoted by $\xrightarrow{*}$ (resp. $\xrightarrow{=}$, $\leftrightarrow$, $\xleftrightarrow{*}$). The set NF of *normal forms* w.r.t. the relation $\rightarrow$ is given by NF $= \{a \in A \mid a \rightarrow b$ for no $b \in A\}$. The relation $\rightarrow$ has *unique normal forms w.r.t. conversion* (denoted by UNC($\rightarrow$)) if $a \xleftrightarrow{*} b$ and $a, b \in$ NF imply $a = b$. The relation $\rightarrow$ is *confluent* (denoted by CR($\rightarrow$)) if $\xleftarrow{*} \circ \xrightarrow{*} \subseteq \xrightarrow{*} \circ \xleftarrow{*}$. When we consider two relations $\rightarrow_1$ and $\rightarrow_2$, the respective sets of normal forms w.r.t. $\rightarrow_1$ and $\rightarrow_2$ are denoted by NF$_1$ and NF$_2$. The following proposition, which is proved easily, is a basis of the *conditional linearization technique*, which will be used in Sects. 3 and 4.

Proposition 1 ([13,22]). *Suppose (1)* $\rightarrow_0 \subseteq \rightarrow_1$, *(2)* CR($\rightarrow_1$), *and (3)* NF$_0 \subseteq$ NF$_1$. *Then,* UNC($\rightarrow_0$).

The set of *terms* over the set $\mathcal{F}$ of fixed-arity *function symbols* and denumerable set $\mathcal{V}$ of *variables* is denoted by T($\mathcal{F}, \mathcal{V}$). The set of variables in a term t is denoted by $\mathcal{V}(t)$. A term t is *ground* if $\mathcal{V}(t) = \emptyset$. We abuse the notation $\mathcal{V}(t)$ and denote by $\mathcal{V}(e)$ the set of variables occurring in any sequence e of expressions. The *subterm* of a term t at a *position* p is denoted by $t|_p$. The root position is denoted by ϵ. A *context* is a term containing a special constant $\square$ (called *hole*). If C is a context containing n-occurrences of the hole, $C[t_1, \ldots, t_n]_{p_1, \ldots, p_n}$ denotes the term obtained from C by replacing holes with $t_1, \ldots, t_n$ at the positions $p_1, \ldots, p_n$. Here, subscripts $p_1, \ldots, p_n$ may be abbreviated if it can be remained implicit. The expression $s[t_1, \ldots, t_n]_{p_1, \ldots, p_n}$ denotes the term obtained from s by replacing subterms at the positions $p_1, \ldots, p_n$ with terms $t_1, \ldots, t_n$ respectively. We denote by $|t|_x$ the number of occurrences of a variable x in a term t. Again, we abuse the notation $|t|_x$ and denote by $|e|_x$ the number of occurrences of a variable x in any sequence of expressions e. A term t is *linear* if $|t|_x = 1$ for any $x \in \mathcal{V}(t)$. A *substitution* σ is a mapping from $\mathcal{V}$ to T($\mathcal{F}, \mathcal{V}$) with finite dom(σ) $= \{x \in \mathcal{V} \mid \sigma(x) \neq x\}$. Each substitution is identified with its homomorphic extension over T($\mathcal{F}, \mathcal{V}$). For simplicity, we often write $t\sigma$ instead of $\sigma(t)$. A *most general unifier* σ of terms s and t is denoted by mgu(s, t).

An *equation* is a pair $\langle l, r \rangle$ of terms, which is denoted by $l \approx r$. When we do not distinguish the lhs and rhs of the equation, we write $l \dot{\approx} r$. We identify equations modulo renaming of variables. For a set or sequence Γ of equations, we denote by $\Gamma\sigma$ the set or the sequence obtained by replacing each equation $l \approx r$ by $l\sigma \approx r\sigma$. An equation $l \approx r$ satisfying $l \notin \mathcal{V}$ and $\mathcal{V}(r) \subseteq \mathcal{V}(l)$ is a *rewrite rule* and written as $l \rightarrow r$. A rewrite rule $l \rightarrow r$ is *linear* if l and r are linear terms; it is *left-linear* (*right-linear*) if l (resp. r) is a linear term. A rewrite rule $l \rightarrow r$ is *non-duplicating* if $|l|_x \geq |r|_x$ for any $x \in \mathcal{V}(l)$. A *term rewriting system* (*TRS*, for short) is a finite set of rewrite rules. A TRS is linear (left-linear, right-linear, non-duplicating) if so are all rewrite rules. A *rewrite step* of a TRS $\mathcal{R}$ (a set Γ of equations) is a relation $\rightarrow_{\mathcal{R}}$ (resp. $\leftrightarrow_\Gamma$) over T($\mathcal{F}, \mathcal{V}$) defined by $s \rightarrow_{\mathcal{R}} t$ iff $s = C[l\sigma]$ and $t = C[r\sigma]$ for some $l \rightarrow r \in \mathcal{R}$ (resp. $l \dot{\approx} r \in \Gamma$) and context C and substitution σ. The position p such that $C|_p = \square$ is called the *redex position* of the rewrite step, and we write $s \rightarrow_{p, \mathcal{R}} t$ to indicate the redex position explicitly.

A *rewrite sequence* is (finite or infinite) consecutive applications of rewrite steps. A rewrite sequence of the form $t_1 \;_{\mathcal{R}}\!\leftarrow t_0 \to_{\mathcal{R}} t_2$ is called a *local peak*.

Let $l_1 \to r_1$ and $l_2 \to r_2$ be rewrite rules such that $\mathcal{V}(l_1) \cap \mathcal{V}(l_2) = \emptyset$. Let $\sigma = \mathrm{mgu}(l_1, l_2|_p)$ with $l_2|_p \notin \mathcal{V}$. A local peak $l_2[r_1]_p\sigma \;_{p,\mathcal{R}}\!\leftarrow l_2\sigma \to_{\epsilon,\mathcal{R}} r_2\sigma$ is called a *critical peak* of $l_1 \to r_1$ over $l_2 \to r_2$, provided that $p \neq \epsilon$ or $(l_1 \to r_1) \neq (l_2 \to r_2)$. The pair $\langle l_2[r_1]_p\sigma, r_2\sigma \rangle$ is called a *critical pair* in $\mathcal{R}$. It is *overlay* if $p = \epsilon$; it is *inner-outer* if $p \neq \epsilon$. The set of (overlay, inner-outer) critical pairs from rules in a TRS $\mathcal{R}$ is denoted by $\mathrm{CP}(\mathcal{R})$ (resp. $\mathrm{CP}_{out}(\mathcal{R})$, $\mathrm{CP}_{in}(\mathcal{R})$).

Let $l \approx r$ be an equation and let Γ be a finite sequence of equations. An expression of the form $\Gamma \Rightarrow l \approx r$ is called a *conditional equation*. Conditional equations are also identified modulo renaming of variables. If $l \notin \mathcal{V}$, it is a *conditional rewrite rule* and written as $l \to r \Leftarrow \Gamma$. The sequence Γ is called the *condition part* of the rule.

A conditional rewrite rule $l \to r \Leftarrow \Gamma$ is linear (left-linear) if so are rewrite rule $l \to r$. A finite set of conditional rewrite rules is called a *conditional term rewriting system* (*CTRS*, for short). A CTRS is linear (left-linear) if so are all rules. A CTRS $\mathcal{R}$ is said to be of *type 1* if $\mathcal{V}(\Gamma) \cup \mathcal{V}(r) \subseteq \mathcal{V}(l)$ for all $l \to r \Leftarrow \Gamma \in \mathcal{R}$.

Let $l_1 \to r_1 \Leftarrow \Gamma_1$ and $l_2 \to r_2 \Leftarrow \Gamma_2$ be conditional rewrite rules such that w.l.o.g. $\mathcal{V}(l_1, r_1, \Gamma_1) \cap \mathcal{V}(l_2, r_2, \Gamma_2) = \emptyset$. Let $\sigma = \mathrm{mgu}(l_1, l_2|_p)$ with $l_2|_p \notin \mathcal{V}$. Then $\Gamma_1\sigma, \Gamma_2\sigma \Rightarrow \langle l_2[r_1]_p\sigma, r_2\sigma \rangle$ is called a *conditional critical pair* (*CCP*, for short), provided that $p \neq \epsilon$ or $(l_1 \to r_1 \Leftarrow \Gamma_1) \neq (l_2 \to r_2 \Leftarrow \Gamma_2)$. Here, $\Gamma_1\sigma, \Gamma_2\sigma$ is the juxtaposition of sequences $\Gamma_1\sigma$ and $\Gamma_2\sigma$. It is overlay if $p = \epsilon$; it is inner-outer if $p \neq \epsilon$. The set of (overlay, inner-outer) CCPs from rules in a CTRS $\mathcal{R}$ is denoted by $\mathrm{CCP}(\mathcal{R})$ (resp. $\mathrm{CCP}_{out}(\mathcal{R})$, $\mathrm{CCP}_{in}(\mathcal{R})$). A CTRS $\mathcal{R}$ is *orthogonal* if it is left-linear and $\mathrm{CCP}(\mathcal{R}) = \emptyset$.

In this paper, we deal with *semi-equational* CTRSs. The conditional rewrite step $\to_{\mathcal{R}} = \bigcup_{n \in \mathbb{N}} \to_{\mathcal{R}}^{(n)}$ of a semi-equational CTRS $\mathcal{R}$ is given via auxiliary relations $\to_{\mathcal{R}}^{(n)}$ $(n \geq 0)$ defined like this: $\to_{\mathcal{R}}^{(0)} = \emptyset$, $\to_{\mathcal{R}}^{(n+1)} = \{\langle C[l\sigma], C[r\sigma]\rangle \mid$

$l \to r \Leftarrow s_1 \approx t_1, \ldots, s_k \approx t_k \in \mathcal{R}, \forall i\ (1 \leq i \leq k).\ s_i\sigma \overset{*}{\leftrightarrow}_{\mathcal{R}}^{(n)} t_i\sigma)\}$. The *rank* of a conditional rewrite step $s \to_{\mathcal{R}} t$ is the least n such that $s \to_{\mathcal{R}}^{(n)} t$.

Let $\mathcal{R}$ be a TRS or CTRS. The set of normal forms w.r.t. $\to_{\mathcal{R}}$ is written as $\mathrm{NF}(\mathcal{R})$. A (C)TRS $\mathcal{R}$ is UNC (CR) if $\mathrm{UNC}(\to_{\mathcal{R}})$ (resp. $\mathrm{CR}(\to_{\mathcal{R}})$) on the set $\mathrm{T}(\mathcal{F}, \mathcal{V})$. Let $\mathcal{E}$ be a set or sequence of equations or rewrite rules. We denote $\approx_{\mathcal{E}}$ the congruence closure of $\mathcal{E}$. We write $\vdash_{\mathcal{E}} l \approx r$ if $l \overset{*}{\leftrightarrow}_{\mathcal{E}} r$. For sets or sequences Γ and Σ of equations, we write $\vdash_{\mathcal{E}} \Sigma$ if $\vdash_{\mathcal{E}} l \approx r$ for all $l \approx r \in \Sigma$, and $\Gamma \vdash_{\mathcal{E}} \Sigma$ if $\vdash_{\mathcal{E}} \Gamma\sigma$ implies $\vdash_{\mathcal{E}} \Sigma\sigma$ for any substitution σ.

A TRS $\mathcal{R}$ is said to be *right-reducible* if $r \notin \mathrm{NF}(\mathcal{R})$ for all $l \to r \in \mathcal{R}$. Although it is straightforward, we did not noticed the following claim having appeared in the literature:

Proposition 2. *Right-reducible TRSs are UNC.*

Example 1 (Cops ♯126). Let $\mathcal{R} = \{f(f(x,y),z) \to f(f(x,z),f(y,z))\}$. The state of the art confluence tools fail to prove confluence of this example. However, it is easy to see $\mathcal{R}$ is right-reducible, and thus, the UNC property is easily obtained automatically.

3   Conditional Linearization Revisited

In this section, we revisit the conditional linearization technique.

3.1   Conditional Linearization

A conditional linearization is a translation from TRSs to CTRSs which eliminates non-left-linear rewrite rules, say $f(x, x) \to r$, by replacing them with a corresponding conditional rewrite rules, such as $f(x, y) \to r \Leftarrow x \approx y$. Formally, let $l = C[x_1, \dots, x_n]$ with all variable occurrences in l displayed (i.e. $\mathcal{V}(C) = \emptyset$). Note here l may be a non-linear term and some variables in $x_1, \dots, x_n$ may be identical. Let $l' = C[x'_1, \dots, x'_n]$ where $x'_1, \dots, x'_n$ are mutually distinct fresh variables and let δ be a substitution such that $\delta(x'_i) = x_i$ ($1 \le i \le n$) and $\mathrm{dom}(\delta) = \{x'_1, \dots, x'_n\}$. A conditional rewrite rule $l' \to r' \Leftarrow \Gamma$ is a *conditional linearization* of a rewrite rule $l \to r$ if $r'\delta = r$ and Γ is a sequence of equations $x_i \approx x_j$ ($1 \le i, j \le n$) such that $x'_i \approx_\Gamma x'_j$ iff $x'_i\delta = x'_j\delta$ holds for all $1 \le i, j \le n$, where $\approx_\Gamma$ is the congruence closure of Γ. A conditional linearization of a TRS $\mathcal{R}$ is a semi-equational CTRS (denoted by $\mathcal{R}^L$) obtained by replacing each rewrite rule with its conditional linearization. We remark that any result of conditional linearization is a left-linear CTRS of type 1.

Conditional linearization is useful for showing the UNC property of non-left-linear TRSs. The key observation is $\mathrm{CR}(\mathcal{R}^L)$ implies $\mathrm{UNC}(\mathcal{R})$. For this, we use Proposition 1 for $\to_0 := \to_\mathcal{R}$ and $\to_1 := \to_{\mathcal{R}^L}$. Clearly, $\to_\mathcal{R} \subseteq \to_{\mathcal{R}^L}$, and thus the condition (1) of Proposition 1 holds. Suppose $\mathrm{CR}(\mathcal{R}^L)$. Then, one can easily show that $\mathrm{NF}(\mathcal{R}) \subseteq \mathrm{NF}(\mathcal{R}^L)$ by induction on the rank of conditional rewrite steps. Thus, the condition (2) of Proposition 1 implies its condition (3). Hence, $\mathrm{CR}(\mathcal{R}^L)$ implies $\mathrm{UNC}(\mathcal{R})$.

Now, for semi-equational CTRSs, the following confluence criterion is known.

Proposition 3 ([5,15]). *Orthogonal semi-equational CTRSs are confluent.*

A TRS $\mathcal{R}$ is *strongly non-overlapping* if $\mathrm{CCP}(\mathcal{R}^L) = \emptyset$. Hence, it follows:

Proposition 4 ([13,22]). *Strongly non-overlapping TRSs are UNC.*

This proposition is subsumed by the UNC of non-ω-overlapping TRSs [10].

3.2   UNC by Conditional Linearization

We now give some simple extensions of Proposition 4 which are easily incorporated from [8], but does not fall within the class of non-ω-overlapping TRSs. For this, let us recall the notion of parallel rewrite steps. A *parallel rewrite step* $s \dashrightarrow_\mathcal{R} t$ is defined like this: $s \dashrightarrow_\mathcal{R} t$ iff $s = C[l_1\sigma_1, \dots, l_n\sigma_n]$ and

$t = C[r_1\sigma_1, \ldots, r_n\sigma_n]$ for some rewrite rules $l_1 \rightarrow r_1, \ldots, l_n \rightarrow r_n \in \mathcal{R}$ and context C and substitutions $\sigma_1, \ldots, \sigma_n$ ($n \geq 0$). Let us write $\Gamma \vdash_\mathcal{R} u \rightarrow v$ if $\vdash_\mathcal{R} \Gamma\sigma$ implies $u\sigma \rightarrow_\mathcal{R} v\sigma$ for any substitution σ. We define $\Gamma \vdash_\mathcal{R} u \twoheadrightarrow_\mathcal{R} v$, etc. analogously.

The following notion is a straightforward extension of the corresponding notion in [8,19].

Definition 1. *A semi-equational CTRS $\mathcal{R}$ is* parallel-closed *if (i) $\Gamma \vdash_\mathcal{R} u \twoheadrightarrow v$ for any inner-outer CCP $\Gamma \Rightarrow \langle u, v \rangle$ of $\mathcal{R}$, and (ii) $\Gamma \vdash_\mathcal{R} u \twoheadrightarrow \circ \overset{*}{\leftarrow} v$ for any overlay CCP $\Gamma \Rightarrow \langle u, v \rangle$ of $\mathcal{R}$.*

We now come to our first extension of Proposition 4, which is proved in a way very similar to the one for TRSs.

Theorem 1. *Parallel-closed semi-equational CTRSs of type 1 are confluent.*

Corollary 1. *A TRS $\mathcal{R}$ is UNC if $\mathcal{R}^L$ is parallel-closed.*

Example 2. Let $\mathcal{R} = \{@(@(@(S, x), y), z) \rightarrow @(@(x, z), @(y, z)), @(@(K, x), y) \rightarrow x, @(I, x) \rightarrow x, @(@(D, x), x) \rightarrow x, \mathsf{app}(K, x) \rightarrow @(I, x), \mathsf{app}(x, K) \rightarrow x\}$. Since $\mathcal{R}$ is non-terminating, non-shallow, and non-right-ground, previous decidability results for UNC does not apply. Furthermore, since $\mathcal{R}$ is overlapping and duplicating, previous sufficient criteria for UNC does not apply. Also, previous modularity results for UNC does not properly decompose $\mathcal{R}$. Note that the TRS consisting of the first 4 rules is a famous non-confluent example ([12]); one can prove that $\mathcal{R}$ is non-confluent in a similar way. We have $\mathrm{CCP}_{in}(\mathcal{R}^L) = \emptyset$ and $\mathrm{CCP}_{out}(\mathcal{R}^L) = \{\emptyset \Rightarrow \langle @(I, K), K \rangle, \emptyset \Rightarrow \langle K, @(I, K) \rangle\}$. Thus, $\mathcal{R}^L$ is parallel-closed, and from Corollary 1, it follows that $\mathcal{R}$ is UNC.

Next, we incorporate the strong confluence criterion of TRSs [8] to semi-equational CTRSs in the similar way.

Definition 2. *A semi-equational CTRS $\mathcal{R}$ is* strongly closed *if $\Gamma \vdash_\mathcal{R} u \overset{*}{\rightarrow} \circ \overset{=}{\leftarrow} v$ and $\Gamma \vdash_\mathcal{R} u \overset{=}{\rightarrow} \circ \overset{*}{\leftarrow} v$ for any CCP $\Gamma \Rightarrow \langle u, v \rangle$ of $\mathcal{R}$.*

Similar to the proof of Theorem 1, the following theorem is obtained in the same way as in the proof for TRSs.

Theorem 2. *Linear strongly closed semi-equational CTRSs of type 1 are confluent.*

Corollary 2. *A TRS $\mathcal{R}$ is UNC if $\mathcal{R}^L$ is linear and strongly closed.*

We remark that the results of conditional linearization are not unique. Although the rewrite relation $\rightarrow_{\mathcal{R}^L}$ is independent of the results of conditional linearization, the CCPs may be different depending on $\mathcal{R}^L$. Thus, the applicability of Theorems 1 and 2 changes by the choice of $\mathcal{R}^L$. This is exhibited in the next example, where the first 5 rules are from [8].

Example 3. Let

$$\mathcal{R} = \begin{cases} H(F(x,y)) \rightarrow F(H(R(x)),y) & F(x,K(y,z)) \rightarrow G(P(y),Q(z,x)) \\ H(Q(x,y)) \rightarrow Q(x,H(R(y))) & Q(x,H(R(y))) \rightarrow H(Q(x,y)) \\ H(G(x,y)) \rightarrow G(x,H(y)) & K(x,x) \rightarrow R(x) \\ P(y) \rightarrow C & C \rightarrow K(C,C) \\ F(x,R(y)) \rightarrow G(C,Q(y,x)) \end{cases}.$$

There are two variants of conditional linearization of the sixth rule, namely $K(x_1,x_2) \rightarrow R(x_1) \Leftarrow x_1 \approx x_2$ and $K(x_1,x_2) \rightarrow R(x_2) \Leftarrow x_1 \approx x_2$. Depending on the choice of the variants, one obtains two kinds of CCP—namely, $\langle F(x,R(y)), G(P(y),Q(z,x)) \rangle$ and $\langle F(x,R(z)), G(P(y),Q(z,x)) \rangle$. The former is strongly closed as $F(x,R(y)) \rightarrow G(C,Q(y,x)) \leftarrow G(P(y),Q(z,x))$. On the other hand, the latter is not. Actually, the CTRS obtained by the former linearization is strongly closed, while the CTRS obtained by the latter linearization is not strongly closed.

3.3 Automation

Even though proofs are rather straightforward, it is not at all obvious how the conditions of Theorems 1 and 2 can be effectively checked.

Let $\mathcal{R}$ be a semi-equational CTRS. Let $\Gamma \Rightarrow \langle u, v \rangle$ be an inner-outer CCP of $\mathcal{R}$, and consider to check $\Gamma \vdash_{\mathcal{R}} u \twoheadrightarrow v$. For this, we construct the set $Red = \{v' \mid \Gamma \vdash_{\mathcal{R}} u \twoheadrightarrow v'\}$ and check whether $v \in Red$. To construct the set Red, we seek the possible redex positions in u. Suppose we found conditional rewrite rules $l_1 \rightarrow r_1 \Leftarrow \Gamma_1, l_2 \rightarrow r_2 \Leftarrow \Gamma_2 \in \mathcal{R}$ and substitutions θ_1, θ_2 such that $u = C[l_1\theta_1, l_2\theta_2]$. Then we obtain $u \twoheadrightarrow C[r_1\theta_1, r_2\theta_2]$ if $\vdash_{\mathcal{R}} \Gamma_1\theta_1$ and $\vdash_{\mathcal{R}} \Gamma_2\theta_2$, i.e. $s \overset{*}{\leftrightarrow}_{\mathcal{R}} t$ for any equation $s \approx t$ in $\Gamma_1\theta_1 \cup \Gamma_2\theta_2$. Now, for checking $\Gamma \vdash_{\mathcal{R}} u \twoheadrightarrow v$, it suffices to consider the case $\vdash_{\mathcal{R}} \Gamma$ holds. Thus, we may assume $s' \overset{*}{\leftrightarrow}_{\mathcal{R}} t'$ for any $s' \approx t'$ in Γ. Therefore, the problem is to check whether $s' \overset{*}{\leftrightarrow}_{\mathcal{R}} t'$ for $s' \approx t'$ in Γ implies $s \overset{*}{\leftrightarrow}_{\mathcal{R}} t$ for any equation $s \approx t$ in $\Gamma_1\theta_1 \cup \Gamma_2\theta_2$.

To check this, we use the following sufficient condition: $s \approx_\Gamma t$ for all $s \approx t \in \Gamma_1\theta_1 \cup \Gamma_2\theta_2$. Since congruence closure of a finite set of equations is recursive (e.g. [4]), this approximation is indeed automatable.

Example 4. Let

$$\mathcal{R} = \begin{cases} P(Q(x)) \rightarrow P(R(x)) \Leftarrow x \approx A & Q(H(x)) \rightarrow R(x) \Leftarrow S(x) \approx H(x) \\ R(x) \rightarrow R(H(x)) \Leftarrow S(x) \approx A \end{cases}.$$

Then, we have $\mathrm{CCP}(\mathcal{R}) = \mathrm{CCP}_{in}(\mathcal{R}) = \{S(x) \approx H(x), H(x) \approx A \Rightarrow \langle P(R(x)), P(R(H(x))) \rangle\}$. In order to apply the third rule to have $P(R(x)) \twoheadrightarrow_{\mathcal{R}} P(R(H(x)))$, we have to check the condition $S(x) \overset{*}{\leftrightarrow}_{\mathcal{R}} A$. This holds, since we can suppose $S(x) \overset{*}{\leftrightarrow}_{\mathcal{R}} H(x)$ and $H(x) \overset{*}{\leftrightarrow}_{\mathcal{R}} A$. This is checked by $S(x) \approx_\Sigma A$, where $\Sigma = \{S(x) \approx H(x), H(x) \approx A\}$.

$$\frac{}{\Gamma \sqcup \{u \approx v\} \Vdash_{\mathcal{R}} u \sim_0 v} \qquad \frac{}{\Gamma \Vdash_{\mathcal{R}} t \sim_0 t} \qquad \frac{\Gamma \Vdash_{\mathcal{R}} t \sim_i s}{\Gamma \Vdash_{\mathcal{R}} s \sim_i t} \qquad \frac{\Gamma \Vdash_{\mathcal{R}} s \sim_i t \quad \Sigma \Vdash_{\mathcal{R}} t \sim_j u}{\Gamma \sqcup \Sigma \Vdash_{\mathcal{R}} s \sim_{i+j} u}$$

$$\frac{\Gamma \Vdash_{\mathcal{R}} s \sim_i t}{\Gamma \Vdash_{\mathcal{R}} C[s] \sim_i C[t]} \qquad \frac{\Gamma_1 \Vdash_{\mathcal{R}} u_1 \sim_{i_1} v_1 \quad \cdots \quad \Gamma_n \Vdash_{\mathcal{R}} u_n \sim_{i_n} v_n}{\bigsqcup_j \Gamma_j \Vdash_{\mathcal{R}} \langle u_1,\ldots,u_n\rangle \sim_k \langle v_1,\ldots,v_n\rangle} \quad k=\sum_j i_j$$

$$\frac{\Gamma \Vdash_{\mathcal{R}} s \to_i t}{\Gamma \Vdash_{\mathcal{R}} s \sim_i t} \qquad \frac{\Gamma \Vdash_{\mathcal{R}} \langle u_1\sigma,\ldots,u_n\sigma\rangle \sim_i \langle v_1\sigma,\ldots,v_n\sigma\rangle}{\Gamma \dashv\vdash_{\mathcal{R}} C[l\sigma] \to_{i+1} C[r\sigma]} \quad l \to r \Leftarrow u_1 \approx v_1,\ldots,u_n \approx v_n \in \mathcal{R}$$

Fig. 1. Inference rules for ranked conversions and rewrite steps

4 Automating UNC Proof of Non-duplicating TRSs

In this section, we show a slight generalization of the UNC criterion of the paper [21], and show how the criterion can be decided. First, we briefly capture necessary notions and notations from the paper [21].

A *left-right separated (LR-separated) conditional rewrite rule* is $l \to r \Leftarrow x_1 \approx y_1,\ldots,x_n \approx y_n$ such that (i) $l \notin \mathcal{V}$ is linear, (ii) $\mathcal{V}(l) = \{x_1,\ldots,x_n\}$ and $\mathcal{V}(r) \subseteq \{y_1,\ldots,y_n\}$ (iii) $\{x_1,\ldots,x_n\} \cap \{y_1,\ldots,y_n\} = \emptyset$, and (iv) $x_i \neq x_j$ for all $1 \leq i,j \leq n$ such that $i \neq j$. Here, note that some variables in $y_1,\ldots,y_n$ can be identical. A finite set of LR-separated conditional rewrite rules is called an *LR-separated conditional term rewriting system* (*LR-separated CTRS*, for short). An LR-separated conditional rewrite rule $l \to r \Leftarrow x_1 \approx y_1,\ldots,x_n \approx y_n$ is *non-duplicating* if $|r|_y \leq |y_1,\ldots,y_n|_y$ for all $y \in \mathcal{V}(r)$.

The LR-separated conditional linearization translates TRSs to LR-separated CTRSs: Let $C[y_1,\ldots,y_n] \to r$ be a rewrite rule, where $\mathcal{V}(C) = \emptyset$. Here, some variables in $y_1,\ldots,y_n$ may be identical. Then, we take fresh distinct n variables $x_1,\ldots,x_n$, and construct $C[x_1,\ldots,x_n] \to r \Leftarrow x_1 \approx y_1,\ldots,x_n \approx y_n$ as the result of the translation. It is easily seen that the result is indeed an LR-separated conditional rewrite rule. It is also easily checked that if the rewrite rule is non-duplicating then so is the result of the translation (as an LR-separated conditional rewrite rule). The LR-separated conditional linearization $\mathcal{R}^S$ of a TRS $\mathcal{R}$ is obtained by applying the translation to each rule.

It is shown in [21] that semi-equational non-duplicating LR-separated CTRSs are confluent if their CCPs satisfy some condition, which makes the rewrite steps 'weight-decreasing joinable'. By applying the criterion to LR-separated conditional linearization of TRSs, they obtained a criterion of UNC for non-duplicating TRSs. Note that rewriting in LR-separated CTRSs is (highly) non-deterministic; even reducts of rewrite steps at the same position by the same rule are generally not unique, not only reflecting semi-equational evaluation of the conditional part but also by the $\mathcal{V}(l) \cap \mathcal{V}(r) = \emptyset$ for LR-separated conditional rewrite rule $l \to r \Leftarrow \Gamma$. Thus, how to effectively check the sufficient condition of weight-decreasing joinability is not very clear, albeit it is mentioned in [21] that the decidability is clear.

For obtaining an algorithm for computing the criterion, we introduce ternary relations parameterized by an LR-separated CTRS $\mathcal{R}$ and $n \in \mathbb{N}$ as follows.

Definition 3. *The derivation rules for $\Gamma \Vdash_{\mathcal{R}} u \sim_n v$ and $\Gamma \Vdash_{\mathcal{R}} u \to_n v$ are given in Fig. 1. Here, $n \in \mathbb{N}$ and Γ is a multiset of equations.*

Intuitively, $\Gamma \Vdash_{\mathcal{R}} u \sim_n v$ means that $u \overset{*}{\leftrightarrow}_{\mathcal{R}} v$ using the assumption Γ where the number of rewrite steps is n in total (i.e. including those used in checking conditions). Main differences to the relation $\underset{\Gamma}{\sim}$ in [21] are twofold:

1. Instead of considering a special constant •, we use an index of natural number. The number of • corresponds to the index number.
2. Auxiliary equations in Γ are allowed in our notation of $\Gamma \Vdash_{\mathcal{R}} u \sim_n v$ (i.e. not all equations in Γ need not be used). On the contrary, Γ in $\underset{\Gamma}{\sim}$ in [21] does not allow auxiliary equations in Γ.

The former is useful to designing the effective procedure to check the UNC criteria presented below. The latter is convenient to prove the satisfiability of constraints on such expressions.

The following slightly generalizes the main result of [21].

Theorem 3. *A semi-equational non-duplicating LR-separated CTRS $\mathcal{R}$ is weight-decreasing joinable if for any CCP $\Gamma \Rightarrow \langle s, t \rangle$ of $\mathcal{R}$, either (i) $\Gamma \Vdash_{\mathcal{R}} s \sim_{\leq 1} t$, (ii) $\Gamma \Vdash_{\mathcal{R}} s \leftrightarrow_2 t$, or (iii) $\Gamma \Vdash_{\mathcal{R}} s \to_i \circ \sim_j t$ with $i + j \leq 2$ and $\Gamma \Vdash_{\mathcal{R}} t \to_{i'} \circ \sim_{j'} s$ with $i' + j' \leq 2$.*

Thus, non-duplicating TRSs $\mathcal{R}$ are UNC if all CCPs of $\mathcal{R}^S$ satisfy some of these (i)–(iii).

Thanks to our new formalization, decidability of the condition easily follows.

Theorem 4. *The condition of Theorem 3 is decidable.*

Proof. We show that each condition (i)–(iii) is decidable. Let Γ be a (finite) multiset of equations, s, t terms, and $\boldsymbol{s}, \boldsymbol{t}$ sequences of terms. The claim follows by showing the following series of sets are finite and effectively constructed one by one: (a) $\mathrm{SIM}_0(\Gamma, s) = \{ \langle \Sigma, t \rangle \mid \Gamma \backslash \Sigma \Vdash_{\mathcal{R}} s \sim_0 t \}$, (b) $\mathrm{SIM}_0(\Gamma, \boldsymbol{s}) = \{ \langle \Sigma, t \rangle \mid \Gamma \backslash \Sigma \Vdash_{\mathcal{R}} s \sim_0 \boldsymbol{t} \}$, (c) $\mathrm{RED}_1(\Gamma, s, t) = \{ \Sigma \mid \Gamma \backslash \Sigma \Vdash_{\mathcal{R}} s \to_1 t \}$, (d) $\mathrm{SRS}_{010}(\Gamma, s, t) = \{ \Sigma \mid \Gamma \backslash \Sigma \Vdash_{\mathcal{R}} s \sim_0 \circ \to_1 \circ \sim_0 t \}$, (e) $\mathrm{SIM}_1(\Gamma, s, t) = \{ \Sigma \mid \Gamma \backslash \Sigma \Vdash_{\mathcal{R}} s \sim_1 t \}$, (f) $\mathrm{SIM}_1(\Gamma, \boldsymbol{s}, \boldsymbol{t}) = \{ \Sigma \mid \Gamma \backslash \Sigma \Vdash_{\mathcal{R}} s \sim_1 \boldsymbol{t} \}$, and (g) $\mathrm{RED}_2(\Gamma, s, t) = \{ \Sigma \mid \Gamma \backslash \Sigma \Vdash_{\mathcal{R}} s \to_2 t \}$. □

Example 5. Let

$$\mathcal{R} = \left\{ \begin{array}{ll} f(x, x) \to h(x, f(x, b)) & f(g(y), y) \to h(y, f(g(y), c(b))) \\ h(c(x), b) \to h(b, b) & c(b) \to b \end{array} \right\}$$

Since $\mathcal{R}$ is non-terminating, non-shallow, and non-right-ground, previous decidability results for UNC does not apply. Furthermore, since $\mathcal{R}$ is overlapping and duplicating, previous sufficient criteria for UNC does not apply. Also, previous modularity results for UNC does not properly decompose $\mathcal{R}$. By conditional linearization, we obtain

$$\mathcal{R}^S = \begin{cases} f(x_1, x_2) & \to h(x, f(x, b)) & \Leftarrow x_1 \approx x, x_2 \approx x \\ f(g(y_1), y_2) \to h(y, f(g(y), c(b))) \Leftarrow y_1 \approx y, y_2 \approx y \\ h(c(x), b) & \to h(b, b) & c(b) \to b \end{cases}.$$

We have an overlay CCP $\Gamma \Rightarrow \langle h(x, f(x, b)), h(y, f(g(y), c(b))) \rangle$, where $\Gamma = \{(a) : y_1 \approx y, \;\; (b) : y_2 \approx y, \;\; (c) : g(y_1) \approx x, \;\; (d) : y_2 \approx x\}$. (Another one is its symmetric version.) Let $s = h(y, f(g(y), c(b)))$ and $t = h(x, f(x, b))$. To check the criteria of Theorem 3, we start computing $\mathrm{SIM}_0(\Gamma, s)$ and $\mathrm{SIM}_0(\Gamma, t)$. For example, the former equals to

$$\begin{cases} \langle \{(a), (b), (c), (d)\}, h(y, f(g(y), c(b))) \rangle & \langle \{(b), (c), (d)\}, h(y_1, f(g(y), c(b))) \rangle \\ \langle \{(b), (c), (d)\}, h(y, f(g(y_1), c(b))) \rangle & \langle \{(b), (d)\}, h(y, f(x, c(b))) \rangle \\ \langle \{(a), (c), (d)\}, h(y_2, f(g(y), c(b))) \rangle & \langle \{(a), (c), (d)\}, h(y, f(g(y_2), c(b))) \rangle \\ \langle \{(a), (c)\}, h(x, f(g(y), c(b))) \rangle & \langle \{(a), (c)\}, h(y, f(g(x), c(b))) \rangle \\ \langle \{(c), (d)\}, h(y_1, f(g(y_2), c(b))) \rangle & \langle \{(c), (d)\}, h(y_2, f(g(y_1), c(b))) \rangle \\ \langle \{(c)\}, h(y_1, f(g(x), c(b))) \rangle & \langle \{(c)\}, h(x, f(g(y_1), c(b))) \rangle \\ \langle \{(d)\}, h(y_2, f(x, c(b))) \rangle & \langle \emptyset, h(x, f(x, c(b))) \rangle \end{cases}.$$

We now can check $s \sim_0 t$ does not hold by $\langle \Gamma', t \rangle \in \mathrm{SIM}_0(\Gamma, s)$ for no Γ'. To check $\Gamma \Vdash s \to_1 t$, we compute $\mathrm{RED}_1(\Gamma, s, t)$. For this, we check there exist a context C and substitution θ and rule $l \to r \Leftarrow \Gamma \in \mathcal{R}^S$ such that $s = C[l\theta]$ and $t = C[r\theta]$. In our case, it is easy to see $\mathrm{RED}_1(\Gamma, s, t) = \emptyset$. Next to check $\Gamma \Vdash s \sim_1 t$, we compute $\mathrm{SRS}_{010}(\Gamma, s, t)$. This is done by, for each $\langle \Gamma', s' \rangle \in \mathrm{SIM}_0(\Gamma, s)$, computing $\langle \Sigma, t' \rangle \in \mathrm{SIM}_0(\Gamma', t)$ and check there exists $\Sigma \in \mathrm{RED}_1(\Sigma', s', t')$. In our case, for $\langle \emptyset, h(x, f(x, c(b))) \rangle \in \mathrm{SIM}_0(\Gamma, s)$ we have $\langle \emptyset, t \rangle \in \mathrm{SIM}_0(\emptyset, t)$, and $\emptyset \in \mathrm{RED}_1(\emptyset, h(x, f(x, c(b))), t)$. Thus, we know $h(x, f(x, c(b))) \to_1 h(x, f(x, b))$. Hence, for these overlay CCPs, we have $y_1 \approx y, y_2 \approx y, g(y_1) \approx x, y_2 \approx x \Vdash_{\mathcal{R}} h(y, f(g(y), c(b))) \sim_1 h(x, f(x, b))$. We also have $\mathrm{CCP}_{in}(\mathcal{R}^S) = \{ \emptyset \Rightarrow \langle h(b, b), h(b, b) \rangle \}$. For this inner-outer critical pair, it follows that $\Vdash_{\mathcal{R}} h(b, b) \sim_0 h(b, b)$ using $\langle \emptyset, h(b, b) \rangle \in \mathrm{SIM}_0(\emptyset, h(b, b))$. Thus, from Theorem 3, $\mathcal{R}^S$ is weight-decreasing. Hence, it follows $\mathcal{R}$ is UNC. We remark that, in order to derive $\Vdash_{\mathcal{R}} h(b, b) \sim_0 h(b, b)$, we need the reflexivity rule. However, since the corresponding Definition of $\sim$ in the paper [21] lacks the reflexivity rule, the condition of weight-decreasing in [21] (Definition 9) does not hold for $\mathcal{R}^S$. A part of situations where the reflexivity rule is required is covered by the congruence rule, and the reflexivity rule becomes necessary when there exists a trivial critical pair such as above.

5 Equivalent Transformation for UNC

In this section, we present a transformational approach for proving and disproving UNC.

Addition

$$\frac{\mathcal{R}}{\mathcal{R} \cup \{l \to r\}} \quad l \notin \mathrm{NF}(\mathcal{R}), l \stackrel{*}{\leftrightarrow}_{\mathcal{R}} r, \mathcal{V}(r) \subseteq \mathcal{V}(l)$$

Elimination

$$\frac{\mathcal{R} \cup \{l \to r\}}{\mathcal{R}} \quad l \notin \mathrm{NF}(\mathcal{R}), l \stackrel{*}{\leftrightarrow}_{\mathcal{R}} r$$

Reversing

$$\frac{\mathcal{R} \cup \{l \to r\}}{\mathcal{R} \cup \{l \to l, r \to l\}} \quad r \notin \mathrm{NF}(\mathcal{R} \cup \{l \to r\}), \mathcal{V}(l) \subseteq \mathcal{V}(r)$$

Disproof-1

$$\frac{\mathcal{R}}{\bot} \quad l, r \in \mathrm{NF}(\mathcal{R}), l \stackrel{*}{\leftrightarrow}_{\mathcal{R}} r, l \neq r$$

Disproof-2

$$\frac{\mathcal{R}}{\bot} \quad r \in \mathrm{NF}(\mathcal{R}), l \stackrel{*}{\leftrightarrow}_{\mathcal{R}} r, \mathcal{V}(r) \not\subseteq \mathcal{V}(l)$$

Fig. 2. Inference rules for equivalent transformation and disproof

5.1   Equivalent Transformation and Disproof

Firstly, observe that the conditional linearization does not change the input TRSs if they are left-linear. Thus, the technique has no effects on left-linear rewrite rules. But, as one can easily see, it is not at all guaranteed that left-linear TRSs are UNC.

Now, observe that a key idea in the conditional linearization technique is that the CR property of an approximation of a TRS implies the UNC property of the original TRS. The first method presented in this section is based on the observation that one can also use the approximation other than conditional linearization. To fit our usage, we now slightly modify Proposition 1 to obtain the next two lemmas, whose proofs are easy.

Lemma 1. *Suppose (1)* $\to_0 \subseteq \to_1 \subseteq \stackrel{*}{\leftrightarrow}_0$ *and (2)* $\mathrm{NF}_0 \subseteq \mathrm{NF}_1$. *Then,* $\mathrm{UNC}(\to_0)$ *iff* $\mathrm{UNC}(\to_1)$.

Lemma 2. *Suppose (1)* $\stackrel{=}{\leftrightarrow}_0 = \stackrel{=}{\leftrightarrow}_1$ *and (2)* $\mathrm{NF}_0 = \mathrm{NF}_1$. *Then,* $\mathrm{UNC}(\to_0)$ *iff* $\mathrm{UNC}(\to_1)$.

These lemmas are made into first three transformation rules in Fig. 2.

Definition 4. *Let* $\mathcal{R}$ *be a TRS. We write* $\mathcal{R} \rightsquigarrow \alpha$ *if* α *is obtained by one of the inference rules in Fig. 2.*

The next lemma immediately follows from Lemmas 1 and 2.

Lemma 3. *Let* $\mathcal{R}$ *be a TRS and* $l \to r$ *a rewrite rule.*

1. *Suppose* $l \stackrel{*}{\leftrightarrow}_{\mathcal{R}} r$ *and* $l \notin \mathrm{NF}(\mathcal{R})$. *Then,* $\mathrm{UNC}(\mathcal{R})$ *iff* $\mathrm{UNC}(\mathcal{R} \cup \{l \to r\})$.
2. *Suppose* $r \to l$ *is a rewrite rule and* $r \notin \mathrm{NF}(\mathcal{R} \cup \{l \to r\})$. *Then* $\mathrm{UNC}(\mathcal{R} \cup \{l \to r\})$ *iff* $\mathrm{UNC}(\mathcal{R} \cup \{l \to l, r \to l\})$.

Applying Lemma 3 (1) to the Addition and Elimination rules, and Lemma 3 (2) to the Reversing rules, we obtain:

Theorem 5. *Let $\mathcal{R}$ be a TRS and suppose $\mathcal{R} \overset{*}{\rightsquigarrow} \mathcal{R}' \neq \bot$. Then, $\mathcal{R}'$ is a TRS, and $\mathrm{UNC}(\mathcal{R}')$ iff $\mathrm{UNC}(\mathcal{R})$.*

Note that the relation $\rightsquigarrow$ is not well-founded; we will present some strategies for automation in the next subsection. We next show the correctness of the Disproof-1/2 rules.

Theorem 6. *Let $\mathcal{R}$ be a TRS and suppose $\mathcal{R} \overset{*}{\rightsquigarrow} \bot$. Then $\neg\mathrm{UNC}(\mathcal{R})$.*

Proof. Then we have $\mathcal{R} \overset{*}{\rightsquigarrow} \mathcal{R}' \rightsquigarrow \bot$ for some $\mathcal{R}'$. From Theorem 5, we have $\mathrm{UNC}(\mathcal{R}')$ iff $\mathrm{UNC}(\mathcal{R})$. Thus, it remains to show $\neg\mathrm{UNC}(\mathcal{R}')$. Suppose $\mathcal{R}' \rightsquigarrow \bot$ by Disproof-1. Then $l \overset{*}{\leftrightarrow}_{\mathcal{R}'} r$, $l, r \in \mathrm{NF}(\mathcal{R}')$, and $l \neq r$. By the definition of UNC, $\mathcal{R}'$ is not UNC. Suppose $\mathcal{R}' \rightsquigarrow \bot$ by Disproof-2. Then $s \overset{*}{\leftrightarrow}_{\mathcal{R}'} t \in \mathrm{NF}(\mathcal{R}')$ and $x \in \mathcal{V}(t) \setminus \mathcal{V}(s)$. Take a fresh variable y and let $t' = t\{x := y\}$. Clearly, from $t \in \mathrm{NF}(\mathcal{R}')$ we have $t' \in \mathrm{NF}(\mathcal{R}')$. By $t' \overset{*}{\leftrightarrow}_{\mathcal{R}'} s \overset{*}{\leftrightarrow}_{\mathcal{R}'} t$, $\mathcal{R}'$ is not UNC. $\qquad\square$

5.2 Automation

The correctness of equivalent transformation itself does not give us any hint how to apply such transformations. Below, we give two procedures based on the equivalent transformation.

First one employs the Reversing rule, the Elimination rule, and an ordering $>$ as a heuristic (not to loop).

Definition 5 (Rule reversing transformation). *Let $\mathcal{R}$ be a TRS. We write $\mathcal{R} \hookrightarrow \mathcal{R}'$ if $\mathcal{R}' = (\mathcal{R} \setminus \{l \to r\}) \cup \{l \to l, r \to l\}$ for some $l \to r \in \mathcal{R}$ such that $l < r$, $r \notin \mathrm{NF}(\mathcal{R})$ and $r \to l$ is a rewrite rule, or $\mathcal{R}' = \mathcal{R} \setminus \{l \to r\}$ for some $l \to r \in \mathcal{R}$ such that $l = r$ and $l \notin \mathrm{NF}(\mathcal{R} \setminus \{l \to r\})$. Any transformation $\mathcal{R} \overset{*}{\hookrightarrow} \mathcal{R}'$ is called a rule reversing transformation.*

It is easy to see that the relation $\hookrightarrow$ is well-founded, by comparing the number of increasing rules (i.e. $l \to r$ such that $l < r$) and the number of rules lexicographically. The correctness follows from Theorem 5.

Theorem 7. *Let $\mathcal{R}'$ be a TRS obtained by a rule reversing transformation from $\mathcal{R}$. Then, $\mathrm{UNC}(\mathcal{R})$ iff $\mathrm{UNC}(\mathcal{R}')$.*

Next, we consider constructing an approximation $\mathcal{S}$ of a TRS $\mathcal{R}$ by adding auxiliary rules generated by critical pairs. To guide the procedure, we consider two predicates φ and Φ such that the following confluence criterion holds:

Suppose that TRS $\mathcal{S}$ satisfies $\varphi(\mathcal{S})$. If $\Phi(u, v)$ holds for all critical pairs $\langle u, v \rangle$ of $\mathcal{S}$, then $\mathcal{S}$ has the CR property.   (A)

Multiple criteria in this form are known: one can take $\varphi(\mathcal{S})$ and $\Phi(u, v)$ as '$\mathcal{S}$ is left-linear' and '$\langle u, v \rangle$ is development-closed', respectively [16] and as '$\mathcal{S}$ is linear' and '$\langle u, v \rangle$ is strongly closed', respectively [8]. The idea is that if one encounters a critical pair $\langle u, v \rangle$ for which $\Phi(u, v)$ does not hold, then (check whether one can apply Disproof rules and) apply the equivalent transformation so that $\Phi(u, v)$ is satisfied.

Definition 6 (UNC completion procedure).

> **Input:** TRS $\mathcal{R}$, predicates φ, Φ satisfying (A).
> **Output:** UNC or NotUNC or Failure (or may diverge)

> **Step 1.** Compute the set $\mathrm{CP}(\mathcal{R})$ of critical pairs of $\mathcal{R}$.
> **Step 2.** If $\Phi(u, v)$ for all $\langle u, v \rangle \in \mathrm{CP}(\mathcal{R})$ and $\varphi(\mathcal{R})$ then return UNC.
> **Step 3.** Let $S := \emptyset$. For each $\langle u, v \rangle \in \mathrm{CP}(\mathcal{R})$ with $u \neq v$ for which $\Phi(u, v)$ does not hold, do:
>   (a) If $u, v \in \mathrm{NF}(\mathcal{R})$, then exit with NotUNC.
>   (b) If $u \notin \mathrm{NF}(\mathcal{R})$ and $v \in \mathrm{NF}(\mathcal{R})$, then if $\mathcal{V}(v) \nsubseteq \mathcal{V}(u)$ then exit with NotUNC, otherwise update $S := S \cup \{u \to v\}$.
>   (c) If $v \notin \mathrm{NF}(\mathcal{R})$ and $u \in \mathrm{NF}(\mathcal{R})$, then if $\mathcal{V}(u) \nsubseteq \mathcal{V}(v)$ then exit with NotUNC, otherwise update $S := S \cup \{v \to u\}$.
>   (d) If $u, v \notin \mathrm{NF}(\mathcal{R})$ then find w such that $u \xrightarrow{*}_{\mathcal{R}} w$ $(v \xrightarrow{*}_{\mathcal{R}} w)$, and $\mathcal{V}(w) \subseteq \mathcal{V}(v)$ (resp. $\mathcal{V}(w) \subseteq \mathcal{V}(v)$). If it succeeds then update $S := S \cup \{v \to w\}$.
> **Step 4.** If $S = \emptyset$ then return Failure; otherwise update $\mathcal{R} := \mathcal{R} \cup S$ and go back to Step 1.

Again, the correctness of the UNC completion procedure follows immediately from Theorems 5 and 6.

Theorem 8. *The UNC completion procedure is correct, i.e. if the procedure returns UNC then* $\mathrm{UNC}(\mathcal{R})$, *and if the procedure returns NotUNC then* $\neg\mathrm{UNC}(\mathcal{R})$.

Example 6. Let $\mathcal{R} = \{a \to a, f(f(x, b), y) \to f(y, b), f(b, y) \to f(y, b), f(x, a) \to b\}$. Since $\mathcal{R}$ is non-terminating, non-shallow, and non-right-ground, previous decidability results for UNC does not apply. Furthermore, since $\mathcal{R}$ is overlapping and $\mathcal{R}^L = \mathcal{R}$ is non-confluent, previous sufficient criteria for UNC does not apply. Also, previous modularity results for UNC does not properly decompose $\mathcal{R}$. Now, let us apply the UNC completion procedure to $\mathcal{R}$ using linear strongly closed criteria for confluence. For this, take $\varphi(\mathcal{R})$ as $\mathcal{R}$ is linear, and $\Phi(u, v)$ as $(u \xrightarrow{*} \circ \xleftarrow{=} v) \wedge (u \xrightarrow{=} \circ \xleftarrow{*} v)$. In Step 3, we find an overlay critical pair $\langle f(a, b), b \rangle$, for which Φ is not satisfied. Since $f(a, b)$ is not normal and b is normal, we go to Step 3(b). Thus, we update $\mathcal{R} := \mathcal{R} \cup \{f(a, b) \to b\}$. Now, the updated $\mathcal{R}$ is linear and strongly closed (and thus, $\mathcal{R}$ is confluent). Hence, the procedure returns UNC at Step 2.

6   Implementation and Experiment

We have tested various methods presented so far. The methods used in our experiment are summarized as follows.

(ω) UNC($\mathcal{R}$) if $\mathcal{R}$ is non-ω-overlapping.
(**pcl**) UNC($\mathcal{R}$) if $\mathcal{R}^L$ is parallel-closed.
(**scl**) UNC($\mathcal{R}$) if $\mathcal{R}$ is right-linear and $\mathcal{R}^L$ is strongly closed.
(**wd**) UNC($\mathcal{R}$) if $\mathcal{R}^S$ is non-duplicating and weight-decreasing joinable.
(**sc**) UNC completion using strongly closed critical pairs criterion.
(**dc**) UNC completion using development-closed critical pairs criterion.
(**rr**) UNC($\mathcal{R}$) if $\mathcal{R}$ is right-reducible.
(**cp**) ¬UNC($\mathcal{R}$) by adhoc search of a counterexample for UNC($\mathcal{R}$).
(**rev**) Rule reversing transformation, combined with other criteria above.

For the implementation of non-ω-overlapping condition, we used unification algorithm over infinite terms in [9]. For (**sc**) and (**dc**), we approximate $\overset{*}{\to}$ by the development step $\multimap\to$ (e.g. [16]) in Step 3(d). We employed as the heuristic ordering > for (**rev**) the comparison in terms of size. For (**cp**), we use an adhoc search based on rule reversing, critical pairs computation, and rewriting.

We tested on the 242 TRSs from the Cops (Confluence Problems) database[3] of which no confluence tool has proven confluence nor terminating at the time of experiment[4]. The motivation of using such testbed is as follows: If a confluent tool can prove CR, then UNC is obtained by confluent tools. If $\mathcal{R}$ is terminating then CR($\mathcal{R}$) iff UNC($\mathcal{R}$), and thus the result follows also from the result of confluence tools. Thus, we here evaluate our UNC techniques on such testbed.

Table 1. Test on presented criteria

without (rev)	(ω)	(pcl)	(scl)	(wd)	(sc) 1/2/3	(dc) 1/2/3	(rr)	(cp)	all
YES	10	8	3	3	4/10/12	3/9/12	45	0	62
NO	0	0	0	0	24/49/59	24/49/59	0	68	87
YES+NO	10	8	0	0	28/59/71	27/58/71	45	68	149
timeout (60 s)	0	0	0	0	13/20/53	15/23/70	0	0	–
time (min)	0	0	0	0	13/21/60	16/25/79	0	2	–
with (rev)	(ω)	(pcl)	(scl)	(wd)	(sc) 1/2/3	(dc) 1/2/3	(rr)	(cp)	all
YES	6	4	1	1	26/44/47	26/37/41	45	0	75
NO	0	0	0	0	25/52/60	25/53/61	0	60	84
YES+NO	6	4	1	1	51/96/107	51/90/102	45	60	159
timeout (60 s)	0	0	0	3	14/19/47	14/19/60	0	0	–
time (min)	0	0	0	4	15/20/54	15/21/70	0	0	–
both	(ω)	(pcl)	(scl)	(wd)	(sc) 1/2/3	(dc) 1/2/3	(rr)	(cp)	all
YES+NO	10	8	3	3	53/102/112	52/96/106	45	68	171

In Table 1, we summarize the results. Our test is performed on a PC with 2.60 GHz cpu with 4G of memory. The column headings show the technique

---

[3] Cops can be accessed from http://cops.uibk.ac.at/, which consists of 1137 problems at the time of experiment.

[4] This was obtained by a query 'trs !confluent !terminating' in Cops at the time of experiment.

used. The number of examples for which UNC is proved (disproved) successfully
is shown in the row titled 'YES' (resp. 'NO'). In the columns below **(sc)** and
(dc), we put $l/n/m$ where each l, n, m denotes the scores for the 1-round (2-
rounds, 3-rounds) UNC completion. The columns below '*all*' show the numbers
of examples succeeded in any of the methods.

The columns below the row headed '*with (rev)*' are the results for which
methods are applied after the rule reversing transformation. The columns below
the row headed '*both*' show the numbers of examples succeeded by each technique, where the techniques are applied to both of the original TRSs and the
TRSs obtained by the rule reversing transformation.

3 rounds UNC completions **(sc)**, **(dc)** with rule reversing are most effective,
but they are also the most time consuming. Simple methods **(rr)**, **(cp)** are also
effective for not few examples. Although there is only a small number of examples for which criteria based on conditional linearization are effective, but their
checks are fast compared to the UNC completions. Rule reversing **(rev)** is only
worth incorporated for UNC completions. For other methods, the rule reversing
make the methods less effective; for methods (ω), **(pcl)**, **(scl)** and **(wd)**, this is
because the rule reversing transformation generally increases the number of the
rules. In total, the UNC property of the 171 problems out of 242 problems have
been solved by presented methods. The details of the experiment are found in
http://www.nue.ie.niigata-u.ac.jp/tools/acp/experiments/frocos19/.

7   Tool

ACP originally intends to (dis)prove confluence of TRSs [3]. ACP integrates
multiple direct criteria for guaranteeing confluence of TRSs; it also incorporates several divide-and-conquer criteria. We have extended it to also deal with
(dis)proving the UNC property of TRSs.

Like its confluence proving counterpart, ACP first tries to decompose the
UNC problem of the given TRS into those of smaller components. For this, one
can use the following modularity results on the UNC property, where we refer
to [3] for the terminology:

Proposition 5 ([2]). *Suppose* $\{\mathcal{R}_1, \dots, \mathcal{R}_n\}$ *is a persistent decomposition of*
$\mathcal{R}$. *Then,* $\bigcup_i \mathcal{R}_i$ *is UNC if and only if so is each* $\mathcal{R}_i$.

Proposition 6 ([1]). *Suppose* $\{\mathcal{R}_1, \dots, \mathcal{R}_n\}$ *is a layer-preserving decomposition*
of $\mathcal{R}$. *Then,* $\bigcup_i \mathcal{R}_i$ *is UNC if and only if so is each* $\mathcal{R}_i$.

After possible decomposition, multiple direct criteria are tried for each component. For the direct criteria, we have incorporated (ω), **(pcl)**, **(scl)**, **(wd)**,
(rr), **(cp)** without rule reversing, and **(sc)**3 and **(dc)**3 with rule reversing. These
methods are tried one method after another. We also add yet another UNC check,
namely that after the Steps 1–3 of the UNC completion using development-closed
critical pairs criterion, the confluence check in ACP is performed.

Other tools that support UNC (dis)proving include CSI [14] which is a confluence prover supporting UNC proof for non-ω-overlapping TRSs and a decision

Table 2. Comparison of UNC tools

	ACP	ACP(direct)	CSI	FORT
YES	83	83	86	38
NO	92	92	65	34
time	62m	62m	78m	2m

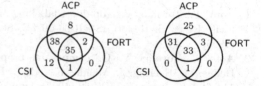

procedure of UNC for ground TRSs (at the time of CoCo 2018[5]), and FORT [18] which implements decision procedure for first-order theory of left-linear right-ground TRSs based on tree automata. Our new methods are also effective for TRSs outside the class of non-ω-overlapping TRSs and that of left-linear right-ground TRSs. We use the same testbed in the previous section, to compare our tool with the latest versions of CSI (ver. 1.2.2) and FORT (ver. 2.1), also test the effect of the divide-and-conquer criteria. The result is shown in the Table 2.

There is no example in the testbed that fails when decomposition techniques are inactivated (ACP (direct)). For the next example, however, our tool succeeds only if the decomposition techniques are activated.

Example 7. Let $\mathcal{R} = \mathcal{R}_1 \cup \mathcal{R}_2$, where $\mathcal{R}_1 = \{f(f(x,y),z) \to f(f(x,z),f(y,z))\}$ and $\mathcal{R}_2 = \{ \ @(@(@(S,x),y),z) \to @(@(x,z),@(y,z)), \ @(@(K,x),y) \to x, \ @(I,x) \to x, \ @(@(D,x),x) \to x \ \}$. By the persistency decomposition, UNC($\mathcal{R}$) follows UNC($\mathcal{R}_1$) and UNC($\mathcal{R}_2$). Since $\mathcal{R}_1$ is right-reducible, UNC($\mathcal{R}_1$) holds. Since $\mathcal{R}_2$ is non-ω-overlapping, UNC($\mathcal{R}_2$) holds. Thus, one obtains UNC($\mathcal{R}$).

The techniques in the present paper mainly contributed to make our tool ACP win the UNC category of CoCo 2018. The details of the competition can be seen at http://project-coco.uibk.ac.at/2018/. The version of ACP for CoCo 2018 (ver. 0.62) is downloadable from http://www.nue.ie.niigata-u.ac.jp/tools/acp/.

8   Conclusion

In this paper, we have studied automated methods for (dis)proving the UNC property of TRSs. We have presented some new methods for (dis)proving the UNC property of TRSs. Presented methods have been implemented in our tool ACP based on divide-and-conquer criteria.

Acknowledgements. Thanks are due to the anonymous reviewers of the previous versions of the paper. This work is partially supported by JSPS KAKENHI No. 18K11158.

---

[5] The recent version of CSI had been extended with some other techniques.

References

1. Aoto, T., Toyama, Y.: Top-down labelling and modularity of term rewriting systems. Research Report IS-RR-96-0023F, School of Information Science, JAIST (1996)
2. Aoto, T., Toyama, Y.: On composable properties of term rewriting systems. In: Hanus, M., Heering, J., Meinke, K. (eds.) ALP/HOA -1997. LNCS, vol. 1298, pp. 114–128. Springer, Heidelberg (1997). https://doi.org/10.1007/BFb0027006
3. Aoto, T., Yoshida, J., Toyama, Y.: Proving confluence of term rewriting systems automatically. In: Treinen, R. (ed.) RTA 2009. LNCS, vol. 5595, pp. 93–102. Springer, Heidelberg (2009). https://doi.org/10.1007/978-3-642-02348-4_7
4. Baader, F., Nipkow, T.: Term Rewriting and All That. Cambridge University Press, Cambridge (1998)
5. Bergstra, J.A., Klop, J.W.: Conditional rewrite rules: confluence and termination. J. Comput. Syst. Sci. **32**, 323–362 (1986)
6. Dauchet, M., Heuillard, T., Lescanne, P., Tison, S.: Decidability of the confluence of finite ground term rewrite systems and of other related term rewrite systems. Inf. Comput. **88**, 187–201 (1990)
7. Gramlich, B.: Modularity in term rewriting revisited. Theor. Comput. Sci. **464**, 3–19 (2012)
8. Huet, G.: Confluent reductions: abstract properties and applications to term rewriting systems. J. ACM **27**(4), 797–821 (1980)
9. Jaffar, J.: Efficient unification over infinite terms. New Gener. Comput. **2**, 207–219 (1984)
10. Kahrs, S., Smith, C.: Non-ω-overlapping TRSs are UN. In: Proceedings of 1st FSCD. LIPIcs, vol. 52, pp. 22:1–22:17. Schloss Dagstuhl (2016)
11. Klein, D., Hirokawa, N.: Confluence of non-left-linear TRSs via relative termination. In: Bjørner, N., Voronkov, A. (eds.) LPAR 2012. LNCS, vol. 7180, pp. 258–273. Springer, Heidelberg (2012). https://doi.org/10.1007/978-3-642-28717-6_21
12. Klop, J.: Combinatory Reduction Systems, Mathematical Centre Tracts, vol. 127. CWI, Amsterdam (1980)
13. Klop, J.W., de Vrijer, R.: Extended term rewriting systems. In: Kaplan, S., Okada, M. (eds.) CTRS 1990. LNCS, vol. 516, pp. 26–50. Springer, Heidelberg (1991). https://doi.org/10.1007/3-540-54317-1_79
14. Nagele, J., Felgenhauer, B., Middeldorp, A.: CSI: new evidence – a progress report. In: de Moura, L. (ed.) CADE 2017. LNCS (LNAI), vol. 10395, pp. 385–397. Springer, Cham (2017). https://doi.org/10.1007/978-3-319-63046-5_24
15. O'Donnell, M.J. (ed.): Computing in Systems Described by Equations. LNCS, vol. 58. Springer, Heidelberg (1977). https://doi.org/10.1007/3-540-08531-9
16. van Oostrom, V.: Developing developments. Theor. Comput. Sci. **175**(1), 159–181 (1997)
17. Radcliffe, N.R., Moreas, L.F.T., Verma, R.M.: Uniqueness of normal forms for shallow term rewrite systems. ACM Trans. Comput. Logic **18**(2), 17:1–17:20 (2017)
18. Rapp, F., Middeldorp, A.: Automating the first-order theory of rewriting for left-linear right-ground rewrite systems. In: Proceedings of 1st FSCD. LIPIcs, vol. 52, pp. 36:1–36:17. Schloss Dagstuhl (2016)
19. Toyama, Y.: Commutativity of term rewriting systems. In: Fuchi, K., Kott, L. (eds.) Programming of Future Generation Computers II, North-Holland, pp. 393–407 (1988)

20. Toyama, Y.: Confluent term rewriting systems. In: Giesl, J. (ed.) RTA 2005. LNCS, vol. 3467, p. 1. Springer, Heidelberg (2005). https://doi.org/10.1007/978-3-540-32033-3_1. Slides at http://www.nue.ie.niigata-u.ac.jp/toyama/user/toyama/slides/toyama-RTA05.pdf
21. Toyama, Y., Oyamaguchi, M.: Conditional linearization of non-duplicating term rewriting systems. IEICE Trans. Inf. Syst. **E84-D**(4), 439–447 (2001)
22. de Vrijer, R.: Conditional linearization. Indagationes Math. **10**(1), 145–159 (1999)

Transforming Derivational Complexity of Term Rewriting to Runtime Complexity

Carsten Fuhs[(✉)]

Department of Computer Science and Information Systems,
Birkbeck, University of London, London, UK
carsten@dcs.bbk.ac.uk

Abstract. Derivational complexity of term rewriting considers the length of the longest rewrite sequence for arbitrary start terms, whereas runtime complexity restricts start terms to basic terms. Recently, there has been notable progress in automatic inference of upper and lower bounds for runtime complexity. We propose a novel transformation that allows an off-the-shelf tool for inference of upper or lower bounds for runtime complexity to be used to determine upper or lower bounds for derivational complexity as well. Our approach is applicable to derivational complexity problems for innermost rewriting and for full rewriting. We have implemented the transformation in the tool APROVE and conducted an extensive experimental evaluation. Our results indicate that bounds for derivational complexity can now be inferred for rewrite systems that have been out of reach for automated analysis thus far.

1 Introduction

Term rewrite systems (TRSs) are a classic computational model both for equational reasoning and for evaluation of programs with user-defined data structures and recursion [5]. A widely studied question for TRSs is that of their *complexity*, i.e., the length of their longest derivation (i.e., rewrite sequence) as a function of the size of the start term of the derivation. From a program analysis perspective, this corresponds to the worst-case time complexity of the TRS.

In the literature, commonly two distinct notions are considered for the set of start terms. On the one hand, the *derivational complexity* [21] of a term rewrite system considers arbitrary terms as start terms that need to be regarded, including terms with several (possibly nested) function calls. This notion is inspired by the notion of termination of a rewrite system, which also considers whether all rewrite sequences from arbitrary start terms terminate. Derivational complexity is a suitable measure for the number of rewrite steps needed for deciding the word problem in first-order equational reasoning with the help of a terminating and confluent term rewrite system to rewrite both sides of the conjectured equality to normal form.

On the other hand, the notion of *runtime complexity* [18] of a term rewrite system restricts the set of start terms that are regarded to what is known as *basic terms*: intuitively, these are terms where a single function call is performed on constructor terms (i.e., data objects) as arguments. The motivation for this restriction comes from program analysis, where one is usually interested in the running time of a function when it is invoked on data objects.

These notions have been particularly studied for term rewriting with arbitrary rewrite strategies ("full rewriting") and for term rewriting restricted to innermost rewrite strategies ("innermost rewriting"). The latter notion is closely related to call-by-value evaluation in programming languages and λ-calculi.

Both for the derivational complexity and the runtime complexity of rewriting, and both for innermost and full rewriting, fully automatic push-button tools have been devised to determine asymptotic upper and lower bounds on the derivational complexity and the runtime complexity of term rewriting. Examples include the tools APROVE [14], CAT [23], MATCHBOX [34], and TCT [4].

However, as far as the author of this paper is aware, the two strands of research on derivational and on runtime complexity have essentially stayed separate thus far. While an upper bound on derivational complexity also implies an upper bound on runtime complexity and a lower bound on runtime complexity also implies a lower bound on derivational complexity, these implied bounds are seldom tight. A translation that would allow for applying tools for analysis of runtime complexity to analysis of derivational complexity (or vice versa) to infer potentially tight bounds is still missing. This paper aims to close this gap. We propose a transformation between rewrite systems such that the runtime complexity of the transformed rewrite system is the same as the derivational complexity of the original rewrite system. This transformation is applicable both for innermost rewriting and for full rewriting.

This paper is organized as follows. In Sect. 2, we give preliminaries on term rewriting and on notions of complexity. Sect. 3 proposes our novel transformation (Definition 5) and proves its correctness (Theorems 12 and 14). In Sect. 4, we discuss related work for complexity analysis of rewriting and for transformational approaches to analysis of rewrite systems. Sect. 5 provides a detailed experimental evaluation of our contributions on a large standard benchmark set. Sect. 6 concludes.

2   Preliminaries

In the following, we assume basic knowledge of term rewriting [5]. We recapitulate (relative) term rewriting as well as the notions of derivational complexity and runtime complexity.

Definition 1 (Signature, term, term rewriting, defined symbol, constructor symbol, basic term). *We write $\mathcal{T}(\Sigma, \mathcal{V})$ for the set of terms over a finite signature Σ and the set of variables $\mathcal{V}$. For a term t, $\mathcal{V}(t)$ denotes the set of variables occurring in t, and if t has the form $f(t_1, \ldots, t_n)$, we write $\mathrm{root}(t) = f$.*

A term rewrite system (TRS) $\mathcal{R}$ is a set of rules $\{\ell_1 \to r_1, \ldots, \ell_n \to r_n\}$ with $\ell_i, r_i \in \mathcal{T}(\Sigma, \mathcal{V})$, $\ell_i \notin \mathcal{V}$, and $\mathcal{V}(r_i) \subseteq \mathcal{V}(\ell_i)$ for all $1 \le i \le n$. Its rewrite relation is given by $s \to_{\mathcal{R}} t$ iff there is a rule $\ell \to r \in \mathcal{R}$, a position $\pi \in \mathcal{Pos}(s)$, and a substitution σ such that $s = s[\ell\sigma]_\pi$ and $t = s[r\sigma]_\pi$. Here, the term $\ell\sigma$ is called the redex of the rewrite step.

For two TRSs $\mathcal{R}$ and $\mathcal{S}$, $\mathcal{R}/\mathcal{S}$ is a relative TRS, and its rewrite relation $\rightarrow_{\mathcal{R}/\mathcal{S}}$ is $\rightarrow_\mathcal{S}^* \circ \rightarrow_\mathcal{R} \circ \rightarrow_\mathcal{S}^*$, i.e., rewriting with $\mathcal{S}$ is allowed before and after each $\mathcal{R}$-step. We define the innermost rewrite relation by $s \xrightarrow{i}_{\mathcal{R}/\mathcal{S}} t$ iff $s \rightarrow_\mathcal{S}^* s' \rightarrow_\mathcal{R} s'' \rightarrow_\mathcal{S}^* t$ for some terms s', s'' such that the proper subterms of the redexes of each step with $\rightarrow_\mathcal{S}$ or $\rightarrow_\mathcal{R}$ are in normal form w.r.t. $\mathcal{R} \cup \mathcal{S}$. We may write $\rightarrow_\mathcal{R}$ instead of $\rightarrow_{\mathcal{R}/\emptyset}$ and $\xrightarrow{i}_\mathcal{R}$ instead of $\xrightarrow{i}_{\mathcal{R}/\emptyset}$.

For a relative TRS $\mathcal{R}/\mathcal{S}$, $\Sigma_d^{\mathcal{R}\cup\mathcal{S}} = \{\text{root}(\ell) \mid \ell \rightarrow r \in \mathcal{R} \cup \mathcal{S}\}$ and $\Sigma_c^{\mathcal{R}\cup\mathcal{S}} = \{f \mid f \in \Sigma \text{ occurs in some rule } \ell \rightarrow r \in \mathcal{R} \cup \mathcal{S}\} \setminus \Sigma_d^{\mathcal{R}\cup\mathcal{S}}$ are the defined (and constructor, respectively) symbols of $\mathcal{R}/\mathcal{S}$. We write $\Sigma^{\mathcal{R}\cup\mathcal{S}} = \Sigma_d^{\mathcal{R}\cup\mathcal{S}} \uplus \Sigma_c^{\mathcal{R}\cup\mathcal{S}}$. A term $f(t_1,\ldots,t_k)$ is basic (for a given relative TRS $\mathcal{R}/\mathcal{S}$) iff $f \in \Sigma_d^{\mathcal{R}\cup\mathcal{S}}$ and $t_1,\ldots,t_k \in \mathcal{T}(\Sigma_c^{\mathcal{R}\cup\mathcal{S}}, \mathcal{V})$. We write $\mathcal{T}_{\text{basic}}^{\mathcal{R}/\mathcal{S}}$ for the set of basic terms for a relative TRS $\mathcal{R}/\mathcal{S}$.

In the following, ω is the smallest infinite ordinal, i.e., $\omega > n$ holds for all $n \in \mathbb{N}$, and for any $P \subseteq \mathbb{N} \cup \{\omega\}$, $\sup P$ is the least upper bound of P, where $\sup \emptyset = 0$.

Definition 2 (Size, derivation height, derivational complexity dc, runtime complexity rc [18,21,37]). The size $|t|$ of a term t is defined as $|x| = 1$ if $x \in \mathcal{V}$ and $|f(t_1,\ldots,t_k)| = 1 + \sum_{i=1}^k |t_i|$, otherwise.

The derivation height of a term t w.r.t. a relation $\rightarrow$ is the length of the longest sequence of $\rightarrow$-steps starting with t, i.e., $\text{dh}(t,\rightarrow) = \sup\{e \mid \exists t' \in \mathcal{T}(\Sigma,\mathcal{V}). t \rightarrow^e t'\}$ where $\rightarrow^e$ denotes the eth iterate of $\rightarrow$. If t starts an infinite $\rightarrow$-sequence, we write $\text{dh}(t,\rightarrow) = \omega$.

To define the intended complexity notions, we first introduce a generic complexity function compl parameterized by a natural number n, a relation $\rightarrow$, and a set of start terms $\mathcal{T}$: $\text{compl}(n,\rightarrow,\mathcal{T}) = \sup\{\text{dh}(t,\rightarrow) \mid t \in \mathcal{T}, |t| \leq n\}$.

The derivational complexity function $\text{dc}_{\mathcal{R}/\mathcal{S}}$ maps any $n \in \mathbb{N}$ to the length of the longest sequence of $\rightarrow_{\mathcal{R}/\mathcal{S}}$-steps starting with a term whose size is at most n, i.e., $\text{dc}_{\mathcal{R}/\mathcal{S}}(n) = \text{compl}(n, \rightarrow_{\mathcal{R}/\mathcal{S}}, \mathcal{T}(\Sigma^{\mathcal{R}\cup\mathcal{S}}, \mathcal{V}))$. The innermost derivational complexity function $\text{idc}_{\mathcal{R}/\mathcal{S}}$ is defined analogously for innermost rewriting: $\text{idc}_{\mathcal{R}/\mathcal{S}}(n) = \text{compl}(n, \xrightarrow{i}_{\mathcal{R}/\mathcal{S}}, \mathcal{T}(\Sigma^{\mathcal{R}\cup\mathcal{S}}, \mathcal{V}))$.

The runtime complexity function $\text{rc}_{\mathcal{R}/\mathcal{S}}$ maps any $n \in \mathbb{N}$ to the length of the longest sequence of $\rightarrow_{\mathcal{R}/\mathcal{S}}$-steps starting with a basic term whose size is at most n, i.e., $\text{rc}_{\mathcal{R}/\mathcal{S}}(n) = \text{compl}(n, \rightarrow_{\mathcal{R}/\mathcal{S}}, \mathcal{T}_{\text{basic}}^{\mathcal{R}/\mathcal{S}})$. The innermost runtime complexity function $\text{irc}_{\mathcal{R}/\mathcal{S}}$ is defined analogously: $\text{irc}_{\mathcal{R}/\mathcal{S}}(n) = \text{compl}(n, \xrightarrow{i}_{\mathcal{R}/\mathcal{S}}, \mathcal{T}_{\text{basic}}^{\mathcal{R}/\mathcal{S}})$.

Our transformation will preserve and reflect derivation height precisely. However, many analysis techniques for derivational complexity and runtime complexity of rewriting consider asymptotic behavior. The following definition is standard.

Definition 3 (Asymptotic notation, $\mathcal{O}$, Ω, Θ). Let $f,g : \mathbb{N} \rightarrow \mathbb{N} \cup \{\omega\}$. Then $f(n) \in \mathcal{O}(g(n))$ iff there are constants $M, N \in \mathbb{N}$ such that $f(n) \leq M \cdot g(n)$ for all $n \geq N$. Moreover, $f(n) \in \Omega(g(n))$ iff $g(n) \in \mathcal{O}(f(n))$, and $f(n) \in \Theta(g(n))$ holds iff both $f(n) \in \mathcal{O}(g(n))$ and $f(n) \in \Omega(g(n))$ hold.

Example 4 (plus). Consider the relative TRS $\mathcal{R}/\mathcal{S}$ with the following rules in $\mathcal{R}$:

$$\mathsf{plus}(0, x) \to x$$
$$\mathsf{plus}(\mathsf{s}(x), y) \to \mathsf{s}(\mathsf{plus}(x, y))$$

and with $\mathcal{S} = \emptyset$. Here 0 and s are constructor symbols, and plus is a defined symbol. We have $\mathrm{rc}_{\mathcal{R}/\mathcal{S}}(n) \in \Theta(n)$ (so both $\mathrm{rc}_{\mathcal{R}/\mathcal{S}}(n) \in \mathcal{O}(n)$ and $\mathrm{rc}_{\mathcal{R}/\mathcal{S}}(n) \in \Omega(n)$ hold) and $\mathrm{irc}_{\mathcal{R}/\mathcal{S}}(n) \in \Theta(n)$. Moreover, we have $\mathrm{dc}_{\mathcal{R}/\mathcal{S}}(n) \in \Theta(n^2)$ and $\mathrm{idc}_{\mathcal{R}/\mathcal{S}}(n) \in \Theta(n^2)$.

3 From Derivational Complexity to Runtime Complexity

In this section we present the main contribution of this paper, an instrumentation of a relative TRS $\mathcal{R}/\mathcal{S}$ to a relative TRS $\mathcal{R}/(\mathcal{S} \uplus \mathcal{G})$ with the same (innermost or full) runtime complexity. Moreover, we provide a proof for its correctness. The idea is to encode the set of arbitrary start terms that is considered for derivational complexity into a set of corresponding basic terms of the same size that can be analyzed for runtime complexity. This is accomplished by adding further constructor symbols cons_f that represent the defined symbols f from $\mathcal{R}/\mathcal{S}$. We also add an "instrumentation" in the form of relative rewrite rules $\mathcal{G}$ that generate the original start term for $\mathcal{R}/\mathcal{S}$ from its encoding as a basic term for $\mathcal{R}/(\mathcal{S} \uplus \mathcal{G})$, but do not lead to additional derivation height. The root symbol for these basic terms will be called enc_f for f a defined or a constructor symbol for $\mathcal{R}/\mathcal{S}$ (note that the root symbol of a start term for derivational complexity with maximum derivation height is not necessarily a defined symbol, e.g., consider the rewrite rule $\mathsf{a} \to \mathsf{c}(\mathsf{b}, \mathsf{b})$). We will also introduce an auxiliary function symbol argenc for recursive application of the additional rewrite rules.

For example, a start term $\mathsf{plus}(\mathsf{plus}(\mathsf{s}(0), 0), x)$ for derivational complexity will be represented by a basic term $\mathsf{enc}_{\mathsf{plus}}(\mathsf{cons}_{\mathsf{plus}}(\mathsf{s}(0), 0), x)$. Here $\mathsf{enc}_{\mathsf{plus}}$ will be a defined symbol and $\mathsf{cons}_{\mathsf{plus}}$ a constructor symbol. Rewriting using $\xrightarrow{i}_{\mathcal{G}}$ then restores (an instance of) the original start term.

Definition 5 (Generator rules $\mathcal{G}$, runtime instrumentation). *Let $\mathcal{R}/\mathcal{S}$ be a relative TRS. We define the* generator rules $\mathcal{G}$ *of $\mathcal{R}/\mathcal{S}$ as the set of rules*

$$\mathcal{G} = \{\mathsf{enc}_f(x_1, \ldots, x_n) \to f(\mathsf{argenc}(x_1), \ldots, \mathsf{argenc}(x_n)) \mid f \in \Sigma^{\mathcal{R} \cup \mathcal{S}}\}$$
$$\cup \{\mathsf{argenc}(\mathsf{cons}_f(x_1, \ldots, x_n)) \to f(\mathsf{argenc}(x_1), \ldots, \mathsf{argenc}(x_n)) \mid f \in \Sigma_d^{\mathcal{R} \cup \mathcal{S}}\}$$
$$\cup \{\mathsf{argenc}(f(x_1, \ldots, x_n)) \to f(\mathsf{argenc}(x_1), \ldots, \mathsf{argenc}(x_n)) \mid f \in \Sigma_c^{\mathcal{R} \cup \mathcal{S}}\}$$

where $x_1, \ldots, x_n$ are variables and where all function symbols argenc, cons_f, and enc_f are fresh (i.e., they do not occur in $\mathcal{R} \cup \mathcal{S}$). We call the relative TRS $\mathcal{R}/(\mathcal{S} \uplus \mathcal{G})$ the runtime instrumentation *of $\mathcal{R}/\mathcal{S}$. Moreover, we call terms over the signature $\{\mathsf{enc}_f \mid f \in \Sigma^{\mathcal{R} \cup \mathcal{S}}\} \cup \{\mathsf{cons}_f \mid f \in \Sigma_d^{\mathcal{R} \cup \mathcal{S}}\} \cup \Sigma_c^{\mathcal{R} \cup \mathcal{S}}$* generator terms *for $\mathcal{R}/\mathcal{S}$ (they are the intended start terms for $\mathcal{R}/(\mathcal{S} \uplus \mathcal{G})$).*

Example 6 (Example 4 continued). Continuing Example 4, we obtain the following generator rules $\mathcal{G}$:

$$\text{enc}_{\text{plus}}(x, y) \rightarrow \text{plus}(\text{argenc}(x), \text{argenc}(y))$$
$$\text{enc}_0 \rightarrow 0$$
$$\text{enc}_{\text{s}}(x) \rightarrow \text{s}(\text{argenc}(x))$$
$$\text{argenc}(\text{cons}_{\text{plus}}(x, y)) \rightarrow \text{plus}(\text{argenc}(x), \text{argenc}(y))$$
$$\text{argenc}(0) \rightarrow 0$$
$$\text{argenc}(\text{s}(x)) \rightarrow \text{s}(\text{argenc}(x))$$

To reason about our transformation, we introduce several helper functions to encode and decode arbitrary terms for $\mathcal{R}/\mathcal{S}$ as basic terms for $\mathcal{R}/(\mathcal{S} \uplus \mathcal{G})$.

Definition 7 (Constructor variant, basic variant, decoded variant).
Let $\mathcal{R}/\mathcal{S}$ be a relative TRS and let $\mathcal{R}/(\mathcal{S} \uplus \mathcal{G})$ be its runtime instrumentation.
For a term $t \in \mathcal{T}(\Sigma^{\mathcal{R} \cup \mathcal{S}}, \mathcal{V})$, we define its constructor variant $\text{cv}(t)$ inductively as follows:

- $\text{cv}(x) = x$ *for* $x \in \mathcal{V}$
- $\text{cv}(f(t_1, \ldots, t_n)) = f(\text{cv}(t_1), \ldots, \text{cv}(t_n))$ *for* $f \in \Sigma_c^{\mathcal{R} \cup \mathcal{S}}$
- $\text{cv}(f(t_1, \ldots, t_n)) = \text{cons}_f(\text{cv}(t_1), \ldots, \text{cv}(t_n))$ *for* $f \in \Sigma_d^{\mathcal{R} \cup \mathcal{S}}$

For a term $t = f(t_1, \ldots, t_n) \in \mathcal{T}(\Sigma^{\mathcal{R} \cup \mathcal{S}}, \mathcal{V})$, we define its basic variant $\text{bv}(f(t_1, \ldots, t_n)) = \text{enc}_f(\text{cv}(t_1), \ldots, \text{cv}(t_n))$.
Finally, for a term $t \in \mathcal{T}(\Sigma^{\mathcal{R} \cup \mathcal{S} \cup \mathcal{G}}, \mathcal{V})$, we define its decoded variant $\text{dv}(t) \in \mathcal{T}(\Sigma^{\mathcal{R} \cup \mathcal{S}}, \mathcal{V})$ as follows:

- $\text{dv}(x) = x$ *for* $x \in \mathcal{V}$
- $\text{dv}(f(t_1, \ldots, t_n)) = g(\text{dv}(t_1), \ldots, \text{dv}(t_n))$ *for* $f \in \{g, \text{cons}_g, \text{enc}_g\}$ *with* $g \in \Sigma_d^{\mathcal{R} \cup \mathcal{S}}$
- $\text{dv}(f(t_1, \ldots, t_n)) = f(\text{dv}(t_1), \ldots, \text{dv}(t_n))$ *for* $f \in \Sigma_c^{\mathcal{R} \cup \mathcal{S}}$

The following lemmas address properties of our helper functions that we will use in the proofs of our theorems.

Lemma 8 (Basic variants of function applications are basic terms).
Let $\mathcal{R}/\mathcal{S}$ be a relative TRS, let t be a term from $\mathcal{T}(\Sigma^{\mathcal{R} \cup \mathcal{S}}, \mathcal{V})$.

(a) We have $\text{cv}(t) \in \mathcal{T}(\Sigma_c^{\mathcal{R} \cup \mathcal{S} \cup \mathcal{G}}, \mathcal{V})$.
(b) The term $\text{bv}(t)$ is a basic term for the runtime instrumentation $\mathcal{R}/(\mathcal{S} \uplus \mathcal{G})$.
(c) $|\text{bv}(t)| = |t|$.

Proof. Claims (a) and (b) follow directly from the definitions of cv, of bv, and of generator rules, and claim (c) follows by induction over the definitions of bv and cv. □

In the following lemmas and proofs, we will need a particular substitution σ_t that maps each variable x of a term t to $\mathsf{argenc}(x)$, so we introduce corresponding notation.

Definition 9 (σ_t). *For a term t, we define the substitution σ_t by $\sigma_t(x) = \mathsf{argenc}(x)$ for $x \in \mathcal{V}(t)$ and $\sigma_t(x) = x$ otherwise.*

Lemma 10 (argenc reduces constructor variants innermost to instances of their originals). *Let $\mathcal{R}/\mathcal{S}$ be a relative TRS and $\mathcal{R}/(\mathcal{S} \uplus \mathcal{G})$ its runtime instrumentation. Then for all $t \in \mathcal{T}(\Sigma^{\mathcal{R}\cup\mathcal{S}}, \mathcal{V})$, $\mathsf{argenc}(\mathrm{cv}(t)) \xrightarrow{\mathrm{i}}^{*}_{\mathcal{R}\cup\mathcal{S}\cup\mathcal{G}} t\sigma_t$ is an innermost rewrite sequence that moreover uses only rules from $\mathcal{G}$.*

Proof. By induction over the structure of t. Let $t \in \mathcal{V}$. Then $\mathrm{cv}(t) = t$, and $\mathsf{argenc}(\mathrm{cv}(t)) \xrightarrow{\mathrm{i}}^{*}_{\mathcal{R}\cup\mathcal{S}\cup\mathcal{G}} t\sigma_t$ in zero steps.

Now let $t = f(t_1, \ldots, t_n) \in \mathcal{T}(\Sigma^{\mathcal{R}\cup\mathcal{S}}, \mathcal{V})$. By induction hypothesis, we have $\mathsf{argenc}(\mathrm{cv}(t_i)) \xrightarrow{\mathrm{i}}^{*}_{\mathcal{R}\cup\mathcal{S}\cup\mathcal{G}} t_i\sigma_{t_i}$.

If $f \in \Sigma_c^{\mathcal{R}\cup\mathcal{S}}$, we have $\mathrm{cv}(f(t_1, \ldots, t_n)) = f(\mathrm{cv}(t_1), \ldots, \mathrm{cv}(t_n))$. By applying the induction hypothesis, we get the desired innermost rewrite sequence:

$$
\begin{aligned}
&\mathsf{argenc}(\mathrm{cv}(t)) \\
={}& \mathsf{argenc}(f(\mathrm{cv}(t_1), \ldots, \mathrm{cv}(t_n))) \\
\xrightarrow{\mathrm{i}}_{\mathcal{R}\cup\mathcal{S}\cup\mathcal{G}}{}& f(\mathsf{argenc}(\mathrm{cv}(t_1)), \ldots, \mathsf{argenc}(\mathrm{cv}(t_n))) \\
\xrightarrow{\mathrm{i}}^{*}_{\mathcal{R}\cup\mathcal{S}\cup\mathcal{G}}{}& f(t_1\sigma_{t_1}, \ldots, t_n\sigma_{t_n}) \\
={}& t\sigma_t
\end{aligned}
$$

If $f \in \Sigma_d^{\mathcal{R}\cup\mathcal{S}}$, we have $\mathrm{cv}(f(t_1, \ldots, t_n)) = \mathrm{cons}_f(\mathrm{cv}(t_1), \ldots, \mathrm{cv}(t_n))$. By applying the induction hypothesis, we get the desired innermost rewrite sequence:

$$
\begin{aligned}
&\mathsf{argenc}(\mathrm{cv}(t)) \\
={}& \mathsf{argenc}(\mathrm{cons}_f(\mathrm{cv}(t_1), \ldots, \mathrm{cv}(t_n))) \\
\xrightarrow{\mathrm{i}}_{\mathcal{R}\cup\mathcal{S}\cup\mathcal{G}}{}& f(\mathsf{argenc}(\mathrm{cv}(t_1)), \ldots, \mathsf{argenc}(\mathrm{cv}(t_n))) \\
\xrightarrow{\mathrm{i}}^{*}_{\mathcal{R}\cup\mathcal{S}\cup\mathcal{G}}{}& f(t_1\sigma_{t_1}, \ldots, t_n\sigma_{t_n}) \\
={}& t\sigma_t
\end{aligned}
$$

□

Lemma 11 (Basic variants reduce innermost to instances of their originals). *Let $\mathcal{R}/\mathcal{S}$ be a relative TRS and $\mathcal{R}/(\mathcal{S} \uplus \mathcal{G})$ its runtime instrumentation. Then for all $t \in \mathcal{T}(\Sigma^{\mathcal{R}\cup\mathcal{S}}, \mathcal{V})$ of the form $f(t_1, \ldots, t_n)$, $\mathrm{bv}(t) \xrightarrow{\mathrm{i}}^{*}_{\mathcal{R}\cup\mathcal{S}\cup\mathcal{G}} t\sigma_t$ is an innermost rewrite sequence that moreover uses only rules from $\mathcal{G}$.*

Proof. Let $t \in \mathcal{T}(\Sigma^{\mathcal{R}\cup\mathcal{S}}, \mathcal{V})$ of the form $f(t_1, \ldots, t_n)$. Then we have $\mathrm{bv}(t) = \mathrm{enc}_f(\mathrm{cv}(t_1), \ldots, \mathrm{cv}(t_n))$. The only possible rewrite step uses the rewrite rule $\mathrm{enc}_f(x_1, \ldots, x_n) \rightarrow f(\mathsf{argenc}(x_1), \ldots, \mathsf{argenc}(x_n))$ in $\mathcal{G}$ for $\mathrm{bv}(t) \xrightarrow{\mathrm{i}}_{\mathcal{R}\cup\mathcal{S}\cup\mathcal{G}} f(\mathsf{argenc}(\mathrm{cv}(t_1)), \ldots, \mathsf{argenc}(\mathrm{cv}(t_n)))$. By Lemma 10, we have:

$$
f(\mathsf{argenc}(\mathrm{cv}(t_1)), \ldots, \mathsf{argenc}(\mathrm{cv}(t_n))) \xrightarrow{\mathrm{i}}^{*}_{\mathcal{R}\cup\mathcal{S}\cup\mathcal{G}} f(t_1\sigma_{t_1}, \ldots, t_n\sigma_{t_n}) = t\sigma_t
$$

□

Now we are ready to prove the first theorem:

Theorem 12 (Derivational complexity via runtime complexity). *Let $\mathcal{R}/\mathcal{S}$ be a relative TRS and let $\mathcal{R}/(\mathcal{S} \uplus \mathcal{G})$ be its runtime instrumentation. Then for all $n \in \mathbb{N}$, we have $\mathrm{dc}_{\mathcal{R}/\mathcal{S}}(n) = \mathrm{rc}_{\mathcal{R}/(\mathcal{S} \uplus \mathcal{G})}(n)$.*

Proof. We show the two directions of the theorem separately.

(1) $\mathrm{dc}_{\mathcal{R}/\mathcal{S}}(n) \leq \mathrm{rc}_{\mathcal{R}/(\mathcal{S} \uplus \mathcal{G})}(n)$.

For $n = 0$, there are no terms of size $\leq n$. Thus, let $n > 0$ and let $t \in \mathcal{T}(\Sigma^{\mathcal{R} \cup \mathcal{S}}, \mathcal{V})$ be an arbitrary term with $|t| \leq n$ starting a $\to_{\mathcal{R}/\mathcal{S}}$-rewrite sequence

$$t = t_0 \to_{\mathcal{R}/\mathcal{S}} t_1 \to_{\mathcal{R}/\mathcal{S}} t_2 \to_{\mathcal{R}/\mathcal{S}} \cdots$$

of maximal length for all terms of size at most n, i.e., (i) $\mathrm{dh}(t, \to_{\mathcal{R}/\mathcal{S}}) = \mathrm{dc}_{\mathcal{R}/\mathcal{S}}(n)$.

By Lemma 11, we have $\mathrm{bv}(t) \to_{\mathcal{G}}^* t\sigma_t$. Since $\to_{\mathcal{R}/\mathcal{S}} \subseteq \to_{\mathcal{R}/(\mathcal{S} \uplus \mathcal{G})}$ and since rewriting is closed under substitutions, we have

$$\mathrm{bv}(t) \to_{\mathcal{G}}^* t\sigma_t \to_{\mathcal{R}/(\mathcal{S} \uplus \mathcal{G})} t_1\sigma_t \to_{\mathcal{R}/(\mathcal{S} \uplus \mathcal{G})} t_2\sigma_t \to_{\mathcal{R}/(\mathcal{S} \uplus \mathcal{G})} \cdots$$

which yields

$$\mathrm{bv}(t) \to_{\mathcal{R}/(\mathcal{S} \uplus \mathcal{G})} t_1\sigma_t \to_{\mathcal{R}/(\mathcal{S} \uplus \mathcal{G})} t_2\sigma_t \to_{\mathcal{R}/(\mathcal{S} \uplus \mathcal{G})} \cdots$$

and thus (ii) $\mathrm{dh}(t, \to_{\mathcal{R}/\mathcal{S}}) \leq \mathrm{dh}(\mathrm{bv}(t), \to_{\mathcal{R}/(\mathcal{S} \uplus \mathcal{G})})$.

By Lemma 8, $\mathrm{bv}(t)$ is a basic term for $\mathcal{R}/(\mathcal{S} \uplus \mathcal{G})$ with $|\mathrm{bv}(t)| = |t| \leq n$. Thus, $\mathrm{dh}(\mathrm{bv}(t), \to_{\mathcal{R}/(\mathcal{S} \uplus \mathcal{G})}) \leq \mathrm{rc}_{\mathcal{R}/(\mathcal{S} \uplus \mathcal{G})}(n)$. Using equality (i) and inequality (ii), we can conclude that the claim indeed holds.

(2) $\mathrm{dc}_{\mathcal{R}/\mathcal{S}}(n) \geq \mathrm{rc}_{\mathcal{R}/(\mathcal{S} \uplus \mathcal{G})}(n)$.

For $n = 0$, there are no terms of size $\leq n$. Thus, let $n > 0$ and let $t \in \mathcal{T}(\Sigma^{\mathcal{R} \cup \mathcal{S} \cup \mathcal{G}}, \mathcal{V})$ be an arbitrary basic term for $\mathcal{R}/(\mathcal{S} \uplus \mathcal{G})$ with $|t| \leq n$ starting a $\to_{\mathcal{R}/(\mathcal{S} \uplus \mathcal{G})}$-rewrite sequence

$$t = t_0 \to_{\mathcal{R}/(\mathcal{S} \uplus \mathcal{G})} t_1 \to_{\mathcal{R}/(\mathcal{S} \uplus \mathcal{G})} t_2 \to_{\mathcal{R}/(\mathcal{S} \uplus \mathcal{G})} \cdots$$

of maximal length for all terms of size at most n, i.e., $\mathrm{dh}(t, \to_{\mathcal{R}/(\mathcal{S} \uplus \mathcal{G})}) = \mathrm{rc}_{\mathcal{R}/(\mathcal{S} \uplus \mathcal{G})}(n)$.

We will now show that there exists a term $s \in \mathcal{T}(\Sigma^{\mathcal{R} \cup \mathcal{S}}, \mathcal{V})$ of size at most n that has at least the same derivation height, witnessed by a "simulation" of the above $\to_{\mathcal{R}/(\mathcal{S} \uplus \mathcal{G})}$-derivation using $\to_{\mathcal{R}/\mathcal{S}}$.

If $\mathrm{root}(t) \in \Sigma_d^{\mathcal{R} \cup \mathcal{S}}$, t does not contain argenc or enc_f for any f since t is a basic term. Moreover, no rewrite sequence starting with t can use the rules in $\mathcal{G}$ since none of the rules reachable from t introduce any of the symbols argenc or enc_f for some f. Therefore, the above $\to_{\mathcal{R}/(\mathcal{S} \uplus \mathcal{G})}$-sequence starting from t is an $\to_{\mathcal{R}/\mathcal{S}}$-sequence of the same length. To get a term s over the original signature $\Sigma^{\mathcal{R} \cup \mathcal{S}}$, we replace all occurrences of function symbols cons_f by the corresponding $f \in \Sigma_d^{\mathcal{R} \cup \mathcal{S}}$, i.e., we set $s = \mathrm{dv}(t)$. Thus, we have $\mathrm{dh}(t, \to_{\mathcal{R}/(\mathcal{S} \uplus \mathcal{G})}) \leq \mathrm{dh}(s, \to_{\mathcal{R}/\mathcal{S}}) \leq \mathrm{dc}_{\mathcal{R}/\mathcal{S}}(n)$.

Now consider $\mathrm{root}(t) = \mathsf{argenc}$, i.e., $t = \mathsf{argenc}(u)$ for a constructor term $u \in \mathcal{T}(\Sigma_c^{\mathcal{R} \cup \mathcal{S} \cup \mathcal{G}}, \mathcal{V})$. We can simulate the $\to_{\mathcal{R}/(\mathcal{S} \uplus \mathcal{G})}$-derivation starting with t from the term $s = \mathsf{dv}(u)$. In this simulation, we omit the $\to_{\mathcal{G}}$-steps from the original $\to_{\mathcal{R}/(\mathcal{S} \uplus \mathcal{G})}$-derivation and obtain a $\to_{\mathcal{R}/\mathcal{S}}$-derivation with the same number of $\to_{\mathcal{R}}$-steps and hence the same derivation height. As $|s| \leq n$ ($|\mathsf{dv}(u)| = |u|$ can be shown analogously to Lemma 8), we have $\mathrm{dh}(t, \to_{\mathcal{R}/(\mathcal{S} \uplus \mathcal{G})}) \leq \mathrm{dh}(s, \to_{\mathcal{R}/\mathcal{S}}) \leq \mathrm{dc}_{\mathcal{R}/\mathcal{S}}(n)$.

Finally, let $\mathrm{root}(t) = \mathsf{enc}_f$ for some $f \in \Sigma_d^{\mathcal{R} \cup \mathcal{S}}$ and thus $t = \mathsf{enc}_f(u_1, \ldots, u_k)$ for some terms $u_1, \ldots, u_k \in \mathcal{T}(\Sigma_c^{\mathcal{R} \cup \mathcal{S} \cup \mathcal{G}}, \mathcal{V})$. By construction, the first rewrite step in the above $\to_{\mathcal{R} \cup \mathcal{S} \cup \mathcal{G}}^*$-derivation must be $t \to_{\mathcal{G}} f(\mathsf{argenc}(u_1), \ldots, \mathsf{argenc}(u_k))$. We again obtain $s \in \mathcal{T}(\Sigma^{\mathcal{R} \cup \mathcal{S}}, \mathcal{V})$ as the start term for our simulation from $f(u_1, \ldots, u_k)$ as $\mathsf{dv}(f(u_1, \ldots, u_k))$, and analogously to the case $\mathrm{root}(t) = \mathsf{argenc}$, we again have $\mathrm{dh}(t, \to_{\mathcal{R}/(\mathcal{S} \uplus \mathcal{G})}) \leq \mathrm{dh}(s, \to_{\mathcal{R}/\mathcal{S}}) \leq \mathrm{dc}_{\mathcal{R}/\mathcal{S}}(n)$. □

To prove the corresponding theorem for *innermost* derivational complexity, we use an additional lemma which lets us simulate innermost rewrite steps $s \xrightarrow{i}_{\mathcal{R}/\mathcal{S}} t$ via $s\sigma_s \xrightarrow{i}_{\mathcal{R}/(\mathcal{S} \uplus \mathcal{G})} t\sigma_s$. (This is a priori not completely obvious since innermost rewriting is not closed under substitutions nor under addition of rewrite rules.)

Lemma 13 (Innermost simulation with generator rules). *Let $\mathcal{R}/\mathcal{S}$ be a relative TRS and let $\mathcal{R}/(\mathcal{S} \uplus \mathcal{G})$ be its runtime instrumentation. Let $s, t \in \mathcal{T}(\Sigma^{\mathcal{R} \cup \mathcal{S}}, \mathcal{V})$. Let σ be a substitution with $s\sigma = s\sigma_s$.*

(a) If $s \xrightarrow{i}_{\mathcal{R} \cup \mathcal{S}} t$, then $s\sigma \xrightarrow{i}_{\mathcal{R} \cup \mathcal{S} \cup \mathcal{G}} t\sigma$.
(b) If $s \xrightarrow{i}_{\mathcal{R}/\mathcal{S}} t$, then $s\sigma \xrightarrow{i}_{\mathcal{R}/(\mathcal{S} \uplus \mathcal{G})} t\sigma$.

Proof. (a) Let $s, t \in \mathcal{T}(\Sigma^{\mathcal{R} \cup \mathcal{S}}, \mathcal{V})$ such that $s \xrightarrow{i}_{\mathcal{R} \cup \mathcal{S}} t$. Then we also have $s \xrightarrow{i}_{\mathcal{R} \cup \mathcal{S} \cup \mathcal{G}} t$ since s, t do not contain any defined symbols from $\mathcal{G}$. Moreover, we have $s\sigma \xrightarrow{i}_{\mathcal{R} \cup \mathcal{S} \cup \mathcal{G}} t\sigma$ since the introduced function symbol argenc does not occur in $\mathcal{R} \cup \mathcal{S}$, since argenc does not occur below the root of a left-hand side of $\mathcal{G}$, and since argenc occurs in $s\sigma$ only in subterms of the shape $\mathsf{argenc}(x)$ for variables x, whereas all argenc-rules in $\mathcal{G}$ require a function symbol below the root of a potential redex.

(b) Follows directly from (a).

Theorem 14 (Innermost derivational complexity via innermost runtime complexity). *Let $\mathcal{R}/\mathcal{S}$ be a relative TRS and let $\mathcal{R}/(\mathcal{S} \uplus \mathcal{G})$ be its runtime instrumentation. Then for all $n \in \mathbb{N}$, we have $\mathrm{idc}_{\mathcal{R}/\mathcal{S}}(n) = \mathrm{irc}_{\mathcal{R}/(\mathcal{S} \uplus \mathcal{G})}(n)$.*

Proof. (1) $\mathrm{idc}_{\mathcal{R}/\mathcal{S}}(n) \leq \mathrm{irc}_{\mathcal{R}/(\mathcal{S} \uplus \mathcal{G})}(n)$.

The proof for this direction of the theorem is analogous to the one for Theorem 12. The only difference is that Lemma 13 is required to show that $t_i \xrightarrow{i}_{\mathcal{R}/\mathcal{S}} t_{i+1}$ implies $t_i\sigma_t \xrightarrow{i}_{\mathcal{R}/(\mathcal{S} \uplus \mathcal{G})} t_{i+1}\sigma_t$.

(2) $\mathrm{idc}_{\mathcal{R}/\mathcal{S}}(n) \geq \mathrm{irc}_{\mathcal{R}/(\mathcal{S} \uplus \mathcal{G})}(n)$.

Let $n \in \mathbb{N}$ and let $t \in \mathcal{T}(\Sigma^{\mathcal{R} \cup \mathcal{S} \cup \mathcal{G}}, \mathcal{V})$ be an arbitrary basic term for $\mathcal{R}/(\mathcal{S} \uplus \mathcal{G})$ with $|t| \leq n$ starting a $\xrightarrow{i}_{\mathcal{R}/(\mathcal{S} \uplus \mathcal{G})}$-rewrite sequence

$$t = t_0 \xrightarrow{i}_{\mathcal{R}/(\mathcal{S} \uplus \mathcal{G})} t_1 \xrightarrow{i}_{\mathcal{R}/(\mathcal{S} \uplus \mathcal{G})} t_2 \xrightarrow{i}_{\mathcal{R}/(\mathcal{S} \uplus \mathcal{G})} \cdots$$

of maximal length for all terms of size at most n, i.e., (i) $\mathrm{dh}(t, \xrightarrow{i}_{\mathcal{R}/(\mathcal{S} \uplus \mathcal{G})}) = \mathrm{irc}_{\mathcal{R}/(\mathcal{S} \uplus \mathcal{G})}(n)$.

We will now show that there exists a term $s \in \Sigma^{\mathcal{R} \cup \mathcal{S}}$ that has at least the same derivation height, again witnessed by a simulation of the above $\rightarrow_{\mathcal{R}/(\mathcal{S} \uplus \mathcal{G})}$-derivation using $\rightarrow_{\mathcal{R}/\mathcal{S}}$.

If $\mathrm{root}(t) \in \Sigma_d^{\mathcal{R} \cup \mathcal{S}}$, no rewrite sequence starting with t can use the rules in $\mathcal{G}$ since none of the rules reachable from the basic term t introduce any of the symbols argenc or enc_f for some f. Therefore, the above $\xrightarrow{i}_{\mathcal{R}/(\mathcal{S} \uplus \mathcal{G})}$-sequence is an $\xrightarrow{i}_{\mathcal{R}/\mathcal{S}}$-sequence of the same length.

For our simulation, we still need to obtain a start term over the original signature $\Sigma^{\mathcal{R} \cup \mathcal{S}}$. Simply replacing all cons_f by f as in the proof of Theorem 12 might introduce new $\mathcal{S}$-redexes that, due to innermost rewriting, could prevent further steps in the derivation using $\mathcal{R}$ and lead to a shorter $\xrightarrow{i}_{\mathcal{R}/(\mathcal{S} \uplus \mathcal{G})}$-derivation. Thus, to obtain a term s over $\Sigma^{\mathcal{R} \cup \mathcal{S}}$, we replace all maximal "alien subterms" u of t with regard to the signature $\Sigma^{\mathcal{R} \cup \mathcal{S}}$ by corresponding fresh variables x_u. (An alien subterm u of a term t with regard to a (sub-)signature Σ is a subterm of t with a root symbol $h \notin \Sigma$. Here $h = \mathrm{cons}_g$ for some $g \in \Sigma_d^{\mathcal{R} \cup \mathcal{S}}$ may occur.)

The obtained rewrite sequence from s has at least as many $\xrightarrow{i}_{\mathcal{R}/\mathcal{S}}$-rewrite steps as the original $\xrightarrow{i}_{\mathcal{R}/(\mathcal{S} \uplus \mathcal{G})}$-rewrite sequence had steps from t, and so we have $\mathrm{dh}(t, \xrightarrow{i}_{\mathcal{R}/(\mathcal{S} \uplus \mathcal{G})}) \leq \mathrm{dh}(s, \xrightarrow{i}_{\mathcal{R}/\mathcal{S}}) \leq \mathrm{idc}_{\mathcal{R}/\mathcal{S}}(n)$.

The cases $\mathrm{root}(t) = \mathrm{argenc}$ and $\mathrm{root}(t) = \mathrm{enc}_f$ are analogous to Theorem 12. Note that by construction, here argenc is always applied to constructor terms as arguments. $\qquad\square$

We finish the section by presenting an example that (to the author's knowledge) was out of reach for automated analysis tools for derivational complexity so far, but can now be handled using an off-the-shelf tool for automated inference of runtime complexity bounds. This example is taken from the *Termination Problems Data Base (TPDB)* [36], a collection of examples used at the annual *Termination and Complexity Competition* [16,35].

Example 15 (Derivational_Complexity_Full_Rewriting/AG01/#3.12, TPDB). Consider the following set of rewrite rules $\mathcal{R}$:

$$\mathrm{app}(\mathrm{nil}, y) \rightarrow y$$
$$\mathrm{app}(\mathrm{add}(n, x), y) \rightarrow \mathrm{add}(n, \mathrm{app}(x, y))$$
$$\mathrm{reverse}(\mathrm{nil}) \rightarrow \mathrm{nil}$$
$$\mathrm{reverse}(\mathrm{add}(n, x)) \rightarrow \mathrm{app}(\mathrm{reverse}(x), \mathrm{add}(n, \mathrm{nil}))$$
$$\mathrm{shuffle}(\mathrm{nil}) \rightarrow \mathrm{nil}$$
$$\mathrm{shuffle}(\mathrm{add}(n, x)) \rightarrow \mathrm{add}(n, \mathrm{shuffle}(\mathrm{reverse}(x)))$$

Using our transformation to a runtime instrumentation, APROVE adds the following generator rules $\mathcal{G}$:

$$\mathsf{argenc}(\mathsf{nil}) \rightarrow \mathsf{nil}$$
$$\mathsf{argenc}(\mathsf{add}(x_1, x_2)) \rightarrow \mathsf{add}(\mathsf{argenc}(x_1), \mathsf{argenc}(x_2))$$
$$\mathsf{argenc}(\mathsf{cons}_{\mathsf{app}}(x_1, x_2)) \rightarrow \mathsf{app}(\mathsf{argenc}(x_1), \mathsf{argenc}(x_2))$$
$$\mathsf{argenc}(\mathsf{cons}_{\mathsf{reverse}}(x_1)) \rightarrow \mathsf{reverse}(\mathsf{argenc}(x_1))$$
$$\mathsf{argenc}(\mathsf{cons}_{\mathsf{shuffle}}(x_1)) \rightarrow \mathsf{shuffle}(\mathsf{argenc}(x_1))$$
$$\mathsf{enc}_{\mathsf{nil}} \rightarrow \mathsf{nil}$$
$$\mathsf{enc}_{\mathsf{add}}(x_1, x_2) \rightarrow \mathsf{add}(\mathsf{argenc}(x_1), \mathsf{argenc}(x_2))$$
$$\mathsf{enc}_{\mathsf{app}}(x_1, x_2) \rightarrow \mathsf{app}(\mathsf{argenc}(x_1), \mathsf{argenc}(x_2))$$
$$\mathsf{enc}_{\mathsf{reverse}}(x_1) \rightarrow \mathsf{reverse}(\mathsf{argenc}(x_1))$$
$$\mathsf{enc}_{\mathsf{shuffle}}(x_1) \rightarrow \mathsf{shuffle}(\mathsf{argenc}(x_1))$$

Then APROVE determines $\mathrm{dc}_{\mathcal{R}/\emptyset}(n) \in \mathcal{O}(n^4)$ and $\mathrm{dc}_{\mathcal{R}/\emptyset}(n) \in \Omega(n^3)$. (A manual analysis reveals that $\mathrm{dc}_{\mathcal{R}/\emptyset}(n) \in \Theta(n^4)$.)

For the inference of the upper bound, first a sufficient criterion [12] is used to show that this TRS belongs to a class of TRSs where runtime complexity and innermost runtime complexity coincide. To analyze innermost runtime complexity, the approach by Naaf et al. [30] is applied. Here the search for an upper bound for innermost runtime complexity is encoded as the search for an upper bound for the runtime of integer transition systems. The proof is completed using the tools CoFloCo [10,11] and KoAT [6] as backends for complexity analysis of integer transition systems.

For the inference of the lower bound, APROVE uses a technique based on rewrite lemmas [13].

4   Related Work

Derivational Complexity Analysis. There is a significant body of work on automated analysis of derivational complexity [21] of term rewriting systems. Early techniques are based on observations on the induced maximal derivation height by a direct termination proof via reduction orders [20,22,27,28,31]. Later work also considers modular techniques [37].

Runtime Complexity Analysis. In recent years, techniques to infer bounds on the runtime complexity of rewrite systems [18] have become a subject of intensive study, both for full and for innermost rewriting strategies [2,3,13,18,30]. We can use these techniques to analyze the runtime instrumentations generated from our transformation. In this way, we can now analyze of derivational complexity indirectly, e.g., using amortized complexity analysis [29], adaptions of the dependency pair method [18,32], and further transformational techniques discussed below (see also Example 15).

Transformational Approaches for Proving Properties of TRSs. Transformational approaches for proving properties of TRSs have been introduced successfully in the literature before.

For instance, for termination, techniques like semantic labeling [38] or dependency pairs [1] transform rewrite systems in a way that preserves and reflects termination and that often makes the resulting system more amenable to (automated) termination proofs.

For termination of rewriting with different rewrite strategies, a number of transformations have been devised. For example, transformations to context-sensitive rewriting [25] have been proposed for innermost rewriting [8] (later adapted to innermost runtime complexity [19]) and for outermost rewrite strategies [7]. Here termination of the resulting rewrite system w.r.t. a context-sensitive strategy implies termination w.r.t. the original strategy. Similarly, for context-sensitive rewriting, a number of transformations to full rewriting have been proposed [9,15,24,39] such that termination of the transformed TRS w.r.t. full rewriting implies termination of the original TRS w.r.t. the original context-sensitive rewrite strategy. In particular, Giesl and Middeldorp [15] propose a transformation such that termination of the transformed system is equivalent to termination of the original system w.r.t. its context-sensitive rewrite strategy. These transformations often encode aspects of the context-sensitive rewrite strategy by means of rewrite rules. We follow a related idea, but in contrast to the rewrite strategy, in this paper we encode the set of *start terms*.

For complexity analysis, dependency pairs have been adapted in the form of weak dependency pairs [18] and dependency tuples [32]. Further transformational approaches with term rewriting as target formalism for complexity analysis of programming languages have been investigated, e.g., for Prolog [17] and for Java [26]. Here upper bounds on the (innermost) runtime complexity of the obtained TRS (possibly with constraints) are used to draw conclusions on upper bounds for the worst-case time complexity of the input program. Our approach is related in that it also encodes a complexity problem for a source language (here: term rewriting) to a runtime complexity problem.

Similar to us, Frohn and Giesl [12] also relate different complexity properties. They identify a sufficient criterion to identify TRSs where runtime complexity of innermost rewriting and of full rewriting coincide.

However, to the best of the author's knowledge, so far complexity properties for *different sets of start terms* for the same TRS have not been related. This is where the present work comes in.

5   Implementation and Experimental Evaluation

Of course, to make the point that an instrumentation technique such as the present one is of practical interest, automatic analysis tools need to be able to actually prove useful statements about the output of the technique on standard examples. Thus, to assess the practical usefulness of our contributions, we implemented our transformation in the termination and complexity analysis tool AProVE [14]. First the runtime instrumentation of the derivational complexity problems is computed, and then this generated problem is processed further by existing techniques to find upper or lower bounds for runtime complexity of innermost or full rewriting. The corresponding configurations are labeled "APROVE instrumentation irc" and "APROVE instrumentation rc" in Tables 1, 2, 3 and 4.

As the state of the art against which to compare our contributions, we used the complexity analysis tool TcT [4] from the Termination and Complexity Competition in 2018[1] (for the competition of 2019, no tools had been submitted to analyze derivational complexity of rewriting) to analyze derivational complexity for innermost and for full rewriting. The corresponding tool configurations are labeled "TcT direct idc" and "TcT direct dc" in Tables 1, 2, 3 and 4. Thus far, APROVE featured only rudimentary techniques for analysis of derivational complexity. Therefore, we did not use APROVE as a reference implementation for analysis of derivational complexity, and we deactivated the existing rudimentary techniques for direct analysis of derivational complexity in our experiments.

Additionally, we wanted to assess whether our runtime instrumentation technique could be useful also for existing state-of-the-art tools like TcT for analysis of derivational complexity. To this end, we extracted the runtime instrumentations for the derivational complexity benchmarks and then conducted experiments on the resulting runtime complexity inputs for innermost and for full rewriting using TcT. The time needed for computing the runtime instrumentations themselves is negligible, so we believe that this is a fair comparison that can inform whether it might be worthwhile to add our transformation technique to the portfolio of techniques to analyze derivational complexity in an established tool like TcT.

For inferring lower bounds for dc, it is sound to use lower bounds for irc or rc for the same set of rewrite rules. Similarly, a lower bound for idc can be obtained directly from a lower bound for irc for the same set of rewrite rules. Thus, for computation of lower bounds, we ran the tools APROVE and TcT on corresponding versions of the rewrite systems (configurations "APROVE direct irc", "APROVE direct rc", "TcT direct irc", and "TcT direct rc" in Tables 2 and 4). The purpose of including these configurations was to see to what extent the addition of our generator rules facilitates the search for lower bounds.

As benchmark set, we used the derivational complexity families of the TPDB, version 10.6 [36]. For technical reasons, we restricted ourselves to the 2664 benchmarks for innermost rewriting[2] and the 1754 benchmarks for full rewriting[3] whose rewrite rules satisfy the conditions from Definition 1 that left-hand sides

---

[1] Available at:
https://www.starexec.org/starexec/secure/details/solver.jsp?id=20651.
[2] Benchmark family: Derivational_Complexity_Innermost_Rewriting.
[3] Benchmark family: Derivational_Complexity_Full_Rewriting.

Table 1. Upper bounds for derivational complexity of innermost rewriting

Tool	$\mathcal{O}(1)$	$\leq \mathcal{O}(n)$	$\leq \mathcal{O}(n^2)$	$\leq \mathcal{O}(n^3)$	$\leq \mathcal{O}(n^{\geq 4})$
TcT direct idc	1	368	468	481	501
TcT instrumentation irc	3	465	555	626	691
APROVE instrumentation irc	13	598	769	827	833

of rewrite rules must not be variables and right-hand sides of rewrite rules must not contain variables that do not occur in the corresponding left-hand sides.[4]

Table 2. Lower bounds for derivational complexity of innermost rewriting

Tool	$\geq \Omega(n)$	$\geq \Omega(n^2)$	$\geq \Omega(n^3)$	$\geq \Omega(n^{\geq 4})$	EXP
TcT direct idc	0	0	0	0	0
TcT direct irc	913	10	10	10	10
APROVE direct irc	1047	205	140	140	139
TcT instrumentation irc	893	10	10	10	10
APROVE instrumentation irc	1082	169	135	135	134

We ran our experiments on the STAREXEC compute cluster [33] in the all.q queue with a timeout of 300 s per example.

Tables 1, 2, 3 and 4 give an overview over our experimental results. For each considered configuration, we state the number of examples for which the corresponding asymptotic complexity bound could be inferred. More precisely, a row "$\leq \mathcal{O}(n^k)$" means that the corresponding tools proved a bound $\leq \mathcal{O}(n^k)$ (e.g., in Table 1, the configuration "TcT direct idc" proved constant or linear upper bounds in 368 cases). The column "EXP" in Tables 2 and 4 refers to an unspecified exponential.

Upper Bounds for Innermost Rewriting. Table 1 provides our experimental data for inference of upper bounds for innermost rewriting. As evidenced by the results, both TcT and APROVE benefit significantly from using our instrumentation rather than relying on existing techniques. For example, the 2018 version of TcT inferred constant or linear upper bounds for 368 TRSs. In contrast, TcT with our instrumentation found constant or linear upper bounds for 465 TRSs, and APROVE found constant or linear upper bounds for 598 TRSs. This indicates that our technique is particularly useful for finding upper complexity bounds.

---

[4] Version 10.6 of the TPDB contains 60 further examples for derivational complexity of innermost rewriting and 55 further examples for derivational complexity of full rewriting that violate these restrictions.

Table 3. Upper bounds for derivational complexity of full rewriting

Tool	$\mathcal{O}(1)$	$\leq \mathcal{O}(n)$	$\leq \mathcal{O}(n^2)$	$\leq \mathcal{O}(n^3)$	$\leq \mathcal{O}(n^{\geq 4})$
TCT direct dc	1	366	466	479	499
TCT instrumentation rc	1	203	224	304	304
APROVE instrumentation rc	1	328	386	398	399

Lower Bounds for Innermost Rewriting. In Table 2 we present our data for the inference of lower bounds for innermost rewriting. Here the analysis of innermost runtime complexity of the runtime instrumentation and the analysis of the original TRSs are roughly on par. In particular, approximately the same numbers of exponential bounds could be found.

Table 4. Lower bounds for derivational complexity of full rewriting

Tool	$\geq \Omega(n)$	$\geq \Omega(n^2)$	$\geq \Omega(n^3)$	$\geq \Omega(n^{\geq 4})$	EXP
TCT direct dc	0	0	0	0	0
TCT direct rc	415	0	0	0	0
APROVE direct rc	451	73	68	68	68
TCT direct irc	345	0	0	0	0
APROVE direct irc	426	59	54	54	54
TCT instrumentation rc	378	0	0	0	0
APROVE instrumentation rc	456	68	65	65	65

Upper Bounds for Full Rewriting. Table 3 presents our data for upper bounds of derivational complexity for rewriting with arbitrary strategies. Here we observe that the 2018 version of TCT scores noticeably better than our instrumentation-based approach. We conjecture that this is because a number of advanced techniques (e.g., [19,29,30,32]) for analysis of runtime complexity are available only for innermost rewriting. Still, Example 15 shows that also here bounds on derivational complexity can now be found that were out of reach before.

Lower Bounds for Full Rewriting. Table 4 shows the results for our experiments with respect to lower bounds for arbitrary rewrite strategies. Similar to innermost rewriting, also here the precision of the analysis with and without the generator rules is roughly on par (note that for lower bounds, high bounds are better).

Overall we can conclude that in particular for upper bounds of (innermost) derivational complexity, our instrumentation-based approach provides a good addition to state-of-the-art techniques.

Our experimental data from STAREXEC is available at the following URL:

http://www.dcs.bbk.ac.uk/~carsten/eval/rcdc/

6   Reflections and Conclusion

In this article, we have introduced a transformation technique that allows one to analyze derivational complexity problems in term rewriting via an off-the-shelf analysis tool specialized for the analysis of runtime complexity. We have proved correctness of the technique, and we have performed extensive experiments to validate the practical usefulness of our approach.

We recommend that a complexity analysis tool should use this approach and existing techniques in parallel. For complexity analysis tools specialized to (innermost) runtime complexity, our transformation can provide an avenue to broadened applicability.

In general, the approach of using instrumentations by rewrite rules to generate the set of "intended" start terms from their representation via "allowed" start terms appears to be underexplored in the analysis of properties of rewrite systems. We believe that this approach is worth investigating further, also for other properties of rewriting.

Acknowledgments. The author wishes to thank Florian Frohn and Jürgen Giesl for valuable discussions and the anonymous reviewers for suggestions and comments that helped to improve the paper.

References

1. Arts, T., Giesl, J.: Termination of term rewriting using dependency pairs. Theor. Comput. Sci. **236**(1–2), 133–178 (2000). https://doi.org/10.1016/S0304-3975(99)00207-8
2. Avanzini, M., Eguchi, N., Moser, G.: A path order for rewrite systems that compute exponential time functions. In: Proceedings of RTA 2011, LIPIcs, vol. 10, pp. 123–138 (2011). https://doi.org/10.4230/LIPIcs.RTA.2011.123
3. Avanzini, M., Moser, G.: A combination framework for complexity. Inf. Comput. **248**, 22–55 (2016). https://doi.org/10.1016/j.ic.2015.12.007
4. Avanzini, M., Moser, G., Schaper, M.: TcT: tyrolean complexity tool. In: Chechik, M., Raskin, J.-F. (eds.) TACAS 2016. LNCS, vol. 9636, pp. 407–423. Springer, Heidelberg (2016). https://doi.org/10.1007/978-3-662-49674-9_24
5. Baader, F., Nipkow, T.: Term Rewriting and All That. Cambridge University Press, Cambridge (1998). https://dblp.uni-trier.de/rec/bibtex/books/daglib/0092409
6. Brockschmidt, M., Emmes, F., Falke, S., Fuhs, C., Giesl, J.: Analyzing runtime and size complexity of integer programs. ACM Trans. Program. Lang. Syst. **38**(4), 13:1–13:50 (2016). https://doi.org/10.1145/2866575
7. Endrullis, J., Hendriks, D.: Transforming outermost into context-sensitive rewriting. Logical Methods Comput. Sci. **6**(2) (2010). https://doi.org/10.2168/lmcs-6(2:5)2010

8. Fernández, M.-L.: Relaxing monotonicity for innermost termination. Inf. Process. Lett. **93**(3), 117–123 (2005). https://doi.org/10.1016/j.ipl.2004.10.005

9. Ferreira, M.C.F., Ribeiro, A.L.: Context-sensitive AC-rewriting. In: Narendran, P., Rusinowitch, M. (eds.) RTA 1999. LNCS, vol. 1631, pp. 286–300. Springer, Heidelberg (1999). https://doi.org/10.1007/3-540-48685-2_24

10. Flores-Montoya, A., Hähnle, R.: Resource analysis of complex programs with cost equations. In: Garrigue, J. (ed.) APLAS 2014. LNCS, vol. 8858, pp. 275–295. Springer, Cham (2014). https://doi.org/10.1007/978-3-319-12736-1_15

11. Flores-Montoya, A.: Upper and lower amortized cost bounds of programs expressed as cost relations. In: Fitzgerald, J., Heitmeyer, C., Gnesi, S., Philippou, A. (eds.) FM 2016. LNCS, vol. 9995, pp. 254–273. Springer, Cham (2016). https://doi.org/10.1007/978-3-319-48989-6_16

12. Frohn, F., Giesl, J.: Analyzing runtime complexity via innermost runtime complexity. In: Proceedings of LPAR 2017, EPiC, vol. 46, pp. 249–268 (2017). https://doi.org/10.29007/1nbh

13. Frohn, F., Giesl, J., Hensel, J., Aschermann, C., Ströder, T.: Lower bounds for runtime complexity of term rewriting. J. Autom. Reason. **59**(1), 121–163 (2017). https://doi.org/10.1007/s10817-016-9397-x

14. Giesl, J., et al.: Analyzing program termination and complexity automatically with AProVE. J. Autom. Reasoning **58**, 3–31 (2017). https://doi.org/10.1007/s10817-016-9388-y

15. Giesl, J., Middeldorp, A.: Transformation techniques for context-sensitive rewrite systems. J. Funct. Program. **14**(4), 379–427 (2004). https://doi.org/10.1017/S0956796803004945

16. Giesl, J., Rubio, A., Sternagel, C., Waldmann, J., Yamada, A.: The termination and complexity competition. In: Beyer, D., Huisman, M., Kordon, F., Steffen, B. (eds.) TACAS 2019. LNCS, vol. 11429, pp. 156–166. Springer, Cham (2019). https://doi.org/10.1007/978-3-030-17502-3_10

17. Giesl, J., Ströder, T., Schneider-Kamp, P., Emmes, F., Fuhs, C.: Symbolic evaluation graphs and term rewriting: a general methodology for analyzing logic programs. In: Proceedings of PPDP 2012, pp. 1–12 (2012). https://doi.org/10.1145/2370776.2370778

18. Hirokawa, N., Moser, G.: Automated complexity analysis based on the dependency pair method. In: Armando, A., Baumgartner, P., Dowek, G. (eds.) IJCAR 2008. LNCS (LNAI), vol. 5195, pp. 364–379. Springer, Heidelberg (2008). https://doi.org/10.1007/978-3-540-71070-7_32

19. Hirokawa, N., Moser, G.: Automated complexity analysis based on context-sensitive rewriting. In: Dowek, G. (ed.) RTA 2014. LNCS, vol. 8560, pp. 257–271. Springer, Cham (2014). https://doi.org/10.1007/978-3-319-08918-8_18

20. Hofbauer, D.: Termination proofs by multiset path orderings imply primitive recursive derivation lengths. Theor. Comput. Sci. **105**(1), 129–140 (1992). https://doi.org/10.1016/0304-3975(92)90289-R

21. Hofbauer, D., Lautemann, C.: Termination proofs and the length of derivations. In: Dershowitz, N. (ed.) RTA 1989. LNCS, vol. 355, pp. 167–177. Springer, Heidelberg (1989). https://doi.org/10.1007/3-540-51081-8_107

22. Koprowski, A., Waldmann, J.: Max/plus tree automata for termination of term rewriting. Acta Cybern. **19**(2), 357–392 (2009)

23. Korp, M., Sternagel, C., Zankl, H.: CaT (complexity and termination). http://cl-informatik.uibk.ac.at/software/cat/

24. Lucas, S.: Termination of context-sensitive rewriting by rewriting. In: Meyer, F., Monien, B. (eds.) ICALP 1996. LNCS, vol. 1099, pp. 122–133. Springer, Heidelberg (1996). https://doi.org/10.1007/3-540-61440-0_122
25. Lucas, S.: Context-sensitive computations in functional and functional logic programs. J. Funct. Logic Program. **1998**(1), 1–61 (1998)
26. Moser, G., Schaper, M.: From Jinja bytecode to term rewriting: a complexity reflecting transformation. Inf. Comput. **261**, 116–143 (2018). https://doi.org/10.1016/j.ic.2018.05.007
27. Moser, G., Schnabl, A.: Proving quadratic derivational complexities using context dependent interpretations. In: Voronkov, A. (ed.) RTA 2008. LNCS, vol. 5117, pp. 276–290. Springer, Heidelberg (2008). https://doi.org/10.1007/978-3-540-70590-1_19
28. Moser, G., Schnabl, A., Waldmann, J.: Complexity analysis of term rewriting based on matrix and context dependent interpretations. In: Proceedings of FSTTCS 2008, LIPIcs, vol. 2, pp. 304–315 (2008). https://doi.org/10.4230/LIPIcs.FSTTCS.2008.1762
29. Moser, G., Schneckenreither, M.: Automated amortised resource analysis for term rewrite systems. In: Gallagher, J.P., Sulzmann, M. (eds.) FLOPS 2018. LNCS, vol. 10818, pp. 214–229. Springer, Cham (2018). https://doi.org/10.1007/978-3-319-90686-7_14
30. Naaf, M., Frohn, F., Brockschmidt, M., Fuhs, C., Giesl, J.: Complexity analysis for term rewriting by integer transition systems. In: Dixon, C., Finger, M. (eds.) FroCoS 2017. LNCS (LNAI), vol. 10483, pp. 132–150. Springer, Cham (2017). https://doi.org/10.1007/978-3-319-66167-4_8
31. Neurauter, F., Zankl, H., Middeldorp, A.: Revisiting matrix interpretations for polynomial derivational complexity of term rewriting. In: Fermüller, C.G., Voronkov, A. (eds.) LPAR 2010. LNCS, vol. 6397, pp. 550–564. Springer, Heidelberg (2010). https://doi.org/10.1007/978-3-642-16242-8_39
32. Noschinski, L., Emmes, F., Giesl, J.: Analyzing innermost runtime complexity of term rewriting by dependency pairs. J. Autom. Reason. **51**(1), 27–56 (2013). https://doi.org/10.1007/s10817-013-9277-6
33. Stump, A., Sutcliffe, G., Tinelli, C.: StarExec: a cross-community infrastructure for logic solving. In: Demri, S., Kapur, D., Weidenbach, C. (eds.) IJCAR 2014. LNCS (LNAI), vol. 8562, pp. 367–373. Springer, Cham (2014). https://doi.org/10.1007/978-3-319-08587-6_28
34. Waldmann, J.: A tool for match-bounded string rewriting. In: van Oostrom, V. (ed.) RTA 2004. LNCS, vol. 3091, pp. 85–94. Springer, Heidelberg (2004). https://doi.org/10.1007/978-3-540-25979-4_6
35. Wiki: The International Termination Competition (TermComp). http://termination-portal.org/wiki/Termination_Competition
36. Wiki: Termination Problems DataBase (TPDB). http://termination-portal.org/wiki/TPDB
37. Zankl, H., Korp, M.: Modular complexity analysis for term rewriting. Logical Methods Comput. Sci. **10**(1) (2014). https://doi.org/10.2168/LMCS-10(1:19)2014
38. Zantema, H.: Termination of term rewriting by semantic labelling. Fundamenta Informaticae **24**(1–2), 89–105 (1995). https://doi.org/10.3233/FI-1995-24124
39. Zantema, H.: Termination of context-sensitive rewriting. In: Comon, H. (ed.) RTA 1997. LNCS, vol. 1232, pp. 172–186. Springer, Heidelberg (1997). https://doi.org/10.1007/3-540-62950-5_69

Author Index

Printed in the United States
By Bookmasters